Everyday Life in the Balkans

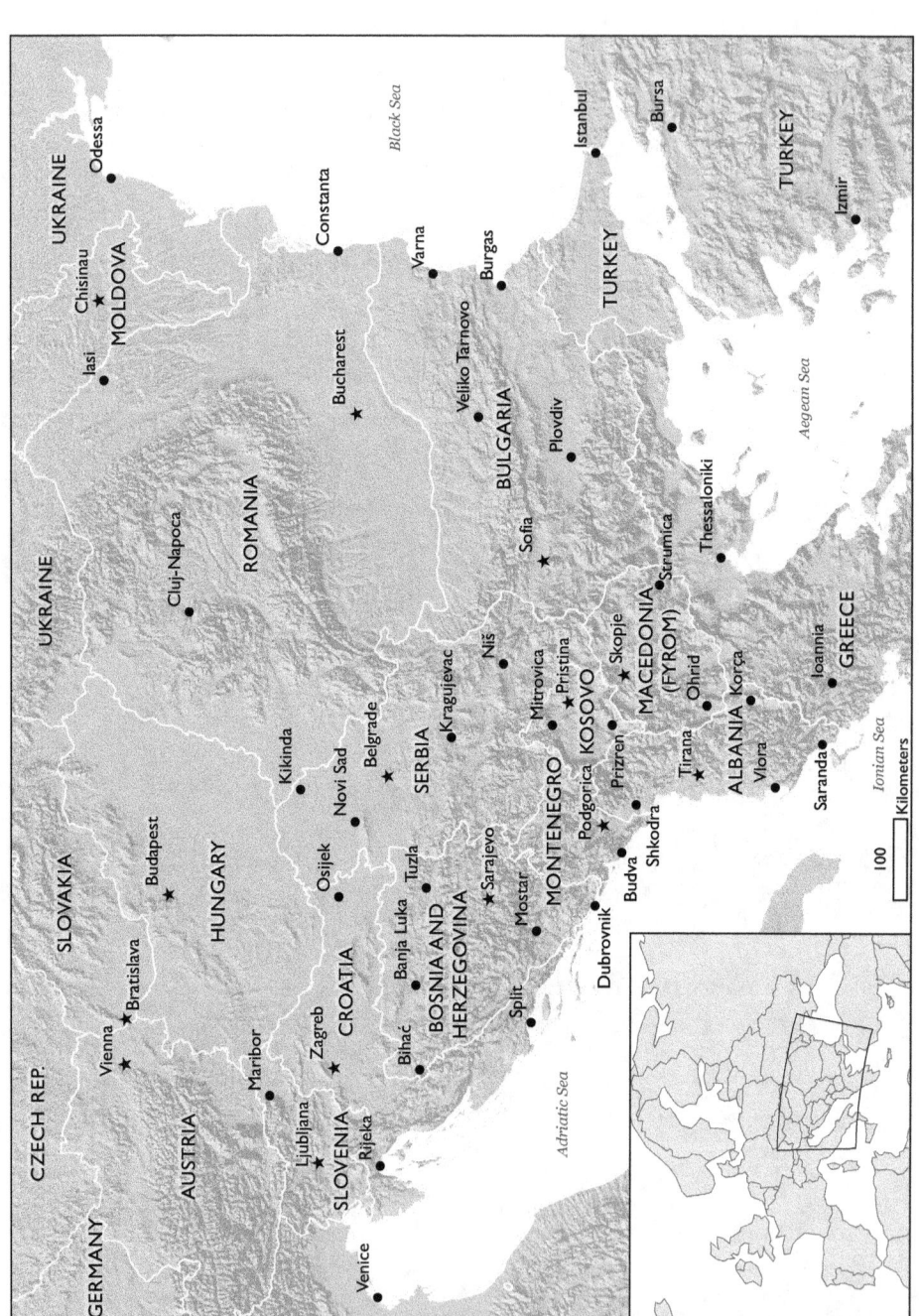

Map of the Balkans, by Theresa Quill.

EDITED BY
DAVID W. MONTGOMERY

Everyday Life in the Balkans

INDIANA UNIVERSITY PRESS

This book is a publication of

Indiana University Press
Office of Scholarly Publishing
Herman B Wells Library 350
1320 East 10th Street
Bloomington, Indiana 47405 USA

iupress.indiana.edu

© 2019 by Indiana University Press
All rights reserved

No part of this book may be reproduced or utilized in any form or by any means, electronic or mechanical, including photocopying and recording, or by any information storage and retrieval system, without permission in writing from the publisher. The paper used in this publication meets the minimum requirements of the American National Standard for Information Sciences—Permanence of Paper for Printed Library Materials, ANSI Z39.48-1992.

Library of Congress Cataloging-in-Publication Data

Names: Montgomery, David W., 1968- editor.
Title: Everyday life in the Balkans / [Thirty-five authors] ; Edited by David W. Montgomery.
Description: Bloomington, IN : Indiana University Press, c2018. | Includes bibliographical references and index
Identifiers: LCCN 2018048030 (print) | LCCN 2018049206 (ebook) | ISBN 9780253038203 (web PDF) | ISBN 9780253026170 (hardback) | ISBN 9780253038173 (pbk.) | ISBN 9780253038197 (ebook epub) Subjects: LCSH: Balkan Peninsula—Social life and customs.
Classification: LCC DR23 (ebook) | LCC DR23 .E94 2018 (print) | DDC 949.6—dc23
LC record available at https://lccn.loc.gov/2018048030

1 2 3 4 5   23 22 21 20 19 18

To our friends...
Kushtuar miqve tanë...
На нашите приятели...
Našimp prijateljima...
Για τους φίλους μας...
Prietenilor noştri...
Нашим пријатељима...
Našim prijateljem...
На нашите пријатели...
Sevgili dostlarımıza...

...and to Sarah.

Contents

Preface xi
Acknowledgments xiii

   1. Seeing Everyday Life in the Balkans   1
      David W. Montgomery

Section I: The (Historical) Context of Everyday Life   7

   2. Early Balkan Everyday Life   9
      Andrew Wachtel

   3. Crimes and Misdemeanors: Scenes of Everyday Life among the Gendarmerie in Ottoman Macedonia, ca. 1900   22
      İpek K. Yosmaoğlu

   4. It's What's Inside That Counts: Furnishing the Modern in the Apartments of Socialist Yugoslavia   31
      Patrick Hyder Patterson

   5. Consuming Lives: Inside the Balkan *Kafene*   44
      Mary Neuburger

   6. *Burek, Da!* Sociality, Context, and Idiom in Macedonia and Beyond   52
      Keith Brown

Section II: The Home(s) of Everyday Life   61

   7. Kinship and Safety Nets in Croatia and Kosovo   63
      Carolin Leutloff-Grandits

   8. "This Much We Know": Domestic Remedies and Quotidian Tricks since Tito's Bosnia   76
      Larisa Jašarević

   9. Femininity, Fashion, and Feminism: Women's Activists in Bosnia and Herzegovina   86
      Elissa Helms

  10. That Black Cloud upon Our Family: Everyday Life of Gays and Lesbians in Slovenia   96
      Roman Kuhar

11. Between Past and Future: Young People's Strategies for Living a "Normal Life" in Postwar Bosnia and Herzegovina   107
    Monika Palmberger

12. "But Where Else Could They Go?" The State, Family, and Private Care in a Bosnian Town   117
    Azra Hromadžić

Section III: The Livelihoods of Everyday Life   131

13. Cars, Coffee, and "The Crisis": Balkan Migration in Precarious Times   133
    Ana Croegaert

14. "We Don't Belong Anywhere": Everyday Life in a Serbian Town Where Immigrants Are Former Refugees   145
    Mila Dragojević

15. Neoliberal Spaces of Immorality: The Creation of a Bulgarian Land Market and "Land-Grabbing" Foreign Investors   155
    Deema Kaneff

16. Making Ends Meet in a Rural Community: The Life and Times of Aleksandar Živojinović   168
    Andrew Konitzer

17. A Lot of Sweat, a Little Bit of Fun, and Not Entirely "Hard Men": Worker's Masculinity in the Uljanik Shipyard   179
    Andrea Matošević

18. Perceptions of Balkan Belonging in Postdictatorship Greece   188
    Daniel M. Knight

Section IV: The Politics of Everyday Life   199

19. Neither the Balkans nor Europe: The "Where" and "When" in Present-Day Albania   201
    Nataša Gregorič Bon

20. Growing Up in Montenegro: A Story of Transformation and Resistance   211
    Jelena Džankić

21. War Criminals, National Heroes, and Transitional Justice in Macedonia   220
    Vasiliki P. Neofotistos

22. A Lively Border: Bosnia and Herzegovina and
    Serbia on the Shifting Banks of the Drina   230
    Čarna Brković and Stef Jansen

23. "Politicians Are All Crooks!": Everyday Politics
    in Bulgaria   239
    Emilia Zankina

24. Life among Statues in Skopje   251
    Ilká Thiessen

Section V: The Religion(s) of Everyday Life   263

25. "The Hardest Time Was the Time without
    Morality": Religion and Social Navigation
    in Albania   265
    David W. Montgomery

26. Ramadan in Prizren, Kosovo   278
    Frances Trix

27. The Cross at the Crossroads: The Feast of *Slava*
    between Faith and Custom   289
    Milica Bakić-Hayden

28. Boundaries of Freedom, Boundaries of
    Responsibility: Everyday Religious Life of
    Croatian Catholic Women   299
    Slavica Jakelić

29. Religious Boundaries, *Komshuluk*, and Sharing
    Sacred Spaces in Bulgaria   311
    Magdalena Lubanska

30. The Everyday of Religion and Politics in
    the Balkans   321
    Albert Doja

Section VI: The Art of Everyday Life   337

31. Unintentional Memorials: Everyday Places of
    Memory in Post-Transition Bucharest   339
    Alyssa Grossman

32. Between East and West, Folk and Pop,
    State and Market: Changing Landscapes of
    Bulgarian Folk Music   351
    Carol Silverman

33. Mothers in Balkan Film   363
    Yana Hashamova

34. Memories of Foreign Love   372
    Ervin Hatibi

35. The Sound of Charcoal Rustling:
    Drawing from Life in Belgrade   384
    Marko Živković

Postface   397
David W. Montgomery

Index   399

Preface

Somewhat prosaically, the title of this book—*Everyday Life in the Balkans*—gives the reader a sense of what it is about. But each reader no doubt brings his or her own understanding (and corresponding biases) as to why either "everyday life" or the "Balkans" matter. Thus, some explanation about the composition is required, for therein one can see how the various chapters constitute windows into a way of seeing the world that is sorely needed if we have any hope of understanding it.

This is a large book and the chapter topics are diverse. Each author was approached to write on a specific topic corresponding to her or his expertise, with country, discipline, and thematic diversity being central to the project. All contributions are original and were not intended to be a review of the literature so much as a critical engagement with some aspect of everyday life—broadly framed—from the perspective of those living it. The writing is intended to be felicitous to the lay public, yet the approach of bringing so many topics to bear on the character and depth to the picture of the Balkans should have relevance to regional specialists whose commitment to certain disciplinary approaches can obscure the interdisciplinary environment in which people live. This gets us to the importance of everyday life, for it is here that most of life is lived.

Most of our days are spent in familiar environments with which we seldom critically engage. The commonplace, after all, is "known," and thus its subtle yet formative role in our becoming who we are is easily overlooked. This applies also to our understanding of—or at least our attempts to understand—others: in failing to appreciate the everyday of their lives, we risk missing the more indirect engagements that give culture character and behavior clarity. As such, an implicit argument of this volume is that more empathic and thoughtful engagement with others comes from an appreciation of their lifeworlds and those factors that help explain what is valued and why.

Seeing everyday life requires us to look to places and relationships that are not commonly associated in regional introductions. Having an appreciation for the context in which people live forces us to know a bit about the diverse groupings that constitute this book: an understanding of history and tradition, the political face of quotidian life and its home, the nature of work and religion, and the role the aesthetic plays in local belonging. Brief introductions to each section explicate how the chapters fit within a section, but it is always the case that in life little exists in isolation. History, home, politics, education, labor, religion, and so on, are categories that offer each other reciprocity in the everyday, so one should read the chapters not simply as self-contained but also as speaking across sections. The work we do can be political; religion can be art; home has history. Everyday life is dynamic and syncretic, and we must see this if we have any hope of understanding the Balkans or anywhere else.

Acknowledgments

While created in moments of solitary composition, all books are collective endeavors, with this volume even more collective than most. It would not have been possible without the chapter authors, who turned to their research with the intent of drawing out the everyday of the places where they have invested so much of their work and observation. In many ways, this was both a reflective and reflexive process made possible by the generosity of our various interlocutors, who shared with us their hopes and fears as they allowed us to be part of their daily lives. Thus it is collectively that we acknowledge, in the many languages in which we work, that this book is "to our friends" who have made this possible and made our time in the region meaningful.

Alongside the general acknowledgment of those about whom we write, there are some who were especially helpful to me over the course of this project, from recognizing the need to bring a discussion of everyday life to focus on the Balkans to bringing this final product together. My appreciation for the Balkans began with Bela Blasszauer, Darina Kokona, Sanja and Borislav Starčević, Sashka Popova, and Valentin Haş—to each, in various ways, I owe a great debt. Others who offered friendship and insight on the region include Jasmina and Andrew Konitzer, Suzanna and Robert Kokona, Ervin Hatibi, Mentor Mustafa, Rudina Verdha, Armela Bega, Armida Tola, Laura Shimili, Florian Ravoniku, Enton Derraj, Eno Muho, Elona Saro, Jorida Cila, Dorina Nikolla, Denalda Kuzumi, Irma Vuci, Shqipe Hajredini, Virgjil Kule, Shpresa Fuga, Artan Fuga, Rusmir Mahmutćehajić, Alma Mrgan-Slipicevic, Marija and Zivojin Budovalcev, Lowell Lander, Natasha Korn, Adam Seligman, Rahel Wasserfall, and Milena Katsarska. As well, special recognition and gratitude go to Roska Vrgova, who commented on many of the chapters and contributed significantly with the photos used in the volume. Also, thanks to Theresa Quill for creating the Balkan map used in this volume. There are many others I have failed to mention, but hopefully they will see their influence in what is written, and that their insights were noticed and appreciated.

Research was supported by grants from the American Councils for International Education, the University of Pittsburgh's Center for Russian and East European Studies, and the Global Studies Center, also at the University of Pittsburgh. As well, CEDAR (Communities Engaging with Difference and Religion), which held its first program in Bosnia and Herzegovina, Croatia, and Montenegro in 2003—and continues to have an ongoing presence in the Balkan Summer School on Religion and Public Life and other initiatives that have evolved from those programs—has been central to my engagement in the region.

In closing, I acknowledge the generosity and selflessness of my parents, Dee and Luke Montgomery, who supported me even when I know they wished I was closer to home; in every way, they made this work possible by instilling a deep appreciation for the joys of quotidian life. Thanks also to Jennifer, Nathan, Lauren, and Reed Tegtmeyer and Denise, Tim, and Deirdre Ligget. Lastly, I deeply thank my wife, Sarah; the love and support she has provided throughout the writing and editing of this work made it all more manageable—writing is a process that takes place while the everyday unfolds, and her presence, in great and at times unnoticed ways, enriches the world we navigate together. It is my hope that as parents we will successfully impart an appreciation for everyday life upon our son, Gabriel—born during the last stages of the book's production—and that he will grow to see this work as useful.

Everyday Life in the Balkans

1 Seeing Everyday Life in the Balkans

David W. Montgomery

We all encounter the world with incomplete knowledge, and this is no less the case when we approach the Balkans—a region characterized by orientalists as backward yet understood by residents as home. How we come to understand the Balkans is thus heavily dependent on the sources we prioritize and the narratives we privilege. To schoolchildren in the West, it is taught that both world wars began in the Balkans, there was repression under socialism, and the years after socialism were difficult, as the violence of war and the struggle to figure out life in a postsocialist world were fraught with uncertainty. The majority of what is taught and learned—through textbooks and modern media—focuses on the actions of both elites and nations as actors; but this is only part of the story. Indeed, it is only part of what one needs to know to understand anywhere. The more complete story—one that conveys the affective richness of life—comes in understanding the stories of the everyday, stories where the taken-for-granted aspects of the ordinary define what it means to belong to a certain locale, where well-being can be seen in neighborly relations despite the struggles of life, and where the quotidian nature of existence is recognized for what it is: part mundane and part tragic, yet also at times heroic.

Often, the full context of what connects people to their worlds is occluded when we focus on a region or a particular event. What defines any place must be understood in relation to what makes it home for those who reside there or otherwise remain connected to the area. The boundaries of these connections are, however, often fluid and ambiguous, requiring a nuanced, interactive relationship with others to contextualize meaning. This can be seen even in the very way a generalizing term like *Balkans* holds baggage and implies varying categories of identity. The importance of interrogating the implications of such a catchall term cannot be understated,[1] for implicit prejudices can be pernicious when outsiders see locals as less than equals. But in starting to see local ways of creating meaning and value in everyday life, we are afforded the opportunity to appreciate the range of struggles and joys that capture what it means to be in relationship with others, that make sense only in relation to the everyday negotiations that constitute life.

The Ambiguity of *Balkan*

To appreciate the complex nature of everyday life in the Balkans, I turn to the ambiguity of the regional moniker itself. Here I opt for an indirect way of doing so because it is more reflective of what takes place in social interactions than the conventions of scholarly writing that advocate for clarity and directness. Thus, as so many days begin in the region, I begin with coffee.

Coffee is an important part of everyday life in the Balkans. The first coffee of the day begins a morning at home. The second and third may be with friends or colleagues midmorning and midafternoon. Another may be had after dinner with friends. More may be had in between. Covered by the filigree of tradition, coffee is a conduit of social relations, an invitation that brings people together to share stories, anxieties, hopes, and all that grows out of people coming together. Meeting for coffee creates a space where the ambiguities of life can be worked out (or managed) and as such comes to represent a social characteristic of the region.

To the outsider, the invitation to coffee is not always straightforward. Meeting someone for coffee often means a drink of roasted, finely ground coffee beans that are boiled in a *cezve* (*ibrik*) and served in a small cup in which the grounds settle prior to drinking. Yet meeting for coffee can also mean lunch, dinner, or even a beer, anytime throughout the day. The invitation to "meet for coffee" has multiple meanings that are contextually understood without the need to distinguish the details of what the meeting will entail. Misunderstandings may still emerge, but generally people know the context without everything needing to be worked out beforehand.

Balkan is a similarly ambiguous term that has come to hold political, cultural, and geographical characteristics, all used contextually yet as if the uses were widely agreed on. As such, when the term is used, it takes context to know if it implies a geographical setting—either as the Balkan Peninsula or Southeast Europe—or a cultural setting, suggesting cultural similarities within the region that are distinguishable from those beyond the region. People from different places may be talking about two very different things—much like the meaning of coffee can be differently interpreted by the outsider unfamiliar with the nuances—and thus it becomes all the more important for people with roots outside the Balkans to appreciate the local context of the Balkans. To this end, the various uses of the term—and how the political, cultural, and geographical aspects of life within the region get animated in the everyday—are employed throughout this volume.

The main goal of these contributions is to convey what life is like for people who understand their home as being within the Balkans. The focus, thus, is not the elite newsmakers of the region, but rather those toiling closer to the land in which they live, whose lives are often seen as unexceptional. It is the everyday of these lives that best captures the dynamism of any place.

Nonetheless, cognates associated with the region, like *balkanized* and *balkanization*, are commonly used to imply a process of political fragmentation and uncooperative hostility. This is, of course, an unfortunate and inaccurate representation of the people who live here that says more about the prejudices of those using such terms than it does about any specific population in the Balkans.

Because of the pejorative connotations the term sometimes holds, many from the region prefer the regional identifier of Southeast Europe, despite colloquially talking about the region as "the Balkans." On multiple occasions, several of my interlocutors from throughout the region have advocated identifying the region as Southeast Europe, yet in informal settings referred to the region in terms that are both ubiquitous and ambiguous, such as "Balkan culture" or "Balkan mentality" or "historically Balkan"—all terms that captured something meaningful and cohesive yet not easily bounded. Within a geospatial sense, in relation to the European continent, Southeast Europe works somewhat neutrally to convey a bounded region. But in terms of holding the ambiguity of boundaries and belonging within a local context of understanding, *Balkans* remains useful.

What I mean by this utility is that the boundaries implied in the term *Balkans* are inherently ambiguous and thus also a metaphor for understanding the context of everyday life. At times, people identify as belonging to a particular group, and at other times they may not. Named after a mountain range that forms the watershed between the Adriatic and Black Seas, the Balkan Peninsula includes those lands bounded by the Adriatic, Ionian, Aegean, Marmara, and Black Seas and the Danube and Sava Rivers. The cultural boundaries of what is within the Balkans is imprecise. The fluidity of where one group ends and another begins is locally understood and yet in a way obscured by titular nation-states. Where the Balkans end is fuzzier than where southeast Europe ends (though southeast Europe has its own problems of precision), and perhaps part of the challenge to understanding the region is to be held in that fuzziness.

Within this volume, the fuzziness of what constitutes the in- and out-groups can be seen. The various authors' contributions cover Albania, Bulgaria, Bosnia and Herzegovina, Croatia, Greece, Kosovo, Macedonia, Montenegro, Romania, Serbia, and Slovenia, with reference to Ottoman Turkey. Yet some parts of Greece do not self-categorize as Balkan despite falling within the Balkan Peninsula. Sometimes Slovenians consider themselves Balkan in relation to their Yugoslav experience, and other times they distance themselves by claiming themselves as central European; likewise, Romanians move between Balkan and central European. These are some of the peripheries of the Balkans and are included because it is along the periphery that the precision of a category can be appreciated for its fluidity. All chapters engage with populations connected to a Balkan identity and collectively convey the types of variation and exchange found by people across the region. As such, the chapters also come together to connect the everyday to the variability of experience across the region. After all, while any term may be complicated or have seemingly political ends, understanding the context in which people live means we also must look at the more quotidian environment of struggles and meaning-making.

The Everyday of Life

Much of the context of life's stories comes from the everyday. The everyday is common yet also exceptional in its ability to influence the trajectory of our days. It is the home where most of life takes place, and yet its place as an object of discussion is often a second-level analysis for those concerned with specific events; everyday life underlies all major events yet is often overlooked for its seeming banality and unremarkability.[2] But the significance of the ordinary and commonplace becomes relevant when we think about notions of what makes a life worth living and how people come to value their surroundings.

Collectively, this volume focuses on the "everyday-ness"—both affectively and popularly—of experience in the Balkans. There is both poetry and urgency in the everyday, and part of what these chapters convey is a context for understanding the free verse quality common to life. The urgency should be apparent to anyone (self-)reflective about life and its conditions, poignantly captured in the dictum attributed to the playwright William Archer: "Drama is anticipation mingled with uncertainty." What makes life dramatic for our interlocutors—though also for ourselves—is that in the everyday, events unfold organically, situated as they are in a specific time and place. And they unfold with some need for response, for engagement. There is ambiguity here, but it is made manageable through connection with others.

In this book, we focus on the nature of the everyday to see the drama and the context as life unfolds. All people have dramatic—and meaningful—lives, even when it may not seem as such to those on the outside. When we put a frame around home and contextualize it in a larger setting—that setting being the everyday of life—we can more easily make sense of what is going on in a place and how people are thus relating experience and events to the story of their lives. Speaking of the everyday and everyday life is a way of seeing more holistically what goes into making life.

Seeing Everyday Life in the Balkans

In some respects, this book captures a moment in time, or rather, particular moments in particular times. It shows the specific as a way to make sense of the general, in part by saying that without the specific, the general becomes disassociated from the very actors for whom events are personal. After all, it is when experience is personal that it becomes meaningful. As such, this book conveys everydays as they are experienced from different perspectives to show the diverse character constituent of the region. In looking at the quotidian details of the Balkans, we can come to appreciate the more affective contexts in which people exist. The everydays of our interlocutors evolve across a lifetime, and we see this evolution in these chapters. Tomorrow is different from both today and yesterday, even as antecedents of the latter permeate—at times, even define—the former, yet coherence remains within a life's trajectory.

The structure of this book reflects a way of seeing everyday life around six loosely categorized and interrelated topics of engagement and meaning-making. Beginning with the historical context of everyday life in the region, we are reminded that origins evolve, in varied ways, into presents that both reflect and obscure the past. This is played out in subsequent sections, where aspects of home, work, politics, religion, and art convey the dynamic context in which relationships emerge. As the chapters collectively express, to live in any place is to hold multiple interests across topics that engage in the present that surrounds us. This is true for those in the Balkans as well as people anywhere else and thus serves as a touchstone from which more empathic modes of understanding may prevail.

All this is a way of saying that this is a book that not only speaks to the local context of the region but also recognizes the varied components of everyday life that give a way for making sense of change and how it is both brought about and lived through. This is a book about the people living in the Balkans, but it is also about the centrality of seeing the seeming mundanity of the everyday as crucial to understanding any population. Both celebration and toil—and everything in between—take place in relationships that begin in the everyday of ordinary time.

Notes

1. See Bakic-Hayden 1995; Todorova 2009.
2. While the book largely concerns itself with the ethnographic task of seeing life unfold in daily contexts, and this contributes implicitly to framing the everyday as a way to see the world, more explicit engagement with theories of everyday life can be found in the work of, among others, Berger and Luckmann (1966), Bourdieu (1977), de Certeau (1984), Felski (1999), Heller (1984), Highmore (2002, 2011), Lefebvre (2014), Schutz (1970), and Schutz and Luckmann (1973, 1989). As such, there is a theoretically rich debate in the literature that shows how the varied ways of understanding the everyday affect the ways in which it is made sense of analytically. De Certeau sees the everyday as filled with acts of resistance and subversion whereas more sociological and phenomenological accounts, such as those offered by Schutz—and his students, Berger and Luckmann—look at the everyday as a space of information and information making. Felski offers a useful definition that combines the works of Heller, Lefebvre, and Schutz to ground everyday life in "three facets: time, space, and modality. The temporality of the everyday, I suggest, is that of repetition, the spatial ordering of the everyday is anchored in a sense of home and the characteristic mode of experiencing the everyday is that of habit" (Felski 1999, 18).

References

Bakic-Hayden, Milica. 1995. "Nesting Orientalisms: The Case of Former Yugoslavia." *Slavic Review* 54 (4): 917–31.
Berger, Peter L., and Thomas Luckmann. 1966. *The Social Construction of Reality: A Treatise in the Sociology of Knowledge*. New York: Anchor Books.
Bourdieu, Pierre. 1977. *Outline of a Theory of Practice*. Translated by Richard Nice. Cambridge: Cambridge University Press.
de Certeau, Michel. 1984. *The Practice of Everyday Life*. Translated by Stephen Rendall. Berkeley: University of California Press.
Felski, Rita. 1999. "The Invention of Everyday Life." *New Formations* 33: 15–31.
Heller, Ágnes. 1984. *Everyday Life*. London: Routledge and Kegan Paul.
Highmore, Ben, ed. 2002. *The Everyday Life Reader*. London: Routledge.

Highmore, Ben. 2011. *Ordinary Lives: Studies in the Everyday*. London: Routledge.
Lefebvre, Henri. 2014. *Critique of Everyday Life*. Translated by John Moore. London: Verso.
Schutz, Alfred. 1970. *On Phenomenology and Social Relations*. Chicago: University of Chicago Press.
Schutz, Alfred, and Thomas Luckmann. 1973. *The Structures of the Life-World*. Vol. 1. Translated by Richard M. Zaner and H. Tristram Engelhardt, Jr. 2 vols. Evanston: Northwestern University Press.
Schutz, Alfred, and Thomas Luckmann. 1989. *The Structures of the Life-World*. Vol. 2. Translated by Richard M. Zaner and David J. Parent. 2 vols. Evanston: Northwestern University Press.
Todorova, Maria. 2009. *Imagining the Balkans*. Updated ed. Oxford: Oxford University Press.

DAVID W. MONTGOMERY is Director of Program Development for Communities Engaging with Difference and Religion (CEDAR) and Associate Research Professor at the Center for International Development and Conflict Management at the University of Maryland. He is author of *Practicing Islam: Knowledge, Experience, and Social Navigation in Kyrgyzstan* and of *Living with Difference: How to Build Community in a Divided World* (with Adam Seligman and Rahel Wasserfall).

Section I: The (Historical) Context of Everyday Life

The space that constitutes the everyday has a history that precedes our usage of it. Put another way, history has both latent and manifest functions that provide context to sociality. But history is a long narrative, and within the context of this volume, we can allude to only some of the ways its arc has brought us to where we are. As such, this section covers a great deal of ground to remind the reader that events begetting events are part of the progressions through which the everyday is navigated.

Andrew Wachtel lays the groundwork for understanding the contemporary Balkans by exploring the relationship between history and everyday life, from the Roman colonization of the peninsula through the migration of the Slavs and the effect of Christianization on how people live. Within the early historical record, it is hard to find reference to everyday life, but he nonetheless shows how these varied shifts in history have left a mark that remains evident today. Discussing the challenge of locally maintaining security, İpek Yosmaoğlu turns our attention to everday instances of misconduct—and the shifting mores of what is considered "misconduct"—during the Ottoman period. Patrick Patterson describes how Yugoslavs during the socialist period managed the physical spaces in which they lived. And both Mary Neuburger and Keith Brown add depth and context to our seeing the café and *burek* as aspects of everyday consumption that are laden with social and political meanings rooted within a historical context.

Together these chapters speak to a dynamic engagement with the past, socially navigated in seen and unseen ways.

2 Early Balkan Everyday Life
Andrew Wachtel

A Roman Land

It is often said that history is written by the victors. It could equally be added that history has generally been written by the rich and powerful and records their interests. As a result, capturing the texture of the everyday life of normal people in ancient times is quite difficult. In the last few decades, however, more attention has been paid to the history of everyday life, and new tools, particularly archaeological ones, have allowed for a surprisingly broad understanding of how people lived their daily lives.[1] This is particularly the case for the Roman Empire, which, in addition to a wide range of written sources, left a well-documented material heritage behind, at least if we speak about major centers. When we turn to provincial areas such as the Balkans, however, our vision gets increasingly hazy, and we have to extrapolate from what we know of life in the metropolitan centers.

Beginning in the first century AD, the Roman Empire became the earliest organized political group to colonize both the coast and the interior of the Balkans. As a result, the Roman presence was felt almost everywhere on the peninsula and remains visible today. Among the cities the Romans founded, or enormously expanded, were Emona (Ljubljana), Singidunum (Belgrade), Serdica (Sofia) Philippopolis (Plovdiv), Spalatum (Split), and Dyrrhachium (Durrës). The greatest Roman engineering feat in the region was the construction of the 520-mile-long Via Egnatia, the first major road built outside Italy, which linked Dyrrhachium with Byzantium. Along with a more northerly route that followed river valleys from Emona through Singidunum, Philippopolis, and Adrianople, these remain the main lines of communication through the Balkans to this day.

The Romans also colonized the Balkans extensively. Although most of the region would lose its Roman character in the wake of the barbarian invasions that began in the fourth century AD, some coastal cities of the Adriatic (Dubrovnik, Split, Zadar) still contained Latin-speaking populations until the Renaissance. Curiously, the Roman presence lasted longest in one of the most marginal parts of the empire: the Dacian provinces, which were annexed after Trajan's victory over the Dacians in AD 106. The Romans killed off the local nobility, exiled or enslaved much of the native population, and encouraged

Figure 2.1. Ruins in Butrint, a World Heritage site in Albania that was an ancient Greek and later Roman city before coming under Byzantine administration and later abandoned in the Middle Ages, 2013. Photograph by David W. Montgomery.

colonization of the province by settlers from other parts of the empire. Although barbarian invasions forced the Romans to pull back to the Danube a mere 150 years later, the colonists, who presumably had mingled in time with the remaining Dacian population, stayed behind to become the ancestors of today's Romanians.

Perhaps the most influential person to be born in the Balkans during Roman times was the future emperor Constantine. In the course of a series of brilliant military campaigns between AD 312 and 325, he reunited the Roman Empire, which had been split in half by his predecessors. In the course of these campaigns, he also converted to Christianity, though his Christianity was rather unorthodox, mixing the still not fully formed doctrines of the church with a pagan sun cult. Nevertheless, he encouraged the church and donated enormous sums for its expansion, and it was as a Christian that he took up residence in his capital Constantinople (today's Istanbul), formally dedicated in AD 330. Built on the site of an older Greek settlement called Byzantion, the city is located in a supremely strategic position athwart the land and sea routes connecting Europe and Asia. Constantine's decision to locate the seat of his power here was to have a momentous effect on the entire Roman world. It signified a turning away from the West, from Latin and pagan Rome, toward the Greek and Christian East.

The city grew rapidly. Under Emperor Theodosius in the early fifth century, massive walls were constructed to protect the city from attacks from the north. They would serve their purpose for over one thousand years. By the reign of Justinian, which began in 527, Constantinople was the largest city in Europe, with a population approaching half a million. In this period, many of the most famous early Byzantine monuments were built, including the Church of Holy Wisdom (Hagia Sophia).

The civilization centered in Constantinople was a curious amalgam of old and new. Though the empire is conventionally called the Byzantine, its inhabitants never used the term, calling themselves instead Rhomaioi (Romans) and considering themselves the heirs of the moribund Western city. They spoke primarily Greek, however, which replaced Latin as the main language of the empire by the mid-sixth century. Though the empire would suffer ups and downs, it managed to retain its integrity until Constantinople was captured by Catholic crusaders in 1204. Even after this catastrophe, it rebounded, though never fully recovered, before its final destruction in 1453.

The empire's strength derived from its unique blend of secular and religious institutional power. It was first and foremost a Christian state, whose basic doctrines were defined by the church fathers, the church councils, and the decisions of various Byzantine emperors. Although during the early centuries the church was racked by heresies and doctrinal disagreements, after the final victory of the icon venerators in 843, the doctrine of the Eastern Orthodox Church became essentially fixed. By comparison to Catholicism, Orthodoxy was a static religion that placed great stock in liturgy and ritual and tended to be less concerned with individual achievements. The emperor, chosen by God, was more powerful than any Western ruler. It was he, not the patriarch (the spiritual leader of the Orthodox church), who presided over church councils and expounded dogmatic pronouncements. While Catholic popes had the authority to bend even the most powerful kings to their will at times, the Byzantine patriarch was appointed by the emperor and could be dismissed by him. When one eleventh-century patriarch tried to challenge this arrangement, he was arrested, beaten, and thrown into prison, where he died before his trial.

Although Byzantine society changed and evolved in the course of its millennium-long existence, one of the great illusions propounded by this civilization was that change was unnecessary. Harmony, order, precedent, symmetry, and stasis were supreme values, as can be seen most clearly perhaps in the classic lines of a building like Hagia Sophia, the beautifully preserved mosaics in Ravenna, or the incantatory melodies of Byzantine church music. Defending the multitude of Byzantine ceremonies to his son in the tenth century, Emperor Constantine VII remarked: "If the body of a man were not gracefully formed, and if its members were casually arranged and inharmoniously disposed, one would say that the result was chaos and disorder. The same is true for the institution of empire; if it not be guided and governed by order, it will in no way differ from vulgar deportment in a private person."[2]

Order was preserved not merely by a complex series of secular and religious rituals, but also through the efforts of an enormous bureaucracy. Byzantine bureaucrats were generally highly educated, both in theology and in the Greek classics (rhetoric and poetry particularly), and they frequently vied with the empire's military leaders, who were based primarily in outlying territories where they exercised extensive civil and military control. Both bureaucrats and military men were supported by the labor of farmers, who made up the bulk of the population. Farmers worked primarily on small plots, producing sufficient food to support their families and to pay taxes. Many tilled land owned by monasteries, and in later periods, many worked on the extensive estates of provincial lords. In the cities, craft industries were regulated by guilds, including organizations for butchers, fishmongers, bakers, and producers of silk goods, jewelry, and perfumes. Not surprisingly in such an orderly state, prices were strictly controlled by the state.

Although much of the Balkan Peninsula would be lost during various ebbs of Byzantine power, the empire and its culture nevertheless exerted a crucial influence on developments in the Balkans between the seventh century, when the Slavic invasions destroyed Roman urban life in the central and northern Balkans, and the thirteenth century, by which time the Slavic invaders had converted to Christianity.

Three central processes dominate the history of the Balkans from the sixth century until the beginning of the Ottoman conquest in the latter half of the fourteenth. The period is marked by the migration of the final "permanent residents" of the Balkan Peninsula to the region: these were, most important—because eventually most numerous—the Slavs, but also the Turks (first Bulgars and then Ottomans) to the south and east, the Magyars (Hungarians) in the north, and finally the Roma (Gypsies). These new peoples joined those already present in the region—the Greeks, the Illyrians (likely ancestors of the Albanians), and the Romanized Dacians. With their arrival, the basic ethnic and linguistic composition of the Balkans was fixed.

It was also during this period that many of these peoples formed their first political states. Though they had arrived as a motley array of loosely organized tribes, under the influence of Byzantine models between the eighth and thirteenth centuries, the Bosnians, Bulgarians, Croats, Hungarians, Romanians, and Serbs would each develop an independent, though generally fragile, state. They were all to lose their political independence after the Ottoman conquest, but hazy memories of medieval glory, preserved in religious institutions, architectural monuments, and oral peasant culture, would remain to be marshaled by nineteenth-century nation-building intellectuals and politicians.

Finally, this period saw the Christianization of the majority of the Balkan peoples. While many Balkan inhabitants had probably been Christians in the fifth century, after the Slavic invasions the peninsula was again pagan, with the exception of Constantinople, Salonica, and the walled cities on the Adriatic coast. In the course of some three hundred years, the newcomers would be evangelized by missionaries from either Constantinople or Rome. The competition for influence between the two main Christian centers was fierce, and ultimately the region was split, approximately along the line of division between the former eastern and western halves of the Roman Empire: the northern and western Balkans became primarily Catholic, while the southern and eastern Balkans were primarily Orthodox. Conversion to Christianity, initially by the highest political elites and later by the common folk, brought enormous changes, for Christianity permeated daily life (though never entirely destroyed the vestiges of older, pagan traditions). Rituals connected with saints' days, festivals, and solemn church holidays, intimate events such as baptisms, marriages, and funerals, all took on a new coloration. Furthermore, Christianity brought literacy, at least to the elites, and by making available Christian and some classical learning, opened new possibilities for cultural development. Finally, the architectural and artistic monuments of Christianity were visible to all and can still be seen throughout the Balkans.

A Slavic Land

In its heyday, the Roman Empire controlled the entire Balkan Peninsula. And while the Balkan provinces had never been of central concern to the empire, they were crisscrossed by imperial highways and dotted with significant urban centers, both along the coasts and inland. By the sixth century, however, weakened by hundreds of years of invasions from the north and east, the eastern half of the then definitively split empire controlled the peninsula only as far north as the Danube River. Beginning in the early years of that century, raids across the Danube by peoples the Greeks had never before encountered became endemic. The Byzantine chroniclers, unsure as to who exactly these invaders were, called them "Huns, Sclavenes, and Antes." By the mid- to late seventh century, scarcely 150 years later, Slavs had settled practically the entire peninsula. Byzantine settlements remained only along the coasts and in the lands immediately surrounding the capital.

From the surviving records, it is clear that the Slavs wreaked havoc on the Balkan urban infrastructure, as the following account by John of Ephesus (written in about 585) indicates: "The accursed people the Slavs arose and passed through the whole of the Hellades, through Thessaly and Thrace, conquering many towns and forts, wasted and burnt, looted. They overcame the country and settled it freely without fear as if it were their own, and strange to say to the present day inhabit it."[3] He seems particularly surprised that the Slavs remained and this was indeed something new in the Byzantine experience. Previous invaders had been nomads on horseback who attacked swiftly and then withdrew, but the Slavs came to stay. They began to farm the land, using simple wooden and then iron plows to cultivate grains, vegetables, and fruits; keeping herds and flocks of domestic animals; and brewing beer and making wine.

The Slavs reintroduced paganism throughout the Balkans. Because pagan practices were vigorously suppressed after the Slavs themselves were Christianized, we know little about the religious traditions of these then illiterate peoples, but it appears that the Slavs had a well-developed set of beliefs concerning the world of evil spirits (many of which survived in rural areas into the early twentieth century). Demons could inhabit any place, from the home to the fields, forests, and streams, and had to be placated. The dead were particularly dangerous, including those who became "vampires," blood-sucking spirits whose name is apparently of Balkan origin. Festivals took place at strategic points of the year, in particular midsummer's eve. The tradition of lighting a bonfire on this night and dancing and singing around it, still practiced today, derives from this festival.

Compared with the rich material culture of late antiquity, that of the early Slavs in the Balkans was poor. Archaeologists have recovered large quantities of handmade pottery, but the invaders do not appear to have used potter's wheels. By the tenth century, however, the Slavs had developed a professional pottery industry, with wheel-made objects fired in closed kilns at relatively high temperatures. Early Slavs were skilled smiths as well and produced a wide variety of iron implements, from knives to plowshares. The inventory of objects used by the Slavs was not, however, as limited as the archaeological evidence suggests. For where Balkan dwellers in late antiquity had used ceramics and metals intensively, the Slavs employed cloth, skins, and wood. Unfortunately, these are far more perishable. Nevertheless, some pictorial and written descriptions of daily life do exist, and their accuracy has been confirmed by finds of objects that were buried deep in bogs. Men appear to have worn a kind of knee-length long-sleeved tunic fastened at the waist by a leather belt. Underneath they wore tight breeches and leather shoes or boots. Women wore linen or woolen dresses. Earrings, rings, and bracelets of silver and semiprecious stones frequently found in graves attest to a love of adornment.

After they settled down, the Slavs constructed houses. These were usually sunken-floored one-story huts with an oven, used for heating and cooking, in one corner. Such houses were not built to last. Most probably, fields nearby would be intensively cultivated for some years and then abandoned as the land became less productive, for the early Slavs do not appear to have practiced crop rotation or fertilization. They did not have to develop these techniques because the abundance of available land in these sparsely populated areas allowed them simply to move a short distance away, clear new land and rebuild their simple homes.

The Slavic invaders had no experience with urban life. Lacking any complex political organization, the invaders, led by a chief and his military retinue, plundered whatever territory they could and then settled down to a life of subsistence farming supplemented by occasional raids. Having been looted repeatedly, the majority of the Balkan towns were abandoned in the course of the seventh and eighth centuries, with urban life reduced to Constantinople, Salonica, and the coastal cities, including Ragusa (Dubrovnik) and Spalatum (Split). From this time on, a relative paucity of cities, especially in the core Balkan region, would remain a feature of life until modern times. The economy also contracted. Although archaeologists find coins from the late antique period all over the Balkans, almost no Byzantine coinage from the seventh and eighth centuries has been uncovered, suggesting that subsistence farming and barter became the norm, and that long-distance land-based trade all but disappeared.

By the ninth century, however, the Byzantine Empire, which had almost collapsed in the two previous centuries, was again expanding. Enterprising merchants began to venture out on the Roman roads. Sea traffic, though harried by piracy, revived along the Adriatic and Black Sea coasts. Under the influence of a revitalized Byzantine Empire, the once barbarian Slavs and Bulgars began to form centralized kingdoms and to rebuild urban areas, generally around the courts of local princes. These included Pliska and Preslav in Bulgaria as early as the ninth century and Ras in Serbia in the eleventh. Cities stimulated trade in the interior of the Balkans, which slowly grew, despite the almost constant warfare characteristic of this period. By the twelfth century, mining reappeared, particularly in Serbia and in Bosnia, as the names of new towns such as Srebrenica and Olovo (Silverton and Leadville) attest. To develop mines, rulers encouraged foreigners, including German-speaking Saxons, to settle on their lands. Nevertheless, throughout the medieval period and well into the twentieth century, the average Balkan dweller remained a farmer.

Although most contemporary Balkan countries trace their ancestry back to medieval predecessors, the states that grew up in the Balkans beginning around the ninth century were not like modern nation-states. Medieval states were primarily the creation of charismatic rulers, who exerted nominal political control over as large a territory as possible. They generally incorporated local lords in adjacent lands, with either carrots (the promise of continued local autonomy and booty as the kingdom expanded at the expense of neighbors) or sticks (threats of being deposed and replaced by others more loyal). All states were, from a modern perspective, multinational, for they contained speakers of multiple languages and cultures. Although the highest elites in a given medieval state would likely speak the same language, no medieval ruler made any attempt to coerce his subjects to accept the customs or language of the sovereign.

The Byzantine Empire was undoubtedly the model for all the Balkan medieval kingdoms. Although it had been in crisis when the Slavs and Bulgars entered the region, in comparison to the motley group of invading tribes, Byzantium was still a well-ordered bureaucratic state with a functioning royal court, military, tax collection system, and centralized religion. Even as they competed with Byzantium, the Slavs and Bulgars learned from it and ultimately created, in effect, a series of mini-Byzantiums. In imitation of the Byzantine emperor, powerful local rulers attempted to develop among their subjects a feeling of loyalty. They built rich capital cities and established elaborate court rituals. They accepted Christianity for themselves and their subjects, and encouraged the appearance of state churches loyal to the ruler and often dependent on his patronage.

The first Balkan group to create its own state was the Bulgars. As early as 681, the marauding Bulgar chief Isperikh forced the Byzantines to cede territory south of the Danube to him. The Turkic-speaking Bulgars themselves appear not to have been very numerous, perhaps no more than ten thousand warriors who took over the leadership of a larger group of Slavs. By the early ninth century, the

Bulgars had created a centralized and powerful state. It was ruled primarily by a Turkic aristocracy, which over the next few hundred years became thoroughly Slavicized. In the period between the reigns of Khan Krum (803–14) and King Symeon I (893–927), this state expanded from a relatively small territory straddling the Danube to an enormous kingdom that controlled almost the entire Balkan Peninsula.

One can get a hint at the splendor of Simeon's court from the account of John the Exarch, written in the early tenth century:

> When some poor foreigner from afar approaches the Tsar's city and sees it, he is awed. And when he gets to the gates, when he enters and sees the buildings on both sides, embellished with stones and carved wood, he is amazed. And when he enters the compound and sees the tall roofs and churches, abundantly ornamented with precious stones, inlaid wood and velvets, enters the palace—with its marble and copper, silver and gold—he realizes that he does not know what to compare this to ... but if he should happen to see the Tsar inside, sitting, wearing his mantle set with pearls, with the golden necklace about his neck, and bracelets on his arms, girdled with his purple belt with his sword hanging at his side, flanked by his boyars wearing their golden necklaces, belts and bracelets—well, when he returns home if someone asks "what did you see there," he will answer "I can find no words for it."[4]

In the late twelfth century, a Serbian state began its ascent in the southwest Balkans. Beginning from the humble principality of Zeta (more or less today's Montenegro), the Serbs expanded rapidly between 1190, when King Stefan I Nemanja (reigned 1166–96) removed the Serbs from Byzantine control, and the mid-fourteenth century, when, under the rule of Stefan Uroš IV Dušan (1331–55), the Serbs controlled large territories in what is today southern Serbia, Kosovo, Albania, and Greece. Like Symeon of Bulgaria, Dušan dreamed not merely of controlling a great Serbian kingdom but of inheriting the Byzantine Empire itself. Having moved his capital from Raška (in the south of today's Serbia) to Skopje, Dušan proclaimed himself emperor of the Serbs, Greeks, Bulgarians, and Albanians. The law code he promulgated in 1349, clearly derived from Byzantine sources, illustrates the high level of sophistication of Serbian feudal society. Though it mandated cruel punishments for many offenses, it was liberal regarding the rights and privileges of non-Serbians in Dušan's lands, allowing Greek and Saxon towns to live under the laws they followed before being conquered.

When the Slavs overran the Balkan Peninsula, they were unable to capture the walled cities along the Adriatic coast. During the medieval period, one of them, Ragusa (Dubrovnik), grew into a small but powerful city-state. Though the city's leaders remained mostly Latin and later Italian speakers, Dubrovnik's populace was from an early period a mixed group including Slavs and Latin speakers. Inhabitants of a small city-state (the walled city itself probably never had a population greater than seventy-five hundred), Dubrovnik residents relied on their wits to survive. Politically, Dubrovnik was an oligarchy, led for much of its existence by some one hundred noble families. Dubrovnik was able to exploit its protected site and favorable geographic position as the last major port between the Adriatic and the Mediterranean, and as the terminus of land routes from Bosnia and Serbia to the sea, to develop into a leading commercial center by the eleventh century. Ragusan merchants traveled extensively, taking advantage of their republic's independent foreign policy to carve out trading opportunities. In the twelfth and thirteenth centuries, the Ragusans specialized in such products as skins, wool, honey, and salt. By the fourteenth and fifteenth centuries, they were busy trading lead and silver mined in Serbia and Bosnia.

A Christian Land

It is difficult to re-create a picture of everyday life in the late medieval period. What we do know for certain is that the majority of the population was involved one way or another with agriculture. Whether farmers were slaves, serfs, or freemen, most probably never ventured very far from the places they were born, and they used agricultural techniques and implements that were little changed from Roman times, which can be seen either as a sign of stagnation or a recognition that such agricultural practices were effective, if not exceptionally productive. According to Jacques Lefort, the average peasant household in the Balkans would have consisted of around five people, who would have had a single ox, a cow, a pig, four goats or sheep, and poultry.[5] They would have lived in relatively simple wooden houses surrounded by small plots of land on which they grew cereals, fruits, and vegetables. In coastal regions, olive and grape production was common. Peasant families paid a variety of taxes to local landlords, monasteries, or directly to the state, and in general, we can guess that even in the best of times peasant families did not produce significantly larger amounts than required to pay taxes and what was necessary for their own survival.

None of the medieval Balkan kingdoms would survive directly into the early modern period, as all were overrun by the Ottoman Empire between the late fourteenth and late fifteenth centuries. As a result, beyond vague memories of bygone glory, little was passed down to posterity from the medieval Balkan political experience. What did endure, however, was the cultural and religious legacy of Christianization.

Christianity had a number of advantages that ensured its eventual triumph over paganism. For one thing, it was well organized. With a strong hierarchy centered in either Constantinople or Rome, it could send a coherent and consistent message to the people over a long period. After an early period of hesitation, Christianity was usually supported by local political leaders, who saw it as a unifying ideology, and who therefore encouraged and supported the work of the well-organized clerics. Furthermore, Christianity was flexible in its ability to incorporate preexisting practices, thereby making the transition from paganism to Christianity relatively smooth. Finally, it produced lasting texts, both visual and literary. Most obvious were imposing and copiously decorated church buildings, which came to dominate the landscape of both the few urban areas and rural centers. Churches, in turn, sponsored the production of literary texts, which, even despite low levels of literacy, provided a permanent tradition that the illiterate pagan priests could not match.

Although the formal split between the Eastern and Western churches would not occur until 1054, deep divisions between them appeared much earlier. Thus, when evangelization was undertaken in the eighth and ninth centuries, Rome and Byzantium were rivals for converts among the Balkan pagans. In the end, the line of cleavage between the Latin (Roman Catholic) and the Greek (Orthodox) churches would run through the middle of the peninsula. This seemingly neat picture, however, masks a more complex reality. One can view the process of Christianization in the Balkans as a triangular struggle in which local Slav leaders attempted to achieve as much control over local church affairs as possible by playing Rome and Constantinople against each other. In principle, a medieval ruler who accepted Christianity ceded control over the religious life of his kingdom. Nevertheless, Balkan rulers realized they could exploit their position between the two great Christian religious centers. By threatening to convert to whichever branch of the church offered the most autonomy, they pressed for, and often received, powers usually reserved for Rome or Constantinople, such as the authority to appoint bishops and the right to use their own language for the liturgy.

Monasticism was a central part of Byzantine and later Balkan Christian life. The first monastery in Constantinople was founded in the late fourth century, and there were already almost thirty monasteries in the city by the mid-sixth century. As opposed to the Western church where monks were mostly bound to centralized orders, Byzantine monastic life was centered in individual monasteries. In the cities, monks provided extensive social services, manning hospitals, inns, and schools. Those in the countryside generally formed self-sufficient agricultural communities, in some cases richly supported by noble patrons through gifts of lands and serfs. Monks, who had to remain celibate and from whom the higher clergy were exclusively drawn, were considered holier and more spiritual than parish priests, who by contrast were required to marry.

Powerful monasteries were founded throughout the Balkans. When Bulgaria became Christianized, for example, a number of the disciples of Cyril and Methodius, particularly St. Kliment and St. Naum, founded monastic centers in today's Macedonia. John of Rila moved from a monastery near the then–capital Preslav to the inaccessible Rila Mountains to lead a solitary life. Other monks followed, however, and by 930, his disciples had founded a monastic house that exists to this day. Although there were both male and female monasteries, the greatest center of Orthodox monastic life was the exclusively male Holy Mountain (Mount Athos), on a peninsula in northern Greece. This self-governing community is the only institution to have survived from the Balkan Middle Ages to the present. The first monks came to Athos in the early ninth century, living an ascetic life on this rocky peninsula. By the middle of that century, there were sufficient monks to necessitate the construction of a lavra (an arrangement in which monks live in separate though nearby cells but come together for prayer). By the tenth century, coenobitic monasteries (in which all property was held in

Figure 2.2. Excavations at the Church of Saints Clement and Panteleimon in Ohrid, Macedonia, 2007. Photograph by David W. Montgomery.

common and monks performed duties collectively) were organized, and Athos was recognized as a self-governing monastic community under an elected head. Although the first Athonite monks spoke Greek, in time other branches of the Orthodox Church founded or took over existing monasteries. By the end of the Byzantine period, tens of thousands of monks inhabited Mount Athos. Today, only a few thousand remain, but they still live according to the ancient monastic laws as a self-regulating community.

The most visible effect of Christianization, however, was in art and architecture. Although the first artists who built and decorated churches in the Balkans were undoubtedly imported from Constantinople, the appearance of hybrid works of art and architecture that blend typical Byzantine styles with local particularities indicate that native artists emerged quickly. One striking example is the haunting icon of St. Theodore (in the National Museum in Sofia), made of painted ceramic tiles. While the saint's austere face and piercing gaze are typical of Byzantine painting, the tiles are an artistic material more typical of Central Asia than of Byzantium and probably reflect the oriental roots of the Turkic Bulgars.

In the long run, however, the most important long-term influence of Christianization was its contribution to the advent of literacy among the Slavs. The first alphabet for writing a Slavic language was developed by the missionary brothers Cyril and Methodius, who had been raised in a bilingual Slav-Greek environment near Salonika. The language into which Cyril and Methodius translated the basic texts necessary for the purposes of evangelical work, now called Old Church Slavic, proved comprehensible across the entire Slavic medieval world, and it remains the religious language of Slavic Orthodox Christians to this day. An Old Church Slavic literary culture gradually developed throughout the Balkans during the medieval period, flourishing at the courts of various rulers and in the great monastic centers. This culture easily crossed existing political boundaries, and itinerant Orthodox monks carried texts as far afield as Russia.

While most written work was purely religious in character, with saint's lives and sermons being the most widespread genres, there is also evidence of secular writing. The most touching text of the pre-Ottoman period is a lament for her dead son written by the Serbian noblewoman Jefimija (Jelena Mrnjavčević, 1349–1405) and preserved on the back of an icon now kept at the Hilander Monastery on Mount Athos. This lovely poem indicates that, whatever historical distance may separate us from the Middle Ages, some emotions remain universal: "Little icon, but a great gift, which bears the most holy images of the Lord and the most pure Mother of God, presented by a great and holy man to my baby boy, Uglješa, who in his innocent infancy was taken into the eternal family and his body, created in sin, was buried in the grave. Grant, Lord Christ, and You, O pure Mother of God, to me, miserable, that I should see the rising of my soul, and that I see the souls of those who bore me and of my little son whom I bore, for whom grief ever burns in my heart, overcome by the bonds of motherhood."[6]

Notes

1. See, for example, the five-volume series *Histoire de la vie Privée*, edited by Philippe Ariès and Georges Duby (Paris: Seuil, 1985–87). Published in English between 1987 and 1891 as *A History of Private Life* (Cambridge: Harvard University Press).
2. Quoted in Speros 1997, 8.
3. Quoted in Barford 2001, 61.
4. Dinekov 1969, translation by Andrew Wachtel.
5. Lefort 2002.
6. Original text at https://otacmilic.com/stihovi-jefimije-prve-srpske-pesnikinje-tuga-za-mladencem-ugljesom/ Accessed June 11, 2018, translation by Andrew Wachtel.

References

Barford, Paul M. 2001. *The Early Slavs: Culture and Society in Early Medieval Eastern Europe*. London: British Museum.
Dinekov, Petr, ed. 1969. "Six Days," *Iz starata b'lgarska literature*. Sofia: B'lgarski pisatel.
Evans, Helen C., and William D. Wixom, eds. 1997. *The Glory of Byzantium: Art and Culture of the Middle Byzantine Era, A.D. 843–1261*. New York: Metropolitan Museum of Art.
Laiou, Angeliki E., ed. 2002. *The Economic History of Byzantium: From the Seventh through the Fifteenth Century*. Washington, DC: Dumbarton Oaks.
Lefort, Jacques. 2002. "The Rural Economy, Seventh–Twelfth Centuries." In *The Economic History of Byzantium: From the Seventh through the Fifteenth Century*, edited by A. E. Laiou, 231–314. Washington, DC: Dumbarton Oaks.

Vryonis, Speros P., Jr. 1997. "Byzantine Society and Civilization." In *The Glory of Byzantium: Art and Culture of the Middle Byzantine Era, A.D. 843–1261*, edited by H. C. Evans and W. D. Wixom, 4–19. New York: Metropolitan Museum of Art.

Wachtel, Andrew Baruch. 2008. *The Balkans in World History*. Oxford: Oxford University Press.

ANDREW WACHTEL is Rector of Narxoz University in Almaty, Kazakhstan. He is a fellow of the American Academy of Arts & Sciences, a member of the Council on Foreign Relations, and an active translator from multiple Slavic languages.

3 Crimes and Misdemeanors: Scenes of Everyday Life among the Gendarmerie in Ottoman Macedonia, ca. 1900

İpek K. Yosmaoğlu

In an episode of Comedy Central's award-winning show *Key and Peele*, the actors satirize a Macedonian café owner's (over)reaction when the customers demand to know the difference between the restaurant's specialty, *kebapi*, and *cevapi*, served at the Albanian café across the street. Obviously offending the owner's sensibilities about Macedonian cuisine, the terrified diners run away as the man starts stabbing the map on the wall with a chef's knife, repeatedly screaming: "They [Albanians] are there; we [Macedonians] are here!" At the Albanian café, where they take refuge, the couple is welcomed with a similar reaction at their suggestion that the two dishes seem essentially the same. The episode ends as they make haste to the nearest McDonald's.[1] Keegan-Michael Key and Jordan Peele may overestimate the average TV viewer's appreciation for the finer points of European geography and culinary culture, but the sketch is universally appealing because it so successfully pokes fun at a universal scourge: what Freud called "the narcissism of small differences."[2]

Macedonia, and the Balkan Peninsula as a whole, is unfortunately associated with all sorts of ills stemming from the narcissism of small differences, such as endemic and atavistic violence, political fragmentation, and civil strife, making the imaginary Macedonian café owner an all too probable character. This is due in large part to the wars that have afflicted the region, but also in no small measure to a specific way of representation employed by western European scholars and travelers in the region who sought to present it as exotic, foreign, and close yet distant, or as "the West of the East."[3] But violence in the Balkans, just like violence in any other part of the world, is neither timeless nor irrational; it has context-specific reasons and a historical background. The kind of violence that we tend to identify as specifically "Balkan"—namely, ethnic violence—has its roots in the nineteenth century and, by most accounts, in the scramble for territory during what in hindsight seems to be the inexorable collapse of the Ottoman Empire.

It is hard to imagine the details of "everyday life in the Balkans" during this period when continuous waves of wars and the violent process of nation-state formation rocked the region, not least because the everyday deeds and woes of ordinary people rarely leave their mark in the historical record. For this reason, I have chosen to present here examples that illustrate not the shocking and the extraordinary but the mundane, petty details of life as a small contribution toward our imaginary of normal concerns of normal people in the Balkans. More specifically, I present a few vignettes of life among the Ottoman gendarmerie, a group of people who were assigned the impossible task of maintaining peace and security in the war-torn region of Macedonia—a task that their very presence made even harder.

The Gendarmerie

The first gendarmerie force in the Ottoman Empire was formed in 1879 based on the earlier *asâkir-i zaptiye* (military police) organization.[4] The gendarmes that concern us here, however, belonged to a different group established in 1904 as an auxiliary force of the regular army, modeled after the Italian carabinieri, and under the command of an Italian general, Degiorgis Pasha. From the beginning, the new gendarmerie force was met by suspicion and even hostility by members of the Ottoman Third Army stationed in Macedonia. The new "reformed" gendarmerie was the direct result of the Mürzsteg Reform program, initiated or, as far as the Ottomans were concerned, imposed by the European powers following the Ilinden Uprising against Ottoman rule in Macedonia in the summer of 1903.

Recruits into the reformed gendarmerie joined the force voluntarily. They were local men who often served in areas close to their place of birth, distinct from regular army conscripts who came from various parts of the empire and were subject to obligatory conscription. The typical recruit was a poor and illiterate young man from the countryside for whom the promise of a salary, however meager and irregularly paid, made up for the hardships the job involved.[5] As we shall see later in this chapter, there were also certain "fringe benefits" associated with the position that made it seem like a reliable occupation in an environment with few other prospects for upward social mobility. The select few who were able to read and write were immediately hired with the rank of sergeant.

Since the new gendarmerie's mission was to promote peace and security in an area where the majority of the population consisted of Christians (albeit of fractious sects), the initiative required that Christians should be included among its numbers. Even though hundreds of Christians did indeed join the new gendarmerie force—due in some measure to specific incentives, such as the "exemption from [the] military exemption tax" normally paid by non-Muslim males—their representation never reached the desired levels, and an esprit de corps did not develop sufficiently to resolve the mutual suspicion between Muslim and Christian gendarmes entirely.[6]

Muslim and Christian members of the reformed gendarmerie attended the school in Salonika, donned their new uniforms, and bore the brunt of resentment on the part of regular soldiers as well as the "older" gendarmerie together. Upon graduation, they were dispatched as auxiliary forces to different garrisons in the region, and while some must have dutifully performed their tasks, the deeds of those who did not were more likely to have left a written record, which constitutes most of the material for this chapter. It is for this reason that one may get an impression of the gendarmes as an unruly bunch as likely to misbehave and loot as any others with access to means of violence at the time, but one should take the following examples with a grain of salt.

Tobacco and Everyday Crimes

Since the focus of this chapter is "everyday" forms of misbehavior rather than more egregious infractions, I will not mention acts of violence committed against the civilian population by the gendarmes other than noting that while these were regular occurrences, members of the reformed gendarmerie were relatively better disciplined and not involved in such crimes to the same extent that the older gendarmerie units, irregulars, and common soldiers were.[7] Most common among their misdeeds was tobacco smuggling. This was a frequently and widely committed crime perpetrated not only by members of the gendarmerie, reformed and otherwise, but also by soldiers, civilians, and career criminals. In fact, the volume of smuggled tobacco circulating in the local markets rivaled the legal product according to some estimates.

Tobacco was not an ordinary consumer good; it was as essential as bread to men and women (and even some children) in the Balkans. It had first been introduced into the Ottoman Empire in the sixteenth century. By the seventeenth century, the use of tobacco was widespread, but the legality of its consumption remained dubious. Just like the coffee it usually accompanied, tobacco was viewed by some scholars of Islam and members of the ruling elite as a dangerous substance, not only because of its effects on the mind and body but also because of the social anxieties it produced thanks to its use in public places of gathering, fostering new forms of sociability in the early modern Ottoman Empire.[8] By the nineteenth century, however, none but the extreme purist considered tobacco a sinful substance; cigarettes had replaced the more cumbersome pipes and hookahs, and tobacco had taken root, literally and figuratively, all over the Ottoman Empire. The coffeehouses where it was widely consumed were places where Muslims, Christians, and Jews met and intermingled. Its cultivation, preparation, and trade constituted a lucrative business in the Balkans, especially in Bulgaria, Greece, and Ottoman Macedonia.[9]

The cultivation and sale of tobacco was strictly regulated in the Ottoman Empire by a state monopoly that dispensed banderoles to producers to be affixed to tobacco products, just like the small holographic stamps on cigarette packages today. After the Ottoman Empire declared insolvency of its public debt in 1879, an international consortium was established to oversee the payment of its foreign

Figure 3.1. Tobacco and shisha culture remain popular throughout the region. Here, a young Bosnian woman blows smoke rings in Sarajevo, 2014. Photograph by Roska Vrgova.

creditors. The Ottoman Public Debt Administration (OPDA), or *la Dette*, as it was commonly known, collected certain revenues of the Ottoman state and earmarked them for servicing the public debt. After 1883, the OPDA transferred the tobacco concession to another international consortium called the Régie des Tabacs de l'Empire Ottoman, which would still pay the OPDA the fixed amount of 750,000 Turkish Liras per year and leave the collection of the tobacco tithe from the cultivators to the OPDA.[10]

The Ottoman government was antagonistic toward the Régie and allowed the sale of contraband tobacco to continue more or less unchecked despite repeated pleas and protests of the Régie administrators until the revolution of 1908, after which government forces controlled tobacco smuggling more effectively. Considering the attitude of the government and the small cultivators, joined in their resentment against the Régie, and the vital role cigarettes played in the lives of people, including gendarmes and soldiers who were supposed to prevent smuggling, it should come as no surprise that the sale of contraband tobacco rivaled that of the banderoled product. Carrying guns and wearing uniforms made the soldiers and gendarmes more, rather than less, likely to engage in tobacco smuggling. They did, however, occasionally find themselves on opposing sides of this profitable trade, as was the case one summer day in 1907, when a gendarme, suspicious of the load a soldier was carrying, searched him and seized the banned product. Instead of receiving a reward, he was beaten up by the smuggler's fellow soldiers.[11] This conscientious gendarme was the exception rather than the rule, as attested by documents produced by the command of the reformed gendarmerie forces in Salonika. Two, for instance, from the gendarmerie division in Cuma-i Bâlâ (contemporary Blagoevgrad) were caught taking bribes from smugglers in March 1907. Both were discharged from the gendarmerie, and one was sentenced to one month in prison.[12] According to General Degiorgis, this was not sufficient punishment for smugglers and those who facilitated their activities; he recommended that they be sent to Yemen after their dismissal from the force—a punishment that was often tantamount to death at the time, as the Ottomans were fighting a hopeless insurgency in the region. The frequency of complaints against gendarmes engaging in the contraband tobacco trade suggests, however, that the incentives remained greater than the potential for punishment.[13]

Drunk and Disorderly Conduct and Other Misdemeanors

Another social activity that often got the gendarmes into trouble was drinking. Despite the injunction against drinking in Islam, consumption of alcohol in the Ottoman Balkans was never limited to the non-Muslims. Taverns, just like coffeehouses, were public places where Muslim and non-Muslim males mixed, if under the shunning gaze of their more pious neighbors. By the nineteenth century, in port cities like Salonika, beer gardens and cafés where men and women mixed had sprung up along fashionable avenues. Such establishments were usually not the kinds of places where gendarmes and common soldiers frequented. They could more often be seen in taverns where the crowds were of more modest backgrounds and jugs of wine cost considerably less. The combination of guns and alcohol rarely results in fortuitous outcomes, however, and countless of these men found themselves at the brink of being court-martialed for brandishing a weapon or getting into fights after a night of heavy drinking.[14]

A particularly Ottoman venue of socialization was the *muhallebici*, the "pudding shop," that was not as seedy as the tavern but not quite as respectable as the European-style cafés. Such a pudding shop was evidently the setting for an incident that the Italian general Degiorgis could only describe as "detestable." The incident that so shocked him concerned a certain Yusuf Ziya, a corporal employed as a teacher in the gendarmerie school, and Ahmed Ali, one of the pupils in the school. Several people at the school had noticed that Yusuf Ziya called on Ahmed Ali rather frequently and on at least one occasion after the sounding of the curfew. Their behavior raised an alarm after one of the students reportedly overheard the two setting up a rendezvous at a pudding shop in Salonika. Rıza Adem, a student and former telegram clerk, was also accused of misconduct because he had served as an "intermediary" between the two according to the report. More specifically, Yusuf Ziya had asked Rıza Adem to read the words he had scribbled in Morse code on the blackboard. The coded message read, "I am burning for this lad; if you can convince him, I will pay you a Lira." Yusuf Ziya then handed Rıza Adem a letter, presumably to be delivered to Ahmed Ali.[15]

Figure 3.2. Kino Bosna, a former cinema turned into an occasional bar and music venue—especially popular on Mondays—in Sarajevo, continues the tavern tradition, 2013. Photograph by Roska Vrgova.

General Degiorgis was scandalized by the conduct of the three and demanded an investigation. When students and other gendarmes of higher rank at the school confirmed the rumors, he personally wrote to the inspector general of the three provinces of Rumeli for the direct dispatch of all three to Yemen after their dismissal from the school. "In order to present an effective example to the students, the gendarmes, and the teachers" he wrote, "the severest punishment is absolutely necessary and desirable for the morale and the discipline of the school and its men."[16] It is not clear, however, whether his wish was granted as speedily, or if at all, since the response of the Inspectorate noted that such decisions were "under the authority of the General Command" and added simply that General Degiorgis's request had been thence transferred.[17]

Even though we do not know how exactly this incident was resolved, it still provides important clues about the shifting spectrum of acceptable behavior and normative conception of morality at the time—not only among the gendarmes in the Balkans but also in the broader Ottoman world. Several things are worthy of note here, especially considering how one might assume this incident would be interpreted under current understandings of normal sexual behavior and relations between teacher and student. For instance, we would consider the excessive and implicitly sexual attention Yusuf Ziya showered on Ahmed Ali a case of sexual harassment. We may also find General Degiorgis's reaction predictable, if not entirely reasonable, based on the assumption that homosexuality was anathema, especially among men in uniform at the time.

There are certain issues that complicate the picture, however. First, we do not know for sure if Ahmed Ali considered himself to be harassed. His conversation with Yusuf Rıza, at least as it was related in the report, is the only (weak) hint that he may have actually been a willing participant:

[Yusuf Rıza] "Would you meet with me some place today?"

[Ahmed Ali] "Yes, I would"

[YR] "Where can I find you?"

[AA] "At the pudding shop"

[YR] "Do you have any money"

[AA] "No"

[YR] "Then let me give you some."

It was this apparent willingness to go along with Yusuf Rıza that ultimately got the young gendarme into trouble. "Because he did not inform any of his superiors of the treatment he received," the report concluded that he was "of low morals."[18] Even though our scant knowledge of this "sordid affair," as General Degiorgis would call it, is not enough to conjecture about Ahmed Ali's agency in his presumed seduction by his superior, we do know from a soldier's diary during the First World War that harassment was common enough among the Ottoman military at a comparable time and place.[19] Unfortunately, there is no diary among the documents in question here, which means Ahmed Ali's own opinions on the matter will remain a mystery.

The second, and more important, issue that complicates our interpretation of this incident a hundred years on is the fact that the spectrum of acceptable sexual behavior in the early modern Ottoman Empire was much wider than in modern times. While "homosexuality" as we understand it today did not quite exist as a separate social category in the early modern Ottoman Empire, male homosexuality was considered within the normal realm of human sexuality—if not openly condoned.[20] Starting in the nineteenth century, however, the modernization of social norms and practices redefined the borders of acceptable sexual behavior, and male homosexuality was pushed to the margins of respectable society. By the turn of the twentieth century, the prevailing public opinion shunned sexuality outside the heteronormative and familial framework, and organizations such as schools and the military were expected to enforce these new norms under pain of punishment even as social practice evidently continued as before.[21] The incident described here took place at the cusp of the emergence of a new morality that did not tolerate male homoeroticism and viewed it as an affront to modern society. General Degiorgis and the Inspector General's Office agreed that the involved gendarmes should be disciplined, but it is worth noting that the response of the inspectorate was muted compared with Degiorgis's apparent disgust, and its referral of the matter to the General Command without comment instead of moving forward with repeated demands of dismissal and dispatch to Yemen reveal a level of equanimity in striking contrast with the Italian general's reaction.

Everyday Mischief

Smoking, drinking, getting in fights, and setting up dates: these are acts that imply ordinariness by their very definition. Yet these were not ordinary times in Ottoman Macedonia. The region was in the middle of an insurgency, violence was endemic, and the Ottoman Empire's rule was about to come to a bloody end. But people, even those with some form of agency in the turmoil that changes political systems and shifts boundaries, such as the gendarmes we have seen here, commonly gravitate toward the familiar and the mundane. This is why we can easily recognize their concerns, desires, and petty fights as our own, even if we cannot locate Salonika on a map or understand a word of the languages they spoke. This is also why the sketch by Key and Peele is universally hilarious: we can all see the folly in the narcissism of small differences regardless of time and place—even as we rationalize the violence that they cause as "ethnic conflict."

Notes

1. Comedy Central, *Key and Peele,* Season 4, Episode 5, October 22, 2014.
2. Freud 1961, 72.
3. Skopetea, 1992; Todorova 2009.
4. Alyot 1947, 113.
5. Basbakanlik Osmanli Arsivleri (Prime Ministry Ottoman Archives, Istanbul, Turkey, BOA), General Degirogis to the General Inspectorate of Rumeli, May 12, 1907, TFR.I.AS 54/5318.
6. Gülsoy 2000, 124–126.
7. For examples see Yosmaoğlu 2014, 267–287.
8. Grehan 2006.
9. Neuburger 2013.
10. Birdal 2010.
11. BOA, TFR.I.AS 49/4852, Degiorgis Pasha's letter, Salonika, July 24, 1907.
12. BOA, TFR.I.AS 49/4867, Degiorgis Pasha to Hüseyin Hilmi Pasha, June 1, 1907.
13. BOA, TFR.I.AS 49/4867, Memorandum of Reformed Gendarmerie Command, Salonika, May 8, 1907.
14. BOA, TFR.I.AS 56/ 5516, Degiorgis Pasha to Hüseyin Hilmi Pasha, January 30, 1907; TFR.I.AS 49/4867, Degiorgis Pasha to Hüseyin Hilmi Pasha, July 2, 1907.
15. BOA, TFR.I.AS 49/4867, undated report.
16. BOA, TFR.I.AS 49/4867, Degiorgis Pasha to Hüseyin Hilmi Pasha, June 27, 1907.
17. BOA, TFR.I.AS 49/4867, Inspectorate to Degiorgis Pasha, June 29, 1907.
18. BOA, TFR.I.AS 49/4867, undated report.
19. Tamari 2011.
20. Ze'evi 2006; el-Rouayheb 2009.
21. Students at the Public Charity School (Dâr-ül-Aceze) risked termination of their enrollment if they engaged in "immoral" acts, BOA, MF.MKT 896/55 (February 2, 1906). Even being a tribal notable's son at the Imperial Tribal School did not protect one against such punishment, as was the case for a boy who let himself "be kissed" and another who visited his friend's cot "in the middle of the night."; BOA, MF.MKT 873/26 (July 29, 1905).

References

Basbakanlik Osmanli Arsivleri. Prime Ministry Ottoman Archives. BOA. Istanbul, Turkey.
Alyot, Halim. 1947. *Türkiye'de Zabıta*. Ankara: İçişleri Bakanlığı Yayınları.
Birdal, Murat. 2010. *The Political Economy of Ottoman Public Debt*. London: I. B. Tauris.
Comedy Central. *Key and Peele*. Season 4, Episode 5, October 22, 2014.
el-Rouayheb, Khaled. 2009. *Before Homosexuality in the Arab-Islamic World, 1500–1800*. Chicago: University of Chicago Press.
Freud, Sigmund. 1961. *Civilization and Its Discontents*. New York: W. W. Norton.
Grehan, James. 2006. "Smoking and 'Early Modern' Sociability: The Great Tobacco Debate in the Ottoman Middle East (Seventeenth to Eighteenth centuries)." *American Historical Review* 111: 1352–1377.
Gülsoy, Ufuk. 2000. *Osmanlı Gayrimüslimlerinin Askerlik Serüveni*. Istanbul: Simurg.
Neuburger, Mary. 2013. *Balkan Smoke: Tobacco and the Making of Modern Bulgaria*. Ithaca, NY: Cornell University Press.
Tamari, Salim, ed. 2011. *The Year of the Locust: A Soldier's Diary and the Erasure of Palestine's Ottoman Past*. Los Angeles: University of California Press.
Skopetea, Elli. 1992. *Ē Dysē tēs Anatolēs*, Athens: Gnōsē.
Todorova, Maria. 2009. *Imagining the Balkans*. Oxford: Oxford University Press.
Yosmaoğlu, İpek. 2014. *Blood Ties: Religion, Violence, and the Politics of Nationhood in Ottoman Macedonia, 1878–1908*. Ithaca, NY: Cornell University Press.
Ze'evi, Dror. 2006. *Producing Desire: Changing Sexual Discourse in the Ottoman Middle East, 1500–1900*. Berkeley: University of California Press.

İPEK K. YOSMAOĞLU is Associate Professor of History at Northwestern University. She is author of *Blood Ties: Religion, Violence, and the Politics of Nationhood in Ottoman Macedonia*.

4 It's What's Inside That Counts: Furnishing the Modern in the Apartments of Socialist Yugoslavia

Patrick Hyder Patterson

Present-day travelers to the places that once made up communist Europe often find the classic structures of socialist-era housing distinctly unappealing. Tall, forbidding apartment blocks executed in concrete and metal with a modernist hostility to adornment and (especially when new) not much softened with landscaping and greenery, these "ugly" constructions have become fixed in the imagination of the Western public as stereotypical symptoms of the insensitivities and inadequacies of Marxist-Leninist rule. During communist times, such buildings were the object of jokes and complaints among outsiders, and they seem no better liked by visitors today, a quarter century after the collapse of communism, when their dated style is aggravated by serious signs of age and weathering. As Kimberly Elman Zarecor observes in her history of Czechoslovakia's experimentation with new, mass-scale housing developments, "Few building types are as vilified as the socialist housing block."[1]

Building Blocks: Apartments as Progress

It is critical to recognize that when structures like these were new—and when socialism still appeared to be, for all practical purposes, the only way forward for Eastern Europe—they were genuinely welcomed at home as real accomplishments: comfortable, sensible, contemporary solutions to a lingering housing crisis. They offered many things that ordinary citizens in the socialist states wanted, and apartments in these buildings were highly sought after.[2] In the prosperous West, however, they got a decidedly different reception. Especially when judged against the styles favored by the more affluent classes of the United States, the most assertive exemplar of capitalism's achievements, they could look woefully inadequate. The new socialist developments bore little resemblance either to the colorful, buzzing, pedestrian-friendly streetscapes of what American urbanites have tended to think of as "real" cities or to the sheltered single-family retreats of the postwar American Dream in the suburbs. And so while the expert

Figure 4.1. A socialist architecture apartment complex in Belgrade, Serbia, 2014. Photograph by Radmila Vankoska.

opinions of architects and urban planners have often been much more forgiving, at times even celebratory, the big apartment blocks have remained, for the most part, a much-derided emblem of socialism.[3]

New block developments frequently appeared on the peripheries of expanding cities where open space was readily available. But a similar material and aesthetic divide can be found in the urban cores as well, where residential streets frequently mixed the flat concrete functionalism of socialist new construction with holdovers from earlier architectural periods. By 1989, many of these buildings were often in a state of decay and disrepair, due in part to the straitened finances of socialist governments and their citizens. Compounding the problem (if it is truly fair to call this a problem, since much of what is at issue here is a matter of differing habits, expectations, and tastes) was the comparative lifelessness of shopping streets in the communist world. To people accustomed to the flash and bang of the consumer economies of capitalism, something was missing. If the buildings themselves were thought to be "ugly," the overall environment was, in a word, "gray." Western commercial areas of the time were remarkable for the proliferation of bold advertising, colorful signage, and other attention-grabbing visual maneuvers meant to lure customers in a highly competitive environment. Their communist-zone counterparts, with some exceptions, seemed remarkable for the lack of these things.

The commercial amenities of socialist housing blocks, which the planners regularly outfitted with modest grocery stores and other small-scale services in adjacent ground-level structures meant to serve first and foremost the residents of the complex, did not do much to counter the outward impression of lifelessness.

Yet outward impressions can be misleading: for those living in the apartments nearby, these stores were, in fact, very convenient and often quite popular. Where these outlets have managed to survive in a new capitalist business landscape that now depends more on the economies of scale and cost-cutting efficiencies that socialism decided to do without—in order to provide full employment and more traditional neighborhood-based services—they are still well liked today. But they have never been able to offer the lively experience of concentrated consumer abundance that announces vitality in the dense High Street/Main Street urban cores and bustling shopping centers and malls of the West.

In the territories that used to make up socialist Yugoslavia, as in communist southeastern Europe more generally, big new housing blocks rose as a standard element of the state's effort to deliver an acceptable solution to insufficient and substandard housing. Even today, their distinctive appearance remains a prominent feature of urban centers across the region. But here, too, appearances can be deceiving: in some of the ex-Yugoslav republics, the proportion of citizens now living in detached homes is, on a countrywide basis, actually at the high end of the European spectrum.[4] Curiously, the big blocks have somehow become stereotypical without being truly typical. This was by no means the way everyone lived but rather a phenomenon of the cities and towns that were undergoing rapid expansion in socialist times and, indeed, prevalent in only certain parts of those urban areas.

That said, apartment living was extraordinarily important in Yugoslavia, particularly for new arrivals to towns and cities and for younger residents, especially couples, who were living for the first time away from the homes in which they grew up. As they moved in to their new apartments, they encountered a considerable range of building designs—a diversity still visible on the ground today. In contrast to other socialist states, the Yugoslav building and planning industry did not stipulate a narrow range of uniform, standardized apartment-building models to be deployed nationwide using prefab concrete panels.[5] Coupled with the distinctive Yugoslav system of enterprise autonomy through "worker self-management," the thoroughgoing decentralization of economic processes down to the level of the republics and municipalities led to far greater variety and "inadvertently saved the country" from the cookie-cutter uniformity of its socialist neighbors, so that Yugoslavia ended up in some ways "defying the stereotype of drearily monotonous prefabricated neighborhoods."[6] Nevertheless, even some of the most carefully planned housing block developments ended up disappointing their new residents, as happened with the high-profile New Belgrade (Novi Beograd) project in the 1960s, where the promised amenities and services fell far short of what residents expected, a problem that, as Brigitte Le Normand notes, "continued to plague New Belgrade throughout the socialist era."[7]

Outward Appearances: Residential Exteriors and Common Disregard

In the Yugoslav developments, as elsewhere in the communist world, a tendency toward rather stark, barren, and uninviting exterior spaces prevailed.

Under socialism (and in many cases, after socialism), the exterior environments of the big blocks and other apartment buildings were not just poorly outfitted, sparsely landscaped, and disconnected from a more sociable, intimate, human scale from the outset. They quite often ended up disregarded, little-used, and badly maintained later on as well. Why this neglect? Clearly, some of it was more or less "built-in" by design choices. In other cases, a failure to deliver on amenities and exterior improvements that actually had been planned made matters worse.[8] But there was another critical cause. Simply put, there was not much that Yugoslav apartment dwellers could do about the outward presentation or the broader exterior surroundings of the buildings in which they lived.

For the most part, ordinary citizens in socialist Yugoslavia seemed remarkably unconcerned with the way their apartment buildings looked from the outside. In the broader public discourse on housing issues, exterior appearances only rarely came up as a topic of reportage, advice, conversation, or debate. Instead, there seemed to be a generally shared agreement—in other words, a cultural principle—that individual residents would not be held accountable for the communal parts of their shared structures. Residing in a building that showed the public an unappealing face did not entail any serious charge against one's personal status. The architects' functionalist modernism may or may not have accorded well with the personal style of the residents, but no one much cared. My own time living in Yugoslavia, during what turned out to be the latter years of socialism in 1988–89, confirms that conclusion: while there was enormous attention and energy devoted to furnishings, decor, and other interior improvement projects, no one was especially worried about the exterior surfaces, grounds, and common spaces of their apartment houses. How all these non-private spaces looked when they were brand new was, for better or worse, someone else's responsibility. And how they ended up looking after they were lived in and used was someone else's problem.

Here it is instructive to note one stark contrast to the culture that developed around larger multi-unit structures: those who were comfortable enough to have a vacation home (*vikendica*; *vikendice* [pl]; Slovenian *vikend*) paid lots of attention to exterior appearances and landscaping. Some of this was no doubt due to the distinctive modes of use that such dwellings offered. Whether they were on the coast or in the mountains or countryside, these *vikendice* were typically meant to be enjoyed from the outside, too, so outdoor living spaces and external aesthetics mattered a great deal. Just as important, however, was the simple fact that as private proprietors, those who had such homes *could* do something about how their weekend getaways looked and felt from the outside. Here, homeowners themselves could shape exterior appearances in a personal and immediate fashion. Weekend homes occupied a big place in the public imagination—and sometimes even in the political commentary of Josip Broz Tito and other communist leaders, who wrestled with the question of whether *vikendice* were a sign that Yugoslav citizens, in their pursuit of a "Yugoslav Dream" of material abundance, had been seduced by consumerist values and developed an unhealthy attachment to comfort, luxury, status symbols, and inappropriate, un-socialist displays of wealth.⁹ In the end, though, the interest in vacation homes continued more or less unchecked by political pressures. Spending power was the real limitation. When it was not possible to build or to buy, it was still possible to plan and to dream, and the popular press frequently presented construction plans and photo essays featuring vacation homes and building layouts, like the dozens of designs and finished projects set forth in full color in *Lepe kuće* (Beautiful Houses), a special 1980 issue of the popular current affairs magazine *Duga* (Rainbow), published in Belgrade and read around the country.

But in the multi-unit structures that made up an increasingly important share of the housing stock available to urban Yugoslavs, it was usually difficult if not impossible for any particular resident to exert a direct influence on external appearances, even if that person happened to have strong ideas about these matters. And so, in apartment complexes, attention turned inward. The exteriors and landscaping of these buildings remained *socialized* space: common property subject to joint regulation and governance and only enhanced through communal action and shared expense—which, understandably, many were reluctant to offer, since there seemed to be little to gain by investing in improvements and not much to lose by just letting things go. Indoors, away from the common spaces, the situation was different. Here, the gains arising from new improvement projects would be effectively *privatized*. What was achieved in interior, personal space might indeed accrue to one's own individual status. The overriding principle was this: it's what's inside that counts.

What's Inside: Displaying the Value of the Individual in Interior Spaces

So if the exteriors of apartment buildings were largely ignored, what were Yugoslav citizens doing in—and doing with—the indoor spaces that they could control? How did they learn about and talk about their options, and how can we learn today about the choices they faced? As they set about furnishing and decorating the interiors of their homes, ordinary Yugoslavs found a rich collection of designs, models, and ideas in the mass media, one of the most important sources for understanding home life under communism. As mirrors of everyday experience, these media materials are not without their problems—not least because of their tendency to represent prescriptive argumentation about how things *should be*, rather than descriptive documentation of how things actually *were*, and the related worry that they may record only officially sanctioned views. Yet even in a society like communist Poland, where the media were under substantially greater pressure from government authorities than in Yugoslavia, popular magazines reporting on housing issues ultimately managed to move beyond serving as mere mouthpieces for the party-state's "interest in disciplining the home" to offer instead some degree of opposition, becoming venues in which "private homes were made public to assert individual histories over collective futures."[10]

Figure 4.2a and b. The deteriorating facade of a typical apartment building showing neglected maintenance common to the socialist period, and the inside of one of its apartments, where detail and care given show how residents value the interior space, 2017. Photograph by Adis Novic.

Especially in subject areas that were not highly sensitive, the Yugoslav press under communism operated with a comparatively high degree of autonomy, surprisingly unburdened by strict, top-down party directives or sharp prepublication censorship. This freedom was even more evident for publications and coverage concerned with fairly "safe" topics like home improvement and interior design or consumer affairs more generally. In fields like these without immediate links to high politics, perceived excesses might occasionally trigger some ideological pushback and in-print debate, but there is little evidence to indicate that media presentations of residential living were geared in a slavish, mechanical way to any party line. The mass media's images and ideas of home life were consequently much more than a set of prescriptive behavioral guidelines. Moreover, business enterprises operating autonomously in the system of self-management no longer followed the dictates of centralized production planning but were instead, to a notable extent, trying to respond to consumer demand. The home furnishings and related products that were featured (and in many cases, heavily advertised) in the Yugoslav mass media should therefore be seen as far more reflective of what manufacturers and retailers thought customers *did want* than what party ideologists thought they *should want*.

Feature films and television programming, for example, often sought to capture the look and feel of residential culture across the country—in other words, how "real" Yugoslavs were living—with careful attention to the details of home and apartment interiors. Some of the country's most popular television series in the 1970s and 1980s, for example, depicted the efforts of more-or-less ordinary citizens to equip dwellings in the new blocks with all the trappings of the consumerist Good Life: impressive furniture, stylish decor, modern appliances, and fashionable accessories.[11] But the richest collection of evidence about the arrangement of home interiors comes from the many mass-circulation magazines that relied on engaging, up-to-date reporting and colorful graphics to connect consumers with the latest styles, trends, and products in the stores. The most important of these was *Naš dom* (Our Home), a Ljubljana-based monthly that appeared in both Serbo-Croatian and Slovenian editions and was the most widely read home-improvement publication at the time. Features, news items, and promotional pieces on residential furnishings and decor, along with increasingly sophisticated advertising in these fields, also appeared in a wide range of news, current affairs, and lifestyle periodicals, including some targeted at particular market segments, such as the popular women's magazines *Praktična žena* (Practical Woman), *Svijet* (The World), and *Naša žena* (Our Woman). Together these products of the mass media serve as an invaluable guide to what was happening, and what people hoped to make happen, within the walls of the country's private residential spaces.

One unavoidable conclusion that emerges from the media of the times is that the transformation of the Yugoslav home was, from the 1960s onward, big business and a major topic of public attention and conversation. The pages of *Naš dom*, for example, were notable for their extensive advertisements, many of them in color, and for the way that even ostensibly informational coverage called attention to the products of Yugoslav enterprises. From the outset, advertising was in fact such a prominent feature of the periodical that one reader wrote to complain: "I hope that the magazine will not with time turn into one big advertisement. Every time I look at it, there are always more of them."[12]

As that comment suggests, the broader public conversation about the quality of residential life in Yugoslavia reflected a wide range of opinions and tastes. There were competing values and, with them, disagreements at times. Yugoslavia was a notoriously complicated society, and its citizens used and improved their homes in ways so rich and diverse that they defy any clear-cut, comprehensive characterization. Nevertheless, some useful generalizations will hold, and in the end, it is possible to identify a prevailing *ethos of the contemporary home* that took shape under Yugoslav socialism, one strongly influenced by the distinctive experience of urban apartment living.

Private Spaces, Shared Values: Socialist Yugoslavia's Ethos of the Contemporary Home

In speaking of a dominant ethos here, I mean to stress that in towns and cities (and in rural households that aspired to urban models), the *expressive, communicative quality* of residential life—in other words, what people were saying with their homes—was commonly marked by a set of recurring primary points of emphasis. These five key cultural complexes were centered on rationality, culture, modernity, individuality, and status.[13] Linked with each of these were several related subsidiary values, all of which were frequently expressed in the way residential interiors were outfitted:

- Rationality: economy, efficiency, practicality, time savings, scientific planning
- Culture: informed judgment, good taste, simplicity, moderation, modesty, harmony
- Modernity: progress, continual improvement, freshness, fashion, Europeanness
- Individuality: expressiveness, creativity, style, resourcefulness, problem-solving
- Status: wealth, comfort, achievement, sophistication, distinction, worldliness

We must be careful, of course, not to approach the categories identified here in a rigid, reductionist way. The specifications are not exhaustive, and the classifications are not exclusive. In some cases, there may be considerable overlap among the groupings. Inventive resourcefulness, for example, could sometimes be as much a manifestation of rationality as of individuality, while designing one's apartment with a self-consciously "European" aesthetic might simultaneously communicate a sense of not just modernity but rationality, individuality, status, and culture as well. But with such caveats in mind, this summary can serve as a good and generally reliable guide, for it captures many of the principal values and purposes that Yugoslav apartment-dwellers had in mind as they set about furnishing and decorating their homes—in other words, what counted for them in the spaces they inhabited, and how they made what was inside count.

The strong emphasis on rationality in the ethos of the contemporary home that emerged in socialist Yugoslavia reflected to some extent the spread of the dominant values of the country's communist leadership, with its scientific, materialist, rationalist, and technocratic bent. When mass media sources on interior design sought to act as expert guides and arbiters of taste—which happened fairly often, even in the absence of strict party dictates—they offered up visions of praiseworthy indoor spaces that demonstrated the virtues of economy, efficiency, practicality, time savings, and scientific planning. But the culture of the rational contemporary home was not simply a top-down projection of elite tastemakers. In many ways, it also accorded well with the values and needs of ordinary apartment-dwellers, and it was their endorsement and their practical application of such values that made the principle of rationality something genuinely shared and expressed—that is, something truly *cultural*.

Perhaps most importantly, the emphasis on rational, thoughtful, efficient interiors proved well suited for the twofold economic reality that ordinary Yugoslavs encountered: remarkable advancements coupled with ongoing frustrations over the gap between what was desired and what was really attainable. There was no escaping the fact that no matter how much they desired to beautify their homes, ordinary citizens were constantly bumping up against the considerable restrictions imposed by their incomes. Consequently, home improvement culture was keyed to pragmatic solutions in the face of constraints. How to do a lot with a little was a recurring theme. Most critically, space itself was limited. Along these lines, a Belgrade reader of *Praktična žena* shared her desire to work out a pleasant living environment in cramped quarters, a dilemma typical of many Yugoslav apartment residents: "I live in a two-bedroom apartment of 63 square meters [678 square feet] with my husband, daughter, son-in-law, and two-year-old grandson. I would like the apartment to be comfortable, functional, and beautiful. Please help me with the arrangements."[14] The architect brought in by the magazine suggested a design that carefully maximized available space, using modern, multipurpose furniture, including a day-use sofa that converted into the young couple's bed at night, with a separate sleeping corner and play area for their child.

Space limitations were, in the end, a function of economic limitations. The culture of rational interior design acknowledged this and sought to make the most of the opportunities available in what was habitually referred to as "our specific conditions," that is, in an economy that had seen encouraging growth but did not yet rise to the standards of the developed capitalist world. Life in the new block complexes posed problems that demanded some solution. "When we get an apartment in a block, we are usually very happy," one writer for *Naš dom* observed. "But how quickly we find out that, as a rule, an apartment in a block is already too small for us and that another square meter or so would be very welcome. With practical furnishings, however, we can make an apartment that seems too small somewhat bigger. It is important that we use the available space as rationally as possible and that everything which is in the apartment is, above all, functional."[15] Thoughtful use thus appeared as a way to avoid disappointments and feel good about what was possible in the here and now.

An emphasis on the ideal "cultured" quality of living spaces was another way in which the values associated with socialist residential customs in Yugoslavia resembled those that developed in other communist countries. As with the stress on rationality, this particular element of the ethos of the contemporary home tended to surface more often in the work of writers, reporters, designers, architects, and other professional and expert tastemakers than in evidence that came from ordinary citizens. One architectural engineer instructed her readers, for instance, that a correct understanding of "the culture of the home" meant that living space and everything in it should be conceived and executed according to design principles that acknowledged "the human being as the measure and as the goal," with each room and item apportioned in a recognition that "the parts of the human body are the basis of all units of measurement."[16] Naturally, it could be difficult at times to convert abtractions like this and similar refined notions of taste into broadly held social codes. But other elements of the insistence that homes display "culture" did translate well enough. As with the emphasis on rationality, the stress on simplicity, moderation, and modesty meshed nicely with the demands of a tight budget and thus could readily be incorporated into a widely shared set of values and attitudes.

An enthusiasm for modernity, while clearly not universal, was widely shared by tastemakers and ordinary apartment dwellers alike. Of course, there was nothing necessarily socialist about modernity in general or modernism in particular, but socialist official culture embraced both. Given Yugoslav shoppers' customary excitement for fashion and their keen interest in international consumer trends, furniture and decor that seemed suitably modern were often met with both public and elite approval. Along these lines, it is noteworthy that Scandinavian styles and designs—and Scandinavian ways of living more generally—attracted considerable attention and admiration. In the simple, forward-looking, and ultimately affordable design culture of the Nordic states, with their comfortable standard of living and their generous (some said socialist) provision of welfare benefits, there was a fashion that could unite cultural elites and ordinary citizens. One multipage photo spread in *Naš dom* showcased the products of the Swedish furniture industry with the proclamation "This Is How the Swedes Live—Simply—Modestly—Functionally."[17] That phrase was later picked up as ad copy for the major furniture manufacturer Slovenijales (Sloveniawood) and used to advance the message that the company's designs were bringing to Yugoslav customers the same high standards and commendable values that served as the foundations of Swedish home life. Similar themes marked another feature on "Danish residential culture," which was likewise presented as reflecting refinement, progress, and modern, up-to-date elegance.[18] With its indisputably progressive and European quality, this was contemporary style, industrially produced, for everyone. "Modern" sold well.

While certain aspects of the ethos of the contemporary Yugoslav home promoted participation in widely held patterns—a general appreciation of rationality, a common recognition of what it meant to be cultured, a shared excitement over the possibilities of the modern—one element cut in the other direction and against any narrow conformity. If the exteriors of their apartment buildings were typically impersonal, and hopelessly so, what might happen inside was another matter entirely. Here there was ample opportunity to privatize and humanize the mass-scale structure, to transform a generic and standardized *unit* into a *home*. Perhaps surprisingly, even the mass media not only acknowledged but also actively encouraged the view that "my home is my castle," a mindset that, it was said, Yugoslav readers tended to share with the English. According to *Naš dom*, success in transforming even a small one- or two-bedroom flat into "your own personal 'little castle' by yourself, following your own wishes and ideas" depended on the observance of certain essential rules: "First of all: the apartment is yours. You live in it. Not your neighbor. Accordingly, you have to buy the furniture that you like. Not any specific kind of furniture."[19] The attitude reflected here—that interior space could be and should be a personal, individual, expressive domain, with ample opportunities to demonstrate a resident's own style, creativity, resourcefulness, and problem-solving talents—constituted a key part of the way Yugoslavs approached apartment living. In the midst of an official and public sphere that persistently reinforced socialist values of solidarity, collective action, brotherhood, and unity, the residential interior provided a critical setting in which a countervailing social agreement could be lived out: a place where it was not merely permissible but indeed desirable to be an individual, to be distinctive, to be different.

With the place created for individuality came another point of emphasis that likewise ran counter to socialist values. For it was clear that the ethos of the contemporary Yugoslav home recognized the significance of personal status. Apartment dwellers joined those who resided in other housing types in using their dwellings to signal their achievements. Having only interior spaces to work with, they did what they could. A comfortable life thus became something to be displayed and admired. In defiance of officialdom and those tastemakers who upheld socialist egalitarianism, this set of values emerged more or less "from below." Not surprisingly, the Yugoslav mass media did not promote the quest for status to any great extent—or at least not explicitly. Quite to the contrary, status-seeking and the broader problem of "social differentiation" were often the subjects of polemics and lamentations. Nevertheless, it was undeniable that many ordinary Yugoslavs approached interior design and decor as a way to express their wealth, sophistication, distinction, and worldliness. The country's advertising industry understood this reality and frequently tried to play to it. And if public commentary and the media were hesitant to endorse this tendency openly, an indulgence of it still tended to creep in implicitly, and the polemics were softened with a recognition, often humorous, that if this was a sin, it was one that many Yugoslavs shared.

In socialist systems, the government's ultimate responsibility for providing satisfactory living conditions massively raised the stakes of housing policy. Residential life could be profoundly politicized in numerous ways, and this was all the more true for the big apartment blocks that were the grand models of modern socialist construction. This politicization of everyday life was widespread. It was certainly evident, for example, in the German Democratic Republic, where residential culture in general, and interior furnishings in particular, became the focus of what Paul Betts has called an ideological and aesthetic "reform crusade" in which individual apartments became crucial sites for the party-state's efforts at education and consciousness-building, targets of a "reform spirit to reengineer both private spaces and private citizens."[20] But if more rigid communist states like East Germany ended up maintaining a heavy-handed regime of pressure, surveillance, and intense party-sponsored messaging on issues of residential culture—with the result that "private life was never all that private"—the remarkably decentralized and far looser Yugoslav system gave its citizens something rather different.[21] To be sure, ordinary Yugoslavs did end up embracing some of the values such as rationality, modernity, and "cultured" refinement on which those in power hoped to build a reliably socialist culture and reliably socialist people. But they often did so as an expression of their own individual, personal interests, and they managed to create within their apartments and homes a private life that was, in fact, genuinely private, one in which values such as individuality and even the need for status might also find shelter. In Yugoslavia, individuals ended up with a significant freedom to determine what was inside their homes—and to make what was inside count.

Notes

1. Zarecor 2011, 1. Zarecor's analysis in certain ways rehabilitates these buildings, challenging traditional accounts and stereotypes of the big apartment blocks as offensive failures.
2. The public response was not universally or perpetually welcoming. On the repudiation of the vaunted "Socialist Modern" styles as "a devalued *Socialist Generic*" by Hungarian apartment residents, see Fehérváry 2012, 619.
3. For a generally appreciative account of the aims and achievements of the country's modernist housing projects, see Kulić, Mrduljaš, and Thaler 2012, 174–180.
4. In recent years, Croatia and Slovenia have been the European Union states with the highest percentage of the population living in detached homes, at 73.0 and 66.6 percent, respectively. These figures, from 2012, far exceed the average for the EU-28 countries, at 34.1 percent (European Commission 2015). In 1981, individual ownership of residential units accounted for 69.4 percent of the overall Yugoslav tenure structure (Tsenkova 2009, 42).
5. Kulić, Mrduljaš, and Thaler 2012, 176.
6. Ibid., 176, 174.
7. Le Normand 2014, 137.
8. Ibid., 128–138.
9. Patterson 2011, 207.
10. Crowley 2002, 189, 201–202.
11. Patterson 2011, 275–282.
12. Kušar 1968, 4. All translations from foreign languages are those of the author.
13. As regards "culture," I have in mind the term *kultura*, which in addition to the obvious primary meaning may connote "the state of being cultured" or "the quality of having culture." Soviet ideology tended to invoke "culturedness" (*kul'turnost*), but the analogous noun (*kulturnost*) was only rarely used in Serbo-Croatian (and only slightly more so in Slovenian).
14. Jovović 1974, 64.
15. "Stanovanje v bloku," 7.
16. Đokić 1980, 74.
17. "Tako stanujejo Švedi," 5–8.
18. "Danska stanovanjska kultura," 12–14.
19. "Moj dom je moja tvrdnjava," 34.
20. Betts 2008, 99–100. On related developments in the USSR, see Harris 2013, esp. chs. 6–7.
21. On East Germany, see Betts 2008, 123.

References

Betts, Paul. 2008. "Building Socialism at Home: The Case of East German Interiors." In *Socialist Modern: East German Everyday Culture and Politics*, edited by Katherine Pence and Paul Betts, 96–132. Ann Arbor: University of Michigan Press.

Crowley, David. 2002. "Warsaw Interiors: The Public Life of Private Spaces, 1949–65." In *Socialist Spaces: Sites of Everyday Life in the Eastern Bloc*, edited by David Crowley and Susan E. Reid, 181–206. Oxford: Berg.

"Danska stanovanjska kultura." 1967. *Naš dom* 1, no. 5 (September): 12–14.

Đokić, Svetislava. 1980. "Prostor u kome živimo—čovek kao mera i cilj." *Praktična žena* 25, no. 623 (May 3): 74.

Fehérváry, Krisztina. 2012. "From Socialist Modern to Super-Natural Organicism: Cosmological Transformations through Home Decor." *Cultural Anthropology* 27, no. 4 (November): 615–640.

Harris, Steven E. 2013. *Communism on Tomorrow Street: Mass Housing and Everyday Life after Stalin*. Baltimore: Johns Hopkins University Press; Washington, DC: Woodrow Wilson Center.

European Commission. 2015. "Housing Conditions." Eurostat: Statistics Explained. February11.http://ec.europa.eu/eurostat/statistics-explained/index.php/Housing_conditions#Main_statistical_findings.

Jovović, Gorica. 1974. "Uredjujemo stan zajedno s vama: dve porodice u dvosobnom stanu." *Praktična žena* 18, no. 463 (March 16): 64.

Kulić, Vladimir, Maroje Mrduljaš, and Wolfgang Thaler. 2012. *Modernism In-Between: The Mediatory Architectures of Socialist Yugoslavia*. Berlin: Jovis.

Kušar, Meta. 1968. Letter to the editor. *Naš dom* 2, no. 4 (April): 4.

Le Normand, Brigitte. 2014. *Designing Tito's Capital: Urban Planning, Modernism, and Socialism*. Pittsburgh: University of Pittsburgh Press.

"Moj dom je moja tvrdnjava." 1967. *Naš dom* 1, no. 1 (May): 34.

Patterson, Patrick Hyder. 2011. *Bought and Sold: Living and Losing the Good Life in Socialist Yugoslavia*. Ithaca, NY: Cornell University Press.

"Stanovanje v bloku." 1967. *Naš dom* 1, no. 5 (September): 6–9.

Tako stanujejo Švedi." 1967. *Naš dom* 1, no. 2 (June): 5–8.

Tsenkova, Sasha. 2009. *Housing Policy Reforms in Post Socialist Europe: Lost in Translation*. Heidelberg: Physica-Verlag.

Zarecor, Kimberly Elman. 2011. *Manufacturing a Socialist Modernity: Housing in Czechoslovakia, 1945–1960*. Pittsburgh: University of Pittsburgh Press.

PATRICK HYDER PATTERSON is Associate Professor of History at the University of California, San Diego. He is author of *Bought and Sold: Living and Losing the Good Life in Socialist Yugoslavia*.

5 Consuming Lives: Inside the Balkan *Kafene*

Mary Neuburger

If you have not been to Etera—a "village museum" in the Central Balkan Mountains of Bulgaria—you should really go. Fresh air and a roaring stream greet visitors to this carefully curated, yet somehow natural-feeling, Balkan "main street" nestled in an alpine setting. Traditional buildings that have been gathered, taken apart, reassembled, and arranged evoke a quieter, simpler, Bulgarian past—namely, the nineteenth-century National Revival era. A favorite spot for Bulgarians to while away the day is Etera's *kafene* (café), stocked with Turkish coffee, Turkish delight, and a range of other regionally consumed sweets. It strikes no one as remarkable that this Bulgarian café is filled with Turkish coffee and sweets. Indeed, the kafene evokes a traditional Bulgarian past that is remembered precisely for its "Oriental" style. It is this flavor of the Orient, in fact, that arouses a sense of Bulgarian (or Balkan) authenticity, as it differentiates that which is local, Bulgarian, or Balkan from what is European, Western, or more generically modern.

In the Balkans, as elsewhere, food, drink, and their modes and venues of consumption mark everyday lives in a profound way. There is arguably nothing so vital, so all-consuming and consumable, so embedded in everyday sensory experience and memory of the past than the flavors, textures, and smells of food and drink. These memories are further embedded in social life—family life, the home, seasonal change, holidays, and places of public gathering, like the kafene. Bulgarians, like most people living in the Balkans, embrace the kafene, past and present, as a quintessential part of everyday life. On the one hand, the five hundred years of Turco-Ottoman rule in the Balkans (from the fifteenth to nineteenth century) is generally rejected wholesale as a period of slavery and oppression or, at least, an aberration from a presumed "European" historical trajectory. Yet the legacies of Ottoman everyday life, like tastes and smells, the Turkish sweets and dense coffee of the kafene, and other kinds and modes of food and drink, are generally embraced, even romanticized, as part of an authentic Bulgarian past.

The kafene, in all its old and new incarnations, remains a quintessential part of Bulgarian life. Bulgarians love coffee. But *not* in the way Americans do. The American way of consuming coffee—grabbing it "to go" through drive-through windows, drinking it while walking, or simply having it for the caffeine-induced buzz—is still rare, if not utterly foreign, to Bulgarian consumers. For coffee consumption in the Balkans, traditionally as well as today, is less about the substance of the cup and more about the substance of life. Admittedly, this is not just a Balkan phenomenon but more a European one. Of course, consumers in Sofia do often grab a small coffee from a street kiosk and sip it standing at the counter, but this is not by preference.[1] The norm for coffee drinking is that it punctuates the day, offering repose and social interaction. It takes *time*. This is not to say that kafene culture, or Bulgarian/Balkan culture is totally static or stuck in time. On the contrary, the kafene provides a window into historical transformations that reshaped the Bulgarian everyday. But there is a palpable connection between the kafene culture of today and meanings evoked by the Etera kafene, symbolic of the kafene of the past. The smells and sensations of the Etera kafene evoke a *return* to a Balkan history in which the kafene provided an oasis from the worries of the world and a venue in which everyday life unfolded.

Café culture is iconic, even elemental, in a number of southern and central European cultures—for example, French, Italian, Viennese. But for some reason, the Balkan kafene is less well known outside the region, even though it is an as deeply embedded part of social life in the Balkans as it is in these better-known café cultures.[2] Although the café is often romanticized in the West as quintessentially European, it is *not* of European but rather Near Eastern origins. More precisely, the café was born of the habits and products of the long-lived and sprawling Ottoman Empire, where the coffee beans native to Ethiopia were profitably roasted, ground, and brewed in gathering places called *kahve hane* (Turkish for coffeehouse) since the sixteenth century.

Since the fourteenth century, the Balkans were under Ottoman rule. Thus, when the kahve hane (which in Bulgarian became "kafene") became commonplace in the empire, so too did it spread, beginning in the sixteenth and seventeenth centuries, throughout the Balkans. Yet significantly, the kafene was primarily Muslim until the mid-nineteenth century, often adjacent to the mosque and central to both Muslim social life and social infrastructure of city neighborhoods, villages, and towns. Non-Muslims, including local Christians and Jews, were more likely to gather at the *krŭchma* (tavern) and/or *bakal* (store), where alcohol and food, but not coffee, were traditionally consumed. Still, city neighborhoods and village cafés, taverns, and stores served a number of functions, including local administration, dry goods supply, post office, and dentist. By the nineteenth century, Balkan Christian men—and it was exclusively men in these spaces in that period—began to establish their own kafenes as meeting places across the empire, in an archipelago of cities from the imperial capital of Istanbul to Plovdiv, Varna, Sofia, and Ruse and in smaller "revival" towns in the Balkan mountains such as Gabrovo or Karlovo. Local bakals and krŭchmas across the region began to serve coffee by day and alcohol by night, while patrons smoked tobacco night and day. The big three globally consumed drugs of the twentieth century—alcohol, nicotine, and caffeine—had established themselves in every Bulgarian village by the later nineteenth century, with tobacco and alcohol being produced locally. There was a large degree of interaction, though little integration, between Muslims, Christians, and Jews in the Balkans. They entered each other's spaces and frequently conducted business or settled local administrative matters in shared cafés and market places. They had daily exposure to the gathering places and consuming habits of other ethnic groups.[3]

This phenomenon was depicted, for example, in Ivan Vazov's *Pod Igoto* (*Under the Yoke*), read in school by virtually every Bulgarian. In *Pod Igoto*, set in late Ottoman Bulgaria, Ganko's kafene provides the stage on which the novel unfolds: "Ganko's *kafene* as usual, filled with noise and smoke. It was the meeting place of old and young alike, where public matters were discussed, and the Eastern Question too, as well as all the domestic and foreign policy of Europe. A miniature parliament one might say."[4] While Ganko's clientele is primarily Bulgarian, the reader is also invited to experience the patchwork of Balkan culture inside of a kafene in a neighboring Turkish village. On the run from the Ottoman authorities, the young revolutionary hero Ivan Kralich stops for the night at a rustic inn in this village. Dressed incognito as a "common Turk," Kralich enters through the inn's kafene and is taken aback to see that it was crowded with *agas* (Ottoman officers):

> To leave immediately was awkward. He decided to sit down, and made his salaam [hello], which they politely returned. As he had lived long among the Turks he knew their customs and their language very well. They were squatting on straw-mats, their shoes off, pipes in hand. A dense fog of smoke filled the room.
> "A coffee!" he said sternly to the host.
> And he started filling his pipe, bending low over it to hide his features as much as possible.[5]

Kralich does his best to remain invisible, "furiously sipping his third cup of coffee, while at every other moment he blew out a cloud of smoke."[6] Kralich's familiarity with the "habits and language" of the Turks, his ability to "pass" for Turkish, is striking. But so too is the author's own ability to portray the Balkan kafene as somehow both public and intimate, as a place of ethnic separation and yet grounds for a shared cultural intimacy. Indeed, the place of the kafene in the Bulgarian past is largely a product of its prominence in Bulgarian literature, as well as memoir.[7] As depicted by Vazov, the kafene is embraced as a part of the fabric of Bulgarian life under the Ottomans, even as the Ottoman system is critiqued and rejected.

As in literature, memoirs from the late Ottoman period are nostalgic about a time in which the kafene was an integral part of Balkan everyday life. In chronicles of nineteenth century Ottoman cities, the rich cultural life of these ethnically mixed cities is most vividly depicted though kafene interaction. The urban Muslim coffeehouse, which spilled onto streets of cities like Istanbul, was part and parcel of the color of the vibrant, cosmopolitan Ottoman tapestry of which Bulgarians were a strand. As lovingly described in the memoir by Khristo Brŭzitsov, *Once in Istanbul*, which describes the late nineteenth-century city: "In front of Akhmed Topal's *kafene*, hidden from a red ribbon of baking sun, sat the Turks in

Figure 5.1. A man pouring himself coffee in Sarajevo, Bosnia and Herzegovina, 2014. Photograph by Roska Vrgova.

their holiday clothes.... They sipped steaming coffee out of large *fildzhans* [a type of cup], filling the entire pot with coffee, and the *narghiles* [hookahs] were well-supplied."[8] Non-Muslim Bulgarians experienced the Muslim café not just from the street view. During the Muslim festival of Ramadam Bairam, for example, people of *all* religions and ages gathered in Muslim coffeehouses to watch playful shadow puppetry.[9] By the 1840s, Armenians, Greeks, and Slavs, and later Jews, began to appear on guild registries as kafene owners, and non-Muslim coffeehouses proliferated in the course of the century. Urban coffeehouses in particular tended to cater to specialized, self-selecting clientele based on ethnicity, class, political affiliation, and village of origin (for recent migrants).[10] And the traditional kafene generally had a multitude of functions—barbershop, dentist office, inn, restaurant, bar, and opium den, as well as center of male itinerant merchant and artisan culture.[11]

Significantly, the memoir genre tended to highlight the colorful, traditional Balkan kafene just as it was slowly and unevenly transforming it into a "European" café. The gradual dissolution of the Ottoman Empire brought in its wake the creation of nation-states—including Serbian, Greek, Romanian, and Bulgarian—and mass migration, exile, and expulsion of peoples over the course of the nineteenth and twentieth centuries. This brought dramatic change to the ethnic landscape of the newly formed and expanding Balkan states, including Bulgaria—autonomous as of 1878 and independent in 1908. This unmixing of Balkan peoples was accompanied by a "Europeanization" of cityscapes, trade

Consuming Lives 47

Figure 5.2. "Putnik" café bar, normally visited by men, in Novi Pazar, Serbia, 2011. Photograph by Roska Vrgova.

orientations, and material culture (clothing, furniture, etc.), in and outside the kafene. Such changes provoked a sense of loss among many Bulgarians, who looked wistfully to the places where aspects of Bulgarian-Ottoman culture still survived.[12] In the immediate post-1878 period, the Bulgaria principality concentrated "Europeanization" efforts on Sofia, the new capital. In contrast, in Plovdiv—integrated into autonomous Bulgaria only in 1885—"Europeanization" was slower, thwarted perhaps by efforts to embrace and maintain the Ottoman everyday past.[13]

The memoirs of Nikola Alvadzhiev describe the richly textured Balkan cityscape of early post-Ottoman Plovdiv. With a delicious intimacy, Alvadzhiev details the quarters of Plovdiv, the "aromas" and "kefove" (pleasures) of their cafés, but also restaurants and taverns, inhabited by colorful characters. The city's complex web of ethnic and social relations unfolds as groups gather separately or intermingle within the multitude of neighborhood kafenes.[14] Alvadzhiev's describes, for example, the numerous kafenes on Dzhumaia Street, where "in the summer all the tables were full on the little square and even on the street." He continues: "For hours the Bulgarians, Turks, Greeks, Armenians, drank coffee, smoked, and chatted about everything imaginable."[15] In short, the old-style kafene persists, even as new kinds of kafenes appear. As Alvadzhiev describes, many of the kafenes of Plovdiv's were filled with newly educated and politically engaged youth, who "oiled-back their long hair, dressed in black and sported beards in imitation of the Russian nihilists. They read Gorky, Tolstoy, and Bakunin as they drank coffee and smoked into the night."[16] Certain kafenes became known for allegiance to a particular political party and many even functioned as party headquarters. To be sure, Bulgarian socialism fermented in the café environment, at home and abroad.

In Sofia, Ottoman-style kafenes were even more quickly replaced with myriad political clubs, luxurious "European" cafés, as well as beer halls, cabarets, restaurants, and other urban establishments. The fabric of Sofia's urban life was rewoven after 1878 into a self-consciously European city, home to a fashionable and famous café set of literati and notable personages. By the interwar period, Sofia's writers had come into their own, and they met, held court, and even wrote their masterworks in Sofia's dense web of old- and new-style kafenes—from gleaming to dinghy, rich to poor, right wing to socialist. Even when the Bulgarian economy was at a low point, Bulgarian journalist Khristo Brŭzitsov noted that the cafés of Sofia were full, though people were lingering more than buying.[17] Brŭzitsov's other memoir, *Niakoga in Sofia* (Once in Sofia), is less an account of his own life than a thick ethnography of Sofia's kafene life, which he maps with precision, from the cramped and stuffy to the airy and gleaming, frequented according to literary taste and political or social leanings. It was at such establishments that men met, wrote, networked, and retired.

Women, however, were rarely a part of this kafene life. Generally, memoirs written by women on the prewar period are devoid of references to the kafene or depict an intimacy of the kafene world from the outside. Raina Kostentseva's memoir describing the early twentieth century, for example, features observations of a male-dominated kafene as it spilled onto the streets of Sofia in mild weather.[18] Certain women would have been present in some of these establishment, either presumably "loose" or "fallen women" or, in a few cases, newly prominent intellectual women who became regulars in respectable kafenes, like the famous "Tsar Osvoboditel."[19] Many women however, participated in food- and drink-centered kinds of social networking outside the café setting, in homes, salons, public baths, and the church.[20] They also frequented other new kinds of consumption venues (restaurants, beer halls, taverns), where "respectable" women were welcome, as long as they were accompanied by male family members.[21]

World War II and the new communist system in postwar Bulgaria brought dramatic change to kafene life. At least initially, the communist regime decried kafene life (and, even more so, tavern life) as idle and bourgeois, a vestige of the capitalist past. But kafenes did not disappear entirely. Indeed, in the period after Stalin's death—when so-called de-Stalinization swept through Eastern Europe—there was an explosive growth in state-built and run kafenes and other kinds of venues for public consumption like restaurants, *sladkarnitsas* (sweet shops), street kiosks, and even taverns and bars. The clientele was vastly more diverse, including men, women, and youth.

In line with global trends in public consumption of food and drink (and tobacco), the old-style Bulgarian kafene was eclipsed by a plethora of options from the modern Sofia kafene to the newly tourist Black Sea coast—even more ensconced in leisure than its urban counterpart. Such abundance and its varied clientele, was quite new to postwar Bulgarians. It was part and parcel of communist attempts to provide the Good Life to its citizens and restore its sagging legitimacy. Any such efforts, of course, would pale in relation to the explosive growth of gleaming hip cafés, bars, and restaurants of postcommunist Bulgaria.

Today upscale kafenes line the streets of Sofia and other Bulgarian cites, which are also still dotted with little kiosks with one or two worn out tables. But through all this change, the kafene ritual—the meeting of friends and colleagues for a hot, bitter coffee, some sweets, or a smoke—with its more lavish sensibility of time is still in place. Perhaps this is not peculiarly Bulgarian but rather, more broadly, Balkan. But it is worth noting that the kafene in Etera, nestled in a reconstructed Bulgarian village from the late Ottoman past, still draws visitors to the luscious tastes and smells of its Turkish coffee and sweets. In a certain sense, it is time itself that people of the Balkans are buying and savoring at the kafene. This is what the past has to offer the present.

Notes

1. For more general work on coffeehouses, see, for example, Reato 1991 and Ellis 2004.
2. Recent Bulgarian scholarship has begun to offer in-depth discussion of the historical phenomenon of the kafene and the Bulgarian everyday. See, for example, Kraev 2005; Gavrilova 1999.
3. Alvadzhiev 1971, 182.
4. Vazov 1971, 110. It is unclear whether Vazov was familiar with Balzac's famous novel *The Peasants*, in which he called the café the "parliament of the people," but it is entirely likely that we would have been exposed to the work of the French writer.
5. Ibid., 164.
6. Ibid.
7. In another Vazov novella, *Chichovtsi: Galeriia ot tipove i nravi Bŭlgarski v Tursko vreme* (Uncles: A Gallery of Bulgarian Types and Morals in Turkish Times), satire mixes with the burlesque in cutting representations of Bulgarian archetypal social figures, in and around the kafene.
8. Brŭzitsov 1966, 40.
9. Kirli 2001, 156. Kirli explains that the well-known Karagöz (meaning "black-eye" in Turkish) shadow puppet phenomenon took place in Muslims cafés, but drew a mix of ethnicities and religions, even women and children.
10. Iankovo and Semov 2004, 388.
11. Kirli 2011, 11.
12. Bakurdzhieva 2001, 141.
13. Kozhukharov 1967, 191–192.
14. Alvadzhiev 1971, 93.
15. Ibid., 49.
16. Ibid., 226.
17. Brŭzitsov 1970, 67–68.
18. Kostentseva 2008, 124–125, 231.
19. Brŭzitsov 1970, 69; Konstatinov 1976, 144.
20. Leslie 1933, 47, 60.

21. Who was a "respectable" versus "fallen" women at the time was in the eye of the beholder. But in general, respectable women were married and always accompanied by husbands or fathers in public consumption venues. Fallen women may have been actual prostitutes, or simply women who did not marry at the socially prescribed age and frequented public establishments unaccompanied. See Neuburger 2011.

References

Alvadzhiev, Nikola. 1971. *Plovdivska khronika*. Plovdiv: Izdatelstvo na "Khristo G. Danov," Bakurdzhieva, Teodora. 2001. "Vlianie na Evropeĭskite modeli v organiziraneto na svobodnoto vreme na Rusensti v kraĭ na XVIII-70te godini na XIX vek," Evropeĭstika, Evropeĭski identichnosti: Tom 3, Seria 1. 141.

Brŭzitsov, Khristo. 1966. *Niakoga v Tsarigrad*. Varna: Dŭrzhavno izdatelstvo.

Brŭzitsov, Khristo. 1970. *Niakoga v Sofiia: Spomeni 1913–1944*. Sofia: Bŭlgarski pisatel.

Ellis, Markman. 2004. *The Coffee-House: A Cultural History*. London: Weidenfeld and Nicholson.

Gavrilova, Raina. 1999. "Sv. Kliment Okhridski." *Kolelota na zhivota: Vsekidnevieto na Bŭlgarskiia vŭzrozhdenski grad*. Sofia: Universitetsko izdatelstvo.

Iankovo, Ivanka and Mincho Semov, 2004. "Sveti Kliment Okhridski." *Bŭlgarskite gradove prez vŭzrazhdaneto: Istorichesko, sotsiologichesko i politichescko izsledvane, chast pŭrva*. Sofia: Universitetsko izdatelstvo.

Kirli, Cengiz. 2001. "The Struggle over Space: Coffeehouses of Ottoman Istanbul, 1780–1845," PhD diss., State University of New York, Binghamton.

Kostentseva, Raina. 2008. "Riva." *Moiat roden grad Sofiia v kraia na XIX–nachalo na XX vek i sled tova*. Sofia.

Konstantinov, Konstatin, 1976. "Georgi Bakalov." *Pŭtuvane kŭm vŭrkhovete: Portreti, spomeni, eseta*. Varna: Knigodatelstvo.

Kozhukharov, Georgi. 1967. *Bŭlgarskata kŭshta prez pet stoletie: Kraia na XIV vek–kraia na XIX vek*. Sofia: Bŭlgarskata akademiia na naukite.

Kraev, Georg ed. 2005. *Kafeneto kato diskurs*. Sofia: Nov Bŭlgarski universitet.

Leslie, Henrietta. 1933. *Where East Is West: Life in Bulgaria*. Boston: Houghton Mifflin.

Neuburger, Mary. 2011. "The *Krŭchma*, the *Kafene*, and the Orient Express: Tobacco, Alcohol, and the Gender of Sacred and Secular Restraint in Bulgaria, 1856–1939," *Aspasia: International Yearbook of Central, Eastern, and Southeastern European Women's and Gender History* 5(1): 70–91.

Reato, Danilo. 1991. *The Coffee-House: Venetian Coffee-Houses from 18th to 20th Century*. Venice: Arsenale.

Vazov, Ivan. 1971. *Under the Yoke*. New York: Twayne Publishers.

MARY NEUBURGER is Professor of History, Director of the Center for Russian, East European, and Eurasian Studies (CREEES), and Chair of Slavic and Eurasian Studies at the University of Texas of Austin. She is author of *The Orient Within: Muslim Minorities and the Negotiation of Nationhood in Modern Bulgaria* and *Balkan Smoke: Tobacco and the Making of Modern Bulgaria*. She is editor with Paulina Bren of *Communism Unwrapped: Consumption in Cold War Eastern Europe*.

6   *Burek, Da!* Sociality, Context, and Idiom in Macedonia and Beyond

Keith Brown

In Milčo Mančevski's award-winning film from 1994, *Before the Rain*, the graffito "BUREK, DA!" (Burek, yes!) appears on screen for approximately three seconds.[1] It occurs around one minute into the sequence charting the passage of the main character, Aleks, through the Macedonian capital city, Skopje, on his way from London to his native village. The camera records Aleks's point of view: The phrase is clearly legible on a wall to the right of a young couple in argument, the man gesticulating angrily, the stylishly dressed woman taking a step back. Mančevski cuts away immediately to a reaction shot of Aleks smiling.

Victor Friedman, one of the more astute and acute readers on the film (as well as Macedonian culture), explained the graffito to outsiders in the following way:

> Burek (from Turkish börek) is an oven-baked savoury pastry made from very thin sheets of oiled, unleavened dough layered with ground meat, cheese, or spinach. It is popular throughout the Balkans and traditional burek-shops fulfill the function of Western fast-food restaurants. In a country where graffiti are often used in political functions (both government-sponsored and antigovernment), such a graffito has multiple resonances. A slogan praising a local food item rather than a political leader, party or movement is a parodic rejection of political slogans in general. At the same time, however, the choice of burek for such praise is a kind of proud assertion of Balkan identity and, given the function of burek shops in Macedonia and the opening of a McDonald's a few blocks from the location of the graffito, it can also be taken as [rejecting] the cultural hegemonic homogenization of global (read: western) capitalism. Thus the slogan can be read as both locally apolitical and globally political.[2]

Friedman thus points out several of the layers of meaning on display here—provided by the filmmaker Mančevski and consumed, we may imagine (on the basis of his smile), by Aleks, as well as by knowing viewers.[3] Friedman here, though, runs the risk that anthropologists and other cultural analysts always face—the criticism of overanalysis, often made by comparison to Freud's cigar. Isn't a savory pastry, after all, sometimes just a savory pastry? Perhaps; however, recent years have seen several works in Slovenia on the topic. Peter Stanković argued there was much to be learned in the ethnographic and sociological tradition by reflection on this everyday food.⁴ In 2010, Stanković supervised a thesis by Bojana Rudović Žvanut entitled "The Meanings of Burek in Slovenia" that attracted some critical press coverage.⁵ Elsewhere, Jernej Mlekuž completed a doctoral thesis on burek at the University of Nova Gorica.⁶ These Slovenian transformations of Balkan pastry into theoretical capital inspire this short reflection on why and how burek still matters, in more ways than ever, twenty years after Mančevski's film.

Burek: Slicing Intra-Yugoslav Politics

One aspect of the slogan that Friedman mentions in a footnote is its explicit intertextuality. Rather than existing in isolation—or in relation only to hegemonic Western capitalism—the single-language phrase "Burek, Da!" (Burek, yes!) and Stankovic's code-switching choice of title for his 2005 column, "Burek, Ja, bitte!" (Burek, yes please!), are both in fact ripostes to another earlier graffito, reportedly seen on the street in Ljubljana in the late 1980s. The phrase, mixing Serbo-Croatian or Macedonian with German, was "Burek? Nein, danke."⁷

In his witty and irreverent 2007 book chapter with that title, Jernej Mlekuž makes the case that in late 1980s Slovenia, the burek—or, in his terms, the meta-burek—became a symbol of the underdeveloped Balkans, freighted with the metageographical baggage of "South" or "East" and juxtaposed with an emerging Slovenian self-image as northern/western, Europe-facing, and modern. He sketches a brief history of burek's physical presence in Slovenia—introduced, he argues, by Albanian vendors for the "underclass" market of migrant laborers and soldiers on national service from elsewhere in Yugoslavia. He then discusses burek's semiotic career within a Slovene discourse that increasingly took on nationalist, exclusionary qualities. Burek, available in Slovenia from the 1960s onward, was part of a larger, polluting presence of Yugoslav fellow-nationals in Ljublana and other Slovenian cities; in altering the urban foodscape, burek was tangible evidence of trends that, in the words of one Slovenian author, were transforming Ljublana into "Bajazit's and Murat's amusement park."⁸ In this regard, "Burek? Nein, danke" sits alongside a playful, yet edgy, discourse of humor that reflected the socioeconomic distinctions between more and less developed republics and regions of Yugoslavia.⁹ Federal efforts to close the gap, including the Fund for the Accelerated Development of the Undeveloped Republics and Kosovo (FADURK) program of centrally funded subsidies for Bosnia, Montenegro, Macedonia, and Kosovo, caused increasing resentment in Slovenia and Croatia, where leaders and emergent publics considered "their" money was being wasted on handouts.¹⁰

Mlekuž provides his own archaeology of the graffito, pointing to the West German antinuclear slogan "Atom, nein danke" as providing the frame. He also notes that burek captured widespread attention during the 1984 Winter Olympics in Sarajevo, where the Slovenian skier Jure Franko won Yugoslavia's first winter Olympic medal, prompting the slogan "Volimo Jureka, više od bureka" ("We love Jurek more than burek").¹¹ As reported by these two commentators,

Figure 6.1. A woman serving burek in Sarajevo, 2017. Photograph by Roska Vrgova.

that phrase was disemic. Chanted by Sarajevans, or by enthusiasts for Yugoslav solidarity, it appears it is a sign of inclusive affection for the skier ("We love you alongside, and even more than, our shared favorite dish"). Adopted by Slovenian nationalists, it takes on a negative, adversarial cast ("We prefer 'our' world-recognized skier to 'your' cheap, greasy, Balkan fast food").

Although it is tempting to accept this clear distinction, one core element of everyday sociality in the Balkans is people's widespread facility with wordplay that preserves ambiguity rather than collapsing it straightforwardly. To be sure, jokes often have an edge, but the same jokes, or dueling variations, can be told across social and political frontiers and, in fact, as Keith Basso argued in a very different context, serve to stitch together social fabric at risk of tearing.[12] The very different careers of Slovenia and its former fellow republics since 1991 have served to obscure the intimate nature of the various social relations that bound them together. The divergent histories of the new sovereign states since 1991 have also hidden the degree to which the "fault lines" of East/West, North/South, and autonomism/interdependence were replicated at multiple scales within Yugoslavia.

In her compelling and intricate discussion of the Greek-Albanian borderland, Sarah Green enlists the language of fractals to represent this aspect of the Balkans—in her own reiterated phrasing, "bumps upon bumps upon bumps."[13] The point, Green stresses, is to be sensitive to the quality of the relation generated by the "repeated clashes of scalar domains."[14] In that spirit, it is significant that in Slovenia's capital, Ljubljana, in the 1970s and 1980s, burek's market quickly spread beyond the southern conscripts and migrant workers and—as in Macedonia—quickly included young high school and college urbanites. Of particular importance, was burek's late-night availability, which combined with its reputed alcohol-absorbing properties to make it a popular way to round off a night of drinking before returning to one's home (usually shared with one's parents). Younger Slovenes, then, perhaps experienced burek as adding variety rather than threatening essence. In this same period, Ljubljana also served as a hub for human rights activism within Yugoslavia, in which the situation of Kosovo's Albanians was of particular concern and a potential source of solidarity against Serbian hegemonic aspirations. The opinion expressed in the graffito "Burek? Nein, danke"—if we insist on reading it as anti-Muslim or anti-Albanian—was perhaps not as widely shared as it has come to appear in hindsight.

Acknowledging these layers of meaning in Yugoslav-era Slovenian discourses of burek serves as a useful corrective to the illusion that "BUREK, DA!" conveys a single, stable message to those who can read it. This is especially important in light of Macedonia's own pathway out of the wreckage of Yugoslavia and the enduring importance of relations between Macedonians (who constitute a majority of the republic's population) and Albanians (who in the last official census, conducted in 2002, represented 25 percent of the country's population).[15] Having detailed part of the prehistory of the limiting phrase "Burek? Nein, danke!" in the Yugoslav space, I now turn to consider the more recent resonances of its affirmative double, "Burek, da!," in the Republic of Macedonia.

Burek, Ajvar, and the Ethnicization of Politics

Although ethnic tensions between Macedonians and Albanians capture international attention, burek has not been widely pressed into service as a marker of difference. One colleague did report, in 2008, seeing the graffito "Burek da, Ajvar ne" in Skopje—which is also the title of a Macedonian song recorded in 2001 and available on YouTube.[16] *Ajvar* is a winter preserve made from roasted red peppers and eggplant; people generally agree that commercially made ajvar is a poor substitute for the homemade (*domašen*) version. At least until the late 1990s, at the time of the pepper harvest, ajvar production was a communal event in residential neighborhoods across Skopje, as people set up small stoves outside to make the preserves and, often, drink and share *rakija*—homemade brandy—in the process. Regulations, presumably introduced in the interests of health and safety, outlawed this practice in Skopje, and families now contract with friends or neighbors elsewhere in the country to get their ajvar.

When she brought up the graffito, the colleague suggested there was in fact an ethnic connotation, as "burek is not from here, while ajvar is." The imputed meaning of the phrase, then, was an ironic commentary on the multiple denials of Macedonian autonomy and identity and the growing power and presence of Albanian interests. The year of the song's release, 2001, was also, of course, the year when an Albanian armed insurgency in western Macedonia changed the country's political landscape.[17]

Burek, Cigarettes, and Manhood

Yet this is not the limit of the idiomatic career of burek in modern Macedonia. Rather, the pastry continues to feature in turns of phrase that mark out the contours of what Michael Herzfeld has termed "cultural intimacy."[18] As a nonnative speaker and student of Macedonian for the past twenty years, I still learn new idioms on every visit. Most recently, reading *Toa Sum Jas*,[19] a memoir by a key political figure in Macedonia's post-Yugoslav transition, Ljupčo Georgievski, I was struck by a phrase he referenced while describing some of the preliminary meetings in 1990 that led to the formation of Internal Macedonian Revolutionary Organization–Democratic Party for Macedonian National Unity (VMRO–DPMNE). Georgievski was the first president of the party, serving until May 2003, when he was succeeded as premier by Nikola Gruevski. More recently, Georgievski has emerged as a critic of VMRO–DPMNE's national leadership, which in 2012 prompted a series of revisionist accounts of the party's formation.

Toa Sum Jas is a response to these revisionist accounts, mostly produced by figures who belittle Georgievski's role and claim a leading role for themselves—including Branislav Sinadinovski, Vlado Golubovski, Vlado Tarantalovski, and Todor Nanev.[20] Among the phrases used to signal Georgievski's junior status is that at the critical, foundational meetings he was "sent out for burek and cigarettes." The phrase encodes both masculinist modalities of doing serious and dangerous business and the rigidities of hierarchy built into those practices. VMRO–DPMNE came into being, this asserts, in smoke-filled rooms late at night, beyond the gaze of the existing communist authorities and without access to the lavish hospitality that was habitual in Yugoslavia, as in other socialist and communist economies of favors.[21] Instead, these protracted senior male conversations and negotiations were fueled by their younger aides or hangers-on acting as errand boys. Through what might seem like an innocuous reference to a practical activity, Georgievski's enemies did not just deny his leadership, but questioned his manhood.

This aspect of burek's meaning, signaling gender and power inequalities, is also manifest in another idiom I first learned when I started asking people for their burek stories. When someone sees or is talking about a couple who are mismatched in height, then reportedly they might say, "She is tall enough to eat burek off his head." In this case, the image conjured is more self-evidently absurd (and funny). Again, though, it invokes—and thereby authorizes as normative—a particular cultural context of gender division. In Macedonia (unlike Slovenia, where burek is often served in paper and eaten in the hand, as one might eat takeout pizza), people generally consume burek from a plate, either with a knife and a fork or with two forks. Burek shops either have regular tables and chairs or higher counters, where customers eat either seated on a stool or standing. I have seldom observed women eating burek standing at a counter. So the image of a woman eating burek off her boyfriend's head is not just funny but also culturally transgressive. The pastry's specific location in the quip is an emphatic reminder to all concerned that there is a proper order to things.

Figure 6.2. Two men eating burek at a café in Old Town, Skopje, 2016. Photograph by Roska Vrgova.

(Don't) Eat Burek!: Cheap Food, Cheap Talk

As noted above, when working on this chapter I asked friends and colleagues for their own burek stories and idioms. By far the most common response was to invoke the phrase "Ne jadi burek"—which often expresses frustration at a speaker's tone or topic and, in a polite translation of idiomatic Macedonian, means "Don't talk nonsense." People will use the term in everyday conversation to interrupt someone who is engaging in rumor, speculation, conspiracy theorizing, flights of fancy, or tendentious reasoning. These are all staples of informal social chitchat—what Macedonians call *muabet*. "Ne jadi burek" extends that spirit— it is more often used in a tone of affectionate amusement than sharp reproach. If Shakespeare's Romeo were a Macedonian-speaker, he might well have cut off Mercutio's extended riff on Queen Mab with "ne jadi burek," where in the authorized English text he says, "Peace, peace, Mercutio, peace! Thou talk'st of nothing."

In this case—as we have seen in other burek phrases—the term has spawned a well-known riposte of its own. Among the most enduring late-night talk shows on Macedonian TV is Janko Ilkovski's *Jadi burek*, which has been broadcast for around a decade and at the time of writing airs nightly on Sitel 3. The show attracts a wide audience; as well as featuring high-profile guests (including, on several occasions since 2006, Prime Minister Nikola Gruevski) and political and other topics chosen by the host, it is built around Ilkovski's conversations with members of the public calling in response to his invitation to "eat burek"—that is, talk nonsense or talk of nothing. The show has a loyal following in the Macedonian-language segment of Macedonia's fragmented media landscape, as Ilkovski plays the role of everyman and fosters an informal atmosphere of exchange very much aligned with Macedonians' habits of sociable conversation, which tend to be highly performative and range over domestic and foreign political scandals, European sport, American popular culture, and elaborate conspiracy theories of how the world is run.[22] The show is often criticized by Macedonian media analysts as populist and facile. But by maintaining a folksy style, while striving to cultivate the impression of journalistic objectivity, analytical virtuosity, and worldly playfulness, Ilkovski has turned *Jadi burek* into a distinctive brand of its own.

Burek, Da!

When speaking with Macedonians about their burek stories, I expected more enthusiasm than I received—perhaps because, unlike people who grew up with burek in their lives, I have still not learned to take its presence for granted. My own romanticized relationship with burek, I realized, was heavily influenced by the liberating context in which my early encounters occurred: I was conducting ethnographic fieldwork and archival research in a vibrant city where the social and physical capital amassed by its residents during the Yugoslav years had not yet been destroyed by the wars of secession/succession. Burek—its taste and texture and the familiar rituals of placing an order and watching as it is deftly sliced and served—speaks to me of youth, discovery, and friendship in a city and a country in which I have learned to feel at home. And over the years, I have also come to relish the continuing learning experience of uncovering the rich and evolving idiomatic life of burek, even as the country's foodways adapt. It was striking, and strangely comforting, on my most recent visit to Skopje to observe that the city's McDonald's restaurants—in business for over a decade, but more as destinations for children's birthday parties than go-to fast food—had recently closed down. Meanwhile, although the new monuments and neoclassical façades have transformed the feel of the squares and boulevards of the city center and skyrocketing real estate prices have led some small shop owners to cash in, burek joints remain in business. Beginning with mothers buying a takeout breakfast treat for their families on a Saturday morning, through the office workers taking a quick shared lunch break during the week, and ending with the teenagers grabbing a snack and reliving the adventures of the evening past on their way home from the clubs in the early morning, the foot-traffic around any *burekdzilnica* serves as enduring evidence of the intense sociality that remains key to everyday life in Macedonia. Or—to make the point more succinctly—BUREK, DA!

Notes

1. In *Before the Rain*, the graffito appears in all capitals.
2. Friedman 2000, 138–39.
3. Brown 2005, 31; see also Brown 1998.
4. Stanković 2005.

5. Rudovič Žvanut 2010.
6. Mlekuž 2008; see also Mlekuž 2007.
7. Mlekuž 2007, 179.
8. Štih, cited in Mlekuž 2007, 176. Bajazit and, especially, Murat, are recurring names in Yugoslav-era jokes and anecdotes, immediately recognizable to Yugoslav audiences as Bosnian and Muslim.
9. Brown 1995; see also Živković 2011.
10. Ramet 2006, 276–79.
11. Mlekuž 2007, 178; see also Nuhefendić 2014.
12. Basso 1976.
13. Green 2005, 128–58, partially following Irvine and Gal 2000.
14. Green 2005, 146.
15. Population Census, State Statistical Office, Republic of Macedonia, accessed March 1, 2017, http://www.stat.gov.mk/OblastOpsto_en.aspx?id=31.
16. "Ajvar—Ajvar, Ne, Burek Da," accessed June 20, 2014, https://www.youtube.com/watch?v=5YJtn2DLOmg.
17. Phillips 2004; Siljanovska-Davkova and Nikolovska 2001; Neofotistos 2012. "Ajvar ne, burek da" can also carry a commentary on continuing Slovene-Macedonian relations. Slovenia reportedly tried to patent the name "Ajvar"—used not only in Macedonia but also across the western Balkans—with an eye to securing a monopoly on the brand in the international specialty food market. See Nikolovski 2008.
18. Herzfeld 1997.
19. Georgievski 2012.
20. See, for example, Sinadinovski 2012. The front and back covers of Sinadinovski's book can be viewed on a Canadian-based online form, Kotle Forum, http://kotle.ca/forum/showthread.php?tid=153&pid=51145#pid51145, accessed June 3, 2014. Sinadinovski announced the promotion of his book in Skopje in April 2012; the book is not available through library services in the United States, and I was unable to locate a copy in Skopje's bookstores in 2013. Sinadinovski's claims for his own standing are made in the text on the back cover; the discussion of the content here is based on references to the text made by Georgievski and his interviewer in *Toa Sum Jas*.
21. Ledeneva 1998; Yang 1994.
22. Brown and Theodossopoulos 2003.

References

Basso, Keith. 1976. *Portraits of "The White Man": Linguistic Play and Cultural Symbols among the Western Apache*. Cambridge: Cambridge University Press.
Brown, Keith. 1995. "Political Realities and Cultural Specificities in Contemporary Macedonian Jokes." *Western Folklore* 54 (3): 197–212.
Brown, Keith. 1998. "Macedonian Culture and Its Audiences: An Analysis of *Before the Rain*." In *Ritual, Performance, Media*, edited by F. Hughes-Freeland, 160–176. London: Routledge.
Brown, Keith. 2005. "The Knowable City: Interpretation, Science, and Activism in Urban Anthropology." *Ethnologia Balkanica* 9: 25–42.
Brown, Keith, and Dimitris Theodossopoulos. 2003. "Rearranging Solidarity: Conspiracy and World Order in Greek and Macedonian Commentaries of Kosovo." *Journal of Southern Europe and the Balkans* 5 (3): 315–335.

Friedman, Victor. 2000. "Fable as History: The Macedonian Context." *Rethinking History: The Journal of Theory and Practice* 4 (2): 135–146.
Georgievski, Ljupčo. 2012. *Toa Sum Jas*. Skopje: Leks Legis.
Green, Sarah. 2005. *Notes from the Balkans: Locating Marginality and Ambiguity on the Greek-Albanian Border*. Princeton, NJ: Princeton University Press.
Herzfeld, Michael. 1997. *Cultural Intimacy. Social Poetics in the Nation State*. London: Routledge.
Irvine, Jill, and Susan Gal. 2000. "Language Ideology and Linguistic Differentiation." In *Regimes of Language: Ideologies, Polities, and Identities*, edited by P. V. Kroskrity, 35–84. Santa Fe, NM: SAR Press.
Ledeneva, Alena. 1998. *Russia's Economy of Favours: Blat, Networking and Informal Exchange*. Cambridge: Cambridge University Press.
Mlekuž, Jernej. 2007. "Burek, Nein Danke: The Story of an Immigrant Dish and a Nationalist Discourse." In *Historical and Cultural Perspectives on Slovenian Migration*, edited by Drnovšek, Majan, 173–202. Ljubljana: ZRC.
Mlekuž, Jernej. 2008. "Artefact as Actor? The Case of the Burek in Slovenia." PhD diss., University of Nova Gorica, Slovenia.
Neofotistos, Vasiliki. 2012. *The Risk of War: Everyday Sociality in the Republic of Macedonia*. Philadelphia: University of Pennsylvania Press.
Nikolovski, Zoran. 2008. Macedonia Tries to Trademark Popular Balkan Food as National Dish. *Southeast European Times*, February 2, 2008. Accessed June 1, 2014. http://www.setimes.com/cocoon/setimes/xhtml/en_GB/features/setimes/features/2008/02/07/feature-03.
Nuhefendić, Azra. 2014. "Sarajevo 1984, Yugoslavia's Olympic Games." Osservatorio: Balcani e Caucaso, Transeuropa, May 31, 2014. http://www.balcanicaucaso.org/eng/Regions-and-countries/Bosnia-Herzegovina/Sarajevo-1984-Yugoslavia-s-Olympic-Games-147078.
Phillips, John. 2004. *Macedonia: Warlords and Rebels in the Balkans*. New Haven, CT: Yale University Press.
Ramet, Sabrina. 2006. *The Three Yugoslavias: State-Building and Legitimation, 1918–2005*. Bloomington: Indiana University Press.
Rudovič Žvanut, Bojana. 2010. *Pomeni bureka v Sloveniji: diplomska naloga* (The meanings of burek in Slovenia: Diploma thesis) (in Slovene, with an English abstract). Faculty of Social Sciences, University of Ljubljana. Accessed June 27, 2014. http://dk.fdv.uni-lj.si/diplomska/pdfs/rudovic-zvanut-bojana.pdf.
Siljanovska-Davkova, Gordana, and Natalija Nikolovska. 2001. *Transition in Deficiency: From Unitarian to Bi-National State*. Skopje: Magor.
Sinadinovski, Branislav. 2012. *Boris Zmejkovski: Sovremeniot Damjan Gruev*. Skopje.
Stanković, Peter. 2005. "Burek? Ja, Bitte!" *Dnevnik* 55: 36–37.
Yang, Mayfair. 1994. *Gifts, Favors and Banquets: The Art of Social Relationships in China*. Ithaca, NY: Cornell University Press.
Živković, Marko. 2011. *Serbian Dreambook: National Imaginary in the Time of Milošević*. Bloomington: Indiana University Press.

KEITH BROWN is Director of the Melikian Center: Russian, Eurasian and East European Studies and Professor in the School of Politics and Global Studies at Arizona State University. His books include *Loyal Unto Death: Trust and Terror in Revolutionary Macedonia* and *The Past in Question: Modern Macedonia and the Uncertainties of Nation*.

Section II: The Home(s) of Everyday Life

Home is many things in many contexts. It is a residence, a structure, a repository of memories, and a library of reference. It is a place where we rest our heads and where we imagine our hearts to be. It is a place and a feeling, and we think of it in both concrete and conceptual terms, with interchangeable fluidity. Its centrality to everyday life cannot be understated because home is the reference point from which we make sense of the world and the place where our daily joys and struggles most often play out.

In this section, we see the aspects of what makes a home—aspects that are often overlooked but are always salient to individual interpretations of comfort, security, and even morality. Carolin Leutloff-Grandits looks at the network of family relationships within the environment of caregiving. In examining the interrelated nature of kinship, family, and the state, she gives us a framework for understanding family in rural and urban areas. Larisa Jašarević looks at how neighbors help take care of each other's health—using medicinal plants, home recipes, and offering advice—and the various strategies people employ to make ends meet. These give us a sense of the micro context out of which the concept of *home* evolves.

But home is also a place that exists in relation to elsewhere. Despite the seeming ubiquity of globalization, places of home negotiate their own relationship to outside influences. In her chapter on women activists, Elissa Helms shows how the tension between femininity and fashion is one that—despite international pressures—plays out locally: women can be feminists without having to succumb to foreign expectations. And in talking about the challenges of gay and lesbian life, Roman Kuhar examines how understandings of sexuality interface with liberal ideals of openness and acceptance. In both chapters, we see how home implies a dynamic, and not always easy, relationship with others.

Ultimately, however, home is about caring for others: parents caring for children; children, for parents; neighbors, for neighbors. In Monika Palmberger's chapter, we see how young people try to negotiate their present in relation to the past they have inherited. Although we often focus on the lives of adults, here we are reminded that adulthood begins with youth and at home. On the other end of the spectrum, Azra Hromadžić shows us the full challenge of providing elderly care amid the breakdown of traditional family structures and the effect of neoliberal reforms. As the obligations of home shift, so does the very concept that is central to our being within the everyday.

7 Kinship and Safety Nets in Croatia and Kosovo

Carolin Leutloff-Grandits

In southeastern European societies, kin members and acquaintances take up various tasks in the provision of care. With this, they are not different from other societies, as, in fact, the provision of care by kin members and close ones is one of the anthropological universalities found around the globe. The way kin care is provided, however, differs. These variations are closely linked to local conditions, the state provision of social security, existing social networks and their underlying caring norms, and global processes. As southeastern European societies are known for their tradition of patriarchal family forms, their socialist past, and the neoliberalization of their economy since the fall of socialism—which created, among other things, high unemployment—it becomes relevant to understanding the region to see how these contexts influence contemporary kin-based care.

To make sense of the patterns of kin-based safety networks, I discuss three contemporary cases in two countries of the former socialist Yugoslavia. The cases demonstrate the variety of kin-based care networks and their distinctive ways of relating patriarchal family forms, the socialist past, and the current societal conditions. The three contexts are the suburban, socialist-built quarter of Travno in Zagreb, the capital of Croatia; the rural region of Bjelovar in Croatia; and the rural region of Opoja in the south of Kosovo, in which migration to German-speaking European Union countries has long been the main form of economic provision and social security. In order to pay attention to local differences of kin care provision, I integrate a short historical perspective as well as take note of current sociopolitical circumstances. Before turning to the case studies, however, I overview some theoretical considerations necessary to understanding kin-based safety networks in southeastern Europe.

On Kinship Networks and Care

In order to understand kin-based forms of care, I take a functional approach which differentiates various forms of care—such as practical assistance, material and financial support, and emotional and moral support. The latter highlights the fact that one's sense of security is often less dependent on the material

Figure 7.1. Grandparents taking care of grandchildren in Skopje, 2011. Photograph by Roska Vrgova.

provision of goods than on the quality of relations one has and the fulfillment of expectations of the social world in general and of relatives in particular.[1]

Care provided by kin members can be based on a time-delayed reciprocity, on direct reciprocity, and/or on cultural conceptions of certain duties, which may or may not imply reciprocal provisions. Kin care may include child- and elderly care as well as educational support—which is seen as vital to social mobility and integration—material transfers over the course of a lifetime, and inheritance from one generation to another. Kin care is often gendered, as certain tasks, like the provision of instrumental care, may be seen as female domains, while other tasks, like financial support, may be seen as male. Kin care may take intergenerational forms, like taking place between parents and children, or intragenerational patterns, like between siblings. It is therefore useful to explore which care forms are provided by whom, how care is negotiated within kin networks, and on which conditions and values the provision of care is based. As kin care takes place not only within the frame of kin networks but also in a societal frame in which the state provides care, it is necessary to explore how the two main providers of care—the state and the family—relate to each other.

In the early history of Western social anthropology, it was assumed that modern societies relied on a state, while premodern societies (or, more appropriately, communities) were based on kinship. This opposition was used to create spatial temporal divides between western and southeastern Europe: While western Europe was characterized by the nuclearization of the family, the decline of kinship, and the growing importance of modern state structures as well as a civil society, southeastern Europe was historically characterized by patrilocal families and multiple and complex family households, as well as weak state structures, therewith lagging behind western Europe. This view is criticized because of its colonial perspective, but for a long time it was not really questioned and research on the meaning of the family in Europe remained meager; answers were already assumed.[2]

However, a recent comparative research project about kinship and social security in eight European countries, which combined a historical as well as a sociocultural anthropological approach, has shown that throughout Europe the state and the family are not competing social security providers.[3] Rather, the state and family supplement, support, and even strengthen each other, as they take up different roles. Of course, the relations of kin care and state care are very different from country to country and from location to location. Kin and family members may, for example, engage in daily childcare, like in Croatia and Italy, or may take over crisis intervention and spend joint ritualized holidays in a "family house" in the countryside, as in Sweden or France. In cases in which the state provides only little social security (in the form of pension payments, health care, kindergartens, and so on), as in Kosovo, or reduces the provision of state social security—as experienced by many countries in the Balkans after the fall of socialism—the question arises about whether this leads to a rise or fall in family-based social security. In what follows, I look at kin-based care in three different contexts to better understand the processes at play.

Travno: Re-Creating Proximate Family Care in Suburban Croatia

Travno is a quarter of New Zagreb that houses today about twelve thousand inhabitants and—along with nine other settlements of similar structure—was built in the 1970s, following a socialist urbanization and modernization plan. It consists of a twenty-seven-story-high "Mammoth building" of about one thousand apartments, as well as several smaller block buildings circling around a green park. The average size of most apartments is fifty to eighty square meters. The first-generation inhabitants were mainly of rural background, having become employees in the nearby state firms, from which they also received tenant rights to the socially owned apartments.

In contrast to the widespread, extended, three-generational village households with distinct gender roles from which most of the tenants originated, the settlement was designed for "modern" nuclear families and provided various daycare facilities for children. This enabled both spouses to work, therewith "equalizing" gender relations within the family. As housing, education, childcare, and financial support was provided by the state and the socially owned firms, the provision of kin care beyond the core family seemed to become obsolete.

The new inhabitants, who were often already acquainted with common workplaces, however, soon established intimate social ties among neighbors, which partly took up kin-like relations. This included emotional as well as practical care for each other, like sharing food and inviting each other to life-stage festivals, as well as relying on each other for childcare. In fact, several women in the settlement remained at home and offered private childcare to neighbors—partly because public childcare facilities were crowded, but also partly because the inhabitants preferred such private childcare arrangements for small children; such private care arrangements had a more family-like feel than did the public care facilities. Women who watched younger children became a kind of surrogate kin, with the female neighbors serving traditional roles of kin caregivers and even being called aunt (*teta*).[4]

After the collapse of Yugoslav socialism, kin-based care increased again and took on new meanings. This was first based on the new spatial proximity of three generations of family members, which developed as grown-up children partly remained in the settlement while the first-generation inhabitants turned elderly. Although various young adults made a deliberate decision to remain close to their parents, others were "forced" to do so because they had difficulties securing housing. They therefore continued to share an apartment with their parents until they earned enough money to buy their own apartment. As state-owned housing had been privatized—and subsidized housing was limited—it could be years after marrying and starting a family before a couple could get an apartment. This differed from the practice during socialism, when socially owned apartments were distributed to the employees of socialist firms.

Today, acquiring housing has often become a joint project between adult children and their parents. When middle-aged parents are well off enough to secure private housing property, they often either financially support their children in buying an apartment or leave their apartment to their child and child-in-law and move to a smaller apartment in the neighborhood. In other cases, however, middle-aged and elderly parents are not able to provide their children with an apartment; they may even need financial support themselves if they remained unemployed after the former state-owned firms were closed down. In these cases, grown-up children end up partly supporting their parents, and this can, in some instances, strain intergenerational relations.[5]

Intergenerational support, however, is not limited to only housing or monetary help. The main source of intergeneration support is childcare, provided by grandparents, especially grandmothers; taking care of grandchildren is one reason why close relatives decide to live near each other. Due to the new economic conditions of the neoliberal nation-state—which not only demand that both spouses take a full labor position in order to earn the income but also create an increased flexible and insecure labor market—parents often have longer working hours, as well as weekend and evening shifts, and public childcare is seldom sufficient. In such situations, grandparents take up the care for their grandchildren as soon as they are able bodied, have the necessary time (e.g., being unemployed or retired or not having entered the labor market), and live near enough. They bring grandchildren to and from the nearby nurseries, kindergarten, and schools and look after them on weekends or when they are ill. Doing so enables parents to work extra shifts or to have spare time of their own.

Such "grandma services," as they are locally referred to, have become the desired solution for rearing small children after the collapse of socialism and reflect the still underlying values that children are best cared for within the family circle. This finds support in conservative political parties that promote an idealized image of women staying at home to care for children and look after the household. In this line of thought, mothers who "can afford" to remain at home and to engage in childcare, as well as the grandmothers who take up this obligation, do not see this as a burden but as a gift. Such care affords grandmothers the possibility to create relatedness and transmit their own values to their (grand)children, therein fostering family unity. However, such practices do not necessarily support patrilineal family structures, as mothers often prefer to rely on the support of their own mothers and not on their mothers-in-law. Thus, they foster "relatedness" between matrilineal kin, juxtaposing patrilineal kin ties.[6]

Grandmothers are also engaged in the provision of food for their children (in-law) and grandchildren. They invite them for lunch on weekends and prepare various precooked foods in boxes to be heated up at home in order to save time and money. Preparing food also has a social and emotional component, bringing the family together regularly and reinforcing intergenerational ties. Here again, support from mothers to daughters and their families seems easier to accept than from mothers-in-law. Such a reorientation toward the close family within the neoliberal atmosphere, however, goes not only hand in hand with the privatization of the building space and economic life but also with the deterioration of neighborhood relations; the former kin-like neighborhood relations are often fragmented or not being newly created.

But it is not only a matter of childcare. Care of the elderly is (still) largely performed within the close family network in Travno—and throughout Croatia—and it is often based on the housing proximity of the related generations.[7] However, taking care of the elderly is no longer based on gendered patriarchal values of duty and respect only, which required that daughters-in-law would take up this task. Rather, now it is based on reciprocity, availability, and the quality of the emotional relations between the elderly parents and their adult children (in-law). The fact that grandparents take care of their grandchildren fosters their chances to be cared for by their own children (in-law)—in many cases their daughters. But there is a gap between the expression of willingness to care for close elderly relatives and its implementation, as many adult children are fully employed and do have not time to provide the necessary care. Furthermore, not all grandparents want to be cared for, as they do not want to be a burden for their children, who are busy with other obligations. The elderly often try to manage their household independently as long as possible. Others rely on those friendship and neighborhood relations developed during socialism that had substituted (and partly still are substituting) kinship relations. However, in view of the deteriorating neighborly relations in neoliberal times, such possibilities do not always exist. As the elderly become frail, many prefer to move to a nursing home, an institution gaining significance in postsocialist Croatia. Nursing homes are slowly losing their negative image as a place for those without family or with bad family relations. However, such institutional care is expensive and can partly be financed only with the support of the children.[8]

Bjelovar: The Fragmentation of Patrilocal Family Care in Rural Croatia

The municipality of Bjelovar consists of the town of Bjelovar, which has approximately twenty-seven thousand inhabitants, as well as about thirty smaller villages, ranging from a few dozen to a few thousand inhabitants. It is about a one-and-a-half-hour drive northeast of Zagreb. Like other rural regions in Croatia, the region became marginalized through the war and the postsocialist transformation in the 1990s and is characterized by outmigration. However, Bjelovar has fared better than most due to its relative economic prosperity in socialism and its relative quick recovery from war and the postsocialist economic devastation of the late 1990s.

Different from suburban settings like Travno, where the proximate intergenerational helping relations were basically a phenomenon that developed after socialism, the helping relations in rural Bjelovar mainly follow "traditional" patrilocal family patterns based on partible male inheritance.[9] This means that at least one son stays at home after marriage, builds a residential economic unit with his parents, and inherits the house; daughters marry into the house(hold) of their husband (and his parents) and do not inherit immovable property.[10] Although today the number of three-generation households in the villages around Bjelovar is rather small, there are often two patrilineally related households under one roof, or sons who have built their family house close to the one of their parents.[11] In other cases, and usually for economic reasons, children have started to move to the town of Bjelovar or even farther away to the Croatian capital of Zagreb. This has resulted in the fragmentation of traditional helping relations. As well, poverty and family conflicts have a negative effect on caring relations among family members.

With the economic crisis since the fall of socialism, the number of women engaged in wage work—which was rather low during socialism—has dropped considerably, and today, most women are at home. Because there are no childcare facilities in the villages, which is typical for rural Croatia, women care for their children and engage in housework and small-scale agriculture. With the availability of mothers at home, the need for a "grandma-service," as it is done in urban areas like Travno, is limited. This again affects intergenerational relations and partly reduces the willingness of young women to care for their elderly parents (in-law). Such a provision of care is, however, still expected by the elderly generation and many middle-aged women care for elderly relatives. But conflicts around this care are increasingly common, as women question their duty of caring for their mothers-in-law, especially as they may not feel emotionally close to them. Because of limited economic possibilities for women in the rural areas, as well as their many (unpaid) family obligations, there has been a continuous outmigration of young women into the cities, where they hope to achieve a better, more independent life. In many cases, such young women are supported by their mothers, who finance their education with their small-scale agriculture and do not envision such traditional caregiving roles as the best future for their daughters.

Because of this outmigration of young women, young village men, thus, remain unmarried and the elderly stay behind. As soon as they become fragile and ailing, the elderly often end up living in dismal conditions, because without the daily support of their children, they have difficulty caring for themselves. As in urban areas, the provision of elderly care is (still) clearly seen as a family affair; also, neighbors are often no substitute in this sense. In rural areas, however, caring for oneself can be even more challenging than in urban areas, because in the villages one has to cut fire wood in order to heat the home, and one has to go to town to go shopping or to the doctor.[12]

Opoja: Shifting Translocal Care Networks in Rural Kosovo

Opoja is a rural region in Kosovo's mountainous south. During socialism, it was an economically marginal region, and from the 1960s on—when international labor migration treaties were concluded between socialist Yugoslavia and western European states—young men migrated to western European countries in order to send remittances to their families in Kosovo. These migrant workers were, in general, members of patrilocal and complex families at home. Being abroad for decades, leaving their wives and children in the parental home (under the leadership of their father, uncle, or brother) allowed them to not only finance the patriarchal household but also support the patriarchal value system at home.[13]

Since the early 1990s, however, migration paths and household structures have changed. Due to the escalating conflict along ethnic sides of Serbs and Albanians in Kosovo in the 1990s, men started to take their wives and (now often already teenage or adult) children abroad to create neolocal, nuclear households. At the same time, opportunities for legal labor migration ceased though the economic and political need to migrate was still pressing for many Albanian families. Therefore, family reunion as well as asylum applications became the primary avenue for legal migration. In most cases, migrants still counted as family members in joint households in the village in Kosovo and mostly remained quite strongly oriented toward home. They worried about their family members at home and therefore tried to save money to send to their families, mainly their

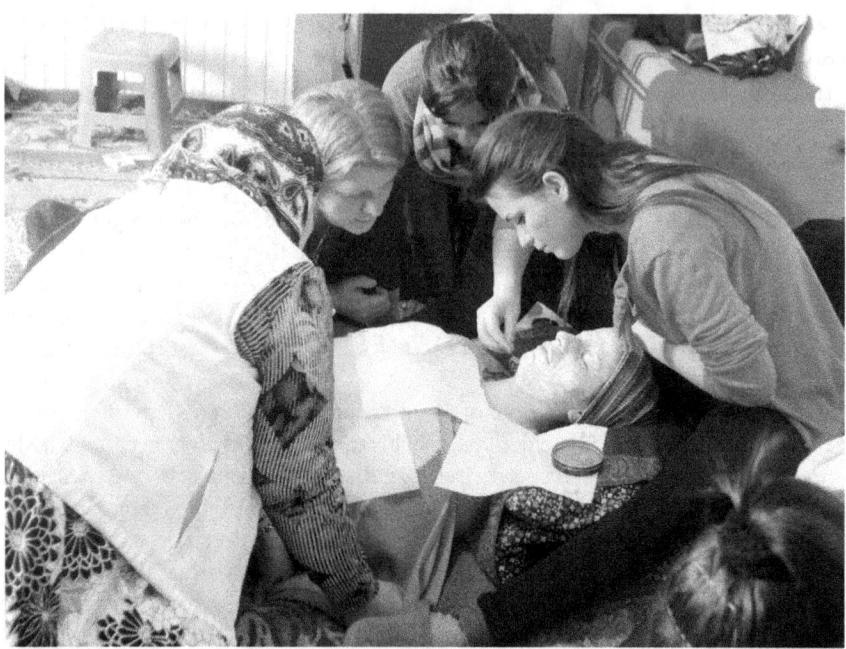

Figure 7.2. Bridal face painting is a traditional rite for the Kosovo Bosniak community living in Gornje Ljubinje and other villages of the Zupa-Zhupe Valley, Prizren municipality. The traditional rite is dying out as there are only a few elder women still practicing the tradition. The photograph depicts Majka Aziza teaching young girls the art of face painting on a bride-to-be, 2013. Photograph by Sehida Miftari.

parents or (male) siblings. In fact, in the time of ethnic conflict and flight, family solidarity with those at home played an important role and homogenized many individual differences among migrants within translocal families.

However, years after the end of the war in 1999, the economy in Kosovo was still sluggish, with very high unemployment rates of 30 to 50 percent—and even higher among the youth—and socioeconomic differences increasing. Many people live at or below the poverty line and the state social security provision is largely insignificant. The pension payments are extremely low,[14] public health care is inadequate, and unemployment insurance or social assistance to the poor is minimal.[15] While kin-based social security is of greatest importance in such situations, both globalization and liberalization have affected family relations in Kosovo. Such family relations, however, are often strained and characterized as much colder and more fragmented than before the end of the war in 1999. Elderly people say that younger people no longer show respect toward them, which had been a guiding feature of social order and solidarity before the war. One young, university-educated man even spoke about an "ice age of family relations" developing after the war, wherein formerly close relatives lose contact with each other and no longer practice kin care because they lack time and follow their own plans.

This rather depressing economic and social picture supports the willingness of Kosovo Albanians to emigrate for good in order to start a perceived Good Life in western countries. However, possibilities to emigrate and receive permanent residency abroad became even fewer after the end of the violent conflict in the summer of 1999. As asylum ceased to be a feasible way to migrate, options to legally immigrate to western Europe were reduced to family completion and marriage migration and, for a small minority, higher education. What about kin-based family care then? Are migrants still supporting their families at home, and is this still based on patrilocal values of seniority and respect toward male members of the family?

What can be observed are often highly ambivalent processes of translocal family care. While on the one hand those migrants who left Kosovo in the 1990s and established themselves as family households there partly reduce their financial support to family members at home and concentrate their payments on their children (and not on their parents and brothers) and other investments in their immigration destinies.[16] For the organization and advancement of their lives abroad, family members in Kosovo are only of minor importance.[17] As such, the main financial investment at home may go into the construction of a house designed for their nuclear family.

On the other hand, however, migrants often strongly invest in social relations "at home" in Opoja. When they come home for their yearly holidays or family festivals like circumcisions and weddings, they pay visits to their relatives, bring gifts, and invite them for drinks, picnics, and other activities that affirm success and generosity toward kin. These investments in social and emotional ties enable migrants to remain an active part in the local kinship network, which can give migrants identity, status, and even a future perspective of returning home in their old age. This, however, also affects the kin network itself. As one villager expressed it, "Migrants keep us together, because as soon as they come, we pay each other visits and celebrate jointly." And in fact, some villagers claimed that everyday visits of neighbors and kin have diminished after the war, partly because they are too busy, but also because they increasingly withdraw to their own family circle.

Even more striking, many migrants hope that their children, socialized within Western European countries, will marry "at home" (meaning the region of Opoja from which migrants originate) —ideally to a partner from home. Such translocal marriage practices facilitate the wish of many villagers who want to migrate themselves. They enable new migrations from the village abroad, and those new migrants often feel indebted to their parents and siblings and send remittances, thereby replacing those relatives abroad who stopped sending remittances to family members in the village as they turn to investing in their own homes (in Kosovo and abroad) while still visiting for a vacation. In this way, translocal weddings are a means to renew family solidarity and obligations across geographical spaces. However, family reunion and marriage migration also effect changes in gender relations, which, of course, affect the caring relations of those at home. In fact, many migrant women take up wage work and earn money abroad, which enables them to send remittances to relatives of their choice and become a provider—and gain status—in their translocal family network.

Also, many male villagers migrate abroad via marriage. They therefore establish neolocal households, often in proximity to the parents of their wives and their wives' brothers, who often also establish close networks of everyday care, turning the patrilocal village relations upside down.[18] And when sons leave through marriage migration, their parents sometimes are left at home, alone. This poses a problem for elderly care in Opoja similar to Bjelovar; in the rural regions, caring for the elderly is still clearly seen as a family responsibility, and there are no readily available substitutes for family care.

On Taking Care of Kin

In all three cases, kin care matters and its meanings have by no means shrunk. The majority of care takes place among first-order relatives and is not expected to be immediately reciprocated. As a rule, material and practical help among close kin is offered in a vertical direction, between children and their parents and grandparents. In Kosovo, care may also be horizontally provided, among siblings (and here especially among brothers, but increasingly also sisters). The provision of kin care relates not only to existing values but also to the care offered by the state as well as the socioeconomic situation prevailing in the locality itself. This implies that rationalities of kinship differ between the urban and rural field sites in Croatia, as well as the rural field site in Kosovo.

When assessing kinship relations in postsocialist Travno, it becomes clear that spatial proximity of the parents and their adult children has become more widespread again and fosters daily helping relations, especially from grandmothers to their grandchildren. This feeds into conservative family values like the one of intrafamilial childcare. But at the same time, care provided by grandparents enables young women to participate in the labor market and families to react to the new flexibility of the working life, as well as to the growing demands for individualism, thus contributing to the financial success of women and their families.

In rural Bjelovar, this connection between intrafamilial care and coping with new flexibilities of the labor market, as well as with female employment, is far less pronounced. Because of the constraints of the labor market in rural areas, caring tasks bind women to the house. This is a reason why women increasingly move to urban areas, therewith fragmenting local caring relations.

The rural region of Opoja in the south of Kosovo gives again another example of kin-based care. It shows the translocal dimensions of family-provided social security in a situation where the state provides only limited security and migration became a way of providing a livelihood for the local household. While these translocal kin networks of care have been based on certain patrilocal family values, such caring networks have become fragile in the last decades, largely because of changing migration and economic systems. The kin networks of Opoja have as well been transformed through marriage migration and partly even feminized, indicating the high flexibility of such relations.

In fact, all three field sites show that kin care is first and foremost based on social relations, which need to be lived and maintained and which are in constant transformation.[19] This means that neither spatial closeness nor a certain "kinship system" automatically create the basis of care. Instead, care can be provided with spatial distance, as soon as relatives invest in these relations and can take nonpatriarchal forms.

Notes

1. Benda-Beckmann and Benda-Beckmann 1994; Baldassar 2007, 276.
2. Leutloff-Grandits and de Pina Cabral 2012.
3. Grandits 2010; Heady and Schweitzer 2010; Heady and Kohli 2010; Heady 2010a, 2010b; Segalen 2010; see also Kohli 1999. The sociocultural anthropological research was based on participant observation, narrative interviews, and a computer-based kinship network questionnaire.
4. Rubić and Leutloff-Grandits 2015.
5. Leutloff-Grandits and Rubić 2010.
6. See Thelen and Leutloff-Grandits 2010.
7. The percentage of elderly in dedicated homes—less than 3.0 percent in the year 2000—is negligible. In socialism, these numbers were even smaller: only 1.3 percent of all pensioners at the end of the 1980s (see Grandits 2010a; Zavod za mirovinsko osiguranje 2002, 60).
8. See Leutloff-Grandits and Rubić 2010.
9. In fact, inheritance was more or less equally divided among sons. In some cases, each son had a house or floor of a house in the village, but based on the general phenomenon of outmigration, often also only one son remained; others received money as compensation.
10. Buchowski 2010, 299, 301; Čapo Žmegač 2000; Grandits 2002; Kaser 2000.
11. For a description of Slavonia in the 1980s, see Olson 1989.
12. See Leutloff-Grandits, Birt, and Rubić 2010; Leutloff-Grandits 2012.
13. Reineck 1991.
14. Persons who are registered residents of Kosovo and are sixty-five years or older are eligible to receive a basic pension of seventy-five euros per month (See Kosovo Agency for Statistics, 2016. Social Welfare Statistics. http://ask.rks-gov.net/media/3204/social-welfare-statistics-2016.pdf, accessed April 10, 2017.
15. Shaipi 2005, 7–12.
16. Hockenoes 2006.
17. Dahinden 2005.
18. Leutloff-Grandits 2014; 2015.
19. See Drotbohm 2009, 133, 147.

References

Baldassar, Loretta. 2007. "Transnational Families and Aged Care: The Mobility of Care and the Migrancy of Ageing." *Journal of Ethnic and Migration Studies* 33 (2): 275–292.
Benda-Beckmann, Franz von, and Keebet von Benda-Beckmann. 1994. "Coping with Insecurity." *Focaal—Journal of Global and Historical Anthropology* 22/23: 7–31.

Buchowski, Michał. 2010. "Family in Europe: Urban and Rural Contexts Compared." In *Family, Kinship and State in Contemporary Europe*, vol. 3, *Perspectives on Theory and Policy*, edited by Patrick Heady and Martin Kohli, 295–314. Frankfurt: Campus.

Čapo-Žmegač, Jasna. 2000. "From Local to National Community: Peasant Social Structure." In *Croatian Folk Culture at the Crossroads of Worlds and Eras*, edited by Z. Vietz and A. Muraj, 495–540. Zagreb: Gallery Klovićevi dvori.

Dahinden, Janine. 2005. *Prishtina—Schlieren. Albanische Migrationsnetzwerke im transnationalen Raum*. Zürich: Sexism.

Drotbohm, Heike. 2009. "Horizons of Long-Distance Intimacies: Reciprocity, Contribution and Disjuncture in Cape Verde." *History of the Family* 14(S): 132–149.

Grandits, Hannes. 2002. *Familie und sozialer Wandel im ländlichen Kroatien (18.-20. Jh.)*. Wien: Böhlau.

Grandits, Hannes. 2010. "Kinship and the Welfare State in Twentieth-Century Croatian Transitions." In *Family, Kinship and State during the Century of Welfare*, vol. 1, *The Century of Welfare: Eight Countries*, edited by Hannes Grandits, 249–281. Frankfurt: Campus.

Heady, Patrick. 2010a. "Family, Kinship and State in Contemporary Europe: A Brief Overview of the Three-Volume Series." In *Family, Kinship and State in Contemporary Europe*, Vol. 2, *The View from Below: Nineteen Localities*, edited by Patrick Heady and Peter Schweitzer, 9–11. Frankfurt: Campus.

Heady, Patrick. 2010b. "Introduction: Care, Kinship and State in Contemporary Europe: The View from Below." In *Family, Kinship and State in Contemporary Europe*. Vol. 2, *The View from Below: Nineteen Localities*, edited by Patrick Heady and Peter Schweitzer, 13–60. Frankfurt: Campus.

Heady, Patrick, and Martin Kohli, eds. 2010. *Family, Kinship and the State in Contemporary Europe*. Vol. 3, *Perspectives on Theory and Policy*. Frankfurt: Campus.

Heady, Patrick, and Peter Schweitzer, eds. 2010. *Family, Kinship and the State in Contemporary Europe*. Vol. 2, *The Views from Below: Nineteen Localities*. Frankfurt: Campus.

Hockenoes, Paul. 2006. "Cutting the Lifeline. Migration, Family and the Future of Kosovo." European Stability Initiative, Berlin, Istanbul, September. http://www.esiweb.org/pdf/esi_document_id_80.pdf.

Kaser, K. 2000. *Macht und Erbe. Männerherrschaft, Besitz und Familie im östlichen Europa (1500–1900)*. Wien: Böhlau.

Kohli, Martin. 1999. "Private and Public Transfers between Generations: Linking the Family and the State." *European Societies* 1 (1): 81–104.

Leutloff-Grandits, Carolin. 2012. "Kinship, Community and Care: Rural-Urban Contrasts in Croatia." *Ethnologie francaise* 42 (1): 65–78.

Leutloff-Grandits, Carolin. 2014. "Migrantisierung und Entmigrantisierung der Familie: Ein kritischer Blick auf Migration aus dem Kosovo in die EU." *Berliner Blätter* 65(S): 62–76.

Leutloff-Grandits, Carolin. 2015. "Transnationale Ehen durch die Linse von Gender und Familie: Heiratsmigration aus Kosovos Süden in Länder der EU." *IMIS Heft* 46: 163-193.

Leutloff-Grandits, Carolin, Danijela Birt, and Tihana Rubić. 2010. "Two Croatian Localities." In *Family, Kinship and State in Contemporary Europe*, vol. 2, *The View from Below: Nineteen Localities*, edited by Patrick Heady and Peter Schweitzer, 129–168. Frankfurt am Main: Campus.

Leutloff-Grandits, Carolin, and João de Pina Cabral. 2012. "The Importance of Kinship in Contemporary Anthropological Research." *Ethnologie francaise* 42 (2): 374–380.

Leutloff-Grandits, Carolin, and Tihana Rubic. 2010. "Kinship and Social Security in Urban Croatia: The Example of Travno, Zagreb." In *Family, Kinship and State in Contemporary Europe*, vol. 2, *The View from Below: Nineteen Localities*, edited by Patrick Heady and Peter Schweitzer, 135–150. Frankfurt: Campus.

Olsen, Mary Kay Gilliland. 1989. "Authority and Conflict in Slavonian Households: The Effects of Social Environment on Intra-household Processes." In *The Household Economy. Reconsidering the Domestic Mode of Production*, edited by R. Wilk, 149–170. Boulder, CO: Westview Press.

Reineck, Janet. 1991. "The Past as Refuge: Gender, Migration, and Ideology among the Kosova Albanians." PhD diss., University of California, Berkeley.

Rubic, Tihana, and Carolin Leutloff-Grandits. 2015. "Creating a Familiar Space after Post-Socialist Crisis: Childcare, Kinship and Community in Zagreb's Satellite Town." In *Narrating the City. Everyday History and Urban Networks*, edited by W. Fischer-Nebmaier, M. P. Berg, and A. Christou, 219–242. New York: Berghahn Books.

Segalen, Martine. 2010. "The Modern Reality of Kinship: Sources and Significance of New Kinship Forms in Contemporary Europe." In *Family, Kinship and the State in Contemporary Europe*, vol. 3, *Perspectives on Theory and Policy*, edited by Patrick Heady and Martin Kohli, 249–270. Frankfurt: Campus.

Shaipi, Kustrim. 2005. "Report on the Present State and Future of Social Security in Kosovo." Kosovar Research and Documentation Institute (KODI Institute), LPO, August 1. Accessed August 28, 2012. http://www.coe.int/t/dg3/sscssr%5CSource%5CCRepAnn1KosEN.PDF.

Thelen, Tatjana, and Carolin Leutloff-Grandits. 2010. "Self-Sacrifice or Natural Donation? A Life Course Perspective on Grandmothering in New Zagreb (Croatia) and East Berlin (Germany)." *Horizontes Antropologicos* 16 (34): 427–452.

Zavod za mirovinsko osiguranje. 2002. *80 godina mirovinskog osiguranja u Hrvastkoj 1922–2002*. Zagreb: Hrvatski Zavod za mirovinsko osiguranje.

CAROLIN LEUTLOFF-GRANDITS is Postdoctoral Research Fellow and Scientific Coordinator at the Viadrina Center B/ORDERS IN MOTION, European University Viadrina in Frankfurt (Oder). She is author of *Claiming Ownership in Postwar Croatia: The Dynamics of Property Relations and Ethnic Conflict in the Knin Region* and editor of *Migrating Borders and Moving Times: Temporality and the Crossing of Borders in Europe* (with Hastings Donnan and Madeleine Hurd.)

8 "This Much We Know": Domestic Remedies and Quotidian Tricks since Tito's Bosnia

Larisa Jašarević

I have been so often told about medicinal resources in northeastern Bosnia that, supposedly, "everyone knows." This abundant common knowledge of homemade, herbal, and dietary remedies is readily rehearsed and just as easily mobilized at the signs of someone's discomfort or sounds of complaint. Complain that you are unwell to an old acquaintance you bump into on the street, to fruit vendors in the market, or to your companions over whiffs of cigarettes and strong, grainy coffee and see what happens. Health advice is likely to rain, and your symptoms, carefully interrogated or hastily assumed, will be traced to possible visceral malfunctions and sources of stress. Most importantly, you will receive instructions on how to proceed with specific dietary regimes, how to use or avoid pharmaceuticals and herbal medicine, and how to grind, mix, soak, steep, ferment, cook, and concoct medicine at home.

Moreover, if health complaints seem grave enough or your intimates and interlocutors are proactive, the advice is quickly followed with samples: a jar of pomade, a pinch of tea, some medicinal mushrooms or probiotic cultures, cuttings, seeds and seedlings, herbal oils, honey mixtures, and a family's own precious fruit butters, juices, or brandy. I spent hours in a yard of a suburban neighborhood of Tuzla, examining and recording the many remedies and homemade products that one family used, prepared, and stored. One afternoon together, they listed some thirty items and brought for examination at least half of those they used or "would recommend to everyone" (*svakom bi preporučili*). Jasmina was the family's designated pharmacist—after all, she has been actively collecting, receiving, and experimenting with *materia medica* ever since she was diagnosed with malignant tumors on her breast and small intestine in 2002 and underwent two surgeries and chemotherapy. She starts a day taking fresh leaves of *čuvarkuća* (*Sempervivum tectorum*) on an empty stomach, followed by a spoonful of honey mixed with *žara* (stinging nettle) tea; takes a glass of medicinal petroleum distillate in the course of the day; prepares two of her own mixtures of teas for the stomach and urinary tract; consumes several glasses of home-brewed probiotic; and cooks meals with medicinal ingredients, including sunchoke (*čičoka*) or *Bosanac*, a variety of corn.

As Jasmina described her dietary routines, it became obvious that her husband, Ramiz, and their adult daughter kept good track of Jasmina's medical self-care. They remembered recipes, contributed to their preparation, and reminded Jasmina of the details of their application. They helped pick herbs from the meadow or the garden to spread out on the table, next to stashes of dried and fresh plants, jars, and bottles, all fetched to help me better catalogue them. They also had a fair share of their own experiences with efficacious—and not so efficacious—substances and concoctions. A large jar, one-third full, with whitish, clumpy salve that smelled oddly of part pharmacy and part auto repair shop, was a cure Ramiz introduced as not only tried and true but also "medically verified." Not too long ago, he suffered debilitating pain in his right knee which doctors attributed to a dislocated bone fragment and recommended surgery. The pain overwhelmed him. He reduced his mobility, gave up bicycling, and would groan loudly in pain. He prepared and tried a salve of ground roots and crushed berries of an ivy whose violet blossoms decorate many neighborhood yards. This was highly recommended to him by two people, but he found no relief. But then an auto-body mechanic in the nearby workshop dictated this recipe: "Using a glass bottle as a roller, grind 20 *Andol 100* (a regional brand of Acetylsalicylic acid medication) to dust; grade *kabash* (a traditional laundry soap made of bovine gelatin) and add both to a jar of home-brewed *šljivovica* (plum brandy); shake it well and wait for a cream to form. Apply before going to bed." After two applications, Ramiz's pain was gone. His orthopedic specialist, having heard him boast about the "old women's magic" (*babine gatke*, literally "grandmothers' spells") had the pomade analyzed in a lab and concluded that each ingredient's therapeutic effects were enhanced when combined.

As the table surface filled with various forms, scents, and substances—there were leaves of *Miloduh*, long and soft like rabbit's ears and smelling very sweet; yellow and pink *Kantarion* flower sprays; fine feathery fingers of *Božije drvce* bush; a tight pack of plump Tibetan mushrooms, submerged in pinkish liquid like layers of pancakes; and so on—my hosts traced some of the more unusual items to people in the neighborhood or across the town who brought them at the news of Jasmina's illness and left the provenance of others unspecified, since everyone, supposedly, knows where and how to get them. I was brought to this household by a dear aunt, Slavica, who was an invaluable intermediary and companion in my field visits, even as she often dampened my research enthusiasm with flat remarks such as: "What is there to talk about? It's common knowledge!" or "There's nothing to see: it's *pekmez* [Turkish for liquid fruit butter or molasses]." But Slavica's casualness recommended her as a knowledgeable guide to home medicine and her cordial relationship with the residents of one outlying district of Tuzla opened many doors in the summer of 2013. Moreover, Slavica strongly suggested a broader reading of self-care practices when she said matter-of-factly, while poking a little spoon about a thick, dark paste of pekmez, almonds, walnuts, and black cumin seeds she made to improve her bone density and stored in a recycled dairy plastic container: "After the war, I started developing periodontitis and all of that because I didn't pickle any cabbage that autumn."

Taking seriously the implication behind this remark, I unfold the anatomical logic that connects disorders of the skeletal frame via (disrupted) seasonal customs of pickling and preserving. In what follows, I suggest that there is much to appreciate about the tone of this etiological inference as it delivers significant clues about the local sense of bodily being and the casual nature of the substantial quotidian knowledge.

Pekmez, Tibetan Mushrooms, and Japanese Quails Are Good for Everything

Like many others, Jasmina and Ramiz have intensified home production of food and medicine since the end of socialism and the war. Both held employment in "Tito's state," as they put it—Jasmina was a professional cook and Ramiz a doorkeeper—and farmed only on the side. With mass layoffs from state enterprises, forced early retirement plans, high unemployment and the informalization of work for minimum wage and often deferred payment, Bosnians are increasingly cultivating land and keeping livestock, as well as harvesting wild fruits and plants. Urbanites are also finding their ways to food production, whether in their country homes, on their relatives' land, or simply entering in crop and livestock sharing arrangements.

The times of postsocialist and postwar precariousness have revalued the domestic food economies but the homemade (*domaće*) has long been enjoyed and praised and never quite displaced by the convenient industrial foods appearing during the Yugoslav period: Soup or salad made of wild, bitter greens (*žara* or *srijemoš*, wild garlic) initiate spring in households. Powdery flowers of a mature weed bush, *zova* (elder), are boiled into juice at the turn of the summer, while brewing, preserving, and pickling of fruits and vegetables fills the air of homes and hamlets with the smell of autumn: rich fruity aromas of jams and butters bubbling for hours in cauldrons, preferably over open fire. Later still, rancid or fiery scents of vegetables pickling or stewing foreshadow winter's arrival. It is a rare household that does not produce some form of domaće, which is always meant to be not only delicious but also nutritionally and medicinally potent. With a serving of jam or zova juice, with an offer of žara soup, you will most likely be reminded or taught just how, specifically, each one is good for you ("everyone knows" that zova is packed with vitamins and a cure for the kidneys and respiratory organs or that nettle cleanses blood and is rich in iron).

Given the long tradition of folk medicine, it is not surprising that homemade foods and medicines are emphasized as alternatives to commercial foods and drugs. Numerous scandals from food poisoning to questionable ingredients found in imported and national brands, are taken to prove not only the new state's indifference toward the citizens' well-being but also the popular suspicions that the pharmaceutical and food industries are in the business of making profit, by whichever means. Many Bosnians are finding ways to avoid or replace

Figure 8.1. A man selling homemade pekmez and herbs outside of Sarajevo, 2017. Photograph by Roska Vrgova.

pharmaceutical drugs—the prescription and self-medication of which is on the rise since the 1990s, according to the regional pharmacists—and not only because of their cost. Jasmina proudly listed a number of natural remedies that she uses instead of prescribed medicine and store-bought supplements. And Slavica told me frankly that she reluctantly uses drugs, except for an over-the-counter fever reducer and a common cold medicine.

Domaće is literally everywhere in Bosnian homes and diets: there are stashes of herbs drying for tea, jars of preserves in pantries, bottles of home-brewed plumb brandy, which also has various medicinal uses (ranging from simple inflammation compresses to digestive aids to preparation of herbal tinctures). It presumes time-consuming and labor-intensive production as well as an immediate working relationship with "clean" land, plants, and animals and potent, highly varied produce.

Pekmez is an iconic domaće item.[1] Cooked over a slow fire for as long as it takes the juice of crushed apples or pears to thicken, sometimes as long as forty-eight hours, it is a product of both general and singular processes. There are simple instructions on how to treat the few elements of its production—fruits, fire, caldron, and stirring spoon—but variations are inevitable to the point that a family's product varies from one season to the next and no two jars of one batch are the same. Organically produced fruits taste different from year to year and from heap to heap; cooking fire always burns with its own flickering logic; stirring lends itself to various interruptions and habits of persisting at the task. Furthermore, canning seals the product's peculiar destiny, depending on the amount of trapped air and fermentation processes that continue below the lid. Production

Figure 8.2. A woman selling homemade preserves in Stragari, Serbia, 2015. Photograph by Zeljko Stevanović.

of home medicine and food relies on what anthropologist Nadia Seremetakis calls the memory of the senses: tastes entangled in textural densities of objects known from the tip of the tongue or picked up by nostrils, fingertips, or belly that provide traction to historical changes and market trends, stay attached to seasons and idiosyncratic, nonmarket flavors.[2]

Domaće, however, is also presented among family and friends and bought in the market where there is always a danger of a counterfeit—produce diluted with sugar, made of commercial ingredients or spoiled by synthetic pesticides and fertilizers, or otherwise "unclean"—unless one has developed discriminating strategies or established trusted sources of supply. As one woman puts it, "I don't like buying that from a stranger [od nepoznatog]."

Home medicine goes beyond authentically local produce to include more exotic remedies, variously domesticated through the local market or gifting circles: aloe plant, sunchokes, black cumin seed, fermentation agents known as Tibetan or Japanese mushrooms or simply "little mushrooms" (the gift of which I found advertised in the municipal yellow pages), and Japanese quail eggs (recommended to cancer patients), to name a few. The vernacular knowledge is casually cosmopolitan; people take into account global nutritional trends, borrow across medical traditions, and methodically submit medicine to home trials, mixing, adjusting, improving, and monitoring their effects on the bodies of recipients.

This ethnographer learned, sometimes in frustration, that substances are most commonly described as "good for everything" (*dobro za sve*), or "good for the organism," "recommended to everyone," or else "good for the stomach." Such imprecision skips over many details that people learn through experience and practice but do not share as spontaneously as the reference itself; instead, only in the expert talk of one user or producer to another do more specific instructions surface as knowable or mentionable. In the popular anatomy, furthermore, stomach seems to be the sensuous epicenter of the Bosnian being. In people's stories, the gut is where life tends to happen most intensely: distress is initially registered, stress accumulated, and other disorders manifested.[3] Hence an overwhelming number of items are at least initially described as "good for the stomach." But try and complain of a headache hoping for a quick tip, and you will be surprised with a deliberate silence, followed by hesitant queries to uncover first what causes it, whether sinuses, skeletal-muscle issues, or blood pressure. Compared to the lengthy recipes published by some of the region's favorite herbalist—whose advice can be discouragingly elaborate and precise about the amounts and frequency of use, cooking, and steeping methods—folk advice clearly counts on practice to figure out the details while accounting for particular responses of each trying body that calls for further adjustments. Properties and application of home remedies are a form of knowledge that Bosnians call "od oka."

We All Know This

Literally, "by means of an eye," *od oka* registers a judgment shot from the hip, trusting the expertise of one's senses. There is no set time, for instance, for the boiling of pekmez; it lasts until one can tell it's done by smelling, tasting, and assessing its consistency by how reluctantly it drops from the spoon in dark, viscous threads. This is a form of knowledge that one embodies and learns while trying to make or procure food and remedies. It is diffused and elusive if you start asking, as I did, where it comes from—"everyone knows;" "we all consume that (*trošimo*);" "we all exchange these knowledges;" "no one told me, it is written everywhere;" "people say" (*narod* or *svijet kaže*)—but readily available once you begin searching for or complaining of a particular something, be it a dieting trick, cooking recipe, or medicine.[4] At times, items are traced to a particular giver and the solemn occasion when someone, meaning well and hearing of someone's health disorder, brought this or that. Jasmina's medicinal repertoire was full of such specimens, brought by neighbors and friends who heard of her cancer. A number of textual, televisual, and digital sources contribute to this oral tradition. Most often cited are books by three folk herbalists from the early twentieth century—Sadiković 2002 [1928]; Mijatović 1982; Pelagić 2008 [1888]—alongside a number of popular magazines devoted to health, beauty, or gardening, television shows, and internet sites that tend to gather followers and contributors from across the ex-Yugoslav region.[5]

Furthermore, this popular practice handles an impressive volume of references to medical anatomy, function of organs and glands, as well as the biochemical and microbial composition of a human body. For instance, people read each other's comprehensive lab tests with facility, demystifying acronyms and medical units and metrics for values of blood and urine and evaluating risks and comfort zones surrounding the norms of vital fluids composition, sedimentation, coagulation, acidity, et cetera. It is this generalized form of biomedical knowledge that people sometimes draw on when they evaluate folk medical claims. Slavica once clarified žara. "People say it cleanses blood. As the matter of fact," she said, "it cleanses liver, because liver processes blood. That much we know."

Home health care is always in conversation with biomedical and pharmaceutical authority, often reverently, sometimes defiantly.[6] It is circulated and cited from within clinics and waiting rooms as well as by medical professionals. But the knowledge it presumes and produces is also fantastically improvisational, inventive, and experimental, as practitioners regularly tinker with the received recipes, add or replace items, refine or simplify processing times, and adjust the consumption according to their own sense of what feels right.

The Organic Self

Home medicine also testifies to the seasonal and ordinary pleasures and rhythms of caring for the self and others and so directs our attention to practices that intervene in, shape, tone, recover, relax, refresh, revive, and preserve body and being. Simply put, home medicine offers insights into how historical subjects are conceived, made, and remedied through seemingly inconsequential quotidian affairs. Illness complaints do not lead us to the narratives of war trauma and its psychosomatic effects—as one might expect given the history of the 1990s violence and so much writing on the region since—but, rather, the stories emphasize efficacies and difficulties on a smaller scale. Remember Slavica, who linked the onset of periodontitis to the lack of pickled cabbage, which she failed to make in the fall after the war ended, either because the cabbage was too expensive or "the human was preoccupied with too many things to attend to the self properly." Attending to the self (*pozabavit se sobom* or *posvetit se sebi*) presumes a broad definition of health and an array of care practices to achieve it, from beauty treatments to groomed appearances. "Attending to the self" aims for no less than happiness or the much idealized but rarely achieved disposition of tranquility. Moreover, the self invoked in this vernacular is not primarily conceived as the subject but more broadly, as a composite human being. Being an organism, it is a part of nature and as all beings, it exercises dispositional and sensuous orientations.

Zlata, for instance, a lively seventy-year-old lady who runs a boutique of handicrafts, is very clear on smells and foods that suit her. She keeps track of substances that make her skin glow and is keen on relating the environmental conditions—air pressure, moisture, draft, the time of the day, the phase of the moon—to her sense of wellness and her shifting moods. From here, she easily leaps to broader conclusions: according to Zlata, the Tibetan mushroom too has discernable inclinations: it prefers black or linden tea over all others and likes to dwell in glass as opposed to plastic containers. Successful fermentation is taken as a sign of the mushroom's comfort and pleasure. Furthermore, being a body, one is a visceral intricacy whose organs function or malfunction in relation to the natural and the historical circumstances within which the sense of being and being embodied is imbedded or misplaced. These multiple domains are interlinked to the point where visceral organs and vital flows are presumed to be affected by the existential circumstances and exposed to the diffused threats and irritants as readily as is skin to the pressure of a thumb. All living forms, be they human, fungal, or microbial, are equally exposed and handled with due attention to the inseparability of their insides and outsides. Nurturing and remedying, thus, always proceeds remotely, reworking and knitting together the subtle and the superficial, touching the apparently withdrawn via the points that are readily surfacing.[7]

No One Can Tell the Difference

The knowledge that frames everyday care in Bosnia is not sterile, fixed, or rigidly concerned with principles. Rather, because it is rooted in and revised through practice—and adjusted by subtle, situated discernments of something as trainable, but intuitive and contingent, as the knowing eye (od oka)—it allows for compromises and is receptive to surprises and uncertainties. Thus domestic and homemade can mingle, more or less comfortably, with the quintessentially opposite qualities: industrial, plastic, artificial, or alien. Jasmina shows me around a traditional wooden storehouse where she keeps her herbal teas in paper bags, because, she says, "We all know that plastic is not healthy [as a container]." But next, from within paper she pulls out a rustling bunch of *Kantarion* in a placental wrapping of a recycled plastic sack. Another time Zlata tells me a secret: how adding diced carrots and parsley leaves to a bag of instant soup "make domaće out of an artificial [meal]." Or, similarly, how she procures commercial *ajvar*, a prized, vegetable relish, cooked and canned in Bosnian households in autumn, but then processes it further to make *domaći*. "No one can tell / No one knows," Zlata says smiling smartly at the important fact that she can fool the taste buds of the many experts she welcomes at her home.

Disturbed from its homogenized, industrially sealed consistency and combined with separately fried vegetables, then cooked and canned again, *ajvar* is altered: neither quite industrial nor domestic, embodying multiple times and conditions of production. In her own words, Zlata buys "someone else's grinding labor, for cheap," calculating savings in time and money with a memory of Marx's theory of value, but then disguises the product of alienated labor with the addition of her own time of cooking and extra care. Everyday life is full of such kinds of ordinary "magic"—homely transformations and simulations, secrets and surprises that disrupt a little the quotidian fold. Like plastic within paper, the unexpected is a regular guest, or an uninvited visitor, who surprises one in the comfort zone of a well-loved chair. "Did I tell you about the alien?" Zlata asks, startling me a bit after our conversation about comestible counterfeiting.

She sighted an alien visitor one evening by her TV, she goes on, a grayish, smallish figure, staring at her with dark, unblinking eyes while she panicked, pinched herself, and remained perfectly still, reciting silently the Qur'an for protection, until it left. She rarely mentions it, for people will think her mad.

I bring up this sighting, because the way Zlata mentioned it—at once casually and in confidence, doubting, checking, and trusting her eyes (as well as her responses and Qur'anic recitations)—gives precious insight to the ethnographer, who was, admittedly, initially confounded. An alien figure is at home in the everyday life, which, as Ben Highmore thoughtfully suggests, tends to throw our theoretical practices into a crisis and invites attention to the poetic, intractable, and what is leftover in the wake of our attempt to describe and analyze the quotidian reality.[8]

Living by Tricks

The everyday can be strange. Conversations about home medicine invoke domestic spaces and times where misgivings about the contemporary state and economy hang about the homely stuff, ringing alarm about growing health disorders and suicides (of the young, unemployed, and the war veterans), unreliable health care, and ineffective and expensive medicine. Home medicine, in other words, registers bodily health as it is enmeshed in its historical and natural context where nature and domesticity are cherished sites of care and production that nurtures life. Zlata describes various strategies that pensioners use to stretch the inadequate incomes and save money on food and medicine while attempting to eat well and take care of themselves, hoping to minimize the encounters with health care facilities. She calls it "living by tricks." Jasmina proudly listed a number of natural remedies that she used instead of prescribed medicine and store-bought supplements and Slavica, as I mentioned, similarly prefers alternatives to drugs. Marching in and out of the kitchen to show various concoctions for osteoporosis, high blood pressure, diabetes, and urinary infections, she passes by the image of Marshall Tito (Josip Broz), smiling as ever, on a wall calendar displaying the month of August, ages since the page of history of the socialist state turned. A historical reference more than a nostalgic image, Tito hangs on the edge of the calendric time frame that marks seasonal rituals and quotidian affairs of attempting to live in the happiest state of optimal health.

Notes

1. A number of market campaigns that promote domestic food products rely on the polyvalence of domaće (homemade, domestic, local) to further valorize the national product, as in "domaće je najbolje." This strategy sometimes works in reference to a broader natural and industrial context, as when people say that soil, air, and water in Bosnia are pure and special, giving rise to tasteful and healthful foods in comparison to elsewhere in Europe. On the other hand, people tend to assess the different quality of the global products contingent on the market for which they are intended. So, for instance,

in the waiting room of a famous alternative medical practitioner, the savvy receptionist tells me how he exchanges some of his own crop of potatoes for EU-bought Nutella, which his friends residing in Austria bring on their trips. EU Nutella tastes nothing like Nutella for the Bosnian market. The receptionist, an urban resident who insists on producing or procuring domaće by all means, is also concerned about the effects of the globalizing GMO technologies and food standards on Bosnian food production (not least on the home-brewing of plumb brandy), should Bosnia join the European Union.

2. Seremetakis 1996, 1–13.

3. See how novelist Fadila Nura Haver speaks of stomach (2011, 15).

4. Home medicine is not primarily women's domain, although women are most frequently the caretakers. Men also make pekmez and herbal teas and readily exchange cooking tips and advice on herbal remedies. It was, for example, a neighbor's husband who passed a wondrous dieting tip to a household collective concerned with unruly waistlines: one dry fig soaked overnight in apple vinegar.

5. See, for example, Coolinarka, available at www.coolinarika.com, and Prirodni lijek, available at http://prirodni-lijek.blogspot.com/2013/04/kopriva-zara-kao-lijek.html, both last accessed May 20, 2015.

6. Ramiz was very pleased when the doctor's laboratory analysis proved the logic of his remedy and so countered the presumed mistrust of the "old women's magic."

7. Sadik Sadiković, an early twentieth-century herbalist whose books are being reprinted and regularly consulted by medicinal cooks and home caretakers today, writes: "Whoever wants to live long and to preserve a strong body and spirit clear and fresh, must nurture and take care of his stomach" (2002 [1928], 130). Sadiković, in other words, presumes that the digestive and spiritual are inseparable components of human vitality. Ingestion of food is the beginning of a metabolic process that is at once carnal and metaphysical, involving stomach and spirit as complementary rather than opposing categories.

8. Highmore 2001, 3.

References

Haver, Fadila Nura. 2011. *Kijamet Via Vranduk*. Sarajevo: Dobra Knjiga.
Highmore, Ben. 2001. *The Everyday Life Reader*. New York: Routledge.
Mijatović, Jova. 1982. *Travar. Trave i Melemi*. Beograd: Porodica i Domaćinstvo.
Pelagić, Vasa. 2008 [1888]. *Narodni Učitelj*. Beograd: Beoknjiga.
Sadiković, Sadik. 2002 [1928]. *Narodno Zdravlje*. Svjetlost: Sarajevo.
Seremetakis, Nadia. 1996. *The Senses Still: Perception and Memory as Material Culture in Modernity*. Chicago: University of Chicago Press.

LARISA JAŠAREVIĆ is Senior Lecturer in the Global Studies Program at the University of Chicago. She is author of *Health and Wealth on the Bosnian Market: Intimate Debt*.

9. Femininity, Fashion, and Feminism: Women's Activists in Bosnia and Herzegovina

Elissa Helms

Femininity and Feminism

"What do you need feminism for? You're pretty!" Dženana[1] had heard versions of this sentiment many times from her family and friends and others she encountered as an activist at a women's NGO (nongovernmental organization) in a provincial Bosnian town. Her organization, Medica Zenica, explicitly defined itself as feminist, and she was among the activists who identified personally with the label, in defiance of its negative connotations among the general public. Feminists were assumed to be man-hating, frustrated, ugly women with unsatisfying lives. What would a young, attractive woman like Dženana need with an ideology that allegedly denied women their femininity and pushed them to be aggressive, violent, and crass like men or probably even to reject men altogether? This certainly would not help her find a good husband and become a mother, the path many presumed that every woman should want.

NGOs like Dženana's were also associated with foreign women who came to Bosnia and Herzegovina during and after the 1992–95 war to bring aid or join into efforts to support women survivors of wartime atrocities, most notoriously mass rapes. These women, mostly from Western countries and invariably young and childless, tended to have a simpler, less conventionally feminine style than the average woman in Bosnia and Herzegovina; in particular, the feminists who established and later came to work with Medica tended not to wear makeup, high heels, or high-maintenance hairstyles. There were even a few lesbians. For plenty of people from the community, these were just markers of Western difference, but there was also the whiff of suspicion that for Bosnian women to take up similar styles and stances was a threatening and unwelcome consequence of Western intervention after the war. It was no wonder that many Bosnian women's activists distanced themselves from the feminist label. But there was still a core of "brave" women who proudly called themselves feminists—just, they often added, "in a Bosnian way." Negotiating this position involved strategic choices in the way they presented their activist work, but it was also reflected in their personal style and consumption habits. Striking the right balance—distinguishing oneself from both conservative women in the local community and from foreign feminists who, some felt, did not pay enough attention to looking feminine—was a challenge, especially in small towns where fashion choices were limited and very different looks were immediately noticed. What was at stake was not so much the feminist label as a political position but its relationship to femininity, women's "proper" roles, and how the parameters of respectability for women (and men) should be defined.

This chapter is about some of the personal choices and the material, ideological, and social constraints from which activists carved out their everyday self-presentation. My aim is to give a sense of how such everyday details reflected and helped to shape some of the most pressing social and political issues confronting Bosnian society, and especially Bosnian women, after the war and the dissolution of the unique setup of socialist Yugoslavia. Not only were questions of gender ideology and the feminist label points of contention, but personal style and dress were also part of constantly shifting social divisions between rural and urban, public and private, Europe and the Balkans, ethnic or religious exclusivity and multiethnic secularism. My stories and observations come from over twenty years of engagement with the region; I focus on the women I met through their participation in a variety of community associations, NGOs, and activist groups.[2]

This Is What a Muslim Woman Looks Like

Questions of femininity were not the only pressures felt by women like Dženana who belonged in some way to the majority ethnonational group, the Bosniaks. This is how the Muslims of Bosnia and Herzegovina have been referred to with increasing regularity since the name of the group was officially changed at a congress of Bosniak intellectuals, politicians, and clergy during the war. Many people still used the old name, simply "Muslims," in everyday speech, but of course, there was always the possibility of ambiguity—did this mean the ethnic or the religious identity? Catholics were now almost always referred to as Croats and Orthodox Christians as Serbs, making those labels more clearly "ethnic." Further complicating this was the reality that a large part of the population was not particularly religious and many were outright atheists, even while some maintained that the religious part of their heritage was important to them culturally. Many people, especially in urban areas and not only those of "mixed" parentage, simply called themselves Bosnians (or Herzegovinians) to indicate belonging to a multiethnic state and cultural space. During more than forty-five years of Yugoslav socialism, both religious practice and ethnic affiliation had been discouraged, though not eliminated by any means. Then, since the violence of the war had specifically aimed to (re-)*create* ethnic difference and mistrust, suddenly religion, ethnicity, and national belonging had taken on new, politically charged meanings in everyday interactions and especially political discourses.[3] People like Dženana, who had been made a refugee during the war when her hometown was "cleansed" of Muslims—her family subjected to devastating violence, trauma, and loss because of the ethnic and religious belonging signified by their names and local identities—were forced to ask themselves what this part of their identity really meant to them.

At the same time, being a typical twenty-something educated woman in an urban milieu, Dženana was immersed into global and regional popular culture. She cultivated a slightly edgy style, following mainstream trends but always pushing the margins. Tall and thin and strikingly beautiful with a delicate bone structure and jet-black straight shoulder-length hair, Dženana was always dressed fashionably and informally but in interesting and creative combinations of standard fare. Her personality accentuated the drama of her looks—she was frequently excited or agitated about something, which she would make jokes about or angrily dissect over coffee or beer, a cigarette almost always delicately poised between two fingers of an outstretched arm. Knowing her and other then-young female Bosniak activists this way from countless afternoon coffees, evening drinks, and all-night smoked-filled slogs in a local run-down disco, the stories of Dženana's encounters with foreign aid workers were all the more absurd. Once, in the year or two just after the end of the war, two British male hairstylists were visiting Medica on a trip sponsored by aid funds to share their expert knowledge with the NGO women, who would train refugee women to be professional hairstylists as a way to reintegrate them into the community and provide them with a means of earning a living. The two British men spent considerable time hanging out with Dženana and other activists of the organization. At one point, Dženana said she realized they were trying to "educate" her about the history of rock and pop music—they assumed she had never even heard of Aretha Franklin or the Rolling Stones. Dženana shot back that her *mother* had listened to "the Beatles and all those bands!" Yugoslavia had been communist, but it was not closed to global popular culture, especially not in the 1980s of Dženana's childhood. It even had its own vibrant rock scene that these Brits were sure to know nothing about.

Or perhaps these men had internalized the images being put forth by the Western media during the war that portrayed a backward, rural, traditionally patriarchal society of older peasant women in *dimije* (baggy trousers) and headscarves, or young women who strictly guarded their virginity and chastity—as maintained by the many reports on the use of mass rapes as a weapon in this war, especially by Serb forces against Bosniak women.[4] Because, sure enough, after an evening of bar hopping with Dženana and her colleagues, one of the British men said he would really like to "meet and talk with a real Muslim girl." One of the activists of Serb background had smiled and gestured to Dženana with her fashionable, Western persona, "smoking and drinking right in front of him all night!" as Dženana incredulously pointed out, but the man refused to believe in her authenticity, and they got into a heated argument. "People have no idea what Bosnians are like. They have these stereotypes in their heads, especially of Muslims and women," Dženana fumed when she related the story later.

Figure 9.1. Women, some wearing hijab and others not, sharing an iftar meal in Sarajevo, 2012. Photograph by Roska Vrgova.

Like the majority of Bosnians, Dženana and her friends were well aware of how the war and her community was being depicted in the Western press. They watched CNN, too. I met several women from an older generation who were particularly incensed by these depictions. These were educated, professional women who had come of age and established careers and a sense of self under the system of Yugoslav socialism with its formal commitment to gender equality (practice was, not surprisingly, a different story) and its massive modernization project. They belonged to the generations of women for whom higher education, paid work, and state family support had been a given. They firmly held on to their identities as urban intellectuals, above all unquestionably part of a civilized Europe. Their outrage at the media portrayal had even pushed many of them into political and social activism.

One of these women, Mensura, a high school teacher who later became a member of the cantonal assembly as a candidate from the Women's Party active at the time, complained with barely disguised disdain about media images of refugee women "with five scarves on their heads." She wanted the world to know that "we're not just old peasant women like the world media showed!" In terms of personal style, Mensura and the urban women of her generation favored conservative, classic styles of professional women in male-associated arenas for whom it was nevertheless important to retain their femininity, to "remain women," as I heard several of them put it. It was imperative that they not be seen as wanting to *become* men. They wore suits with pants or skirts in pastel colors accessorized with pearls, low heels, and floral scarves (for their necks, of course, not their heads!). They argued in their NGO work and in their political involvement for women's inclusion in political life and the particular qualities they would bring to politics as women, but ultimately they distinguished themselves from men as more responsible, honest, caring, and practical, precisely because of their femininity and roles as mothers, caregivers, and keepers of the home. Women would bring respectability and integrity to politics precisely because of their femininity.

This Is What an Urban Woman Looks Like

As mentioned, these older professional women also distinguished themselves from rural women and the working classes on the basis of their education and positions of responsibility in paid work. This led to some amount of tension as they grappled with a newfound imperative to affirm themselves as Bosniaks since they seemed to locate the essence of Bosniak culture in village life. Several times they told me I should visit a Muslim village to see a true Bosniak woman. This existed simultaneously with their outrage over the depiction of "Bosnian women" as rural refugees in the international media. They wanted the world to know they were not backward, superstitious, ignorant, uncivilized—everything associated with the rural refugee, especially those most prominent in media images, refugee women from the eastern Bosnian region around Srebrenica (from which women, children, and the elderly were expelled in what was ruled by the International Criminal Tribunal for the former Yugoslavia as genocide against Bosniaks perpetrated by Serb forces). Before the war, it had been the practice of Muslim village women to replace their dimije with skirts and more Western, urban-looking clothes when they went to town, making them less visible there.[5] But rural Muslim dress was now a common sight in the towns of Bosniak-dominated areas, too, as this is where refugees from the countryside had sought safety, many of them not to return.

Since the mid-1990s, the renewed importance of ethnic and religious identity incited by the war violence and ethnic polarization, combined with the lifting of state-socialist restrictions on religion, had given rise to increased numbers of urban women who adopted Islamic dress, *hijab*. This was a much different style of covering from the colorful patterned scarves and dimije of the village. Similar to contemporary styles in Turkey, Egypt, or the Persian Gulf states, the colors worn by these pious urban women tended to be more plain and subdued; head and body coverage was more complete than with village dress. There were variations, in turn, among hijab styles that signaled different approaches to Islam and levels of piety.[6] Female Islamic dress in its different forms had in fact become one of the main areas of contestation over the Europeanness and modernity of Bosnian Islam, and of Bosniaks and Bosnians by extension.[7] Not unlike stereotypes in the United States or the rest of Europe, "covered" women in Bosnia and Herzegovina were consistently assumed to be uneducated and subservient to traditional patriarchal values. Several young hijab-wearing women I knew had experienced the surprise of fellow Bosnians or foreign visitors when the women spoke intelligently on political and social issues, especially when they revealed a knowledge of English or argued for women's rights—or spoke out at all. On the other hand, Western dress—or, more accurately, globalized mass-produced styles—was also associated with urban centers, spaces marked especially since the socialist period by the mingling of ethnic groups, a deemphasis on ethnic and religious markers, and even atheism and cosmopolitan orientations. It was this identification with urban modernity and its association with educated, professional women that Mensura and her colleagues were trying to reconcile with an affirmation of Bosniak identity that they continued to associate with village customs.

This Is What a Feminist Looks Like

Nada Ler, one of the only Bosnian veterans of the homegrown feminist movement in socialist Yugoslavia, told me about her reaction to seeing Western feminists for the first time. It was the late 1970s and spaces were opening up for alternative discourses and movements as long as they did not threaten the primacy of the Communist Party. The small and urban but socially well-positioned feminist movement had been reading feminist theory from France and the United States and formulating its own critique within a Marxist framework.[8] They eagerly awaited the Western feminists they invited to the first international feminist conference, Comrade Woman (*Drug-ca*), held in Belgrade in 1978. Nada described her and other Yugoslav women's shock and disappointment at the women who came. Emerging as they had out of counterculture movements of the time, it was the "thing" among Western feminists to reject what society said was acceptable behavior and dress for women, so they showed up unshaven, bra-less, and dressed very casually, with no makeup and natural hair; they sat on the floor with their legs spread out. "We were so taken aback," Nada said, "this was not what we wanted out of feminism." Some of the Western feminists had also insisted that the gatherings be women only, which meant excluding the male allies with whom the Yugoslav feminists had very good relationships.[9]

Similar clashes of style and ideology emerged during my research. In the spring of 2000 at a regional conference on women's human rights held in a typical socialist-era concrete block hotel near Sarajevo, I joined a group of women activists on the terrace for coffee during a break. Tidža, one of the Sarajevo activists, told a story about her encounter with a feminist from Canada who had later reported that she had met the most fantastic lesbian in Sarajevo. And this is how Tidža said she had "become a lesbian," counting on the rest of us to appreciate the irony that this did not describe her at all. She had told the visiting feminist what I had heard her say many times, that every Bosnian woman is born a feminist but in our Bosnian way (*na naš bosanski način*). "We don't want some kind of domination, just equal chances in life," she said. This kicked off a litany of complaints about "women like that," especially by Lidija, an older woman from an elite Sarajevo family who, like many others in her position, remained committed to the Yugoslav socialist concept and used her activism for women's human rights as a way to preserve some of the positive aspects of that system. Lidija was dressed that day as I had always seen her—a dress and blazer with pantyhose and pumps, a pearl necklace, makeup beneath her gold-rimmed glasses, and her shoulder-length blond hair pulled into a ponytail with a black- and gold-beaded bow-barrette. She had been teased several times—"Oh *gospođo* (madam), I see you've gotten dressed up again!"—by a Belgrade lesbian feminist whom Lidija described as wearing shorts and sandals to one of the meetings they attended. Lidija told us she disapproved of "that kind of unwashed, unkempt woman" and the idea that she might be expected to give up her own personal style. "As long as I can remember I've worn makeup and glasses!" she protested. This was part of the reason she was not a feminist, she told the group, making dress and style into a marker of sexuality. One of the Medica activists who also heard this was disappointed by the antigay and antifeminist sentiments expressed during this exchange, but she apparently did not feel comfortable enough objecting to the group. Indeed, Lidija's sentiments took for granted much of the prejudices of Bosnian society about what feminism stood for.

And so personal style was not just an issue of generation and class—Lidija with her pearls and bows was not too much older than the Belgrade feminist in shorts and sandals, and they both came from educated, urban backgrounds. It also reflected these activists' notions of what they were fighting for when they engaged in women's activism. Those who were reluctant to embrace or even vehemently rejected "feminism" seemed to view it as a threat to their femininity and to the established gender order where there was no confusion of roles. They wanted women to be included, for their voices to matter, for them and their expected roles as mothers and caregivers to be treated with respect. But as in the middle-class, urban practice that emerged from socialist Yugoslavia—the reality criticized by the Yugoslav-era feminists—the new model of liberal democracy promoted by international NGOs and donors could easily incorporate entrenched patriarchal gender conventions and the strict separation of men's and women's roles, especially in areas considered private: the home, family, fashion, sexuality, and so on. It was the seeming blurring of those "private" gender conventions, if not outright homophobia, that apparently made many people, including many of the women's activists, uncomfortable.

Being Feminist the Bosnian Way

Let us return to Medica, where a small group of twenty- and thirty-something women working in Infoteka, the documentation and publicity branch of the organization, *did* want to challenge and reformulate commonsense notions and everyday practices of gender and sexuality. This was the last place I expected to be told I should wear makeup and do something with my hair, but this happened on a regular basis. When I wore a skirt one warm day, one of the women looked me over and said that my legs were actually good—I should wear skirts more! There was another young woman from the United States volunteering with Medica at the time. She also felt the pressure and was wearing makeup, jewelry, and skirts more than she had before. This was a reflection of the general climate of female presentation in the region, however; something similar happened to a

Figure 9.2. Different fashion styles in Baščaršija, Old Town, Sarajevo, 2017. Photograph by Roska Vrgova.

fellow anthropologist doing long-term research in neighboring Serbia, and she was not hanging out with feminists. At issue was the particularly local brand of feminism these activists saw themselves nurturing. It was articulated primarily around a long-term strategy of changing social norms as opposed to what they saw as more critical and vocal activism in other countries. Not presenting a radically different persona to the community, and not adopting what many saw as unfeminine styles from the West, was part of this positioning.

At the same time, the activists in Infoteka struggled to distinguish themselves from mainstream styles, to mark themselves as cosmopolitan and critical of provincial norms. Cultivating an alternative style was not easy in a town like Zenica. In neighborhoods and at family gatherings, unusual outfits, like many kinds of differences from the expected patterns, would always be remarked on, often disparagingly. It was also just difficult to find clothing that would make one stand out: all of the market stalls and affordable shops sold more or less the same things in the same colors and styles. There was more choice in the capital city, Sarajevo, but mostly in the form of global chains where clothing was either too expensive for most Bosnians or not too different from what could be found at the outdoor market. Secondhand stores were still associated with humanitarian aid and poverty—something for refugees rather than civilized urbanites (although this has changed over the years, particularly for younger urban generations and in the face of widespread poverty). It was not that the women of Infoteka diverged radically from others in the community (and there were those who did not conform entirely because they did not pay much attention at all to their appearance), but there were several who took pains to find unusual pieces—some funky shoes, an unusually patterned skirt, vintage earrings—or to combine common items in new ways. They also took advantage of trips abroad made as part of their work to acquire interesting accessories. I will always remember one woman, for example, who frequently wore scarves and tunics she got in Sri Lanka while attending a women's conference there. Different and unusual items were always noticed in the Infoteka office; coffee break conversations were just as likely to revolve around where to find an item of clothing or makeup as they were to be about feminist activism (not to mention all the standard forms of workplace gossip and complaints or general commentary about life).

These differences of fashion and style should not be overstated—at the end of the day, it was these activists' words and deeds that really differentiated their political stances. Alternative appearances were far from a guarantee of radical social critique or political courage, as can be seen through fashion and lifestyle trends just about everywhere (from hippies to hipsters). And I sometimes heard quite astute feminist critique come from conventionally dressed professional women or girls in hijab. Many of the associations to different sorts of women's dress were specific to the social and political contests of Bosnia and Herzegovina, but they also participated in and reflected global trends, markets, and ideas from the US and European "West" and the Muslim "East," as well as the socialist past when Yugoslavia attempted to carve a place for itself between those imagined worlds. Like just about everywhere in the world, though, it was women's dress and what it said about their family status, class position, religious affiliation, and most of all sexuality that was scrutinized and was therefore a key part of all kinds of social struggles.

Notes

1. All names given as first names only in this text are pseudonyms.
2. Most of this material relates to the parts of the country that have been dominated politically and demographically since the war by Bosniaks, otherwise known as Bosnian Muslims, although my research took me to all parts of Bosnia and Herzegovina and into contact with people of all possible ethnic and religious backgrounds. For more on this research and on many of the issues raised here, see Helms 2013.
3. See Hayden 1996; Sorabji 1995.
4. See Helms 2013; Žarkov 2007.
5. See Bringa 1995.
6. Mesaric 2013.
7. Helms 2008.
8. See Benderly 1997; Bonfiglioli 2008.
9. The well-known feminist writer from Zagreb, Slavenka Drakulić, who was also a participant at the 1978 conference, has reproduced a similar East-West division based on style in her accounts of those encounters (see "How Women Survived Post-Communism (And Didn't Laugh)," *Eurozone*, June 5, 2015, accessed July 28, 2015, http://www.eurozine.com/articles/2015-06-05-drakulic-en.html, and Drakulić 1992). However, historian

Chiara Bonfiglioli shows these differences were not so clear-cut and did not always fall along East-West lines. Still, Bonfiglioli also documented a sense among some of the Yugoslav participants that both their personal style and their approaches to feminism were markedly different from those of their "Western sisters" (see Bonfiglioli 2008, 87–94).

References

Benderly, Jill. 1997. "Feminist Movements in Yugoslavia, 1978–1992." In *State-Society Relations in Yugoslavia, 1945–1992*, edited by M.K. Bokovoy, J.A. Irvine, and C.S. Lilly, 183–209. New York: St. Martin's Press.

Bonfiglioli, Chiara. 2008. "Belgrade 1978: Remembering the Conference "Drugarica Žena: Žensko Pitanja—Novi Pristup?" / "Comrade Woman: The Women's Question—A New Approach?" Thirty Years After." MA thesis, Utrecht, Netherlands.

Bringa, Tone. 1995. *Being Muslim the Bosnian Way: Identity and Community in a Central Bosnian Village*. Princeton, NJ: Princeton University Press.

Drakulić, Slavenka. 1992. *How We Survived Communism and Even Laughed*. London: Vintage Books.

Hayden, Robert M. 1996. "Imagined Communities and Real Victims: Self-Determination and Ethnic Cleansing in Yugoslavia." *American Ethnologist* 23 (4): 783–801.

Helms, Elissa. 2008. "East and West Kiss: Gender, Orientalism, and Balkanism in Muslim-Majority Bosnia-Herzegovina." *Slavic Review* 67 (1): 88–119.

Helms, Elissa. 2013. *Innocence and Victimhood: Gender, Nation, and Women's Activism in Postwar Bosnia-Herzegovina*. Madison: University of Wisconsin Press.

Mesaric, Andreja. 2013. "Wearing Hijab in Sarajevo: Dress Practices and the Islamic Revival in Post-War Bosnia-Herzegovina." *Anthropological Journal of European Cultures* 22 (2): 12–34.

Sorabji, Cornelia. 1995. "A Very Modern War: War and Territory in Bosnia-Herzegovina." In *War: A Cruel Necessity? The Bases of Institutionalized Violence*, edited by R.A. Hinde and H. Watson, 80–99. London: Tauris Academic Studies.

Žarkov, Dubravka. 2007. *The Body of War: Media, Ethnicity, and Gender in the Break-Up of Yugoslavia*. Durham, NC: Duke University Press.

ELISSA HELMS is Associate Professor in the Department of Gender Studies at the Central European University. She is author of *Innocence and Victimhood: Gender, Nation, and Women's Activism in Postwar Bosnia-Herzegovina* and editor of *The New Bosnian Mosaic: Identities, Memories, and Moral Claims in a Post-War Society* (with Xavier Bougarel and Ger Duijzings).

10 That Black Cloud upon Our Family: Everyday Life of Gays and Lesbians in Slovenia

Roman Kuhar

The annual International Lesbian, Gay, Bisexual, Trans and Intersex Association (ILGA)–Europe's Rainbow map of 2014,[1] which ranks European countries according to their legislation and policies that impact the human rights of LGBT people, did not receive much attention from Slovenian media—but just enough to raise some eyebrows. The Rainbow map ranked Slovenia on a scale from 0 (gross violation of human rights) to 100 (full equality and respect for human rights) at 35 percent (nineteenth out of forty-nine countries). This was just a bit below the European average of 36 percent. However, it is not this information that attracted media attention. Slovenians are used to being "in the golden middle" of European standards, which is also translated into "better than the rest of the Balkan countries." But that was not the case this time: Croatia reached 55 percent; Montenegro 45 percent; and even Albania was better with 38 percent. Although the map does not measure social attitudes toward gays and lesbians—in this regard Slovenia is doing better than all three mentioned countries—the eyebrows were raised for a reason.

In Slovenia, "Balkan" was constructed as the "Other," in an attempt to align itself with the progressive, liberal European culture, based on the rule of law and a respect for human rights. It was this construction, which intensified both in political and everyday life discourses in the late 1980s and early 1990s, that helped establish an independent Slovenian (political and cultural) identity upon the dissolution of Yugoslavia in 1991. At first, Slovenia tried to get rid of any links that tied the country to the Balkan region. A new political identity, springing from the recently achieved political independence, started to emerge as an opposition to "the Balkan culture," which was seen as backward and nondemocratic. With revived nationalism, people from the former Yugoslavia were no longer welcome in Slovenia. They are still not recognized as ethnic minorities, although they outnumber Italians, Hungarians, and Roma people, who are all constitutionally recognized as ethnic minorities in Slovenia. Italians and Hungarians even have their representative among the ninety members of the Slovenian parliament.

However, in the mid-1990s, when the new national identity was no longer seen as being tremendously endangered by the former Yugoslav nations, which were by that time already involved in a horrifying military conflict, new "Others" slowly started to emerge. One of them was the homosexual, "the other within the nation," which put Slovenian identity building between Scylla and Charybdis: on the one hand, gays and lesbians were understood as something non-Slovenian; on the other hand, it became clear that nonacceptance of LGBT people and the recognition of their human rights (as required from EU) would make Slovenian culture Balkan-like. That was exactly the image Slovenians wanted to avoid. It is between these two tensions that Slovenian gays and lesbians experience their everyday life.

The Europeanization process of downloading the European standards of fundamental rights protection into the national legislature has been taking place since the early 1990s and intensified during the EU accession process. The gay and lesbian movement, which had emerged by 1984 and is the oldest such movement in eastern Europe, was rather successful in demanding antidiscrimination policies, often using the "magic catchphrase" European standards. Especially during the last stages of Slovenia's joining the EU, the Slovenian parliament seemed to readily do almost anything to please the supranational organization, including ensuring support for the protection of sexual minorities. However, after 2004, when Slovenia became a full member of the EU, the political readiness to recognize and protect social minorities subsided.

It is such political readiness in relation to the EU accession process that can—at least partly—explain the better legal situation of LGBT people in some Balkan countries. Slovenia regressed not only because it was the first of the former Yugoslav republics to enter the EU but also, primarily, because of the lack of political will to address the next bundle of human rights protections of LGBT people—that of same-sex partnerships and families and, recently, transgender human rights. Politically these issues seem to be harder and riskier to address than antidiscrimination policies, as they intervene with the binary gender system and issues of marriage and family. The latter has always been an ideological and political battleground. The lack of binding EU regulations in this area does not help either: according to article 9 of the EU charter of Fundamental Rights, "the right to marry and the right to found a family shall be guaranteed in accordance with the national laws governing the exercise of these rights."[2]

While the social distance toward gays and lesbians in Slovenia has shortened considerably—from 62 percent of Slovenian citizens who did not want a homosexual to be their neighbor in 1993 to 28 percent in 2016[3]—it seems that the issue of same-sex families is becoming the key litmus test of acceptance and tolerance of homosexuality in the twenty-first century. According to data from the European Value Survey (2008), 18 percent of respondents in Slovenia support the right of same-sex couples to joint adoption, placing Slovenia at the European bottom.

These data and the Rainbow map are a telling illustration of the so-called transparent closet, which will be used in this chapter as a frame concept, describing the painful situation of gays and lesbians in Slovenia who are out but remain socially, politically, or even personally invisible at different levels of their everyday life. This is, however, not to say that the experience of the transparent closet is a unique experience of gays and lesbians in Slovenia. It rather shows how their experiences are comparable to the situation of gays and lesbians throughout the Balkans and elsewhere in Europe.

The Transparent Closet

Both waves of the sociological research into everyday life of gays and lesbians in Slovenia showed that a lot of respondents from the study ended up in a *transparent closet* after coming out to their parents.[4] The transparent closet refers to those situations where one's same-sex orientation is acknowledged after coming out, but parents or the family as such refuse to discuss it further. This shows the relational nature of coming out. Coming out is not just an act or a process that unfolds over many iterations; it is not just a self-contained act, reliant on the sole will of the person who comes out. It is rather something interrelated that affects both the subsequent coming-outs and the relationship with the person to whom one comes out. In other words, the understanding that once one comes out, one is out, is rather limited. Coming out requires acknowledgment, and it needs to be acted on by the other side, the person to whom one comes out. The transparent closet refers to those situations where one comes out of the closet and is then pushed back into it in order to ease the discomfort of those to whom one has come out.

It is precisely this element—the relational effects of coming out—that pushes gays and lesbians back into the closet, as their family members refuse to accept and deal with the consequences and meanings of the new information. As a result, one's coming out also compels their family members to confront the same homophobic society, but family members often "resolve" this tension by creating silence around their daughter's/son's homosexuality. In such a way, homosexuality becomes a "family secret." Maruša (lesbian, twenty-seven), for example, reported: "We haven't talked about it for a long time . . . about how I live. Later, when I heard from others about their coming-outs, I realized that after the first shock parents never ask about anything, no matter if the reaction was positive or negative. . . . This is a sign of certain uneasiness." Similarly, Borut (gay, thirty) said:

> I expressed the wish [to talk about it] several times, for instance, I showed them an article. . . . Mom takes a quick glance and doesn't say anything; then I give it to Father, but he looks away. Then mom starts to yell, like, why do you rub our noses in it. Like, I shouldn't press them, they do not want to talk about it. She didn't say explicitly that they didn't want to talk about it, but just that I shouldn't press with these themes. Now I launch the subject every now and then, but there is no reaction. Mom sometimes says that it is hard now that she knows what I am.

According to the study, there are typically two moments that describe the coming out narratives within the family of origin: the first shock (often accompanied by psychological violence, such as emotional blackmailing) is followed by the consolidation phase. During this phase, the disturbance caused by the new information is resolved through demands that the child's sexual orientation is swept under the carpet, hidden and not discussed. The fact about one's homosexuality is recognized, but its implications are not accepted. As a rule, homosexuality is not discussed within the family any further, or it is discussed with great discomfort. It becomes, as one respondent said, "that black cloud upon our family that we pretend not to see."

As parents find their child's homosexuality shameful, they often try to keep the information to themselves. Fifty-seven percent of the respondents from the 2005 study reported they know or presume that their parents did not talk about their homosexuality with any of their closest friends or relatives or anyone else. Ksenija (lesbian, thirty), for example, reported: "After all these years I've noticed that my mother has not come out to anyone (i.e., as a mother of a lesbian daughter).... I've also noticed that she can hardly bring herself to utter that word."

Some parents eventually do "come out" and confide in someone who they think might offer them some support: "I think that they told a couple of friends, and one reason was that they themselves needed to talk about it. But, for example, my mom told it to her sister only two years later. More than two years later. And she is close to her sister" (Oskar, gay, twenty-four).

Unlike in the West, there are no support groups for parents of gays and lesbians in Slovenia. LGBT nongovernmental organizations tried a few times to start such a group but without any substantial success: after a few initial meetings, when only one or two parents showed up, the group ceased to exist.

The First Coming Out

The respondents from the study were on average nineteen and a half when they first came out, but there is a trend of younger gays and lesbians coming out earlier in their lives. Most of them, nearly 80 percent, first came out to their friends. The majority reported getting support and understanding from the person they came out to, which should be at least partly attributed to the well-considered choice of to whom to come out. In a 2005 study, 75 percent reported a positive reaction to their first coming out, and in 2014 the share was even higher: 85 percent. Only 4 percent in 2005 and 2 percent in 2014 said that the person to whom they first came out rejected them or reacted in a negative way.

The initial coming out in the context of their immediate family occurs on average a year or two later. Gays and lesbians who come out to both parents do that at the age of twenty, on average, although as a rule younger gays and lesbians come out at a much earlier age than did their older counterparts. However, there is still a clear distinction between coming out to one's mother and father. While nearly 70 percent of respondents in both studies reported being out to their mothers, the share of those who are out to their fathers is about 20 percent smaller. On average, after coming out to their mothers, gays and lesbians are more likely to come out to their siblings, classmates, or co-workers before coming out to their fathers.

The fact that younger generations of gays and lesbians in the study are more likely to come out to both of their parents at the same time is a sign of a growing shift away from the patriarchal family model. This might, at least partly explain the fear older generations had in coming out to fathers. They often attributed the reasons for not coming out to their fathers to superficial communication between the alienated father and the child. Sebastjan (gay, thirty-one), for example, explained: "I simply was always closer to my mom than my dad, which means that we could have a good talk. I spent incomparably more time with her than with my father. But I don't have problems with this. I don't think that my father doesn't love me or anything like that." While the images of alienated fathers indicate that the patriarchal order in family relations was present until recently, if only on the symbolic level, and reminiscent of stereotypical images of the "Balkan masculinity," it seems that there is a growing shift away from the patriarchal family model in Slovenia, characterized by the erosion of the father's authority.[5] The results from the second wave of the research on everyday life of gays and lesbians in Slovenia show that it is precisely the family context in which the greatest change was recorded: there is still a distinction between mothers and fathers—fewer people are out to their fathers—but an increasing number of young gays and lesbians come out to both parents, and their reactions are described in more positive terms than only ten years ago.

The Public Transparent Closet

The transparent closet is not only a social situation that can emerge within the family. Similar mechanisms occur in other social contexts, primarily in public space in Slovenia, which remains a heteronormative haven. Any visible sign of homosexuality in public space is often understood as a disturbance of the heteronormative matrix of everyday life. Although we can report on some symbolically important steps forward—such as the decision of Ljubljana's mayor to display a rainbow flag on May 17 (International Day against Homophobia, Transphobia, and Biphobia) outside the town hall and the display of a rainbow flag from Ljubljana's castle during the annual Pride parade[6]—Ljubljana has been only recently introduced to the dominant European culture of cities supporting rainbow events and lifestyles. As such, the heteronormativity of everyday life in Slovenia remains rather intact, particularly outside of the capital.

Similar to the family context where homosexuality is swept under the carpet, in public space gays and lesbians are faced with subtle regulative mechanisms (such as a coercive gaze, name-calling, staring, verbal comments, whistling) or even physical violence, which are all mechanisms of control over sexualities that are constructed as deviant. "You can get one strange gaze in the street," said Amalija (lesbian, twenty-six) "and you will change your mind [about holding hands with your same-sex partner]." The heteronormativity of public space therefore functions as a kind of public panopticon that establishes an awareness among LGBT people feeling continuously watched. The result, as such, is a different form of self-control, which Michel Foucault described by claiming that

Figure 10.1. Marchers in the 2009 Pride parade in Ljubljana, Slovenia. Photograph by Nada Žgank.

Figure 10.2. Marchers in the 2009 Pride parade in front of the Slovenian parliament. Photograph by Nada Žgank.

"there is no need for arms, physical violence, material constraints. Just a gaze. An inspecting gaze, a gaze which each individual under its weight will end by interiorizing to the point that he is his own overseer, each individual thus exercising this surveillance over and against himself."[7]

All this explains why, on an everyday basis, one generally does not see same-sex couples holding hands or expressing other forms of "public intimacy" that heterosexual couples would regularly display in Ljubljana. Most same-sex couples adjust to the heteronormative public space through mimicry, which is a mechanism of self-control and self-protection. The study namely showed that 53 percent of lesbians and gays surveyed had reported being victims of violence due to their sexual orientation at least once (in the second wave of the study, the share dropped to 50 percent). In both studies, about 90 percent reported verbal violence; 25 percent, physical violence; and 6 percent, sexual violence. Most of these violence incidents, over 60 percent, occurred in public spaces and were committed by strangers. Moreover, 68 percent of those experiencing violence due to their sexual orientation reported several such incidents.

In this context, the transparent closet runs along the lines of a private/public divide: gays and lesbians are tolerated as long as they are hidden in the privacy of their homes. The spontaneous gestures—such as holding hands—are disabled by a constant awareness of the heteronormativity underpinning the public space. The private/public divide is transgressed only in some exceptional moments, such as the annual Pride parades or when gays and lesbians believe that the threat of violence is momentarily abolished, as explained by Igor (gay, twenty-seven): "One feels the pressure. You take a look around yourself and if there is no one, then you do it [you hold yours partner hand]. Or you do it if the environment is such that it allows it. If there are no primitive people around you, then you do it. However, I don't walk hand in hand with my boyfriend around Ljubljana, definitely not.... It seems as if all this is already in your DNA, that we live in a heterosexual society with certain rules and that you must not provoke it."

The Black Cloud over the Balkans?

It is hard to appreciate the impact of homophobia on the everyday life of LGBT people in Slovenia and in the rest of the former Yugoslav republics. It is true that Slovenia has always been considered the most progressive and liberal of all former Yugoslav republics. Although these are very general, and to a certain extent also stereotypical, representations of Slovenian society, the empirical evidence somehow supports it as the social distance toward gays and lesbians in Slovenia is nearly half what it is in the other former Yugoslav republics: according to the European Value Study from 2008, there were 65.1 percent of Montenegrins, 58.0 percent of Macedonians, 56.0 percent of Serbians, and 51.8 percent of Croatians who would not like a homosexual to be their neighbor, compared to 34.4 percent of Slovenians who would not like gay neighbors.[8]

But what do these numbers mean for gays and lesbians who have to organize their everyday life in a heteronormative environment? For sure there is an emotional toll to it, as homosexuality in Slovenia often remains an open secret, particularly in the context of family life. For those who organize their life outside of their families of origin—it is not unusual that people live together with their parents until they are thirty or older—the heteronormative legislation might cause numerous complications in terms of housing, inheritance, hospital visits, tax reduction, and so on. It is also true that these problems are being increasingly addressed in public and policy discourse, but it does not mean that homophobia will be instantly swept away.

In his study on the closet in America, Steven Seidman suggests that young generations tend to organize their everyday life beyond the closet, while for older generations the closet represented an inescapable part of their lives.[9] While in Slovenia and elsewhere in the Balkans one can see similar trends, living beyond the closet is still not possible in every aspect of social life: gays and lesbians might be accepted in social circles of close friends and the experience of the transparent closet in the family context might slowly disappear with the younger generations, but structurally the transparent closet and homophobia preserve their powers, primarily in the public sphere.

Homophobia in Slovenia is—unlike in some other Balkan countries (think of notorious homophobic incidents at Pride parades in Belgrade[10])—not very vocal and loud. It is generally also not aimed at the overt exclusion of gays and lesbians. Nevertheless, it is constantly bubbling underneath the alleged "tolerant" Slovenian culture and can be easily triggered to become overt hatred against gays and lesbians, as happened, for example, during the debate on the new Family Code (2009–2012).

In October 2009, the Ministry of Labor, Family, and Social Affairs presented a proposal for a new Family Code, which included essential innovations in the understanding of family and marriage. It showed the determination of the left-wing government not to address same-sex partnerships in a separate law but rather in one general law that would address all types of partnerships and families.

The Family Code changed the definition of a family, basing it on the concept of ethics of care. In other words, the family was defined as a union between one or more children and one or more adults that take care of these children. The definition of a civil marriage was also changed in a way that heterosexual and homosexual couples were put on equal legal footing, including the right to second-parent and joint adoptions.

The public debate on the new Family Code was often narrowed down to the issue of adoption of children by same-sex couples. Scientific arguments from sociological and psychological studies on same-sex families were rarely confronted, and even in those few cases, the scientific arguments were often silenced by the loud and dramatic speeches of political and religious demagogues. Their debates were often a well-orchestrated show of hatred against gays and lesbians, hidden under the guise of caring for children and the future of the Slovenian nation. These groups are part of the increasingly vocal antigender movement in Europe, which is manifested as a populist resistance to marriage equality, abortion, reproductive technologies, LGBT rights, gender mainstreaming, sex education, and even the notion of gender itself.[11]

While the Family Code was adopted by parliament in 2011, the opponents of the code, primarily the Civil Initiative for a Family and the Rights of Children, a satellite organization of the Slovenian Roman Catholic Church, managed to collect the forty thousand signatures needed for a public referendum and eventually the law was rejected by the voters. The referendum took place in March 2012; 45 percent of voters supported the law and 55 percent voted against.

In 2015, Slovenia saw another attempt to pass marriage equality, when an amendment to the old Family Code was adopted, changing the definition of marriage from "a union of a man and a woman" to "a union of two persons." Again, the Civil Initiative collected forty thousand signatures and demanded a public referendum on the adopted law, which was again rejected by the voters in December 2015. However, just two days after this referendum, the MP Jani Möderndorfer introduced a bill to give same-sex couples all the rights of marriage, except joint adoption and in-vitro fertilisation. The law was adopted in April 2016 and came into effect in February 2017, replacing the 2005 act on registered same-sex partnerships, which confered only inheritance and visitation rights to same-sex couples.

Despite the fact that the act on civil same-sex partnership legally and symbolically differentiates (and discriminates) between heterosexual and same-sex couples, it surely placed Slovenia higher on the ILGA's Rainbow map. In 2018 Slovenia was ranked at 48 percent, two places higher than in 2014 (seventeenth out of forty-nine countries).[12] But in the reality of everyday life, gays and lesbians do not care much about this map. All they want—in the words of one lesbian activist—is a "peaceful life and those few rights that our neighbors and friends already have."

Notes

1. ILGA–Europe Rainbow map, accessed June 3, 2014, http://www.ilga-europe.org/rainboweurope/2014.

2. "Charter of Fundamental Rights of the European Union," accessed June 3, 2014, http://eur-lex.europa.eu/legal-content/EN/TXT/?uri=CELEX:12012P/TXT.

3. Toš 2009, 2016.

4. Švab and Kuhar 2005; Kuhar 2014; Švab 2016. The research combined qualitative and quantitative methodology. First, we conducted a questionnaire-based face-to-face survey on a sample of 443 self-identified gays and lesbians. Then seven focus groups were carried out with 36 participants in total. In 2014, the second wave of the study was conducted. The first phase included a quantitative study with an online questionnaire on a sample of 1,145 self-identified gays and lesbians, followed by eight focus groups with 36 participants in total.

5. See Švab 2001.

6. The first Pride parade in Slovenia was organized in 2001 as a reaction to an incident that occurred in front of the allegedly gay-friendly bar Café Galerija. The bouncer at the door refused to let in two gay men, saying that they should get used to the fact that it is not a bar for "that kind of people." While the first Pride parade passed without any homophobic incidents, homophobic attacks would appear in later years. These were not attacks during the parades but immediately after, when people were heading home, or in the evening, after the Pride parade parties. In these attacks, a few gay men and lesbians were injured. The most resounding attack, however, appeared in June 2009, a few days before the parade. A group of eight masked men attacked a gay-friendly bar, Café Open, in Ljubljana. They threw a lit torch into the bar during a

gay literary reading taking place inside. They also physically attacked one gay activist, who happened to be outside of the bar at the time of the attack. They burned his neck with the torch and injured his head. The police arrested three attackers, aged eighteen to twenty-two, who were eventually sentenced to five to seven months imprisonment. This was also the first court case in Slovenia of a hate crime based on sexual orientation.

7. Foucault 1980, 155.

8. Bosnia and Herzegovina was not included in the study. See European Values Study, accessed June 30, 2015, http://www.europeanvaluesstudy.eu/.

9. Seidman 2002.

10. In Serbia, religious beliefs align closely with ethnic and national identity. Individuals with identities that deviate from the norm tend to be targeted for violence, especially where those identities throw into question the dominant patriarchal culture, as homosexuality does. This is most violently manifested during Pride parades in Belgrade. In 2001, a week before the first Pride parade was organized in Ljubljana, the first Pride parade was supposed to take place in Belgrade. However, it turned into a violent antigay demonstration. Serbians—nationalists, football fans, and other protesters—at least partly organized and led by the Serbian Orthodox religious authorities, rioted in the street, beating gays and lesbians and looting stores. Policemen, who were not even equipped to suppress riots, did little to protect the participants who were beaten. The next Pride parade was supposed to take place eight years later, in 2009, but was banned by the Serbian authorities at the very last moment, when the police said that they could not protect the festival attendees.

In 2010, Belgrade finally had its Pride parade—the first one since 2001. However, it turned out to be a total disaster again. Serbian authorities sent thousands of policemen to encircle the small area where the parade would take place. They did this primarily to protect EU officials, including the EU ambassador to Serbia, who were attending the parade, from thousands of Serbians who showed up to violently protest against the Gay Pride Festival. Although the immediate area around the Pride parade was contained, the rest of Belgrade was described as a war zone with fire-bombs and Molotov cocktails thrown in the streets, looters smashing windows and setting fires, and protestors shouting "death to homosexuals!" According to official police reports, 78 policemen and 17 civilians were injured, and 101 people were detained for violent behavior.

In 2011, another Pride parade was scheduled, but the Serbian authorities prohibited it just before it was supposed to take place. Similarly, as in 2009, the Belgrade Police Department issued a statement claiming that "obstruction of public transport, endangering health, public morale or safety of individuals and properties," might take place if the Pride parade was allowed. The practice of banning the parade was repeated in 2013. Although the Serbian authorities first allowed the parade, it was eventually banned only a day before it was supposed to take place.

In 2014, finally the Pride parade took place. It was protected by 7,000 policemen. Although there were some violent clashes around the city, it was the first time the Pride parade went through without any major incidents. However, the Pride parade (i.e., public visibility of homosexuality) remains a dividing issue in Serbia and causes a lot of discomfort, which forces LGBT people deep into the closet.

11. See Kuhar and Paternotte 2017.

12. ILGA–Europe Rainbow map, accessed July 1, 2018, https://www.ilga-europe.org/resources/rainbow-europe/rainbow-europe-2018.

References

Foucault, Michel. 1980. *Power/Knowledge: Selected Interviews and Other Writings 1972–1977.* London: Harvester Press.

Kuhar, Roman. 2014. *Raziskava o pravni podinformiranosti LGBT skupnosti in vsakdanjem življenju gejev in lezbijk: Raziskovalno poročilo.* Ljubljana: DIC Legebitra.

Kuhar, Roman, and David Paternotte, eds. 2017. *Anti-Gender Campaigns in Europe: Mobilizing against Equality.* London: Rowman & Littlefield International.

Seidman, Steven. 2002. *Beyond the Closet: The Transformation of Gay and Lesbian Life.* New York: Routledge.

Švab, Alenka. 2001. *Družina: od modern k postmoderni.* Ljubljana: ZPS.

Švab, Alenka. 2016. "Narratives of Coming Out to Parents: Results of Replicating a Sociological Study on the Everyday Life of Gays and Lesbians in Slovenia (2014–2015)." *Teorija in praksa* 6: 1344–1355.

Švab, Alenka, and Roman Kuhar. 2005. *The Unbearable Comfort of Privacy: Everyday Life of Gays and Lesbians.* Ljubljana: Peace Institute.

Toš, Niko, ed. 2009. *Vrednote v prehodu VIII: Slovenija v srednje in vzhodnoevropskih primerjavah 1991–2011.* Ljubljana: FDV.

Toš, Niko, ed. 2016. *Vrednote v prehodu X: Slovensko javno mnenje 2010-2016.* Ljubljana: FDV.

ROMAN KUHAR is Professor of Sociology at the University of Ljubljana. His books include *Media Construction of Homosexuality*; *Doing Families: Gay and Lesbian Family Practices* (edited with Judit Takács); and of *Anti-Gender Campaigns in Europe: Mobilizing Against Equality* (edited with David Paternotte).

11 Between Past and Future: Young People's Strategies for Living a "Normal Life" in Postwar Bosnia and Herzegovina

Monika Palmberger

Mostar and Its Institutionalized Postwar Division

Mostar, the city where I conducted ethnographic fieldwork in the period 2005–2008, is often referred to as the worst-case scenario of postwar partition.[1] This stands in stark opposition to accounts of prewar Mostar, which depict the city as a showcase for good interethnic neighborliness among Bosniaks,[2] Croats, and Serbs. Mostar, a city located in Herzegovina (the southern part of the country) is beautifully situated along the Neretva River. While Mostar has long been a favored tourist destination, its main attraction, the Old Ottoman Bridge, became known around the world when it was destroyed in 1993. The pictures of the destroyed bridge were then taken as a symbol of the shattered cross-ethnic relations in Bosnia and Herzegovina. Yet in Mostar, in the beginning, Croat and Bosniak armed forces fought together against the Serb-dominated Yugoslav National Army. When the latter finally retreated, the former allies started war among themselves. The war has remained visible in Mostar's cityscape, not least because of the many ruins and the division of the city in a Croat-dominated west and a Bosniak-dominated east side. This division has encompassed most aspects of life: politically, economically, culturally, and also in terms of health care, education, and the media.[3]

The young people this chapter is concerned about were teenagers or in their early twenties when I met them, between two and ten years old when the war started, and between five and fourteen years old when it ended. This means all of them lived more years of their lives in post-wartime than in pre-wartime and thus have been educated in an ethnically divided education system. This postwar division has the effect that the youngest generation is much less familiar with customs, names, and particular expressions associated with the other ethnonational groups, which are part of the older population's common knowledge. An age difference of only a couple of years already matters in this respect.[4] A Bosnian-Croat friend of mine from Mostar, in her late twenties, repeatedly expressed her astonishment about the younger generation this chapter is concerned about. For instance, she once expressed disbelief at the fact that her younger friends are no longer familiar with Bosniak names. Names that for her were typically Bosnian (i.e., not Bosniak) did not sound familiar to her friends who were only a few years younger than her. This unfamiliarity also extends to socialist festivities, prewar rock bands, and *turcizmi*[5] (in the case of Croat youth), which were all common in prewar Bosnia and Herzegovina. For many of those belonging to older generations, prewar Mostar is still the true Mostar while postwar Mostar is a kind of artificial state. Following this line of thought, the youngest generation is pitied for their lack of memory of true (prewar) Mostar.[6]

The division of schools and universities (and even kindergartens) introduced during the war, constitute an effective way of institutionalizing Mostar's division. In Bosnia and Herzegovina, officially three languages are spoken—Bosniak, Croatian, and Serbian—which are, however, very close to each other and the differences used to be first and foremost of a regional (rather than an ethno-national) nature. While during Tito's Yugoslavia schools were shared by Bosniak, Croat, and Serb pupils, today a curriculum for each of them exists. Those in favor of the educational division argue that separate curricula are necessary, particularly in respect to so-called national subjects, such as history, geography, and local language. Due to a lack of space after the war, many school buildings in Herzegovina have hosted two schools, one teaching the Croatian and the other the Bosniak curriculum, one taught in the morning, the other in the afternoon. The best-known example of this kind of schools is Mostar's old grammar school (Stara gimnazija), which was officially reunited in 2004. Although uniting "two schools under one roof" was sold as a big success by the international community at that time, it needs to be said that Bosniak and Croat students attended different classes following different curricula even though they shared the same school building.[7]

History in present Bosnia and Herzegovina is a particularly sensitive subject, not least because it is taken to ground the nation's past and justify the nation's destiny. The different curricula teach history in very divergent ways. Even if the curricula do not cover the period of the war (1992–95), the war is not completely absent from the classroom. The situation presents itself in a similar fashion at the university level. Mostar, while a relatively small city with about 120,000 inhabitants, since the war has two universities, one Croat- and one Bosniak-dominated. During lectures on the history of Bosnia and Herzegovina and Croatia in the twentieth century at the two universities, I witnessed the effort to rewrite history after the fall of Yugoslavia. It was common to teach history in a positivistic way, teaching so-called historical facts whereby professors claimed authority over the interpretation of history. While the 1992–95 war was not part of the books used for the class and little room was given to explicit discussion of this period, the war was still overly present. References were made frequently linking experiences of the recent war with injustices and atrocities each nation experienced earlier in history. The 1992–95 war was thereby presented only as the peak of an iceberg

Figure 11.1. Institutionalized divisions in schools extend beyond Mostar, such as the unique case of a school in Travnik, Bosnia and Herzegovina, where ethnic Bosniaks and Croats attend classes in the same building yet are taught different curricula and are physically separated. Here we see the Croat school on the right side of the fence and the Bosniak school on the left, 2013. Photograph by Roska Vrgova.

of humiliations against one's nation. In order to validate the suffering of their own nation, different historical periods were strung into one coherent narrative, a narrative of victimization and suppression. A history teacher in an interview with me cemented this link between World War II and the 1992–95 war because of the recurring importance of a specific date, which he took as proof that the recent war was a repetition of World War II. He underpinned the connection between the aggression against Bosnia and Herzegovina, against the Bosniak nation (he used the two interchangeably), by fascists during World War II and the war of 1992–1995, by calling attention to the date, November 9: November 9, 1938, the Reichskristallnacht (Night of Broken Glass) and November 9, 1993, the final destruction of the Old Bridge.

The (Un)Spoilt Generation?

Due to their limited (if any) prewar memories and because they spent their childhood in a war-torn country, Mostar's youth was often presented by the older generations as the one most effected by ethno-national hatred. Adults among my interlocutors (locals as well as foreigners) frequently referred to these youth as a "lost generation"—lethargic and disillusioned—that cannot rely on the memory of a better life and thus has fallen subject to manipulation by nationalist propaganda. These stereotypical representations, however, are vehemently rejected by Mostar's youth. In defense against the stigmatization of being trapped in the realm of the "lost generation," my young interlocutors found strategies to "detach" themselves from the legacy of the war.[8] Young people attribute their young age during the war period as the reason for them being less affected by the war. This was the case with Mario, a Croatian in his late teens. Mario claimed that the war would surely have had a completely different effect on his life if it broke out now and he had to take up a rifle and fight. Although the war had a traumatic influence on people, this was not the case for him personally, he told me. Mario's narrative of the war is ambiguous. While he states that this war, like any war, did leave behind many scars, he simultaneously removes himself from that experience by stating he had been too young to understand what was going on. He explained why he was spared any feelings of hate due to his age and his lack of direct war experience: "Because when my town [Mostar] was shelled, I was in Split. I went to excursions on islands. I went swimming. I didn't feel the war, and later on when I came back to my community, I didn't have anything against Muslims or Serbs. . . . Coexistence [*suživot*] is good, especially among young people of my age who didn't feel the war a lot." When narrating the war, Mario distances his personal story, and to some extent also that of his entire generation, from what is often described as a collective experience.

Other interlocutors of his age narrated their war experiences to me in a similar way, especially when they had been evacuated to safer places. This was also the case for Lejla, a sixteen-year-old Bosniak woman. Lejla is from a Mostar family whose members identified themselves as Yugoslavs (a supranational identity) before the war but today declare themselves Bosniaks. Lejla left Mostar with her parents and sister in 1992 for Italy and only returned six years later, while her grandparents, cousins, and other family members remained in Mostar throughout the war. Lejla told me the following: "It is for sure easier for us than for our parents, because they are familiar with everything, with the situation that led to war and everything else, while we were protected from everything; we were just facing some consequences of the war." Here, Lejla, similarly to Mario, clearly expresses what I so often encountered in conversations with young people in Mostar; namely, that they present themselves as the "unspoilt" generation due to their young age and thereby distance their personal experiences from that of the wider society. Lejla did so with phrases like "we were protected from everything" and "we were just facing some consequences of the war." These phrases also show that Lejla (like others of my young interlocutors) speaks of youth in Mostar (at

Figure 11.2. Recent graduates standing outside the United World College in Mostar, 2010. Photograph by Srdjan Jordanovski.

times at least) as a "we"-group, although the lives of young Bosniaks and Croats are separated and points of encounter are rare. This does not mean that Lejla did not see the "indirect" effects of the war on her life. Like others of her generation, Lejla was devastated with the grim job prospects in Bosnia and Herzegovina, which she would eventually face after completing her education. Moreover, she was also not fond of Bosnia and Herzegovina's education system, especially of the old-fashioned teaching and examining methods. Lejla was also very unhappy with the present division of Mostar and thus became active in a youth organization that aims to bridge the division. But not all of my young interlocutors were upset with the division. Several of them even presented the division as if it were natural, with roots in ancient history. This was also the case with Mario, whom I introduced earlier. He did not present the division as artificial and related to the war but as a division between two different "civilizations."9

Returning to the previously described strategy of my interlocutors to remove their personal memories from that of their nation, this strategy also enabled them to remove personal memories from the discourse of victimization, which is a strong element in both the national Bosniak and Croat meta-narratives, as well as in the older generations' narratives. But it would be wrong to say that my young interlocutors denied that their lives were affected by the war altogether. Although they presented themselves as less affected by personal war experiences, as described, their accounts of wartime included personal hardship. Many of them were evacuated to safer places, often outside the country, and remember that time as a time of separation from family members (sometimes even from their parents). Narratives of the war period also include feelings of confusion and insecurity due to a lack of information they received at that time from older family members and other adults about what was going on.

Besides the strategy to distance their past experiences from that of their co-nationals, I encountered a strong tendency among young people in Mostar to dissociate their lives from politics in a more general sense. Young people in Mostar aimed to present the city they lived in, and thereby their lives, as just any other city and any other young person's life. This strategy seemed specifically important to those young people who felt the consequences of war in their personal lives the most: they were the ones who particularly skillfully avoided addressing their experience as related to the wider problems Mostar's society faces today.

I encountered this vividly in Elvira, a twenty-one-year-old woman with whom I became friends at the beginning of my fieldwork and whose life I followed for the three years I was based in Bosnia and Herzegovina. Elvira faced the difficulties of the city's division in her private life more than most others I knew. She had been in a relationship with a Bosniak man but had to keep it entirely secret since she was from a Croat family; neither her friends nor her family were allowed to know about it, as they would have greatly disapproved. Unlike her parents who avoided crossing to the Bosniak-dominated east side of the city, Elvira crossed sides almost every day because she studied at the Bosniak-dominated university. Her parents approved this choice only because the Croat-dominated university did not offer the subject she had chosen. When asked about the experience of being a Croat student at the Bosniak-dominated university, she told me she had not encountered any problems, after a while adding that indeed nobody knew of her Croat origins, as her first and last names are not clearly and exclusively identifiable as Croat. I was surprised she never complained about having to keep the issue about her Croat background as yet another secret.

When from time to time I went for coffee with Elvira and her fellow students in a café on the university campus, I understood how it was possible for her to keep her national identity out of conversations. Elvira and her friends talked about exams, professors, fellow students, fashion, and other topics but avoided conversations about local politics. Their dissatisfaction with Mostar's present situation was expressed mainly through sharing their mutual dissatisfaction with the bad economic situation and bleak job prospects. Almost all of them saw the extremely weak (and corrupt) economy as particularly burdensome for their individual future. Like many others of her generation, Elvira would consider leaving Mostar if the right opportunity presented itself.[10]

It was interesting to see that it was her Bosniak partner who, from time to time, challenged her way of presenting Mostar's reality as removed from the legacy of the war. Once, in a coffee bar at the beginning of my stay in Mostar, Elvira, her boyfriend, and I discussed in which parts of the city it would be good for me and my family to live. Elvira suggested West Mostar (where she lived) since it was greener than East Mostar. Her Bosniak boyfriend, however, found this statement provocative, adding that the east side used to be green as well but during the war, people needed heating material so they had cut down most of the trees. I never felt quite comfortable challenging Elvira's depoliticized presentations in such a way and assumed that once we knew each other better she would share her thoughts on such matters anyway. But I was wrong; all my subtle attempts to engage her in conversation about the political situation of her city failed, even though we met frequently. By offering me only monosyllabic answers she indicated her desire to change the topic and talk about more lighthearted things, such as parties and holiday plans. When once she and I attended a photograph exhibition in the Bosniak-dominated university showing images of a heavily destroyed Mostar, I was sure she would be moved to share her thoughts about Mostar's recent past with me. However, she expressed her feelings with only three words: "That is horrible!" For Elvira, crossing sides when studying at the Bosniak-dominated university and upholding a relation with a Bosniak man seemed only feasible when she detached her private everyday life from the politicized public. One could even argue that only this strategy made it possible for Elvira to cross sides.

Discrepancies between Past and Future

Although there is a general discrepancy between the public sphere in which the war takes a dominant role (e.g., in memorials, commemorations, the media, and speeches of politicians) and private everyday life in which the war is a much less explicit topic, this discrepancy was most pronounced among those who had experienced the war as children. Their narratives included strong elements of silencing and distancing the effects the war may have had on their lives. Although those belonging to older generations sometimes expressed the wish to forget about war atrocities they themselves or their nation had experienced, the war and its aftermath snuck into almost every longer conversation.[11]

In this chapter, I suggested that the phenomenon of distancing personal (generational) memories among Mostar's youth from that of the nation may be interpreted as a strategy used to cope with the legacy of the war and as a defense against stigmatization by the older generations. Even if individuals tend to embed their personal memories into wider officially accepted narratives, one is likely to also encounter dissonance between stories of individual experience and their larger social and historical context. According to Jacob Climo, distancing autobiographic memories from memories of the group one belongs to can be a personal decision.[12] This can occur when it feels too threatening to put oneself into the recognized historical context. So, by separating personal memories from collective memories, the person feels protected from the difficult collective experiences.[13]

Similar observations by Lynne Jones, a psychiatrist working in Goražde and Foča a year after the war had ended, support this understanding: "The fact that for some children, in some situations, distancing is an effective means of coping challenges widely held assumptions about the psychological effect of stressful events. It suggests that we might do well to pay more attention to avoidance as a constructive rather than pathological coping mechanism."[14] This suggests that past events of war are so overwhelming and threatening that young people in Mostar prefer to remove their personal stories from the wider social context and at the same time dissociate their present lives from the politicized public. These strategies are then utilized in order to cope with the legacy of the war and as a defense against stigmatization by the older generations, as well as to create room for hope for the city to which the post-Yugoslavs' lives are inextricably bound. This dynamic is likely to be connected to the post-Yugoslavs' strong orientation toward the present and the future, which also becomes visible in their narratives, which are less past-oriented than those of the older generations.[15] But the relative silence of war experiences may also be connected to the fact that the post-Yugoslavs have not yet found their meta-narrative. Silence, as Connerton rightly reminds us, "is not a unitary phenomenon; there are, rather, a plurality of silences", which seems also to be the case here.[16]

Notes

I would like to express my gratitude to the Austrian Academy of Sciences, the Max Planck Institute for the Study of Religious and Ethnic Diversity, and the Austrian Science Fund (FWF T702-G18) for their generous support. Parts of this chapter have been published in the article "Distancing Personal Experiences from the Collective—Discursive Tactics among Youth in Post-War Mostar" in *L'Europe en formation: Journal of Studies on European Integration and Federalism*.

1. The war in Bosnia and Herzegovina that lasted from 1992 until 1995.
2. *Bosniak* is today the official term for Bosnian Muslims.
3. See Palmberger 2006, Palmberger 2018.
4. See Palmberger 2010.
5. *Turcizam* (pl. *turcizmi*) is the local name for a word of Arabic origin incorporated into what used to be referred to as Serbo-Croatian and is nowadays used mainly by Bosniaks or the older population.
6. See Palmberger 2013a.
7. See Hromadžić 2008, 2015.
8. The act of silencing memories of war in order to reestablish cross-national relationships has been described by several authors working in the region as conducive for postwar coexistence (Eastmond and Mannergren Selimovic 2012; Hayden 2009; Stefansson 2010). By drawing close attention to strategic silences, the "ethics of memory" is a question that emerged at the end of the twentieth century and in which remembering is presented as a virtue and forgetting as a failure (Connerton 2011, 33).
9. See Palmberger 2016.
10. Several opinion polls in Bosnia and Herzegovina have shown a high percentage (more than 70 percent) of young people want to leave their country, especially for economic reasons. See, for example, a report by the Youth Information Agency Bosnia and Herzegovina in 2005 for the UN Review of the World Programme of Action for Youth. It states that 77 percent of youth in Bosnia and Herzegovina want to leave the country, 24 percent of whom want to leave without ever returning.
11. See Palmberger 2008, 2013b.
12. Climo 2002.
13. Ibid., 126; see also Leydesdorff et al. 1999.

14. Jones 2004, 247.
15. See Neyzi 2004.
16. Connerton 2011, 53.

References

Climo, Jacob. 2002. "Memories of the American Jewish Aliyah: Connecting Individual and Collective Experience." In *Social Memory and History: Anthropological Perspectives*, edited by J. Climo and M.G. Cattell, 111–127. Lanham, MD: AltaMira Press.

Connerton, Paul. 2011. *The Spirit of Mourning: History, Memory and the Body*. Cambridge: Cambridge University Press.

Eastmond, Marita, and Johanna Mannergren Selimovic. 2012. "Silence as Possiblity in Postwar Everyday Life." *International Journal of Transitional Justice* 6 (3): 502–524.

Hayden, Robert. 2009. "Comments to Carol Kidron 'Toward an Ethnography of Silence: The Lived Presence of the Past in the Everyday Life of Holocaust Trauma Survivors and Their Descendants in Israel.'" *Current Anthropology* 50 (1): 5–27.

Hromadžić, Azra. 2008. "Discourses of Integration and Practices of Reunification at the Mostar Gymnasium, Bosnia and Herzegovina." *Comparative Education Review* 52 (4): 541–563.

Hromadžić, Azra. 2015. *Citizens of an Empty Nation: Youth and State-Making in Postwar Bosnia-Herzegovina*. Philadelphia: University of Pennsylvania Press.

Jones, Lynne. 2004. *Then They Started Shooting: Growing Up in Wartime Bosnia*. Cambridge, MA: Harvard University Press.

Leydesdorff, Selma, Graham Dawson, Natasha Burchardt, and Timothy G. Ashplant. 1999. "Introduction: Trauma and Life Stories." In *Trauma and Life Stories: International Perspectives*, edited by K. L. Rogers, S. Leydesdorff, and G. Dawson, 1–26. New York: Routledge.

Neyzi, Leyla. 2004. "Exploring Memory through Oral History in Turkey." In *Balkan Identities: Nation and Memory*, edited by Maria Nikolaeva Todorova, 60–76. London: Hurst.

Palmberger, Monika. 2006. "Making and Breaking Boundaries: Memory Discourses and Memory Politics in Bosnia and Herzegovina." In Bufon, Milan et al. (eds.), The Western Balkans: A European Challenge. Koper: Annales, 525–536.

Palmberger, Monika. 2008. "Nostalgia Matters: Nostalgia for Yugoslavia as Potential Vision for a Better Future?" *Sociologija. Časopis za sociologiju, socijalnu psihologiju i socijalnu antropologiju* 50 (4): 355–70.

Palmberger, Monika. 2010. "Distancing Personal Experiences from the Collective—Discursive Tactics among Youth in Post-War Mostar." *L'Europe en formation: Journal of Studies on European Integration and Federalism* 357: 107–124.

Palmberger, Monika. 2013a. "Practices of Border Crossing in Post-War Bosnia and Herzegovina: The Case of Mostar." *Identities: Global Studies in Culture and Power* 20 (5): 544–560.

Palmberger, Monika. 2013b. "Ruptured Pasts and Captured Futures: Life Narratives in Post-War Mostar." *Focaal—Journal of Global and Historical Anthropology* 66: 14–24.

Palmberger, Monika. 2016. *How Generations Remember: Conflicting Histories and Shared Memories in Post-War Bosnia and Herzegovina*. London: Palgrave Macmillan.

Palmberger, Monika. 2018. "Renaming Streets and Nationalizing Public Space: The Case of Mostar, Bosnia-Herzegovina." In *The Political Life of Urban Streetscapes: Naming, Politics, and Place*, edited by R. Rose-Redwoods, D. Alderman, and M. Azaryahu. London: Routledge.

Stefansson, Anders. 2010. "Coffee after Cleansing? Co-Existence, Co-Operation, and Communication in Post-Conflict Bosnia and Herzegovina." *Focaal—Journal of Global and Historical Anthropology* 57: 62–76.

UN Review of the World Programme of Action for Youth. 2005. *Independent Evaluation of the National Youth Policy in Bosnia-Herzegovina*. Accessed June 24, 2015. http://www.un.org/esa/socdev//unyin/documents/wpaysubmissions/bosnia.pdf.

MONIKA PALMBERGER is a research fellow at the Department of Social and Cultural Anthropology, University of Vienna, and at the Interculturalism, Migration and Minorities Research Centre, University of Leuven. She is author of *How Generations Remember: Conflicting Histories and Shared Memories in Post-War Bosnia and Herzegovina* and editor of *Care across Distance: Ethnographic Explorations of Aging and Migration* (with Azra Hromadžić) and *Memories on the Move: Experiencing Mobility, Rethinking the Past* (with Jelena Tošić).

12 "But Where Else Could They Go?": The State, Family, and Private Care in a Bosnian Town

Azra Hromadžić

Vitalis is a nursing home located in the northwestern Bosnian town of Bihać.[1] It is in Vitalis—and numerous other emerging private-nursing homes dotting the Bosnian postwar and postsocialist landscape—that we can grasp the profound effects of the uneven and partial "withdrawal" of the state and family from the care of the elderly and needy in this country. This retreat of the state and family from care that they traditionally delivered prompts the inclusion of some Bosnians who do not have "anywhere else to go" into the emerging, profit-oriented private systems of care. By paying careful attention to these tender and incomplete transformations, we can begin to grasp the terrain of care as a fundamental dimension of postwar political, economic, and social life in Bosnia and Herzegovina, where "lives seem habitually at stake."[2]

In order to elucidate these larger transformations of the state and family as they converge around care, in this chapter I rely on the stories of two Vitalis residents, Kija and Nezira.[3] Their accounts illuminate historically informed, contemporary arrangements of care that are evolving, converging, and reassembling from the ruins of war and socialism. More specifically, by unpacking the fragments of Kija and Nezira's life (hi)stories, I reveal the main change in the current regime of care—*the inability of the Bosnian family to provide for their kinfolk in need*. This "collective scandal"[4] is multipart, but here I focus on two dimensions: physical and material. The first is a phenomenon that arose from the war-produced geographical dispersal of Bosnian families; these families commonly cannot be there to *physically* provide care. Since many younger people left the country during or at the end of the Bosnian war (1992–95), they could no longer take care of their parents, who either chose to stay in Bosnia and Herzegovina or returned there after several years in exile. Therefore, many families abroad find themselves looking for a solution to their transnational problem—taking care of their aging parents and other family members at a distance.[5]

The second dimension pertains to those families who either stayed in Bosnia during the war or returned to Bosnia after several years spent in the war-produced exile. These families face an increasing inability to *materially* provide care because the family itself is not materially supported as it was during socialism. More specifically, the family was fairly secure—financially and socially—during the socialist era, while today, when the official unemployment rate hovers around 20.5 percent (63 percent among youth),[6] families frequently cannot *afford* to take care of their members in need. Thus, family members of those in need are commonly unemployed and often have to live off the pensions of their elderly family members. These massive alterations in providing care are reflective and generative of the "semi-absent state and family" in Bosnia and Herzegovina.[7]

The postwar Bosnian state, which in a typical "postsocialist" fashion continues to aggressively retreat from medical care, welfare, and social services, does not have a solution or an official policy to confront these difficulties of care and neglect. As a result, private institutions, including Vitalis, emerge as places that fill in these ever-increasing gaps in care—material, physical, and emotional.[8] In order to understand the character and effect of these new modalities of care on ordinary lives, however, we first need to address the context that engenders them, including the postwar and (post)socialist politics, policies, discourses, and practices of care and social protection as they unfold in a unique context of Bosnia and Herzegovina in general and Bihać in particular. These processes, experiences, and (hi)stories shape the lives and deaths of people in the Balkans, and they point to the need to bring into conversation what scholarship in the region has treated as separate: postwar and postsocialist transformations and regimes of care, and the narrated and socially embedded subjectivities that these transformations produce.

Socialist and Postsocialist Regimes of Care: The State and Family

Starting in the 1950s, socialist Yugoslavia developed a prolific yet decentralized web of republic-based professional bodies responsible for providing social protection.[9] The infrastructure of Yugoslav social work was rather developed and implemented mostly through a wide network of local Centers for Social Work as well as through the "traditional long-stay residential institutions for children and adults."[10] While the parameters of social protection varied across Yugoslavia's six republics, in all of them the social welfare system included some elements of the socialist self-management system, Bismarckianism, and the engagement of a variety of nonstate actors, such as religious institutions.[11]

As a result of these coordinates of "socialist humanism," the Yugoslav state, and the socialist state more broadly, was experienced as paternalistic[12] or imagined "as a caring parent that provided for its citizen–children."[13] This representation of the caring state created expectations about what the state *should* deliver:[14] the supreme duty of the state, as "the big father,"[15] was to "take care of the society as whole," the process that, according to socialist ideology, would eventually lead to the termination of the need for social help in general, since *everyone* would be taken care of.[16] In order to achieve this, the Yugoslav state, through large-scale technologies of regulation, started to collect information and thus engage in the control of health and well-being of its population. As a result, "the government became responsible for living conditions of the people 'from the birth until the grave' (*od kolijevke pa do groba*)."[17] In harmony with the rest of its citizen-care policies, the socialist state implemented a health care system that provided universal medical assistance that was defined as "rational, progressive and scientific."[18] These "universal" entitlements to social security and health care were central to socialist modernity and the means through which the socialist state demonstrated that it cared for its citizens.[19] The Yugoslav people's response to these socialism-produced novelties was a combination of "enthusiasm and hope, mixed with fear and suspicion."[20]

Economic priority, however, was given to the Yugoslav health care services that focused on maintaining and reproducing a healthy and productive workforce; those seen as "nonproductive" members of the citizen body, including the elderly, were not always guaranteed an equivalent standard of care.[21] Therefore, while the state extended its control and management of populations in all domains of citizen-care and protection, when it came to the care of old people, the state had a strong commitment to avoid creating separate (medical) environments that would solely focus on the elderly. Rather, the decentralized socialist system focused on the creation of comprehensive primary care services and health centers associated with local "self-managing communities of interest... originating in the homes of people's health (*domovi narodnog zdravlja*)."[22] In addition, different republics within Yugoslavia showed a varied distribution of the centers for the elderly; in 1987, Croatia was leading the way with the highest number (120) of special residencies for the elderly (*Dom umirovljenika*—"retirement homes") while Belgrade, the capital of Serbia and the former Yugoslavia, had only 2 of these centers.[23] These discrepancies are reflections of different historical and infrastructural trajectories and of more recent demographic trends: for example, Croatia has seen a more developed infrastructure for the care of elderly while Serbia has harbored the largest number of orphan-care facilities.[24] In addition, rural Croatia witnessed a heavy out-migration of the young, who could not take care of their elderly parents,[25] showing again a strong sociocultural link between the state, family, and eldercare.

The paternalistic relationships and self-projections of the Yugoslav state and its citizens, and the "structures of feeling"[26] they enticed relied heavily on traditional Bosnian approaches to family care; conventionally, Bosnians, especially Bosnian women, took care of their elderly family members. Similar to many East European countries where the state projected an image of a caring institution, it was "the private sphere of kinship, friends and personal networks that became the focus for emotionally inflicted and socially embedded care."[27] Until recently, elderly Bosnians were physically and emotionally cared for by their children and they were often expected to live with (at least) one of them, usually the youngest son and his family. These expectations were based on the cultural notions that stress the communal nature of kinship and symbiotic relationship between generations.[28]

The legal system incorporated this cultural expectation as well. For example, Article 150 of the former Yugoslav constitution defined the care of the elderly as children's responsibility,[29] and Article 190/10 stated: "Members of the family shall have the duty and right to maintain parents . . . and to be mentioned by them, as an expression of their family solidarity."[30] These legal rights and institutionalized expectations of family care were not always legally enforced,[31] but they still continued to shape the vernacular understandings and responsibilities of care. These sociocultural approaches continue to intermingle with the legal register today. For example, in the current Federation of Bosnia and Herzegovina's family law, it is stated that (grand)children are responsible for taking care of their (grand)parents and vice versa.[32] Due to the war-produced geographical fragmentation of family and the devastating reduction of the overall standard of living, family members' ability to fulfill the vernacular and legal expectations of care could not be delivered, however, causing frustration for all parties within the postwar assemblage of care. Furthermore, these massive political, social, and economic restructurings reveal many myths and raptures in ideologies of care, as well as continuities and discontinuities between past and present. More specifically, both socialist and postsocialist regimes, regardless of their very different social policies, ideologies, and ethic of care, *relied heavily on the institution of family for care*. The major differences, however, are that in socialism, (a) family was socioeconomically supported, thus generally able to deliver care to its family members and (b) the state-provided outpatient medical care for the elderly was extensive and free. Today, however, the postsocialist state's medical care system is in shambles, and fragmented and impoverished families cannot deliver on the promise and expectation of care. These converging processes painfully expose a tender zone of cultural intimacy[33]—an increasing neglect of the elderly and needy in Bosnia.

The existing remains of the socialist system of welfare cannot adequately respond to these requirements and expectations of care either: at the end of the 1990s, Bosnia and Herzegovina had ninety-eight locally based, socialism-established Centers for Social Work, "the pillar of statutory social work in the former Yugoslavia."[34] While numerous, these centers were underfunded by the postwar government and frequently bypassed by the extensive international humanitarian and technocratic aid regime inserted into Bosnia and Herzegovina after the war.[35] For example, the government of Denmark worked in partnership with other international (non)governmental agencies and donated money for the opening of four daily centers for the elderly in the Republika Srpska (RS) and five in the Federation of Bosnia and Herzegovina (FBiH).[36] These internationally sponsored, elderly-centered projects largely worked around the local Centers for Social Work, however, thus minimizing and rendering what went before explicitly useless and invisible.[37]

The larger Bosnian postwar political fragmentation and the current bureaucratic maze are especially visible when it comes to caring for the elderly and needy. For example, reflecting the larger splintering of the state, there is no state-level mechanism in Bosnia and Herzegovina today that is tasked with the coordination of eldercare, nor is there a countrywide strategy for the social protection of the elderly and needy. And yet, there is a web of loosely connected laws and provisions that focus on social protections for the elderly population.[38] For example, both FBiH and RS in Bosnia and Herzegovina have laws[39] that name *starije osobe bez porodičnog staranja* (older people—over sixty-five for men and over sixty for women—without family care) as one set of recipients of government social protection. The ability (and willingness) of the state entities to deliver on these legal expectations of care, however, is fully dependent on material conditions, which are dire.[40] These calamitous material circumstances and shifting relations of care took their own, unique form in the context of Bihać and its private nursing home, Vitalis.

Vitalis: Commodification of Love, Care, and Abandonment

The Bihać region, also known as Krajina, with approximately 300,000 residents, is the northwestern pocket of the country and Bosnia's forgotten battlefield.[41] The region suffered terribly during the war in the 1990s. The largest town is Bihać, the sixth-largest Bosnian town, with approximately 50,000 inhabitants. At the beginning of the war, the Serb population of Bihać left the city for other Serb-dominated regions of the country or went abroad. The war began in June 1992 with the Serb army besieging and intensely shelling the town. The region was besieged for over three years but never conquered by the Serb army. Bosniak (roughly 66 percent of the town's population) and Croat (roughly 8 percent of the town's population) armies and civilians defended their town jointly during the siege. In addition, in 1993, the northern part of the besieged region, led by the businessman-turned-politician Fikret Abdić, proclaimed independence from the Bosnian government and its army and started to collaborate with the Serb forces. This created a very difficult situation for the besieged region, which was liberated in the controversial Bosnian-Croatian army offensive in August 1995, soon after which the Dayton Peace Agreement was signed.

In addition to the projects and material objects destroyed by the war, Bihać's postwar reconstruction and the crooked postwar privatization of the state's resources—including the significant socialist industries that employed the majority of the region's prewar citizenry—further exacerbated the war losses and people's pessimistic outlook for the future. The economically and politically calamitous present, which stems out of (post)war and (post)socialist ruins, is possibly most symbolically visible in the war-interrupted 1980s socialist plan to build a *Dom penzionera* (retirement home) on the banks of the Una River in prewar Bihać: the building itself remains unfinished, caught in the incomplete and stale privatization process, which included a land dispute and competing needs of different stakeholders (the city's association of pensioners and the municipal, cantonal, and federal governments).[42] The wraith-like ruins of the building illustrate the combined weakness of late socialist economic infrastructure and the interruption of social life caused by the war. Immediately after the war, this ghostly building was renamed *građa* (the built) by its unintended beneficiaries—troubled youth who until recently (before the building was sealed off due to the legal process) used the ruins to drink alcohol, consume drugs, and have sex.[43] Regardless of its inadequacy, at the time of writing in 2018, *građa* is housing several hundred Syrian refugees.

These physical ruins of the socialist project of eldercare are a potent site that reveals the state's withdrawal and nondelivery of its services in the context where many citizens still remember how the state used to provide for them. As a result, many Bosnians, both at home and abroad, faced with the absence of the state-run institutions of eldercare in Bihać, turn to new, privately owned nursing homes, including Vitalis.

Vitalis is a twenty-five-bed center that opened in June 2011. The owners of Vitalis are Lidija and Ramo, a married couple in their midforties. Originally from Banja Luka,[44] they spent the war years (1992–95) as refugees in Germany. After the war ended, and their hometown was ethnically cleansed, they decided to return to their home country and start a new life in Bihać. Upon their return, the couple recognized that there was a "crisis of care" for elderly; they secured a high-interest bank loan, borrowed money from family and friends, and opened Vitalis.

Intrigued by the anxieties, rumors, and projects articulated around the care of the elderly in this town, I began research at Vitalis in the summer of 2013. During three visits to this home (the summers of 2013 and 2014, and January–July 2015), I was immediately captivated by the life (hi)stories of the people I met at this home, and the multiple meanings, expectations, and horizons of care that their stories encapsulated. For example, traditionally, Bosnians took care of their elderly family members; as recently as twenty years ago, sending them to nursing homes was not socially acceptable.[45] Thus, many of my interlocutors embodied and expressed a real tension between feeling grateful to their family members for worrying about their well-being and paying for their nursing home expenses on the one hand and experiencing a strong sense of societal and intimate abandonment on the other. For example, eighty-one-year-old Lucija said, "I am grateful that they [Lucija's three sons living abroad with their families], are *živi i zdravi* [alive and healthy, thus able to provide for her], but my place is with them, in our house."

Furthermore, I learned that private nursing homes are sites of economic privilege, since they are very expensive in relation to the Bosnian standard of living. The monthly fee is between 750 and 1,050 Bosnian convertible marks (BAM), approximately $500–850, a sum too high for most of the country's older inhabitants, who receive an average monthly pension of 350 BAM. Thus, most of the people at Vitalis had some family member(s), usually their child(ren), living and working abroad, helping to pay their nursing home expenses. These networks of care reveal changing family and intergenerational relationships, and they point at uneven ways in which the social, economic, and emotional support emerges in the transnational context of home and exile. Furthermore, they disclose the private, for-profit regimes of care that emerge in the gaps left behind by the dispersed family and the retreated welfare state.

Figure 12.1 a and b. Residents of a private care home in Bihać, 2017. Photograph by Rosa Vrgova.

Due to this shrinking of the state and war-produced scattering of family, Lidija and Ramo had to perform and embody both the state (by offering paternalistic care and medical services) and family (by offering affection, bodily intimacy, and novel kinship visible in hugs and gentle strokes, proximity, and, importantly, love).[46] In other words, Vitalis's for-profit affective labor was filling the vacuum left in wake of the state's withdrawal and family dispersal.[47] That Lidija and Ramo had to compensate for the vanishing state, albeit for profit, is also visible in the fact that quite a few of the home's residents are not elderly. Rather, they, at the time of my research, included some younger (as young as forty) individuals with special needs, including one case of mental retardation and one of schizophrenia, and others who, due to the semi-absent state and family, did not have anywhere else to go. So they ended up in Vitalis. These two unique stories illustrate the unexpected convergences of state, family, and private care.

Emerging Modalities of Care: Kija and Nezira

Kija is a schizophrenic woman in her midforties, who came to Vitalis after spending most of her life in the Yugoslav socialist institutions of care for mentally disabled youth and adults. The war caught Kija at one of these centers located in eastern Bosnia, which, at the time, was being ethnically cleansed of Bosniaks—a group Kija learned to belong to. After several days of traveling across a country that was exploding in violence and with help received from some kind strangers, Kija reached her hometown of Veliko Polje (pseudonym), located some thirty miles from Bihać. The rest of Kija's family, who returned to Veliko Polje after being internally displaced in central Bosnia for almost a decade, took care of Kija for a while, but when she became too difficult to handle and provide for, they asked Lidija to take her in. Lidija agreed to admit Kija, feeling empathetic toward this impoverished family in which only one of six people was employed.

At the time I started my research at Vitalis, Kija had been living at this home for almost a year. She was easy to spot—significantly younger than most others, skinny, and extremely busy. Her illness required her to be active all the time, so she washed clothes and took care of the garden. Her energy was overwhelming, and it colored the ambiance of the home. It also sometimes resulted in outbursts of massive anger and loud crying. I happened to be at home during one of those outbursts. After the employees and Lidija finally calmed her down by giving her heavy medications, I whispered to one of the nurses, "She does not belong here." The nurse nodded but replied, "Sure, but where else can she go? This canton does not have any institutions for people like her. So we have to take her in." This statement potently articulates the effects of the absent institutions of the state and family and the reason for the emergence of the private home that, albeit in this case temporarily and incompletely, absorbed some of Kija's "terror of being on the wrong side of the (bio)politics of life."[48]

Kija was an "expensive" patient; her condition required a diverse pallet of costly medications, and since she was the only Vitalis resident who was fully on the state/cantonal budget, Lidija had to negotiate Kija's payments with several local institutions. Given the perpetual shrinking of the government's budget allocated to medical and social services, the payments were late, irregular, and incomplete, and Lidija and Ramo often had to pay for Kija's medications out of their own pocket, sinking even deeper into never-decreasing debt.

Ten months after coming to Vitalis, Kija became too dangerous to herself and others; as a result, Lidija, with the help of the Veliko Polje Center for Social Work, arranged for her to be placed in a mental institution in the Republika Srpska. Kija resisted going back to the entity from which she was forcibly expelled at the beginning of the war, but Lidija, maneuvering the vacuum of the state and family, had no other visible solution. In the middle of July 2015, one-and-a-half-years after Kija left Vitalis, the Una-Sana Canton still owed the owners of Vitalis 4,000 BAM (approximately $2,800) for Kija's care, exacerbating their debt.

Kija still sporadically calls Vitalis to tell them that she dislikes being so far away from "home"—her family, Vitalis, and Veliko Polje. The Una-Sana Canton, however, has no institution that would allow for Kija to stay closer to her home, and her family, which was willing but materially, medically, and infrastructurally unable to take care of her; they have not seen Kija since she left Vitalis. The shrinking of the socialist state and impoverished family converged to contribute to yet another dislocation of bodies and souls.

Another resident who did not "really" belong to Vitalis was sixty-three-year-old Nezira, whose life was powerfully marked by the convoluted experiences of war and peace, home and exile. She, together with her husband and two small children, was forced out of her home in Sjenica (pseudonym), located some ninety miles from Bihać, at the beginning of war. After a traumatic refugee experience crossing multiple state borders, the family finally settled in Belgium[49] while longing to return to Bosnia. Nezira's husband died in a small suburb in Belgium; he was in his midfifties, never able to make his return to Sjenica. Nezira, devastated by the premature death of her husband, felt that she had to fulfill her husband's dream of returning to their homeland. In the mid-2000s, she came back to Sjenica, even though that meant that, due to the peculiar type of legal status she had had in Belgium, she could never return to live or use the state services of that country again. Nezira never regretted this decision, not even when her health started to deteriorate in 2014 or when she was in a need of a kidney transplant.

When faced with her unexpected and progressive kidney failure, Nezira realized that she had to be closer to the regional center for dialysis, since the one in Sjenica had been devastated by the war and neither repaired nor reopened. She was eligible, however, to use the cantonal hospital's ambulance—which would, every other day, collect and distribute people from all over the canton who needed dialysis. This option proved to be too complicated, painful, and time-consuming for Nezira: the commute was long, and her progressing arthritis made it very difficult for her to enter and exit the old, unequipped ambulance car without a stair chair or to climb the four stories to get to her flat, located in a socialism-produced, unkempt apartment building without an elevator.

Searching for a solution on the internet, she and her war-displaced children, who still live in Belgium, discovered Vitalis and, given its proximity to the cantonal dialysis center, decided to place Nezira there. Putting Nezira into a private nursing home was the family's way to, however temporarily, confront and maneuver their own physical absence and the state's crumbling medical infrastructure. Nezira's two children—physically distant but materially capable and willing to support Nezira's stay at Vitalis—desperately tried to help their mother return to Belgium and have an urgent kidney transplant. Nezira's returnee status restricted their options, however. While waiting and hoping, caught between home and exile, Nezira died at Vitalis in 2014. Nezira's refugee experience and peculiar legal status, when combined with the fragmented, semi-absent family and the "ever more absent state,"[50] both Bosnian and Belgian, amalgamated to produce her unique predicament, eventually leading to Nezira's possibly preventable, premature death at Vitalis.

The Aging Predicament

Anxieties around the "aging predicament" in contemporary Bosnia and Herzegovina and the shifting roles of family and state in providing care for elderly and needy Bosnians have been exacerbated by postwar and postsocialist transformations. The double-withdrawal of the state and family from care is a result of war-destroyed infrastructure, the state's aggressive retreat from medical care and welfare, and the family's physical (largely due to the war-dispersal) and material (largely due to high unemployment) inability to provide care to their family members in need.

New private institutions, such as Vitalis, are emerging at the intersection of these shifting topographies of care, and they absorb, for profit, an increasing number of Bosnian citizens who do not have anywhere else to go, including Kija and Nezira. These emerging private institutions of care are thus partially substituting for the semi-absent state and family, while never fully filling the gap in care which opened under the changing postwar, postsocialist, and neoliberal conditions. These processes affect many "ordinary lives," as well as more exceptional cases like those of Kija and Nazira. Theirs are stories of war displacement and destruction of lives, bodies, and objects; the weakening, semi-absence, and reformation of the postwar and postsocialist state; families fragmented across continents; new homes and borders; and shifting terrains and expectations of life and death, care and responsibility.

Notes

1. In this chapter, I use Bosnia and Bosnia and Herzegovina interchangeably. Two slightly modified sections of this chapter, "Socialist and Post-Socialist Regimes of Care: The State and Family" and "Vitalis: Commodification of Love, Care, and Abandonment" have been published in Hromadžić (2015) and Hromadžić (2016).
2. Jašarević 2011, 109.
3. All personal names in this article are pseudonyms.
4. I am grateful to Larisa Jašarević for this phrase.
5. See Hromadžić and Palmberger 2018.

6. According to the Bosnian Agency for Statistics, the official unemployment rate, calculated on the basis of ILO methodology is 20.5 percent (see http://www.bhas.ba/?option=com_publikacija&id=1&lang=ba). However, some sources report that the nominal rate of unemployment may be as high as 45 percent (see http://www.novilist.hr/Vijesti/Svijet/Posao-u-BiH-trazi-550.000-ljudi-nominalna-nezaposlenost-44-5-posto).

7. See Hromadžić 2015.
8. See Hromadžić 2016.
9. Zaviršek and Leskošek 2005, 39.
10. Stubbs and Maglajlić 2012, 1177.
11. Ibid., 1176.
12. Manning 2007.
13. Dunn 2008, 247.
14. Dunn 2008.
15. Zaviršek and Leskošek 2005, 40
16. Of course, not everyone was equally deserving of the government's protection and help. Zaviršek and Leskošek (2005, 47–49) explain how the government divided its people into "deserving" and "undeserving," or "ours" and "not-ours," where the latter were mostly former owners of shops, factories, and banks and some Jewish survivors, who were all expropriated by the new socialist government.
17. Zaviršek and Leskošek 2005, 46.
18. Read 2007, 204.
19. Ibid., 203.
20. Zaviršek and Leskošek 2005, 46.
21. Read 2007, 206.
22. Sokolovsky et al. 1991.
23. Ibid.
24. Paul Stubbs, personal communication, October 2014.
25. Ibid.
26. Williams 1977.
27. Read 2007, 206.
28. Simic 1990, 97.
29. Tomorad and Galoguža 1984, 306.
30. See Sokolovsky et al. 1991.
31. Tomorad and Galoguža argue that regardless of the legal right to be taken care of by their offspring, the elderly very rarely used these means to secure these rights, since the emotional basis of the relationship was not present. The authors also argue that children were sometimes materially unable to support their parents (1984, 306n1).
32. Act 128/2 of the FBiH's Family Law states that a "child has a responsibility to help his/her parents" (see http://www.fbihvlada.gov.ba/bosanski/zakoni/2005/zakoni/25bos.pdf).
33. Herzfeld 2005.
34. Stubbs 2002, 7.
35. Stubbs and Maglajlić 2012.
36. Miković 2011, 312n8. Bosnia and Herzegovina is divided into two entities: The Federation of Bosnia and Herzegovina (FBiH), with a 51 percent share of the territory and inhabited mostly by Bosniaks (Bosnian Muslims) and Bosnian Croats, and the Republika Srpska (RS), with 49 percent of the territory and populated almost exclusively by Bosnian Serbs. The FBiH is further divided into ten cantons. Bihać is the administrative center and the largest city in the Una-Sana Canton.

37. Stubbs 2002, 7–8.
38. Miković 2011, 307.
39. Zakon o osnovama socijane zaštite, zaštite civilnih žrtava rata i zaštite porodica sa djecom (FBiH/ čl. 12 and Zakon o socijalnoj zaštiti RS/ čl. 10).
40. Miković 2011, 309.
41. O'Shea 2012.
42. See Hromadžić and Čavkić 2016.
43. Čelebičić 2013.
44. Banja Luka is city of 200,000 people; at the outbreak of the war, the majority of the population was ethnically Serb (roughly 55 percent), with a significant presence of Croats (roughly 15 percent), Bosniaks (around 15 percent), and Yugoslavs (roughly 12 percent). This "mixed" town's habitus, in which different groups intermingled for centuries, was common in Bosnia and Herzegovina and socialist Yugoslavia at large. At the very beginning of the war, the town was ethnically cleansed of its non-Serb population (including Lidija, Ramo, and their families) by the Serb (para)militaries and incorporated into the Serb Republic of Bosnia and Herzegovina (RS) as its capital.
45. Sokolowsky et al. 1991.
46. See Hromadžić 2016.
47. Ibid.
48. Wool 2015, 1.
49. Not the real country of residence; the country was changed to protect the identity of this individual and her family.
50. Muehlebach 2012, 36.

References

Čelebičić, Vanja. 2013. *"Waiting Is Hoping": Future and Youth in a Bosnian Border Town*. PhD diss., Anthropology, University of Manchester, UK.

Dunn, Elizabeth. 2008. "Postsocialist Spores: Disease, Bodies and the State in the Republic of Georgia." *American Ethnologist* 35 (2): 243–258.

Herzfeld, Michael. 2005. *Cultural Intimacy: Social Poetics in the Nation-State*. 2nd ed. New York: Routledge.

Hromadžić, Azra. 2015. "'Where Were They Until Now?' Aging, Care and Abandonment in a Bosnian Town." *Etnološka tribina: The Journal of Croatian Ethnological Society* 45 (38): 3–29.

Hromadžić, Azra. 2016. "Affective Labour: Work, Love and Care for the Elderly in Bihac." In *Negotiating Socialities in Bosnia and Herzegovina*, edited by Stef Jansen, Čarna Brković, and Vanja Čelebičić, 79–93. Ashgate: Southeast European Studies.

Hromadžić, Azra, and Lejla Čavkić. 2016. "Relikvije buduće prošlosti: Dom penzionera u Bihaću" (Relics of the future past: The empty retirement home in Bihać). *Holon: Croatian Integral Society* 6 (1): 77–99.

Hromadžić, Azra, and Monika Palmberger, eds. 2018. *Care Across Distance: Ethnographic Explorations of Aging and Migration*. New York: Berghahn Books.

Jašarević, Larisa. 2011. "Lucid Dreaming: Revisiting Medical Pluralism in Postsocialist Bosnia." *Anthropology of East Europe Review* 29 (1): 109–126.

Manning, Paul. 2007. "Rose-Colored Glasses? Color Revolutions and Cartoon Chaos in Postsocialist Georgia." *Cultural Anthropology* 22 (2): 171–213.

Miković, Milanka. 2011. "Social Status, Needs and Care of Older Persons in BiH." *Yearbook of the Faculty of Political Sciences* 5–6: 303–313.
Muehlebach, Andrea. 2012. *The Moral Neoliberal: Welfare and Citizenship in Italy.* Chicago: University of Chicago Press.
O'Shea, Brendan. 2012. *Bosnia's Forgotten Battlefield: Bihac.* Stroud: Spellmount.
Read, Rosie. 2007. "Labour and Love: Competing Constructions of 'Care' in a Czech Nursing Home." *Critique of Anthropology* 27 (2): 203–222.
Simic, Andrei 1990. "Aging, World View and Intergenerational Relations in America and Yugoslavia." In *The Cultural Context of Aging: World-Wide Perspectives*, edited by J. Sokolovsky, 89–107. New York: Bergin and Garvey.
Škrbić, Milan, Slaven Letica, Boško Popović, Josip Butković and Ante Matutinović 1984. *Socijalna zaštita.* Zagreb: JUMENA.
Sokolovsky, Jay, Zvonko Sosic, and Gordana Pavlekovic. 1991. "Self-Help Hypertensive Groups and the Elderly in Yugoslavia." *Journal of Cross-Cultural Gerontology* 6 (3): 319–330.
Stubbs, Paul. 2002. "Globalisation, Memory and Welfare Regimes in Transition: Towards an Anthropology of Transnational Policy Transfers." *International Journal of Social Welfare* 11 (4): 321–330.
Stubbs, Paul, and Reina Ana Maglajlić. 2012. "Negotiating the Transnational Politics of Social Work in Post-Conflict and Transition Context: Reflections from South-East Europe." *British Journal of Social Work* 42: 1174–1191.
Tomorad, Mirjana, and Antonija Galoguža. 1984. "Stare i nemoćne osobe." In *Socijalna zaštita*, edited by Milan Škrbić, Slaven Letica, Boško Popović, Josip Butković and Ante Matutinović 304–310. Zagreb: JUMENA.
Williams, Raymond. 1977. "Structures of Feeling." In *Marxism and Literature* (Marxist Introductions), 128–135. New York: Oxford University Press.
Wool, Zoe. 2015. "The Terror of Being on the Wrong Side of the (Bio)Politics of Life." *Somatosphere*, April 15. Accessed November 28, 2015. http://somatosphere.net/forumpost/the-terror-of-being-on-the-wrong-side-of-the-biopolitics-of-life.
Zaviršek, Daria, and Vesna Leskošek. 2005. "The History of Social Work in Slovenia." *Research Report.* Ljubljana: University of Ljubljana.

AZRA HROMADŽIĆ is Associate Professor of Anthropology at Syracuse University. She is author of *Citizens of an Empty Nation: Youth and State-Making in Postwar Bosnia and Herzegovina* and *Care across Distance: Ethnographic Explorations of Aging and Migration* (with Monika Palmberger).

Section III: The Livelihoods of Everyday Life

We *make* our own place in the world. This is not to suggest that the act of being or belonging is one done alone or in conditions of our own making; it is not. Rather, there is an ongoing process—a *doing*—that leads to us becoming who we are. The doing is the work, the experience, the striving out of which we come to understand home, history, and the ascribed aspects of ourselves. The environment in which we go about this making is familiar and, in many ways, an extension of home and the everyday of life.

This section begins with chapters looking at the effect of migration and work on understandings of belonging. Ana Croegaert looks at ways families take care of each other while separated and the connecting role remittances play in coping with uncertainty and vulnerability. Mila Dragojević writes of the struggle refugees face in trying to make a home in the place where they live. Work becomes central to integration, but it can also speak to the limits of integration.

While livelihoods can be spaces of integration, as well as separation, they also frequently are of economic significance. In her chapter on the postsocialist land market, Deema Kaneff writes about the moral effect of foreign investment on local populations. In speaking to the postsocialist reality of making ends meet, Andrew Konitzer describes the struggles of Aleksandar Živojinović, striving to provide for his family and be successful within the terms available to him. And Andrea Matošević discusses the relationship of class and masculinity in livelihoods of hard labor. In the last chapter of this section, Daniel Knight looks at how economies—and, in this case, Greece's economic downturn—affect the sense of belonging to the Balkans.

What we do to make ends meet consumes a good part of our lives and as such influences our understanding of the world and immediate surroundings. This is the context of our efforts in making a livelihood.

13 Cars, Coffee, and "The Crisis": Balkan Migration in Precarious Times

Ana Croegaert

Driving

Ajla's straight dark hair whipped about her face and shoulders as her bare arm worked the manual transmission on the black Fiat, maneuvering the sporty car—purchased with the assistance of her uncle in Chicago—through the roads that skirt the Dinaric Alps in the Neretva River valley. Her elastic-waisted white linen pants and olive-colored tank top provided comfort in the dry June summer heat. Aviator sunglasses and lavender leather sandal flats—a gift from her aunt in Sweden—completed the look. We were making our way down from her small town, Stolac, to the regional university in Mostar. But first we had to pick up her friend Amela. We pulled off on the side of the road, with no sign of a residence from what I could see, but Ajla assured me that Amela was nearby. Sure enough, Ajla phoned her and, moments later, she emerged from a well-hidden path, also wearing a tank top, with sporty cropped pants, converse low-tops, and cell phone in hand. She wore her honey-blond hair pulled back in a ponytail, and her warm broad smile revealed slightly crooked teeth.

The young women were university students, and it was time to drop off papers and pick up exams they would turn in at the beginning of July. Once we arrived at the university, we entered the building where the Civil Engineering Department was housed, and Ajla turned in her paper and collected the next assignment. Ajla's parents had met while they were students in the Economics Program at the University of Sarajevo in the late 1960s, and they expected that when she graduated in 2010, she would play a part in the postwar economic development of Mostar. Although the war in Bosnia and Herzegovina had ended officially fourteen years earlier, the postwar governance agreement brokered in the Dayton Peace Accords produced a multilayered bureaucratic infrastructure that often hindered postwar redevelopment efforts. Further, the entire country was under the "oversight" of an externally appointed high representative selected by the Peace Implementation Council (PIC) tasked with assessing the implementation of the terms of the peace agreement.¹ One of the terms that had to be met in order to dispense with the Office of the High Representative was the resolution of state and of defense property. Ajla wanted to participate in the decision-making regarding such properties in Mostar, where property title was highly contested and, as a result, a significant part of the built environment remained in disrepair. But this did not mean that postwar reconstruction was not happening.

Indeed, influxes of support for reconstruction projects came from sources outside of Bosnia and Herzegovina. The iconic Stari Most/Old Bridge over the Neretva River in Mostar is perhaps the most well-known example of such an undertaking. The sixteenth-century Ottoman-era bridge was destroyed in 1993 by Croatian separatists and then reconstructed with funding from Croatia, Germany, Italy, and Turkey. Now a UNESCO World Heritage site, the "new" Old Bridge opened with great fanfare in July 2004 and is the major tourist draw in the city.² Another source of external investment for postwar reconstructions were transnational migrant connections—the links maintained among those who remained in Bosnia and Herzegovina and those who left during the war. In particular, restored and freshly painted homes and religious sites stood in stark juxtaposition to Yugoslav-era government buildings and former mines and manufacturing sites. These new and newly reconstructed buildings were created with assistance from the more than one million wartime refugee-migrants living outside Bosnia and Herzegovina's borders. Nearly a quarter of the country's prewar population resided in nearby Croatia and Slovenia, as well as in Australia, Austria, Canada, Germany, the United States, Sweden, and Turkey.

This chapter looks at what life was like for people after the war by examining the connections among migrants and those who remained in Bosnia and Herzegovina. I explore the ways that people use material culture to sustain relationships with family social relations to obtain support and to provide relief in times of uncertainty.³ In what follows, I discuss two prominent ways in which people used objects to communicate connections across space and time. First, I look at the transformation of remittances—of money—into objects of function and display.⁴ By attending to the relationships people create with and through objects, we see that migrant remittances are not simply economic contributions; they are investments imbued with moral meanings that generate social expectations of reciprocity.⁵ Next, I turn to the objects associated with coffee preparation and service—a shared and storied activity widely documented across the Balkan Peninsula. In their talk about these objects, people emphasize vulnerabilities and hopes and teach us about transformations in labor and status that occurred in their migrant trajectories. Their narratives direct our attention to the challenges of living in the wake of the "double rupture" of postwar reconstruction and political economic transformation.⁶

Linking Labors

Ajla was one transnationally connected woman. As an only child, with a relatively well-established extended family, Ajla was the recipient of more gifts and money from those who had left Bosnia and Herzegovina than were most of her peers, but the existence of transnational ties was not unique to her. Indeed, in nearly every interaction I had with people in Bosnia and Herzegovina, a migrant connection came to light.

On the bus from Zagreb to Mostar, I met nineteen-year-old Nina, who was returning to Ključ from Zagreb, where, she explained, she worked in her cousin's beauty salon because she cannot find work in Bosnia and Herzegovina.[7] She hoped to someday visit her grandfather and uncle, who live in Florida, but was not optimistic about obtaining a travel visa because as a young, single woman, she would be considered a "risk" for overstaying her visa to find work and to secure a livelihood in America. In Mostar, Ajla's teenaged acquaintance Sumeja spoke to us with some resentment of her father, who lives now in Michigan with his "new wife." Her mother spent extended periods of time in Sarajevo for work, while Sumeja stayed with her grandmother; they had not seen Sumeja's father since he left in 1999. This impetus to emigrate was not uncommon in postwar Bosnia; Stef Jansen describes the pursuit of emigration as a strategy to obtain a "normal life" that is unavailable in the postwar state.[8]

I met Memo and his wife, Fadila, several years after they and their three teenage children had relocated as refugees to the United States. In their midsixties, they both continued to work full time in order to support themselves and to send money back to Bosnia and Herzegovina; Memo drove a taxi, and Fadila did accounting work for a small business. Through their family network, I found myself in Stolac, staying in the apartment they maintained after the war.

Memo was Ajla's uncle, and his son Edin had put me in touch with her. The people of Stolac—where Muslims were the majority "narod"[9]—had suffered tremendously during the war, when the entire Muslim population was forced to leave, their homes and neighborhoods looted and destroyed by VRS and HVO militias.[10] All the men were placed in concentration camps, and women and children were deported to areas under control of the Bosnian army.[11] Although many—like Ajla's family—had returned, they made do under quite changed and challenging circumstances. After the war, Ajla's mother, Safija, began to suffer from a severely degenerative autoimmune disease.[12] This meant she needed twenty-four-hour care and assistance—care provided primarily by her sister Tidža, and by Ajla. Memo and his wife also sent money when they could, to assist with Safija's care. Ajla explained to me that although her father was currently sober, he had struggled with alcohol abuse as a way of coping with the violence, displacement, and downward mobility caused by the war and, lately, Safija's decline. The money sent by Memo's family helped to alleviate some of the vulnerability brought about by these hardships, a point that Ajla took great care to illustrate to me.

For example, she described the little Fiat as being from her mother, given to Ajla so that she would have the means to get herself to university and to drive Safija to doctor's appointments and to hospital if need be—all these sites were located down in the valley, in Mostar. The commute from Stolac to Mostar involved a forty-minute descent down the mountain roads, and although buses ran daily, their schedules were rather unpredictable and generally took closer to an hour because of stops along the way. Relying on such transit could mean the difference between life and death for someone in Safija's condition. But there was another layer to Safija's car gift: Ajla's first choice for university was to attend one in Sarajevo. She had declined her admission there and instead enrolled at the university in Mostar in order to be available to her mother. Safija bought the car with funds sent to her from Ajla's uncle, along with money from the meager pension she received.

Through the purchase of the Fiat, Ajla's mom made visible the care, work, and sacrifice the family contributed to her well-being. She demonstrated thoughtful investment of her brother's family's wages, transforming these into a useful object that provided mobility to Ajla and others—like me and Amela. The car also marked the status of the family: it was an economy model—not flashy—but clearly new. It meant that Ajla could travel to and from the university without relying on the bus and could offer rides to her friends. The investment objectified and reaffirmed multiple family and friend relationships: the sibling tie between Safija and Memo, the parent-child tie between Safija and Ajla, the friendship tie between Ajla and Amela, and the new tie established with me that intensified the connection between Memo's and Safija's families and their households. This reaffirmation relied on kinship identities established through engagement with reciprocal giving: Memo to Safija; Safija to Ajla; Ajla to Safija.

The built environment was another domain of migrant investment that reaffirmed kin ties. Ajla invited me over to tour her family's home, so that I could see firsthand how her parents had put their relatives' money to use. We started in the yard—a significant feature of many Bosnian homes. On the lot next to Ajla's home, situated between two pomegranate trees, stood the remains of her neighbors' home. The Roma Muslim family had been forced from town along with the rest of Stolac's Muslims and had never returned. Ajla knew of neither their whereabouts nor well-being. Half of the roof was gone, and window frames and panes were also missing. Weeds had grown to shoulder-height within the structure, suggesting ruptures in the cement floor base. There were many damaged homes dotting the landscape that served as constant reminders of the previous decade's war, but the neighbors' home also offered a daily reminder of what Ajla's home in particular had looked like before reconstruction and repairs. Inside her house, Ajla led me upstairs so I could see where her bedroom walls had been completely destroyed by bombing. The new wall showed no signs of the wartime damage; clearly, all the interior walls had been recently respackled and repainted, and the entryway floor had new tiles. But she most emphasized the repairs and improvements made to the home's exterior.

Ajla's parents built the original home five years prior to the war, in the typical regional Muslim-style emblematic of the socialist era: a two-story square structure of stone and cement, with a slightly sloping tile roof.[13] When we stepped out of the hall from Ajla's bedroom, she led me to another doorway that opened onto a corner veranda adjoining the modest balcony that ran the perimeter of the house's second story. Ajla explained that the veranda was specifically for Safija's use so

Figure 13.1. Ajla on the terrace of her home in Stoac, framed by new construction material, 2009. Photograph by Ana Croegaert.

that she could enjoy the outdoors without having to be carried downstairs. The balcony's original rail—a rust-colored metal geometric frame that resembled a modest art deco design—was to be replaced by prefabricated cement pillars that were on trend with the region's new "villa-style" motifs. From here, Safija could look down on the palm tree and rose bushes Ajla's father had recently planted. Ajla's parents were also responsible for the almond orchard, originally a vineyard that Ajla's grandfather had planted, extending several acres beyond the rear of the house.

Whereas the car purchase highlighted Ajla's active body through her role as the driver, the home improvements highlighted the active bodies of Ajla's father and uncle. The two men together had purchased the building materials and undertaken the labor needed to complete the repairs and renovations. Neither the car nor the home improvements would have been possible to undertake without Memo's family's assistance. Further, Safija's family's care for the car and the house made it possible for Memo to remain connected to the town and to the land his parents had cultivated there. The exchange of money and labor and the procuring of, consumer goods involved in these projects served as embodied and material reminders of the obligations between the two siblings' families.

But the attempt to achieve well-being was increasingly elusive for many migrants living now in the United States. On a typical evening at a café in Stolac, I met twenty-seven-year-old Edin, who had recently moved back to Bosnia and Herzegovina after living in North Carolina, Pennsylvania, and Michigan. When I asked Edin if he missed America, he was quick to reply, "Not at all"; he missed his friends but nothing else. America, he said, is all about "work, eat, sleep; work, eat, sleep; work, eat, sleep." According to Edin, no one from Bosnia would miss America—maybe they would miss the people in America but not the American life.

Edin's description of the drudgery of life in America—"work, eat, sleep; repeat"—aptly captures a dominant sentiment I found among refugee-migrants living in the United States. They felt tremendous responsibility to provide economic support to family and friends who had remained in Bosnia and Herzegovina and simultaneously were woefully underprepared for the hardship of living in the United States during an era of tremendous neoliberal restructuring that severely limited people's access to affordable housing, job security, healthcare, and education opportunities. Many migrants held two to three jobs at a time and significantly reduced their living expenses in order to send money to relatives back home and to make return trips to Bosnia and Herzegovina. When I asked about what life was like now in Bosnia, migrants sometimes responded by saying that people there "just sit around drinking coffee and smoking cigarettes." These evaluations of overly active bodies in America and of sedentary bodies in Bosnia and Herzegovina may be understood also as expressions of desire: for those in Bosnia and Herzegovina, the desire to have what they viewed as more opportunity for work, education, industry—the elements of a "normal life" that were still so tenuous following the devastation wrought by war, and the disaster and mafia capitalism that followed in the wake of war;[14] for those who had left for the United States, the desire for respite from the demands of overwork and the increasing precariousness surrounding well-being in America.

When Coffee Pots Travel

"No one wants to know what our lives were like before the war" was an objection I heard often during my fieldwork among refugee-migrants from Bosnia and Herzegovina in America. Indeed, humanitarian workers' insistent focus on the refugee-as-victim often worked to marginalize refugee-migrants' own attempts to manage their displacements and experiences with trauma.[15] In part as a response to this lack of interest in life before the war, I led a collaborative ethnographic project in 2013 with three generations of refugee-migrants in Chicago. Using a series of questions centered on coffee preparation and consumption—a

Figure 13.2. In the midst of everyday struggles, coffee is a mainstay of Balkan tradition, connecting family and friends through good and bad times and across distances.
Here, Bosnians living in Chicago gather for coffee around a džezva to share their hopes, struggles, and thoughts about home, United States, 2016. Photograph by Elmina Kulašić.

shared and storied activity widely documented across the Balkan Peninsula—young women in their twenties and thirties interviewed women of their mothers' and grandmothers' generations.[16]

Here I center my discussion on several iconic objects associated with Bosnian coffee, often given as gifts. Just as we saw above that remittances are not solely economic contributions, but become most meaningful as they are transformed into material goods that can be used, shared, and exchanged, the gifts that people circulate are not limited to their symbolic qualities but also serve to extend social networks and to remind people of their material well-being. The giving of coffee and Bosnian coffee pots—*džezva*—is one key arena in which social relations are sustained in Bosnia and among the diaspora.

It is impossible to travel in the Balkans, or to visit with immigrants from the region, without being introduced to the ritualistic approach to drinking strong dark coffee in small espresso-size cups.[17] Even households of the most modest means manage to serve this "slow" coffee to a guest, and many middle-class homes keep a coffee set on display; wealthier families have multiple sets that they rotate for entertaining and may combine for elaborate affairs such as weddings.[18]

Bosnian coffee conjures sensory experiences that involve slowing time and shifting space. Forty-six-year-old Zumreta, who lives now in Sweden, describe this coffee as "about the time . . . there was some special magic [*čar*]"; her mother, Tidža, living in Chicago, reported that one took coffee "when you get tired and coffee hits the spot . . . to get some rest." People also emphasize the pleasure of taking coffee—"we knew how to relish [*ćejfit*] it"—and contrasted this to the practice of drinking coffee to-go, or in transit, when people "just gulp it down. . . . You don't relish [the experience] [*ne ćejfis*]."[19] This slow coffee preparation and consumption is also a form of knowledge production.[20] Snežana thirty-eight, remembers observing her grandmother serving coffee to neighbors as they discussed "women's issues" like desire for sex and love and how to approach contraception and address serious problems like domestic violence. Tidža, sixty-six, recalls discussing desires and strategies for how to provide more opportunities for their children, particularly education. But even as women remarked on the familiar sensory powers and pleasures of coffee, and the therapeutic properties of drinking it together, slowly, their interviews included themes of uncertainty and vulnerability.

The presence of džezva and *fildžani*—small porcelain cups—in a home are symbols of movement, change, and migration, marked by the mobility of women. Ismeta, sixty-two, recalls receiving her first set: "When I got married, I remember, I do. I got it from my mother-in-law. Because . . . she told me, she told me how to brew coffee, even though I already knew how, but she also gave me some advice, and she said, here, this is how you will make coffee." It was common at the time of Ismeta's marriage for women to migrate and live with their husband's family. Ismeta had moved from her family's home in Podgorica to Sarajevo, where her husband's mother gifted her the džezva set. A džezva marked the beginning of a new household and family and also was the vehicle through which mothers-in-law would instruct new wives on proper service within the home.

One can imagine that these transitions were difficult in particular for the new wife as she was removed from her familiar social supports and was expected to establish good relations with her husband's relatives. Ismeta's reference to the fact that, although she already knew how to make coffee, her mother-in-law insisted on teaching her, with the directive that "this is how you will make coffee [now that you are here, in this house]" indexes the tensions involved in these household formations. Sometimes new wives were put through hazing procedures that tested their food preparation and service. Rasima recalled being asked by her sisters-in-law to make the lemonade at her own wedding celebration and experiencing embarrassment because she did not know how. After she had been married for a while, her husband's aunt came to visit and asked Rasima to prepare coffee for her. The aunt then refused to drink Rasima's coffee because she had only brought the coffee to a boil once, not twice as was customary in the aunt's family. Coffee service, then, not only was used to bring women together but also served to distinguish status among women.

Not only are džezve symbols of movement and a woman's transformation from single to married, but they also indicate economic status. They are handcrafted from copper and are sometimes finished in silver or gold-plating and thus can be quite expensive. Designers etch džezva with motifs that celebrate regional emblems such as the Herzegovinian pomegranate flower. Ismeta's family and her husband's family were both wealthy, evidenced by several džezva sets she had managed to bring with her to Chicago from Sarajevo and Podgorica. If the presence of džezva was an indication of wealth established by connections among regions, families, and households, the absence of džezva and of coffee indicated risk, vulnerability, and economic precarity. Rasima's father's family had lost much of their property after World War II during the Yugoslav-era land reforms. She remembered the scarcity of coffee during this period, as did Ismeta, who grew up in the same region of northern Bosnia. Now living in the United States and Sweden, following the 1990s wars, women referenced this correlation between absence and vulnerability in noting that their džezva had been stolen when they were forced to flee Bosnia and Herzegovina during the war. Nasiha was forced to leave all her belongings when she was forced from her apartment in Prijedor, and her coffee story alerts us also to women's ongoing vulnerability after being displaced.

Nasiha agreed to be interviewed for the coffee project, but she did not want to talk about džezva or who taught her to make coffee or who she took her coffee breaks with at the office she worked in during the Yugoslav era. Instead, she offered the following story about coffee. When Nasiha left Prijedor in 1992, she was a single mother of a preteen daughter. She fled with her daughter to her sister's small flat in Croatia. Nasiha needed to find work right away, as her sister was already feeling the burden of their elderly parents' sudden arrival several months earlier. Finding a job was a challenge since Nasiha was a refugee and had no Croatian residency or citizenship documents. Her sister's friend helped her get a job at a local coffee roaster, where Nasiha worked full-day shifts in the small-scale industrial operation. She was responsible for every aspect of processing the raw coffee beans for retail sale. This meant transferring baskets of raw beans into the large hot roaster and then standing at the roaster to ensure the beans were evenly and uniformly cooked—in increments lasting from ten to fifteen minutes. Once the beans were roasted, they had to be transferred to cooling bins. After the beans had cooled, she loaded them into large burlap sacks and then carried the coffee sacks—weighing about fifty pounds apiece—up the stairs. In the upper level, she would sort some of the beans out into seven-ounce increments to be ground and packaged for sale. The roaster supplied one of the larger Croatian coffee companies—Mina's—as well as local restaurants and households. Around 3:00 p.m., Nasiha would move to the front of the store to sell the coffee. She was happy to be working, although the labor was intensely physical and constant, and since she was without documents, her wages were very low: "The whole day, if you're working, like eight, eight and half hours, it doesn't matter, for that money, you can just buy a small chicken." In other words, she worked an entire day to have enough income to buy food for the household for that day and nothing more.

Like Nasiha and her family, Mirzet and Tidža had all their possessions stolen when they were forced from their home near Prijedor. Now they live in Chicago, but Bosnian coffee—*pravu kafu* ("the real coffee")—remains a big part of their life; they drank it together every day before or after work, depending on their schedules. When Tidža and Mirzet were interviewed about coffee, they wanted most to show and discuss a hand grinder that Mirzet had made. In Bosnia, Mirzet made over twenty hand grinders for people, including his wife, Tidža, and for his sister to take when she moved to be with her husband in Sarajevo. He also made one for his sister to give to her mother-in-law. He would use some of the scraps and machinery at the steel factory where he worked to forge the pieces. Although hand grinders were rarely used after the introduction of electric grinders, many people kept them, along with džezve, as objects of display. Mirzet was clearly proud of the gifts he had made for some of the women in his life and was especially pleased that his sister had sent one back to him. Because Tidža's had been taken in the war, they had been left with none. The one he had made for his sister's mother-in-law had been returned upon the elder women's death, and it was sent on to Mirzet and Tidža: "It spent time in Herzegovina, spent time in Sarajevo, and arrived in Chicago."

Softening Displacement

People who left Bosnia as a result of the 1990s wars and the people who remained in the country work to soften the experience of displacement and distance by maintaining connections through the circulation of money and objects. People create and convey meaning through sharing activities like driving, home reconstruction, and coffee preparation and drinking, yet people's differential access to these practices and spaces illuminates the tensions and challenges of the postwar period. The availability of work and the option for leisure during a period of great political and economic uncertainties signals the significance of time and space as markers of difference among those living in Bosnia, and those who comprise the diaspora. Although their efforts are heavily circumscribed by the pressure to work more for less in the United States and the limits of social well-being in postwar Bosnia, women's labors and interpretations of the material world connect home and homeland—old and new—collapsing distance through the meaningful exchange and consumption of money and objects.

Postscript

This chapter is dedicated to the memory of Ajla and her mother, Safija.

Notes

1. This governance structure did little to alleviate postwar political tensions and even seemed to facilitate the fracturing of national belonging along ethnic lines.
2. Grodach 2002.
3. I take my cue here from Jansen's call for "a culturally sensitive political economy of displacement and emplacement" (2007, 16). Most of the immigrants I met insisted on referring to the post-2007 crash as "the crisis" and explicitly linked their economic hardships to the intensifying hegemony of state and corporate capitalism.
4. Remittances refer to the wage income migrants set aside to send back to family and friends to support the basic costs of housing, health, and education. In 2007, migrant remittances composed 15 percent of Bosnia and Herzegovina's GDP; in 2014, 15.6 percent (World Bank 2014).

5. Appadurai 1986; Miller 1998.

6. Jansen 2007, 190. My analysis draws on visits to Mostar in 2009 and interviews from a collaborative intergenerational ethnographic project I directed with refugee-migrants in Chicago in 2013 and is also informed by my research among refugee-migrants in the United States since 2003.

7. The official rate of unemployment in 2009 in Bosnia and Herzegovina was 24 percent, while it was 10 percent in the United States.

8. Jansen 2007, 194. See also Croegaert 2011. The case in postsocialist Bosnia and Herzegovina provides some contrast to the discourse of achieving a "normal life" in other postsocialist countries, as Jansen convincingly shows that people used it to evaluate the shortcomings of postwar capitalism by comparing it to the basic benefits produced during the socialist era. Similarly, refugee-migrants in Chicago often used the socialist era as the baseline for a "normal" that in their experience, United States capitalism failed to provide (Croegaert 2011).

9. See Hromadžić (2012) for an extended discussion of the concept of "narod."

10. See Kolind 2007; Hromadžić 2012. VRS and HVO refers to armed forces of Bosnian Serbs (VRS) and of Bosnian Croats (HVO) during the 1992–95 war.

11. According to the 1991 census, the town of Stolac totaled 5,530 people: 62.0 percent Muslim, 20.0 percent Serb, and 11.8 percent Croat (Kolind 2007, 123).

12. Safija had been diagnosed with scleroderma not long after the war. At the time of my visit in 2009, she had already lived well beyond the projected five years following diagnosis and made it to more than ten years before finally passing on in 2013. She was in her early sixties when she died.

13. This regional style is emblematic of Muslim homes and the socialist era, where Muslim homes in the region are typically square, like the mosque, while Catholic homes have rectangular roofs with the longest side facing toward village.

14. See Jansen 2007; Sampson 1996. My interlocutors in the United States located "normal" in time, the Yugoslav state, and in space, in the principles associated with socialist—rather than purely capitalist—development paradigms (Croegaert 2011).

15. Croegaert forthcoming.

16. Bringa 1995; Helms 2010; Croegaert 2011.

17. Džezva and fildžan are Bosnian spellings of Turkish words.

18. Because of its centrality in everyday life, numerous scholars of the region have documented the importance of coffee brewing and service.

19. See Croegaert (2011) for an in-depth discussion of Bosnian coffee and *ćejf*.

20. Gursel also describes coffee grounds fortune-telling as a form of knowledge production—a way of "prognosticating" futures (2012, 8–9)

References

Appadurai, Arjun. 1986. "Introduction: Commodities and the Politics of Value." In *The Social Life of Things: Commodities in Cultural Perspective*, edited by Arjun Appadurai, 3–63. New York: Cambridge University Press.

Bringa, Tone. 1995. *Being Muslim the Bosnian Way: Identity and Community in a Central Bosnian Village*. Princeton, NJ: Princeton University Press.

Croegaert, Ana. 2011. "Who Has Time for Ćejf? Postsocialist Migration and Slow Coffee in Neoliberal Chicago." *American Anthropologist* 113 (3): 463–477.

Croegaert, Ana. Forthcoming. *Gathering Grounds: The Pathos and Promise of Forced Migration*. Chicago: University of Chicago Press.

Grodach, Carl. 2002. "Reconstituting Identity and History in Post-War Mostar, Bosnia-Herzegovina." *City* 6 (1): 61–82.

Gursel, Zeynep. 2012. "Following Coffee Futures: Reflections on Speculative Traditions and Visual Politics." In *Sensible Politics: Visual Cultures of Nongovernmental Activism*, edited by Y. McKee and M. McLagan, 373–393. Brooklyn: Zone Books.

Helms, Elissa. 2010. "The Gender of Coffee: Women and Reconciliation Initiatives in Post-War Bosnia and Herzegovina." *Focaal: Journal of Global and Historical Anthropology* 57: 17–32.

Hromadžić, Azra. 2012. "Once We Had a House: Invisible Citizens and Consociational Democracy in Post-War Mostar, Bosnia and Herzegovina." *Social Analysis* 56 (3): 30–48.

Jansen, Stef. 2007. "Troubled Locations: Return, the Life Course, and Transformations of 'Home' in Bosnia-Herzegovina." *Focaal: Journal of Global and Historical Anthropology* 49: 15–30.

Kolind, Torsten. 2007. "In Search of 'Decent People': Resistance to the Ethnicization of Everyday Life among the Muslims of Stolac." In *The New Bosnian Mosaic: Identities, Memories, and Moral Claims in a Post-War Society*, edited by Xavier Bougarel, Elissa Helms, Ger Duizings, 123–140. Burlington: Ashgate.

Miller, Daniel. 1998. "Why Some Things Matter." In *Material Cultures: Why Some Things Matter*, edited by Daniel Miller, 3–21. Chicago: University of Chicago Press.

Samspson, Steven. 1996. "The Social Life of Projects: Importing Civil Society to Albania." In *Civil Society: Challenging Western Models*, edited by Chris Hann and Elizabeth Dunn, 120–138. London: Routledge.

World Bank Group 2014. "Bosnia-Herzegovina and Herzegovina Partnership: Country Program Snapshot 2014." Washington, DC.

ANA CROEGAERT IS Assistant Professor of Anthropology and Sociology at the University of New Orleans.

14 "We Don't Belong Anywhere": Everyday Life in a Serbian Town Where Immigrants Are Former Refugees

Mila Dragojević

> Once you leave your hometown, you no longer belong anywhere. That is really true. . . . Two years ago, my daughter and I went back to visit some relatives. We walked alone and we didn't even go to see our apartment. . . . It was not the same place, not the same neighbors, not the same people. And, when we come back here, we realize we don't belong here either.
>
> —Former refugee from Sarajevo[1]

The poor conditions at the office of the local commissioner for refugees reflected the circumstances faced by most clients who passed through it. A modest building from the outside, the unpainted room, filled with old filing cabinets, tables, and uncomfortable mismatched chairs, was uninviting. The commissioner's welcoming and friendly demeanor, however, quickly changed the initial impressions; any preconceptions of encountering a discourteous and cold bureaucrat, tired of hearing and having to address refugees' problems, faded. Nikola, the local commissioner for refugees in the Serbian town of Ravnica, began his work with refugees in May 1991.[2] This was shortly after the first outbreak of clashes in Croatia between Serbs and Croats in eastern Slavonia, when the initial waves of refugees started arriving in his town.[3] Most refugees in Ravnica, in the account of the commissioner, arrived from the areas of Croatia and Bosnia and Herzegovina that were affected by violence.

Even though almost two decades had passed since the first wave of refugees arrived in the early 1990s, former refugees continued to represent a significant proportion of the total population in Serbia.[4] In Ravnica, refugees composed the average proportion of the town's population based on the 2002 census.[5] For the first eight months, until December 1991, Ravnica's residents provided housing for most of the refugees. Based on Nikola's account, the locals remembered how they had been displaced in 1941 and had a sense of solidarity with refugees. At first, it was possible to house refugees in individual homes, but when they began arriving massively in December 1991, some had to be placed in a school gym and others in the local cultural center, the spaces that became official "collective centers" or places of temporary residence of refugees designated by the Serbian government's Commissariat for Refugees and the United Nations High Commissioner for Refugees (UNHCR). Local collective centers housed only 650 refugees out of the total number of 6,150 until 2005, when the last official collective center closed down.[6] The first collective center closed in 1998, and three more closed in 2000, according to Nikola.[7] While at the time of the research, there were no official collective centers in the county, one unofficial center remained open after 2005.[8] The county received some assistance from the national Commissariat for Refugees, as well as from international donations, particularly by the Norwegian government.

What Makes Refugees Different from Locals?

After the morning coffee and a short conversation with the commissioner upon my arrival on the first day, clients of the local Commissariat of Refugees started to arrive. It is difficult to define individuals who passed through the office in general terms, as each story was unique and each situation was filled with the sort of obstacles that made the small financial aid this office was able to provide not only inadequate but inappropriate. Their lives were interrupted by the displacement, as well as by the loss of livelihood and property, the tragedies they witnessed were great, and they kept returning even though the refugees at the office knew the aid was insufficient. They did this because at least for a few minutes on that day, someone cared about them. This was at a time when even the former national commissioner for refugees considered the "refugee problem" to be a politicized problem, an "old story."[9] The chance for these refugees to talk to the commissioner, as a representative of the state, was something that many individuals appreciated more than the actual assistance, which in many cases was not possible due to the limited resources of the office. In fact, it was evident from the start that the clients and the commissioner knew each other very well and that an important role of the commissioner was not just to resolve the problem at hand but also to listen and to provide a glimmer of hope that their situation would eventually return to normal.

As mentioned earlier, when refugees began to arrive in 1991, local people helped with what they could, but "nobody could keep guests for fifteen to sixteen years," Nikola commented.[10] In his account, many non-Serbs felt threatened by the arrival of refugees partly because of the demographic change in favor of ethnic Serbs and partly because they expected that these newcomers would have a stronger sense of Serbian national identity than local Serbs as they came from the regions recently affected by ethnic violence.[11] But "luckily," Nikola added, "there were no major clashes along ethnic lines between the newcomers and the

Figure 14.1. A family taking a break after gathering hay in rural Serbia, 2007. Photograph by Željko Stevanović.

locals in the 1990s."[12] According to Nikola, this was notable because Ravnica was ethnically diverse and there were conflicts during World War II between local Serbs and Hungarians.[13] There was, however, one relatively minor incident at the time when refugees first began to arrive in the 1990s. Refugees from Dalmatia protested the local officials' plan to construct a collective center in front of the Catholic church.[14] The refugees' rationale was that Catholics in Dalmatia destroyed Serbs' Orthodox churches and houses and refugees "did not want to see happy people going to church every Sunday and remember their own lost property and churches."[15] On the other hand, locals' perceptions of refugees, if negative at all, were a result of other differences related to their newcomer status in the community.

The tendency of the refugees to see themselves as a "different" social group relative to locals is puzzling—many arrived more than a decade ago (some nearly two) and most refugees share the same Serbian ethnic identity as the local majority. While many refugees found ways to survive in their new homeland—and some even managed to prosper economically—they continued to feel as if they were somehow different from local residents. Indeed, many refugees encountered a cold response when they confided in their new acquaintances about the difficulties of adjusting to a new environment. "We are the refugees in our own country," Andjelka, a local resident, said to emphasize that during the period when

"We Don't Belong Anywhere" 147

Serbia was undergoing severe economic crisis, refugees, in contrast to the local population, at least qualified for humanitarian assistance.[16] Many local residents, in the account of Branka, another local respondent, could not even understand why refugees left their homelands in the first place instead of staying behind and adjusting to new political leadership in Croatia.[17]

Another important difference between refugees and locals was the memories of war and exodus that formed an inextricable part of everyday life for many refugees. Hana, a woman from Bosnia, gave birth to her daughter in December 1992, in the midst of the war, when they had nothing to buy in the stores and one salary could buy only matches.[18] If it were not for agriculture and the resourcefulness of those who knew how to make everything at home, like a homemade dish detergent, they would not have survived during those years in the remote mountainous villages of war-torn Bosnia. Hana remembered the morning they left their home. Her extended family, which had come previously to Hana's home from other parts of Bosnia where the war was more intense, was sleeping when they heard grenades at five in the morning. Fearful of fighting coming to the village, she only took her documents and a few things for the baby. It was raining that morning and the rain was dripping through the roof of their truck, which was "full of children and the elderly."[19] They traveled in a convoy that Hana "could not forget even if she lived to be a hundred years old," not only because of having to leave everything behind and the uncertainty in her destination but also because of the fear for one's life as the road she was crossing was bombed and a pregnant woman died near her.[20] Hana subsisted on temporary agricultural work and on assistance from her extended family. She retained her refugee status for thirteen years, hoping in vain that she would receive some humanitarian aid. In retrospect, she was worse off than applying for citizenship right away and qualifying for state-provided social assistance.

An Uncertain Future

In addition to struggling to socially integrate into their new communities, a number of refugees in Ravnica suffer from depression or post-traumatic stress disorder (PTSD) from the trauma they experienced prior to migration. Some managed to adjust and prosper, while others lost their will—and ability—to overcome the difficult challenges of refugee life. As a result, Nikola described his office database as containing life stories that were so tragic that they resembled characters from Dostoyevsky's novels: There was a man from Bosnia who jumped into a well at an abandoned farm where he lived with his wife and two adult children.[21] There was a refugee, the father of two small children, who committed suicide by electrocuting himself.[22] There was one seventy-year-old refugee who was responsible for caring for his elderly mother.[23] He came to the local Red Cross office one day, with drinks and food to, in his words, "treat everyone since that was his last day alive."[24] The next day, he hanged himself at the entry of the town cemetery.[25] While these were some of the more extreme cases Nikola recounted, the psychological effects of war were an important obstacle—though only one among many—that refugees faced in their efforts to remake their lives in a new place. And to do this amid uncertainty and the new (for many) experience of extreme poverty.

Alongside the psychological traumas people bring, the challenge to meet basic economic needs can feel insurmountable. When Nikola asked Cvjetko, whose wife was killed while he waited for her with his convoy of refugees, if he had found a job, the widower responded: "Who is going to give me a job at my age?"[26] He came to ask for modest, one-time financial assistance to pay for transportation to school for his daughters. Through a local humanitarian program financed by the Norwegian government and aimed at providing housing for the most economically disadvantaged families, Nikola had helped Cvjetko find both his present apartment and a bed for his elderly mother, who lives with him in the apartment. "This year is the most difficult one," Cvjetko said. "My mother is doing badly and needs constant assistance." [27] While the prospect of a better future seems unlikely for Cvjetko, he continues to look for ways to survive and support his family from one day to the next, from one year to the next. Over the course of the seventeen years of working with refugees and learning about the challenges they faced both in the places from which they came and in their new communities, Nikola demonstrated empathy beyond the concern that his job required.

Even though many refugees, especially the younger ones, do not plan to return, the parents of Emil from Croatia returned to their hometown in 1998 to find their house still standing but everything inside stolen.[28] His hometown had been devastated by war. Although Emil may return when he retires, he does not plan to return for now.[29] Very few young people return; agriculture is the mainstay of Emil's hometown and for that reason, young people cannot pursue other career options there. Emil believes his hometown has potential to attract young people again—there is an old factory that could be restarted, for example—but any strategy for return needs to be accompanied by a program aimed at economically reviving the area.[30]

But not all refugees remained in an economically, psychologically, or socially precarious situation. Filipa, fleeing a war-torn city with her husband and their three children, managed to attain economic stability after her arrival in 1993.[31] Mainly because she had a university education and experience as a clerk in her husband's business, she was lucky enough to qualify when a job opportunity opened up.[32] As for many other refugees, the war was a surprise; nobody knew the war would start, and at first they did not know where to go. Filipa and her family decided to settle in Ravnica, where the housing was more affordable than in big cities. They were renting until 2007, when they finally managed to buy their own home with the help of her family who lived abroad.[33] Filipa's husband opened the business, the same as he had before the war. She found a job as a clerk in 1997, when she was able to obtain citizenship, because "laws were such that I could not get citizenship right away; the paperwork took several years."[34] Filipa and her family did not receive any humanitarian aid, donations for refugees, or financial assistance from state institutions and nongovernmental organizations

Figure 14.2. Stragari village center in Serbia, with locals selling produce and socializing, 2017. Photograph by Željko Stevanović.

since they felt that they did not need it, as they could find jobs. Until they found more permanent jobs, they lived from temporary work, their own savings, and remittances from family members who lived abroad. "It was hard in the beginning; everything was new," but it became easier when they started to work and formed a new circle of friends, including many locals.[35]

Establishing a new social network and feeling at home in a new place were challenges for many refugees in the beginning. Katarina worked as a high school teacher when the war started in 1991.[36] She, her husband, and their son arrived in Serbia soon after the start of the war and moved around a lot for twelve years prior to settling in Ravnica, where they now own a small apartment. They, a non-Serb multiethnic couple, had a hard time fitting in anywhere, although she was not sure whether it had to do with their identities: "In the beginning, local people were well-meaning. But later, this turned into animosity. We were somehow guilty for everything bad that was happening to them. . . . I formed friendships with others who arrived from Osijek, Split, and other parts of Croatia or Bosnia and Herzegovina."[37] Katarina's son did not receive Serbian citizenship for ten years even though his father was a citizen: "This was a strange and long story."[38] Despite these difficulties, she rejected any possibility of return: "We would never return, and my mother also left after my father died."[39] Her mother used to receive anonymous threatening phone calls at night. While Katarina occasionally visited her old city and friends, she did not take her son there yet because she did not want to expose him to any situation that would compel him to form a negative image of his hometown.[40]

Like Katarina, Dejan, who arrived from Bosnia and Herzegovina in 1995, had a very difficult time establishing new friendships, or even business partnerships, with locals.[41] He and his wife and two children moved to four places, including a city in Kosovo, where a job that never materialized was promised, prior to settling down in Ravnica in 1998.[42] At first, he could not find a job in Ravnica; he managed to work only through a network of other refugees who collaborated with him to form a company in the agricultural sector.[43] He tried to include locals as well, but locals would not work with him because they distrusted him. Dejan lived in an area of the town inhabited predominantly by other refugees. In 1999, during the NATO bombing campaign, he and his family started constructing their own home. He recalled: "We were building our house here while the planes were flying above us. We were used to bombs in Bosnia already."[44] Five years after arriving in Serbia, in 2000, his family decided to apply for citizenship, which they needed for identification cards, passports, and other documentation. Since that time, he voted regularly. He admitted that at first he voted for "patriotic" parties but later realized that the "democratic" option was more realistic if one was concerned more about the future than about the past. He sounded optimistic even though he recognized that the refugee experience has had a negative effect on his children's education, as they did not complete their university degrees. He did not intend to return to Bosnia: "A return would be a waste of time. In our neighborhood, where we are surrounded by others who came from all over the territories of former Yugoslavia, we feel like locals."[45] Feeling like locals in a community of other newcomers seemed like a sufficient degree of social integration for Dejan, who was surprised by the locals' lack of empathy for the refugees' situation.

Refugees' extended families often offered a support system, sometimes helping with housing. In Ivan's family, three generations of newcomers—parents, three sons, and their children—lived in the same house.[46] The family home was built with humanitarian donations for which they qualified because Ivan's parents had been imprisoned during the war.[47] "Both of my parents were arrested in 1995," Ivan explained. "My mother was let go after a month and a half," and his father was tortured in prison. "Life is back to normal" for them now that they had a place to live and Ivan started his own business.[48]

Even though individual experiences of refugees varied greatly, for most people who overcame an initial period of uncertainty, the economic conditions began to improve somewhat over time. They integrated in the local economy by starting small businesses in the service or hospitality industry, as well as working in agriculture. The town of Ravnica was economically more developed than many other parts of Serbia before the war, prior to the arrival of refugees. While economic crisis and the wars of the 1990s strained the local economy, it is still considered economically strong compared to many other parts of the country. The adjustment to a new place was more difficult for older refugees, as it was harder for them to find employment, build new friendships, and recover from significant material losses later in life. By trying to survive in a situation of uncertainty during a time when both national and international laws lacked clear guidelines or guarantees that their basic rights and needs would be met, many refugees unintentionally set themselves apart from the local population. The locals, on the other hand, perceived themselves to be at a financial disadvantage in their own state compared to refugees, who could claim certain forms of social assistance from two states once their refugee status was removed.

While many newcomers in Serbia were legally no longer refugees, as many became citizens over time, they continued to perceive themselves, or they continued to be perceived in their communities, as refugees. Reasons for this are numerous, as the interviews illustrated. When exile becomes a permanent state, life goes on as normal, or perhaps, a new way of life eventually becomes normal. In the end, many newcomers in this community continued to live both here and there, connected superficially to both their new place and to their old hometown but profoundly to neither.

Notes

1. Ana, a former refugee from Sarajevo (author's interview, number 37–55, September 14, 2008).

2. All proper names of towns, officials, and respondents are changed in order to protect the privacy of the individuals. The information from the commissioner's office is based on the interviews held from October 6 to October 18, 2008, while interviews with refugees, former refugees, or local residents conducted outside of commissioner's office were conducted from August 2008 through June 2009.

3. UNHCR and Commissariat 1996; UNHCR and Commissariat 2001; UNHCR and Commissariat 2007.

4. Based on estimates from the 2002 census, former refugees constituted almost 5 percent of the total population nationally and in some cities, like Šid and Inđija, even more than 20 percent of the local population. Using the category "persons who arrived from Bosnia and Herzegovina and Croatia after 1991" in the 2002 census (National Statistical Office 2002), there were 379,135 individuals residing in Serbia (Ladjević and Stanković 2004, 51–52).

5. Ladjević and Stanković 2004; National Statistical Office 2002.

6. Author's interview with the commissioner, October 8, 2008.

7. Ibid.

8. Ibid.

9. In his article, entitled *Victims of Manipulation*, and in an interview conducted on June 20, 2008, in Belgrade, the former Republican commissioner for refugees (from February 2003 until March 2004) Ozren Tošić asked why there are still "refugees" in Serbia when most of them had the right to receive citizenship by 2008. He argued that the principal reason these individuals wished to maintain their refugee status was because they were actually convinced by both the government of Serbia and the UNHCR that this was a more beneficial status to them compared to any alternative (Tošić 2006).

10. Author's interview with the commissioner, October 8, 2008.

11. Author's interview with the commissioner, October 14, 2008.

12. Ibid.

13. Author's interview with the commissioner, October 8, 2008.

14. Author's interview with the commissioner, October 14, 2008.
15. Ibid.
16. Andjelka, a local resident (author's interview, number 61–86, February 3, 2009).
17. Branka, a local resident (author's interview, number 63–88, February 3, 2009).
18. Hana, a refugee from Bosnia and Herzegovina, commissioner's office (author's interview, number 46–65, October 23, 2008).
19. Ibid.
20. Ibid.
21. Author's interview with the commissioner, October 8 and 14, 2008.
22. Author's interview with the commissioner, October 14, 2008.
23. Ibid.
24. Ibid.
25. Ibid.
26. Cvjetko, a refugee from Bosnia and Herzegovina, commissioner's office (author's interview, number 39–58, October 8, 2008).
27. Ibid.
28. Emil, a refugee from Croatia, commissioner's office (author's interview, number 40–59, October 8, 2008).
29. Ibid.
30. Ibid.
31. Filipa, a refugee from Bosnia and Herzegovina, commissioner's office (author's interview, number 43–62, October 14, 2008).
32. Ibid.
33. Ibid.
34. Ibid.
35. Ibid.
36. Katarina, a refugee from Croatia, commissioner's office (author's interview, number 44–63, October 14, 2008).
37. Ibid.
38. Ibid.
39. Ibid.
40. Ibid.
41. Dejan, a refugee from Bosnia and Herzegovina, commissioner's office (author's interview, number 41–60, October 14, 2008).
42. Ibid.
43. Ibid.
44. Ibid.
45. Ibid.
46. Ivan, a refugee from Croatia, commissioner's office (author's interview, number 50–70, October 23, 2008).
47. Ibid.
48. Ibid.

References

Ladjević, Petar, and Vladimir Stanković. 2004. "The Refugee Population in Serbia Based on the 2002 Census Data." Belgrade: National Statistical Office and Ministry for the Human Rights and Rights of Minorities of Serbia and Montenegro.

National Statistical Office, Republic of Serbia. 2002. "Stanovništvo knj. 9—Popis stanovništva, domaćinstava i stanova iz 2002: Uporedni pregled broja stanovnika 1948, 1953, 1961, 1971, 1981, 1991 i 2002, podaci po naseljima [Population Vol. 9—Census of the population, households, and housing from 2002: Comparative population numbers from 1948, 1953, 1961, 1971, 1981, 1991 i 2002, by municipalities]." Belgrade: Republički zavod za statistiku Republike Srbije.

Tošić, Ozren. 2006. "Victims of Manipulation." *Politika Daily*, January 10, 2006, p. 6, translated by Mirjana Milenkovski.

UNHCR and Commissariat. 1996. "Registration of Refugees." Belgrade: UNHCR and the Commissariat for Refugees of the Republic of Serbia.

UNHCR and Commissariat. 2001. "Registration of Refugees." Belgrade: UNHCR and the Commissariat for Refugees of the Republic of Serbia.

UNHCR and Commissariat. 2007. "Refugee Registration Report in the Republic of Serbia in 2005." Belgrade: UNHCR and the Commissariat for Refugees of the Republic of Serbia.

MILA DRAGOJEVIĆ is Associate Professor of Politics at the University of the South. She is author of *The Politics of Social Ties: Immigrants in an Ethnic Homeland*.

15 Neoliberal Spaces of Immorality: The Creation of a Bulgarian Land Market and "Land-Grabbing" Foreign Investors

Deema Kaneff

> We are now the proud owners of a house we have never seen in a country we flew over once, bizarre ehh![1]

> Friends, we bought quite a few properties in and around Varna. All purchases were blind. This is not because we could not afford the trip in monetary terms, it is because we could not afford the time.[2]

The Booming Market

The above quotes capture some of the frenzy associated with Bulgaria's booming property market that at its peak between 2006 and 2008 constituted one of the hottest property markets in the world. They reflect a particular group of property buyers who, unlike those I have discussed in the rural region of Veliko Tarnovo,[3] engaged in the market largely, if not entirely, for investment purposes.[4] These investors focused their attention on the capital, the Black Sea, and ski resorts in Bulgaria. The quotes indicate not only the importance of foreign players in this market but also the degree of activity, much of which was carried out not by large commercial development companies (although that certainly took place) but by individual citizens shopping for properties over the internet, without ever having visited the country. There were cases reported of investors "buying 10 apartments at a time, just like penny chews."[5] One investor was reported to have bought twenty-five properties from one company.[6] Given the relative cheapness of the properties, western citizens could afford to do so.

The effect was significant in terms of the expansion of the market. In 2007, Bulgaria recorded a rise in house prices of 30.6 percent, giving it the highest

Figure 15.1. A street scene in the laid-back town of Kyustendil, Bulgaria. Although benefiting from its relative closeness to Sofia, the town has not experienced the same high level of foreign investment as resort locations, evidencing the unevenness of international demand for real estate. Photograph by Mina Hristova, 2017.

growth rate in the world, ahead of Shanghai and Singapore, which were in second and third place.[7] Real estate constituted over a quarter of the total foreign direct investment in the country between 2006 and 2008,[8] and it was one of the fastest-growing sectors of the national economy, generating billions of euros in revenue every year.[9]

This market was partly created and driven by the western media. Channel Four in Britain, for example, aired four programs on property buying in Bulgaria between 2001 and 2004, and the emerging market was widely covered in various newspapers, magazines, and the internet. Many of the British with whom I spoke, who unlike the investors in this study had become permanent or seasonal migrants to Bulgaria, identified these TV programs as the source of their interest in Bulgaria. This coincided with the anticipated entry of Bulgaria into the European Union (in 2007), which held the promise of greater investment security. The market was also supported by the local tourist industry, which had a long-established and successful history going back to socialist Bulgaria;[10] cheaper air travel and the opening of new routes by various airline companies to Bulgaria; the development of new infrastructure, including the expansion of Sofia's airport, a venture sponsored financially by the Kuwait Fund for Arab Economic Development, the European Investment Bank, EU programs (PHARE and ISPA), and the Bulgarian state; and the active support of various politicians and government bodies encouraging investment in Bulgaria, including the mayor of Sofia who in 2006 attended the International Real Estate Forum in London.[11]

The growth of the property market had far-reaching consequences in terms of the expansion of related sectors of the economy: on the construction and building industries, which included commercial developers who were behind many of the new housing complexes with their associated golf courses, leisure centers, and so on;[12] on the growth of real estate companies; on businesses offering translators who mediated between the foreign buyers and Bulgarian sellers; on the growth of the legal profession involved in property transfers; and on the banking sector, which gave loans for various commercial projects.

The global crisis in 2008 slowed down much of this expansion; the property bubble burst, and prices plummeted.[13] The situation, however, was temporary and resulted in the emergence of investment from a greater diversity of foreigners: British buyers were joined by Russian and Greek investors, and interest from the Chinese has also been growing. Since early 2014, the property market has been showing signs of a gradual recovery[14] with notable increases in the purchases of investment properties and a growth in the luxury property sector.[15]

Exploiting "Loopholes" in the System: Illegal Foreign Land Ownership

> It is no secret that foreigners, including from non-EU countries, have been buying Bulgarian land for years by different means.[16]

During the period that is the focus of this chapter—2000 to 2015, which largely coincides with the development of the property market—it was illegal for foreigners to own land in Bulgaria (for residential housing, agriculture, or any other reasons). They could, however, acquire ownership over buildings, for example, apartments in which land is not part of the package. In effect, however, most apartment and all house ownership involves partial or full land ownership. So, in reality, land was being bought by foreigners despite legal measures designed to deter this.

The law concerning foreign ownership was part of the negotiated conditions of entry in the EU. As in all other eastern European accession countries, moratoria were agreed. In the case of Bulgaria, a five-year moratorium was negotiated on the foreign ownership of land for residential purposes (expired January 1, 2012) and a seven-year moratorium for the ownership of agricultural or forest land (expired January 1, 2014). After the end of the moratorium period, foreign ownership of land became permissible. The moratorium was intended to stop western Europeans from making big acquisitions of land immediately after accession, as this would increase prices, thereby excluding Bulgarians from engagement in the market.[17] Land prices were, and still are, much lower than in western Europe. The land market is thus skewed strongly toward buyers from EU member states whose higher salaries, higher wealth/assets, and relative greater experience with the market gives them important advantages. Fears about exclusion, and the necessity to level the playing field and give access to Bulgarian citizens, lay behind the moratoria.

Therefore, the literally tens of thousands of property transactions that have taken place since 2000, described above as part of a booming market, have been carried out against the spirit, if not directly against the law, of the Bulgarian Constitution and EU accession laws. During this entire period that foreign ownership was officially illegal, it has been taking place with both the tacit approval of government organs and the unashamed activities of private investors. The process was backed by a multitude of actors: the media enticing people to engage in a new property market and find their "place in the sun"; various levels of government—Bulgaria and the EU—whose drive for accession opened up political, administrative, and economic (i.e., international finance) borders, while corresponding cut backs in state welfare forced individuals to seek their own forms of social security through engaging in the new property market (as buyers or sellers); as well as the private business sector and individual investors keen to make profits.

With such a force behind market expansion, it was little wonder that investors found ways around the laws that, though denying foreign individual citizens ownership, did allow businesses/companies the right to own land. Individuals thus circumvented these laws by registering themselves as limited companies. As Nik, a UK estate agent in Veliko Tarnovo told me in 2004: "It's just a way for the individual to own property; it's not hard to organize, and we do that all as part of the business." So, when buying property with land, foreigners registered themselves as a limited liability company in Bulgaria, in whose name the purchase was then made. This is not, as one internet site notes, "as off putting as it might sound."[18] To the contrary, there are advantages: the company can be set up in a day as part of the purchasing transaction (organized by the estate agent as part of the sales package), and when buying the property, a company pays less tax on eventual sales than individual owners (15 percent versus 25 percent, respectively).[19] The company created does not have to operate or carry out any trade activity; it is simply a way to allow foreign individuals to buy property.

As of January 2014, all restrictions relating to the ownership of land (including agricultural and forest) in Bulgaria by EU nationals were removed.[20] Non-EU citizens can still buy land using the more circuitous method of registering a company. In any case, as already noted, the official legal position that foreign citizens could not acquire land during the moratorium was never a practical restriction; the market boomed precisely during the time when foreign land ownership was officially illegal. Perhaps because of this, toward the end of the agricultural land moratorium, the Bulgarian government tried to extend restrictions on foreign ownership of agricultural/forest land beyond 2014. A law was passed in parliament to extend the moratorium another six years, to 2020. This act was designed to help stabilize agricultural production and protect the interests of local, small-scale farmers who, it was argued, could not compete against foreign capital, especially from multinational agribusinesses set on buying up large tracts of agricultural land.[21] The relatively low prices of the land with respect to the rest of Europe would make foreign domination inevitable while damaging domestic farmers' ability to buy. The government's position was supported by Vesselin Boyadzhiev, a professor in the Department of Social and Economic Geography at Sofia University, who expressed a commonly held fear that "we will wake up on January 1, 2014, only to realize that we have given away our land for free."[22] He pointed out that Bulgaria's land "is just as good as in France in terms of mineral resources and biodiversity, but it is tagged at ten times lower prices."[23] It was seen as a "precious natural resource" that would be plundered and lost.[24]

However, following threats from various EU and Bulgarian quarters,[25] and a successful appeal in the constitutional court in Bulgaria, the law was repealed. It was argued that the extended moratorium violated Bulgarian EU accession commitments and was against the Bulgarian Constitution. Soon after, however, other measures to deter foreign investors from buying agricultural land were introduced by the government with overwhelming support from the public and members of parliament across the political spectrum. Thus, for example, current legislation requires EU individual and company owners to have five years' permanent residency status.[26] Such residency demands have put Bulgaria at loggerheads with the European Commission, which demanded clarification in 2015 of the new laws regulating acquisition of agricultural land, as they "may be considered to restrict the free movement of capital and freedom of establishment" within the borders of the EU—that is, they are seen as a threat to the open market and transborder investment.[27] Unsatisfied with the received response, the European Commission has, more recently in 2016, formally requested Bulgaria to amend its legislation, as it is seen as potentially discriminatory against other EU national investors.[28] Divergent views vis-à-vis the property market remain.

Morality Debates

> Not only is it rather tasteless to take part in some sort of developing-country land-grab, but I can't help feeling that it is financially foolish as well.[29]

While to my knowledge the legality of foreign property ownership was not a topic debated explicitly by individual buyers or at the level of national governments, the topic was broached in the media and various internet sites, in terms of morality.

One theme around which a dialogue of morality was expressed was triggered by an article written by the journalist Rosie Murray-West (see the quote at the beginning of this section) with respect to the high interest shown by the British in buying Bulgarian property. Her accusation of Britons as "land grabbing" and so taking advantage of a "developing" country drew heated comments on internet sites accessed by buyers, whose differing positions often reflected their interests as defined by the nature of their involvement in the market (e.g., as either investors or permanent/seasonal migrants). Some sympathized with her position, agreeing that it was shameful that the main focus was on profit rather than on the effect the sales have on the country and its people.[30] Others pointed out that not all buyers were investors; there were many motives for buying, and many chose to make Bulgaria their home. Yet others emphasized the positive contribution made by foreign investment, which it was argued was "good for the local economy."[31] The majority—in the main, pure investors—were both indignant and angry with the journalist, rejecting the idea that it was somehow "tasteless" to take part in a "developing country land grab." One twenty-four-year-old boldly stated that he was indeed interested in Bulgaria purely for financial gain: "I'm not ashamed of this, and I don't see anything wrong with this. . . . If that means that locals can't afford the properties us 'greedy Brits' are snapping up—such is life. Sorry to sound quite blunt, but that's the way it is."[32] He continued in a further posting: "I will take every opportunity that comes my way—be it financial or otherwise. If that means that others miss out, be they neighbors or even friends—such is life. . . . I put my own welfare first. Which is the most natural thing in the world."[33] His perspective was supported by others who pointed out that "profit is not a dirty word" and that this was the free market at work. Another stated: "The vast majority are looking to increase their own wealth. Buy low, sell high. That's plain common sense so don't be ashamed of it."[34] Exclusion is an accepted "fact" of how this market works: people who can afford to buy do so and prices go up, and others who are disadvantaged by prohibitive prices are either totally excluded from the market or forced to engage in buying property in less sought-after locations that they can afford.

It is precisely this concern of being excluded from the market that seemed to be the focus of most online comments by Bulgarians. The view was that foreign involvement makes the land too expensive and a growth in prices serves to deny access to Bulgarian buyers. As one Bulgarian woman asked: "House prices are set to rise and when everyone has finished their boom buying, who in Bulgaria is going to be able to afford to buy a house in their own country?"[35] Another reinforced this concern, noting that foreigners will buy the best land by the sea, where already ordinary Bulgarians cannot afford to live, and the prices will rise so much that it will be a market "solely between foreigners with their unreachably high prices,"[36] thereby entirely excluding Bulgarians from the market.

A small number of Bulgarians did not seem unduly concerned: "What will they [i.e., British buyers] do, walk off with the land?"[37] One pointed out that we "can't go back to the fifteenth century, when houses were fortified from outsiders and we secretly looked at outsiders only from behind our curtains."[38] Drawing on an image from times when Bulgaria was under Ottoman rule, it conveys the idea that Bulgarians are scared of the consequences of foreign ownership and that this is a very "backward" way of viewing the situation. The basic message was that people need to get used to the contemporary situation of unregulated, that is, "open," markets in which foreigners can freely participate. Arguments underlying economic advantages were used to justify this position: that foreigners will build houses using labor and materials from Bulgaria, and they will spend their money in the country. (This has proven to be only partly true.) They argued against those who preferred to leave the land untended rather than allow foreigners to own and develop it. Supporters of foreign land ownership further pointed out that foreigners will not come and build up industry, investing millions in the country, unless they can also own the land on which the building exists. To encourage investment, foreigners must be able to own land.[39] However, others retorted that land ownership is hardly the crucial factor for investors. Rather, investment possibilities, attractive laws, political climate, opportunities to export profits, and EU membership status are far more significant.[40]

Figure 15.2. Built in 1856, the Shabla Lighthouse is the oldest and tallest lighthouse in Bulgaria. Such stereotypical images of coastal villages are becoming harder to find, as the commercial development of the Black Sea through tourism and property development transforms the landscape. Photograph by Mariya Stoyanova, 2014.

A second theme around which a discussion of morality was articulated was at the level of national and EU politics. A tirade of discussions took place in late 2013, when the Bulgarian government moved to extend the restrictions of foreign ownership of agricultural land a further six years, to 2020. Frequently identified as the poorest member of the EU, the Bulgarian government argued that income standards in Bulgaria are at least ten times lower than in other parts of Europe and the liberalization of the country's land market would put its citizens at a considerable disadvantage when seeking to buy agricultural land, as well as severely reduce the competitiveness of Bulgarian farmers, who would be forced to compete with the foreign agribusiness enterprises that snapped up the low-cost land.

The EU's response to Bulgarian attempts to extend the restriction of foreign ownership of agricultural land was unsympathetic. The European internal markets commissioner was quoted as saying, "Bulgaria's accession treaty did not provide for any extension period.... Therefore we expect Bulgaria to open its market in compliance with its commitments."[41] Ironically, given their prominent anti–European Union stance, the British were the loudest and most vocal in criticizing Bulgaria and demanding it honor EU laws. The UK Tory MP Nigel Mills accused Bulgaria of hypocrisy and pointed out that when the Bulgarian government voted to extend the restrictions of foreign agricultural land ownership to 2020, it breached EU agreements: "Bulgaria hasn't applied the obligations it signed up to. If it isn't satisfying all the terms of the treaty it doesn't deserve the benefits"— a thinly veiled threat to withdraw EU labor and mobility opportunities if Bulgaria

Neoliberal Spaces of Immorality 161

does not fully open its market to foreign investment.[42] This position, expressed by a British politician from a party that in the main opposes EU "interference" in national issues and has a significant membership that largely supports Britain's exit from the EU, is clearly motivated by UK business interests in Bulgaria. Three weeks later, the Bulgarian Constitutional Court ruled that the extension violated Bulgarian commitments to the EU, and the law was repealed—although as noted earlier, the tensions over this matter between Bulgaria and the EU continue today.[43]

Moral dilemmas concerning the loss of access to, and control over, a basic resource with particular national value is an old problem faced by regions entering the global economy. Debates concerning private financial gain versus the common good are a feature of every period of capitalist expansion. Such moral discussions are fueled, in contemporary times, by a form of capitalism that has arguably generated greater inequalities than any other period of capitalist development/exploitation (depending on one's perspective) in living memory.[44]

Global Inequalities and Neoliberal Spaces of Immorality

> There exists a direct correspondence between the advance of globalisation, neoliberalism and the advance of poverty, social inequality and social inequity.[45]

Several years have passed since the moratorium was lifted, yet the property market is still a focus of contestation: with the Bulgarian government attempting—through a degree of regulation—to protect native farmers and its national resource from (large-scale) foreign investors, while the EU's on-going concern is to open the market to all its citizens wishing to exploit market opportunities. The case raises questions about whether it is ever possible to have a truly "open" or "free" market, as it will always be a site in which different actors with different interests engage, and those with greater wealth and power have more freedom and access to control, shape, and participate in it.

In other words, the case I have discussed here provides a concrete example of the types of problems generated by a system that advocates an "open" market system and yet, on paper at least, simultaneously attempts to address imbalances in such a system. Two sets of laws operated in parallel and against each other: laws that privileged business interests (backed up by favorable tax policies) versus laws designed to protect citizens potentially excluded from the market. That different laws advocate different interests is not the concern; it is a commonly met occurrence. What is a concern, however, is the fact that in a democracy, laws are supposed to be equally applicable to all citizens. What we are witnessing is the opposite: laws are unequally implemented and unevenly accessible (dependent on how much capital/assets any actor has), which results in differing access to opportunities. The opening up of Bulgaria and the way in which the market was developed was not a process equally accessible or engaged in by all. Foreigners with capital worked the system to their own advantage, overriding any legal attempts to bring about a level playing field (assuming this is ever attainable). In this system, where one set of laws operates against another, one set of practices clearly dominates: the one that favors business and capital above laws that strive for human equality and inclusion.

The unequal application of laws and unequal participation in the market has two consequences, which I discuss in turn. Firstly, it leads to greater regional and global inequalities. As evident from the example discussed in this chapter, foreign investors with money to spend were advantageously placed and able to engage and speculate in the property market. In the case described, we have a range of actors—namely, those with financial resources—taking advantage of pro-business policies for their own personal interests. In so doing, native Bulgarians were increasingly fearful of being excluded. The wealth differentials increased as investors increased their profit (and later lost it, during the economic crisis), while those unable to engage in the market faced greater poverty and marginalization. Secondly, unequal access to the market is also a process that lacks transparency and thus poses a threat to democratic processes. The many foreigners who registered companies made it impossible to collect official data as to who owns what land in Bulgaria, since foreign companies often used Bulgarian names while Bulgarian-owned companies frequently used foreign names. The inability to monitor these processes made turning a blind eye to irregular activities that operated against the good intentions of laws/moratoria not only easier but also inevitable. Lack of transparency erodes democratic processes, working against a fairer and more equitable society through the loss of taxes for the state, which in the long run impoverishes all citizens living in the country.

Neoliberal policies operate against the previous redistributive economies of socialism (as well as against the welfare capitalism of post–World War II western Europe). They benefit and serve to concentrate resources and power in the hands of investors (advantages reinforced through tax breaks and insufficient market regulation that allows buyers, as we saw, to exploit laws for their own benefit). Once one of the most equal societies in Europe, Bulgaria is now one of the most unequal, fairing worse than the vast majority of other European countries, irrespective of the study or measuring scale one chooses to consult.[46] This is a result, at least in part, of policies implemented over the previous twenty years, including those relating to property, that give (well-off) foreigners privileged access to the market while at the same time increasingly excluding many Bulgarians—that is, privileging business interests and financial elite above the interests of ordinary citizens.[47]

This story of transnational exploitation and rising regional inequalities is replicated throughout the postsocialist world—in the Balkans and across Eastern Europe—where "open" markets have been established in the last couple of decades. The inequalities generated by an uneven playing field that deliberately favors some players above others is not, however, a "natural process," as some of the "land-grabbing" Brits chose to portray the situation. The circumstances are both changeable and challengeable (through, for example, greater regulation).

Although one may take some heart in the fact that debates concerning the morality of "open/free" markets still take place, it is also disturbing how many see inequalities and selfish greed/profit motives as both "natural" and justifiable, as evidenced by the young British man quoted earlier, who has no hesitation in prioritizing his own economic interests of profit making above any of his relationships with "friends" or neighbors. The human cost of neoliberal capitalism and its drive for endless profit is high—many would say too high.

Notes

1. My Bulgaria Forum 2004, October 14, posted by "Malkers" in the Property Advice Forum. These discussions—and others within My Bulgaria Forum—included foreigners and Bulgarians over a period of more than a year, directly addressing morality concerns relating to the buying of property in Bulgaria.

2. Ibid., October 7, posted by "Kam" in the Buying Blind Forum.

3. Kaneff 2009.

4. Fieldwork with this very different group of buyers—investors—is only possible through various online sites where they constitute a virtual "community" on the basis of their shared interest in investing in Bulgarian property. Often, they have never been to Bulgaria, nor do they intend to go, and the internet is the only place that this group comes together.

5. Nurden 2006. Penny chews are a chewy candy that traditionally sold in the UK for a penny.

6. Conradi 2004.

7. BBC News 2008.

8. Global Property Guide 2014.

9. Brunwasser 2006b.

10. Ghodsee 2005.

11. Novinite 2006a.

12. For example, see Novinite 2006b.

13. For example, see Hope and Troev 2008.

14. Global Property Guide 2014.

15. See Novinite 2017.

16. Novinite 2013.

17. Brunwasser 2006a.

18. Black Seas Villas 2005.

19. Brunwasser 2006a.

20. See British government official website that provides guidance to British citizens for buying property in Bulgaria: Foreign and Commonwealth Office 2014.

21. See *Sofia Globe* 2013.

22. Novinite 2013.

23. Ibid.

24. Ibid.

25. For example, see Roth (2013).

26. Novinite 2015.

27. European Commission 2015.

28. Ibid.

29. Murray-West 2005.

30. My Bulgaria Forum 2005, June 18, posted by "Kazz" in the Property Buying/Selling Advice.

31. Ibid., March 27, posted by "Fazal1."

32. Ibid., April 26, posting by "Stevetd" in the Media Coverage Forum.
33. Ibid.
34. Ibid., April 26, posted by "Soarer" in the Media Coverage Forum.
35. Ibid., March 28, posted by "Miraumbd."
36. Kaldata 2007, March 10, posted by "Vobko."
37. Ibid., March 10, posted by "Stanley56."
38. Ibid., March 11, posted by "Shanna."
39. Ibid., March 20, posted by "Nickfox."
40. Ibid., March 21, posted by "Agni."
41. EuroActiv.com with Reuters 2013.
42. PressTV 2014.
43. EUbusiness 2014. The situation has been further complicated by Britain's 2016 referendum that voted to exit the EU. At the time of publication, it is unclear what effects Brexit will have on British property owners in Bulgaria or in other parts of the EU, for that matter.
44. Duménil and Lévy 2005; Wade 2007.
45. UNDP 2010, xv, cited in Petras and Veltmeyer 2011, 59.
46. See, for example, EU Commission. n.d., accessed June 18, 2015. Also see Eurostat (ie statistical office of the European Union): http://ec.europa.eu/eurostat/web/products-datasets/-/tespm151; e.g., "bulgaria and inequalities": http://ec.europa.eu/eurostat/tgm/graph.do?tab=graph&plugin=1&language=en&pcode=tespm151&toolbox=type; and Oxfam: https://policy-practice.oxfam.org.uk/blog/2015/09/an-unequal-union.
47. Harvey 2005; Duménil and Lévy 2005.

References

BBC News. 2008. "Bulgaria Tops House Price League." BBC News, January 7. Accessed June 12, 2015. http://news.bbc.co.uk/1/hi/business/7175429.stm.

Black Seas Villas. 2005. "Analysis of Bulgarian Market by Property Investor." June 27. Includes article by investor Jeremy Cornah. Accessed June 28, 2006. www.blackseavillas.net.

Brunwasser, Matthew. 2006a. "Buying Abroad: In Bulgaria." *New York Times*, April 13. Accessed June 20, 2015. http://www.nytimes.com/2006/03/31/realestate/31iht-reBUYBULG.1476264.html?_r=0.

Brunwasser, Matthew. 2006b. "The Rise and Rise of Bulgarian Property." Novinite, March 27. Accessed June 15, 2015. http://www.novinite.com/articles/61090/The+Rise+and+Rise+of+Bulgarian+Propert.

Conradi, Peter. 2004. "A House for the Cost of a Car." *Sunday Times*, October 3. Accessed June 18, 2015. http://www.bulgarianproperties.com/Bulgaria_articles/a_house_for_the_cost_of_a_car_120.html.

Duménil, Gérard, and Dominique Lévy. 2005. "The Neoliberal (Counter-)Revolution." In *Neoliberalism. A Critical Reader*, edited by A. Saad-Filho and D. Johnston, 9–19. London: Pluto Press.

EuroActiv.com with Reuters. 2013. "Bulgaria Extends Land Purchase Ban despite EU Warning." October 23, last updated January 8, 2015. Accessed June 20, 2015. http://www.euractiv.com/central-europe/bulgaria-extends-land-purchase-b-news-531248.

EUbusiness. 2014. "Bulgarian Court Annuls Ban on Land Sales to Foreigners." January 28. Accessed June 21, 2015. http://www.eubusiness.com/news-eu/bulgaria-property.tcm.

European Commission. N.d. "Research Finding – Social Situation Monitor – Income Inequality in EU Countries." Accessed June 18, 2015. http://ec.europa.eu/social/main.jsp?catId=1050&intPageId=1870&langId=en; http://www.gini-research.org/system/uploads/592/original/GINI_Policy_Paper_3.pdf?1386692133.

European Commission. 2015. "Financial Services: Commission Opens Infringement Procedures against Bulgaria, Hungary, Lithuania and Slovakia on Investor Restrictions for Agricultural Land." Press release. March 26. Accessed February 27, 2017. http://europa.eu/rapid/press-release_IP-15-4673_en.htm.

Foreign and Commonwealth Office. 2014. "How to Buy Property in Bulgaria." Last updated February 6. Accessed February 27, 2017. www.gov.uk/guidance/how-to-buy-property-in-bulgaria.

Ghodsee, Kristen. 2005. *The Red Riviera: Gender, Tourism, and Postsocialism on the Black Sea*. Durham, NC: Duke University Press.

Global Property Guide. 2014. "Bulgarian Housing Market Recovering Slowly." April 7. Accessed June 12, 2015. http://www.globalpropertyguide.com/Europe/Bulgaria/Price-History-Archive/Bulgarias-housing-market-recovering-slowly-127252.

Harvey, David. 2005. *A Brief History of Neoliberalism*. Oxford: Oxford University Press.

Hope, Kerin, and Theodor Troev. 2008. "Bulgaria Loses Allure for UK Buyers." *Financial Times*. February 9. Accessed June 25, 2015. http://www.ft.com/cms/s/0/93d152d8-d66a-11dc-b9f4-0000779fd2ac.html#axzz3e7FTKsv2.

Kaldata. 2007. Разрешиха окончателно чужденци да придобиват земя у нас. Various dates. Accessed June 2015. https://www.kaldata.com/forums/

Knauf, Deema. 2009. "Property and Transnational Neoliberalism: The Case of British Migration to Bulgaria." In *Accession and Migration: Changing Policy, Society, and Culture in an Enlarged Europe*, edited by J. Eade and Y. Valkanova, 59–74. Surrey: Ashgate.

Murray-West, Rosie. 2005. "Snakes and Ladders: Beware the Cheap and Nasty Bulgarian Dream." *The Telegraph*, March 26. Accessed June 18, 2015. http://www.telegraph.co.uk/finance/property/property-market/propertymarketwatch/3340440/Snakes-and-ladders-Beware-the-cheap-and-nasty-Bulgarian-dream.html.

My Bulgaria Forum. 2004. Various dates. Accessed February 2006. http://www.mybulgaria.info/modules.php?name=Forums&file=index.

My Bulgaria Forum. 2005. Various dates. Accessed February 2006. http://www.mybulgaria.info/modules.php?name=Forums&file=index.

Novinite. 2006a. "Mayor Flaunts Sofia Real Estate Assets in London." June 27. Accessed June 15, 2015. http://www.novinite.com/articles/65662/Mayor+Flaunts+Sofia+Real+Estate+Assets+in+London.

Novinite. 2006b. "Spaniards to Build 2 Golf Courses near Sofia." March 24. Accessed June 20, 2015. http://www.novinite.com/articles/60979/Spaniards+to+Build+2+Golf+Courses+Near+Sofia.

Novinite. 2013. "Bulgaria to Lift Ban on Land Sale to Foreigners 2014, Prices 'Ridiculously Low.'" September 16. Accessed June 20, 2015. http://www.novinite.com/articles/153674/Bulgaria+to+Lift+Ban+on+Land+Sale+to+Foreigners+2014%2C+Prices+%27Ridiculously+Low%E2%80%99.

Novinite. 2015. "EU Launches Proceeding on Agricultural Land Ownership Law in Bulgaria." March 26. Accessed June 30, 2018. https://www.novinite.com/articles/167504/EU+Launches+Proceeding+on+Agricultural+Land+Ownership+Laws+in+Bulgaria.

Novinite. 2017. "Vesela Ilieva: Property Purchases for Investment Purposes Increased in Bulgaria in 2016." February 9. Accessed February 28, 2017, http://www.novinite.com/articles/178801/Vesela+Ilieva%3A+Property+Purchases+for+Investment+Purposes+Increased+in+Bulgaria+in+2016.

Nurden, Robert. 2006. "Bulgaria: See the Light." *The Independent*, May 31. Accessed June 18, 2015. http://www.independent.co.uk/property/house-and-home/bulgaria-see-the-light-480357.html.

Petras, James, and Henry Veltmeyer. 2011. *Beyond Neoliberalism: A World to Win*. Surrey: Ashgate.

PressTV. 2014. "Bulgaria Land Law Breaks EU Agreement: Lawmakers." January 6. Accessed June 10, 2015. http://www.presstv.com/detail/2014/01/06/344094/bulgaria-land-law-breaks-eu-agreement.

Roth, Stephanie. 2013. "Bulgaria Extends Ban on Land Acquisition by Non-Nationals." October 24. Accessed June 10, 2015. www.arc2020.eu/front/2013/10/bulgaria-extends-ban-on-land-acquisition-by-non-nationals/.

Sofia Globe. 2013. "Bulgaria 'Plans Restrictions' After Ban on Foreigners Buying Land Is Lifted in 2014." October 11. Accessed June 20, 2015. http://sofiaglobe.com/2013/10/11/bulgaria-plans-restrictions-after-ban-on-foreigners-buying-land-is-lifted-in-2014/.

Wade, Robert Hunter. 2007. "The Causes of Increasing World Poverty and Inequality; Or, Why the Matthew Effect Prevails." In *Neoliberalism, Globalization, and Inequalities. Consequences for Health and Quality of Life*, edited by V. Navarr, 119–141. New York: Baywood Publishing Company.

DEEMA KANEFF is Reader in Social Anthropology at the University of Birmingham and Associate at the Max Planck Institute for Social Anthropology. She is author of *Who Owns the Past? The Politics of Time in a "Model" Bulgarian Village*.

16 Making Ends Meet in a Rural Community: The Life and Times of Aleksandar Živojinović

Andrew Konitzer

If we look beyond the spectacular images of violence accompanying Yugoslavia's collapse, the death of the state produced a quieter but nonetheless devastating social economic upheaval that left lasting marks on the day-to-day lives of people throughout the region. Since the birth of Socialist Federal Republic of Yugoslavia out of the chaos of World War II, millions of Yugoslavs were born into and raised within a relatively stable set of political, economic, and social relations. Within their individual spaces, they learned how the system operated and, in most instances, made life choices aimed at maximizing their success and happiness within that system. Along the way, expectations were built. Certain combinations of *this* type of family, *this* house, *this* wage, *this* career, and *this* daily routine were expected to yield the same outcomes as they had for countless other people throughout the country.

Unfortunately, the events of the late 1980s and early 1990s abruptly set in motion a maelstrom of changes that altered, and more frequently destroyed, entire ways of life. With the rules perpetually in flux, individuals were forced to rely on new coping mechanisms in order to maintain some semblance of stability or even to survive. The skills, character types, and other resources that ensured success in the old system were suddenly less valuable, forcing individuals to identify and cleverly utilize other sets of tools and attributes just to make ends meet. The process remolded, or rather disfigured, individual and community alike. Few who endured this process emerged unchanged.

This chapter provides an account of one such person living in a rural community in what is today the Republic of Serbia. As a rather typical example of a rural member of the Yugoslav "middle class," he illustrates many of the challenges facing people throughout the post-Yugoslav region. For the person in question, the end of the state disrupted a life that up to this point was headed for success and easy retirement. Rather than reaping such benefits, he found himself scrambling to adapt to a rapidly deteriorating situation in ways that fundamentally altered his person, family, and wider social circle.

A Day in the Life

Aleksandar[1] returns home from the vineyard and sits down to a dinner accompanied by a few shots of *rakija*.[2] As usual, he is preoccupied. Tomorrow is evolving into a particularly complex jumble of conflicting obligations. The mason he needs to finish the addition on the village doctor's house announced that he's only available tomorrow, and Aleksandar must quickly locate enough sand to prepare the mortar for the job. He must also deliver a meat grinder to his friend Siniša's restaurant in time to prepare meat for *pljeskavica* that another acquaintance will sell at the Exit music festival in Novi Sad.[3] The meat from the bull that was slaughtered earlier that day is lying on a chopping table in the slaughterhouse, and the combination of flies and high temperatures is likely to make short work of their labors. Siniša also asked him to look at a ventilator whose motor seems to have stopped working. After recent heavy rains, disease is threatening the vineyard, so Aleksandar must also set aside some time to treat the vines with pesticide. Finally, Siniša has invited Aleksandar, his wife (Mila), and his daughter's family (recently arrived from America) to a dinner at his small weekend home on the edge of the nearby city. The thought of the dinner also reminds him that, as foreigners, his *zet* (son-in-law) and children must register with the local authorities by tomorrow at the very latest. This means he must coordinate a visit to the city with his jet-lagged visitors.

Speaking with Mila, the two hatch an elaborate *kombinacija* (plan). At first light, he will drive out to the fields on the edge of town with his portable sprayer to treat the vineyards before the onset of the midday heat. Then he will leave the car with his daughter's family so that they can visit the city and register at the police station. On the way, they can drop the meat grinder off at Siniša's. While they are away with the car, he can walk down to the doctor's house to meet the mason and confirm that the sand was delivered. The two can then work until late afternoon, at which point he can ride into the city with his brother Toma and look at Siniša's ventilator. After that, he can catch another ride back to the village with Toma's daughter when she finishes her shift at the county (*opština*) hospital. Once home, he can take a shower and return to the city with his daughter's family for dinner at Siniša's weekend home.

Partway through the conversation, Mila casually mentions that their grandson, who recently left to stay with his father Igor, was once again in the hospital with a low-grade fever. The boy had been in and out of various facilities since he started complaining of feeling tired and slightly feverish. Several possible diagnoses, ranging from a minor bacterial infection to cancer, were bantered about, but despite an endless string of different tests and examinations, nothing had been found. Mila's news means that Aleksandar will spend hours on the phone tomorrow trying to track down a hospital staff member who can provide an update. The doctors and nurses are frustratingly difficult to reach, and when he did talk to them, they rarely provided any useful information. Tired from a long day, and uninterested in initiating another argument about his troublesome son, Aleksandar retires to his bedroom to fall asleep watching a subtitled spaghetti western.

The next morning, Aleksandar wakes up, loads his aging car, and heads out to the vineyard. He always enjoys the peace and solitude in the fields surrounding the village, and today is a particularly beautiful morning. He looks over the half-completed weekend house that he pieced together from spare and bartered housing materials and confirms that no one has broken in to steal wires or anything else of value. Then he fires up the old portable sprayer, dons his mask, and begins walking the rows, spraying each of the plants. The work goes quickly, and he's home before 9:00 a.m.

He arrives to find that his daughter's family has just awoken and will not be ready to head into town for another half an hour. Seizing an opportunity for a quick errand, he drives over to the home where they had yesterday slaughtered the bull to pick up the cattle gun and return it to his *kum*.[4] With this decision, his plans begin to unravel. His kum offers him a drink of rajika, which quickly becomes three as the conversation moves to the government's failure to pay vaguely promised agricultural subsidies. It's noontime when the rapidly escalating antistate diatribe reaches its thunderous climax. Bidding farewell to his kum, Aleksandar returns home with a heavy head and hands over the car to his annoyed daughter. After a hasty lunch consisting of last night's leftovers, he makes an unsuccessful call to the hospital and sets off to the doctor's house.

At the doctor's, he's greeted by an irritated mason sitting in the yard smoking and drinking coffee. The mason arrived an hour ago to find neither Aleksandar nor the sand for the mortar. Aleksandar calls the young laborer responsible for delivering the sand and discovers that he has no diesel fuel for his tractor. Since there are no working fuel stations in town, Aleksandar calls his brother Toma, who works for a state firm and makes money on the side selling syphoned-off diesel fuel to people in the village. Unfortunately, his brother is still sleeping off a night of heavy drinking, so no fuel will be available for at least a few hours. Aleksandar explains that the situation is not his fault (his version of an apology) and asks the mason to come back tomorrow. Despite the fact that he'd earlier told Aleksandar that he was otherwise occupied for the entire week, the mason utters a few choice phrases and says that he can probably rearrange a few things for tomorrow.

Aleksandar returns home, places another unanswered call to the hospital and remembers with disappointment that he had planned to catch a ride to the city with the still intoxicated Toma. At that moment, another kum arrives unannounced and takes a place at the table on the front terrace. Always the model host, Aleksandar offers the kum a drink, opens one for himself, and settles into another conversation. The two drink several rounds, moving easily from topic to topic until they are interrupted by the return of his daughter's family. Straight from the car, his zet grabs three more beers and joins the conversation. As hope for his elaborate plans fades into a dull torpor, Aleksandar begins a harangue about the difficulty of accomplishing anything in the village. "Three rakija at kum's, then that jackass with the sand, then Toma . . ." He shrugs. "*Jebaš posao* (literally, fuck the job)." It's a very common lament among the more resourceful and restless members of the village. In their eyes, the entire local culture seems geared toward preventing even the smallest amount of progress. Aleksandar is frustrated, but with the alcohol coursing through his veins, he makes one final fruitless phone call to the hospital, collects another round of beers, and looks forward to the dinner at Siniša's. The daily struggle will have to pause until tomorrow.

A Life in the Making

Aleksandar Živojnović was born in the village on October 10, 1950. The town is a settlement of fifteen hundred people in the Banat region of the Autonomous District of Vojvodina. In many respects, it is very typical of small, Serbian settlements in this ethnically mixed part of the country. Residents are predominantly engaged in agricultural work, which today consists of small cash crops, maintaining orchards and vineyards, raising livestock, and other tertiary activities. Aside from agricultural activities, the only enterprises in or near the village are a fishery, a small sawmill, a handful of little groceries and general merchandise shops, an agricultural pharmacy, and a constantly changing number of generally unprofitable cafés. As in most rural communities, the town had a more vibrant life and economy during the socialist era. During these times, it boasted an active house of culture and a larger variety of shops, cafés, and clubs. The postsocialist times witnessed a steady decline paralleled by an equally steady drop in population as the older population died out and younger people left for larger towns or other countries.

While villagers tend to possess a much wider range of basic mechanical skills and practical talents than their urban and certainly Western counterparts, a brief overview of Aleksandar's life history shows that his was a more varied tool kit than most. Aleksandar's father, Dragan Živojinović, was a well-known butcher in the village, and his mother was a housewife who also worked in the butcher shop and slaughterhouse. Altogether, Dragan had three sons. The oldest was Aleksandar, and the younger two were twins born nineteen years later. Each of the boys learned the butcher trade, which they would use to serve both their household needs and as a means of livelihood throughout their lives.

Aleksandar finished high school, and at the very young age of seventeen, he took his first job at Elektrovojvodina, the electric service provider for the Vojvodina district. As the company is a state enterprise, a position at Elektrovojvodina was highly prized. Employees could expect steady work, a respectable and stable wage and an attractive pension. Joining the enterprise at such a young age, Aleksandar could look forward to retirement in his early fifties. Over the coming decades, Aleksandar's work with Elektrovojvodina would take him to different towns throughout the region, working on electrical installations that ranged from basic repairs to the installation of stadium lights in his hometown. He was well liked by his colleagues, a tightly knit group that spent a great deal of time together both in and outside of work. At that time, work was a very social affair, and he frequently hosted his colleagues at his home—including a nearly regular, yet impromptu, weekday lunch that had his wife, Mila, scrambling to

Figure 16.1. A butcher in rural Serbia on New Year's Eve, 2009. Photograph by Andrew Konitzer.

feed a group of hungry workers on very short notice. Working for Elektrovojvodina thus helped Aleksandar build a strong social network and a very diverse set of skills that would be put to good use throughout his life. Aside from learning all the particulars of electrical systems, he also became a competent mason and carpenter. Across different state and economic systems, such skills allowed him to work additional side jobs to supplement his income, situate himself as an important node in village exchange networks, and further establish himself in the community.

Aleksandar prided himself on being "cultured," tasteful, and generally appreciative of the finer things in life. His relationship with people in the region's hospitality industry—particularly his dear friend Siniša—gave him strong opinions about the aesthetics of leisure activities and the myriad village social events (weddings, baptisms, village days, slavas, funerals) that marked any given calendar year. This, combined with his culinary skills, made him a sought-after host, a position for which he made good use of his network of chefs, waiters, and caterers. Aleksandar first met Siniša when the latter was the head chef at the local Radnički Dom (literally, workers house)—a state-owned restaurant and banquet hall in the nearby city. Siniša cooked for Elektrovojvodina company dinners and later organized the wedding for Aleksandar's son, Igor. The two began working together on catering jobs around the region and

Aleksandar would do the occasional electrical or other handyman jobs for Siniša—particularly after Siniša opened his own restaurant. Aleksandar's dabbling in the service industry and his background as a butcher also led to his family's decision to open up a grocery on the ground floor of their home in 1986 and to take over management of the town's largest café, Balkan Ekspres, in 1989. The store was part of the Čelarevo franchise, and it sold food and beverages to mostly local customers. Balkan Ekspres doubled as the main bus stop for intracity buses traversing the main road through the village and was therefore a local gathering place.

Rounding out the list of skills and resources that he acquired over the years, Aleksandar and his family also owned a collection of small and mostly inherited property holdings. These included one of the many vineyards on the edge of town and other small plots where his family grew vegetables, feedstock, and other crops. The family also maintained some poultry and other animals in the pens and sheds, typical to the backyards of most family homes in the village.

Overall, at the start of Yugoslavia's demise, Aleksandar and his immediate family (his wife, Mila; his teenage son, Igor; and his younger teenage daughter, Jelena) were comfortable "middle class" beneficiaries of the Yugoslav socioeconomic system. They owned a sizable home, property holdings, public-sector jobs (Mila was a schoolteacher), an automobile, and the ordinary domestic appliances of the time. The family had sufficient resources to lavishly (by village standards) host all the major social events that marked each year and take family vacations to the Croatian coast and other destinations (Aleksandar and Mila vacationed in Spain in 1989). Their extended family network, an institution that plays a very dominant role in village life, was also stable and well provided for. Much like the country where they lived, they could not foresee the pending difficulties that would threaten their very existence.

A Life Unraveled

The turmoil that accompanied the disintegration of Yugoslavia shattered the economy and tore at the social fabric that had characterized the country for decades. Aleksandar's family, like millions of others, first saw their livelihood threatened and soon after witnessed strains in their interpersonal relations that weakened the family's cohesion in the midst of a seemingly never-ending barrage of misfortune. The family store was the first victim. Amid the period of hyperinflation, Čelarevo went out of business and was sold to a Belgium company. Balkan Ekpres struggled along somewhat longer, with the family finally leaving the business in 2001. At the worst moments of hyperinflation, Mila and Aleksandar recall how most of the working day was spent raising prices to match the spectacularly collapsing dinar. But even after the worst of the inflationary period, the destruction visited on peoples' household finances and the predations of local and national government made private enterprises increasingly losing propositions.

Just as the turmoil lashed away at citizens' well-being, it also tore family structures. In 1992 Jelena left for Florida as an exchange student. Seeing this as an opportunity for her to escape an increasingly dismal situation, Aleksandar sold the family tractor to purchase Jelena's airline ticket. During her year in America, Jelena was terribly homesick and found it rather difficult to adjust to life in the United States. At the end of her time in Florida, she looked forward to moving back to the village and had no intention of returning to America. However, after only six months in the village, she left for Ohio in January 1994 and settled down, found a job, married twice (first to someone from Serbia, then to an American), and had three children from her second marriage.

Jelena's brother, Igor, proved to be a very different case. As a young man during this period of war and political and economic instability, Igor faced his own set of difficulties that would later carry major implications for the entire family. As the only son in the family, Igor was highly favored, and his very affable personality made him popular in the family's various community circles. However, Igor also had a knack for mischief. At an early age, he convinced his younger sister to join him in impersonating members of the Red Cross, and the two went from door to door in the village collecting donations. When Aleksandar and Mila discovered this, they forced the two of them to return to each house, give back the money, and apologize. At first, this made for an amusing piece of family lore, but subsequent behavior recast it as the start of an increasingly destructive series of clever plans, tricks, and get-rich-quick schemes hatched in an environment where it was all too easy for young men to fall into such activities.

Igor married Biljana in 1993, and she gave birth to their first child, Danica, in 1994. Two sons, Zoran and Boris, followed. The marriage itself was quite rocky, and Igor's tendency to get entangled in failed business schemes, shady financial deals, and outright criminal activities only worsened the situation. Unpaid debts to banks and more legitimate agencies gave way to debts to shadier elements, and it was not uncommon for Aleksandar and Mila to receive phone calls threatening to harm or even kill Igor and his family.

The nature of local family structures meant that the negative effect of these activities would extend well beyond Igor. As he and his wife's relationship deteriorated and financial difficulties mounted, the three children moved in with Aleksander and Mila. The physical, psychological, and financial pressures of two grandparents caring for three grandchildren in an increasingly unstable social and economic environment was difficult enough. To make matters worse, Aleksander's attempts to help Igor get out of financial trouble further entangled him in his oftentimes nefarious activities, leaving him with his son's debts and potential legal problems. What Aleksandar did not offer, sometimes Igor would take. At one point, while Aleksandar was visiting Jelena in the United States, Igor quietly sold his father's car. Aleksandar only discovered the car was missing when he returned to an empty garage.

As Igor's problems continued to squeeze Aleksandar and Mila's household, the couple's own relationship worsened. Aleksandar frequently blamed Mila for not "cutting off" their son earlier, even though it oftentimes seemed that Aleksandar was as likely to lend assistance as was Mila. On her side, Mila had to endure Aleksandar's frequent and repetitive ranting about Igor's behavior and the general collapse of society as a whole. Private moments, increasingly rare given the ever-growing workload, were consumed by discussions of financial matters, which frequently spiraled into hurtful arguments.

In 2003 Aleksandar retired from his job at Elektrovojvodina and started receiving what was hoped would be a solid, sustainable pension. Unfortunately, the sustained economic calamity meant that his pension was not nearly as valuable as had been anticipated. Furthermore, debt service, some to pay off obligations accumulated by Igor, further ate away at his monthly deposit. He soon fell into a dangerous cycle, borrowing more money to support new ventures to service existing debt. Sometimes these ventures succeeded; sometimes they failed.

In the immediate term, Aleksandar was more fortunate than many of his fellow villagers because he possessed a collection of skills and strong local, regional, and increasingly international (via Jelena's contacts in Ohio) networks that allowed him to continue to generate extra income, even at great cost in terms of time, energy, and health. Aleksandar's ever-expanding and evolving list of revenue-generating activities included construction jobs, electrical work, plumbing work, concrete work, butchering livestock, selling meat and produce, catering and grilling for local and regional events, and countless other odd jobs. Payment was sometimes made in cash, sometimes in kind, and the complexity of barter arrangements or credits reached absurd proportions. Amid her many other duties of maintaining the household, caring for household animals, and physically assisting Aleksandar on certain jobs, Mila carefully kept the books for this complex web of exchanges.

Aleksandar also took advantage of his overseas connections through Jelena, visiting his daughter on a regular basis and finding odd jobs with construction firms and other businesses. Here, the local Serbian emigrant community proved to be an invaluable resource helping to find jobs and providing company for Aleksandar during off hours. Over time, Aleksandar came to enjoy his time in America more than in the village. Upon his return, he frequently lambasted his old community and boasted about his time in the United States, where all you needed was an "idea and the will to work." The villagers on their part would frequently chide him for his "Americanization," but they also envied his contacts and the fact that he had an outlet that they lacked.

However, as economic conditions continued to slide, Aleksandar's skills, his access to specific resources, and his very (over) confidence in his own abilities to control the situation drew him into risky ventures that others with fewer opportunities might have avoided. A glimpse at the household situation in the early 2000s presented an entity that was delaying its ultimate demise by slowly consuming the very resources necessary to generate revenue and maintain stability.

Things hit rock bottom in 2008. In an apparent lack of judgement, Aleksandar entered into an arrangement with Igor to open a store and butcher shop in Novi Sad. He cosigned a loan for Igor, who was still carrying many poorly understood debts from past ventures. The business worked well for a short time, but as had happened so many times in the past, it soon failed under questionable circumstances, leaving Aleksandar with another major debt. No longer able to service

Figure 16.2. Construction work in a Serbian village, 2007. Photograph by Jasmina Konitzer.

the combined weight of his and his son's obligations, and with his home under constant barrage from creditors and thugs, Aleksandar mortgaged the house and most of his property. This bought only a brief reprieve. Before long, he was behind on his payments, and the last of the family's assets were on the auctioning block. The situation was only saved through a combination of sheer lack of interest in village housing, loans from his daughter's family, another working visit to America, and a steady delaying action with his creditors.

Nonetheless, stories in the village rarely have spectacular endings—cataclysmic or otherwise. After a long period in limbo, the situation gradually eased through a series of coincidences both positive and negative. His oldest granddaughter graduated from high school and left for school in Ohio, where she stayed temporarily with Jelena's family. The two grandsons also left the house, though under less favorable circumstances. Goran moved out to attend the veterinarian school in a nearby town. Despite Aleksandar's considerable efforts to produce both the paperwork and money to make this a reality, Goran failed out during the first year. This proved to be a watershed moment. Aleksandar told Goran not to return home and to instead move in with his father. At around the same time, Boris also failed his courses. To make matters worse, he also began stealing and selling various objects from the house and at one point boldly stole a large sum of Euros from

Aleksandar's wallet. Within weeks, Boris was sent to live with his mother. For the first time since the birth of Igor, Aleksandar and Mila were alone.

The combination of these events, unfolding over the course of one year, created a small opening. With the debt situation increasingly under control (largely through the help of his contacts in America) and only himself and his wife living in the house, Aleksandar's pension was finally enough to cover monthly expenses. Furthermore, with no household dependents and with his brothers available to assist their mother, Aleksandar was freer to make working trips to the United States. In 2014 he finally replaced his aging Peugeot with a twelve-year-old Opel van—as sure a sign as any that the household had stepped back from the very edge of survival.

Today, although the bills are being paid, Aleksandar still insists that he's "had enough" and wants to leave Serbia and settle in with his daughter's family in Ohio. He's still clearly proud of his Serbian identity, but he feels disappointed with his dying village, betrayed by the state and authorities, and constantly set upon by an abstract "other" that is all around him and yet nowhere in particular. Given his penchant for the dramatic, he imagines his escape from a failed situation and victorious reemergence in another, idealized setting. His friends and family may roll their eyes at this latest resolution, but perhaps this time it bears an element of credibility as his obligations to his grandchildren and extended family melt away.

In making the decision to leave, Aleksandar would follow in the footsteps of many others who possessed the skills, nerve, luck, and resources to bid farewell to the community and lifestyle that surrounded their families for generations. Despite his bravado, this break would likely produce its own difficulties. Mila enjoys brief visits to Ohio exclusively for the chance it affords to see her daughter and grandchildren. Otherwise, she is a less adventurous and less restless type who appreciates the pace of village life and her collection of family and friends. For Mila, America is a socially desolate place, and she finds it difficult to kill time in the absence of her household responsibilities and social circle. Mila's response to Aleksandar's plans is simple: "If he goes, he goes without me."

As with many things in this relationship, such "pivotal" moments consistently give way to a sort of muddling through that is virtually indistinguishable from the status quo ante. Aleksandar's relationship with Mila, much like his relationship with the village, is embedded in a complex web of emotions, habits, and traditions that Aleksandar himself only partly understands. Rational urges to escape a place, break a relationship, or cut off a relative are consistently overridden by seemingly irrational feelings of obligation, nostalgia, and even love. In this respect, Aleksandar is little different from many of his fellow Serbs.

Life Goes On

Dinner at Siniša's was a relaxed affair. The guests were well fed, and wine and beer were available in their usual abundance. Another acquaintance stopped by later with a guitar, and the group sat outside, under a vine-covered arbor, and sang nostalgic songs late into the evening. The next morning, Aleksandar woke up a bit later, made yet another unsuccessful attempt to reach the hospital, and then met Toma to fill a container of diesel fuel for the young laborer responsible for delivering the sand. By early afternoon, the sand was in place and work had begun again on the doctor's house. Siniša's ventilator would have to wait another day as Alexander was committed later that evening to collect and stack bails of clover in exchange for the transport of the bull that was slaughtered now two days before.

Thus continues this paradoxically monotonous daily struggle. The details of any two working days are never the same, but each is frustratingly similar in its failure to achieve any fundamental change in the household's financial trajectory or any consistent, and consistently lucrative, path. Every sunrise is merely the starting point for a daily recurring scramble to cobble together sufficient resources to maintain what is left of a once very promising life. This story is certainly not unique to the states of the former Yugoslavia, but such an observation provides little comfort to those who run the race from day to day.

Notes

1. All names in the chapter are pseudonyms.
2. Rakija refers to a broad category of strong liquors usually distilled from fermented fruit. The drink, or some variation on it, is enjoyed throughout the region.
3. Pljeskavica is a regionally popular grilled dish consisting of thin patties of ground meat (usually pork and lamb), onions, garlic, and other spices.
4. A kum is an important family relation who stood as a witness for a wedding or baptism. Despite changes over time (and consistent laments about its demise), *kumstvo* remains a key aspect of the Serbian family structure. Its privileges and obligations are felt particularly strongly in rural communities.

> ANDREW KONITZER is a former Research Scholar at the Woodrow Wilson International Center for Scholars' Kennan Institute for Advanced Russia Studies. He is author of *Voting for Russia's Governors: Regional Elections and Accountability under Yeltsin and Putin*.

17 A Lot of Sweat, a Little Bit of Fun, and Not Entirely "Hard Men": Worker's Masculinity in the Uljanik Shipyard

Andrea Matošević

Many young people from the Croatian coastal regions of Istria, Primorje-Gorski Kotar County, and Dalmatia leave to enroll in Italian universities.[1] This outward movement for education began earlier but intensified in the 1990s, during and after the wars that dismantled Yugoslavia. Although neighboring countries with many historical relations, Croatia was often perceived by Italians, both geopolitically and culturally, as part of the Balkans. It was in this context of the late 1990s that I heard about the "particularities" and distinctiveness of Balkan masculinity—as well as it's rather "loose codification"—for the first time.

It came mostly from my Italian colleagues, who seemed to consider it ambivalent, exotic, and attractive in its geographical nearness and "firm attitudes" but also as a bearer of gender relations that in the West had presumably been overcome. Although they spoke about Balkan masculinity without hiding a certain fascination, attraction, and even "theoretical" interest, it was therefore also considered *a volte un po' troppo grezzo* (sometimes a bit too rough). Whether a "significant coincidence" or a fact of *longue durée*—Alberto Fortis, an Augustinian monk, writer, and naturalist from Padua codified the proto-Balkan character in his two volume book *Viaggio in Dalmazia* (Travel to Dalmatia) published in 1774[2]—the contemporary version of "peninsular" masculinity was given shape and content mostly by prominent movie directors such as Emir Kusturica and Milčo Mančevski.[3] There is an interesting overlap between the "exaggerations" described by Fortis and the self-representational frame[4] in a masculine key developed by the directors that film historian Pavle Levi sees in Kusturica's *Underground* (1995) as "marked by the marathon orgiastic celebrations and the constant presence of trumpeter and frenetic dance . . . that Jean Francois Lyotard describes as an 'enjoyment's sterile consummation of energy' or what a physician would simply describe as 'sterile waste of energy.'"[5]

Although fictional material, the power of movies is embedded in their explanatory potential. Or as historian Robert A. Rosenstone wrote after seeing Mančevski's *Prije kiše* (*Before the Rain*): "Reading books about the region got me nowhere because too many things have happened in Macedonia during centuries for me to be able to absorb them within the limits of history. . . . But *Before the Rain* keeps me awake as it cuts through all the complications and gives me a sort of history in presence, it makes me feel some of the region's problems at the point where books leave me floating in a sea of details."[6] In a similar manner, many of my Italian friends saw these movies as a sort of ex-Yugoslav *pars pro toto* (a part [taken] for the whole), a lightly fictionalized presence/history of the Balkans and the emotional states that were involved in bellicose events during the 1990s. The highly accentuated manhood in these movies had to be a sort of hypervirility triggered by the war. Though hypervirility is often used simply in describing aggressive male behavior, in a larger and more "capillary" sense, it includes a lack of emotional expression, risk-taking attitudes, or negation and minimization of hazardous situations, alongside playing a dominant role in family, sometimes not based on breadwinning but simply on "manliness." Already present in popular images of men in socialism based on Western *scientia sexualis* (sexual knowledge) concerning the Balkans,[7] this "Balkan manhood," as an important part of the "peninsular imagery," shares many commonalities—except the "waste of energy and resources," *stricto sensu* (strictly speaking)—with another type of "trans-regional" virility that was also developed within the very heart of Balkan socialist Yugoslavia: hard industry.[8] Hard industry—such as mining, shipbuilding, and construction—was inseparable from the development of the socialist and proletarian project in the Yugoslav Federation, but its milieus were mostly, with rare exceptions, populated with men. This gave shape and content to a particular kind of gendered socialist economy that also supports the construction of a "distinct" Balkan virility that, seen from the perspective of those within hard industries, ceases to be this peninsula's exclusiveness.

Masculinity in the Shipyard

In their recent publications, oral historians Ronnie Johnston and Arthur McIvor stressed the important influence of hardworking milieus and difficult conditions of work in the construction of "industrial masculinities."[9] Though they were writing about the British working class, the conditions of work they described—risk-taking attitudes toward tasks, a particular sort of masculinity that recently became identified with an excess of life-threatening illnesses and premature death[10]—was very similar to ones I have encountered during research of Yugoslav/Croatian mines and shipyards. The response to these conditions by the manual workers was articulated within a pattern of *mutatis mutandis*—that is, they include the often difficult relationships with foremen, alcohol consummation during working hours, and occasional/situational usage of protective gear that indicated some of the main traits of the highly male-oriented working culture. For example, although alcohol consumption was and is strictly forbidden within all shipyards and mines, it is a rule that is very often transgressed because, as my informants claim, it was one of the ways they could relax and create a sense of a "personalized answer" to a mostly standardized and deindividuated working process. Extreme weather conditions, working under the hot sun in the summer (one of the Uljanik shipyard working sections is tellingly named Sahara) or in the rain, is often both challenged and overcome by alcohol. Even though communalities in working attitudes between mining and shipbuilding can be grasped, here I focus on the Uljanik, one of the biggest and most important of Croatia's shipyards, located in the city of Pula.[11]

One of the first traits of the shipyard's working milieus, protracted through time, is occasional conflict between management and the foreman. Many workers/informants claimed that their foreman pushed them to work beyond regulations, although it was their duty to observe them. For example, Eliđo (born 1931), a retired crane driver, recalled how he was forced to lift a cargo heavier than allowed:

> But we had to lift overloaded cargo, beyond allowed, yes. You will do it, or find another job in another city, that's what they said. Whenever I said, "I will not lift that cargo," their response was "you must." And we came to a compromise: I would do it, but slowly. But once, the entire section that weighed more than thirty tons fell into the water! Directly down! A main motor axle broke. If somebody had been down there it would be a massacre. The misfortune came, but this time without death. "Take care of yourself people, do not walk under cargo" I was always telling the workers, but they didn't listen to me or the siren; they were always walking under. But I never killed a fly in my forty years of work.

This is just one of many examples of how the obvious danger in a shipyard is often denied or minimized by both the foremen and the workers. As Mladen, a welder (born 1978), characterized it: "Listen, the dangers are many, but after a while you get used to it, and you neglect them and the sound of the warning siren. You work by your instinct and do not look around all the time. Having fun, right?"

However, the romantic notion of shipbuilders—expressed, for example, through the famous motto "We don't only build ships, we build men"[12]—could easily be inverted in terms of decay, injury, or death. Or, as Robert (born 1985), a young ship pipe worker summed it up: "This is what they say—every ship takes one death injury, and every year at least one worker dies."

It is rather easy to chronicle black news from the Uljanik shipyard. Examples from some recent cases include the following article: "K.K. (43), a citizen of Serbia died yesterday during welding in a confined space. He probably suffocated from butane gas or was burned alive by the fire that erupted from the contact of gas and spark."[13] Also *Novi list* in 2011 wrote, "Two persons died in Uljanik last year—a welder B.F. was caught by the flames when a spark started a fire. His body was 80 percent burned. He passed away a few days later. During the last days of 2010, a 47-year-old turner M.M. from Pula was badly injured while at work. He also passed away a few days later."[14] These macabre examples, which extend to a large part of hard industry, are reasons why workers very often talk about the conditions of their work in terms of war or hell.[15]

Figure 17.1. Workers in the Uljanik shipyard, Croatia, 1985. Photograph by Angelo Božac.

Facing these immanent hazards should be seen as complementary to the exposure of long-term dangers in asbestos handling that was used for a long time in industry, shipbuilding included.[16] As Eliđo noted, "Many people died from asbestosis; they had these masks, but they didn't wear them all the time. It was impossible; you sweat all the time and you lack air and get very nervous, so people often worked without protective gear whenever bosses were not around."[17]

Masculinity around the Shipyard

While the conditions of employment in the shipyard contribute to masculinizing workers in a particular way, compensation to those working in the shipyard is not equally distributed. A number of enterprises sign contracts, cooperate with the Uljanik shipyard, and hire workers to perform various tasks—such as painting or welding. These contracted employees, informants claim, get 30 to 40 percent lower paychecks than the Uljanik employees. Particularly for those who work within such cooperatives, the relationship with bosses is problematic and profit oriented. It was an attitude that many workers did not appreciate. As Mladen recounted, "I was working for this boss, foreman, for a year and a half as a welder—he did not know my name, he did not make an effort to remember it! Yes. He was calling me 'Buddy'! What can I say about that man? When you are a cooperate worker you are just 'Get lost, you boy.' He was addressing me, 'C'mon buddy this, c'mon buddy that' without knowing my name. These guys were villains; they had a primitive relationship with workers—all they saw was profit." This attitude was potentially very dangerous because, as this informant claims, he never took the preparatory course that was, for Uljanik workers, obligatory and lasted for three months. Mladen continued: "All I had was one day of observation and learning. Immediately they threw me into real work. 'Go work and fulfill your norm and quantity.' This is what matters to them—quantity, not quality."

But the cooperative worker's response was equally antiheroic, implicitly "oppositional but difficult for the bosses to perceive it immediately as such."[18] For example, Mladen was afraid of heights, but he often had to climb to the level equivalent to the third or fourth floor, carrying a thirty-kilo blowtorch. The response to this difficult situation was to "pretend to do the job, but what I did was blurring the task; I covered it a bit, I sprayed it a little, and got the hell out of there!"

Sometimes, however, the difficulties of work are partially "eased" by ignoring the alcohol prohibition. Alcohol is not allowed in industry, but its consummation is always somehow negotiated and thus part of "situational relationships of power," that is, dependent of worker's and foremen's character and their (tacit) agreement.[19] Thus, men often use an interesting mimicry method and drink *rakija* (brandy) from the plastic water bottle to "restore their body minerals," as they jokingly said. This parallels the environment of Scottish shipbuilders, indicative of the construction of hard men in industry; it is almost impossible to avoid alcohol in these environments: "Even the man that didn't want a drink was more or less forced to have one."[20]

Masculinity beyond the Shipyard

Alcohol consumption, difficult relationships with foremen—almost all informants mentioned problematic relationships with "bosses" and foremen, an opposition that rises from "active work," producing by their own hands and skills, that is seen as superior to the mere bossing around and verbal instructions that characterize their superiors—and exposure to the short- and long-term dangers of the shipyard are some of the categories and practices that produced a particular sort of industrial masculinity.[21] What is interesting is that when compared with the Balkan stereotype of masculinity, constructed within previously mentioned feature films and triggered by the war, there is much in common. The already mentioned metaphor of war and hell, very often used by workers' to

Figure 17.2. The characterization of Balkan masculinity and hard work extends beyond the shipyard, such as these brothers making tiles in Stragari, Serbia, 2017. Photograph by Željko Stevanović.

describe their laboring everyday, captures what is shared in the various attempts to characterize Balkan masculinity.

There is a rough edge to hard work industry. For example, Marija (born 1942), a miner's daughter, when describing a mining community from northeast Istria, spoke of the physicality of these working men: "They were constantly fighting; something akin to a display of superiority, a marking out of territory. It was a well-known fact—everybody would come home with their clothes torn, and mother was always stitching clothes."

But there is more to it: a culture of opposition to the authorities, principal androcentricity, activity, physical endurance, ingeniousness, roughness, and occasional chauvinism are characteristics that can be found within the hard industry working milieus and in famous award-winning feature films. However, the possibilities of different approaches must be stressed. What Kusturica does in *Underground* is answer questions "about [the] mentality of [the] Balkan people"[22] in a "region where war is a natural phenomenon in the same way cataclysms are natural."[23] Thus, Kusturica essentializes any possible answer and heads us off precisely in the wrong direction: toward an isolation of the meaning-form aspects of the matter from the practical contexts that give them life.[24]

What an in situ ethnographic approach offers is a more constructivist range of responses; that is, it is the "unpleasant" context that defines and creates a bit "stiffed," risk taking, or *a volte un po' troppo grezzo* masculinity, and not the very nature or mentality of people who work in the shipyard or other industrial milieus. Therefore, roughness can be seen and analyzed as a sort of defense mechanism and way of "survival" in there. But moving the focus from "nature" toward "context" leads us toward another interesting and important comparative possibility. If these "peninsular masculinities" resemble and show a high degree of coincidence, then what we should seek is a stretched "transnational" understanding of Balkan masculinity that can be found in many industrial workshops, construction sites, and plants that are not necessarily geographically linked but defined by the conditions of work and life. Whether we call it Balkan or something else, it means bringing a negated and, in postsocialist countries, ridiculed class focus back into the game.

Notes

1. As a Croatian citizen, I studied for seven years in Padua, Italy, completing BA and MA degrees there. It continues to be popular for young Croatians to seek Italian schools for study, with the northern Italian universities of Trieste, Udine, Venice, Padua, Bologna, Siena, and Florence being among the most desirable for Croatians.

2. It can be designated proto-Balkanistic discourse because the Balkan Peninsula did not have a name until the nineteenth century. It was named *Hämushalbinsel* in 1808 by a German geographer, Johann August Zeune, and only later changed into Balkan (Jezernik 2007, 21). Fortis wrote about Morlaks, Dalmatian inland shepherds within the oppositional framework of "barbarity as opposed to the European altruism and civilization" (Pletenac 2007, 108); for Fortis, they were behaving in a "wasteful way." He explains, "When there was a religious celebration, although they had no bread to eat Morlaks will organize an overabundant and exaggerated feast in an eastern way" (Jezernik 2007, 76).

3. Their movies won many prizes, with Mančevski's *Before the Rain* winning the Golden Lion at the Venice Film Festival in 1994.

4. For self-representation in this region's cinema, see Iordanova (2001) and Pavičić (2011).

5. Levi 2001, 270–271. Kusturica's *Underground*, with many "masculine" representations in dialogues—such as "Do not trust a lying woman, my son" or "Women and revolution do not fit together"—displays a self-representational frame in a masculine key. As such, what implicitly emerges is a theme of gender division, division that, in this case builds upon a distrust toward women.

6. Rosenstone 2000, 189.

7. Škokić 2011, 447.

8. The economist Branko Horvat, for example, claims socialist Yugoslavia to be "the federation of Balkan people" (1988, 186) thus stressing its cohesive potential within the region but also the very realization of the Balkan confederation idea.

9. Johnston and McIvor 2004; 2007.

10. Johnston and McIvor 2004.

11. Pula is a town in the south of Istria region (northwest Croatia), very near the peninsula's promontory. Its modern history is inseparable from the shipyard established on January 1, 1856, as K.u.K. See-Arsenal on a little island named Olivieninsel, Scoglio Olivi, or Uljanik, and has been almost continuously active since. (Since its inauguration, the shipyard has been Austro-Hungarian, Italian, and Croatian—hence three different names are derived from three dominant languages spoken in Pula, Istria.) The city's demographic, cultural, sport, and infrastructural development is

strictly tied to this shipyard that employs two thousand and cooperates with another one thousand workers (see Markulinčić and Debeljuh, 2006). Often entire families found employment in Uljanik, but construction was almost exclusively reserved for male members: grandfathers, fathers, and sons. It was rare for female workers to be found at Uljanik.

12. Bellamy 2001, 199.
13. Glas Istre 2009.
14. *Novi list* 2011.
15. See Matošević 2011, 104–118; Johnston and McIvor 2007, 27–29.
16. Asbestos was widely used as insulation/fireproofing material, but it was banned in EU industrial production in 2005.
17. This was not unique to Yugoslav/Croatian shipyards. The fact was that workers in many shipyards worked with asbestos, to the point that they were called "white mice because they were always covered in asbestos and for that they frequently developed asbestosis, an inflammation of the lungs caused by inhalation of asbestos dust" (Bellamy 2001, 52).

Although mostly androcentric milieus, women also worked in the shipyard's workshops, but female presence was always "news" and newspapers often ran human interest pieces on them. In the context of injuries, for example, Ernesta Antonić, who worked on a drill machine, recalled that "her face was covered in zinc three times and burns caused her loss of sight for a few days" (*Naša Ernesta* 1960, 8). This occasional female presence in heavy industry is quite indicative in the process of the "construction of maleness" that can have a female prefix. This example, among others (see Bellamy 2001, 39), shows that often propagated theory and pseudo-knowledge of a women's psycho-physical incapacity to "complete a man's job" is a very untenable one because when conditions allowed, women were often employed in heavy industry milieus, thus sharing and enduring the same working conditions, as well as injuries, as their male colleagues. There are several female welders employed in Uljanik, but I was unable to interview them.

18. Matošević 2010, 37.
19. Matošević 2011, 117.
20. Bellamy 2001, 106.
21. For the "feminization of authorities" within working-class masculinity, see Willis (1977).
22. Robinson 1996, 12.
23. Kusturica in Žižek 1997, 62.
24. As Geertz notes, objects, events, relations, or phenomenon have meaning, or form, only if contextualized (1983, 48).

References

Bellamy, Martin. 2001. *The Shipbuilders*. Edinburgh: Birlin.
Geertz, Clifford. 1983. *Local Knowledge. Further Essays in Interpretative Anthropology*. New York: Basic Books.
Horvat, Branko. 1988. *Kosovsko pitanje* (Drugo dopunjeno izdanje). Zagreb: Globus.
Iordanova, Dina. 2001. *Cinema of Flames: Balkan Film, Culture and the Media*. London: British Film Institute.
Jezernik, Božidar. 2007. *Divlja Europa. Balkan u očima putnika sa zapada*. Beograd: Biblioteka XX vek.

Johnston, Ronnie, and Arthur McIvor. 2004. "Dangerous Work, Hard Men and Broken Bodies: Masculinity in the Clydeside Heavy Industries, c. 1930–1970s." *Labour History Review* 69 (2): 135–153.

Johnston, Ronnie, and Arthur McIvor. 2007. "Narratives from the urban Workplace: Oral Testimonies and the Reconstruction of Men's Work in the Heavy Industries in Glasgow." In *Testimonies of the City. Identity, Community and Change in a Contemporary Urban World*, edited by Richard Rodger and Joanna Herbert, 23–44. Abingdon, UK: Ashgate.

Levi, Pavle. 2001. "'Underground'. Jedna estetika etno-nacionalističkog uživanja." *Republika*: no. 270–271. http://www.yurope.com/zines/republika/arhiva/2001/270-271/270-271_25.html

Markulinčić, Hrvoje, and Armando Debeljuh, eds. 2006. *Uljanik 1856–2006*. Pula: Uljanik d.d.

Matošević, Andrea. 2010. "Industry *Forging* Masculinity: 'Tough Men,' Hard Labour and Identity." *Narodna umjetnost* 47 (1): 29–44.

Matošević, Andrea. 2011. *Pod zemljom. Antropologija rudarenja na Labinštini u XX. stoljeću*. Pula-Zagreb: Sveučilište Jurja Dobrile u Puli and Institut za etnologiju i folkloristiku.

Naša Ernesta. 1960. Uljanik—List radnog kolektiva brodogradilišta "Uljanik." February 8.

Pavičić, Jurica. 2011. *Postjugoslavenski film. Stil i ideologija*. Zagreb: Hrvatski filmski savez.

Pletenac, Tomislav. 2007. "Ako je Split, tko je *drugi*?" In *Split i drugi. Kulturnoantropološki i kulturnostudijski prilozi*, edited by Ines Prica and Tea Škokić, 105–119. Zagreb: Hrvatsko etnološko društvo i Institut za etnologiju i folkloristiku.

Robinson, David. 1996. "A Tunnel Vision of War: An Interview with Emir Kusturica." *The Times*, May 3, 1996.

Rosenstone, Robert A. 2000. "History of What Has Not Yet Happened." *Rethinking History* 4 (2): 183–192.

Škokić, Tea. 2011. "Što su brkovi bez muškarca." In *Horror-porno-ennui*, edited by Ines Prica and Tea Škokić, 439–457. Zagreb: Institut za etnologiju i folkloristiku.

Willis, Paul. 1981. *Learning to Labor: How Working-Class Kids Get Working-Class Jobs*. New York: Columbia University Press.

Žižek, Slavoj. 1997. *The Plague of Fantasies*. London: Verso.

ANDREA MATOŠEVIĆ is Associate Professor at the Juraj Dobrila University of Pula. He cofounded the Centre for Cultural and Historical Research of Socialism and has published several books in Croatian on the anthropology of work and discourses of Balkan socialism.

18 Perceptions of Balkan Belonging in Postdictatorship Greece

Daniel M. Knight

In 2012, the British School at Athens, the École française d'Athènes, and the British Institute at Ankara launched a joint project entitled "Balkan Futures"[1] aimed at exploring such diverse themes as regional political and economic cooperation, shared histories, heritages and religions, self-identification with the Balkan region, the presence of the European Union in the Balkans, and the effect of the economic crisis that hit southeast Europe in 2009. I was lucky enough to be part of the Balkan Futures project and around the same time I also received a small grant for some scoping study research in Turkey to complement fieldwork on the post-Ottoman Balkans I had been conducting in central Greece since 2003. At the time, I was skeptical about whether local people in Greece and Turkey really felt that they belonged to "the Balkans." In Greece, notions of belonging are complex and constantly shifting in relation to current events, political needs, available cultural forms, and emotional dispositions.

If one travels around Greece, it is obvious that feelings toward the country's place in the Balkans vary greatly depending on the area one is visiting. Partially due to the diverse social history of the various regions, a Greek in the Aegean Islands may identify differently with the Balkans than another in the northern mainland regions of Epirus or Western Macedonia. An Athenian is likely to tell you a different story of Balkan identity than someone from Thessaloniki. A friend of mine, Anita, originating from the town of Trikala on the central plains, recalls that while studying for her degree in Athens in the mid-1990s, fellow students would tease her by reciting the rhyme "pano ap' ti Lamia arxizei i Voulgaria" (north of Lamia begins Bulgaria), insinuating that anywhere north of the town of Lamia was "Balkan," with the associated derogatory stereotypes of underdevelopment and poverty. Now in her forties and a successful professional working in a government job in Athens, she says that at university she was constantly reminded of her peasant status, her likeness to Bulgarians, her Balkan ancestry. Even her high cheek bones were a sign of her Slavic origin, it was insisted. Since the 1980s, Greece had been championed as the beacon of capitalist enlightenment in what was commonly perceived as the quagmire of Balkan premodernity and socioeconomic backwardness.[2] But Greek understandings of Balkan belonging

Figure 18.1. Greek Orthodox Church of Agios Konstantinos with the Ottoman Kursum Tzami in the background, 2014. Photograph by Daniel M. Knight.

are tied up with wider issues of identity formation, such as ambiguous feelings toward a shared Ottoman past and perennial public debate concerning Greece's place between occident and orient.[3] Furthermore, Anita believes that the hostility she encountered as a student in Athens regarding her supposed Balkan heritage was based primarily on fears of the irredentist agenda of Greece's neighbors.

> Of course, in the mid-1990s there was the whole question of the naming of the Former Yugoslav Republic of Macedonia (FYROM) and the general feeling in Greece that our Balkan neighbors were going to claim our land. The fear about the long-term agenda of FYROM in stealing our territory and our history was coupled with perceived threats from Bulgaria and Turkey. To this day, my friend in Serres strongly believes that Bulgaria is the number one enemy of Greece. His grandfather recites stories of Bulgarians coming down from the mountains and massacring Greeks in their borderland villages during the invasions of World War II. In all cases (FYROM, Bulgaria, Turkey) the problem is the shared history and who owns what and I think our Athenian classmates viewed us with suspicion. (Anita, forty-five, Trikala)[4]

Despite promoting multilateralism in the pre-1990 era, Greece was caught "psychologically unprepared for the great transition" of the Balkans after the fall of communism.[5] This feeling was captured in popular slogans, such as the one with which Anita was taunted.[6] In the midst of the Balkan wars of the mid-1990s, debates about Greece's role in the region were raging both in the halls of Athens and Brussels and on the streets of every peripheral town.[7] Fast-forward to 2015, with the effects of six years of economic squalor still rampaging through the nation, and the observant researcher can once again pick up on conversations regarding Greece's belonging in the Balkans, arguments based on history and culture that have been resculptured for the present circumstances.

This chapter overviews how the onset of the now infamous Greek economic crisis has provoked people in the town of Trikala in Thessaly, central mainland Greece, to start rethinking their identification with the Balkans. Since economic turmoil surfaced in 2009—and after 326 billion euros of Troika (European Commission, European Central Bank, and International Monetary Fund) bailout money—unemployment, wage and pension cuts, a plethora of new taxes, fuel shortages, and crippling health service reforms have irrevocably transformed livelihoods in Trikala. With unemployment among people under twenty-five years of age hitting 60 percent in February 2013, increasing redundancies, the breakdown of family support networks, and hunger taking hold in many regions, people have begun to reassess their perception of belonging vis-à-vis western Europe and the Balkans. Much of this social and cultural reimagining is taking place against a background of intense historical consciousness—moments of the past are evoked to provide meaning and direction to the lives of people living through the crisis.[8] Past events, many of which had an impact far beyond the borders of Greece, that are recalled in relation to the current social turmoil include life under former Ottoman landlords,[9] the Balkan wars of the early 1900s, the World War II Axis occupation and subsequent civil war, and the military dictatorship of 1967–74.

The past and collective memory play a significant role in the way people in Trikala experience the current economic turmoil and articulate their notions of belonging in Europe and the Balkan Peninsula. One can use the terms historical consciousness, polytemporality, historicity, or, as I argue elsewhere, the cultural and temporal "proximity" of selective moments of the past helping people understand dramatic social change.[10] Locals find themselves in what Rebecca Bryant calls the "uncanny present," an elongated moment of increased consciousness where the familiar becomes paradoxically somehow unfamiliar yet also very close, a feeling especially prevalent in moments of angst.[11] For Bryant, belonging and temporality are mutually implicated in inextricable ways, making moments of the past "familiar to us, history accepted as ours, or, conversely, what makes it uncanny."[12] Upon these notions of familiar pasts, elongated presents (for many, the six-year crisis feels like a lifetime), and emergent futures do my research participants discuss feelings of identification with western Europe and the Balkans, Occident and Orient, Euro and Drachma, America and Germany, or Russia and China.

Histories and Futures of Belonging

Over the past eight years of crisis, people in Trikala have drawn on earlier moments of social and economic turmoil to help explain increasing social suffering and material poverty. Locals discuss their fears of returning to past epochs of hardship while drawing courage that even the worst crises can be overcome. The fear of returning to times of hunger as experienced during World War II is a common thread in crisis discourse, while a European Union scheme aimed at decreasing national debt by placing solar panels on agricultural land is locally perceived as a return to an era of German or Ottoman occupation.[13] Also, the moments of the past that remain dormant, that are not recalled, are equally important, for they tell us something else about the sociopolitical history of both Greece and the wider Balkan region. An example of this is how accounts of the divisive events of the Greek civil war (1946–49) are not so prominent in how people in Trikala experience the current economic crisis, yet with a forty-minute drive into the Pindos Mountains, the topology of the past changes completely, and the civil war becomes the main event around which people frame their narratives of crisis and suffering. This fits well with Eric Hirsch and Charles Stewart's thesis on "historicity," which "describes a human situation in flow, where versions of the past and future . . . assume present form," giving credence to "the relevant ways in which (social) pasts and futures are implicated in present circumstances."[14]

When I first visited Trikala in 2003, the expanding construction industry, a buoyant public sector, and secure agricultural markets supported by European Union initiatives and Eurozone membership represented thirty years of uninterrupted socioeconomic prosperity. After decades debating their place on the margins of Europe,[15] Greeks had firmly arrived on the European scene. A decade on and my research participants are describing feeling "physically beaten" their "bones crushed" by crisis. A sixty-eight-year-old retired schoolteacher, Dorothea, reflects on the years of prosperity by stating, "That is another lifetime. Those days before the crisis seem so distant now. . . . I live in a different body, see the world through different eyes." She says that she wants to throw up when she sees the faces of Greek politicians and foreign leaders on television. "I change the channel, but you cannot get away from them. . . . Every day I physically retch and my stomach pains from the crisis." Dorothea breaks down in tears as she recalls how her pension has been cut by two-thirds and she has been forced to put her second home in her ancestral village up for sale. "How do they expect us to survive?" she asks. She claims that "the foreigners have taken our lives, taken our food, and have forced us back in time. We thought we were European, but they are treating us worse than dogs." Potently, Dorothea says that "five years ago if you told me that we would be facing famine I wouldn't have believed you. The future was so bright, we all had so much money, so much energy . . . but now I know that I will die having no hope for the future of my grandchildren in Greece."[16]

Dorothea contrasts her notions of European belonging with the alternative of being "part of the Balkans," the former associated with wealth and modernity, the latter with extreme poverty and civil conflict.[17] In the 1930s, Dorothea's father traveled throughout northern Greece, southern Albania, and Bulgaria working as a stonemason before migrating with his family from his village in the mountains of Greek Macedonia to Trikala during the civil war (1946–49), an event that scattered the extended family across the Balkans. Dorothea's parents decided to move to Trikala, some 120 kilometers away, when the fighting between communist guerrillas and groups loyal to the nationalist army became too fierce. Witnessing the cold-blooded slaughter of close friends and relatives, the majority of the villagers decided to flee. But due to divided allegiances, Dorothea's family split; while her parents headed to Trikala on the central plains, her uncle's family left for Bulgaria. Her uncle changed his family surname and settled near the capital city, Sofia. One of Dorothea's aunts decided to stay behind in the village during the conflict: "Aunt Maria stayed behind in the village but her close family was also torn apart. Her son joined the nationalist army and was killed in action. Her husband fought for the communists but never returned home. He was last seen north of the Albanian border. There were some rumors that he had been killed, but eight years later some tradesmen from our village that were on business in southern Albania reported seeing him with a new wife and child. Even Aunt Maria's brothers had different political allegiances and sympathized with opposite sides in the civil war."

Dorothea's story is by no means unique. She was part of a wave of migrants who left their mountain villages during the civil war to set up homes across northern Greece or relocate farther afield to Bulgaria, Macedonia (FYROM), and Romania.[18] Since the outbreak of the economic crisis, Dorothea believes that Greece has become "like the Balkans," saying that she feels she has "slipped back in time" to an era of "premodernity, pre-Europeanization." She expresses deep concern that her grandchildren will be brought up in a nation that can now "seriously be compared to Bulgaria rather than the West; our future belongs to the Balkans." Dorothea feels frustrated with the broken promises of wealth and modernity made by the European Union and Greek politicians throughout the 1980s and '90s, noting that both her family and her nation chose a particular historical trajectory when they committed to Europe rather than the East or the Balkans.[19]

Michael Herzfeld, writing in 1987, perhaps surprisingly captures the sentiment of many people in Trikala in 2015: "The Greeks of today, heirs—so they are repeatedly informed—to the glories of the European past, seriously and frequently ask themselves if perhaps they now belong politically, economically, and culturally to the Third World. Whether as the land of revered but long dead ancestors, or as the intrusive and rather tawdry fragment of the mysterious East, Greece might seem condemned to a peripheral role in the modern age."[20] At the turn of the millennium Herzfeld's perceptions of ambivalence toward Europeanization would have seemed unconvincing. Futuristic technologies, such as the internet, European Union–supported infrastructure schemes, European fiscal unity, and the impending Athens Olympic Games were opening up even the remotest areas to everything the West had to offer. Although since 2009 Greece has certainly not been on the periphery of European political and economic speculation, the question of belonging has resurfaced on local and national stages as people rhetorically pose the questions "Who are we?" "What have we become?" "Where are we now ... *when* are we now?"

The economic crisis has left many everyday Greeks in Trikala questioning their country's geographical, political, and ideological belonging. While Greece has been striving—and regularly overstepping its political and economic capacities—to become modern,[21] the Balkans have always been lurking in the background of popular imagination like an alligator ready to devour its prey should it slip up. In Greece, modernization (*eksygxronismos*) encompasses understandings of economic as well as social advancement and stands for the historical and cultural commitment of the Greek people to the West.[22] Political rhetoric over the past thirty years has revolved around two ambiguous poles—Greeks as the ancestors of modern Europe, and Greeks residing on the margins of the continent, namely the Balkans.[23] With Troika-enforced austerity, failing European fiscal unity, and increasing social poverty, questions of belonging have never been more poignant for my research participants.

The shared Balkan history of the Ottoman Empire was considered by Renaissance Europe as the "embodiment of barbarism and evil," thus historically and culturally speaking, Greece is symbolically both holy and polluted.[24] As Michael Herzfeld once argued, "Modern Greece does not fit comfortably into the duality of Europeans and Others, especially as Greeks are themselves ambivalent about the extent to which they are European."[25] Changes in livelihood practices brought about by the financial crisis, such as the increasing amount of people growing their own fruit and vegetables on small plots of land for greater self-sufficiency and returning to wood-fueled central heating rather than expensive petroleum or gas (Knight 2014), have triggered reflection on images of western European and Balkan "resemblance and difference."[26]

Ambiguous Narratives

Residing in the same neighborhood of Trikala as Dorothea, Vassilis is forty-four-years-old and has recently lost his job working for a telecommunications company. With two young children and an unemployed wife, Vassilis and his family live on a small amount of money provided by his mother's reduced pension. Educated at a Romanian university in the mid-1990s, Vassilis says that he has witnessed firsthand the positives and negatives of life in other parts of the Balkans. I have known Vassilis for nearly a decade, and he regularly recites stories of his life in Romania over a shot of *tsipouro* or a cup of coffee. Many of his stories revolve around the poverty he encountered when living abroad and the relief he felt when returning to "civilization" in Greece, as well as the unprecedented levels of corruption engrained in everyday life in Romania—somewhat ironic given the well-documented attention given by Troika to tackling so-called endemic corruption in Greece. Vassilis narrates,

> I never even finished my degree. In fact, I only spent eighteen months living in Romania and it was a four-year course. I paid a small amount of money to my main professor and also gave him some gold icons from a monastery in northern Greece, and he provided me with a degree certificate in mechanical engineering. The first year we were supposed to learn the language, but did they really expect that

within one year we would be able to speak Romanian to the standard required to complete a degree? I returned home after eighteen months because I couldn't stand being surrounded by the poverty, going back only for the exams, which I didn't understand anyway. I never thought of Greece as part of the Balkans, that was "over there" to the north. Greece was my safe haven of civilization where you could find properly tarmacked roads, warm houses and didn't need to bribe everyone with cigarettes and alcohol. I knew that if I got a degree I could get a stable public sector job back home. But now, during these last few years of economic crisis, I am wondering whether things were ever that different in Greece; I have been rethinking Greece's place in the Balkans. (Vassilis, forty-four, Trikala)

Vassilis says that during the 1990s, there was a cavernous distance between Greece and the rest of the Balkans in public imagination. He talks of Greece as a prosperous, wealthy, and democratic nation, stable within the European Union and international markets, where citizens were sure about their prosperous futures. Romania and the wider Balkans were, for people like Vassilis, the abject opposite, struggling to find their feet after the fall of communism, offering their citizens a less than certain vision of the future.[27] Like many inhabitants of Trikala, over the next ten years Vassilis's excursions into other Balkan nations comprised short trips across the border to Bulgaria to stock up on cheap food and alcohol or fill up large canisters of petrol. But things changed for Vassilis in 2014, when he headed back to Bulgaria in a privately hired lorry to purchase firewood for his newly installed wood-burning stove. That trip to Bulgaria in 2014 really got Vassilis thinking, for he was going over the border to buy cheap firewood because he had been forced by the economic crisis—forced by northern European bureaucrats and his own government—to stop using his more expensive petrol-fueled central heating, which he could no longer afford. He had to heat his home with firewood, generally perceived as an "archaic method." "I was going backwards," he states. "Greece was going backwards in time."

Although Greek politicians and the mass media regularly emphasize Greece's important role in the modern European political project, Vassilis cannot help thinking that soon "Greece will become just another Balkan nation." He continues, "When I studied in Romania, modernity was a distant dream, local people had no home-comforts and they certainly didn't feel European. They had many dreams but were caught between their past and their future. Now Greeks are feeling similar ambiguous emotions about where they truly belong. . . . It cannot be denied that we are now in free-fall back through the decades. I know that when I am freezing to death in my home, queuing at empty ATMs, or reading about food banks in the urban centers." The ongoing discussion about Greece's membership in the European single currency and the so-called Grexit alternative that would signal a return to the Drachma have been overtly framed in the Greek mass media as a choice between Europe and the Balkans. This was especially prevalent during the July 2015 referendum on a new Troika austerity package, where various figures from the Greek government and their European creditors sold versions of referendum politics, social suffering, and material poverty packaged in arguments of Europe versus the Balkans.[28] Furthermore, it is common practice for people in Trikala to compare their wages, pensions, and commodity prices with Bulgaria's—evidently a communal barometer for individual and national poverty. Sometimes such comparisons are explained away as an inevitable part of a shared history of persecution first by Ottomans[29] and then Germans and Americans.

Between Balkan and European

For many of my research participants in Trikala, the Balkans continue to represent shared history on the one hand and stereotypes of poverty on the other, perceptions communicated through personal experiences, collective and intergenerational memories, and "official" institutionalized narratives of the past. But the current economic crisis has provoked many questions about Greece's place in international affairs and over the past six years the question of belonging in the Balkans has regularly pierced local discourse. Thirty years of general socioeconomic prosperity since accession into the European Union in 1981 have abruptly ruptured, ejecting people back into an ambivalent confused state of belonging described by Herzfeld in the mid-1980s. Western Europe is perceived as both working for the people and against them, generously providing and ruthlessly repossessing. The return to wood-burning energy, increasing fears of hunger, fuel shortages, and a potential return to the Drachma signify a challenge to Greece's relationship with Western Europe and the Balkans.

The past plays a significant role in how people think about the Balkans, in terms of shared Ottoman suppression, cultural heritage,[30] and stories of family migratory movement. In the current economic crisis, certain moments of the past are experienced as more proximate, helping to explain the increasing suffering and poverty; some of these events are directly linked to Greece's Balkan history. As such, it is clear that to fully represent everyday life in Greece, it is integral to understand the complex and messy ways people in different Greek locales perceive their relationship with Balkan history, culture, and heritage.

Notes

1. The project description is available at http://balkan.bsa.ac.uk/, last accessed August 27, 2015.
2. Kamaras 2001.
3. See Herzfeld 1987, Faubion 1993.
4. For further anthropological reading on the Macedonian Question, see Danforth (1995), Cowan (2000), and Brown (2003). On the social history of the Bulgarian invasion during World War II, see Featherstone et al. (2011, chap. 3).
5. Veremis 1997, 227.
6. On the power of slogans as a way for Greeks to voice political allegiance and critique neoliberalism and economic austerity, see Knight (2015b).
7. See Sutton 1998, chap. 7; Brown and Theodossopoulos 2000, 2003.
8. Knight 2015a.

9. Like much of the Balkans, during the Ottoman Empire Thessaly was divided into *tsiflikia*, landed estates where peasant workers gave between one-half and two-thirds of their produce to their landlord (see Knight 2015a, chap. 3).

10. Knight 2015a.

11. Bryant 2014, 682.

12. Ibid., 691; see also Stewart 2017

13. Knight 2015a; Argenti and Knight 2015.

14. Hirsch and Stewart 2005, 262–263.

15. Herzfeld 1987; Faubion 1993.

16. Knight 2015a, 2.

17. See Mazower 2002.

18. Danforth and Van Boeschoten (2012) have written on the evacuation of children from northern Greece during the civil war.

19. As Kalyvas (2015, 2) has argued, Greece launched a series of ambitious projects of state building, democratization, and economic development in a quest to achieve modernity, many of which have ended in epic disaster. Yet Greece remains one of the most prosperous nations in the Balkan region and has gained entrance to exclusive European political and economic clubs.

20. Herzfeld 1987, 3.

21. Kalyvas 2015.

22. See Demetracopoulou-Lee 1953; Clogg 1992, 179, 181.

23. Herzfeld 1987.

24. Ibid., 7.

25. Ibid., 2; see also Faubion 1993.

26. Theodossopoulos 2006, 6.

27. See Mazower 2002.

28. Renowned historian Mark Mazower wrote an interesting piece about the referendum in the *New York Times*, citing how particular historical contexts have shaped popular perspectives on both internal and international political relations. Likening the referendum and a potential Grexit to "the collective suicide" of "Greeks who blew themselves up rather than surrendering to Turkish forces two centuries ago," Mazower also supposed that the Greek government might have been playing on people's obsession with civil war resistance heroes, prevalent in popular culture and the education curriculum since the fall of the military dictatorship in 1974 (Mazower 2015).

29. David Sutton (1998) writes at length about how his informants on the Greek Island of Kalymnos viewed the Yugoslav Wars of the mid-1990s. Identifying the Bosnian Muslims with the Ottoman Turks, along with the perceived desire of the Great Powers to break up Yugoslavia for their own gain, Kalymniots generally supported Serbia in the Yugoslav conflict (see also Brown and Theodossopoulos 2000; 2003). He also notes that Greece's stock as holding a strategic position in NATO has diminished significantly since the fall of communist governments in eastern Europe.

30. See Couroucli and Marinov 2015.

References

Argenti, Nicolas, and Daniel M. Knight. 2015. "Sun, Wind and the Rebirth of Extractive Economies: Renewable Energy Investment and Metanarratives of the Crisis in Greece." *Journal of the Royal Anthropological Institute* 21 (4). 781–802.

Brown, Keith. 2003. *The Past in Question: Modern Macedonia and the Uncertainties of Nation*. Princeton, NJ: Princeton University Press.
Brown, Keith, and Dimitrios Theodossopoulos. 2000. "The Performance of Anxiety: Greek Narratives of the War in Kosovo." *Anthropology Today* 16 (1): 3–8.
Brown, Keith, and Dimitrios Theodossopoulos. 2003. "Rearranging Solidarity: Conspiracy and the World Order in Greek and Macedonian Commentaries of Kosovo." *Journal of Southern Europe and the Balkans* 5 (3): 315–335.
Bryant, Rebecca. 2014. "History's Remainders: On Time and Objects after Conflict in Cyprus." *American Ethnologist* 41 (4): 681–697.
Clogg, Richard. 1992. *A Concise History of Greece*. Cambridge: Cambridge University Press.
Couroucli, Maria, and Tchavdar Marinov, eds. 2015. *Balkan Heritages: Negotiating History and Culture*. Farnham: Ashgate.
Cowan, Jane K., ed. 2000. *Macedonia: The Politics of Identity and Difference*. London: Pluto.
Danforth, Loring M. 1995. *The Macedonian Conflict: Ethnic Nationalism in a Transnational World*. Princeton, NJ: Princeton University Press.
Danforth, Loring M., and Riki van Boeschoten. 2012. *Children of the Greek Civil War: Refugees and the Politics of Memory*. Chicago: University of Chicago Press.
Demetracopoulou-Lee, Dorothy. 1953. "Greece: Cultural Patterns and Technical Change." In *Cultural Patterns and Technical Change: A Manual Prepared by the World Federation for Mental Health*, edited by M. Mead, 77–114. Paris: UNESCO.
Faubion, James D. 1993. *Modern Greek Lessons: A Primer in Historical Constructivism*. Princeton, NJ: Princeton University Press.
Featherstone, Kevin, Dimitris Papdimitriou, Argyris Mamarelis, and Georgios Niarchos, eds. 2011. *The Last Ottomans: The Muslim Minority of Greece, 1940–1949*. New York: Palgrave Macmillan.
Herzfeld, Michael. 1987. *Anthropology through the Looking-Glass: Critical Ethnography in the Margins of Europe*. Cambridge: Cambridge University Press.
Hirsch, Eric, and Charles Stewart. 2005. "Introduction: Ethnographies of Historicity." *History and Anthropology* 16 (3): 261–274.
Kalyvas, Stathis. 2015. *Modern Greece: What Everyone Needs to Know*. Oxford: Oxford University Press.
Kamaras, Antonis. 2001. "A Capitalist Diaspora: The Greeks in the Balkans." *Hellenic Observatory Discussion Paper*. 4: 1–57. London: London School of Economics and Political Science.
Knight, Daniel M. 2014. "A Critical Perspective on Economy, Modernity and Temporality in Contemporary Greece through the Prism of Energy Practice." *GreeSE Working Paper Series, Hellenic Observatory*. 81: 1–44. London: London School of Economics and Political Science.
Knight, Daniel M. 2015a. *History, Time, and Economic Crisis in Central Greece*. New York: Palgrave Macmillan.
Knight, Daniel M. 2015b. "Wit and Greece's Economic Crisis: Ironic Slogans, Food, and Antiausterity Sentiments." *American Ethnologist* 42 (2): 230–246.
Mazower, Mark. 2002. *The Balkans: A Short History*. New York: Random House.
Mazower, Mark. 2015. "Don't Bet on Syriza." *New York Times*. July 1. Accessed August 27, 2015. http://www.nytimes.com/2015/07/02/opinion/dont-bet-on-syriza-alexis-tsipras-greece.html?_r=0.
Stewart, Charles. 2017. "Uncanny History: Temporal Topology in the Post-Ottoman World." *Social Analysis* 61 (1): 129–142.

Sutton, David E. 1998. *Memories Cast in Stone: The Relevance of the Past in Everyday Life*. Oxford: Berg.
Theodossopoulos, Dimitrios. 2006. "Introduction: The 'Turks' in the Imagination of the 'Greeks.'" *South European Society and Politics* 11 (1): 1–32.
Veremis, Thanos. 1997. "The Revival of the 'Macedonian' Question 1991–1995." In *Ourselves and Others: The Development of a Greek Macedonian Cultural Identity since 1912*, edited by P. Mackridge and E. Yannakakis, 227–234. Oxford: Berg.

DANIEL M. KNIGHT is Lecturer in Social Anthropology and Leverhulme Fellow at the University of St. Andrews, and Visiting Fellow at the Hellenic Observatory, London School of Economics and Political Science. He is author of *History, Time, and Economic Crisis in Central Greece,* and editor of *Ethnographies of Austerity: Temporality, Crisis and Affect in Southern Europe* (with Charles Stewart).

Section IV: The Politics of Everyday Life

In formal and informal ways, life is political. Sociality requires ongoing engagement with others who have different interests—not always incompatible interests, but sometimes competing rather than best interests. Negotiating stability and progress vis-à-vis interests is done at both the individual and group level. As such, seeing politics in everyday life requires us to look beyond the impersonal of elite political life and appreciate how the personal context of local forms of struggle and desire frame interpretations of the seemingly impersonal character of elite political discourse. In this section, the authors speak to the affective context of politics—where reforms are felt at a local level in ways different from what may have been intended—and the aspirational context, where hopes of what could be are personal.

Much of politics is about perspective and framing, and throughout these chapters, we see this clearly around questions of belonging. Nataša Gregorič Bon shows how Albanians use history and aspirations of joining the European Union to situate themselves as "being European" over Balkan. In her chapter, Jelena Džankić narrates the development of a Montenegrin identity through a political transition from belonging to Yugoslavia to leaving Serbia and becoming a "new" country. And in Vasiliki Neofotistos's chapter on postwar justice in Macedonia, we see how the complexity of ethnicity centers on debates of belonging. In international responses to these debates, we see that local everydays—and narratives of belonging—are not entirely locally constructed, even as the local is the place where international politics are often felt.

In Čarna Brković and Stef Jansen's chapter on the border between Serbia and Bosnia and Herzegovina, we see the ways nature, politics, and the inexactness of ethnicity create challenges for local populations forced to come to terms with the shift from what once was a federal demarcation of minimal obtrusion to the boundary of an independent state based on a river that is altering the local geography. While international borders may seem straightforward to those who make them, the lived experience is otherwise.

And it is here that we see power, the emergence of a distinction between elites and nonelites alongside efforts to define national identity and belonging. Emilia Zankina writes about corruption and the political divide in Bulgaria, played out through political engagement and activism. While in Ilká Thiessen's chapter, the efforts of Macedonia to rebuild its capital to show a history remade for the present is literally pouring into concrete a national identity narrative that is constructed by elites to speak across borders and impact all.

The local is a place where the questions of belonging are experienced in relation to power and identity. Certainly throughout this book we can see politics at play, but here we turn our attention to some of the historical, aspirational, and practical venues where politics are felt.

19 Neither the Balkans nor Europe: The "Where" and "When" in Present-Day Albania

Nataša Gregorič Bon

On a hot afternoon in mid-July, I was sitting in a café called Britania in the Albanian coastal city of Vlora. I entered into a conversation with Bledi, a man who seemed to be in his forties and was sitting at the next table with his sister-in-law and two nieces. Some minutes into our conversation, he became curious about where I was from.[1] My telling him I was from Slovenia elicited his comment: "Oh, then we are all from the same area: the Balkans." Not long after he succinctly added: "Though we [the Albanians] are in fact Illyrians." Bledi further explained that Albanians are descendants of Illyrians, which he claimed to be one of the oldest populations in Europe. This kind of explanation can be heard from any number of Albanians when they try to explain their identity and emplace themselves on the historical, geopolitical, and social map of Europe and the world.

The hypothesis of Albanians originating from Illyrians was promoted in the period of the communist regime when its autocratic leader at the time, Enver Hoxha, turned it into an official historical fact. With this he promulgated the idea of Albanians as "the first civilization" in Europe who have "always" lived in the present state territory, thus glossing over any differences existing between the ancient past and the present. Despite the fact that over two decades have passed since the collapse of the regime in 1991, this idea still has currency and remains part of the Albanian school curriculum.

The communist regime in Albania was arguably one of the most consistently Stalinist regimes in Europe. Political and economic centralization and draconian restrictions imposed on movement (for example, the ban on private cars and any cross-border transportation), including on imports and exports, as well as foreign political partnerships with western European countries—these factors profoundly influenced peoples' perception of their location on the geopolitical map. Many people can still recall how they were absolutely convinced that Albania was one of the most beautiful and prosperous countries in the world, located at its very center. Only in the course of the last years of the communist regime, following Hoxha's death (in 1985) and during the succession of Ramiz Alia (who soon lost power and control over the country), did people start to realize that many countries were in fact economically, politically, and financially much better off than Albania.

Compared to the ex-Yugoslav countries, the meaning of the phrase "the Balkans" (and the phrase itself) appeared relatively late in the Albanian discourse. After the fall of communism, which was largely brought about by the country's economic and political crisis, a lot of nonprofit, governmental, and nongovernmental international organizations from the United States and western Europe flooded the Albanian public space. It was then that many Albanians became aware that Albania was one of the poorest and least developed countries in Europe. Consequently, the phrase "the Balkans" was never fully adopted in everyday parlance, although it was a phrase often used in Europe and America.

"I want Albania to be like Europe (E duam Shqipërinë si Europa)" was an often-repeated slogan that echoed in many street protests against the communist dictatorship by the end of the 1990s. Although more than two decades have passed since, this slogan is still often heard nowadays, especially after the government signed the Stabilization and Association Agreement on June 12, 2006. This event made it to the front pages of all Albanian newspapers as well as other media, with the then Albanian prime minister Sali Berisha underlining the historical importance of this moment with such statements as, "Albania is returning to Europe after a century of unjust and undeserved slashing of its territory, occupations, racism and ethnic cleansing, and a harsh dictatorship that isolated it from Europe."[2] Since that moment onward, the media have been relentless in discussing issues regarding the European Union (EU) accession on a daily basis, despite the fact—or precisely because of it—that after several years of striving it was finally given the status of a candidate state in June 2014.

This chapter addresses the various meanings of Europe as expressed in people's daily conversations as well as in the media and political discourses on the EU accession. It discusses the ways in which people define themselves in view of geographically, politically, and historically shifting borders. The chapter observes how people's feelings of an uncertain and precarious present get replaced with high hopes and expectations for a better future envisioned in Albania's accession to the EU.

Envisioning Europe

Blerta is a young lawyer, born in 1988 in Vlora, who at the time we spoke still lived with her parents. She is the youngest in a family of three children. Her parents own a small grocery shop in one of Vlora's neighborhoods. In comparison to many families struggling to make a living, this has, according to her, made a crucial difference to their lives, allowing them to earn enough money to survive and save money for the future—or, as she put it, "për të mirë dhe për të keq" (for the good and for the bad). After completing her studies at the Law Faculty at the University of Vlora, she got a job as a lawyer at the Municipality of Vlora. She is obliged to follow daily media reports, which she sees as being saturated with

Figure 19.1. Men having coffee in Vlora near the Europa bakery, Albania, 2012. Photograph by Nataša Gregorič Bon.

information about the EU. To the question on what she thinks about the EU and its role for Albania, she responded: "For us, this [the EU] is a great achievement. I was born at the time when the system [communist regime] was entirely closed [any kind of border crossing was forbidden] and I only learned about that life from my family [literally "të afërt" or "the nearest"]. EU is the greatest achievement. They will help us improve jobs, education, development, economy, all perspectives. I am very positive about the EU. . . . My feelings are more than positive. I don't expect us to join soon. But definitely we will join at one point."

Blerta's view is that geographically and historically Albania is already within Europe. In this she refers to the Albanian historians who are arguing that the Albanians are direct descendants of the Pelasgians: "Several historical studies, for example, argue that we originated from Pelasgians who are the most ancient population in Europe and who preceded the Illyrians." This knowledge, which is part of the school curriculum in Albania, generates an important basis for

Neither the Balkans nor Europe 203

people's understanding of Albania's position in Europe. In the continuing discussion, Blerta was complaining about the current political and economic situation in the country, which was distancing Albania from Europe. In contrast to other western European countries, where development was gradual, Albania entered the liberal democratic system abruptly after 1991. Blerta reasons that twenty years is not enough to catch up with the economic, political, and social development characteristic of western European countries. She suggests that the communist legacy "took Albania" out of Europe and located it on its margins. Albania, in her description, has been shifted from "inside" or from the "center" to the "outside" or the "periphery" of Europe, and her merging of Albania's historic preeminence with present-day Albania is on what she bases her hopes for a better future in the EU. Though she is careful to emphasize she "only hopes," she anticipates that moment in no uncertain terms as something that is yet to come.

Similar reasoning was given to me by Spiro, who was born in 1953 and also lives in Vlora. During communism, he worked as an economist in one of the textile factories in Vlora. After the collapse of the regime, he became a financial advisor in one of the trade companies in Tirana. Due to disagreements with his manager, he left his job and opened a private accountant business in Vlora. One October afternoon in 2012, we had a conversation about the economic, political, and social situation in Albania and the meaning of its accession to EU. Like Blerta, Spiro also firmly set Albania historically onto the map of Europe: "Albania is part of the old Europe, not only geographically but also as a nation. We are an old nation.... We are an old nation, and we have contributed to the history of Europe in many periods, such as the period of Skenderbeg. We have many distinguished individuals who have participated in the history of the developed countries of the West. Emperors in Italy, the pope in Rome, the Vizir in the developed Turkey in the middle ages."

Spiro also thinks that media reports are bombarding people with information about the EU on a daily basis, adding that: "The media and politicians write and speak a lot [about Albania's accession to the EU] but mainly they blame one another for the failure to enter the EU so far. They do not explain our weak points or how to avoid them and how to fight them; what efforts and changes could be made to eliminate the problems of the accession procedure. They hardly have anything to say on these points. Politicians are not as interested in joining the EU as they are in political in-fights." Like Blerta, he also thinks that the communist regime "took" Albania "out" of Europe and placed it on its periphery: "We were raised in the socialist system which made us what we are and therefore we cannot change so easily. Our point of view, our way of thinking and our ideas cannot be changed that fast. Therefore we have difficulties. In these twenty years of democracy we have not made any considerable changes. If one compared us with any other developed EU country, our society has certainly developed in comparison to our past, but in comparison to other western European countries we are considerably behind." With these words, Spiro expressed his dissatisfaction with the current political, economic, and social situation in the country.

Spiro's and Blerta's narratives shift not only the location of Albania, from the "center" to the "periphery," but also its temporality, moving it from the present to the future. This generates the "rhythm" of the "where" and "when" of Albania, through which they, as Spiro notes, are able to anticipate a brighter future:

> Well, EU will not bring us higher taxes. It will bring development, and we'll join the rhythm of their development and law implementation, like the other countries. Here we should consider one or two facts. The current inflation in Albania is 6 percent, and it still fluctuates almost to double levels. The EU, on the other hand, has a rule that does not allow for such high fluctuations of inflation. And this depends on the economic policy of the state. Secondly, their [the EU's] debt management does not allow its members to increase the inflation rate above a certain percentage, whereas here, in Albania, inflation usually increases very fast. EU imposes certain limitations. Therefore Greece for example did not declare its debt but kept it secret and tried to lie when it reported the budget balance to the EU experts. And thus it almost came to the brink of collapse.

Despite their negative vision of the present, many residents of Albania express hope for a more positive and optimistic future. Archilea, who was born in 1972 and originates from and lives in the bilingual (Albanian and Greek speaking) area of Himara in southern Albania, elaborated on these expectations in 2010 with the following words: "The problem is that people here are . . . I would not say stupid. . . . I would say naive, or I would say . . . if you promise them wealth and money they will tend to buy it, even though they might understand that it is very unlikely. It is only because they want to believe that their life will become better, that they believe you." To the question of why people believe that the accession of Albania to the EU will bring them prosperity and well-being, Archilea responded: "People believe that if they get into the EU all their troubles will disappear . . . all their problems. They think that the solution to their problems will be found if they get into the EU. They don't believe there is any way that anything will get better under the Albanian government. They lost faith in the Albanian politicians, parties, whatever. The only thing that this country needs to improve its lot is to join the EU. And that is my opinion too." Archilea continued to criticize the current political situation in Albania: "There is nothing that they [the government] does not control. Everything is a monopoly. There is no hope; that's the problem. The only hope for us individuals is to leave [go abroad]. And even the government says that 'the biggest dream for Albanians, which we are going to realize, is the liberation of the visa regime.' Do you understand what that means: we [the government] cannot feed you here, but we can help you go and find help any way you know how somewhere else. Can you imagine that, after twenty years of democracy!"

I was talking to Archilea in September 2010, a couple of months prior to the liberalization of the visa regime, which took place in December and was widely discussed by the political establishment and promoted by the media. Archilea thought that if Albania were going to "enter" the EU, this would happen not because the Albanian economy and policy have improved their standards. As he went on to say,

Figure 19.2. A bus stop showing support for the EU that, ironically, has become less frequently traveled as a new road is constructed nearby, 2017. Photograph by Yllka Fetahaj.

> the EU needs us [the Albanian citizens]—it needs our manual labor workers, because EU countries have realized that they have fewer problems with workers from Albania, Romania, or Bosnia than with migrants from Africa or the Middle East. The EU thinks in the direction that people are young here, they can speak foreign languages, they are Christians by religion, or if they are Muslims they do not strictly follow their tradition. Besides they [the EU] know that if they try to keep them out, they will come illegally anyway. Therefore, it is better to control them and let them enter.

While we were talking, Archilea's wife jokingly noted, "But we are already in Europe, as we are all over it" and added that one-third of the country's population lives in Europe or elsewhere, which means they do not have to "enter" it anymore, as they are already "present" in Europe.

Archilea's reflections on Europe and the EU and his wife's remark express their lack of trust in the Albanian state. Because they both originate from the bilingual area of Himara, they own special identity cards as coethnic Greeks, which enabled them to cross the Schengen Area borders even before the 2010 liberalization of the visa regime. Therefore, they considered themselves as being "mobile" and "free" to cross borders already for years, which makes them different from the majority of the population in Albania.

For Archilea, Europe and the EU reflect, on the one hand, the expression of their uncertainty and dissatisfaction with the present economic situation in their own country, while on the other, they symbolize hope for a better future. Despite the "Euro crisis" in Greece and Archilea's negative opinion on the role of the EU in Greece, he conceptualizes Europe, Europeans, and the EU as the benchmarks of "modernity" and sees Europe as a place where the better future of Albania could be envisioned.

In contrast to my other two interlocutors, Blerta and Spiro, who see Albania's location in Europe as ambiguous, Archilea exposes the interdependence between Albania and Europe—while Albania needs the EU leadership in order to be saved from its political and economic crisis, at the same time the EU needs the Albanian workforce. Europe is thus defined as a space that embodies hope, if not quite the expectations of full well-being.

Re-Turn to Europe

All these visions of the future should be understood in the context of EU politics, the expansion of the Schengen Area, and the introduction of the European Neighbourhood Policy, which has brought Europe, as an idea and as a place, closer to the people's lives. In people's daily conversations, the concept of Europe is often invested with ideas of a more economically successful and stable future, embodied in the country's "entering" (*hyrie*) the EU. As the Albanian historian Armanda Hysa succinctly observes, in contrast to the present situation of economic and social insecurity in the country, Europe is often imagined as the "ultimate structure of freedom and well-being."[3]

The enlargement of the European Union and subsequent redefinition of its polity borders have brought changes to Europe's cartographic map and its social one, particularly for the ways in which the changing political geography of the EU has influenced people's perceptions of particular places seen to be "within" or "outside" Europe. The "free movement" (*lëvizje e lire*), as many Albanians refer to the visa-free crossing of the state borders after Albania's accession to the Schengen Area in December 2010, has changed significantly their understanding of themselves and their location. This shifting location that Albania now occupies in people's imaginaries is interesting because of the tension that has been created between the perceptions that Albania is Europe's "immediate outside" located on the margins of Europe,[4] and those that allocate it a central place and represent it as the "cradle" of the "European civilization" and modernity.

The latter view is propagated across the disciplines of Albanian historiography, archaeology, and other social sciences. Several Albanian and also foreign historians refer to the period of Pelasgo-Illyrians.[5] As already mentioned, many of them contend that modern Albanians are direct descendants of the ancient Pelasgians, the "pre-Indo-European population" who were the first population and direct predecessors of the Illyrians, settling the area of present-day Europe.[6] In her book *The Role of Pellazgo-Illyrians*, Elena Kocaqi defends the European identity of the Albanian nation and identifies its people as the direct descendants of Pelasgo-Illyrians, the first autochthonous population of Europe, with the Albanian language being today's only surviving proof.

The signing of the Stabilisation and Association Agreement between Albania and the EU on June 12, 2006, was one of the hopeful moments for Albania accession. Many saw it as Albania entering Europe with "one foot," as several media outlets have worded it; for example, the daily newspaper *Korrieri* explicitly stated that with this momentous agreement "Albania is with one foot in the EU."[7] On a similar note, the *Standard* titled its front page "Europe Is Opening Its Doors to Albania."[8] Several Albanian politicians talked about the "years of knocking on European doors," wrote about the "return to the maternal continent," and declared the signing of the agreement as the "historical step toward development."

Albanian scholar Gerda Dalipaj states that the aspirations and projections of Europe in contemporary Albanian society have to be understood in its historical context related to the period of the communist regime. After decades of life in isolation and on the periphery of Europe as well as the Balkans, the Albanian people have formed a "poetic quest for freedom" which they associate with "free movement" across European borders.[9] Dalipaj continues that this poetic quest, laden with communist legacy, constitutes the people's "lyrical quest" of becoming "modern Europeans."[10]

In his book *The European Identity of the Albanians*, the world-renowned novelist Ismail Kadare differentiates between the pro- and anti-European versions of Albanian history. The pro-European history is centered on the Albanian language as one of the core mediums that emplaces Albania and the Albanians onto the map of Europe. The anti-European history, on the other hand, is marked by the period of the Ottoman dominance, which "took" Albania "out of Europe."[11] While Kadare aims to "bring" Albania "back to Europe" and reaffirm its "European roots," the Albanian literature scholar from Kosovo, Rexhep Qosja, in the essay entitled "National Identity and Religious Self-Understanding," sets Albania at the crossroads of civilizations, between East and West. One of the main obstacles to the Albanian road toward the EU is not its culture but its political system, which is economically undeveloped, lacks democracy, and is corrupted.[12]

The Kadare-Qosja debate, in a sense, encompasses the full scale of Albania's ambiguous location. It reveals relations and connections between various places and time periods (Antiquity, Byzantine period, Ottoman period, present time) that set Albania sometimes "in," sometimes "outside," and sometimes "not quite" in Europe.

Hoping for a Better Future

Everyday uncertainties facing people living in Albania have given rise to a complex and conceptual space in which a better future is hoped for. Even in the context of current ramifications of economic and fiscal crisis in neighboring Greece, for European relations hopes have not dampened but remain embedded in the country's accession to the EU. In their daily conversations, people rarely refer to or emplace Albania in the Balkans. Through their conceptualizations of the ancient past and their self-identification as direct ancestors of

Pelasgo-Illyrians, they emplace themselves more in the territory of Europe than that of the Balkans. People's narratives, as well as media, political, and intellectual discourses, also underline temporality, with the present lingering between the past and the future. When people reappropriate and redefine the hegemonic discourses about Europe, they generate their understanding of their time, their place, and themselves.

Notes

I am grateful to my interlocutors for their help and confidence. I am indebted to my dearest friends, Juliana Vera, Adrian Piero, Tina Nina, Enea Kumi, Armanda Kodra Hysa, Enriketa Pandalemoni Papa, and Gerda Dalipaj, for their help during my fieldwork and for their insightful conversations on various issues related to everyday life in Albania. I also thank Mentor Mustafa and the editor, David Montgomery, for his invitation to contribute a chapter to this volume. The earlier versions of some parts of this text were published in the *Bulletin of the Slovene Ethnological Society*, 55, nos. 1/2 (2015). I acknowledge the project entitled *Seizing the Future* (J6-7480) which was financially supported by the Slovenian Research Agency. My special gratitude goes to Maja Petrović-Šteger for her insightful comments. I also thank Ana Jelnikar, Nina Vodopivec, Miha Kozorog, and other colleagues and participants of weekly journal clubs organized by Maja Petrović-Šteger.

1. To keep anonymity of my interlocutors all their names are pseudonyms. The ethnographic data presented in this chapter were mainly gathered in the years between 2008 and 2010 when due to liberalisation of the visa regime in Albania (December 2010) the discourse on the role and meaning of the EU and Albania's accession to it was very pertinent. After 2010, this has changed because of the growing numbers of returnees to Albania from Greece and Italy, the countries that were hit most by the fiscal and economic crisis in 2008.
2. "Evropa hap dyert për Shqiptarët," 2006, 2.
3. Hysa 2008.
4. Jansen 2009.
5. See d'Angely 1998; Kokalari 2001; Aref 2003; Kocaqi 2010.
6. Ceka 2005.
7. "Shqipëria më një këmbë në BE," 2006.
8. "Evropa hap dyert për Shqiptarët," 2006.
9. Dalipaj 2008, 82.
10. Ibid., 79–86.
11. Kadare 2006, 25.
12. Qosja 2006.

References

Aref, Mathieu. 2003. *Albanie ou l'incroyable odyssée d'un peuple pré-hellénique*. Paris: Mnémosyne.
Ceka, Neritan. 2005. *The Illyrians: To the Albanians*. Tirana: Migjeni.
Dalipaj, Gerda. 2008. "The Otherness Outside and Within: The Challenge of Shaping and Manifesting a New Image of the Other and of the Self in Post Socialist Albania." In *Dynamics of National Identity and Transnational Identities in the Process of*

European Integration, edited by E. Marushiakova, 76–87. Newcastle: Cambridge Scholars Press.
D'Angely, Robert. 1998. *Enigma*. Tiranë: Toena.
"Evropa hap dyert për Shqiptarët." 2006. *Standard*, June 12, 1–2.
Hysa, Armanda. 2008. "The Religious Identity of Albanians and the European Integration." In *Dynamics of National Identity and Transnational Identities in the Process of European Integration*, edited by E. Marushiakova, 339–352. Newcastle: Cambridge Scholars Press.
Jansen, Stef. 2009. "After the Red Passport: Towards an Anthropology of the Everyday Geopolitics of Entrapment in the EU's Immediate Outside." *Journal of the Royal Anthropological Institute* 15 (4): 815–832.
Kadare, Ismail. 2006. *Identiteti Evropian i Shqiptareve*. Tiranë: Onufri.
Kocaqi, Elena. 2010. *Roli Pellazgo-Ilir. Në formimin e kombeve dhe gjuhëve europeane* (Botimi i tretë). Tiranë: Emal.
Kokalari, M. 2001. *Epiri, kryeqendra e qytetërimit antik në Evropë*. Tiranë: Koha.
Qosja, Rexep: *Realiteti i shpërfillur*. Tiranë: Toena.
"Shqipëria më një këmbë në BE." 2006. *Korrieri*, June 12, 1.

NATAŠA GREGORIČ BON is Research Fellow at the Institute of Anthropological and Spatial Studies of the Research Centre of the Slovenian Academy of Sciences and Arts (ZRC SAZU) and Assistant Professor at the Postgraduate School ZRC SAZU. She is author of *Spaces of Discordance: Ethnography of Space and Place in the Village of Dhërmi/Drimades, Southern Albania* and editor of *Moving Places: Relations, Return and Belonging* (with Jaka Repič).

20 Growing Up in Montenegro: A Story of Transformation and Resistance

Jelena Džankić

Sanja[1] was born in the early 1980s in Cetinje, a town in the Republic of Montenegro, then a part of the Socialist Federal Republic of Yugoslavia. Around the time she started to go to school in the republic's capital, Titograd, everyone was talking about the "young, bright and beautiful." These were the new leaders: three guys in their late twenties—Momir (Momo) Bulatović, Milo Đukanović, and Svetozar (Sveto) Marović. They took over the Communist Party of Montenegro, which later became the ruling Democratic Party of Socialists (*Demokratska Partija Socijalista*, DPS). There was a lot of talk about war, and Sanja often saw people in uniforms around the streets.

There was no war in Montenegro. It was mostly on TV. In 1991, when she was in the fourth grade, some of her peers tore out the first page of their schoolbooks. All first pages of schoolbooks featured a photograph of Josip Broz Tito, the long-ruling president of Yugoslavia who died in 1980. A year later, in 1992, Sanja was told that the city she lived in was no longer to be called Titograd but Podgorica and that "old" Yugoslavia no longer existed. Rather, she lived in a new country, the Federal Republic of Yugoslavia, composed of Serbia and Montenegro. A handful of people protested—"Liberals," as they would call themselves at the time—but hardly anyone supported them.

Growing Up in the Years of War

Some of Sanja's neighbors went to war. One returned and made a huge cross from bullets on the wall of his living room. On each side of the cross there was a Cyrillic letter *S*, because *Samo Sloga Srbina Spasava* (only unity saves the Serbs). He volunteered to go to war, saying that they had enemies in Croatia and Bosnia and Herzegovina. Those enemies would go to slightly different churches, or pray in mosques, he explained. His children attended religious classes in a church. They prayed before bedtime, and he told Sanja and her brother that they had to pray as well. Otherwise, on the judgment day, there would be no food or water for them. They would be very thirsty, and all God would give them would be salty water, to make them more thirsty to punish them.

Sanja and her family ate a lot of pancakes and doughnuts with sugar in those days. That was the easiest thing to make with flour and water. Her mom baked bread because it was easier to make bread than queue to buy it. Sometimes the queue was too long. Sometimes, queuing was dangerous. Once they sent her little brother to queue for bread. He returned without bread and with a bloody forehead. He said a woman hit him with an umbrella to take his place in the queue. So they would buy flour on the street. The people who sold flour called themselves "refugees"; they came from Croatia and Bosnia and Herzegovina. They received "humanitarian aid," which consisted of big bags of flour, tins of feta cheese, liver pate, and milk powder. This aid was given to them by "international organizations." One of the few things the "refugees" did not sell was gasoline. That was sold by the local Albanians, who smuggled gasoline from Albania into Montenegro across Lake Skadar. Sanja's mom explained to her that they could no longer buy gasoline at the gas stations because of the "embargo" and that they had to buy bottles of gasoline in Podgorica's suburb called Tuzi, which is where the majority of the Albanians lived. Gasoline was precious. Sometimes they could afford to buy only a regular "mineral water bottle" (one liter), but on better days, they would fill up a big bottle (twice as big as the first one). Therefore, they had to use gasoline sparingly.

They mostly used their car to go visit Sanja's aunt who lived right next to the hospital. She had electricity almost all the time because the hospital power grid never lost power. Everyone else had "restrictions" of electricity for six hours a day. During summer months, Sanja would not feel the restrictions that much, but Podgorica winters could be cold. Relatives would also come to visit them during wintertime, since they did not have electricity and Sanja's family did. People would make schedules on whom to visit on what days and at what times and when to expect guests. Sanja, however, did not like having guests; they would eat all the pancakes.

Childhood between Inflation and Restrictions

In late 1993, Sanja discovered a new game called "The Bank." She and her brother would collect banknotes and exchange them. It was very easy to get banknotes because people were changing them every day. She and her brother were very "rich"; they had a suitcase filled with banknotes of all sorts. Their favorites were the ones with more than ten zeros. They would stick ten of them together and make a banknote with a hundred zeros. This was something that Sanja's dad called "hyperinflation." It essentially meant that when he would get his salary in Yugoslav dinars, he would have to run to the market and find illegal foreign currency traders to change the dinars to Deutsch Marks (DM). Being a former sportsman, Sanja's dad was quick. He would get twenty DM for his monthly salary and that would get the family through the month.

Some people started opening "shops" in which you could buy old books, marbles, stickers, and all sorts of stuff. There were kid's shops, where Sanja traded her "hyperinflation" banknotes, and shops that her parents would go to and buy

Figure 20.1. Selling fresh fish in Budva, Montenegro, 2003. Photograph by David W. Montgomery.

stuff with normal money (mostly DM). These shops were usually stands handmade from cardboard boxes turned upside down, and people would use them to sell cigarettes, alcohol, various gadgets, and clothes. Most of these things were "imported." The shop owners would travel to Budapest by train or to Istanbul by bus. They would take their *krmača* (pig) bags, and stuff them with clothes and things from the Chinese flea markets. Then, they would come back to Montenegro and sell what they had purchased. All the profit went to the shop owners. Instead of paying custom duties, they offered money or some of the clothes to the customs officers. They did not pay taxes, either. But they did it to survive, and hardly any of them became rich.

Everyone was talking about the difficulties of everyday life, about some sort of a "shadow market," which was supposedly bigger than those shops one could see all over Montenegro. There was a lot of talk about "bananas," "cigarettes," and other goods smuggled into Montenegro with the blessing of local politicians. Other topics were overshadowed by the hardships of everyday life.

A Teenager in a Land of Divided Loyalties

Sanja finished elementary school in 1996, and things started to change. She grew more responsible because of the environment around her. Her friend Marija got married. Marija was only sixteen, but she became pregnant. In patriarchic Montenegro, getting married was the only thing that would save her family's honor.

That year, Sanja realized that while traditions remained, everyday lives began to change. Politics and support for politicians became a topic that was discussed every day in every family. As everyone had expected, the DPS won the elections, again. Yet, two days before Sanja's birthday in 1997, there was big news of Milo—who was prime minister at the time (and on multiple occasions since)—countering Slobodan Milošević, the man whose political footsteps he followed for almost a decade at the time. Milo's criticism of Milošević was not well-received by Momo, the then President of Montenegro. Over the next couple of months, the DPS split in two, and Milo and Momo emerged as competitors for the presidency of Montenegro in 1997. "Who will you vote for?" was the question that echoed in every house, every day, several times a day. Sanja recalls people calling each other names—"Turks" for those who would vote for Milo, who reached out to Albanians and Muslims for political support or "chetniks" for those who would vote for Momo and continue to support Milošević. Both names had negative undertones—the former reminiscing of the struggles during the Ottoman times, the latter of the Serb nationalist monarchist movement that sought to re-create the Great Serbia and used ethnic cleansing for that purpose. Both "chetniks" and "Turks" designated "enemies" of the people of Montenegro.

Milo won the elections. Momo accused him of electoral fraud and called for protests. Sanja's parents did not allow her to go to school on January 14, 1998, because of the riots. Momo's supporters were protesting and demolishing stores and kiosks in the center of Podgorica. Milo was inaugurated as the president of Montenegro the next day. He remained the leader of the DPS, took control of the state, and built his political agenda around countering Milošević. Momo established the Socialist People's Party, Montenegro's opposition, which remained close to the Belgrade authorities. Sanja's friends regrouped into "Miloists" and "Momoists"; Montenegro was split in half, like an apple.

But there were more and more apples those days, more food, and Sanja's mom would no longer buy gasoline in a plastic bottle, but go to the gas station to fill up the tank of her Yugo. At that time, Western countries gave Montenegro a lot of financial aid, because Milo was no longer close to Milošević. Sanja read somewhere that after Israel, Montenegro was the second-highest per capita recipient of US donor aid, at that time, in the world. Madeleine Albright, then US secretary of state, said that the aid was given to keep "a democratic Montenegro in a democratic Yugoslavia."[2] At the time, Milošević was doing some really bad things in Kosovo, and he did not like the fact that Montenegro was drifting from Serbia. He increased the presence of the Yugoslav army in Montenegro; one could see them around. Milo retaliated by building up a militarized police force of twenty thousand men. Sanja remembers that in 1998 and 1999, Montenegro probably had one of the highest numbers of policemen per capita in the world. Even though at that time her parents had normal salaries, including all sorts of foreign products and gasoline, they feared civil war.

Sanja was in the third year of high school in February and March 1999 and, along with her friends, was worried over whether Milošević would accept the "NATO ultimatum." That was the first time she had heard the word "NATO" (North Atlantic Treaty Alliance), and while she did not quite know what it meant, she knew it had to do with the United States and security. She knew from her history classes that the word "ultimatum" meant "you do what I ask you to do, or else." The NATO ultimatum required Milošević to withdraw from Kosovo, a province in Serbia whose autonomy he had withdrawn in 1989. He did not accept the ultimatum. NATO strikes began on the last birthday her maternal grandmother would celebrate alive. They lasted for seventy-eight days.

Compared to Kosovo and Serbia, Montenegro suffered far fewer airstrikes. This was because when the DPS split, Đukanović's ruling party started distancing itself from Milošević. Sanja remembered reading in the newspapers that foreigners no longer needed visas to enter Montenegro, even though visas were required to enter Yugoslavia, and that separate customs regimes were in place, though she was not too sure what that meant at the time. One day, she went out with a cousin of hers, ten years her senior. The cousin was thrilled at seeing Bajadera chocolates in a shop. And when Sanja asked her, "What is that?" the cousin could not believe that Sanja did not remember Bajadera chocolates, which were very famous in the old Yugoslavia. After 1991, it was not possible to buy Bajadera chocolates in Montenegro, because they were produced in Croatia.

However, by 1998, Montenegro had turned to importing goods from Croatia and Slovenia and apologized to Croatia for crimes committed by the Montenegrin soldiers in the attacks against the old coastal city of Dubrovnik. In November 1998, Montenegro also introduced the Deutsch Mark as a parallel currency to the Yugoslav dinar, and a year later, the switch to the Deutsch Mark was complete. As of 1999, it was no longer possible to use the dinar as a legal tender. Sanja's mom took the remaining dinar bills and placed them in that old, dusty suitcase that she and her brother used as the vault of their bank. She put the suitcase in the basement storage room.

Coming of Age in Solania

In September 2000, Sanja volunteered for an NGO that explored interethnic relations in high schools. Together with a friend and colleague, she traveled to various municipalities and asked high school students how they felt about interacting with people of different ethnic and religious backgrounds. The answers were divided, as were the people. On September 20, 2000, as part of the same project, they traveled to the northern municipality of Berane. Little did she know that was the day when, as a part of his election campaign, Slobodan Milošević held a rally in that town. As they rode on the bus, they saw that many people went to the rally to offer support to Milošević. Some even took their children. The sight of a boy of three or four years of age raising three fingers, a symbol of Serbian nationalism, disturbed her. Montenegro officially boycotted the federal presidential elections because Milošević had changed the electoral law, reducing

Montenegro to a federal electoral unit. Since Montenegro was a twelfth the size of Serbia, there was little chance of any candidate from the smaller republic being elected as the federal president. In a way, those who went to the rally pledged allegiance to Milošević.

Milošević was ousted from power in Belgrade after these elections, and it was time for a new beginning. The DPS and the Socialist People's Party (*Socijalistička Narodna Partija*, SNP) lost their central axis of political competition—opposition or support to Milošević. Yet by that time, the ruling DPS had detached from the federal institutions to such a degree that hardly anyone could call Yugoslavia a federation by early 2001. The SNP showed their support to the new Serbian elites and pushed for the reintegration of Montenegro into Yugoslavia. As a result, two political blocs were created: the pro-independence camp, led by the then prime minister Đukanović, and the unionist bloc led by Predrag Bulatović, who substituted his namesake Momir as the leader of the SNP.

By then, it was clear that Sanja's family and friends belonged to two camps. A part of them supported the detachment of Montenegro from Yugoslavia, a process called "creeping independence."[3] Another part remained supportive of the federal state. The former called themselves "independentists" and the latter "unionists." Judging from the electoral results of 2001 and 2002, roughly half of the population of Montenegro supported the camp promoting the country's independence at that time. An almost equal number preferred to stay in the same state with Serbia. After two failed attempts to negotiate the transformation of the federal Yugoslavia with the new Serbian government, the debate on the independence of Montenegro became increasingly heated.

Yet the beginning of the new millennium had hardly brought any peace to the region. The war in Kosovo, followed by a short war in Macedonia, had left the region unstable. Having learned some political science by then, Sanja understood that these were the reasons why the international community would be unhappy if Montenegro had seceded at that time. Instead, Yugoslavia transformed, with the mediation of the European Union's High Representative for Common Foreign and Security Policy Javier Solana into a state union of Serbia and Montenegro. Some people dubbed the state union as "Solania."[4] Solania was an interesting country, founded so that its constituents—Serbia and Montenegro—could cohabit for another three years. Politically, it was a state that ensured that there would be a three-year moratorium on Montenegro's independence, a state with very few competences, and a state that allowed for as much separation as possible between Serbia and Montenegro. And the politics of Serbia and Montenegro by then were so separate that the two states could not decide on the symbols of the union. In 2004, Montenegro changed its tricolored (red, light blue, and white) flag to a red and gold one, adorned with a two-headed eagle with a lion on its chest. Serbia continued to use its red, blue, and white tricolored flag. Since Montenegro and Serbia could not agree on whether the blue on the state union's flag should be the Montenegrin "light blue" or the Serbian "blue," Solania's symbols remained those of the Federal Republic of Yugoslavia (FRY), including the red, blue, and white tricolored flag; a coat of arms with a two-headed eagle featuring emblems of Serbia and of Montenegro; and the old socialist Yugoslav anthem "Hey, Slavs" (*Hej, Sloveni*).

Country United, Identities Divided

With the coming of Solania, not many things changed for the people of Montenegro—they switched to the Euro as the official currency and started to say that they were ethnically "Montenegrin" if they supported independence or "Serb" if they preferred to stay in the common state with Serbia. A census conducted in 2003 reflected that roughly 43 percent of people in Montenegro declared their ethnic identity as Montenegrin and some 32 percent as Serb.[5] That was an incredible change from 1991, when nearly 62 percent of the people self-identified as Montenegrins and just over 9 percent as Serbs. What happened was not an outcome of the demographic changes, as the birth and death rates of the two ethnic communities remained the same. Rather, what it meant to be a Serb and a Montenegrin changed a great deal from 1991 to 2003 as a result of the political developments in Montenegro. The Montenegrins in the early 1990s thought that they could be both Montenegrin and Serb at the same time. By 2003, the two categories became exclusive for those who self-identified as Montenegrin. So those who believed that the Serbs and Montenegrins were the same people started to self-identify as Serbs.

Sanja's neighbors, two brothers, Branko and Jovan, perfectly illustrated this trend. At the time when Yugoslavia was falling apart, Branko and Jovan, then in their early thirties, were vocal Montenegrins. They went to Croatia to wage wars believing that the Serbs were in danger. They thought of themselves as Serbs and Montenegrins at the same time. When the DPS split happened in 1997, Branko continued to support Milo. His brother, believing that Milo was a criminal, decided to side with his opponent Momo. By 2003, only Branko would say that he was a Montenegrin. But then, being Montenegrin for him meant that Montenegrins were different from Serbs and that one could not be both at the same time. Jovan said that he was a Serb and that Montenegrins were a subgroup of the Serb people. At the 2006 referendum, Branko voted for independence. Jovan voted against.

This division between Montenegrins and Serbs in Montenegro, intensified as the referendum date grew closer. Sanja remembers how the national Eurovision Song Contest held in Belgrade in 2006, an apparently marginal event, heated the referendum debate in both Montenegro and Serbia. After a cunning distribution of votes of the Montenegrin representatives, a Montenegrin boy band "No Name" was proclaimed the winner for the second year in a row. During the 2005 contest, when "No Name" performed for the first time in Kiev, the band members adorned themselves with Montenegrin national symbols, clearly displaying the red-and-gold Montenegrin flag, while their song contained ethnic Montenegrin motifs. The runner-up song was performed by "Flamingosi," a band composed of a Serbian and a Montenegrin singer. In the 2006 Eurovision contest, held the night before the Montenegrin referendum on independence, "No Name" symbolized an independent Montenegro, as opposed to "Flamingosi," who stood for the state union. Sanja was unhappy that Serbia and Montenegro remained

Figure 20.2. The village of Perast on the Bay of Kotor is but one reminder of the many empires that laid claim to cities in the Balkans. From the tenth century on, its control moved from the Byzantines to the Serbs, Venetians, Hungarians, Italians, and Yugoslavs until becoming part of Montenegro, 2003. Photograph by David W. Montgomery.

without a representative in Athens. She cheered for Hari Mata Hari, a Bosnian singer whose songs she loved as a child.

Growing into a State

Sanja remembers the referendum day: May 21, 2006. There were more people in Podgorica than ever. The government and the opposition organized free-of-charge transport for their supporters who lived abroad to come and vote at the referendum. People were flying either red-and-gold or red-white-and-blue flags or bearing some sort of markers that would make clear what they would vote for. Sanja recalls the hopes and fears that everyone had. As the Montenegrin politicians could not agree on the rules for the referendum, the EU decided that in order for Montenegro to become independent, 55 percent of the people were supposed to vote "Yes." Every vote was significant, and votes became an expression of identity. Those who called themselves Montenegrins would vote for independence; those identifying as Serbs would vote against it. Just like Branko and Jovan, the closest family members would vote differently. Her own uncle voted differently than her father. She never found out what her brother had voted for. A total of 55.5 percent of votes were cast for the independence of Montenegro, or 2,095 votes above the required threshold.

On June 3, 2006, Montenegro formally declared independence. What followed then was the building of the state, whose population remained divided along the Montenegrin-Serb lines. In practice, this division did not have many consequences on people's everyday lives. Sanja would still have friends who identified as Serb, Montenegrin, Bosniak, Albanian, or Croat. They would still speak to each other, hang out, and help each other out as they used to or fall in love with whoever they wanted to fall in love with. She was happy that nothing changed in the way they communicate, although they now spoke different languages.

The Montenegrin language was codified in 2010. It is the only post-Yugoslav language that changed its alphabet and now contains two more letters than those of Serbia, Croatia, and Bosnia. Sanja had to learn the Montenegrin language, just as she had to learn Serbian when Yugoslavia fell apart and Serbo-Croatian when she was a child. The way she speaks did not changed, despite the name of the language having changed twice. But Sanja is used to this kind of a change—a change where names, labels, and identities transform but everything else remains the same. Just as the city where she grew up changed its name from Titograd to Podgorica, just as the name and composition of the country in which lived changed not once but four times.

Notes

1. All names are pseudonyms.
2. Albright 1999.
3. Roberts 2002, 6.
4. European Stability Initiative 2007.
5. Zavod za Statistiku Crne Gore 2003.

References

Albright, Madeleine. 1999. "US Support for Democracy in Serbia and Montenegro." *Remarks at US-Serbian Opposition Meeting*. Berlin, December 17. Accessed June 10, 2010. https://1997-2001.state.gov/publications/dispatch/Dec1999.pdf.
European Stability Initiative. 2007. "A Short History of 'Solania.'" September. Accessed June 11, 2015. http://www.esiweb.org/index.php?lang=en&id=281&story_ID=10&slide_ID=8.
Roberts, Elizabeth, 2002. *Serbia-Montenegro—A New Federation?*, London: Conflict Studies Research Centre.
Zavod za Statistiku Crne Gore, 2003. *Population Census of Montenegro*. Accessed June 6, 2015. http://www.monstat.org/cg/page.php?id=57&pageid=57.

JELENA DŽANKIĆ is Research Fellow at the Robert Schuman Centre for Advanced Studies and coordinates the work of the EUI's Global Citizenship Observatory. She is author of *Citizenship in Bosnia Herzegovina, Macedonia and Montenegro: Effects of Statehood and Identity Challenges*.

21 War Criminals, National Heroes, and Transitional Justice in Macedonia

Vasiliki P. Neofotistos

Transitional Justice

Following the signing of the internationally brokered Ohrid Framework Agreement (OFA) that put an official end to the six-month armed conflict between the Albanian National Liberation Army (NLA) and Macedonian forces (both army and police) in the Republic of Macedonia in 2001, the International Criminal Tribunal for the former Yugoslavia (ICTY) in The Hague investigated, on the international community's request, several allegations of war crimes.[1] These alleged crimes included the murder of seven Albanian civilians, the serious beating of a group of Albanian civilians, and the deliberate and unprovoked destruction of property during an intense, three-day police operation in the mainly Albanian-populated village of Ljuboten, on Macedonia's northern border with Kosovo, in August 2001. For their roles in the events in Ljuboten, the then Minister of Interior Ljube Boškoski and Johan Tarčulovski, a man largely unknown to the public and leader of the police unit that entered the village, were indicted on charges of violations of the laws or customs of war. Cases of alleged war crimes reviewed by the ICTY also included the NLA Leadership case, in which ten individuals, including high-ranking Albanian officials in the Democratic Union for Integration (DUI), the largest Albanian political party in Macedonia, were suspected of belonging to the NLA leadership and of having partaken in a wide variety of crimes committed by NLA members; the Mavrovo Road Workers case, in which NLA members allegedly kidnapped, beat, and abused a group of five road workers; the Lipkovo Water Reserve case, in which NLA members allegedly shut off the city of Kumanovo's water source; and, the "Neprošteno" investigation, in which NLA members, including Daut Rexhepi, a former member of parliament from the Democratic Party of Albanians (DPA), were accused of allegedly kidnapping, killing, and burying twelve Macedonian civilians in a mass grave near the village of Neprošteno.

The ICTY's investigation into these allegations revealed the United Nations' emphasis on transitional justice—defined as "the full range of processes and mechanisms associated with a society's attempts to come to terms with a legacy of large-scale past abuses in order to ensure accountability, serve justice and achieve reconciliation"—that was widely shared among other international actors, such as NGOs and consultants working in the region.² There is an unstated assumption here that, following the end of a conflict, local actors make direct and concerted efforts to create a factual account of wrongdoings that transpired in the past as a means of restoring relations among all contending parties. Such efforts, however, are nonexistent in Macedonia, or at best they are inadequate in practice if one considers the work done by the Coalition for RECOM, an extra-judicial body established by the states on the territory of the former Yugoslavia and funded by donations, domestic and foreign, and by international organizations.³ Its stated goals include investigating all allegations of war crimes and other serious human rights violations committed from 1991 to 2001 and establishing the facts important for the history and the future of the region. Because RECOM pays attention to cooperation among hostile parties and shared acceptance of "the truth" about the past—values at the core of the transitional justice paradigm—it enjoys great international support. While RECOM's goals appear noble, and on the local level its advocates include a broad spectrum of people—from members of the political elite and government representatives to artists and writers—the prospects for its success are dubious. For instance, the campaign that began in April 2011 to collect one million signatures across the region by June of that year in support of the petition of the establishment of RECOM only succeeded in collecting a little over half a million. Also, with specific reference to Macedonia, RECOM's public advocate Biljana Vankovska resigned in January 2014, citing, among other reasons, obstacles to building a critical mass of supporters across ethnic boundaries, as well as accusations of nationalism leveled against her by extremist circles and media outlets due to her suggestions that some Macedonian high-ranking individuals be considered accountable for crimes committed during the 2001 conflict.⁴ Other efforts to come to terms with the violence perpetrated during the 2001 conflict do not at all involve cooperation between hostile parties, or ensuring that wrongdoers are held accountable. Members of Zora, the association of internally displaced Macedonians from the village of Aračinovo, for example, have persistently demanded that their status be resolved and have focused their energies on receiving reparations for lost or damaged property.

The lack of significant efforts to establish what happened and who committed wrongs during the 2001 conflict in Macedonia is indicative of a widespread belief that one's own ethnic community did not engage in any wrongdoing at all and only those in the "other" community committed abuses. Many Albanians believe that Macedonians have always treated the Albanian population as second-class citizens and that the response of the state to the NLA insurgency was disproportionate with a view to inflicting maximum harm on Albanian civilians, including women and children. For many Macedonians, on the other hand, Albanians enjoyed all rights a minority could possibly enjoy in any state, but were ungrateful and launched an attack against Macedonia's national sovereignty. Frustration with the international community's support of the Albanian demand for so-called greater rights in Macedonia, evinced by the improved position of

Figure 21.1. Men having tea at the Sloga Tea Place, where issues affecting the community are daily topics of conversation, in Skopje, 2010. Photograph by Roska Vrgova.

Albanians after the OFA, and a sense of national humiliation among Macedonians are further obstacles to developing initiatives that focus on dealing with Macedonia's violent past.

While both communities want justice at the current juncture, their objectives not only are widely divergent but also fall outside the transitional justice template emphasizing reconciliation. For Albanians, justice involves the full implementation of the OFA, including controversial constitutional and institutional reforms, but also the ethnically divisive issue of pensions and other benefits for the purpose of rehabilitation for NLA veterans who were wounded (or if killed, their families would receive the benefits) during the conflict. For Macedonians, despite the fact that the post-OFA amended constitution refers to Macedonia's population as "citizens of the Republic of Macedonia," justice involves recognition of an ethnic understanding of the nation, ingrained in the 1991 founding constitution—namely, recognition that Macedonia remains the national state of the Macedonian people and that Macedonians have the allegedly inalienable right to protect the state against all external and internal enemies—including the Albanian minority living in the state.

It is against the background of the lack of societal attempts to come to terms with past abuses committed against civilians during the 2001 conflict and of divergent understandings of justice in post-2001 Macedonia that ICTY intervention in what would otherwise be considered domestic legal affairs (individual prosecutions, truth seeking, and vetting and dismissals) has unfolded.

In what follows, I discuss the previously mentioned allegations of war crimes and the outcome of the investigation into these allegations. I also look at the various ways in which Macedonian and Albanian politicians and their supporters have responded to international intervention to satisfy their own needs and interests in the post-2001 political landscape. My goal is to shed light on the intersections between domestic politics and international judicial processes and structures and, importantly, on the ways such interactions render intelligible everyday experience in present-day Macedonia. I am particularly interested in the additional, significant strain (besides the strain imposed by national and regional politics) that international judicial intervention—despite the ICTY's declared goal to create the circumstances enabling reconciliation—places on ethnic relations at the group level and the ways that people deal with such strain.[5]

The Ljuboten Investigation

Immediately after the ICTY's indictment against Ljube Boškoski and Johan Tarčulovski was made public in March 2005, the Macedonian authorities obligingly arrested and transferred Tarčulovski to the tribunal's custody. Boškoski, a dual Macedonian-Croatian citizen who had fled to Croatia and was jailed there after being charged with involvement in the killing of seven South Asian migrants by Macedonian forces in 2004, was handed by Croatian authorities to The Hague. The two men stood trial in April 2007 for alleged war crimes committed in Ljuboten at their behest. In July 2008, the ICTY acquitted Boškoski on all charges and ordered him released from prison. Tarčulovski received a prison sentence of twelve years, including time spent in custody, but was granted early release for good behavior by the president of the tribunal in April 2013.

The then ruling VMRO–DPMNE (International Macedonian Revolutionary Organization–Democratic Party for Macedonian National Unity) government of Prime Minister Nikola Gruevski and right-wing, nationalist factions of the Macedonian population lent strong financial and moral support to the two men from the day of their arrest in 2005 until Tarčulovski was released from prison in 2013.[6] Specifically, the government provided guarantees on behalf of the accused, in case the accused were to be provisionally released, that it would ensure the appearance of the two men before court and the protection of victims, witnesses, and other persons involved in the proceedings. The government also covered costs associated with the trial, including court costs, fees for domestic and foreign lawyers, and travel expenses for the detained men's families. A delegation of VMRO–DPMNE ministers and members of parliament traveled to The Hague and was present in the courtroom when the verdicts were announced in 2008, while numerous supporters flooded the courtroom in 2010, when the Appeals Chamber of the ICTY dismissed the prosecution's appeal against Boškoski's acquittal as well as all grounds of appeal of Tarčulovski's defense, and again in 2013, when Tarčulovski's release was announced.

Following his acquittal in 2008, Boškoski flew on a government plane to Macedonia's capital, Skopje, where some of his supporters—wearing T-shirts with his photo and the slogan "Victory for Macedonia"—family members, and a government delegation led by then prime minister Gruevski greeted him at the airport and accompanied him to Skopje's main square. Several thousand supporters from around the country had already gathered at the square to participate in a public celebration of the acquittal of Boškoski, to cheer him as he appeared on stage to address them and to give him a hero's welcome. Similarly, but on a grander scale, Tarčulovski's arrival in Skopje in the spring of 2013 was celebrated by the prime minister, government officials, and several thousand supporters who gathered at the airport to welcome Tarčulovski in a euphoric atmosphere. The former policeman was then escorted downtown, laid a wreath at the monument to the dead of 2001, entered the main square through the newly constructed triumphal arch (Porta Macedonia), and attended festivities in his honor—including performances of pop and folk patriotic songs, fireworks, and paragliding—before he took to the stage to address a large crowd of people waving national flags and some waving flags depicting the images of Tarčulovski and Christ.

The public celebrations were organized by Macedonian citizens' associations for the support of Boškoski and Tarčulovski and were warmly endorsed by the government. Both men, but especially Tarčulovski—despite his conviction by the ICTY—were publicly portrayed and praised as men of noble character, willing to sacrifice their lives and personal freedom for the sake of the Macedonian nation, and admired for their alleged courage and achievements during the events that transpired in the village of Ljuboten in August 2001. Boškoski's acquittal and Tarčulovski's early release from prison were heralded as national triumphs and construed as proof that the international judicial system worked and justice had (eventually) been done. Their actions were depicted as morally right and appropriate in the circumstances of the conflict—and as internationally sanctioned—because Boškoski was acquitted and Tarčulovski got out of prison early. Therefore, the still popular view within the Macedonian community that it is the right of the Macedonian nation—defined exclusively in ethnic terms—to defend itself against external and internal aggressors, including Albanians living in the country, was validated. The social construction and celebration of heroes, as is usually the case, were thus political at heart. The then ruling party interpreted the ICTY rulings to its own advantage and used them as a springboard to increase its popularity and incite nationalist feelings at a time when Macedonian national pride had suffered a heavy blow due to the concessions the government had made in Ohrid.

Beyond satisfying political interests—and successfully at that, in light of the massive citizen mobilization and large attendance at the "welcome home" celebrations—the construction and celebration of Boškoski and Tarčulovski as heroes contributed to an accumulating sense of alienation from the state among Albanians and widened the rift between members of the country's two largest groups. For many Albanians, the two men whose actions were investigated by the ICTY were nothing but heinous individuals who had purposefully and with malicious forethought inflicted harm on innocent civilians during the 2001 conflict. Despite the passage of time, many of my Albanian interlocutors from various socioeconomic backgrounds have often described to me the two men as "criminals" (Albanian: *kriminelët*) during my numerous, post-2005 field visits to Macedonia. What is more, feelings of frustration and anger provoked by the triumphalism and perceived arrogance of the then ruling party and its supporters remain potent among Albanians and negative stereotypes against Macedonians as a group, such as their being an "artificial people" (*popull artificial*), have become stronger as a result.

The Cases Involving NLA Members

Like in the Ljuboten investigation, Macedonian authorities fully cooperated with the ICTY and deferred to the tribunal's competence the four cases related to alleged crimes committed by NLA members during the 2001 conflict. In February 2008, the ICTY Prosecutor's Office returned all four cases to Macedonian jurisdiction after then prime minister Gruevski had visited The Hague in September 2006 to discuss with ICTY president Fausto Pocar and Chief Prosecutor Carla del Ponte the return, acceptance, and processing of the cases. A domestic dispute ensued about whether these cases could be tried in Macedonia's national courts or dismissed under the 2002 Amnesty Law, which was passed by the Macedonian Parliament under significant international pressure a few days prior to an international donors' conference for Macedonia held in Brussels by the European Commission and the World Bank. According to this law, amnesty is granted when there is reasonable doubt as to the guilt of persons who are accused of allegedly having planned or committed criminal acts related to and in connection with the 2001 conflict—unless persons have committed criminal acts that are under the jurisdiction of the ICTY and for which the ICTY will initiate proceedings. Since the return of the four cases to Macedonia's national courts, the leaders of the two major Albanian political parties Menduh Thaci (DPA) and Ali Ahmeti (DUI) asserted that the ICTY had not initiated proceedings and thus the amnesty law had to be applied and the cases had to be dismissed. Ahmeti also warned that if the cases were not closed, ethnic grievances would be revived and the country could again become destabilized. For many Macedonians, including Macedonia's chief public prosecutor, Ljupco Svrgovski, the ICTY had initiated proceedings since it had assumed, albeit temporarily, jurisdiction over the four cases, and so the cases should be investigated to ensure that the Macedonian victims would be provided with access to justice.

The only case that ended up reaching Skopje's district court, the "Mavrovo Workers" case, was constantly delayed or postponed, mainly due to the absence of defendants. The "Lipkovo Water Reserve," "Neprošteno," and "NLA Leadership" cases were under consideration by, and awaiting the decision of, the Public Prosecutor. But before progress could be made on the "Mavrovo Workers" case and the remainder of the cases could come to court, in July 2011, after parliamentary elections had taken place and amid widespread speculation that The Hague cases were part of a deal between then prime minister Gruevski and DUI leader Ahmeti to form a coalition government, the Macedonian Parliament amnestied the four cases. Macedonian and Albanian government officials strategically used the international discourse on conflict resolution, reconciliation, and postconflict recovery and construed this move as an attempt to provide a sense of psychological closure and heal the wounds of the past, as well as an opportunity to move closer toward the restoration of friendly relations between Macedonians and ethnic Albanians.

The interpretation of the 2002 Amnesty Law in such a way that it could be applied to the four cases that were returned from the ICTY embittered and angered Macedonian opposition parties and their supporters, many of whom felt that access to justice for the Macedonian victims and their families had been blocked while the perpetrators of the crimes had been appeased. The relatives of the victims in particular, who had a strong emotional stake in the outcome of the cases, requested Macedonia's constitutional court to review and evaluate first, the constitutionality of the Amnesty Law and second, the constitutionality of the parliament's decision. The argument they put forth was that the government's decision was a breach of international humanitarian law, whereby cases of war crimes and crimes against humanity cannot be covered by amnesty and cannot expire as criminal act cases. The constitutional court decided in October 2012 unanimously and by a majority vote, respectively, to reject the two initiatives, thus in essence upholding the parliament's decision not to prosecute the four cases.

At the same time, many members of the Albanian community, politicians and laypeople alike, regarded the ICTY's decision to return the cases to Macedonian jurisdiction and the Parliament's decision to amnesty the cases and exempt the accused from criminal liability as strong evidence in support of the claims that NLA members, unlike members of the Macedonian community who allegedly were without morals, had not committed any criminal acts whatsoever during the 2001 conflict and had engaged in legitimate operations. The return and amnesty of these cases, what is more, strongly supported claims that justice should be administered to Albanians without delay and it should include state pensions and other benefits and privileges for NLA veterans. Such interpretations, especially with regard to the NLA leadership case, helped to boost the popularity of DUI among Albanian voters. The outcome of the cases also lent an aura of approval to commemorative celebrations in honor of the deceased NLA fighters, seen as heroes and martyrs of the nation, deserving pensions and other benefits of state retirees at lavish monuments and memorial complexes. Members of the Albanian community have been building these structures with financial support from DUI and the Albanian diaspora throughout the 2000s in northwestern Macedonia. The commemorations take place yearly and attract many former NLA insurgents and NLA sympathizers as well as friends and family members of the deceased, but to the bitter chagrin of the Macedonian community, given the widely differing viewpoints on the NLA's legacy between the two communities. Many Macedonians also often use such events as evidence to assert the accuracy of popular stereotypes against Albanians as "uncultured" (Macedonian: *nekulturni*) and "wild" (Macedonian: *divi*).

Everyday Life Despite It All

As Macedonia and its people are confronted with the events that transpired during 2001—killings, tortures, kidnappings, population displacement, and destruction of properties—international judicial intervention has consequences for the conduct of national politics and, in turn, for the intensification of stereotypes and the polarization between the Macedonian and Albanian communities. Macedonian and Albanian politicians and their supporters alike tend to use ICTY decisions related to the conflict and the legacies of violence as they see fit. Although the tribunal found Tarčulovski guilty of crimes and the four cases involving NLA members were never prosecuted, after they were returned to Macedonia, members of both communities acted according to their own political needs and interests at the time, proclaiming that justice with regard to past abuses, as members of each community viewed it, had been (in the case of Macedonians) or should legitimately be (in the case of Albanians) served, and increased each other's discontent.

Even though it aimed at advancing ethnic relations and contributing to a so-called lasting peace, international judicial intervention thus somewhat backfired. Increased tensions at the group level notwithstanding, people come to terms with the violent past in their own, creative ways and, in the process, protect everyday interpersonal relations across ethnic lines (for instance, in the market and at the workplace), as has often been the case in the history of Macedonia.[7] To this end, one of the tactics deployed is the evocation of the sharp and irreconcilable distinction between "politics," which is allegedly immoral, and "ordinary people," who are presumed to be disinterested in politics. The use of the distinction, common in other parts of the former Yugoslavia that suffered violence in the 1990s,[8] enables people to explain past abuses as the work of politics and cast themselves as ordinary people. This is not to suggest that everyone who evades discussions of the violent past is interested in protecting relations across ethnic boundaries. Some people choose not to broach the subject of the 2001 conflict because they find it too painful to relive their memories. When, for example, in the summer of 2011 I visited displaced Macedonian families from the village of Aračinovo who had moved into a student dormitory in Skopje, many people were too emotional to recount what had happened in their village, let alone to their houses, ten years earlier. Others told me that they would never want to restore relations with Albanians.

It is worth noting that avoidance of public discussion and debate of issues carrying social and political significance in local daily life, especially but not only as they pertain to interethnic relations, is becoming the hallmark of an increasingly volatile post-2001 Macedonian society. For example, after five Macedonians were killed near a lake on the outskirts of Skopje on Orthodox Easter in 2012, six Albanians were convicted on charges related to terrorism and sentenced

Figure 21.2. Macedonian and Albanian men talking in a market in Strumica, 2011. Photograph by Roska Vgova.

to life imprisonment, though it was unclear how terrorism charges were made (the full text of the Skopje Criminal Court verdict was not released). The convictions sparked angry protests with violent clashes between Albanian demonstrators and riot police. One Macedonian interlocutor, Vedrana, a well-educated woman working with an Albanian colleague in a travel agency in Skopje, echoed in the summer of 2012 a popular view among some Macedonians with Albanian friends or acquaintances that the court might have wanted to blame the killings on terrorism in order to "sweep things [inciting ethnic conflict] under the rug" (*da se zataškа rabota*). Vedrana also argued that the subject of the killings was out of bounds in her discussions across ethnic boundaries. Even those Macedonians who were less skeptical about the truthfulness of the terrorism charges and believed that justice had been served reproduced stereotypes in conversations with coethnics but otherwise avoided broaching the incident. For many Albanians, the terrorism charges were utterly unfounded, but they, too, kept away from discussion outside group boundaries.

All things considered, the goals of international judicial intervention, highlighting reconciliation over past events, are out of synchrony with local understandings of justice, foregoing such reconciliation, in postconflict Macedonia. In the meantime, international judicial intervention has consequences for the conduct of national politics, whereby political parties with a strong ethnic support base advocate the superiority of one ethnic group over the other and mobilize their constituents to advance their own interests, and also for the creation of parameters around what can be openly discussed and debated—parameters within which the reification of group stereotypes and the negotiation of daily life across ethnic boundaries take place. Everyday local life, thus, is not entirely constructed locally. Rather, it can be affected significantly and in unintended ways by international "structures of good intention," such as transitional justice.

Notes

1. The agreement is named after the resort town of Ohrid, where it was signed. For information about the ICTY, see http://www.icty.org/en/about (accessed March 13, 2017).
2. UN Secretary-General, *The Rule of Law and Transitional Justice in Conflict and Post-Conflict Societies: Rep. of the Secretary-General*, U.N. Doc. S/2004/616 (Aug. 23, 2004).
3. For more information about the Coalition for RECOM, including its reports, see http://www.recom.link (accessed March 13, 2017).
4. See http://blog.transnational.org/category/associates-by-name/biljana-vankovska/
5. See, for example, Danforth 1995.
6. I use the term *Macedonians* to indicate people of Macedonian origin living in Macedonia, and the phrase *ethnic Albanians* to indicate members of the Albanian community from, and/or living in, Macedonia.
7. See, for example, Neofotistos 2012.
8. See Kolind 2007.

References

Danforth, Loring M. 1995. *The Macedonian Conflict: Ethnic Nationalism in a Transnational World*. Princeton, NJ: Princeton University Press.

Kolind, Torsten. 2007. "Remembering with a Difference: Clashing Memories of Bosnian Conflict in Everyday Life." In *The New Bosnian Mosaic: Identities, Memories and Moral Claims in a Post-War Society*, edited by X. Bougarel, E. Helms, and G. Duijzings, 123–138. Aldershot: Ashgate.

Neofotistos, Vasiliki P. 2012. *The Risk of War: Everyday Sociality in the Republic of Macedonia*. Philadelphia: University of Pennsylvania Press.

VASILIKI NEOFOTISTOS is Associate Professor of Anthropology at the State University of New York at Buffalo. She is author of *The Risk of War: Everyday Sociality in the Republic of Macedonia*.

22 A Lively Border: Bosnia and Herzegovina and Serbia On the Shifting Banks of the Drina

Čarna Brković and Stef Jansen

The northern stretch of the border between Bosnia and Herzegovina and Serbia is formed by the Drina River—at least, that is what it looks like from a bird's-eye perspective. Yet when we zoom in on people's practical engagements with this border, in particular locations, things get complicated: the Drina River changes its position, multiple border signs are erected, and villagers living around the border make various claims to the two bordering states. This border, it turns out, is altogether "too lively" to be pinned down. In this chapter, we focus on the interplay of two dimensions of that liveliness. Geopolitically, the 1990s post–Yugoslav Wars period saw the upgrading of this border from one that demarcated federal units of the Socialist Federative Republic of Yugoslavia to one that demarcates two independent states; however, the precise border coordinates have not been ratified yet. Geophysically, its precise location is complicated by the unruly currents of the Drina, which eat away at the riverbanks and disturb any firm fixation.

To understand the unruliness of this border as the result of ethnonational relations levels out the complex interaction of its geopolitical and geophysical dimension and makes irrelevant everyday concerns and experiences that did not follow the ethnonational logic. Taking a road trip around this border, the chapter addresses such everyday concerns and experiences, exploring how they emerged from the tensions between the geopolitical and geophysical processes from the perspective of people whose livelihood and leisure practices have long incorporated both banks of the Drina.

Three Border Signs

It is 2010, and the road from Bijeljina to the Drina River, in the far northeast of Bosnia and Herzegovina, offers plenty of excitement. After shopping centers, attracting large crowds from across the state border with Serbia, we pass an ethno-village[1] with a modern hotel—with pool, gym, and sauna—in the shape of a medieval monastery. Not to be outdone, a private university a little farther is flanked by a pair of near life-size elephant statues. The mild disorientation we may feel after witnessing this is compounded by a much less spectacular sight: a brand-new sign on our right, welcoming us to the municipality of Bogatić, with the flag of Serbia fluttering above it. Nothing unusual about that, were it not for a disconcerting déjà vu a few hundred meters farther down the road. As we arrive at a bridge over the Drina River, we are checked by border police and customs officers of Bosnia and Herzegovina on one side and then by those of Serbia on the other. And then, there it is *again*: "Municipality of Bogatić. Welcome!" and a flag of Serbia. The Bogatić municipality is an administrative unit of the Republic of Serbia consisting of a set of villages on the east bank of the Drina. So it is no surprise that, for a number of years, there has been a sign like this just after the border check on the bridge. But why would anyone plant a *new* official welcome sign, with a state flag, a few hundred meters before an already existing one? Why confuse travelers who have not arrived at a state border yet by welcoming them into a municipality across that border?

The waiter in a nearby restaurant overlooking the Drina is not sure who placed the new preriver border sign there or why. The older men who take care of the restaurant's garden, he says, claim that the recent sign marks the correct location of the state border. *That*, they say, is where the border post should actually be. Some of the land near the bridge, on the west bank of the Drina, is owned by people from Badovinci, a village in the Bogatić municipality (Serbia). They used to cross the river in small boats to cultivate it. Nowadays they have to present their documents at the border posts either side of the bridge to get to this land, sometimes several times per day. This was particularly inconvenient for Badovinci farmers, creating administrative difficulties to transport their produce. In fact, long ago, perhaps centuries, some of this land used to be on the river's east bank but became the west bank over time. This is because the Drina's riverbed continuously changes and in this area, over time, it has been "eating away" arable land on the "Serbian" side and leaving ever increasing parts of land on the "Bosnian"[2] side. So, while according to international jurisprudence it is the middle of the Drina that would form the borderline, the shifting riverbed actually makes this a very unstable demarcation. People from Badovinci thus saw the new sign as a "correction" of the current marked location of the borderline at the bridge.

In fact, when stepping off the principal road onto an unpaved one that used to be the main road in this area until 1990, when this bridge was privately constructed by the same couple who own the elephant-flanked university, we find yet another sign. This one, worn and weathered, reads, "Municipality of Bogatić. K.O. Badovinci."[3] People living around here say this sign was put up in the 1980s, marking the administrative boundary between Bijeljina and Bogatić, two municipalities that were, at the time, part of two different republics within the Socialist Federative Republic of Yugoslavia. Even so, to most people in Yugoslavia who were unfamiliar with the local situation, it was the Drina that formed the border between Bosnia and Herzegovina and Serbia in this region. The river had been a border for long periods before that too, in the time of the Ottoman and Habsburg Empires. In the late socialist Yugoslavia that people remembered, the republics

Figure 22.1 a and b. The image on the left represents a trace from the socialist era—a sign marking the former administrative boundary between the municipalities of Bijeljina and Bogatić, and thus the former inter-republican border, which people from the area could recognize from their embodied memories. In the image on the right, we see a sign welcoming people to the municipality of Bogatić. It is located a few hundred meters before the river, the official check point; an almost identical sign appears on the Serbian side of the bridge. Located on the inter-republican border from the socialist era, it was erected to make claims to state bureaucracy, 2010. Photographs by Čarna Brković.

had had great autonomy within the common state, but the borders between them were not policed or even marked.

It was in the early 1990s that this interrepublican border was upgraded to a border between two states: Bosnia and Herzegovina and Serbia. The most popular political party at the first multiparty elections among people in Bosnia and Herzegovina identified as Serbs, SDS (Serbian Democratic Party, or *Srpska demokratska stranka*), together with the government of Serbia, mobilized people to fight this. In Bijeljina, this struggle involved massacres by paramilitaries and the expulsion of virtually all non-Serbs, especially people identified as Bosniaks, who had constituted a majority of the population in the town.[4] The 1995 Dayton Peace Agreement that brought an end to the military violence did recognize the upgrading of the border, but it also consolidated *intra*-state borders that approximately followed former frontlines and legalized wartime conquest into "entities." So, within the state of Bosnia and Herzegovina, Bijeljina is part of the entity Republika Srpska (Serbian Republic), not to be confused with the neighboring state Republic of Serbia. To this day, Bosnia and Herzegovina's internal borders remain more significant in the everyday lives of most of its inhabitants than the interstate border with Serbia.[5] SDS continues to dominate Bijeljina politics and many of its inhabitants still feel little connection with Bosnia and Herzegovina as a state. And even regardless of anyone's preferences on territorial politics, people in Bijeljina live in a setting where political muscle and the provision of services is concentrated in the "entities."[6]

Where Is the Border? Maps and Embodied Memories

The appearance of the new sign welcoming travelers to the municipality of Bogatić under a flag of Serbia, well before the bridge, made the precise location of the state border into a topic of conversation. Where is the border, really? If it is common to think of "the Drina" as the border, where does that locate it if the river itself moves about? To which state do the (dis)appearing river banks belong? Government documents did not give a definite answer, because negotiations to fix the coordinates of the borderline between Bosnia and Herzegovina and Serbia had so far been unsuccessful. Relying on his scientific education, Nikola, a physics student from Belgrade, the capital of Serbia, claimed that the Drina was taking away parts of the east (Serbian) bank, adding to the west (Bosnian) one. The Coriolis force,[7] he argued, made the opposite impossible. Yet local people relied on a different kind of knowledge. In contrast to Nikola, Zoran, a thirty-year-old man who had been living in Bijeljina most of his life, explained that the Drina was constantly moving, eating away parts of the *Bosnian* side and, consequently, widening the Serbian bank. He recounted his memories of a beach on the west side where he used to swim as a boy and celebrate the first of May.[8] That beach, he said, no longer existed; it had been "eaten away" by the Drina. In that way, Zoran offered knowledge that emerged from excursions, walks, childhood play—in brief, from his personal involvement in this environment. Using this space through his body over time, he had accumulated "embodied knowledge" of the Drina's shores.

A man from the *mjesna zajednica* (local community)[9] in Badovinci, on the other side, also relied on his personal, embodied memories. He knew, he said, up to one meter's precision where the old Yugoslav administrative border between the republics had been, although there were no formal landmarks here except the 1980s sign. This man recalled that once long ago, on a hunt, he crossed this border by a few steps and was acutely aware that he had trespassed into another hunting county (the boundaries of which coincided with the administrative border between the Yugoslav republics). Very soon, he was stopped by hunting police and required to justify his crossing of this unmarked "line." In this way, many local people had intimate knowledge of the location of the border at one particular *section* of a particular river bank, where they had spent much time hunting, swimming, or walking or where their family had a house or land.

The mjesna zajednica members of Badovinci mobilized such knowledge to support their pleas to the Bosnian and Serbian governments for a "correction" to the border post location. They even produced a map for this purpose. Yet it was not only people from Badovinci who decided to intervene in the making of this border on the basis of their practical engagements with and intimate knowledge of the Drina's unruly meanderings. A mirror difficulty concerning the location of the border occurred in Janja, a large village to the south of Bijeljina. People from Janja, too, said that the Drina had moved over time. They, too, have been using the Drina's banks for leisure activities, as well as for fishing and harvesting, for a very long time. But here, they said, like Zoran, it ate away parts of the *west* bank, which, over time, left some of their land on the east bank.

In the 1980s, people from Janja had used a small ferry service to get to that land. During the war, in 1994, all inhabitants identified as Bosniaks—many of whom favored the upgrading of the border that would make Bosnia and

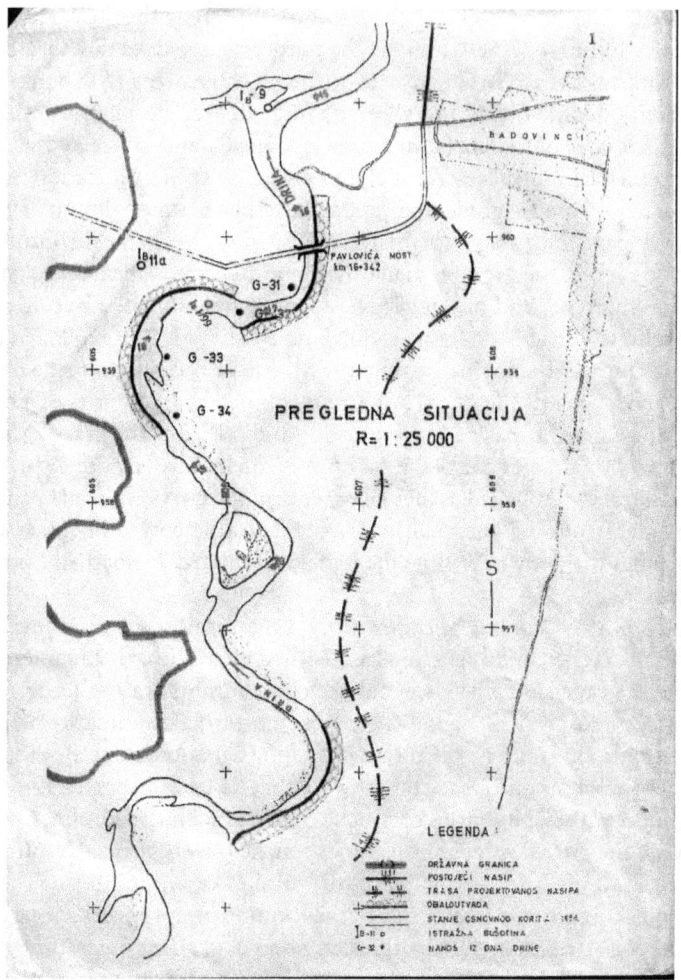

Figure 22.2. The image indicates the shifting location of the Bosnian-Serbian border on different scales. The map was used by people from Badovinci (Serbia) to represent the location of the border (the meandering line at the very left) in relation to the river Drina. It also shows Pavlovića Most, the bridge across the river, with official border checkpoints, 2010. Photograph by Čarna Brković.

Herzegovina into an independent state—were forced to leave. This was almost the entire population. Many of their houses were then occupied by people identified as Serbs, who had fled the violence in other parts of Bosnia and Herzegovina. After 2000, Janja became the only local community in the municipality of Bijeljina where substantial numbers of displaced persons returned. People identified as Bosniaks now formed the majority there again. Yet as so many returnees, they found themselves in a place that had changed much. The ferry service, for one, disappeared during the war. And now that the Drina also constitutes an official interstate border, they are no longer allowed to use their own launches. Instead, in order to reach their land across the river, until recently they had to make a detour of some sixty kilometers via the nearest official border crossing (another bridge to the south). Some of them risked crossing the river in private boats, hoping that the border police would not catch them on such illegal trips. The members of the Janja mjesna zajednica pleaded with the authorities to open a border crossing point for exclusive use by local residents, and in 2010, they received a positive reply. A ferry crossing was officially opened two years later. Demands to demarcate the border several hundred meters into the territory of Serbia, so that it would encompass their land on the east bank, had to wait, just like the similar demands of the people from Badovinci—namely, this is a matter to be decided by the interstate commission established by the governments of Bosnia and Herzegovina and Serbia to agree on the coordinates of the entire stretch of the borderline. People in Janja and in Badovinci should not hold their breath, as the members of this commission have rarely met over the years. Yet life must go on.

Where exactly is the border, if the neighboring municipality—part of another state—begins in at least two, perhaps three, different places? At the border, the territory of one state ends and that of another begins. On the scale of maps and interstate agreements, this seems straightforward enough. On a different scale, people may experience borders in terms of personal knowledge of people and places: they do not just look at it from a bird's-eye view but engage with it from their position on the surface of the earth, as persons moving about in specific locations and pursuing specific life projects. So how are those scales of the border related? One way to think of that question is to focus on how people's everyday routines transgress "official" borders: how their practices can never be captured entirely in official state-related categories. Another way to approach it is to ask how people's engagement reflects state images of borders, how they act in tune with them and invest in them. But do these two routes of investigation help us understand how people from Janja and Badovinci became engaged in efforts to pin down the border on particular coordinates? Ultimately, we suggest, both of these approaches share the same basis: they privilege questions of territorial claims and ethnonationality.

Making Claims to State Bureaucracy

This is nothing new. Disputes about the precise topographical coordinates of borders are often seen through the prism of conflicts between states, and especially of ethnonationalist claims. When the new "Welcome to Bogatić" sign appeared, with its flag of Serbia prominently displayed, this was precisely how it was taken up in the media. A short-lived flurry of reporting erupted in Bosnia and Herzegovina, in Serbia, and even in neighboring Croatia, and some politicians were quick to jump at the occasion to try to score some electoral points. Since the war, most people living on both sides of the Drina perceived themselves in ethnonational terms—as Serbian—and criticized the very existence of this border because it, as they saw it, divided "brothers."[10] Others vehemently objected. In this way, this case was slotted into a broader genre of "ethnonationalist" talk about post-Yugoslav borders, touching also on other complications at the southern stretch of the Bosnia and Herzegovina-Serbia border and at the northern and southern stretches of the Bosnia and Herzegovina-Croatia one. Other commentators, critical of ethnonationalism, presented it as just one more case of the absurd inflexibility of projects to draw precise "nation-state" borders. We saw how, on one level, the post–Yugoslav wars did indeed revolve around the presence or absence, and on the relative status, of borders between polities. Many fascinating anthropological studies have elaborated on such cases to critically analyze the ethnonationalist logics of the making of borders and their (in)significance in people's lives in places all over the world.[11] Yet, as we show here, borders can also become matters of concern in another order altogether.

Had the decision to put up the new sign come from the government in Serbia or in Bosnia and Herzegovina, or even in the entity of Republika Srpska, it would clearly be a case of interstate (mis)communication and, possibly, involve ethnonationalist claims. Instead, embodied memories of the border area as a particular place, and practical questions of livelihood and everyday routines, drove people from Badovinci to put up the new sign in the "correct" spot to the west of the current border post. In Janja, too, such concerns were key in their plea to the authorities for a local border crossing. They remembered how, once, they had simply crossed the river rather than make a sixty-kilometer detour to get to their land. In both cases personalized relationships with places *did* intertwine with official state classifications, but this cannot be grasped as either transgression of or investment in territorial politics. Nor was ethnonationalism key. Intimate and embodied knowledge on the one hand and the logic of statehood on the other *jointly* created the experience of this border among local people. And both shaped their attempted intervention. Through the mjesna zajednica, villagers set out to "correct" the location of the border or to demand an extra border crossing, relying on their personal, practical engagement with places. For those in Badovinci and in Janja, this engagement had been reshaped by the continuous movement of the Drina, by the upgrading to a state border during the 1990s, and, in some cases, by their own war-related movement in and out of the area.

Thus, locals attempted to shape the border in accordance with their embodied memories and everyday life projects. And it was in *that* way that they linked up their concerns with the workings of the state: rather than seeking to stake claims in the order of state territory and nation, they sought to mobilize the bureaucratic apparatus of state provision to facilitate the movements that shaped some important routines in their lives. In other words, they tried to make their claims to state bureaucracy by doing what (in their opinion) it should have done. To make the border on the map compatible with the one of their embodied memories and senses of entitlement, many elements of different orders came together: hunting expeditions, a map, missing beaches, houses and arable land, a new sign, a flag, an old and a new ferry, a local crossing. As indicated on the map from the mjesna zajednica of Badovinci, people thus combined an aerial perspective with one based in practice on the surface. But they knew states only acknowledge claims in their own language, and the sign, the map, and the flag thus played a particular role: through them, people hoped that their concerns would be recognized by state officials in Bosnia and Herzegovina, in Serbia, and beyond.

Notes

1. An ethno-village (*etno selo*) is a form of a live museum and a tourist complex that presents elements of rural folk architecture, cuisine, music, clothes, and so on to interested visitors.
2. Following local use, we use the term *Bosnian* as short for "Bosnian-Herzegovinian."
3. K.O. stands for "Katarska Opština," a unit of cadastral administration in the Socialist Federative Republic of Yugoslavia.
4. Human Rights Watch 2000.
5. Jansen 2008, 2011, 2015.
6. Brković 2016.
7. The Coriolis force is "an apparent force . . . exerted on circulating air and water (or any other moving object) when the motion is evaluated relative to the rotating Earth as a frame of reference. . . . The orientation of Coriolis force has the effect of deflecting motion to the right in the Northern Hemisphere and to the left in the Southern Hemisphere, with the observer facing the direction of the original motion" (Druyan 1996, 205–207).
8. May 1, International Workers' Day, was a holiday in Yugoslavia and remains an official holiday. Many people use it for excursions to mountains, forests, or beaches to barbecue, play games, eat, drink, and generally socialize.
9. An official organ of local self-government.
10. This reference to conationals as brothers is a good example of how nationality is often framed through gendered kinship terms.
11. Bowman 2003, Green 2005.

References

Bowman, Glenn. 2003. "Constitutive Violence and the Nationalist Imaginary: Antagonism and Defensive Solidarity in 'Palestine' and 'Former Yugoslavia.'" *Social Anthropology* 11 (3): 37–58.
Brković, Čarna. 2016. "Scaling Humanitarianism: Humanitarian Actions in a Bosnian Town." *Ethnos* 81 (1): 99–124.
Druyan, Leonard M. 1996. "Coriolis Force." In *Encyclopedia of Climate and Weather*, edited by H. S. Schneider, 205–207. 2nd edition. Oxford: Oxford University Press.
Green, Sarah. 2005. *Notes from the Balkans: Locating Marginality and Ambiguity on the Greek-Albanian Border*. Princeton, NJ: Princeton University Press.
Human Rights Watch. 2000. "Bosnia and Herzegovina. Unfinished Business: The Return of Refugees and DPs to Bijeljina." *Human Rights Watch Report* 12 (7).
Jansen, Stef. 2008. "Troubled Locations: Return, the Life Course and Transformations of 'Home' in Bosnia-Herzegovina." In *Struggles for Home: Violence, Hope and the Movement of People*, edited by S. Jansen and S. Löfving, 43–64. Oxford: Berghahn.

Jansen Stef. 2011. "*Refuchess*: Locating Bosniac Repatriates after the War in Bosnia-Herzegovina." *Population, Space and Place* 17 (2): 140–152.
Jansen, Stef. 2015. *Yearnings in the Meantime: "Normal Lives" and the State in a Sarajevo Apartment Complex*. Oxford: Berghahn.

ČARNA BRKOVIĆ is Lecturer in Cultural Anthropology and European Ethnology at the University of Göttingen. She is author of *Managing Ambiguity: How Clientelism, Citizenship and Power Shapes Personhood in Bosnia and Herzegovina* and coeditor of *Negotiating Social Relations in Bosnia and Herzegovina: Semiperipheral Entanglements*.

STEF JANSEN is Professor of Social Anthropology at the University of Manchester. He is author of *Yearnings in the Meantime: "Normal Lives" and the State in a Sarajevo Apartment Complex* and coeditor of *Negotiating Social Relations in Bosnia and Herzegovina: Semiperipheral Entanglements*.

23 "Politicians Are All Crooks!": Everyday Politics in Bulgaria

Emilia Zankina

Politics in Bulgaria is eventful and in some ways even unique. Between 2013 and 2014, Bulgaria witnessed continued political instability and public discontent: mass protests toppled two governments; two early parliamentary elections failed to produce a stable majority in parliament; and four governments (two of which were caretaker) struggled to address pressing issues in the energy, banking, and social sectors, resulting in inconsistent policy and reform efforts. Despite continued EU monitoring, Bulgaria continues to struggle with endemic corruption (the highest among EU member states)[1] and a dysfunctional judicial system.

The early years of the transition were in no way any better. Bulgaria went through nine governments between 1990 and 1997 and was one of the two countries where the former communists won the first free elections (the other being Romania). Bulgaria is also the country where a former king was elected prime minister, who subsequently formed a coalition with the very same party that dethroned him.[2]

This chapter attempts to make sense of politics in Bulgaria by looking at the political engagement and attitudes of ordinary Bulgarians. How do Bulgarians view politics and politicians? Is politics a significant part of their everyday life and to what extent does it impact them? How much and in what way do Bulgarians engage politically and what are the main motivations behind their political action or inaction? Are new generations different than generations raised under communist rule in their political behavior and outlook? Following a brief account of political developments and political engagement in postcommunist Bulgaria, the chapter makes use of focus group research to address these questions.

Political Dynamics in Bulgaria Following the Collapse of Communism

Among the countries of eastern Europe, Bulgaria was known as the most trusted Soviet ally (twice applying to become the USSR's sixteenth republic) and the country that most closely replicated the Soviet model of one-party rule, a centrally planned economy, nationalization of property, collectivization

Figure 23.1. A protester in Sofia with a sign reading: "I am not paid [to protest]. I hate you for free." The summer 2013 protests (pictured here) against the BSP-MRF coalition government lasted for over a year, ultimately leading to the resignation of the government and early elections in October 2014. Photograph by Rositsa Gradeva.

of agriculture, and control over cultural and social life. Bulgaria was also the country with the longest-standing communist dictator, Todor Zhivkov, who held power for thirty-five years, until the very end of communist rule. Furthermore, Bulgaria experienced a very weak, belated, and poorly organized dissident movement that did not pose serious challenges to the regime. This is not to undermine the heroic acts of Bulgarian dissidents but to establish the fact that Bulgarian dissidence never reached a mass following that could be compared to the 1956 Hungarian Revolution, the 1968 Prague Spring, or the 1980 Polish Solidarity movement.

Given these circumstances, it is no surprise that Bulgaria emerged from communist rule with a very strong *nomenklatura* elite and a weak and poorly organized opposition. Bulgaria was one of the two countries where the former communist party, renamed to the Bulgarian Socialist Party (BSP), won the first democratic elections. Bulgaria was also the only county to start the transition with a constitutional assembly whose main task was the drafting of a new constitution—a process that took a lot of time and energy away from more immediate concerns and one that was dominated by the former communists who held a majority in the first democratically elected parliament.

Politics in the 1990s were characterized by a power struggle between the former communists (BSP) and the democratic opposition (the Union of Democratic Forces, UDF), with outcomes often being determined by a third actor—the ethnic Turkish party, the Movement for Rights and Freedoms (MRF), which would strategically ally with one side or the other, often determining political outcomes. This "regularized" switch of power was combined with unprecedented economic decline and great political instability that resulted in nine governments in the first seven years of the transition and a banking and financial crisis coupled with hyperinflation of over 300 percent in 1996. Lack of effective lustration policies further solidified the position of the former *nomenklatura*, deprived the population from knowing the truth and coming to terms with the past, and fed various conspiracy theories about the role of the former secret service.[3] In addition, the lack of open access to the secret service files made it possible for numerous manipulations vis-à-vis *kompromat*,[4] which would pop up throughout the years, especially around election times. More importantly, the debate around lustration and the secret service continues without any prospects of "settling the score," as was done in other eastern European countries.

The bipolar political model, as Bulgarian scholars and politicians refer to this period,[5] rested on the main division/cleavage within society at the time—that between former communists and anticommunists.[6] Traditional labels of Left and Right had little applicability in the Bulgarian context, where the Left came to be dominated by the former communist party, hence, symbolizing the status quo and the old regime. The Right, in turn, was the only available ideological space for party competition. In the first years, it was represented by an umbrella organization, the UDF, which consisted of an ideological mish-mash—from a green party to a republican party, with anticommunism being the only unifying element. This ideological incongruence, coupled with the domination of the Left by the former communists, would eventually lead to the complete disintegration of the Right in the following decade, with numerous internal splits, regroupings and new actors, all of whom were competing on the Right; all new parties claimed to be right or center right on the political spectrum with none identifying on the left. Aside from the BSP, which relied on its communist-era structures, parties were of the elite type, having little grounding in society—they hardly represented voters' preferences and did not enjoy large membership. Party organizations were weak with no stable internal procedures either for recruitment or nomination of candidates. Government policy in that period was changing direction with every new government and switching back and forth between the decommunization agenda and shock therapy of the UDF and BSP's gradualism approach and forgive-and-forget rhetoric. The result was low trust in political parties and mass disillusionment both with the BSP and the UDF.

After a decade of political instability and economic hardship, Bulgarians were overcome by transition fatigue, disillusioned with politicians, and impatient with the democratic process.[7] They were looking for a savior. It was at this moment that the former king Simeon II of Saxe-Cobourg-Gotha made his precipitous appearance. Exiled by the newly established communist regime in 1946 at the age of nine, Simeon ultimately settled in Spain, becoming the symbol of the lost monarchy and Bulgaria's brief precommunist experience with democracy in the interwar period. He returned to Bulgaria in 2001, several months before the parliamentary elections to form a party that scored an unexpected victory with 43 percent of the votes and proceeded to head a coalition government. His return to Bulgarian politics abruptly did away with the bipolar political model, marking the birth of populism in postcommunist Bulgarian politics and legitimizing the personalist party model.[8] Following Simeon's unprecedented success, many parties and leaders adopted the populist/personalist formula, which led to a fragmented and unstable party system marked by internal divisions, regroupings, and political nomadism. The nationalist ATAKA (Attack) Party made it to parliament in 2005, and in 2009, replicating Simeon's success,[9] the newly formed populist GERB (Citizens for European Development) won the elections. This trend of new parties riding on big promises had an effect on voting behavior as well. Voters became less mature in their choices, continuously looking for the next savior, and less patient with government performance, ousting incumbent governments and frequently switching party affiliations. The 2008 global economic crisis also led to increased nationalist sentiments and rising Euroscepticism. Recent years have been even more volatile, with three early elections between 2013 and 2017, no viable majorities in parliament, and a total of five governments.

But there have been some positive developments as well. Despite a prolonged transition, Bulgaria ultimately joined NATO and the EU, though not with the first wave of eastern enlargement. EU membership has had a disciplining effect on Bulgarian politicians and institutions and a very positive effect in terms of economic development. Twenty-five years after the fall of communism, Bulgaria is no longer a gray and forgotten place but a "successful laggard," as some have termed it,[10] and a member of the rich countries' club.

Political Engagement

Political engagement during communism was forced and regimented, described as reluctant participation in ritualistic acts of public dissimulation.[11] The regime mandated active political participation through membership in the Communist Party or its subsidiary organizations and participation in various party-organized activities, from manifestations[12] to party meetings at the working place and place of residence. Children were also mobilized at an early age, being organized in various youth communist organizations and fed with communist ideology. On the other hand, any political activity that was not mandated by the regime was strictly prohibited and harshly persecuted. Elections did take place, but they consisted of casting the only available ballot—that of the Communist Party.

Following the collapse of communism and the end of political repression, political participation reached its peak. The first free elections registered voter activity of over 90 percent. There were frequent demonstrations, marches, and strikes, gathering people in the thousands. Opposition parties were building a

Table 23.1. Voter turnout at parliamentary elections (in percentages)

1990	1991	1994	1997	2001	2005	2009	2013	2014	2017
90.30	83.87	75.23	58.87	**66.63**	55.76	**60.64**	52.49	48.66	**54.07**

Source: Bulgarian Central Electoral Commission (www.cik.bg).

*In bold: voter turnout results in years when populist parties won the elections and an increase in voter turnout compared to previous election was observed.

membership body, whereas the former communist party experienced a sharp drop in membership as a large portion of its members reverted to the opposition. The excitement gradually subsided as subsequent governments failed to bring about economic reform and ensure political stability. Disillusionment turned into apathy, leading to a decrease in voter turnout, reaching a record low of 48.66 percent in the 2014 elections, and slightly increasing in the 2017 elections (see table 23.1). Decreasing voter activity has been attributed to transition fatigue and disillusionment with corrupt politicians. It has also been the source of great concern, posing questions of democratic deficit, effect of vote buying, and legitimacy of the political establishment. As a result, obligatory voting was discussed in parliament in 2015 and a referendum was held in 2016, with 62.00 percent of those who voted supporting mandatory voting.

Party membership is not common among Bulgarians: in 2006, only 3.5 percent of the voting population held membership in a party.[13] Before the collapse of communism, the Bulgarian Communist Party had a membership of 1 million from an 8 million population. The high number, however, was a function of the fact that the party was the main avenue for professional development. Currently, party members of all parties combined number 350,000, and the membership of the former communists (BSP) has shrunk to under 150,000. The early opposition barely gathers 20,000 members today, whereas new parties such as GERB attract about 80,000.[14] Overall, parties have adopted a strategy of voter mobilization around elections, not relying as much on membership. Populist parties, such as the NDSV in 2001 and GERB in 2009, have managed to mobilize voters more effectively, resulting in a slight increase in voter activity. At the same time, the success of populist parties has been coupled with an increased share of undecided voters at the expense of a decrease of loyal supporters for any party. This has led to great political instability and unpredictability of political processes, as with every new election a new populist party appears, attracting a portion of the undecided electorate.

Protest voting has been the norm in Bulgaria. Bulgarians do not vote governments in, they vote them out. For the twenty-five years of free elections, no single party has been able to win elections and form a government twice in a row. In addition, the electorate has become more and more fragmented, which has also resulted in a more fragmented parliament (there were eight political formations in the 2014–2017 parliament), greater difficulty in forming government coalitions, and, therefore, political instability.

Figure 23.2. A student from the Faculty of Journalism and Mass Communication at Sofia University holding a sign quoting the famous Bulgarian revolutionary poet Hristo Botev. The poem, published in 1870 and titled "Elegy," opens with "Tell me, tell me, o unhappy people, Who lulls you in the cradle of slavery?" and refers to the inaction of the Bulgarian people and their failure to fight the oppressor. The reference hints that corruption exists today, because the Bulgarian people put up with it, 2013. Photograph by Rositsa Gradeva.

Bulgarians do not have a culture of protest or at least not to the extent that the French, for example, have. There have been three waves of political protests since the fall of communism. The first wave followed the collapse of the communist regime. Those were the most massive and inspired protests unleashing long-repressed political energy. The second wave of protests was triggered by the 1996 severe banking and financial crises and led to the resignation of the BSP government. These protests truly mark a break point in Bulgarian politics. They put an end to inconsistent foreign and domestic policy by bringing about the first government to fulfill its four-year mandate and decisively reorient the country toward the Euro-Atlantic partnership. The last wave of protests was the longest, lasting almost uninterruptedly from February 2013 to September 2014. It included anti- and pro-government protests, making political and economic demands. The global economic crisis and endemic corruption were the main triggers of the protests. This last wave also showed a different culture of protesting and organizing. Protesters effectively used social networks to organize and invented creative ways of protest, including improvised performances and enactments, masks, symbols, and more. The protests further evolved into a number of civil society organizations with genuine links to society.

Until the latest wave of protests, civil society organizing has been rather week. For over a decade, civil society organizations were financed externally and promoted an imported agenda.[15] As a result, grassroots organizations were slow to emerge, leaving the third sector largely divorced from domestic constituencies and concerns. The latest wave of protests has had a very positive effect on grassroots organizing. Civil society organizations have reached deeper in the population and have started to forward agendas dictated from below.

Increasing civil society mobilization, however, is coupled with an ever-decreasing voter turnout. This speaks of a wider gap between social strata and the various ways in which these strata engage politically, as well as of ever greater doubts about the ability of common people to influence political outcomes. Politics is largely understood by Bulgarian constituencies as a complex yet not always honorable business that can hardly be influenced by common people.[16]

Political Generations and Their Attitudes toward Politics

Like most postcommunist societies, Bulgaria is struggling to come to terms with its communist past. Socialist nostalgia is on the rise, producing contested readings of the communist era, the democratic transition, and current realities alike.[17] Such nostalgia is but one form of expression of political attitudes, which starkly differ among former communists and anticommunists and winners and losers of the transition. In addition, there is a generational divide. Such a divide would be normal in any context, except for the fact that in Bulgaria different generations were politically socialized under different regime types.[18] This allows us to question what the effect of communist rule and indoctrination on current political attitudes is—or, in other words, to examine the effect of the communist legacy. To gage this legacy and the generational effect, I conducted focus group research. Two groups of ten to fifteen people were composed, one consisting of young people ages eighteen to thirty and one of people age fifty and above. The younger group included mostly students but also unemployed and working young adults, all of whom were born in the last years of communist rule or after its collapse. The older group included employed, self-employed, and unemployed people who lived and worked under communism and who, as the research revealed, have diametrically opposed political views. The groups were asked similar general questions, leaving participants to freely debate their political views and opinions.

The Young

The young group demonstrated a very vague understanding of political processes, democracy, and democratic institutions—something that is not unusual for young people anywhere. At the same time, such superficial understanding is coupled with democratic values and a very pronounced sense of civic duty.

"One must vote" agreed every participant in the group and indeed every one of them did vote. "You have a duty toward society even when society does not give back what you expect," stated another participant. This group also demonstrated great tolerance toward diverging opinions and an understanding that those need to be respected. In that regard, young people seem to be much more aware of the "social" in all of its aspects than the old, as seen in the older respondents. Although their "technical" knowledge of politics is poor or lacking, their normative understanding of democracy is not.

The group was very unconfrontational and conformist in its discussions. Participants seemed to agree on everything, using a lot of clichéd phrases, and did not seem to have strong opinions. As it turned out, they favored different political parties but did not argue over their different views. This is perhaps because they were united in their disappointment with politics and politicians in general. "Our politicians are laughable," said one participant. "They are corrupt, but moreover incompetent. Not like Western politicians."

Overall, the view of politicians and the political system is very critical. The political system is ill-conceived—we need a blank ballot option in order to express disagreement with all parties and we need experts, not parties, to govern. The idea of expert governance was broadly discussed among this group. Although none could articulate what a party-less system would look like, all considered this to be a realistic alternative and a question of finding the right formula. Politicians, in turn, cannot be trusted. They are "crooks" pursuing their own interests. It does not really matter who is in power; they are all the same.

This combination of outright disgust with politics and politicians on the one hand and a sense of democratic duty on the other, leads to a peculiar type of political engagement. Among the participants in the group, all vote and all practice protest voting, none are members of a party, and most participated in the summer 2013 protests. This speaks of distrust in politicians, but belief in the democratic process. The results are a constant comparison with the West and resorting to individual strategies of survival. "Being politically engaged in a 'normal' country [i.e., in the West], makes sense, but here it does not," stated one participant. Yet they do engage politically and much more so than the older group.

By and large, the young view politics as something happening on the side and not directly affecting their everyday lives. There is an understanding that politics has some effect on them, especially in the economic realm, but such understanding is not internalized. All participants were convinced that their individual strategies would determine their future and that they can be successful despite the corrupt government and politicians. At the same time, they kept reciting memorized arguments that "political processes are a function of economic interests"—no doubt a view adopted from their parents and very much resonating with Marxists indoctrination. Low income and unchanged mentality were repeatedly pointed out as the main reasons for weak institutions and effective governance, yet somehow they felt they could get around that on their own.

The young group exhibited a superficial and inconsistent understanding of politics, yet a commitment to democratic values. Though disappointed with politics and politicians, none demonstrated extremist views or sought revenge. They envision a system that would allow them to pursue their goals but not a paternalistic state that would provide for them. Despite residual Marxist overtones in their views, this generation has clearly broken with the communist past, viewing themselves as the crafter of their futures and not blaming the state or politicians for individual failures; this is a view very different from the one exhibited from the older generation.

The Old(er)

The words that best describe the older group are bitter, cynical, and skeptical. They have a very good understanding of political processes and the various elements of democratic governance. Yet they continue to view politics in Marxist terms—that is, economic interests dominate politics—and are skeptical at best about democracy. They understand democracy cannot function without political parties, yet they harbor extreme antiparty sentiments. They acknowledge the need for radical reform, but disagree on what this reform should entail. They trust no one and hate all, yet they expect someone to come and sort it all out—someone else, not them. They seem to be torn between the democratic discourse and the years of communist indoctrination and propaganda.

Like the young, the older group has a very critical view of politicians and the political system. There is a general disillusionment with democratic politics and a sense of "lost years" and "life robbed of social safety nets"—the system does not deliver. Politicians, in turn, are viewed as people who have failed professionally and therefore resorted to politics. The elite is of low quality, they say.

The old are disillusioned with politics, and therefore apathetic and passive. Most have stopped voting, despite previous, and in some cases even current, party membership. They are cynical about political action. The protests, they are convinced, were not spontaneous and genuine. They were staged by political parties who were paying people to protest. Though this is not untrue, as there were paid protesters from all sides in the 2013–2014 wave of protests, such all-encompassing cynicism discards any possibility for genuine societal organization and collective action.

The disappointment with democracy also breeds in them authoritarian tendencies and a desire for revenge. "We need a Pinochet to fix us," said one supporter of the extreme right. "We need to shoot them all [the politicians]," echoed another participant with otherwise moderate views, at which point they shook hands happy to discover they both agree democracy does not work.

There is plenty the group disagreed on. The group was split between the anticommunists and those nostalgic for the communist past, and those positions determined their views and anything they had to say. Arguments on the communist past quickly deteriorated to ideological clichés. One side defended the Marxist view that "the social and material being determines the consciousness," while the other argued that communism breeds loafers. There was disagreement on the need to vote and on the type of government system, some arguing for the need for presidential rule, which provides for clear accountability. The discourse was aggressive and intolerant to diverging opinions, quickly escalating into a fight. One participant even started crying, but even that did not cool emotions. Every participant was convinced he or she had the answers to everything and could solve it all and that the others did not. They could not agree on anything. The uniqueness in their views and opinions were in fact the party line—their party's line.

What is striking about both the Left and Right supporters is their extremism and inability to cooperate. "A real revolution should have taken place; blood should have been shed" was the dominant view, as well as the need for a clean slate: "All politicians should be put in jail." When asked for a solution, they were no better able to articulate one than the young group. In fact, they said the young people, who are not party affiliated, are the solution.

The old group exhibited opinions that were clearly marked by the communist past—total distrust in the system yet dependency on that system; apathy and passivity in terms of political engagement yet highly politicized views; understanding how democracy works but utter skepticism about its viability. They agreed on one viewpoint: politicians are crooks who have stolen our lives; it is their fault for everything that is happening to us, and we are completely helpless.

Politics within Everyday Life

Situating politics within the everyday life of Bulgarians gives an understanding of how average Bulgarian citizens view politics and politicians: very negatively is the resounding answer. According to both young and old, the political system is dysfunctional and politicians are crooks. Is politics a significant part of ordinary Bulgarian's everyday life? Certainly politics occupies a very marginal place in the life of young people who nevertheless are politically informed and engaged. As to the old, everything is political to them, yet they are politically disengaged. They are stuck on the need for retribution, revenge, and compensation for their "lost years," yet they are cynical and apathetic.

To what extent do politics matter? Both groups showed a very Marxist understanding of politics—that is, political processes are a function of economic interests. The young are aware that politics affect them but believe individual (not collective) strategies are the best way to deal with that. The old, on the other hand, are stuck in a state of complete dependency, seeing their lives as the result of political decisions and the behavior of particular politicians yet doing nothing about it.

The motivations for political action among the two groups also greatly differ. The young engage in political action in order to protest. The old are ideologically motivated yet also vulnerable to populist discourse, constantly looking for the next savior who will fix it all without their having to do anything.

Political attitudes among members of the old generation, who were politically socialized during communist rule, and the young generation, who grew up after communism, differ starkly. Although both groups are disillusioned with politics, the old are bitter and cynical. The young have internalized democratic values and are more likely to cooperate, especially outside politics. The old are very much a product of communist indoctrination and stuck in the anticommunist/socialist nostalgia discourse. They are skeptical about democracy, harboring deep-rooted authoritarian sentiments. They care a great deal about politics. Politics is on their mind at all times, yet they are apathetic and unable to cooperate.

The attitudes observed among the two focus groups indicate a lack of political culture that is supportive of democracy. Although we see the emergence of a civic culture among young people who have a sense of civic duty, social capital and trust in government remain extremely low. This poses yet an additional challenge to democratic institutions, which are squeezed between corrupt politicians and a distrustful public. Though few people would question Bulgaria's democratic future, democracy is often taken for granted. Democratic backsliding in countries such as Hungary, for example, reminds us of the fragility of democracy and the need to reaffirm democratic values every day. In that sense, politics matter a great deal and the place of politics in everyday life matters just as much. An attitude of "politicians are all crooks" is subversive to democratic institutions, and it paves the way for populists who have been making gains across Europe and across the political spectrum. It is these attitudes that have made it possible for populist parties in Bulgaria to appear and succeed. Hence, parting with old mentalities and innate skepticism are key for the success of the democratic project in Bulgaria.

Notes

1. European Commission 2014.
2. King Simeon II was dethroned and exiled following the establishment of communist rule in Bulgaria in 1944. A referendum on the abolition of the monarchy was held in 1946, the legality of which has been questioned (Crampton 2007). In 2005, the king's party participated in a government coalition led by the Bulgarian Socialist Party (BSP), a successor of the Bulgarian Communist Party (BCP).
3. During its rule, the UDF put forward three lustration legislative proposals that were blocked by the constitutional court. As revealed by the secret service files, three of the constitutional court judges at the time were secret service "agents," or, in other words, recruited and affiliated with the former state security services.
4. *Kompromat* is the communist-era term for blackmail.
5. Karasimeonov 2010; Spirova 2007, 55–99.
6. Raichev and Todorov 2006.
7. Ghodsee 2008.
8. Gurov and Zankina 2013.
9. "Replicating" is quite literal here, as both parties—Simeon's NDSV and GERB—won the 2001 and 2009 elections, respectively, with 43 percent.
10. Noutcheva and Bechev 2008.
11. Dimitrov 2014.
12. "Manifestations" were in fact organized by the party demonstration in support of communist rule. They very much resembled the 2008 Chinese Olympics with grandiose performances and synchronized marching and displays. They were labeled

"manifestations" because they were, in a way, a manifest of ideology and support for the regime.
13. Raichev and Todorov 2006.
14. Andonova 2012.
15. Tzenkov et al. 2010.
16. Raichev and Todorov 2006.
17. Koleva 2013.
18. Raichev and Todorov 2006.

References

Andonova, Zdravka. 2012. "350,00 Българи в партиите [350,000 Bulgarians Party Members]." *Trud*, November 12. Accessed June 2, 2015. http://www.trud.bg/Article.asp?ArticleId=1632304.

Crampton, Richard. 2007. *Bulgaria*. New York: Oxford University Press.

Dimitrov, Martin K. 2014. "What the Party Wanted to Know: Citizen Complaints as a 'Barometer of Public Opinion' in Communist Bulgaria." *East European Politics and Societies* 28 (2): 271–295.

European Commission. 2014. EU Anti-Corruption Report. Accessed June 19, 2015. http://ec.europa.eu/dgs/home-affairs/e-library/documents/policies/organized-crime-and-human-trafficking/corruption/docs/acr_2014_en.pdf.

Ghodsee, Kristen. 2008. "Left Wing, Right Wing, Everything: Xenophobia, Neo-Totalitarianism, and Populist Politics in Bulgaria." *Problems of Post-Communism* 55 (3): 26–39.

Gurov, Boris, and Emilia Zankina. 2013. "Populism and the Construction of Political Charisma: Post-Transition Politics in Bulgaria." *Problems of Post Communism* 60 (1): 3–17.

Karasimeonov, Georgi. 2010. *The Bulgarian Party System*. Sofia: RK Nik.

Koleva, Daniela. 2013. "Hope for the Past: Socialist Nostalgia 20 Years Later." In *Bulgarian Communism: Debates and Interpretations*, edited by M. Gruev and D. Mishkova, 105–124. Sofia: Center for Advanced Studies and "Riva" Publishing.

Noutcheva, Gergana, and Dimitar Bechev. 2008. "The Successful Laggards: Bulgaria and Romania's Accession to the EU." *East European Politics and Societies* 22 (1): 114–144.

Raichev, Andrey, and Antony Todorov. 2006. "Bulgaria: Democratic Orientations in Support of Civil Society." In *Democracy and Political Culture in Eastern Europe*, edited by H-D. Klingemann, D. Fuchs, and J. Zielonka, 336–354. New York: Routledge.

Spirova, Maria. 2007. *Political Parties in Post-Communist Societies: Formation, Persistence, and Change*. New York: Palgrave.

Tzenkov, Emil, Todor Yalamov, Todor Galev, Pavel Antonov, Svetla Encheva, Boyko Todorov, Yanita Georgieva, and Teodora Georgieva. 2010. "Civil Society in Bulgaria: Trends and Risks." Center for the Study of Democracy. Sofia. Accessed June 19, 2015. http://www.isn.ethz.ch/Digital-Library/Publications/Detail/?lang=en&id=132579.

EMILIA ZANKINA is Associate Professor of Political Science and Provost of the American University in Bulgaria.

24 Life among Statues in Skopje

Ilká Thiessen

In 2012 I was sitting with some good friends at the main square—Macedonia Square—in Skopje, drinking Turkish coffee and discussing the changes happening around us. To our left, a new sculpture had been raised overnight, yet when I asked whom the sculpture portrayed, no one could answer. Perhaps the most disconcerting thing, however, was that none of us stood up to see the statue or its description. We realized it did not matter who or what the statue represented; the government rebuilding project known as "Skopje 2014" was a top-down effort aimed at giving the city a more classical feel that in turn would propagate the "nationalist" ideology of the ruling party, the Internal Macedonian Revolutionary Organization–Democratic Party for Macedonian National Unity (VMRO-DPMNE). What mattered was that city space be "covered" with sculptures telling the story of the city and country in which it sits.

When walking through great European cities like Paris, London, or Berlin, one sees statues and learns about famous men, women, or events in history; the statues act as reminders, warnings, and directions recalling past struggles and a legacy of greatness on which the pride of present generations can be built. Yet in the context of the café where friends meet to explore their everydays as past, present, and future, Skopje 2014 is experienced more through how it hinders or "stops" the space of sociality. Skopje 2014 is about transforming space, space that used to contribute predominately to the social environment in which the inhabitants of Skopje interacted; it is not just about reconstructing the visual landscape of the city but about both using the statues to frame nationalist views and at the same time altering the social space where people may come together to question the agenda of the VMRO-DPMNE.

Framing History for the Present

To appreciate the political context of Skopje 2014, it is imperative to see the politics of history out of which modern Macedonia emerged. Its oldest known settlements date back approximately nine thousand years, but in the middle of the fourth century BC—when the kingdom of Macedon became the dominant power in Greece and the neighboring regions—it made a lasting mark on world civilization. Out of this period emerged the country's most eminent historical claim as the

Figure 24.1. A man walks his dog in the winter slush in Macedonia Square, with the Monument of Gotse Delchev, a leader of the Internal Macedonian Revolutionary Organization, and the Monument of the Gemidzii, memorializing a Bulgarian anarchist group that launched a bombing campaign for Macedonian independence in Ottoman Thessaloniki in 1903. The Archaeological Museum of Macedonia is in the background. Skopje, 2014. Photograph by Robert Atanasovski.

home of Alexander the Great, a claim that over two thousand years later remains a point of contention between Macedonia and its southern neighbor, Greece.

For contemporary Greeks, the kingdom of Macedon and those who resided there—including Alexander the Great—were Greeks. Contemporary Macedonians, however, reframe the ancient Greek world in light of its ethnic contemporaries: as king of Macedon, Alexander was Macedonian, even if Macedon, at the time, was part of the Greek empire. Such disputes are part of contemporary politics. While Greece recognizes the country, the constitutional name "Republic of Macedonia" is not recognized by Greece and, by extension, the European Union because Greece claims historical ownership over the name "Macedonia" and the heritage of Alexander the Great. Because of such pressures, the Republic of Macedonia was only admitted to the United Nations using a provisional name that Greece was willing to accept: the Former Yugoslav Republic of Macedonia (FYROM).[1]

It is never the case, however, that history is a straightforward path. The ancient Macedonian kingdom included parts of contemporary Albania, Greece, and the Republic of Macedonia, whereas the modern geographical region of Macedonia covers portions of Albania, Bulgaria, Greece, Kosovo, Serbia, and the entire Republic of Macedonia. The considerable way Macedonia's boundaries—both as a historical region and contemporary national legacy—have changed leads to different (and competing) claims of historical legitimacy. But narratives of influence and belonging are not simple. For example, in 148 BC, the Macedonian territory became part of the Roman Empire; in the late Roman Empire, it became the diocese of Macedonia; and between the late 700s and the early 800s, it became a province of the Byzantine Empire. At the end of the late fourteenth century—and for roughly five hundred years—Macedonia was part of the Ottoman Empire, before being annexed to Serbia after World War I and eventually becoming part of Yugoslavia after World War II.

The complications of history, however, come not only from the epochs of a people but in the varied minor events that become central to future narratives. The Kruševo Republic—seen as the prelude to the Republic of Macedonia—established short-lived independence from the Ottoman state in 1903. When Yugoslavia was formed by the communist partisans in 1944, they declared, at the Anti-Fascist Assembly for the National Liberation of Macedonia (ASNOM), that the northern part of Macedonia was the Socialist Republic of Macedonia. Early in the Yugoslav Wars (1991–2001), Socialist Macedonia, not wanting to become South Serbia or part of Bulgaria, declared independence from Yugoslavia as the Republic of Macedonia (Republika Makedonjia) on September 8, 1991.[2]

Independence was endorsed by a referendum, but this referendum was boycotted by the large ethnic Albanian minority in the country that wanted the country to be a republic of Macedonians and Albanians. Since that boycott by Albanians, there have been severe tensions between the Albanians and Macedonians in the Republic of Macedonia. While Macedonia managed to stay out of the Yugoslav Wars of the early 1990s, it became seriously destabilized by the Kosovo War in 1999, when an estimated 360,000 ethnic Albanian refugees from Kosovo took sanctuary in Macedonia. The refugees were not greeted kindly, and in 2001, Albanian nationalists started to pursue securing minority rights for the Albanian-populated western areas of Macedonia.[3]

This aforementioned history shows how precarious the social belonging of the people living in the geographical territory called Macedonia is and has been. People have lived through traumatic changes, being part of different empires at different times in history, always trying to negotiate their present in relation to their surroundings and relevant historical antecedents. When I first traveled to Yugoslavia in the 1980s, my Macedonian friends and their families were proud to be Yugoslavian and never spoke about Alexander the Great. They saw themselves as Yugoslavs and descendants of the Slav migration. However, with Greece's efforts at the 2008 NATO Summit in Bucharest to block Macedonia's membership into NATO and the EU, the political climate in Macedonia dramatically changed, becoming more aggressively nationalistic in its state policies. This has changed not only the political landscape but the built landscape as well.

The VMRO–DPMNE has become the largest and leading party in Macedonia. Upon independence, Macedonia was pro-European and pro-NATO, but since 2006, VMRO–DPMNE has won each election—in part—because it refused to change the country's name as demanded by Greece. In 2006, VMRO-DPMNE

Life among Statues in Skopje 253

won the election on issues, but in 2008, it began winning on the basis of rhetoric that has become increasingly nationalist, with the VMRO–DPMNE proclaiming itself as the protector of Macedonian identity, values, and "Macedonianness" (*Makedonshtina*). This is likely in large part due to its continued veto and blocking by Greece for EU and NATO membership. Greece's demands are based on the belief that Greece has exclusive rights to use the word *Macedonia*, and since Macedonia wants to use the same name, Greece claims that the "Republic of Macedonia" has territorial aspirations and wants to hijack parts of ancient history related to ancient Macedonia. This was characterized in the early 1990s as such:

> Greek national identity was created out of a European cosmology that placed Ancient Greece at the summit of the ancestry of Western Civilization. The establishment of a particular history was the work of identity construction, both for Europe and for Greece as an emergent periphery in the European world system. Greek nationalists found their past in the institutional memory of expanding Europe. The Greek past was not opposed to the expansionism of the present but was seen as its democratic, individualist, and commercial foundation. Ancient Greece was the essence of the modern, of everything that was positive in the present and hoped for in the future, its philosophy and science as well as its politics.[4]

To this claim of origin, the VMRO–DPMNE responded with Skopje 2014, aimed at asserting—through an architectural makeover of the capital city—its nationalist claims to the heritage of Alexander and the country's place as the "true" cradle of European civilization,[5] Today, part of the reason the VMRO–DPMNE wins elections is because it presents itself as defender of the state and guardian of national pillars that are under attack: the Macedonian Orthodox Church (under attack by Serbia), the language (under attack by Bulgaria), and the name and territory (under attack by Greece). Architecturally, the VMRO–DPMNE has conjured a lowbrow artificial "European identity" creation for Skopje, and despite the intolerable expenditure of creating a new city on top of the old socialist Skopje, it has united themes of antiquity, neoclassical, and baroque styles with "European" elements to frame history for the VMRO–DPMNE's nationalist present.

Skopje 2014

Skopje 2014 was supposed to create a city whose new European identity was assigned, crafted, and poured into concrete. As such, it is an ideological construction (project) intended to influence national identities and narratives of belonging. The project had its inception in 2008, with the objective of giving the capital European appeal. This "rebuilding or restructuring" of Skopje was supposed to be finished by the year 2014, hence Skopje 2014.[6] The project, officially announced in 2010, consists mainly of the construction of museums and government buildings, the building of new façades, and the erection of monuments depicting historical and classical figures. As Andrew Graan notes, "The counter argument on Skopje 2014's kitschiness has not been limited to activist critiques of the project but extends across everyday talk and dominates popular writing on the project. Throughout, the indictment of Skopje 2014 as a kitschy knockoff of other nations' architectural styles has been linked to anxieties over the project's reception among consequential outside audiences."[7]

But the greatest controversy surrounding Skopje 2014, however, has been its cost—estimated to be over 671 million Euros, though the true figures remain hidden by the government.[8] One reason the costs can only be estimated by the public is the fact that the tenders for the art pieces are not always publicly announced.

I have walked the streets of Skopje for many years, for the first time in 1988, meeting up with friends to go to different cafés around town. I still remember the pain of walking in high heel shoes—as all young women did—from around 10:00 p.m. to 4:00 a.m., standing in or around crowded cafés, dense with cigarette smoke. We were part of the city; perhaps an annoying part of the city to some—sometimes people living above the noisy cafés threw water or tomatoes at us—but still part of what gave the city life. When a law passed in the 1990s forcing cafés to close at 11:00 p.m., young people drove to the Vodno Mountain, where members of parliament lived, and played their car radio as loud as they could, turning quiet tree-lined streets into a place to party. The city belonged to the people: during the day people were walking the city in search of general household items and food; during the night, the city was young and exuded an amazing energy and hope. Changes in the city impact such atmospheres and where people gather.

One comes to understand Skopje 2014 when walking the city as part of the everyday. It is not what the statues portray, or even how artful or lowbrow the art pieces are; it is the fact that the flow of space is being hindered in new ways. Walking around downtown Skopje, one is forced to walk around statues, a feel that is markedly different from the openness of public space created by the Yugoslav urban planners. Often the scale of these Skopje 2014 statues is so extreme, viewers cannot see what is being portrayed—you feel not only dwarfed but at times forced into submission. King Samuel or Emperor Justinian the First, for example, sit atop big blocks of concrete that hinder people's movement through the city square. The blocks are so big, and statues mounted so close, that it becomes nearly impossible to walk around single monuments; instead one must walk around the whole square.

The concrete is a solid way of changing people's means of social becoming in the city of Skopje. The story of Skopje 2014 is one both of nostalgia and of how lives get altered by state construction, leading people to adapt in different ways. Where once we walked straight, now we must walk around; where once we looked straight, now we must look up. There is a whole new world becoming where concrete and humans intermingle.

Lifestyle

In today's political and social climate, "becoming" is on the agenda. A new Macedonian is being created—every person must think about how to become Macedonian; one is not simply Macedonian because one lives in the territory of

Macedonia. Many different groups live in Macedonia—including Roma, Albanians, Vlachs, Turks, and Muslim Macedonians—but this does not make them all Macedonian, at least not Macedonian in the Skopje 2014 construction of a nationalist identity. During socialist times, all went to the same schools and same holiday camps; they lived in the same areas, worked in the same jobs, and went to the same vacation spots. However, today, through the use of the "cradle of Europe" imagery, practices of othering are created anachronistically.

When Macedonia erected the Millennium Cross atop the Vodno Mountain towering over the city and lit it up with thousands of lights, it became a marker of religious (and political) distinction and Macedonian differentiation. The cross was erected in 2002, the same year that Erdoğan's Islamist AKP (Adalet ve Kalkınma Partisi) seized power, and Turkey's integration into the EU became more unlikely.[9]

EU politicians have often argued that Turkey is unfit to become a member of the EU because Turkey is not based on modern Christian values.[10] Since then, Macedonia has plunged into an architectural frenzy that has taken over the entire country. Macedonians build new churches, Albanians in Macedonia build mosques, and for each church it seems a new mosque is built; crosses appear on mountaintops, followed closely by minarets. Never mind, of course that while the airport is named after Alexander the Great and a gigantic statue of him—officially named *Warrior on the Horse* (Воин на коњ), the statue is widely believed to depict Alexander on a horse—stands in the center of the city, his (pagan) religion is never mentioned as part of his contribution to the country's narrative.

Sculpture after sculpture, Ottoman and Yugoslav history are being erased (and rewritten) and the space is transformed—willingly or not—into Christian Orthodox and European. Street names are changed—Boulevard Marshall Tito became Makedonjia Street and Majka (Mother) Teresa replaced the leaders of socialism as the archetypal Macedonian hero—and sculptures are built to honor every single person who fought heroically against the Ottomans in 1903, achieving ten days of independence for the Kruševo Republic in the western part of Macedonia.

New Ways of Being

Reading today's cartography of Skopje, the new spaces between sculptures point people to new ways of being. Macedonians are not only Slavs—and also neither Turk nor Greek—but as descendants of Alexander the Great, they are the first Europeans. However, in this "creation of concrete belonging," whole population groups are literally excluded from the public imagination of space. While Macedonians are becoming European, Christian, and ancient through the creation of a new "old" cityscape, Roma and Albanian residents of Macedonia are excluded and pushed to the edge of this new space.[11] Hence, the public spaces that once belonged to the young people in Skopje, to all citizens of Skopje and the whole of Macedonia—that once presented itself as the center of a new, socialist, liberal, and free era for all—are being erased or "written over."

Figure 24.2. Children playing in the water fountains at Macedonia Square in Skopje, with the *Warrior on a Horse* statue looking on in the background, 2016. Photograph by Roska Vrgova.

Within all this, there has been silence, a frightening silence, among citizens who fear the secret police will overhear them criticizing the changes in the country. Belonging to the wrong political faction has brought even TV and radio stations to the ground and made journalists or university professors who have voiced any kind of criticism lose their employment. Anybody who is against the VMRO-DPMNE is at the same time against a moral order that is understood (or at least constructed) to have evolved from the legacy of Alexander into the idea of Macedonia's centrality in the origin of modern Europe. As such, the reconfiguration of space mandated by the VMRO-DPMNE's Skopje 2014 instantiates a new way of being, a new Macedonian nationalism that, through manipulating the narrative of public space—a story of both inclusion and exclusion—people become accustomed to life among the statue, including their implicit and explicit meanings.

Political Agendas and Reactions

"Today someone asked me if I knew a good place to buy jeans, and to my horror I said, 'Yes, just around to the side of the Arc de Triomphe,'" a friend told me one night. I knew what she meant. When wanting to take a taxi to town, I ask the driver to drop me off at the Arc de Triomphe; very few drivers correct me and tell me that they would drop me off at Porta Makedonijia—everyone knows what

I mean. It is apparent to all that Porta Makedonijia is not about Macedonia at all—neither are the British double decker buses, the Brandenburg Gate, and the Victory Pillar. Similarly, everybody knows that the centerpiece of Skopje 2014 on the banks of the Vardar River is not just a warrior on a horse, as the official title suggests, but Alexander the Great. If nothing else, it is seen in reference: on the other side of the Vardar, Alexander's father, Philip II of Macedon, is waving his greetings with Alexander's proud mother, Olympia, in line of sight.

Certainly some must support Skopje 2014, but the majority with whom I interacted are not among them. Skopje 2014 has been labeled landscape pollution or kitsch—inside and outside of Macedonia—and many criticize the enormous expenditure in one of Europe's poorest countries. However, it is not enough to just have an opinion about Skopje 2014. The question it raises is a political one—why has the VRMO seen it fit to spend billions of euros on recreating and rebuilding a new city on top of the old one?—told in the relationship of material space to ideological intent.

Skopje was rebuilt—literally from rubble—in 1963 after a strong earthquake destroyed most of the city. There was tremendous solidarity after the earthquake, and it was decided by politicians that Skopje was to be rebuilt as a sign of solidarity among the nonalignment movement; it was to be a proud socialist city. There is a lot to be said about this socialist city—though not all flattering—where monotonous boulevards and apartment buildings stand side by side more eccentric constructions like the post office that resembles a fairy tale poured in concrete or the train station that itself partially resembles a train. Close to the City Park, there is a monument that celebrates the victory of the partisans against fascism, and nearby is the old train station, whose clock stopped at the time of the earthquake and reminds the city to forget neither the earthquake nor the tremendous sacrifice it took to rebuild Skopje. From everywhere in the country, young people streamed into the city to help rebuilt it, literally cementing their belief that socialism would bring a better life. A lot of emotion was built into the "new" 1963 Skopje.

But the designers of Skopje 2014 were less concerned with building a new city than in remaking a socialist one. Skopje had a glorious history in antiquity and even within the Ottoman Empire, though the latter is not a popular sentiment in contemporary Macedonia. However, for the longest time it had to be admitted that after the earthquake—and even so today—the area of the city called Carsjia (it used to be the Turkish Carsjia, but after independence in 1991, it was dubbed the old Carsjia) is the liveliest, most interesting, and oldest part of town. Once, walking through Carsjia with two Canadian students of mine, I overheard one of the students sigh with astonishment, admiration, and wonder: "Wow! That is Europe." For her, the Ottoman bequest was firmly European, even if it was the pre-socialist architecture that led her to see the "old" as European. After all, the socialist architecture, while often seen as uninspiring, was still Europe, albeit Eastern Europe.

My student had not yet grown to appreciate the everyday of Skopjeans or how they sought to explain and cope with the struggles they faced. But in Carsjia, she saw the incredible lively, rich, and beautiful pulse of the city—as I did when I first visited as a student in the 1980s—that reflected a past of movement unimpeded by the statues. It is this pulse that is contested by the buildings, monuments, and statues of Skopje 2014. Maybe Skopje 2014 will be able to bring this pulse back to the city. But maybe its legacy will be as an ideological process that covered it over.

Notes

1. On June 12, 2018, it was announced that an agreement was reached between Greece and Macedonia to change the name of FYROM to the Republic of North Macedonia. Macedonian prime minister Zoran Zaev characterized the agreement with his Greek counterpart Alexis Tsipras by saying, "Our bid in the compromise is a defined and precise name, the name that is honorable and geographically precise – Republic of North Macedonia." (https://www.npr.org/2018/06/12/619294020/macedonia-gets-new-name-ending-27-year-dispute-with-greece) Hours after the announcement, Macedonian president Gjorge Ivanov stated that he would not agree to the name change: "My position is final and I will not yield to any pressure, blackmail or threats." (https://www.theguardian.com/world/2018/jun/13/macedonia-rejects-treaty-greece-name-row-zoran-zaev) On July 5, 2018, the Macedonian parliament endorsed the name change for a second time. (https://www.reuters.com/article/us-greece-macedonia/macedonias-parliament-endorses-name-deal-with-greece-for-second-time-idUSKBN1JV1MP) As of the time this volume was going to print, the twenty-seven-year dispute over the official name of Macedonia had not been resolved.

2. Additional political problems arose between Republika Makedonjia, Greece, and the EU over the issue of EU membership despite the fact that Robert Badinter, head of the Arbitration Commission of the Peace Conference on Yugoslavia, recommended in January 1992 Macedonia and Slovenia as the most likely former Yugoslav Republics to gain European Community (EC) recognition. (Before the Lisbon Treaty came into effect in 2009, the EU and the EC were two separate bodies, operating under different rules. This means in practical terms that since December 1, 2009, all EU legislation is referenced as EU. However, before 2009, legal decisions are referenced as made by the EC since it was only the EC that made legal decisions.)

3. Vrgova (2015) characterizes the process as such:

> Following the dissolution of Yugoslavia the country created a Constitution which defines it as primarily the state of the Macedonian people, in which full equality as citizens and permanent coexistence with the Macedonian people is provided for Albanians, Turks, Vlachs, Roma and other nationalities living in the country. According to Daskalovski, this put the "ethnic Macedonians in a superior position vis-à-vis the rest of the population," and as result the Albanian minority found this formulation discriminatory. During this period the Albanians were attempting to address the Albanian interest in autonomy; accompanied with independence for Kosovo, the federalization of Macedonia into an Albanian and a Macedonian entity, within a bilingual state. While the interest in increased autonomy has been a key interest of many Albanian parties for some time, the strategy of framing this demand in terms of federalism has been increasingly evident in the post-Ohrid period, whereas prior to the conflict the main focus of the Albanian parties was recognition of the Albanians as

a second constituent nation, as well as language and education rights in the country. The Macedonian leadership was strongly promoting the idea of a unitary—not federal—state. (113–114)

4. Friedman 1992.

5. The argument for this has been fueled by somewhat dubious and unclearly defined research parameters by a Spanish genetic lab whose research is widely cited in many internet fora, arguing that the Macedonians in the republic had a 40 percent genetic link to Alexander the Great and his people, whereas Greeks only had a 2 percent link. (See Arnaiz-Villena et al. 2001.) It is further propagated in popular interactions, such as a text message from T-Mobile Macedonia that greeted me on arrival at the airport in 2012 and began: "Welcome to Macedonia, the cradle of civilization. During your stay we strongly recommend that you visit the Museum of the Macedonian Struggle and the Memorial House of Mother Teresa in Skopje, the Memorial Center of Toshe Proeski in Krushevo, the Museum on Water...."

6. At the time of writing in 2016, the project is still taking place.

7. Grann 2013, 172. In explaining these activists critiques, Graan writes in a footnote: "To my knowledge, no demographic data exist on Skopje 2014 supporters and opponents. By local stereotype, project supporters are seen as likely to be rural, older, and male; ethnic Macedonian supporters of Prime Minister Nikola Gruevski and his right-leaning party. In contrast, project opponents are seen as likely to be urban, young, educated, and left leaning, or as members of the country's minority groups" (2013, 177).

8. See "Skopje 2014 Uncovered," accessed February 25, 2017, http://skopje2014.prizma.birn.eu.com/en.

9. The EU demanded certain political criteria from Turkey, including a stable democracy, the rule of law, respect for human rights, and protection of the rights of minorities.

10. See, for example, Delfs 2014.

11. Živković (2011) reminds us that Serbians—in a fashion similar to Macedonians and the Illinden Uprising against the Ottomans in Krushevo in 1903—portray themselves as victims of an arrogant Europe and heroes of Blackbird Field (Battle of Kosovo) in today's Kosovo, where Serbian warriors dwarfed the Ottoman onslaught on Christian Europe through great sacrifice. Likewise, nationalist Macedonians portray themselves as descendants of Alexander the Great's empire and fighting the ancient struggle between Christianity and Islam.

References

Arnaiz-Villena, A., K. Dimitroski, A. Pacho, J. Moscoso, E. Gómez-Casado, C. Silvera-Redondo, P. Varela, M. Blagoevska, V. Zdravkovska, J. Martínez-Laso. 2001. "HLA Genes in Macedonians and the Sub-Saharan Origin of the Greeks." *Tissue Antigens* 57: 118–127. http://www.makedonika.org/processpaid.aspcontentid=ti.2001.pdf.

Delfs, Arne. 2014. "Turkey Unfit to Join EU Says Merkel Europe Parliament Candidate." *Bloomberg*. April 10. Accessed April 19, 2016. http://bloom.bg/1D30iKb.

Friedman, Jonathan. 1992. "Myth, History, and Political Identity." *Cultural Anthropology* 7 (2): 194–210.

Graan, Andrew. 2013. "Counterfeiting the Nation? Skopje 2014 and the Politics of Nation Branding in Macedonia." *Cultural Anthropology* 28 (1): 161–179.

Vrgova, Roska. 2015. "Census, Identity, and the Politics of Numbers: The Case of Macedonia." *Contemporary Southeastern Europe* 2 (2): 107–125.

Živković, Marko. 2011. *Serbian Dreambook: National Imaginary in the Time of Milošević.* Bloomington: Indiana University Press.

ILKÁ THIESSEN is Professor of Anthropology at Vancouver Island University. She is author of *Waiting for Macedonia: Identity in a Changing World*.

Section V: The Religion(s) of Everyday Life

While religion means different things to different people, most everyone has an opinion about it. It brings together and divides communities. It is a space of comfort and contestation. It is what some say is wrong with the world and others say can save the world. Most often, what people think of religion is not along such extremes, but their views are also not equally consistent. In reality, there is a great deal of variation in how people make sense of religion, but one of the more straightforward ways of doing so is to see it as a moral framework that both guides actions and helps us make sense of lifecycle events. It plays such a role in the Balkans, and alongside that, in this section, we see how communities emerge around religious identity, are shaped by those of different faith traditions (and none at all), and engage in historical revisionism to political ends. Religion is not a topic relevant to only the religious, for society writ large, whether an individual is religious or not, is shaped by the views of tradition and the future that even in their most secular forms, have antecedents in some religious frame.

In his chapter, David Montgomery looks at how Albanians socially navigate their relationship with religion and make sense of social change in ways that are understood as moral in context. Perhaps one of the most evident times where the presence of religion can be seen is during holiday periods, which we see in both Frances Trix's chapter on Ramadan in Kosovo and Milica Bakić-Hayden chapter on *Slava* in Serbia. They show how Muslims and Serbian Orthodox Christians, respectively, draw on the practices of religious tradition to guide actions, define identity, and instantiate connection to place and past. In both, as well, we see that special, set aside times like holidays have their own routine, rhythm, and rituals, with an everyday character intended to influence behavior across more mundane periods.

Discussions of moral behaviors and identity revolve around community, and we see this in the chapters by Slavica Jakelić, Magdalena Lubanska, and Albert Doja. In her chapter on Catholic women in Croatia, Jakelić looks at the coexistence of individualized religious experience with traditional and collectivist forms of religious identity. Lubanska turns to patterns of coexistence and neighborliness among Bulgarian Muslims and Orthodox Christians in the Rhodopes

Mountains. And Doja looks more broadly across the region to show how history can be repurposed to politically manipulate the present.

Across all the chapters here, it becomes clear that religion has ongoing relevance. It is a place where history gives context to home and both livelihoods and politics have meaning with roots extending beyond present concerns. In religion, we see the interdisciplinarity of everyday life's struggles and some sources of its hope.

25 "The Hardest Time Was the Time without Morality": Religion and Social Navigation in Albania

David W. Montgomery

Religion is a good way into *seeing* everyday life. This may seem an incongruous statement in a world accustomed to looking for religion only among the "religious" or to assuming religion matters only in those places known for fervent religiosity, but understanding public and private relationships with religion is a window into understanding the dynamics of community and moral striving. Life is a complicated affair that we socially navigate in relation to histories, moral frameworks, and the potentialities that surround us. Religion plays a role in this everyday negotiation, serving as a resource that frames relationships and visions of how life should be lived. And it does this even for those uncomfortable with the very idea of religion. What I mean by religion here is something very fluid, not the static characterization of certainty assumed central to formal religious traditions, but the dynamic engagement of one striving to make sense of how to be in the world.

The story of religion in Albania is complicated but one that captures the process of navigation at the heart of all social engagement. Albania was a place that the Apostle Paul Christianized, the Ottomans Islamized, and the socialists made atheist. Today, it is characterized as a secular country with a Muslim majority and a large Christian minority yet where religion has minor contemporary relevance. The messiness of all this can be seen in the census data. Though never viewed as reliable, the pre–World War II census gave a demographic breakdown of religion in the country as 70 percent Muslim, 20 percent Eastern Orthodox, and 10 percent Roman Catholic.[1] In 1967, Albania became the world's only officially atheist state, and at least in principle these numbers drastically declined. The 2011 census broke down the population as 59 percent Muslim (57 percent Sunni and 2 percent Bektashi), 17 percent Christian (10 percent Roman Catholic, 7 percent Eastern Orthodox, and less than 0.25 percent Protestants and other Christians), 2.5 percent Atheists, over 5 percent who identified as believers without a denomination, nearly 14 percent preferred not to answer, and over 2 percent who felt the question was not relevant.[2] All these numbers give a sense of something, but they say very little about what religion means and how it is employed in the everyday.

One of the challenging aspects of talking about religion in Albania is that so many are quick to assure you that it is "irrelevant" or "not really important to Albanians," reflecting a long-standing mantra that Albanians do not care about religion. Seeing religion as of secondary importance to Albanians has roots in the Albanian National Awakening movement of the 1870s, most emblematically characterized in a verse from Pashko Vasa's poem, "O Moj Shqypni" (Oh Albania): "Feja e Shqyptarit asht Shqyptaria" (the religion of the Albanian is Albanianism).[3] Vasa was critical of religious and political factionalism and advocated ethnicity as terms for unity. Later, in 1967, when Albania was decreed atheist under Enver Hoxha, religion fell even further from the profile of everyday life.

But of course, the reality of religion in Albania is a more complex, largely private affair that is complicated by the past and the uncertainties of the present. In the mid-2000s, while traveling with three acquaintances who had been close friends for over a decade since high school, I asked what religion meant to them and their families. Elira reacted somewhat condescendingly, for she felt I had been in Albania long enough to "know Albanians [were] not religious." She went on, saying that her family name was a Muslim name, but it was only her paternal grandfather who considered himself Muslim. She continued to describe the surnames of her other two friends' families—Manjola had a mother with an Orthodox Christian name and a father with a Muslim name whereas the Mirjeta's parents had Catholic names. To understand Albania, Elira said, I needed to know that Albanians are not religious, and that she and her friends were prime examples of that; they neither knew the religions of their ancestors nor cared to practice it. Manjola agreed. But Mirjeta confessed that she and her family went to Mass every Sunday and religion was important to her. This was a surprise to Elira and Manjola, because they saw themselves as close friends with Mirjeta. It was not that Mirjeta was hiding anything; rather Elira and Manjola's assumptions about religion led them to assume its absence among those they knew. In many ways, this highlights the role personal biases and assumptions play in characterizing religion. The point is not to overstate the story of religion in Albania but merely to make sure that it is not understated. So often what passes as understanding is shaped by those for whom religion is not a lived category and thus not always appreciated for the role it plays in everyday life.

Shifting Religious Landscapes

When it comes to religion, history plays a curious role. People draw on history to legitimate the present by rooting it in the past, but this is not done without bias. We all have biases, so pointing this out is merely acknowledging that historical roots are less objective than they are directive of particular outcomes. Thus when drawing connections to the legacy of a religious past, two things should be kept in mind: first, a person learns religion within her lifetime, and second, what facilitates any leaning toward a particular religion—or none at all—is fostered by the social and moral structure the tradition offers. As such, there is always a tension between the lived realities of the present and the presumed continuity with a morally valued past able to offer guidance in managing contemporary struggles. Thus it is relevant to note aspects of Albania's religious past that are presented by my interlocutors as relevant to understanding the country's contemporary religious and social environment.

Commonly, Albanians speak of the Illyrians as the ancestors from whom both their language and territorial claims derive. And it is within this context that we see canonical indications of Christianity's presence in the region, as the Apostle Paul writes: "As far around as Illyricum I have fully proclaimed the good news of Christ" (Romans 15:19). Christianity supplanted Greek and Roman cosmologies early, and as the Christian church split in 1054, the southern tribes maintained allegiance to the church in Constantinople while the northern tribes became more closely aligned with Rome.[4] This led to the prominence of Orthodoxy in the south and Catholicism in the north, with regional religious factionalism still present today.

As the Ottoman Empire spread throughout the Balkans in the fourteenth and fifteenth centuries, so too did Islam. The process of Islamization was slower in Albania than other regions of the Balkans, continuing into the nineteenth century. While the Ottoman Empire allowed tribal autonomy and local privileges to be maintained,[5] the fifteenth century rebellion led by Gjergji Kastrioti, known as Skanderbeg, was an expression of a desire for autonomy that carried some religious undertones. As an Albanian nobleman serving in the Ottoman Empire, Skanderbeg converted to Islam as a teenager. But in 1443, he deserted the Ottoman army, converted back to Christianity, and led a twenty-five-year resistance movement to Ottoman expansion.[6] The Ottomans eventually prevailed, but the story of Skanderbeg's resistance became a myth central for the Albanian nationalist narrative of the nineteenth and twentieth centuries and a statue of him is prominent today in Tirana's central plaza—Skanderbeg Square.

As the Ottomans brought Sunni Islam to Albania—which predominates today—so too arrived the Bektashi Tariqat, a Shi'a Sufi Order active across Anatolia and the southern Balkans, especially in Albania, Bulgaria, and Macedonia.[7] The mystic order was supported by both Ali Pasha—an Ottoman official governing the empire's European territory—and Naim Frashëri, a nineteenth-century leader in the Albanian National Awakening movement. In 1925, when the Turkish Republic was created, Atatürk banned all Sufi orders and the Bektashis moved their headquarters to Tirana. There, Bektashism flourished until the communists took power in 1945, when it came under pressure and was eventually banned with other religions in 1967. The tradition survived in exile—with the establishment of a Bektashi tekke in the United States, near Detroit[8]—and reestablished itself in Albania in 1990, when the ban on religion was rescinded.

It was these four confessional traditions—Catholicism, Orthodoxy, Sunni Islam, and Bektashism—that were all seen as threatening to the communist government. While the banning of religion in 1967 was consistent with communist ideology, the motives were less ideological than pragmatic. Hoxha's move to outlaw religion was one way to control the various regional factions whose tribal affiliations were seen as concomitant with their religious identification. The campaign against religion was brutal.[9] Churches and mosques were destroyed or otherwise repurposed, and people wanting to be religious were forced into secrecy. Mirjeta described how her mother forced the children to secrecy about baking pastries at Christmas or the need to finely break up egg shells at Easter so as not to be seen practicing religion. As atheism became the ideology of the state, all forms of religious practice were forced into secrecy and the private realm, which is why Mirjeta grew up not talking about her religion with friends.

In 1990, when communism ended and the restrictive policies toward religion eased, new opportunities for religious life emerged. This was met with the reopening of churches and mosques that were attended by people without familiarity of the tradition to which their ancestors identified. Guidance came from abroad. As noted, Bektashis came from the United States; Orthodox came from the United States—where the Autocephalous Orthodox Church of Albania was founded in Boston in 1922 by Fan Noli (Noli also led both efforts for Albanian unification after World War I and Albania's successful bid to join the League of Nations)—and Greece; Catholics came from Italy; and Sunni Muslim support came—to varying degrees—from the nearby Muslim world. So too, however, came Protestant missionaries from the West. All groups came offering visions of what a better Albania could be.[10]

Religion and Everyday Life

The opening of religious opportunity took place amid broader social change from socialism. Erion, who came of age with the end of socialism, has many complaints about Albania and the direction the country is moving. For more than a decade since graduating from university, he has been critical of what Tirana, the capital, has become. With a large influx of migrants from rural areas—not to mention the outflow of migrants to Italy and Greece—there is overcrowding and an urban infrastructure ill-equipped to handle it. There is also nepotism and, because his family comes from a rural background, many of the opportunities to which he aspires seem inaccessible to him. He notes how the city has multiple layers of complexity, where access to resources are dependent less on one's merits than on one's connections. Erion is talented but claims much of his professional success was a result of the contacts of his wife's family.

Erion left Vlorë, a coastal city in the south where his parents still live, for university in Tirana. He has been successful but is also bitter and complains about the "village mentality of clans" that makes where someone is from important. He does not reminisce about the past—currently in his midforties, he experienced the last years of communism and the turbulent years of transition—and is angered by what he sees as corruption everywhere. He longs to leave for western Europe, where he envisions there being more opportunity, and like Elira he is dismissive of religion. He sees it as both irrational and something "simple" people engage in. He is not atheist—because he is not that certain—but identifies as agnostic and is uncomfortable with any discussion about religion. For him, it is contrary to the notion of progress, and he sees religion as an antiquated way of seeing the world; being modern, being European, is for religion to be relegated to the private spaces of life, to the customs of traditional life cycle events—by which he mostly means burial, though even here too he is a bit dismissive. All in all, he worries about how the country's new openness to religion will impact it.

Like Elira, Erion often quotes Vasa to show that ethnic Albanian identity matters more than religion. He is so certain of religion's irrelevance in the country that he misses the dynamics of social change around him. He presumes a manipulative role of religion and also that it is something a properly educated person would not embrace. When I talked with him about Ramadan and juma prayers at one of the mosques in Tirana, he insisted that only old people go to the mosque, because they do not have anything better to do and are poorly educated. When I told him that I observed juma prayers earlier that day and that the majority of people there were under the age of thirty, he struggled to believe it. The way he talked about religion and saw it (or failed to see it) was as much a reflection of his relationship to religion as it was of how he saw it as outmoded and perhaps even a bit dangerous.

* * *

Besnik is one of the young men from the mosque that Erion imagined geriatric. Besnik is from a village east of Puka, in the northern mountains of the country, and was living in one of Tirana's nearby unregulated settlements. Unlike some of his high school friends that migrated to Italy for work, he stayed, largely because he could not get a work visa. Growing up in the unregulated settlement, he, like Erion, struggled with being accepted by those who grew up in the city. Through one of his friends, he ended up getting a job delivering pizza on a moped for a halal pizza shop. While Besnik was from a Muslim village, he did not know much about religion until recently, when he would talk with coworkers between waiting for delivery orders. In these slow times, a group of three to four would talk about their hopes for future opportunities. They were concerned with not only employment opportunities but also questions of meaning and purpose. Their conversations ranged from sports and women to cars and houses being built back in the home village with remittance money from Italy.

Islam entered into their conversations but seldom as theology. Rather, Besnik and his friend would contrast the moral problems they saw surrounding them—corruption in business, people going out and partying while they were working, the absence of respect for others—with their friends at the mosque. It was there that Besnik said he found a community where he felt he belonged and had value. He confessed that he was still working on being a better Muslim, which he saw in terms of more regular prayer and finding a wife from the community with whom he could raise a family. In the pizza shop, there was a picture of Mecca that he would referentially point to in speaking of his aspiration to go on hajj.

* * *

Like Erion and Besnik, Genti also moved to Tirana in his youth. His family was from Durrës, the second-largest city in the country, and he moved to study business in university. While at university, Genti began taking English lessons at one of the new private language schools offering English as a means to success in the postsocialist world. The school, established by Protestant missionaries, afforded Genti opportunities: his English improved, he gained an appreciation of how to work with foreigners, and he developed a network of friends that made his integration into living in Tirana more manageable. He had attended the church service at the school a few times, and liked the Americans working there, but took use of the language lessons more pragmatically. A few of his friends became active in the Evangelical church, referring to themselves as having been "saved." But outside of the group, Genti confessed to seeing himself somewhere in between. His time around the missionaries led him to appreciate religious people as a positive force in the county; however, this also pushed him toward Catholicism, for he believed that was the tradition he had inherited. His parents said they were Catholics but had only been to a Catholic church for weddings, and he was not ready to give it up even if he was not active.

When describing himself to others, Genti never began by saying he was Christian. Privately, he told me that he was not sure if he could call himself Christian or what religion meant to him; he was working it out in a context of other relationships. Some things about the Evangelical church appealed to him, such as the kindness of the community and its willingness to help others who were not related to each other. But he also attended the Catholic church on occasion. He described the service there as a bit more formal and distant but he was also as a bit more comfortable in the distance. He wanted to be "good" like some of those he met at church, but church was also not a regular habit. He sees himself within a broader milieu of people figuring out the options before them—both as professional opportunity and as moral community.

It is of course the case that religious identification should not lead one to assume religious competency. Erion, Besnik, and Genti have limited knowledge about religion and what it means within their own communities. Their relationships to religion are characterized in relation to their understandings of what they have experienced in their everydays and a sense of how they want their community to be. They do not know details of religious life or practice much beyond the communities to which they have contact, but that does not prove problematic. In looking at their own engagement, we see religion as part of a negotiating process, a figuring out, that is rooted within and dependent on the everyday, even for those who, like Elira and Erion, are not religious.

Religion and Social Change

Jonida's relationship with religion reflects both internal and external struggles in her life. She grew up in a village near Himarë, part of the Albanian Riviera in the south of the country, between the Ceraunian Mountains and the Ionian Sea. With nearby beaches of postcard beauty, it is a popular tourist

Figure 25.1. Lighting candles at a rural church in southern Albania, 2007. Photograph by David W. Montgomery.

destination. As a divorced mother in her thirties, Jonida lives with her parents and works in a hotel restaurant. Her life moves between work and taking care of her daughter, whom her parents watch when she is at work. She married just out of high school, was divorced a few years later, and has accepted that she is unlikely to remarry or have a social life outside of her family. Her ex-husband left to work in Greece and has little to do with the raising of their daughter.

In the hills near where she lives, about a thirty-minute hike, is a small old Orthodox chapel overlooking the sea that she has regularly visited since childhood. It remains a place she visits to find peace and composure. She attributes the chapel to helping her through the difficult times of her life and speaks of it as belonging to her village. She identifies as a Bektashi, yet going to a chapel to pray does not strike her as unusual or contradictory. She avoids going to the chapel on important Christian holy days, because then the church is for the Christians. She went once to light a candle when service was going on, and she simply stayed back until everyone had left so as not to get in the way.

If asked about her religion, she says she is Muslim. If asked what that means to her, she is vague and unclear. It is a religion she inherited, but she knows very little about how it is distinguished from Christianity or why such distinctions matter. She prays in front of the icons at the chapel and would pass as an Orthodox were it not for her excluding herself from services. The village knows her family as Muslim, and thus it would be noticed and met with skepticism if she began participating in services. So she does not but still considers the chapel hers as much as theirs.

During the communist period, the chapel fell into disrepair. Villagers took care of it as best they could and continued to visit it in their own way, never saying they were going to pray or for a service, but rather being discrete, having a reason to claim other purposes for going: shepherds would stop while tending their sheep and others would stop ostensibly on their way to somewhere else. Though it was part of village life, little was made of the chapel. According to Jonida's father, the chapel did not have a roof for between forty and fifty years, until repairs were undertaken by the church in the early 2000s.

Jonida described the repairs as part and parcel of Greek efforts to assert influence over the southern region of Albania—the northern Epirus region to which Greeks still lay claim—through repairing churches, restoring Orthodoxy, and encouraging Greek to be spoken. In the mid-2000s, this was largely discussed around Albanians in the south being able to claim pensions of 300 Euro per month, if they could prove they were ethnic Greek. The markers for such claims were relatively crude: Greek lineage could be expressed by affirming lineage from northern Epirus, speaking Greek, and being Orthodox. Thus Greekness became a visible trend in Himara. Graffiti began to appear in Greek and shop owners began speaking Greek to Albanian tourists from the north, even though they had spoken to these same tourists in Albanian years earlier—and would still speak to me, as a foreigner, in Albania. Religion got folded in with changing political and aspirational environments.

Such complications between religious life and social change can be seen everywhere: from Jonida's seemingly idiosyncratic visits to a sacred site without any definitive working out of what religion meant to her and Besnik, between delivering pizzas, speaking to his newfound aspiration to go on hajj, to broader struggles within local religious communities attempting to formulate moral responses to contemporary issues. This can be seen at both the local and the national levels that touch on the narratives of Jonida and Besnik but also remain removed from anything that concerns them.

As Besnik works to make sense of the world changing around him, he encounters those striving to do so through a religious frame. While he visits the mosque and socializes with Muslim friends, his engagement is at a more affectual than intellectual level. There are pockets of Islamic intellectualism in Tirana, where sophisticated discussions occur about Islamic scholars, Muslim thought, and how Islam can holistically address the pressures on—and waywardness of—life in Albania. Such elite discussions, however, most frequently are brought back in terms that Besnik could sympathetically embrace.

One parable-like example emerging in such contexts is the story of a man whose father was a socialist and helped tear down a mosque. Afterward, the father raised his hands to show they were intact, that God had not punished him. For the father, this proved the fallacy of faith: if God were alive and real, he would have been punished. Some years later, his granddaughter was filmed being raped as traffickers unsuccessfully tried to get her out of the country. The person

Figure 25.2. Friday prayers at the Ethem Bey Mosque in Tirana, as car traffic continues, 2013. Photograph by David W. Montgomery

charged with the crime was put in jail but got out in 1997 when the government collapsed.

The man who destroyed the mosque saw no connection between his actions and the suffering and sorrows brought on his family. For those skeptical of Islam, such stories are fables reflecting the quaintness of religious belief, that there is no cosmological truth in the story; life events simply happen. But to Besnik and people of faith, the story is understood in the context of social collapse, where one remains humble about the causal implications of failing in one's faith.

* * *

Dëfrim is an Orthodox priest in Tirana who believes God's work can be understood in world events. When I spoke with him about the relevance of religion in contemporary Albania, he began cautiously, arguing that the church gave its parishioners the path to God's forgiveness, as it had since Paul's travels to Illyricum. As the conversation progressed and took a more theological orientation, Dëfrim spoke more freely and passionately about the role of the church in advocating for what he saw as the moral truths of faith. He explained the need for religion to be firm in its moral teachings and traditions and be willing to oppose those pushing it otherwise. For him, sexuality in general, and homosexuality in particular, was an example where he felt compelled to speak against more liberalizing notions of morality that he blamed on the West. He preached against promiscuity and for the value of heterosexual marriage and felt that was a position widely accepted, even expected, from the church.

He became firm, however, in speaking of the church as distinct from the state, arguing its need to uphold morality in face of the state's waywardness. The case in point for him, was same-sex marriage. As Albania looked to bolster its candidacy for European Union membership, Dëfrim described how some political leaders had met with church leaders to tell them to publicly accept same-sex marriages because it would help the country's image, showing the Albanians as progressive and concerned with human rights. While he believes homosexual behavior a sin, Dëfrim accepted parishioners who were homosexual. But the fact that the state told the church to accept something contrary to its moral tenets was, for Dëfrim, an example of why the church was both relevant and essential: people needed a foundation of tradition to discern value from greed and to navigate both changes in society and life itself. And these concerns were, at a more basic level, what explained the tensions over the diversity of moral visions advocated by the religious and the areligious.

Social Navigation and Everyday Morality

At its most fundamental level, religion provides a framework for understanding moral behavior, for knowing how to be in community in the world. Religions give a context for understanding all of life, from birth to death and everything in-between. Religion is not the only thing providing moral structures for society, and in no way do I wish to reduce its significance by suggesting that is all that it does. Rather, how it provides a structure for coping with the existential challenges we face can be understood by the religious practitioner as the very essence of being. We need moral structures, and this is yet another way we see religion playing a role—at times contested—in everyday life. This can perhaps be seen most clearly in the transitional period of the 1990s.

It is not uncommon for postsocialist societies to, a quarter of a century beyond socialism, become nostalgic about the social services—especially pensions—the state once provided in light of the uncertainties many pensioners face today. And in the case of Albania, one must be cautious romanticizing the Hoxha period, for many suffered and many were killed. From a distance, it seems appropriate to look back at the oppressive rule of Hoxha as a dark bit of history for the country; and this is not wrong. But we also must see it is slightly more complicated, as the hope and optimism of the early 1990s gave way to a rupture of social order where gangs and mafias took control of commerce and the pyramid schemes that led to rebellion in 1997 caused many to feel the bottom had fallen out.[11]

Tomor, a pensioner who spent his career as a midlevel functionary of the state, characterized the transitional years of the 1990s as a "time without morality." As closed and tightly regulated as the state was under Hoxha, the parameters of accepted social behavior were generally clear; people knew the restrictions placed on them and that actions outside of the ideological positions of the state had consequences. The most difficult years through which to live, according to Tomor, were those of the 1990s where the rules of social order were seemingly absent.

The 2000s were easier, as the state regained order and legitimacy, becoming able to reassert regulatory control over public space. For many, this return of authority meant people could walk the streets again at night, be it for an evening stroll through the center of town or meeting for coffee with friends.

But the postsocialist reality of Albania was, at many levels, a markedly different one for Tomor and his family. With few options available for employment, Tomor's son migrated to Italy where he has been for a decade.[12] As such, Tomor and his wife feel absent from their grandchildren's lives, seeing them only once or twice a year, and he laments how the respect for family and the elderly was lost with the rupture of postsocialist change. A proud man, he sees the absence of his relevance as part of a broader crisis of morality. In meeting with his friends, he often recounted the fable of when the young killed their fathers when the fathers became old, yet one son hid his father away and took care of him. One day, there was a competition among the young men, and the son who had saved his father won, because he had consulted his father before the competition. Then people realized the wisdom of the elders, stopped killing the fathers when they became old, and began heeding their advice.[13] Tomor characterized the young discarding the insights of their parents who lived through the socialist years as those who killed their fathers in spite of themselves.

Tomor described the present in aspirational terms of wanting the "better" parts of the past back. For him, it was framed in terms of security—not wealth—and family. Besnik and Dëfrim speak of social well-being in talking about religion, a process of socially navigating—of moving and responding in the midst of change—to a "better." For them, the churches and mosques, the missionaries and outreach, teachings and traditions, play a role in ascribing value and meaning to life. For Tomor, who does not know what to do with religion or talk about religion—he believes in ghosts and a divine spirit, but sees organized religion as unnecessary—better comes through the always fluid benchmark of traditional values, which would include having his son return home with his family. The striving to some point of equipoise felt as better, morally and otherwise, is varied but rooted in the experience of the everyday.[14]

To struggle is common, yet in seeing the context of people striving it should always be kept in mind that all places have more to them than suffering. The emotions my interlocutors encounter run the gamut, and even in speaking about topics of despair, they also experience happiness in many parts of their lives. There are struggles, and sometimes a heaviness over life—a fatalism that the Albanian poet Migjeni captures: "The more I know, the more I suffer."[15] But it is not all darkness; there are close friendships and a pride of place. In all, there is a struggling for a better life that occurs within the everyday and in which religion plays a role.

There is a spectrum along which people engage with religion: Besnik is learning to be Muslim while Dëfrim is teaching how to be Orthodox; Jonida is fashioning her own way between Islam and Christianity while Tomor is calling on tradition not in religion as much as in culture; and Erion and Elira are averse to religion whereas Mirjeta and Genti are quiet in their support of it. But in its presence and absence, religion remains relevant to thinking through the dynamics of everyday life in Albania and how people face the moral context of social change. Social life among friends is constituted across myriad connections—some that have been maintained since the early years of school; some brought by location; some created at work; some emerging out of discussions about (or against) religion—and the boundaries are not clean.

Once, over lunch near Lake Shkodra in the northern part of the country, I sat with four friends whose views on religion were diverse and exemplary of the Albanian context. One identified as a Christian without a church, one as an atheist, one as a Muslim, and one was simply unsure what religion meant to her. They were thoughtful, caring, and morally concerned, each working things out in their own ways. There was much on which they disagreed, much in which they shared, and all were trying to make it in a world they wanted to be better.

Notes

1. The population at the end of World War II was to around 1,180,500, with there being around 626,000 Sunni Muslims (53 percent), 200,000 Bektashi (17 percent), 212,500 Eastern Orthodox (18 percent), and 142,000 Roman Catholics (12 percent) (see Keefe et al. 1971, 115). There were myriad problems with the census, but it does provide a context for how the population was described.

2. For the 2011 Albanian census, see http://www.instat.gov.al/media/3058/main_results__population_and_housing_census_2011.pdf, accessed June 30, 2018.

3. Elsie and Mathie-Heck 2008; see also Bayraktar 2011; Duijzings 2002

4. For more on the ethnic and tribal histories of Albanians, see Jacques 1995 and Elsie 2015.

5. Gawrych 2006.

6. Hodgkinson 1999.

7. Norris 2006.

8. Trix 1993.

9. See, for example, Gardin 1988.

10. An ironic indication of how drastically things changed is that small Christian worship and religious activities now take place in the former residence of Hoxha (see Thomas 2005; Blanchard 2010).

11. On the pyramid schemes and their context, see Musaraj (2011).

12. On the issue of migration, see King and Mai (2011).

13. This is a version of the folktale of "How the Killing of Old Men Was Stopped" (see Georgevitch 1918).

14. Even the environment of these everydays changes. Before the end of socialism, most people would socialize over coffee at home or the homes of others. As bars and cafés became ubiquitous, people less frequently visited each other at home and instead met out. The coffee culture moved from the private to the public.

15. Migjeni 2002.

References

Bayraktar, Uğur Bahadır. 2011. "Mythifying the Albanians: A Historiographical Discussion of Vasa Efendi's 'Albania and the Albanians'." *Balkanologie* 13 (1–2). http://balkanologie.revues.org/2272.

Blanchard, John. 2010. "Newsline: Four-Monthly Notes and News of His Ministry from John Blanchard." January. http://www.johnblanchard.org/pdf/Newsline%20Jan%202010.pdf.

Duijzings, Ger. 2002. "Religion and the Politics of 'Albanianism': Naim Frashëri's Bektashi Writings." In *Albanian Identities: Myth and History*, edited by S. Schwandner-Sievers and B. J. Fischer, 60–69. Bloomington: Indiana University Press.

Elsie, Robert. 2015. *The Tribes of Albania: History, Society and Culture*. London: I.B. Tauris.

Elsie, Robert, and Janice Mathie-Heck, eds. 2008. *Lightning from the Depths: An Anthology of Albanian Poetry*. Evanston, IL: Northwestern University Press.

Gardin, Giacomo. 1988. *Banishing God in Albania: The Prison Memoirs of Giacomo Gardin, S.J.* San Francisco: Ignatius Press.

Gawrych, George W. 2006. *The Crescent and the Eagle: Ottoman Rule, Islam and the Albanians, 1874–1913*. London: I. B. Tauris.

Georgevitch, T.R. 1918. *Folk-Lore: A Quarterly Review of Myth, Tradition, Institution, and Custom* 29: 239

Hodgkinson, Harry. 1999. *Scanderbeg*. London: Learning Design.

Jacques, Edwin E. 1995. *The Albanians: An Ethnic History from Prehistoric Times to the Present*. Jefferson, NC: McFarland.

Keefe, Eugene K., Sarah Jane Elpern, William Giloane, James M. Moore Jr., Stephen Peters, and Eston T. White. 1971. *Area Handbook for Albania*. Washington, DC: US Government Printing Office.

King, Russell, and Nicola Mai. 2011. *Out of Albania: From Crisis Migration to Social Inclusion in Italy*. New York: Berghahn Books.

Migjeni. 2002. *Vepra*. Tirana: Cetis

Musaraj, Smoki. 2011. "Tales from Albarado: The Materiality of Pyramid Schemes in Postsocialist Albania." *Cultural Anthropology* 26 (1): 84–110.

Norris, H. T. 2006. *Popular Sufism in Eastern Europe: Sufi Brotherhoods and the Dialogue with Christianity and "Heterodoxy."* London: Routledge.

Thomas, Geoff. 2005. "Visit to Albania and Greece." *Banner of Truth: Biblical Christianity Through Literature*. May 25. https://banneroftruth.org/us/resources/articles/2005/visit-to-albania-and-greece.

Trix, Frances. 1993. *Spiritual Discourse: Learning with an Islamic Master*. Philadelphia: University of Pennsylvania Press.

DAVID W. MONTGOMERY is Director of Program Development for Communities Engaging with Difference and Religion (CEDAR) and Associate Research Professor at the Center for International Development and Conflict Management at the University of Maryland. He is author of *Practicing Islam: Knowledge, Experience, and Social Navigation in Kyrgyzstan* and *Living with Difference: How to Build Community in a Divided World* (with Adam Seligman and Rahel Wasserfall).

26 Ramadan in Prizren, Kosovo

Frances Trix

We were sitting at a table that looked out on one of the arched cobblestone bridges that were so much a part of the distinctive local landscape that had struck me ever since I had first come to Prizren in my student days. The Sinan Pasha Mosque, an important mosque of the city, was to our left. Usually in such a central setting—with the Sharr Mountains of southern Kosovo in the background and the sound of the Bistrica River flowing through the city in the foreground—the tables by the river would have been full of people. It was late afternoon in midsummer, but there were few people in the outdoor café. It was the Muslim month of Ramadan, and in Prizren many people were fasting.

Ibrahim, a university student from Prizren, sat at the table with us. He was taking a summer workshop in photography and had come to ask the professor from Turkey in charge of the workshop several questions. The professor was impressed with the extra work Ibrahim was putting in this late in the afternoon.

Like most young people in Prizren, Ibrahim was fasting. That meant that he did not eat or drink anything from sunup to sundown for the thirty days of Ramadan. Since Muslim holidays are lunar, they come about eleven days earlier each year according to the solar calendar. Every thirty-three years, the holy month makes a complete cycle of the solar year. In 2013, Ramadan began the second week in July and ended the second week of August. People stopped eating and drinking around three in the morning when the sun rose and did not break the fast until the sun went down after eight.

I asked Ibrahim how he kept such a long fast each day in hot weather. He told me, "It is easier if you keep busy." He enjoyed the photography workshop that met in the morning hours. And he liked to keep working in the afternoon as well. His city of Prizren was photogenic; it is a center of tourism for Kosovo due to the preservation of its Ottoman character in a handsome physical setting. Kosovo had been part of the Ottoman Empire from 1455 to 1912. But Ibrahim was also interested in learning how to photograph fireworks.

After the breaking of the fast each evening, there was much life on the streets, including music and fireworks. The photography professor explained the problems of capturing fireworks on film. Indeed, nightlife during Ramadan went on well past midnight and was full of energy. Ibrahim explained that Ramadan had a way of upending the usual time frame of life—that is, instead of the usual emphasis on daytime hours, during Ramadan people coped during the day but truly came alive after dark.

Immediately I realized that following people's lives during Ramadan in Prizren would be challenging. The time frame alone would be extensive. And I needed to see if what Ibrahim had said was true for others as well. Did Ramadan upend their daily lives and in what ways? Recall, Ibrahim still did a photography class in the morning, not unlike his university classes during the academic year. Maybe what he was also telling us was the intensity of the socializing after dark was what was significant for him, something that did not take place during the rest of the year.

Before exploring other citizens' experiences of Ramadan, it is important to establish what is special about the city of Prizren in Kosovo. I will also present the larger religious context of Islam in Prizren and how attempts to destroy its heritage in the twentieth century were foiled by the people.

Contrasts with Other Cities in Kosovo and Background on Prizren

Prishtina is the capital city of Kosovo. As a graduate student, I lived there for an entire academic year when it was still part of Yugoslavia. It has many blocks of buildings from the socialist period, with few mosques from earlier Ottoman times. I also lived a month in Mitrovica, a city in the north known for its mines. I stayed multiple times in Gjakova, a city in western Kosovo known for the intensity of its communist politics and the extent to which its leaders were targeted during the 1998–99 war. None of these cities were known for religion, let alone celebrating Ramadan the way Prizren did throughout the twentieth century and continues to do so into the twenty-first.[1]

Prizren is the second-largest city of Kosovo. It stands out among Kosovar cities for its many mosques, churches, and traditional Ottoman two-story homes in the city center. It also stands out for its ethnic diversity and the multilingualism of its people; many people in Prizren speak Turkish as well as Albanian and Serbian.

In Kosovo as a whole, Albanian Muslims long formed the majority and now constitute about 93 percent of the population. During Serbian and Yugoslav times, which extended from 1918 to 1999, Serbs of Orthodox Christian descent were a minority but in political power. There was a carefully conducted census in Kosovo in 2011, but the Serbs boycotted it in the north. There can only be estimates of the Serb population at 3 percent, with the remaining 4 percent of the population made up of Bosnians, Turks, Roma of different groups, and Gorani, a Slavic-speaking Muslim group.

Yet with such a relatively small number of Turks, how did Prizren retain the Turkish language? Recall how the photography professor from Turkey knew the students in Prizren would understand him. And how did Prizren keep its more traditional appearance when all other Kosovar cities lost theirs?

When I tried to find answers to these questions, I learned that the special character of Prizren drew from the earlier history of the city. It also drew from how its citizens had responded to more recent challenges.

Historically, Prizren was the cultural center of Kosovo. It was on a Roman military road that connected it to the Adriatic Sea to the west. It was important in medieval times when Serbian king Stefan Dushan held court there. Under the Ottomans, it reached commercial heights in the sixteenth and seventeenth centuries, when its marketplace and expert silversmiths, leatherworkers, and sword- and gunsmiths flourished. It was an Ottoman administrative center into the nineteenth century.[2]

Urban Ottoman culture permeated the different ethnic groups that lived in Prizren: Turks, Albanians, Serbs, Vlachs, and Bosnians, all of whom also spoke Turkish. Traditionally Turkish had been the language of the marketplace throughout Ottoman rule and well into the twentieth century. It was also the language of Balkan urban life during this time.

When the Ottoman Empire was pushed out of most of the Balkans and the new borders of Kosovo were set in 1912, Prizren found itself on the margin. Commercially, it was cut off from its markets to the south and east. Politically, it was no longer important and was relatively far from Kosovo's capital of Prishtina. In its marginal position, its diversity of people retained their urban Ottoman culture, which they associated with the Turkish language. It was their civic identity. While Prizren still has the largest Turkish population in Kosovo, most of the people who speak Turkish as their home language there are not Turks.[3]

Islam in Prizren and Attempts to Destroy Its Heritage

There are thirty-three mosques in Prizren, of which twenty-seven are from Ottoman times. In the twentieth century such mosques were vulnerable. During the First World War, Prizren was occupied by the Bulgarians, who stored ammunition in its mosques. The Begzade Mosque exploded and was destroyed at this time. After the First and the Second World Wars, the Serbs, who had taken control of Kosovo, attempted to destroy the important Sinan Pasha Mosque, but the citizens of Prizren rallied and stopped them.

In the early 1960s, a commission came from Belgrade, the Yugoslav capital, to redesign the city of Prizren. There were three options: demolish the Ottoman monuments, apply for UNESCO world heritage status, or destroy the Ottoman monuments on the right side of the river. The third option won out; the sixteenth-century Arasta Mosque in the center of town was destroyed and a bank put in its place. But the people of Prizren were furious, so the mosque's minaret was retained. It does look strange to see a tall stone minaret without a mosque, standing silently next to a bank. No more buildings were destroyed, however.

Most Muslims in Prizren are Sunni Muslims. Prizren now has a *medrese*, which is a secondary school that has regular secondary classes along with classes on religion for male students, as well as a similar medrese for female students. Sufi orders—the mystics of Islam—have long been active in Prizren. These include the Halveti, Rufa'i, Kadiri, Sinani, and Saadi orders.[4] There are also Melamis, a group distinguished by their musical knowledge, spiritual camaraderie, and intellectual acumen. When I was in Prizren, I was honored by a private concert on one of the hottest days of July by Melami musicians. It is experiences like this that make research so unforgettable but also shows the active role of Islam in Prizren life.

Preparing for Ramadan, Its Meaning over the Year, and Fasting

How do people prepare for Ramadan? I asked people this in Prizren. One man told me that people had to save money for Ramadan. He said, "If you want to have good food for *iftar*, the evening meal to break the fast, you need to have extra funds. You will be thinking of what good food you can have all day. So, to make sure you have the money to buy this food when Ramadan rolls around, you have to save." Another man in Prizren told me he got ready for Ramadan by stopping drinking alcohol two months in advance. That way when Ramadan came, it was easier not to drink at all. These are practical ways in which Ramadan affects people before the actual month of fasting begins.

People also mentioned that the discipline to fast gave them strength during the rest of the year as well. It reinforces their Muslim identity. Fasting at Ramadan is one of the five pillars of Islam, and as a major Islamic observance carried out across the Islamic world, it also links Muslims in Prizren with other Muslims. Giving to those in need, which is a major part of Ramadan, is also a feature of Muslim holidays and Muslim practices across the rest of the year. In a sense, Ramadan is an intensification of Muslim values of charity, community, and family that are practiced throughout the entire year.

I asked people how they coped with fasting when the days were so long. In a bookstore late one afternoon, there were three young women working. I asked them if they were fasting. "Yes," they said. "How do you do it?" I asked. "We ask that God give us help," answered one of them simply. "And how old were you when you started fasting the full month?" I asked. "Around fourteen," said another.

People often explained that they started fasting for part of a day when they were young. They would see their parents fasting and wanted to do it too. They would fast from early morning to early afternoon one day. Then they would fast from early afternoon to the evening the next day. "Our grandmothers would say they would sew the two half days together for us," they said smiling. The next year they might fast one whole day, and then eat and drink the next day. Gradually they worked into fasting the full thirty days.

The president of the Islamic Community in Prizren, Lütfi Ballek, said that fasting was a private matter. Before the war in 1998–99, almost all Muslims in Prizren fasted for Ramadan.[5] And before the martial law of the 1990s, the Serbs in Prizren would not eat or drink in public during Ramadan out of respect for their Muslim neighbors. Since the war there are many newcomers to Prizren, but still around 80 percent of Muslims in Prizren fast, including most young people. Indeed, Prizren is known across Kosovo as the most traditional city, and its Ramadan practices are a main expression of this.

Figure 26.1. Bosnian and Albanian women celebrating iftar together in Prizren, 2013. Photograph by Frances Trix.

I want to emphasize the two time periods that Lütfi Ballek gives us here. The earlier one is the period before martial law, that is, before 1990, when even Serbs in Prizren respected Muslims' fast by not eating in public during Ramadan. (Unfortunately, in current times, I watched a Serbian priest eat and drink openly on the street during Ramadan in Prizren. He was young and not from Prizren.) The other period is before the war of 1998–99, that extended the earlier period during which almost all Muslims in Prizren fasted. What Lütfi Ballek has noted is that everyday life during Ramadan in these times was one in which Muslims of Prizren fasted.

Essentially, before the recent war, Prizren was able to maintain its Ottoman traditions of Ramadan fasting of almost all Muslims, despite opposition by the secular communist regime in Belgrade and Prishtina. This was remarkable. It gave the city a special identity in Kosovo. Even after the war when many people from outside Prizren moved in, still 80 percent of Muslims fast, which is a high percentage, and most young people fast as well.

Food at the Edges of a Day in Ramadan

A professional woman who works for the city of Prizren explained the importance of the main meals of Ramadan. Very early in the morning, before sunrise, families gather for *sahur*, the morning meal. This is a full meal that must sustain family members throughout the day, so it often includes soup, bread, cheese, vegetables, meat, and a fresh fruit drink with plenty of natural sugar. After this meal, people pray that God will give them the strength to keep the fast for the entire day. Then many return to bed.

During the day people live as normally as possible. They go to work, study, clean the house, take care of children, or go shopping for the evening meal. People nap if possible because they do not sleep enough during the night. Women prepare the iftar, the meal for breaking the fast in the evening.

There is a special food for Ramadan known as *pitajka*. It is a pita bread that is baked fresh daily at the local bakeries, which use only wood-burning ovens. Every neighborhood has its own bakery, and around an hour before the end of the daily fast, a woman from each family will go to the local bakery with a tray, a towel, and a container of special sauce for her pitajka. The sauce is made of cream cheese, eggs, black sesame seeds, and parsley.

The skilled baker, who has been preparing for this rush all day, slides balls of pitajka dough on a pallet into the traditional oven with a different sauce on top of the dough for each woman. The women wait in line with their trays until their pitajka is baked. Then the women carry their fresh-baked pitajka home from the bakery on a tray covered by a towel to keep it warm. The pitajka is the main bread at iftar dinners. Children wait each year for pitajka, and it is widely considered delicious.

At one of these traditional bakeries I asked the baker how many loaves of pitajka he baked each day of Ramadan. He announced without stopping working, "We bake fourteen hundred loaves a day." And this was only one of many bakeries in Prizren.

People then wait for the end of the fast that day. The table is set in every household, and the family gathers. The atmosphere before the end of the fast is special. There are different kinds of salad on the table. The fresh pitajka from the bakery is there, along with soup and all sorts of other food. People wait for the call from the mosque announcing the end of the fast for the day.

Raif Vırmiça, a well-known journalist and writer of Prizren, told me that they used to shoot a cannon from the old fortress on the mountain over the city to announce the end of the fast for the day. This was done in Ottoman times and even in communist times into the early 1970s. The muezzin from the Bajrakli Mosque, the main mosque in town, then called out from the minaret, followed by muezzins from other mosques all over town announcing the end of the fast.

Lights went on in the minarets as they do today. The cannon stopped when loudspeakers were installed in the minarets. In old times—and still today—there were also drummers who beat their drums at the end of the fast. Of course now one can check the internet and get the exact time to the minute of the end of the fast for each day of Ramadan, though people still prefer the call from the minaret.

At the table, people give a prayer of thanks that they were able to hold the fast for the day and there were no problems. If possible, they break the fast first with dates and water as did the Prophet Muhammad fourteen centuries ago. Then people eat a long-awaited meal and drink much water and often lemonade. After the meal, which is extensive, there is evening prayer.

Two hours after sunset, there is a special Ramadan prayer known as *Teravih*. Its name implies a prayer of relaxation. It is celebrated in all the mosques of Prizren and includes twenty *raka'ats*, or prostrations. Women do not usually go to the mosque the way men do on Friday for noon prayers, but women often go to the courtyards of mosques for Teravih during Ramadan. It is quite beautiful in the late evening to hear verses in Arabic and then prayers in Turkish or Albanian or Bosnian, depending on the imam and his congregation.

My first night in Prizren during Ramadan, I went to Teravih at the Emin Pasha Mosque. There was a whole busload of women who had been driven up to Prizren from Skopje in Macedonia because they knew Teravih was so special in Prizren. We prayed in the summer night air and listened to the imam pray in Arabic, in Turkish, and in Albanian. He gave a short sermon, but mostly it was the prayers that people came for. They were peaceful and fulfilling and no one wanted to leave at the end of the service.

After the iftar meal, and after Teravih, there is much life on the streets in Prizren. Everyone is out walking, or gathering in cafés, or in discotheques with music. Families bring small children in strollers. Young people move in groups along with the crowds. They wear casual summer clothes, similar to what we wear in America, only the girls tend to wear dresses more than shorts, while the young men do not have untrimmed facial hair. There is corn on the cob, grilled by the side of the pedestrian walks, French-fried potatoes, cotton candy, ice cream cones of all flavors, soft drinks, and pizza. It is like a summer fair that goes on and on. There are street musicians who play clarinets and drums, and others who play accordions. Other years there were rock concerts, I was told. There are fireworks from beyond certain mosques and sometimes there are so many people walking along that you cannot even see the cobble-stoned walkways underfoot.

The Meaning of Ramadan and Recent Changes

The imam of the Emin Pasha Mosque, Hafiz Daoud, reiterated what I had seen throughout the city during the holy month. But where the student Ibrahim emphasized the nightlife, Hafiz Daoud saw Ramadan as bringing families together. At other times of the year, people might eat dinner at different times. But during Ramadan, they all come together to eat at the same time for iftar in the evening and sahur in the early morning, too. This is of course also true at the end of Ramadan when there is a three-day holiday with much feasting and visiting of family and neighbors.

There is also the charity of the fast. People are expected to give to the poor during Ramadan. As Hafiz Daoud put it, the fast does not reach heaven if there is no charity. However much people spend on their two meals of sahur and iftar in a day, this much, times the number of people in their family, they should give to the poor at the end of the month. People understand that they are fasting for one month, but the poor often go hungry throughout the entire year. So fasting makes them more aware of the poor.

In Prizren, since its people have defined themselves for decades as keeping Ramadan, the time of Ramadan is a time of civic solidarity. People told me that Prizren has "the feel of Ramadan." It is "a special place," "more traditional." This is clear in the evening after the iftar meal when the whole city seems to be walking out on the streets. I noticed only a light police presence at this time and no trouble, despite the large numbers of people and the late hours. When I asked a local police team, made up of a policeman and a policewoman, about this, they responded that many fewer people drink alcohol during Ramadan. This helped explain the peaceful nature of the crowds.

I should mention that during the Kosovo War (1998–99), most Muslims in Prizren were expelled from their homes. Serbian military and paramilitary tried to force Albanians out of Kosovo from January to June 1999. Fully eight hundred thousand Kosovar Albanians were expelled south to Macedonia or Albania, or west to Montenegro. An estimated ten thousand were killed, while an estimated twenty thousand women and girls were raped, according to the World Health Organization and the Center for Disease Control.[6] People from Prizren ended up in Albania; the trek over the mountains was not easy. They returned as soon as possible after the war ended, mostly in the summer of 1999. When Ramadan came later that year, it began on December 9, 1999. People were most grateful to be home again in Prizren, where they could celebrate the holy days.

There have been changes in Ramadan observances since the end of the war in 1999. One of the main changes is the appearance of public iftar dinners, offered for those in need. Many people lost much in the war. After the war, the factories that used to support many families were privatized and then closed; unemployment is officially 32.8 percent, although it is much higher among the young. These public iftar meals became a way of addressing public needs.

In the first year after the war, Turkish NATO troops, known as Turkish KFOR, began offering iftar dinners in Prizren for 250 to 300 people in a long tent every evening of Ramadan. They have continued this ever since. People begin gathering several hours before the meal. The Turkish troops serve a nutritious meal of pitajka, pepper stuffed with meat and rice, cabbage slaw, and *helva*. They have local musicians from the Balkan Music Association, under Prizrenli composer Aluş Nuş, playing local instruments and singing religious songs. While the festivities can bring happiness, as one woman pointed out in speaking of her worry about her children who had university degrees but not work, the anxieties of everyday life remain.

The next night, I found another set of tents that served iftar meals throughout Ramadan for another 150 people in Prizren. These meals were paid for by a province near Ankara in Turkey. They were coordinated by the mayor's office in Prizren through Orhan Lopar, the assistant mayor for communities. I sat with Bosnian women of Prizren and had iftar. Another evening, the iftar dinner there was just for young people.

A more local change is the eating of iftar dinner in restaurants instead of just in the family home. Families gather in restaurants with the table full of food. But they wait just as they would at home for the call from the minaret announcing the end of the fast. This is a special treat for the women in the family.

Final Note on Prizren, Dokufest, and Ramadan

As noted above, when I was a student, I visited Prizren. What stood out in my mind then, besides the beauty of the city, were all the shops for silver filigree work.[7] I spent time there and learned that there had long been guild organizations of skilled craftsmen and businessmen in Prizren. This made sense, for Prizren had long been a center of trade and commerce.

Much has changed politically since those times. Yugoslavia no longer exists as a country and Prizren is now in independent Kosovo. But the civic leaders of Prizren, both young and mature, clearly still have organizational strengths as shown in their abilities to carry out Ramadan festivities. Each year participation and the communal dinners and entertainments grow stronger and more various. The young people are definitely part of the Ramadan fast in different ways. Considering the disruption of the 1998–99 war and the lack of employment for youth, this is a remarkable achievement. But Ramadan is not the only way that the young in Prizren in recent times have shown their mettle and civic pride.

In 2002 two young men of Prizren bemoaned the loss of the cinema in their city. They used to have cinema, but with the difficulties of the 1990s and the war, they had lost all their theaters. So they decided they needed to find a way to have films come again in Prizren. This was the beginning of what became known as Dokufest, a Festival of International Documentaries and Short Films.

They started with eleven films. In 2013 there were twenty-three hundred applications and two hundred films from 150 countries selected. The theme was Breaking Borders. The films were shown on open-air screens all over the city—in the fortress, along the quays of the river, and in sports stadiums. It is now among the top twenty-five of such festivals in the world.

Young people work as volunteers throughout the nine days of the festival, which also includes workshops and panels on documentary filmmaking. Since it is very difficult for Kosovars to get visas to travel to other countries in Europe, Dokufest brings the world to Prizren. And this brings economic benefit to their city as well as people who come for the documentary festival, stay in hotels, eat in restaurants, and buy souvenirs of its historic mosques and bridges. In 2013, with Ramadan during the hottest time of the summer, helping plan for Dokufest during the day helped young people who were fasting pass the time.

But let us return to Ramadan and Imam Daoud. Imam Daoud suggested that we should remember Ramadan for several months after it has passed, and then we should look forward to its coming again. Thus, we live this life tied to Ramadan, that is, close to God, to the Qur'an, and to the poor. Many people remember different years by when Ramadan came—in the summer or in the spring, the winter or the fall—when they felt especially close to their families and their city. These memories became especially poignant for all those of Prizren when they

Figure 26.2. Two men talking to each other on a bridge in Prizren during Ramadan, 2013. Photograph by Frances Trix.

were expelled during the war. When they returned, everyday life and the annual holidays of Prizren became even sweeter to them.

Notes

1. See Warrander and Brandt's Guide to Kosovo (2013) for different cities in Kosovo.
2. See Malcolm 1997, 104, 193.
3. See Ismajli and Kraja (2011) on languages in Kosovo, pp. 423–433, and especially on Turkish, p. 432.
4. Duizings 2000.
5. For the period of the 1990s, the war, and its aftermath, see Trix (2010, 358–376).
6. Smith 2000.
7. Siqeca (2002) with English summary, p.75

References

Duizings, Ger. 2000. *Religion and the Politics of Identity in Kosovo*. London: Hurst & Company.

Ismajli, Rexhep, and Mehmet Kraja, eds. 2013. *Kosova: A Monographic Survey.* Prishtina: Kosova Academy of Sciences and Arts.

Malcolm, Noel. 1997. *Kosovo: A Short History.* New York: New York University Press.

Siqeca, Shpresë. 2002. *Perlat e Etnisë Shqiptare në Prizren* ("Ethnic Albanian Pearls in Prizren"). Pejë, Kosova: Dukagjini.

Smith, Helena. 2000. "Rape Victims' Babies Pay the Price of War." Special Report. *The Guardian.* April 16. https://www.theguardian.com/world/2000/apr/16/balkans.

Trix, Frances. 2010. "Kosova: Resisting Expulsion and Striving for Independence." In *Central and Southeastern Europe since 1989*, edited by S. Ramet, 358–376. New York: Cambridge University Press.

Warrander, Gail, and Verena Knaus. 2011. *Kosovo, the Bradt Travel Guide.* Bucks, UK: Bradt Travel.

FRANCES TRIX is Professor Emerita of Anthropology and Linguistics at Indiana University, living in Detroit. Her most recent books are *Urban Muslim Migrants in Istanbul: Identity and Trauma among Balkan Migrants* and *Europe and the Refugee Crisis: Local Responses to Migrants.*

27 The Cross at the Crossroads: The Feast of *Slava* between Faith and Custom

Milica Bakić-Hayden

The connection between nationalism and politics is the common focus of much of the scholarly literature on Orthodox Christianity. In the case of the Serbian Orthodox Church, this was particularly acute during the violent disintegration of Yugoslavia in the early 1990s. While justified in certain historical moments, this emphasis on the political has often been at the expense of a more general understanding of the role religion and the church, as an institution, play in the daily life of both those who consider themselves Orthodox Christians and those of Orthodox heritage who reject Orthodoxy as a significant marker of their national and/or personal identity. In this chapter, we look at how Serbians of Orthodox Christian heritage understand and practice their religion today. Specifically, we see how Serbs relate to *Slava*, an annual feast honoring the family's patron saint. A religious holy day, widely perceived by the Serbs to be a unique feature of Serbian Orthodoxy, Slava plays an important role in the construction of Serbian identity, not simply religious, but also ethnic and personal. Thus examining Slava provides good background for understanding wider issues of religious (dis)continuity and change, postcommunist revival, and the invention or rejection of certain aspects of religious practices, as well as the role media plays in strengthening and subverting these processes.

There is little doubt that observers of the fall of communism in Eastern Europe witnessed the reemergence of religion as a powerful marker of national and personal identity, competing for its place in the public square. This is not surprising, because at times of change and transition, humans—individually and collectively—seek to (re)connect with what they perceive to be their (symbolic) roots in order to brace themselves for the uncertainty of the future. In most postcommunist societies, the gradual process of democratization led the voices of traditional religious institutions to become more audible, and thus increasingly subject to public scrutiny. Public responses ranged from toleration to enthusiastic support for those who saw religion having a role in public life and from sharp criticism to open rejection by those warnings against the "clericalization" of society. While close analysis of such perceptions is beyond the scope of this chapter, our focus on Slava provides an illustration of the transformation of certain religious practices in contemporary Serbian society.

Origins of Slava

The origin of Slava is not clear. Some scholars, mainly ethnologists, folklorists, and archaeologists, point to the similarities that exist between Slava and the Greek cult of heroes, such as a yearly sacrificial ritual honoring the ancestors in which boiled wheat and wine were used (Vasić 1985). This Greek connection is supported by the fact that both wheat and wine are indispensable items in Slava and that the Serbian word for wheat, *koljivo*, is derived from the Greek *koliva* or *kolivon*, meaning grain, especially grain of wheat. Another common term for wheat in Serbian is *žito*. Others speculate that Slava actually has origins either in a Roman cult of hero-ancestors—guardians of the hearth and other domains of life known as Lar or Lares[1]—or is a variation on a widespread form of Roman celebration that includes the "breaking of the cake" and toasting, both being the elements of Slava. Those who support this view argue that while this custom of breaking the cake and toasting is also found among some Serbs and Albanians of Catholic faith, mainly in the coastal areas of the Adriatic, it is not recorded among other Balkan Orthodox peoples. This suggests the direction of its spreading from the west to the east, where it became accepted and preserved in the Slava practice of the predominantly Serbian Orthodox population.[2] Another popular ethnological interpretation of Slava, traces its origin to pre-Christian Slavic (Serbian) cults of the mythical ancestors and the cult of the dead where commemoration of the departed ancestors is always accompanied with a sacrificial offering, such as that of wheat and wine.[3]

Today, however, it is widely accepted that Slava, as celebrated among the Orthodox Serbs, was established sometime around 1207 or 1208, by St. Sava (1174–1236), founder of the autocephalous Serbian Orthodox Church and its first archbishop. Some see it as St. Sava's way of reinforcing Christian faith by reinterpreting certain aspects of Serbian folk religion and customs to make it more consistent with Orthodox Christianity. Analysis of manuscripts from the thirteenth to fourteenth century indicate that St. Sava sanctioned the ancient pre-Christian practice of sacrificial offering of animals for the departed souls in the vicinity of the church, and moved the social aspect of the accompanying feast to people's homes. As a result, the religious (i.e., Christian) and the preceding pagan folk customs eventually merged into one practice.[4] While this integration of formal Christian and popular pre-Christian folk practices helped preserve the Orthodox faith during the centuries of Ottoman rule in the Balkans, it also contributed to a complete (con)fusion of religious and ethnonational identities by treating them as interchangeable. In contrast to this view, theologians explain that those elements of the feast that ethnologists and folklorists tend to interpret as pre-Christian may be traced to the Old Testament or are simply universal enough in character to be also found in pagan religions of the Greco-Roman world. However, such elements by themselves cannot explain the parallel that exists between the liturgical and Slava offerings—namely, the religious significance of the Slava celebration is in thanksgiving to God and in the veneration of a saint who is considered to be both protector of the family and mediator of God's grace to the family. The saint is then understood only to be a facilitator of that connection, so that Slava without Christ in mind would be *anthropolatria* (worship of a human being), not a glorification of God.[5] Interestingly, because the protective role of the saint is so emphasized in a Slava, belief in the protective role of guardian angels is not as prominent among those who celebrate Slava as it is among those who do not.[6]

The feast is variously referred to in literature: as *baptismal* Slava (*krsna Slava*) or *family* Slava (*porodična Slava*), but in popular parlance it is simply Slava. As baptismal, Slava commemorates the day associated with a particular saint on whose day, as per liturgical calendar, a family or a clan was baptized, that is, when it accepted the Christian faith. It is patrilineal (handed down from father to son) but in a practice referred to as *preslava*, it is not uncommon for daughters to continue to celebrate (even if not to the same extent) their natal family Slava in addition to the one they adopt through marriage. As a family holy day, Slava not only gathers together extended family and friends in honor of the patron saint but also commemorates the deceased family members—all of whom are understood to be still part of the church. Slava thus differs from name day or birthday celebrations found in other traditions precisely because it is focused on *family* rather than individual. There is also a parallel here between the family and the church, in that both are dedicated to and/or named after saints, so that the celebration of Slava functions as an extension of the liturgical celebration from church to one's home consistent with St. Paul's "the church in their house" (Rom. 16:5; Cor. 16:19).[7] Therefore, the meaning of the feast is not simply to eat and drink but to do so in a ritual manner, because as a ritual feast, Slava is meant to glorify God and venerate the saint after whom it is named. From the perspective of a family who celebrates it, Slava is primarily done for the good health of the living, with an understanding that the celebration is done also in general remembrance of the souls of the departed family members.

Symbolism in Slava

For each item used in Slava and each ritual action associated with the feast, the church has a symbolic religious interpretation and order of rites to follow. A few days before Slava, the celebrant's house must be blessed. The priest, preferably surrounded by the family members, performs the blessing of the water: the celebrant fills a dish with (tap) water into which the priest puts holy oil while reading prayers over it. This is done in front of the icon and a lit candle. Using dried basil stalks, he then sprinkles every room in the house with the blessed water. He also sprinkles family members who are present with the holy water, wishing each of them individually (by saying their names) good health and prosperity. This ritual sanctifies, that is, "purifies," the house of the impurities of daily life that "naturally occur in the fallen world."[8] The holy water is saved and often used for the preparation of the Slava *kolač*, a special round cake (or bread) made especially for this occasion, symbolizing the family's sacrificial offering to God. While the decorations on the top of the cake may vary, they should include a square seal with the inscription IC XC NIKA, Greek for "Jesus Christ Conquers."[9] Wheat preparation (žito or koljivo) is made with boiled whole wheat kernels mixed with sugar or honey and ground walnuts. The wheat itself symbolizes the eternal cycle of renewal, the resurrection, and a similar wheat preparation is also commonly used in the memorial service for those who have "fallen asleep in the Lord." In Slava, it serves the same commemorative purpose, but also to honor the patron saint of the family, for whose protection and good health the family prays. The wheat symbolically represents a connection between the living members of the family and the departed ones, both of whom are believed to be alive in God.

On the day of Slava, the kolač and žito, along with some red wine, are blessed either at the church or the celebrant's home. In either case, the priest begins by first using the censer to sanctify the icon of the saint with incense, an act that has a prayerful meaning ("and the smoke of the incense rose with the prayers of the Saints from the hand of the angel before God" [Revelations 8:3–4]). The offerings of žito, *slavski kolač* (Slava cake), red wine, and candle are all placed on the table facing east. The priest then lifts the kolač while saying prayers and cuts the sign of the cross with a knife on the bottom of it. In some families, the round bread is then turned by the hands of all who are present; when there are greater numbers of people gathered, they keep their right hand on the shoulder of a person who is touching the Slava cake. This signifies participation in eternity, of which the circle is understood to be a symbol. Then the priest pours the wine on the bread in the shape of the cross and having broken it into two halves, he kisses each half and says, "Christ is among us." After this, he offers the bread to the celebrant, who responds by saying, "He is, and will be" and kissing the two halves of the bread. Appropriate *tropars* (short hymns dedicated to the saint) are sung and the feast is thus inaugurated. Without this explicitly religious dimension of Slava, the rest of the celebration—including regional variations in the custom of toasting for good health of the family members and giving thanks to God—would resemble other forms of social gatherings and celebration.[10]

Hospitality of Slava

As guests arrive, they are first treated to a spoonful of žito (or the ritual offering) and a drink of water, wine, or brandy (plum, quince, apricot). Afterward, they are offered the rest of the food prepared specifically for Slava. Depending on the day in the liturgical calendar with which a saint is associated, Slava may be *mrsna*—with no restrictions on food—or *posna*, which means that the holy day falls during one of the fasts. For example, one of the most common Slavas is for St. Nicholas (Sv. Nikola), celebrated on December 19. As this is during the forty-day Christmas fast, it is a posna Slava. In Eastern Orthodox tradition, this translates into abstaining from eating meat, eggs, and dairy products but not fish.¹¹ There are very elaborate menus for posna Slava so that the food is no less festive than during the mrsna one, when there are no food restrictions and dishes with meat and cheese abound.

As an institution of hospitality, Slava has always had an important social role. Historically, the Slava celebration is considered to strengthen relations and closeness within the nuclear as well as the extended family. It facilitates "spiritual balance" within a family by smoothing over conflictual situations and relations. In that sense, it may be seen as a form of social control and regulation.¹² Because of its periodic and reciprocal character, Slava also ensures continuity in relations with other families and friends in the immediate and wider social circle. People generally know who celebrates what Slava, and it was understood in the past (and still is in many rural communities to this day) that no special invitations need to be sent for people to come to Slava. While the celebrant is expected to receive and treat his guests with the utmost hospitality, the amount and kind of food and drink offered for Slava often serves to show off the status of the family. Of course, that is not the religious meaning behind hospitality, but in practice, this social aspect rivals the religious one in dominance and importance. Understood today as a family and national custom, Slava remains the only exclusively family holiday in which the family members as a unit interacts with their social environment, friends, and neighbors.¹³

In communist times, Slava celebrations tended to be downplayed and "private." In some respects, its celebration carried an implicitly political connotation—a discreet subversiveness—since party members, in principle, did not celebrate it, rejecting its religious character. If they did discretely mark their Patron Saint's Day, it was interpreted as a "national custom" and reduced to a family dinner, often with no items with religious connotation, such as an icon of the saint, candle, or Slava cake and wheat.¹⁴ Thus ideas (beliefs) about the patron saint as a protector of and intercessor for the family started to fade away, especially in the cities, where the processes of secularization and modernization were more prominent. In the rural areas, this was not as much the case and many more traditions related to Slava were preserved. In some communities, the ties to the land and association of a particular saint with a particular locality (such as a spring or a cave) were still prominent. Thus, for example, in the early 1960s, when the residents of a village on the Danube by the Serbia-Romania border, where a construction of a huge dam (hydroelectric plant Đerdap) was taking place, had to be dislodged from their inherited ancestral lands and moved to other parts of the country, many stopped celebrating their family Slava. The reason was that in their mind, that particular patron saint was associated with that particular plot of land and not the land to which they were moved by the state, implying that the efficacy of the saint as protector is lost. For some scholars, this is an indication of the agricultural roots of Slava; and the fact that in addition to being passed from father to son, Slava and the patron saint could also be inherited with the land or acquired by its purchase.¹⁵ There exist no data about whether the population in question adopted another patron saint or not, for generally in this period, records about Slava were few: the communist state had no interest in it, and the Church was not likely to keep records of those who celebrate Slava in order not to jeopardize the position of the faithful who kept the feast going.[16]

Slava as Serbian

While the communist period was generally characterized by marginalization or downright suppression of religion, the postcommunist transition to democracy opened up possibilities for religious renewal. This transition became intertwined with a strong nationalist awakening wherein the reemergence of religion was perceived as political. It was noted that "although religious nationalism is only part of the nationalist endeavour, religion highlights ethnic and national boundaries."[17]

With the end of socialism, religion became for many a prime identity marker, with the Serbian Orthodox Church profiling itself as the dominant moral and spiritual authority for the Serbs. The most important religious holidays (such as Christmas and Easter) became observed and officially celebrated, with the state television broadcasting the church services, now also attended by politicians and other prominent public figures. But since the decades of secularization left big gaps in the basic knowledge about religions in the area, in the first several years after the end of socialism clergy was engaged to explain to TV viewers the basic meaning of religious holidays, liturgy, and related church practices. The New Year's Tree of socialist times became again the Christmas tree of pre–World War II times whereas popular Father Frost (Deda Mraz), though associated with the bygone socialist times, retained his secular charm even though the church kept reminding the public that this beloved figure is actually based on a fourth-century saint known as St. Nikola. Additionally, Christian symbols started (re)appearing in public spaces and on all kinds of nonreligious items—from magnets and key chains to wine and brandy labels.

Slava, too, gained in prominence in this religious and national self-rediscovery—and not just as a family *holy day*. Once again, the saints became protectors of the professional associations, cities, villages, and schools.[18] St. Sava's Day, celebrated on January 27, emerged as the most publicly visible Slava. St. Sava is also known as the "Enlightener" for having laid foundations for education in Serbia, so the day is observed as the school Slava. Even though the schools remain open on that day, there are various programs that students prepare for the celebration of their patron saint. The public celebration of St. Sava as school Slava was first introduced to the Kingdom of Serbia in 1840, when it was certainly functioning as a form of national self-affirmation in the light of recently obtained autonomy from the Ottomans.[19] While the renewed celebration of Slava in postsocialist times may also be seen as an act of religious self-affirmation, with the church reclaiming public space from which it was excluded for decades, there is an additional dimension of ethnoreligious neotraditionalism that is evident with this revival. The media, in particular, helped the church achieve greater visibility and participation in public life and thus ultimately consolidate the church's influence.[20] Since the family celebration of Slava does not lend itself to broadcasting,

Figure 27.1. Children celebrating Slava at their school, 2014. Photograph by Željko Stevanović.

it is the Slavas of cities, churches, or professional associations that have come into the televised gaze. As such, news coverage would include social aspects of Slava like the largest Slava bread—over one and a half meters in diameter—made by a small town's bakery for the Guinness World Records or would record how students of a certain school "break" and share the Slava cake with their principal, and so on.

On the home front, and especially in the urban centers, Slava has become for many yet another social opportunity in which the notion of hospitality has been transformed into showing off in front of one's neighbors, colleagues, or business partners. In the midst of extensive food preparation, often the actual reason for the celebration is forgotten. One indicator that the feast is getting detached from its religious meaning is that the Slava cake, traditionally made by the wife of the celebrant, may now be purchased in bakeries and pastry shops, along with the wheat preparation and other food items for the ceremony. The ritual whereby a woman would take a bath and say the Lord's Prayer before making the Slava cake is in such cases left out. As well, the religious meaning and participation in the process of making the ritual offering is now mediated and often lost to the celebrant. In various accounts of Slava from the late nineteenth century to right after World War II, however, it was precisely the mother's kneading of the dough for Slava cake and the joy of anticipation of the celebration that were given special prominence in the lives of children, thus emphasizing the family character of the holy day.[21] However, nowadays this image of family members with their duties and activities related to the preparations for Slava appears almost romantic and out of sync with reality. As elsewhere, the changed pace and style of life in Serbia—in which women are increasingly part of the workforce and children spend more time in daycare centers and schools than in their homes—are redefining the way people go about celebrating this holy day.

In that sense, Slava epitomizes wider trends in religiosity of the Serb Orthodox population that point to both the secularization of religious holidays and practices and, in seeming contradiction to this secularization trend, a steady rise in intellectual interest behind some of the Orthodox religious practices in this postsocialist time. For example, a recent study showed that during the wars of Yugoslav disintegration, certain segments of the population, riding on the ethnoreligious nationalistic revival of the 1990s, put an emphasis on religious rather than ethnonationalistic revival. These people, many of whom were young at the time, took up religion out of their own search for the meaning of life. They educated themselves about it and began to practice it in a much more committed way than those who adhered to it for nationalistic reasons: they exhibited significantly more theological competence and appreciation for the Orthodox Christian tradition so that, perhaps for the first time in the recent history of the Serbian Orthodox Church, a more competent lay following may be forming.[22]

In the end, whether with the full knowledge of what Slava is about or not, the fact that certain aspects of the religious celebration of Slava are clearly being secularized do not prevent people who do not even consider themselves religious, from calling themselves Orthodox Christian. The Slava cake may be bought from the specialty pastry shop rather than made, the meaning of the symbolic decorations on the top of it may or may not be known to the celebrant, the cake may or may not be even blessed by the priest, and there may not even be toasts and prayers to the saint. But if on that particular day in the church calendar devoted to that particular saint with whom the family name is associated, and if family and friends are gathered together—for the celebrant, it would still be Slava. And even if they are not your regular churchgoing folks, or particularly sophisticated in their knowledge and understanding of Christian doctrines, the fact that they keep their family Slava alive affirms them both as Orthodox and Serbian. For as the old folk saying goes, "Where there is a Serb, there is Slava."

Notes

1. Skarić 1912; Truhelka 1985.
2. Skarić 1912.
3. Čajkanović 1940.
4. Kalezić 2000; Vryionis 1988.
5. Kalezić 2000, 9; Grujić 1985.
6. Kalezić 2000.
7. Ibid.
8. Ibid., 59.
9. The Christogram ΙΗΣΟΥΣ ΧΡΙΣΤΟΣ—usually transliterated as "ΙΗCΟΥC ΧΡΙCΤΟC"—signifies the first and the last letter of each word and is widely used in Eastern Orthodox iconography to identify the image of Christ. The term for this seal is

prosfornik and is directly related to *prosfora* (Greek for the liturgical bread used for the Eucharistic meal in the Divine Liturgy), a bloodless offering to God that developed in early Christianity. A common folk term for it is *poskurnjak*.

10. Sinani 2012.
11. There are variations to this basic rule among different Orthodox churches: some abstain from the fish, too, while monastic communities tend to have even stricter rules of fasting (with no oil, etc.).
12. Mandić 2013.
13. Bandić 1986; Sinani 2012.
14. Sinani 2012.
15. Vlahović 1998.
16. There are, however, church records with the number of families celebrating Slava in Belgrade before communist times. For example, records indicate that between the two world wars, about 68–70 percent of families either invited the priest to their home or came to the church for the blessing of the Slava cake. Interestingly, a recent study showed a similar percentage of the Orthodox Serbian population celebrating Slava today (Antonić 1995).
17. Perica 2005, 131.
18. For example, the patron saint of doctors and medical professionals are Sts. Cosmas and Damian, twin brothers who were physicians; St. Panteleimon, also a physician and healer, is patron of pharmacists, and so on (Antonić 1995).
19. Kalezić 2000.
20. At the same time, the media has exposed the church to greater public scrutiny, for which the church was not always prepared. The increased access to media, particularly the World Wide Web, has also posed a challenge to the authority of the church, for the faithful are no longer limited to or dependent on a local parish priest to learn about their faith. The virtual exposure to global Orthodoxy, as well as to other religous ideas and practices, has resulted in a more sophisticated understanding of the faith and a more critical stance toward church leaders, on the one hand, and the strenthening of the conservativism or neotraditionalism, on the other.
21. Antonić 1995.
22. Đorđević 1998; Raković 2013.

References

Antonić, Dragomir. 1995. "Koliko Srba u Beogradu slavi Slavu." *Glasnik Etnografskog Instituta* SANU 44: 207–221.

Bandić, Dušan. 1986. "Funkcionalni pristup proučavanju porodične slave." *Glasnik Etnografskog Instituta* SANU 35: 9–20.

Čajkanović, Veselin. 1940 "Krsna Slava," *Srpski glas*, April 25, 1940.

Đorđević, Dragutin. 1998. "Slava u Srba kao religiozni i profani praznik na kraju 20. veka—sociološki uvid." *Etno-kulturološki zbornik* 4. Svrljig: Etno-kulturološka radionica.

Grujić, Radoslav. 1985. "Crkveni elementi krsne slave." In *O krsnom imenu*, Zbornik radova, 407–485. Beograd: Prosveta.

Kalezić, Dimtrije. 2000. *Krsne slave u Srba*. Beograd: Narodna knjiga.

Mandić, Ivana. 2013. "Krsna slava kao tradicionalni porodični obred u srpskom pravoslavlju." Magistarski rad. Univerzitet u Beogradu, Filozofski Fakultet, Odelenje za Sociologiju.

Perica, Vjekoslav. 2005. "The Sanctification of Enmity: Churches and the Construction of Founding Myths of Serbia and Croatia." In *Myths and Boundaries in South-Eastern Europe,* edited by Pal Kolsto, 130–157. London: Hurst.

Raković, Slaviša. 2013. "Potreba za etnografskim istraživanjem svetova posvećenih vernika SPC." *Antropologija* 13 (2): 103–119.

Sinani, Danijel, 2012. "O proučavanjima krsne slave u Srbiji." *Etnološko-antropološke sveske* 19 (8): 175–192.

Skarić, Vladislav. 1912. "Postanak Krsnog imena." *Glasnik zemaljskog muzeja* 32: 45–277.

Truhelka, Ćiro. 1985. "Larizam i krsna slava." In *O krsnom imenu*, Zbornik radova, 342–406. Beograd: Prosveta.

Vasić, Miloje. 1985. "Slava—krsno ime." In *O krsnom imenu*, Zbornik radova, 209–260. Beograd: Prosveta.

Vlahović, Petar.1998. "Krsna slava i njena uloga u porodičnom i društvenom životu kod Srba." *Etno-kulturološki zbornik* 4, Svrljig: Etno-kulturološka radionica.

Vryionis, Spero. 1988. "The Byzantine Legacy in the Folk Life and Tradition in the Balkans." In *The Byzantine Legacy in Eastern Europe*, edited by Lowell Clucas, 107–145. New York: Columbia University Press.

MILICA BAKIĆ-HAYDEN teaches at the Department of Religious Studies, University of Pittsburgh.

28 Boundaries of Freedom, Boundaries of Responsibility: Everyday Religious Life of Croatian Catholic Women

Slavica Jakelić

When a 2014 Croatia Airlines flight from Frankfurt to Dubrovnik was rerouted several times due to a summer storm, the Swedish minister of foreign affairs Carl Bildt, who was on the airplane, wrote on his Twitter page: "This remains the region of surprises."[1] Had the airlines been German or Swedish or Dutch, Bildt probably would have lamented bad weather. In the case of Croatia Airlines, the problem was not nature but the nature of the region where the airlines originated.

Bildt's comments express quite well a widely held, and still publicly acceptable, Western view of the Balkans as a disordered, disorganized, and unpredictable place that, paradoxically, does not change. The Western perceptions of the Balkans have long been a contentious topic, and, with some exceptions,[2] scholars and journalists still discuss this region without much nuance. This includes the writings about religious life in the Balkans as well. Here, the focus is either on what has "always" characterized the Balkan religious experiences or what is now dramatically changing. What is generally overlooked is the complicated relationship between the traditional and new forms of religious life—the links between one's sense of belonging to a religious group and the more individualistic forms of religious experience, between the sense of being born into some religion and the capacity to choose religious identity.[3]

Maintaining these possibilities only as dichotomies has several problematic implications. One such implication is that the way in which the studies centered on continuities in the religious life of Balkan societies reaffirms the view of these religions as intolerant and as sources of conflict. The scholarship that explores religious continuities, for example, often highlights the links between religious and national identities, seeing such links as a negative pattern.[4] The latter perspective is often supported by the still dominant and deeply unreflexive notion of "religion" as a belief rather than as an identity or cultural phenomenon; it also leaves out the examples of collectivistic religions that shape group identities but remain open to, and inclusive of, religious others.[5] As a result, the perspective

Figure 28.1. From within the old city walls, looking out to the Adriatic Sea, stands Dubrovnik Cathedral and St. Blaise's Church, indicating the long-standing significance of Catholicism in Dubrovnik, 2003. Photograph by David W. Montgomery.

in question reaffirms the essentialized notion of the Balkans as a place ruled by tribalisms and of Balkan religions as bastions of exclusivistic, intolerant group identities.[6]

The studies focused on religious changes also entail an essentialized view of Balkan religions. The scholarship about transformations of religion in the Balkans appears to dispel the stereotypes about the region: it proposes that Balkan societies *are* changing and moving toward religious individualism as a symbol of modernity.[7] In so suggesting, however, the scholarship in question interprets Balkan religious traditions and those religions that are collectivistic in character as remnants of the past—it portrays them as not modern, or not modernized, enough.

This chapter explores the coexistence of individualized religious experience with traditional and collectivistic forms of religious identity in contemporary Croatia.[8] It traces the intertwined relationship between on the one hand, religious identities that one is born into and that are organized around strong institutional authorities and, on the other hand, more personalized approaches to religious ideas, rituals, and symbols. The chapter uses as its interpretative framework the idea that modernity is not of one form but many. Most often expressed in the notion of "multiple modernities," this perspective suggests that modernity entails not a radical break from but a continuity with tradition.⁹ Modernity, furthermore, is not only about the victory of universal identities; it is also about the various configurations of the old and new particular identities.

The idea of multiple modernities has significant repercussions for the study of religion in the Balkans. First, it requires that we reject or at least problematize the long-held view that the individualization of religion is a universal process that will win against traditional, or collectivistic, forms of religious identification. Second, the concept of multiple modernities encourages the empirical examination of the relationship between collective and individualized forms of religious life. Third, this notion enables us to attend to the complicated link between tradition and change without seeing this as a peculiarly Balkan phenomenon, one which represents a deviation from some universal path toward what is perceived as truly modern religions.

In this chapter, I consider the relationship between tradition and change by looking at the practices and meanings the everyday religious lives of women in a small Catholic parish in Croatia. Through observations of the parish religious activities, and especially through interviews with women who have long been active in the daily life of the parish, I offer a snapshot of contemporary Croatian Catholicism as an embodied and embedded religion.

Everyday Catholic Life in Croatia: The Parish in Question

In the summer of 2014, I conducted interviews with women of a Catholic parish situated in a Croatian urban center. I have been aware of this parish for a while; parish members who know me, and who know I study religion, have long been telling me about the enthusiastic religious rituals and observances that occur daily in the parish church, sometimes even late at night.

The parish in question exemplified a vibrant Catholic community even in the period of communism. To some extent, this is not surprising. Like the Polish Catholic Church, the Croatian Catholic Church not only maintained but strengthened its reputation as the main institutional opposition to the communist regime. Yet while reflecting the resilience and strength of the Croatian Catholic Church as a whole, the parish in question is unique. Its church is very small, and due to communist prohibitions, it had to look like a residential building rather than a sacred structure. Despite these aesthetic and spatial constraints, the parish's activities were relentless—from the always-full catechism classes held in the women's convent adjacent to the church to the frequent and loud singing of the church choir and the constant commotion of students who attended music classes led by the nuns.¹⁰

In the postcommunist and postwar period, the parish avoided an exhaustion felt in much of the Croatian Catholic Church. Not only did it not experience the smaller Mass attendance as was the case elsewhere,¹¹ it actually underwent a religious revival. For many parish members, including the women I interviewed, this revival was due to the new young priest who came to the parish ten years ago.¹² He brought with him a Catholicism that many would identify as charismatic. He

Figure 28.2. Nuns hanging laundry to dry in Split, 2012. Photograph by Roska Vrgova.

structured parish religious life around energetic and enthusiastic homilies delivered even during daily Mass and focused his energies on forming and supporting the small prayer communities, especially Rosary groups, which meet regularly in the church and in private homes. The new priest also opened the church building for the activities of the neo-catechumen groups, initiated spiritual renewals (gatherings of believers often led by charismatic Catholic priests), and organized numerous pilgrimages to famous Catholic sites all over the world. During my visits to the parish in the summer of 2014, I found a busy and engaged community. On any given day, approximately 80 congregants celebrated the evening and 40 congregants celebrated the morning Mass—this in a building that could comfortably accommodate only about 150 people. On Thursday evening, the day of the Eucharistic adoration, the church was overflowing with people from the parish and beyond (many of them standing outside the church building, on the stairwell and outside balcony). Women constituted about 90 percent of participants in all the daily masses as well as during other organized parish activities.

The preponderance of women in the daily Mass could easily account for this chapter's focus. But the everyday life of parish women—women whose roles are still predominantly defined by their family duties but who nonetheless partake in all forms of daily religious rituals—became the center of this chapter for more substantive reasons. The women's understanding of how and why they lived their religious faith is particularly illuminating for understanding the links between tradition and change, responsibility and freedom, institutional and individualized religiosity.

My conversations with the parish women were guided by two sets of concerns. The first had to do with the ritualized forms of women's everyday religious life—enthusiastic prayers and observances that remained embedded in church doctrines, traditional rituals (such as saying the Rosary or Eucharistic adoration), and the authority of the parish priest. Are these everyday ritual actions devoid of creativity and merely an indication of women's subjugation to routine daily activities? Or are the aforementioned everyday ritual practices realms of resistance in which women, otherwise consumed by family and professional obligations, are able to subvert the usual order of things?[13] Second, I wanted to explore the language that the parish women used to talk about Catholic tradition. What does that language tell us about their religious identities? Are these identities experienced as ascribed, chosen, both, or neither?

For the purposes of this chapter, I conducted seven in-depth individual interviews and two in-depth group conversations with women who have been participating in the daily life of the parish for ten or more years. Due to the focus on long-term involvement, the age of interviewed women ranged from forty to eighty years. In all my interviews, I asked women to tell me, in their own words, about their religious experiences. I asked them about the contents and logistics of their daily religious practices, family lives, and professional preoccupations. Most women I interviewed were eager to discuss the meanings of religious rituals, especially in relation to how they used to practice their faith and how they practice it now. All the women enjoyed talking about their spiritual experiences, and all linked these experiences to their personal histories.

The Everyday of Croatian Catholic Women: Practice, Belief, and Conversion

Ana is a forty-year-old woman from a big Catholic family who originally lived in a rural area of the country.[14] "What was the place of religion in your life when you were growing up?" I asked her. "We worked, we struggled, and we prayed," Ana responded. "Rosary was an evening ritual for us. God and priests were part of our family life."

Although Catholicism and Catholic practices have always been present in Ana's life, she emphasizes one year as crucial for her own faith. "The year 2000 was the year of my conversion," she explains, "after a period of aimlessness. . . . When I was in the Croatian army [during the war in the 1990s], I served on the front lines of conflict but I always felt I belonged; I had a strong sense of purpose. . . . My aimlessness after the war was caused by the loss of togetherness; it was caused by the fact that everyone in Croatia seemed to have moved on. People lost respect for those who defended the country when it was under attack. And who came to power? Those who were against Croatia's existence," says Ana, referring to the election victory of the leftist parties in 2000.

That year, Ana took part in a seminar with a Catholic charismatic priest in the parish. This was the moment of her conversion—the moment when she began to understand "that everything I was doing before, from confession to communion to praying the Rosary, all that was not what it should have been." In her life, Ana explains, "there is before and after my conversion. After conversion, I had my first true confession—I confessed in humility and not in arrogance. After conversion, Mass was not just a Mass; it was a sign that Jesus is alive. Before my conversion, faith was something I used to *do*, it was what I used as I needed it."[15] After conversion, Ana says, "I learned how to pray, how to kneel."

As a younger woman, including the time when she was a soldier, Ana noted, "I was very much a leader and I was very much against men's special rights. Women in my family were hardworking, competent, unprotected but very strong. . . . I am still vocal about my opinions, but now I always place myself before God and God's mercy. I know now that everything, my aimlessness and my conversion, all that was part of God's plan. Who I am is not me, it is not my choice. Everything I am, everything I do, everything I can—everything is through God," says Ana, paraphrasing one of the popular Marian devotional prayers.

For the past fourteen years, Ana has been going to Mass every day and taking communion daily, no matter what is going in her life. "That is my way of tackling my insufficiencies—by immersing myself into eternity." Also, for more than a decade Ana has been participating in the weekly Eucharistic adorations, has been a leader of the prayer groups that meet regularly during the week, and has been attending spiritual renewals and retreats.

"My four children," Ana says, "are often irritated by my going to church so much. They tell me, 'God is everything to you!' and 'You think you can resolve everything with your prayer.' My husband used to say that I should have become a nun instead of getting married." Several years ago, her husband's views changed: like Ana, he had gone to a spiritual retreat and then started to attend daily Mass. This, Ana believes "transformed him as a father. It transformed our relationship as well. Our life is now organized by full sacramental living—we live sacraments not just in words, but also in body and in spirit."

* * *

Mara is a single woman in her late fifties. She was raised Catholic but "that was the time of communism, and my parents never talked about God."

"It was my grandmother who kept faith in our family," she continued. "This is why I love John Paul II—he is the one who gave us permission to talk about God and to get rid of the power of the devil," Mara tells me, referring to the communist regime.

Although Mara had "always loved going to church" and "felt wonderful" while in church, in 1991 her faith was transformed. "It was only with the first war siren in our city that I had a true experience of God. This was the moment of my conversion—the first time I really called for God, the first time I actually talked to God, in the moment of complete powerlessness." When the new priest came to her parish, Mara says, "the Holy Spirit opened our mouths, people started having visions, miracles were happening. With the new state of my soul, I also started seeing the Holy Spirit.... I had to talk about my faith, to share it with others—I received a huge mercy from God."

For Mara, her conversion not only changed her, it also changed the way she relates to others. "In communism," Mara explains, "all Serbs got on my nerves. ... but the New Testament is a love letter God left to us. Jesus teaches me that he loved even the Roman soldier. So I don't judge or blame any more; I only feel sorry that atheists cannot find peace."

Mara does not speak of her daily religious practices as routine. To the contrary, for her, "every day—every prayer, every Mass—is a conversion experience." In Mara's view, the role of laity in the Catholic Church is to be involved in the life of the church—to go to daily Mass, to go to confession, to participate in Marian devotions. But the laity's role is also to fully employ their spiritual powers. "I see Jesus in the Holy Sacrament, I feel his warmth.... At one spiritual renewal, with Zlatko Sudac," Mara tells me, referring to a renowned Croatian charismatic priest, "we prayed all night, and talked to Jesus. Eight or nine years ago, after prayer group in my house, this was what remained of the burning candle." Here she showed me a photo of what looks like a candle in the shape of a popular representation of Mary.

Her grown-up daughters, Mara reports, say that her faith saved her: "They say, 'You did not need to find anyone, you did not have to go anywhere to find peace.'"

* * *

Zorica has always been a religious person. As a sixty-year old woman, mother of two grown-up sons, she never had any hesitation in asserting her Catholic identity. So even though she married into a family that was not religious, and her new father-in-law was a member of the communist party, Zorica got married in church, baptized her children, and sent them to catechism classes through confirmation.

Yet just like other women I interviewed, Zorica sees and understands her religious life, her beliefs and practices, in relation to the moment of her transformation. "I have always been religious and I have always gone to church regularly," Zorica tells me, but "my faith gained a very new meaning about ten years ago." She and her husband, a former officer in the Croatian army, were going through a very difficult period due to his extramarital affair. "My marriage survived because of my faith," Zorica believes. "During our crisis, my husband would see me pray Rosary and he'd say: 'Pray, pray, like that will save you.' ... But I became stronger as I've accepted my cross. My cross was given to me so that I can know God more fully. I gained strength not only to pray for my marriage, for my husband. I gained strength to pray Rosary for his mistress. It was through Mary that I came to Jesus."

Since the new priest came to her parish, Zorica tells me, "I've learned from him how to truly pray. I have always taken Holy Communion regularly, but it used be a routine for me. Now, every day when I go to Mass, I go with some intention, with some special dedication. Now I see and understand the deeper meaning of Holy Communion. In it, Jesus Christ puts everything that separates

Boundaries of Freedom and Responsibility

us from each other. Holy Communion purifies us, and that's how I go into daily life. It helps me see my own sins; it cleanses me of my own sins."

Zorica thinks that her faith is constantly growing and that she can never fully understand it. But when she speaks of her everyday religious rituals—attending Mass, taking communion, praying the Rosary—she frames all that with the ideal of personal sacrifice. The main goal of life, Zorica says, "is to give oneself to others. The problem today is that nobody wants to make any sacrifices. I know I have my duties to my husband, my children, my parents. To be a Christian, and to live my faith, means not to ask about the other person's sin but to see my own. It is to ask yourself: 'Did I have to say that?' It is to repent for what *I* have done."[16]

"My husband," Zorica concludes, "is not a very religious man, but he is a good man. He fought for Croatia, but he did it because he loves his homeland and he never asked for anything in return. He actually refused privileges and rewards for his service.... He made a mistake in our marriage, but he asked me and asked the church for the forgiveness of his sins." Her two sons are not particularly religious either, and they both—"rightly," according to Zorica—"resist the politics in the homilies of many priests." Zorica does think that her parish priest is different because he cares about faith and not about politics, but she does not ask her husband or her children to go to the parish church. Her way is different. "During the whole period of Lent," Zorica reveals, "I prayed for their conversion. My tool is my prayer."

The Everyday Religious Life of Croatian Catholic Women and the Problem of Agency

All the women I talked to spoke of the new parish priest as central for how they approached their everyday religious practices, how they engaged tradition, and how they understood their personal lives in light of that tradition. The priest's uniqueness, women told me, was especially in his approach to Catholicism—Catholic doctrine and liturgies. He revived what so often looked and sounded like a dry tradition; he turned his homilies into living and feeling events. For the parish women, the priest's authority was grounded not only in his office but also in his personable approach to parish women. Some talked of the priest as a friend who listened to them and was not afraid to give them a hug, "not even in public," as the fifty-year-old Tanja said. For Tonka, an eighty-year-old widow, the parish priest transformed her faith practices but also gave her the courage to speak—"to start believing that I had something worth saying when it came to faith."

At the same time, the women spoke with utmost respect—sometimes even subservience—about the priest's authority to determine the content, structure, and tenor of their everyday religious practices. Ana, for example, who spoke eloquently and without reservation of her spirituality, and who has several leadership roles in the parish groups, initially told me that for any conversation I wanted to have with parish women about their religious life, I first had to ask the priest's permission.

The everyday life of the parish women, then, remains firmly organized with, and within the bounds of, church traditions and doctrines. Even as some women spoke of the spiritual powers of laity as needed for church life, the authority of the priest or the church as an institution was never contested. And when during our group conversations some of the women addressed the problem of sexual abuse in church, they stated that their parish priest was correct when he told them that the problem was that believers did not pray for their priests anymore.

Notwithstanding the high level of obedience to the church, its clergy, and its teachings, the women kept insisting—indeed, this was the underlying trope of all my interviews—that their engagement with Catholic tradition through Mass, prayer groups, or Marian devotions, was anything but routine.[17] On the one hand, everyday religious rituals were always interpreted in light of women's conversion experiences—the moment in which the religious tradition given to them was appropriated in a new way. The ideas and practices of the church, most women emphasized, gained a deeper or truer meaning through their sincere and absolute personal commitment to specific religious observances, enabled by the experience of conversion. That experience is something, women said, that they work to renew every day.

The emphasis that women place on sincerity in their ritualized behavior gains another layer of meaning when we understand how the women I spoke to use everyday rituals to negotiate the brokenness of their private and social worlds.[18] All seven interviews suggested, and the three stories of everyday religious life presented here showed quite clearly, that women's internalization and individualization of ritualized practices was also the framework for their response to the challenges of life—whether those challenges were presented by the fall of communism and the outbreak of war, by the loss of purpose in new and always changing political contexts, or by serious family crises. The everyday religious life of Catholic women in Croatia thus emerges as particularly central for how these women negotiate the relationship between their past, present, and future, and the recent dramatic history of the region looms large in the background of the women's religious commitments and sensibilities.

The stories I heard about the everyday religious life of Croatian Catholic women problematize the usual approaches to religious identities in the Croatian context as either traditional or modern, ascribed or chosen. The women's words reflected their attachment to the church as an institution and their strong sense of patriotism and belonging to the Croatian national group; the way that women sometimes spoke betrayed a patronizing stance toward nonbelievers, which cannot be separated from the recent experience of communism. Still, women I interviewed also emphasized the need to love others, even those who did them wrong, whether these were the members of some group (as in the case of the recent war between Croatia and Serbia) or individuals who harmed them and negatively affected the lives of their families. Zorica's case suggests that this view of love is not just some abstract theological notion: her radical commitment to the Christian ideal of sacrifice is best manifested in her insistence that the child her husband had with another woman regularly visits their home. Put differently, the collectivistic and particularistic sides of women's religious identities go hand in hand with the universalistic Christian values and commandments of love.

Similarly, when women described the Catholicism they were born into and how they made it their own, they did not speak of discarding their religious past but rather of rediscovering it. The nuances shaping the women's views of tradition and transformation suggest that ascription and choice, legacies and shifts in their religious life are deeply intertwined.[19] The women's Catholic identities thus emerge as constitutive rather than attributive in character.[20] Or, as Ana and Mara tell us in their stories, thus pointing to the theological meaning of Catholic identities: who they were in terms of their religious life could not be their choice to begin with; it could only be received.

Understanding the Catholic Identities of Croatian Women

When explored in the context of the everyday religious lives of Catholic women interviewed for this chapter, the religion that one is born into cannot be interpreted simply as a carryover from the past. Rather, it must be regarded in relation to individualized religious experience and can be interpreted as an element of contemporary religious pluralism. When the question of women's agency is placed in the same context, agency does not simply mean freedom to exert one's will, but integrates in complex ways the relationship between freedom and responsibility. Women I spoke to submit to the institutional authority of the church and the authority of tradition, and they especially emphasize how they fulfill their duties to their children, husbands, parents, and friends. Yet the everyday religious life of the parish women also, even if inadvertently, becomes the realm of resistance to their usual family routine. The daily ritual observances require both space and time that the parish women had to carve out for themselves, sometimes regardless of family members' objections. It is possible to think of the agency of the women I interviewed in terms not of their capacity to resist but their capacity to inhabit and embody given norms and traditions.[21] This interpretation counters some of the dominant understanding of what it means to act freely; it also does not fully align with my own theoretical view of religious agency as a capacity to both assent to, and dissent from, the authority of traditions and institutions. Such interpretive possibilities notwithstanding, it is important to see that the religious experiences of the Croatian Catholic women should not be understood as antimodern. To the contrary, they should be taken as a challenge that we develop a more expansive view of what it means to be religious in a truly pluralistic world.

Notes

1. See Jutarnji Vijesti 2014.
2. See Todorova 1997; Bakić-Hayden 1995.
3. One of the recent examples of bridging these dichotomies is Zrinščak (2014).
4. On the dynamics of the public role of religions in postcommunist societies, see Partos (1997), Sells (1998), Vrcan (2001), Perica (2002).
5. For the discussion of these religious traditions, see Jakelić (2010, 2014).

6. For a discussion that brings into conversation the social scientific theories of nationalism and religious studies scholarship, especially theories of religion, see the first chapter of Jakelić (2010).

7. The idea that the Balkan religious identities are not modern enough due to their collectivistic features becomes even more powerful when placed in the context of claims about the exceptional character of western Europe, as secularized and secularizing. For one version of this idea, see Berger (1999). For the transformations of the religiosity among Croatian youth, see Mandarić (2009).

8. One caveat is needed at the outset, which adds to the "messiness" of the discussions about the Balkans: some Croats think Croatia is part of the Balkans, others that it is part of central Europe or of the Mediterranean region, and still others that it is all of the above.

9. This counters the ideas long held by social scientists. For a classic articulation of the notion of modernization, see Durkheim (1984) or Weber (2009); for a more recent reflection on modernity and religion, see Berger (1980). For the theoretical accounts of multiple modernities, see Casanova (2006, 14) and Eisenstadt (2000, 2).

10. The parish never lacked eager members, mostly Catholics who recently moved to the city from rural areas. For these new urban dwellers, the active religious life was an indispensable part of upbringing and family life that they treasured. Since their private family houses bordered with the high-rises inhabited by the families of Yugoslav, mostly atheist, military officers, the parish church quickly grew into a symbol of the Catholic resistance to communist atheism.

11. Some of the challenges come from the pluralization of religious scenes: for the appeal that the new religious movements have in central and eastern Europe, see Borowik and Babinski (1997).

12. I wrote the first version of this chapter in the summer of 2014. Since then, the priest mentioned here was moved to another parish.

13. For the everyday as the realm of victimization, or of resistance and subversion, see Felski (2000, 17).

14. I am using pseudonyms for all the interviewed parish women.

15. Italics are mine.

16. Zorica emphasized this word.

17. Felski 2000, 16.

18. Seligman, Weller, Puett, and Simon 2008, 181.

19. For one of the most nuanced discussions of this phenomenology, see Cadge and Davidman (2006).

20. Sandel 1998, 150–151.

21. See Mahmood 2005.

References

Bakić-Hayden, Milica. 1995. "Nesting Orientalisms: The Case of Former Yugoslavia." *Slavic Review* 54 (4): 917–931.

Berger, Peter L. 1980. *The Heretical Imperative: Contemporary Possibilities of Religious Affirmation*. New York: HarperCollins.

Berger, Peter L., ed. 1999. *The Desecularization of the World: Resurgent Religion and World Politics*. Grand Rapids, MI: William B. Eerdmans.

Borowik, Irena, and Grzegorz Babinski. 1997. *New Religious Phenomena in Central and Eastern Europe*. Krakow: Nomos.

Cadge, Wendy, and Lynn Davidman. 2006. "Ascription, Choice, and the Construction of Religious Identities in the Contemporary United States." *Journal for the Scientific Study of Religion* 45 (1): 23–38.

Casanova, José. 2006. "Rethinking Secularization: A Global Comparative Perspective." *Hedgehog Review* 8 (1–2): 7–22.

Durkheim, Emile. 1984. *The Division of Labor in Society*. Translated by W. D. Halls. New York: Free Press.

Eisenstadt, S. N. 2000. "Multiple Modernities." *Daedalus* 129 (1): 1–30.

Felski, Rita. 2000. "The Invention of Everyday Life." *Cool Moves: A Journal of Culture /Theory/Politics* 39: 15–31.

Jakelić, Slavica. 2010. *Collectivistic Religions: Religion, Choice, and Identity in Late Modernity*. Aldershot: Ashgate.

Jakelić, Slavica. 2014. "Beyond Religious Nationalism." *The Immanent Frame: Secularism, Religion, and the Public Sphere*. Accessed June 8, 2015. http://blogs.ssrc.org/tif/2014/03/04/beyond-religious-nationalism/.

Jutarnji Vijesti. 2014. "Bildt ljut na Croatia Airlines 'Umjesto u Dubrovniku, završio sam u Splitu!'" *Jutarnji list*, July 11, 2014. Accessed August 1, 2014. http://www.jutarnji.hr/template/article/article-print.jsp?id=1205465.

Mahmood, Saba. 2005. *Politics of Piety: The Islamic Revival and the Feminist Subject*. Princeton, NJ: Princeton University Press.

Mandarić, Blaženka Valentina. 2009. *Mladi: integrirani i(li) marginalizirani*. Zagreb: Glas Koncila.

Partos, Gabriel. 1997. "Religion and Nationalism in the Balkans: A Deadly Combination?" In *Religion, Ethnicity, and Self-Identity: Nations in Turmoil*, edited by M. Marty and R. S. Appleby. Hanover, NH: University Press of New England.

Perica, Vjekoslav. 2002. *Balkan Idols: Religion and Nationalism in Yugoslav States*. Oxford: Oxford University Press.

Sandel, Michael. 1998. *Liberalism and the Limits of Justice*. Cambridge: Cambridge University Press.

Seligman, Adam B., Robert P. Weller, Michael J. Puett, and Bennett Simon. 2008. *Ritual and Its Consequences: An Essay on the Limits of Sincerity*. Oxford: Oxford University Press.

Sells, Michael A. 1998. *The Bridge Betrayed: Religion and Genocide in Bosnia*. Berkeley: University of California Press.

Todorova, Maria. 1997. *Imagining the Balkans*. Oxford: Oxford University Press.

Vrcan, Srđan. 2001. *Vjera u vrtlozima tranzicije*. Split: Glas Dalmacije, Revija Dalmatinske Akcije.

Weber, Max. 2009. *The Protestant Ethic and the Spirit of Capitalism with Other Writings on the Rise of the West*. Translated by Stephen Kalberg. 4th ed. Oxford: Oxford University Press.

Zrinščak, Siniša. 2014. "Re-Thinking Religious Diversity: Diversities and Governance of Diversities in 'Post-Societies.'" In *Religious Pluralism. Framing Religious Diversity in the Contemporary World*, edited by G. Giordan and E. Pace. New York: Springer.

SLAVICA JAKELIĆ is Associate Professor of Humanities and Social Thought at Christ College at the Honors College of Valparaiso University. She is author of *Collectivistic Religions: Religion, Choice, and Identity in Late Modernity* and editor of *The Future of the Study of Religion* (with Lori Pearson) and *Crossing Boundaries: From Syria to Slovakia* (with J. Varsoke).

29 Religious Boundaries, *Komshuluk*, and Sharing Sacred Spaces in Bulgaria

Magdalena Lubanska

In the Rhodope Mountains of Bulgaria, Bulgarian-speaking Muslims, and Christians have coexisted side by side for centuries. They nurture good neighborly relations, and one can readily see the overlapping cultural influence of Islam and Orthodox Christianity. Both groups are Slavs indigenous to the Rhodopes, and thus the religious life of Bulgarian-speaking Muslims (Pomaks)[1] and Orthodox Christians is best understood through looking at patterns of coexistence.

It is estimated that there are between 150,000 and 240,000 Bulgarian-speaking Muslims in Bulgaria, with the majority living in the Rhodopes.[2] Smaller groups of them are dispersed in several villages of the central range of the Stara Planina between Lovech and Teteven .[3] In many ways, Bulgarian-speaking Muslims are a population in-between: because they are Muslims, they are seen to be close to the Turks, but because they speak Bulgarian, they are closer to the Bulgarians. The controversy of to whom they belong emerges in the narrative of their conversion.

The process of Islamic conversion in the Rhodopes remains contested, but recent historiography suggests that Bulgarian-speaking Muslims (for the most part) converted to Islam voluntarily, motivated by aspirations of economic and social mobility (since Muslims were exempt from the *jizyah*).[4] According to Antonina Zhelyazkova, Islamicization began with isolated individual conversions in the sixteenth century and gradually intensified over the seventeenth century (particularly in its second half). In the Rhodopes, the process continued until the eighteenth century.[5] In the western Rhodopes, particularly in the Chech region located along the middle of the Mesta Valley, the earliest isolated conversions took place in the third quarter of the fifteenth century.[6]

However, from the late nineteenth century up to 1990, the dominant understanding was that Bulgarian-speaking Muslims were forced to convert under the Ottomans. The thesis about their forced conversions was popularly reinforced in the etymology of the ethnonym "Pomaks," deriving it from the word *pomŭcheni*, meaning people who have been "tortured" or "persecuted" (implicitly, by the Turks) when Bulgaria was part of the Ottoman Empire. The explanation of this term is still popular among Christians in the Rhodopes but treated with ambivalence by the Muslims.[7] These narratives of conversion, however, have implications for belonging.

Komshuluk: A Strategy of Coexistence

When I was in the field (intermittently between 2002 and 2009),[8] I was impressed by how often Muslims and Christians were talking about the importance of *komshuluk*, a word of Turkish origin referring to "good neighborly relations."[9] Komshuluk implies a closeness in separation and the efforts to maintain it; the Muslims and the Christians rarely intermarry and avoid talking about religion in each other's presence. There is also a Slavic term for "neighborhood" (*sŭsedstvo*), but this has a more neutral connotation and is used less frequently in the Rhodopes. Despite different linguistic origins, both words for neighbor—komshiya and sŭsed—are viewed as Bulgarian.

When I asked Muslims and Christians living in the Rhodopes how they get along with each other they told me: "We stick together"; "They [Muslims] are like our people"; "We live like brothers"; "We're all the same"; or "Our life here together is very good." They tend to take pride in their peaceful neighborly relations and emphasize their communal ties with neighbors of a different religion. In the Rhodopes, the roots of komshuluk as a positive unifying force are religious—seen as applicable to both Islam and Christianity—as well as pragmatic, given that locals are often reliant on assistance from neighbors. This pragmatism is often reinforced by religion, especially in Islam, which puts a special emphasis on the unique relationship with one's neighbor.

Rhodopes Muslims commonly say, "Your neighbors include people from the nearest forty households." They emphasize that departed souls are queried in the next world about the relations with their neighbors, and if those relations were bad, they get punished. The dealings with one's neighbor are part of the judgment over the soul of a deceased person that takes place in the grave and involves a series of questions—posed by the angels Munkar and Nakir—relating to one's life.

Pomaks in the Rhodopes often tell stories about the Prophet Muhammad's attitude toward his neighbors of a different religion and view these as examples of how they themselves should behave. For example, according to one *hodzha*[10] in Ribnovo,

> The Prophet himself practiced this. The Prophet had a neighbor—a Jew—who used to put rubbish in Muhammad's yard when he wasn't home. One day the Prophet was astonished to see no rubbish, and he concluded that his neighbor must be ill. He went to pay him a visit, to see his neighbor. The neighbor asked him, "How did you know I was not well?" He answered: "Every day you leave your rubbish in my yard, but I saw no rubbish today. I guessed you must be ill, so I came to see you." This is why he [Muhammad's neighbor] later converted to Islam.

Hodzhas in the Rhodopes often cite the example of Muhammad and his life as the source on which the practice of good relations between neighbors is based. What is more, it is said that Muhammad received the teachings about the importance of komshuluk from the angel Jibra'il (Gabriel).

Likewise, Christians in the Rhodopes recognize komshuluk as intrinsically positive, though they are less likely to invoke religious narratives to justify it. They tend to discuss relations with neighbors in terms of charity and the commandment to "love thy neighbor."[11] They say that "you mustn't walk past [ignore] your neighbor."

The moral imperative of komshuluk manifests itself in the everyday practices of greetings and associations, as well as the acts of neighbors of different religions attending each other's weddings and funerals, offering each other festive foods during religious holidays, and helping each other in times of need. Christians and Muslims in the Rhodopes come together in reciprocity—*do ut des* (Latin: I give that you may give)—confirmed daily through a series of routine and ritual neighborly obligations dependent on a degree of symmetry in their mutual dealings.[12] For the local religiously heterogeneous community, ritual exchanges make their peaceful intentions known through messages confirming that both groups may rely on each other's help in daily life in tasks such as unloading hay, sharing medicine, or returning a cow to a neighbor's cow shed.

Komshuluk exists in reciprocity, practices of gift exchanges and sharing festive foods, and sharing and helping in important life events—childbirth, marriage, burial. We see such practices on an annual basis on religious holidays throughout the year; for example, on the Feast of Kurban Bayrum (Feast of Sacrifice, Arabic: 'Id al-Adha), Muslims often offer meat and sweets to their Christian neighbors, and on Easter, Orthodox Christians offer Easter cake and red eggs to their Muslim neighbors. Importantly, though, neighbors realize that such food sharing practices are subject to certain restrictions and must be done with respect toward the other group's religious sensibilities. Christians, for example, believe it would be inappropriate to offer Muslims foods such as *kolivo* (sweet boiled grain),[13] which is given out as part of a religious practice performed for the dead.

When offered food during the religious holiday of the other, or when greeting another on the holiday, the response often draws on secular phrases—seen as neutral—such as *Chestit praznik* ("Best holiday wishes") or *Blagodarya. Zhivi i zdravi da ste! Do godina pak da ni cherpite!* ("Thank you. May you be alive and well, and offer us more next year!"). Notably, religious greetings, though familiar to members of each group, are not used. This is because when uttered, religious phrases are associated with certain gestures that might lead to assimilation, an undesirable outcome for each group.

Ritual exchanges of komshuluk take place throughout an individual's life cycle: from birth—when close female neighbors visit the mother and child several days after the delivery, bringing food (*ponuda*)—until death, when non-coreligionist neighbors attend funerals or wakes in the deceased person's home. Such expressions of komshuluk are so important to my interlocutors that they are prepared to bend the rules of their own religion to perform them. As Marcel Mauss observed about the importance of exchange, relations of mutuality, though outwardly voluntary, are in fact obligatory; neglecting them threatens

Figure 29.1a-b. Figure 29.1a: An Orthodox Christian family lighting candles in a church in the Rhodope Mountains; Figure 29.1b: Two Muslim men talking before prayers in a mosque in the Rhodope Mountains, 2015. Photographs by David W. Montgomery.

"private or open warfare."[14] Such sentiments were common among my interlocutors, as reflected in a conversation with Hamid, a Pomak hodzha:

HAMID:[15] As a rule, every religion needs to be tolerant toward others.

M. L.: How exactly is that tolerance expressed?

HAMID: They shouldn't be snubbed. Say, a Muslim makes *banitsa* or *baklava*[16] and takes some to share with a neighbor who's Christian or Jewish, or whatever. If that neighbor does not accept it, they will feel unwanted. And you get an atmosphere of intolerance, something like hatred. But if you accept the gift, then you get an affinity between them, like between good neighbors. And you get mutual understanding, as required by Islam, rather than enmity or hatred.

When neighbors no longer exchange gifts, visit each other at important times in their lives, or greet each other in the street, the neighborly relations become less predictable and transparent. But when two religious groups care to preserve their peaceful relationship, they need a way of communicating this intention: a role played by the relationships of reciprocity, which is in turn the foundation of komshuluk.

Mutual Fears and Resentments

It would be a mistake, however, to analyze komshuluk without taking into consideration the relationships of power between Muslims and Christians in the region, and the historical shifts in dominance and subservience that have taken place. Today, Bulgarians are the dominant group at the state level, while Muslims mostly predominate in the western Rhodopes. Muslims were the dominant group in the period of Ottoman rule, only to become marginalized after Bulgaria was liberated in 1878 (1912 in the Rhodopes). Both Christians and Muslims experienced intermittent persecution under different regimes in which they were marginalized, and as a result both groups harbor mutual fears, rooted in the collective memory (or post-memories) of past violence.[17] In speaking to past suffering, Christians in the Rhodopes reference the Batak massacre of 1876,[18] while Muslims reference the Satovcha massacre of 1912.

It is interesting to note the role of komshuluk in discussing past violence. So long as there was a Muslim woman in the company, my Christian interlocutors told me about the close ties and peaceful relations between neighbors. But when the Muslim woman left, they changed the topic to the massacre in Batak and their fears. According to a group of old Christian women from Satovcha, with whom I spoke about the 1876 massacre in Batak, the 1912 massacre of Bulgarian-speaking Muslims in Satovcha was "very nearly" a massacre of Christians instead:

ALBENA: Now listen, there was a time when they [the Bulgarian-speaking Muslims] were sharpening their knives to turn against us. We had [in this house] an old woman, a relative. She told me that. They were sharpening their knives over there, we're telling you, there used to be stones there, and willow trees.... And the Turks were sharpening their knives because they wanted to come here and make a massacre, to massacre our village. But...

BLAGA: Right, but they [the Bulgarian-speaking Muslims] went to Batak instead, to massacre people [there]. If you went there you would see those things. Little hands and everything, they massacred tiny babies. They closed the church, and massacred all the people with knives.

ALBENA: The church, the Turks closed the church and they would [kill] little children, men, women, everybody. There was blood in the yard and tiny heads...

The connection that the old women made with the Batak massacre is unsurprising. The massacre in Batak is an important event shaping the collective imagination of the Ottoman occupation.[19] Batak is seen as a "site of extermination," "a shrine," or "the Bulgarian Golgotha."[20]

Likewise, Bulgarian-speaking Muslims remember themselves as victims of Christian violence. During one of the interviews in Satovcha, I was told about a massacre against them that took place there in 1912. Supposedly organized by the local Bulgarians to exterminate the local Muslim elites prior to a campaign of forced Christianization in the same year, it is characterized as an example of underlying Christian brutality toward the Muslims:

> FATME: One way or the other, they [Christians] came for . . . those who belonged to the Muslim elites. . . . There were Muslims in it [Satovcha] who were richer, smarter, and more active. They took them all, our local Bulgarians did. They said they were taking them to a meeting. They [the Pomaks] went to that meeting and they were trussed up with ropes. There is a hill opposite called Bojnov Rid; that's where they slaughtered all of them. Fifty people standing in a row, all slaughtered.

The private narratives of the Pomaks and the Orthodox Christians reflect an underlying fragility and fear; komshuluk is not always easy, for the narratives of past conflicts recall how violence can (re)emerge when trust erodes. Often, resentment for how past ancestors were believed to have been treated leads to underlying distrust, as actual events blend with historical myth. In contrast to the narrative of komshuluk, the resentment narrative—the "narrative of past wrongs"—is shared only within the group, consisting of topics and problems kept out of conversations with non-coreligionists. In contrast to the strategies for preferred patterns of coexistence, it reveals mutual fears about what the non-coreligionist neighbors might do if and when they achieve political or demographic dominance.

Thus, positive relations between neighbors are a good to which the local community aspires, despite the legacy of resentment existing between the two groups. And while it is true that the trauma of historical events has led to the occasional rupture of good neighborly relations, komshuluk has always been restored because neighbors in the Rhodopes realize the need for affinity between one another. As a result, the reciprocity that regulates the relations between Christians and Pomaks leads to a situation where each group is encouraged to retain their distinctive identity, one in contrast to the lifestyle represented by the neighbor of a different religious faith. When neighbors no longer exchange gifts, visit each other at important times in their lives, or greet each other in the street, the neighborly relations become less predictable and transparent. In the Rhodopes, both groups seem to be aware of the fragile nature of komshuluk and its vulnerability to external political factors. They think that the neighbors could betray the ideals of komshuluk if the political situation becomes volatile. When both religious groups seek to preserve a peaceful relationship, they need a way of communicating this intention, a role played by reciprocity, which is in turn postulated and upheld by the narratives of good relations between neighbors.

Religious Boundaries and Sharing of Sacred Spaces

Living side by side, Muslims and Christians in the western Rhodopes try to cherish both their komshuluk and their distinct religious identities. Central to this is how difference is understood: one interlocutor claimed "the difference between Christianity and Islam is like an onion skin. It's so small. So there aren't any important differences." But while using the metaphor of an onion skin suggests closeness, it does not mean there are no boundaries. Rather, separation, albeit small and at times seemingly insignificant, is a foundational characteristic of komshuluk, of bringing two religious groups together and defusing their potentially destabilizing differences.

There is a practice of tolerance between the groups that is underpinned by a desire to protect group boundaries and a mistrust of (still infrequent) mixed marriages—as a local proverb puts it, "Every frog knows which puddle it belongs in," and neither Christians nor Muslims seem eager to join each other in the same puddle. This is because while komshuluk can embrace the onion skin metaphor, religious differences are still seen as differences that matter.

To my Muslim interlocutors, Christianity is a religion based on a false understanding of the sacred, bearing the original taint of the sin of *shirk* (idolatry) and stemming from a long series of misunderstandings. They view Christianity as a cult of the cross that involves a misinterpretation of Jesus's (Isa's) relationship with God (Allah), seen for example in how Jesus entered heaven after his death. Muslims refer to the "assumption" of Jesus—wherein he was carried into heaven by the will of Allah—because they view Jesus as a prophet. Christians, on the other hand, understand it as the "ascension" of Jesus—which implies entry into heaven was under his own power—because they view Jesus as the son of God and thus an extension of God.[21]

These differences of understanding are manifest in rituals of everyday practice. For example, many of my Muslim interlocutors view Christianity as a religion invented by the apostle Paul, who, according to them, distorted the teachings of Isa (Jesus) and by abandoning ritual ablution (*abdest; wudu*)—a ritual introduced by Adam and Hawwa (Eve)—broke the promise made by the souls in Paradise. Such understandings show that Pomaks have a rather anti-syncretic attitude toward Christianity, which is ironic considering that Christians often think of their Muslims neighbors as crypto-Christians who only superficially confess Islam, deeply in their heart cherishing their old (Christian) beliefs. For Christians in the Rhodopes, the fact that some Muslims visit the Christian Orthodox priests and the famous Christian monastery of St. George in Hadzidimovo is seen as proof of the Pomak neighbors' crypto-Christianity.

But Christians in the Rhodopes also seek guidance from Muslims—visiting, for example, Muslim healers like *dzhindzhiya hodzhas* (hodzhas who are exorcists)—but do not view themselves as crypto-Muslims because of that. In practice, members of both religious groups occasionally visit the holy places and healers of the different religion and do not see themselves as secret supporters of the other tradition. In such cases, Muslims and Christians are equally indifferent to the actual content of the prayer written down for them by a priest or the amulet (*amaliyka*) received from a hodzha. Still, the practice involves a certain cathartic effect accompanied by a sense of fear and fascination with the alien sphere of the (other's) sacred. In this sense, such experiences, though not motivated by an interest in the other religion, do not rule out the numinous experience.

For example, Muslims staying at the church of St. George during Gergiovden (St. George's Day) in Hazdidimovo are very cautious about what they do. They sleep in the church for health as the Christians do, but their attendance in the vespers is rather passive: they simply sit by in the side naves. Some kiss the icons of St. George, the Mother of God, and Christ (as they are all heroes mentioned in the Islamic tradition) or light candles before them; others believe that such gestures are prohibited. They are aware of their distinct religious identity and thus never remain in the church for the Christian liturgy that begins at dawn on May 6. They do not come to venerate Christian saints or to seek an alternative path to salvation but mainly to be freed from the pernicious effect of "Christian jinns" (*rusalkas, samovilas*).

Both Muslims and Christians in the Rhodopes visit healers of the other religion because it is often believed that the only antidote to the harm caused by the demons of another religion can be found within that religion. From the perspective of ordinary believers, seeking healing in the other religion has the double attraction of effectiveness and mystery. Because they are more incomprehensible than one's own traditions, alien practices are paradoxically closer to the awe-inspiring experience that transcends understanding.

But such things are not always straightforward. The same gesture may be performed because it is considered as an effective healing practice or because it fosters better relations with one's neighbors of a different religion. A good case in point is a Muslim woman who lights a candle for the deceased daughter of her Christian friends, a traditional Christian practice she performs during the wake in their home to show sympathy and solidarity. She describes her gesture not as religious but rather as motivated by komshuluk.

The everyday experience of living side by side, and the syncretic relationship that emerges, plays an important role in understanding religion in the Rhodopes. When the declarative level ("We live like brothers") differs from the actual feelings felt for members of the other religion ("We fear them"), the "syncretic behaviors" occurring in the two groups tell only part of the story. Visiting holy places of one's non-coreligionist neighbor may indicate an appreciation of another's religious cosmology, it may serve the purpose of maintaining good relations, or it may be some combination of which even the visitor is not fully certain. But as we see in the idea of komshuluk, living with one's neighbors in the Rhodopes is not so much a given as it is a task requiring continued commitment.

Notes

The findings in this article are based on intermittent ethnographic fieldwork conducted in years 2005–2009 in the Bulgarian Rhodopes and devoted to the studies on Muslim-Christian coexistence and religious (anti)syncretism. The author thanks Piotr Szymczak for his assistance translating this chapter and De Gruyter Open Publishing House for permission to draw on the argument made in her earlier published work, *Muslims and Christians in the Bulgarian Rhodopes: Studies on Religious (Anti)Syncretism* (Lubanska 2015).

1. I use two terms interchangeably: "Bulgarian-speaking Muslims" and "Pomaks." I prefer the phrase "Bulgarian-speaking Muslims" because it is seen as being the most politically correct (Brunnbauer 2007, 94, Neuburger 2004). However, I do not resign completely from the exo-ethnonym Pomaks because of its widespread prevalence in the literature of the subject.

2. Mancheva 2001, 358.

3. Ibid.

4. An obligatory tax levied in the Ottoman Empire on non-Muslim population, perceived as a form of subjection to the state.

5. Zhelyazkova 1997, 52.

6. Radushev 2005, 434.

7. It is worth mentioning that the Bulgarian post-memory of conversion to Islam is shaped to a great extent by Anton Donchev's well-known novel *Vreme razdelno* (Time of parting, 1964), which was required reading in Bulgarian schools. It presents a Christian priest who has to make a decision whether to accept conversion to Islam and decides to side with life. Ludmil Staikov made the book into a film, *Vreme na nasilie* (Time of violence) that was notoriously used as a propaganda tool during the so-called revival process in the 1980s. The decision to convert is portrayed in the novel as an act of heroism intended to protect Pomak women from rape and thus to preserve the purity of Bulgarian blood.

8. My field research was funded by the Polish Ministry of Science and Higher Education (Project NN 109176334).

9. It is a word deriving from Turkish *komşuluk*. According to the Bulgarian sociologist Ivan Hadziyski, the word *komshuluk* is also used to refer to wicket gates separating neighboring homesteads, which were always kept unlocked (Georgieva 2003, 9), unlike the tall, locked gates facing the streets, a familiar element of Ottoman architecture.

10. An Islamic teacher nominated by a mufti (head of the Muslim community, an expert in Islamic law). In the Rhodopes, this term also often indicates the "Islamic teacher," not necessarily nominated by mufti, but regarded as a person of a great knowledge in Islam by his community.

11. Both "charity" and the commandment to "love thy neighbor" (which is Mark 12:31) make this seem like a religious justification. In Bulgarian and other Slavic languages, there is a different word for someone who is close (близък [blizŭk]) but not necessarily one's neighbor (съсед [sŭsed]). In the Bulgarian Bible, one is obliged to love your "blizhniya." Thus, loving one's neighbor is a moral, not religious, obligation, whereas in Islam and Judaism, and even in Anglophone Christianity, it is a religious obligation mentioned in the Bible.

12. This issue of reciprocity is developed more fully in Mauss (1966).

13. Partly because this food is traditionally shared in churches after a *panikhida*—an Orthodox Christian memorial service—which Muslims do not attend.

14. Mauss 1966, 3.

15. All names of interlocutors are pseudonyms.

16. A different type of *kori* pastry with a sweet filling consisting of nuts and syrup.

17. See Hirsch 2012. In an interview, Hirsch explains that post-memory "describes the relationship that the 'generation after' bears to the personal, collective, and cultural trauma of those who came before—to experiences they 'remember' only by means of stories, images and behaviors among which they grew up" (https://cup.columbia.edu/author-interviews/hirsch-generation-postmemory [accessed June 22, 2018).

18. This is a reference to a massacre of the Christian population of Batak at the hands of Pomaks from the village of Barutin. Some of the victims were women and children who fled to a church for safety. The skulls of the victims kept in Batak are considered by Bulgarians to be national relics. For more, see Baleva and Brunnbauer (2007).

19. Szwat-Gyłybowa 2009, 8.

20. See Troeva 2007, 128.

21. The reference to Jesus's entry into heaven is described in Acts 1:1–14 and mentioned in Mark 16:19–20 and Luke 24:50–53, using the words "He was taken up to heaven." The distinction between assumption and ascension thus reflects the understanding of Jesus as prophet or God, respectively.

References

Baleva, Martina, and Ulf Brunnbauer, eds. 2007. *Batak kato myasto na pametta*. Sofia: Iztok-Zapad.

Hirsch, Marianne. 2012. *The Generation of Postmemory: Writing and Visual Culture After the Holocaust*. New York: Columbia University Press.

Lubanska, Magdalena. 2015. *Muslims and Christians in the Bulgarian Rhodopes: Studies on Religious (Anti)Syncretism*. Translated by P. Szymczak. Warsaw: De Gruyter Open.

Mancheva, Mila. 2001. "Image and Policy: The Case of Turks and Pomaks in Inter-War Bulgaria 1918–44 (with special reference to education)," *Islam and Christian-Muslim Relations* 12 (3): 355–374.

Mauss, Marcel. 1966. *The Gift: Forms and Functions of Exchange in Archaic Societies*. Translated by I. Cunnison, London: Cohen & West.

Georgieva, Ts. 2003. "Hristiyani i myusyulmani w bŭlgarskoto prostranstvo." In *Balkanski identichnosti*, part 4, edited by C. Georgijeva and S. Fetbadzhiyeva, 7–29. Sofia: Fondaya Otvoreno Obshtestvo Sofia.

Radushev, E. 2005. *Pomatsite, hristyanstvo i islyam w Zapadnite Rodopi i dolinata na r. Mesta, XV-30-te godni na XVIII vek*. Part 1. Sofia: Narodna Biblioteka Sv.Sv. Kiril i Metodiy Oryentalski Otdel.

Szwat-Gyłybowa, G. 2009. "Batak. Miejsce pamięci w bułgarskiej świadomości zbiorowej." *Borussia. Kultura. Historia. Literatura* 46: 7–27.

Troeva, E. 2007. "Pameti za Batak." In *Batak kato myasto na pametta*, edited by M. Baleva and U. Brunnbauer, 125–130. Sofia: Iztok-Zapad.

Zhelyazkova, A. 1997. "Formirane na na myusyulmanskite obshtnostite i kompleksite na Balkanskite istoriografii." In *Myusyulmanskite obshtnosti na Balkanite i w Bŭlgaria. Istoricheski eskizi, Sŭdbata na myusyulmanskite obshtnosti na Balkanite i v Bŭlgariya*, vol. 1, edited by A. Zheljazkova, 11–56. Sofia: IMIR.

MAGDALENA LUBANSKA is Assistant Professor at the Institute of Ethnology and Cultural Anthropology at the University of Warsaw. Her most recent book is *Muslims and Christians in the Bulgarian Rhodopes: Studies on Religious (Anti)Syncretism*.

30 The Everyday of Religion and Politics in the Balkans

Albert Doja

The deeply social and political significance of religion becomes apparent when looking at how different religious traditions can challenge coexistence and tolerance in everyday life.[1] Ideology—expressed in discourse and doctrine,[2] religious meaning, and moral values[3]—undergirds identity politics. As such, it is important to understand the place of religion in the social organization and transformation of a given society.[4] Above all, discriminatory and stereotyping ideologies behind the categorizing processes of religious affiliations are inherent to any context, whether local, regional, or international.[5] Southeast Europe provides a colorful display of the relationship between religion and politics at the level of religious leaders, state actors, intellectual elites, and ordinary people in everyday interactions. The importance of native language in religious offices and the passion for historical incursions in the everyday life of public discussions—in print media and online networks—shows the intricate interconnectedness of religion and politics. In everyday conversation, people commonly raid history to their own end, convinced that religious movements and political movements have something in common.

Historical Incursions in Everyday Life

People often repurpose history to legitimate their view of how the world was, is, and should be. Though such forays into history may seem innocent, often their impact on political and everyday life is not. In February 2012, the Vatican organized a world conference to commemorate the 1,700th anniversary of the Battle of the Milvian Bridge (October 28, 312) and the legacy of Emperor Constantine's conversion to Christianity. In October 2013, the Serbian Orthodox Church also organized in Nish, the birthplace of Constantine, an even larger world conference to commemorate the importance of the Edict of Milan, in which Constantine established the Christian movement as another official religion of the Roman Empire. The story of Constantine's acceptance of Christianity became important both to the growth of early Christianity and to the growth of Constantine's power, but it also embedded a narrative of providence within a political act that would later serve as a foundation for contemporary claims to the Balkan peoples being foundational to Christendom.

Such moves are neither neutral nor unilateral. Ordinary Albanians are quick to remember June 28, 1989, when Serbian president Slobodan Milosevic used the six-hundredth-anniversary commemoration of the Kosovo Battle of 1389 to strengthen his power by exploiting the myth of the battle,[6] probably not unlike Constantine did with the myth of his own dream. The narrative of a "Muslim" victory—despite both sides suffering heavy losses—is reinterpreted by Serbian nationalist politics, from the nineteenth century until today, as the emblematic Christian Serbian sacrifice at the hands of Ottoman armies. Gatherings to commemorate this myth served to justify the boundaries of Serbian holdings and any means needed to enforce them. Not surprisingly, they also glorified and sanctified the ethno-homicidal criminals who best served Serbian identity politics.[7]

Such celebrations point to the mutually reinforcing—and locally contextualized—nature of religion and politics and the ease with which nationalist tropes emerge as ordained and legitimate. Routinely, one hears support for the blending of religion and politics: ordinary Albanians may recall some imam in Prishtina running for president,[8] or some Kosovar politicians may advocate women wearing Muslim headscarves to gain support among certain voters.[9] Similarly, the Serbian patriarch stated that "Kosovo is the sacred land of Serbia" on Albanian national TV, on June 1, 2014, after the inauguration of the Orthodox Cathedral in Tirana,[10] where the Serbian flag was also briefly displayed.[11] Many ordinary Albanians characterized this as a "brutal and unscrupulous provocation."[12] The Albanian prime minister was outraged and offended, and at his meeting with the patriarchs and primates of world Christian Orthodoxy, he demonstrably pointed his finger to the Serbian patriarch: "Your colleague abused our hospitality, he derogated our religious celebration day and he changed the evidence of our religious coexistence into an outdated political issue."[13]

Regardless of how outdated such moves may seem, incursions into history hold political clout to the extent they make the present seem purposeful. Histories, however, are not without bias. Serbs can look to the churches and monasteries built by the Nemanic dynasty to claim a territorial holding,[14] just as they look to the Kosovo myth to speak of a Serbian sacrifice.[15] Similarly, Albanians look to the efforts of the Greek Orthodox Church during the mid-nineteenth century in squelching the use of Albanian language as an example of systematic oppression.[16] There is an interconnectedness between religion and politics that represents both the imagined and the real state of everyday life.

Religious Realpolitik

On the Easter Saturday 2015 (April 11), when Orthodox Christians celebrated the resurrection of Christ in the Cathedral of Tirana, a prominent Albanian politician expressed his regret in the national press because the Greek archbishop of the Albanian Orthodox Church, Anastasios Yanoulatos, officiated not in Albanian but in Greek.[17] Many deacons rose to the archbishop's defense

Figure 30.1. The Resurrection Cathedral in Tirana, as construction nears completion, 2013. Photograph by David W. Montgomery.

by attesting to the archbishop's theological credentials,[18] but the issue was less about religion than it was about language. To some, the archbishop opting to celebrate Easter in Greek is seen as part and parcel of the Greek Orthodox Church's dismissiveness of the Albanian language and identity. This is well understood especially in the context of the everyday exchanges of Albanian immigrants in Greece, who have adopted Greek language and converted to Greek Orthodoxy. These acts obviously aid integration into Greek society, but if Orthodox Albanians are acquiring more and more Greek at the expense of their native language, something political is at stake.

Such debate about the politics of language behind the religious service is not without historical context. On September 9, 1906, an armed band of Orthodox Albanians fighting for independence from Ottoman rule killed the Greek Metropolitan bishop of Korca, Photios Kalpidhis, on the grounds that one year before he had ordered the murder of an Albanian priest, Papa Kristo Negovani, who officiated in Albanian and taught his believers to read and write Albanian. This unusual event of religious believers killing their own religious leader is still subject to everyday discussions and debates in Albanian public opinion.[19] If Greek clerics exerted ruthless pressure supporting the grecization of Orthodox Albanians, the latter struggled to escape this influence through the arduous path to autonomy and autocephaly of the Albanian Orthodox Church—work led by Theofan (Fan) S. Noli, an Albanian cleric who in 1908 dissociated the Albanian Orthodox liturgy from the Greek Church. This move became important not only to the establishment of the Albanian Orthodox Church but also to advancing the legitimacy of the Albanian language and, in time, the Albanian state.

Another iteration of political-religious entanglement came in 1945, when the communist regime succeeded to enlist the leadership of Orthodox Christians, Sunni Muslims, and Bektashi Albanians in service to the state. Enver Hoxha also called the Albanian Catholic archbishop Vinçenc Prenushi to ask him for the secession of the Albanian Catholic Church from the Roman Papacy. The rejection of the Catholic Albanian leadership resulted in ruthless violence being unleashed in the 1960s on the religious people of all faiths—Catholics, Orthodox Christians, and Muslims alike—which still captivates everyday discussions and debates. The context of this allegiance to Rome is sometimes understood to prove the threat the Catholics posed to the state, as well as their divided loyalty to the nation. Regardless of the fact that the archbishop "was a very good man and great writer, the Dictator was right to separate the Albanian Church from the Papacy. Muslims were independent and Fan Noli founded the Albanian Orthodox Church. Only the Catholics would not be separated from the Papacy! That is why the atheist Communists found an excuse in the attitude of Albanian Catholic leadership and they massacred all religions in Albania."[20]

Undoubtedly, the act of the Albanian Catholic Archbishop, a rightful martyr of the Roman Catholic Church, was a profoundly political, religious, and anticommunist act. Surely, Albanian Catholics could not separate from the Roman Church and remain in communion with Catholicism. What Hoxha characterized as representing an external political threat from Rome, Archbishop Prenushi would have characterized as central to maintaining the religious integrity of his flock. The implications of the political tensions over religion were catastrophic. Nevertheless, compared to the activity of Bishop Fan Noli and other Orthodox Albanians to secede from the Greek Orthodox Church, the rejection of secession from the Roman Catholic Church by Albanian Catholics—despite contemporary religious propaganda and politically motivated endorsements—may still be regarded by some as a political antinational act. In any case, acts of reformation or opposition to religious secession from external religious authorities are always acts of religious politics.

Antinational Identity Politics

Given the tumultuous past, it is no wonder that in the case of the current Greek archbishop of the Albanian Orthodox Church, there are many who question whether his religious politics is related to the political interests of the Albanian Orthodox Christian community or those of the Greeks. To many Albanians, the concern is less about religious credentials than political implication—a concern that his work is not national or nationalistic politics but rather anti-Albanian politics. According to the late Kristo Frasheri, a leading historian and an Orthodox who was active both in church history and in church affairs, the Greek archbishop was not elected by a Saint Synod of the Albanian Orthodox Church, which did not exist at that time. Rather, Anastasios Yanoulatos was appointed by the patriarch of the Greek Orthodox Church with the support of the Greek government at a time when the Albanian government was in a position of no choice but to accept the nomination.[21] The appointment was meant to be a temporary mission to assist the reconstruction of the Albanian Church and some Orthodox clearly supported it. But to the mind of other Orthodox Albanians, these were only Greek-minded Orthodox who took over the Albanian Orthodox Church. Many protesting Orthodox Albanians even opposed massively his enthronement ceremony on August 2, 1992, by shouting nationalist slogans and proclaiming the names of Kristo Negovani and Fan Noli.[22] Because of protests, the so-called enthronement ceremony was forced to move from the church to conclude in a hall at the Hotel Tirana International. For many Orthodox Albanians, and according to church canons, the fact that the ceremony took place outside of a church made the enthronement of the Greek archbishop at the See of the Albanian Orthodox Church illegitimate.

On August 29, 1992, according to Kristo Frasheri, who participated in the event, "a large meeting of Orthodox Christians, attended by representatives of Tirana and delegates of other districts, was held to re-examine the intolerable situation created by the violation of the Orthodox Church canons that enthroned the Greek Archbishop Anastasios Janullatos."[23] The meeting expressed forcefully the general determination that the church must be recovered on the basis of its sacred Albanian and Orthodox traditions. As a result, a sort of schism can be observed among the Orthodox Albanians led by Father Nikolla Marku, of St. Mary Church of Elbasan.[24] The faction led by Father Marku opposes the authority of the Greek archbishop and denounces the usurpation of the Albanian Church by the Greeks. In turn, the official church does not recognize the breakaway faction, simply because Father Marku is ordained by the Macedonian Orthodox Church, which is reminiscent of Fan Noli being ordained by the Russian Orthodox Church before he founded the Albanian Church independent from the Greek Church.

Many Albanians claim that the reconstruction of Orthodox churches advanced by the Greek archbishop of the Albanian Church is an act of religious politics aimed at preserving Greek influence over Orthodox Albanians. Despite the publicly endorsed intentions of Anastasios, the actual actions of the church suggest to many that it is interested less in religious objectives than in political ones. Some claim the reconstruction activism tries deliberately to Grecize the external appearance and architectural style of worship buildings in Albania,[25] and it is reminiscent of the activity of the early Greek Church in Albania. There are similarities here with the ideological education of the so-called new man and the creation of the "new people's culture" or "new folklore" movement during the communist regime.[26] And parallels to this "ideological education" can be found within the militant fundamentalism advocated for by a small minority of Albanian Muslims in Kosovo and Macedonia.[27]

Political tensions between Greece and Albania continue to play out in an overtly religious context, seen in a conflict culminating on August 26, 2015, after much debate between government and Orthodox authorities, with the demolition of an illegal building on the foundations of an old church in Dhermi, in southwest Albania. The same day, the Greek archbishop of the Albanian Orthodox Church had a meeting with the Greek prime minister Alexis Tsipras. Even though "the meeting was planned in advance,"[28] Anastasios was portrayed by the Greek media as having complained about an interference of the Albanian state into the affairs of the Albanian Orthodox Church.[29] Not only did Greek media heap scornful abuse upon Albania and the Albanians but the Greek government also took a tougher stance toward Albanian authorities. The Greek newspaper *Kathimerini* wrote that Athens was expected to lodge an official complaint with Albanian authorities and the international community.[30] Greek Foreign Ministry spokesperson Konstantinos Koutras equated Albanian authorities with jihadists: "The destruction of holy sites and objects of worship took place, at least until recently, in the wider region of the Middle East and North Africa, at the hands of jihadists, but today we also saw such an act carried out in our neighboring country, Albania."[31]

On his part, the Albanian prime minister Edi Rama considered it unacceptable that the senior cleric of the Albanian Church could complain to the prime minister of a foreign country and not to the prime minister of the country whose church leader he is. In a long Facebook posting, extensively reprinted in Albanian media, Rama wrote that Greece

> must be aware that any issue or problem of the Albanian Orthodox Church or the Orthodox Albanians has no connection with Greece. Orthodox Albanians are Albanian citizens who have their own state and the space where they practice their faith is not a protectorate of any other state. Any problem that the Albanian Orthodox Church might have had, might still have, or will have with the state is handled and will be handled with the Albanian state and its institutions. Any intervention in this context is an unacceptable interference in the internal affairs of Albania. Albania is the country where the Orthodox Church is at home and not at the neighbor's home.[32]

The ground on which the shapeless building was demolished in Dhermi is said to have been an early seventeenth-century Uniate church built by Basilian monks and the tomb of an important Roman Catholic missionary who was the archbishop of Durres in 1693. Albanian authorities have expressed a commitment to restoring the site,[33] but the argument in everyday discussions among Albanians remains unchanged, seemingly refighting the same century-old political battles between the Greek-Byzantine Orthodox Church and the Roman Catholic Church. While the Roman Catholic Church is believed by some to have instigated the emergence of an Albanian identity,[34] some interpret the Greek

Orthodox influence as a threat to Albanian identity.³⁵ The claim here is that through the soft power of cultural and religious influence, by means of building Orthodox churches and imagined cemeteries, Greece is trying to nurture its own legitimacy—both in history and in identity—to nationalist claims to a greater Northern Epirus that includes much of the Albanian south as belonging to Greece and its sphere of influence.³⁶

Everyday Balkan Politics

Questions about the primacy of different churches and cultural heritages are often answered with political ends in mind. This brings us back to the 1,700th anniversary of the Battle of the Milvian Bridge and the legacy of Emperor Constantine to Christianity. In May 2012, the first international conference on faiths in Kosovo was organized by the American University in Kosovo to celebrate these events.³⁷ Beyond the old story of the mutual consolidation of imperial power and church authority in the fourth century, one must question why such a conference was organized in Kosovo. Of course, Constantine was of Balkan origin and Dardanian descent, being born in Naissus (modern Nish in present-day Serbia), located within the Illyrian province of Dardania, which corresponds approximately to present-day Kosovo. In fact, this reason was stated very clearly during the conference. Similar events were also organized the following year in Tirana and again in Prishtina, receiving great acclaim in Albanian and Kosovar local media and public opinion.

On April 27, 2013, a symposium titled "Constantine: 1700th Anniversary of the Edict of Milan and the Religious Freedom" was organized in Tirana at the initiative of the Catholic Church in Albania. In his address to the symposium, the Albanian prime minister Sali Berisha acclaimed of Constantine the Great: "Illyrian in origin, Dardanian in descent, in this anniversary, he makes every Albanian proud."³⁸ Another three-day symposium on Constantine and the Edict of Milan was organized in Prishtina for September 3–5, 2013, again at the initiative of the Catholic Church in Kosovo. The explicit aim was to show that "the historical legacy of Constantine the Great and the Edict of Milan are relevant to the historical memory of Kosovo and its European identity." In his address to the symposium, Kosovo foreign minister Enver Hoxhaj stressed the fact that Constantine was a native of Illyrian Dardania: "Given the Western scientific conviction about *our* Illyrian origin, as one of the oldest nations in Europe, Constantine the Great is part of the historical consciousness of the citizens of Kosovo and the Albanians wherever they live." Many other participants made similar declarations, emphasizing that Constantine is "the symbol of *our* European roots" and that his legacy "is very precious for *our* Illyrian-Albanian world."³⁹

During the conference lunch in Prishtina, the Serbian translator, who was from Nish, the birthplace of Constantine in present-day Serbia, told me that people in Nish know where the palace of Constantine is located and some want to dig it out to rebuild a new monument, but they do not have yet the necessary funding. It could be argued that today's Serbs in Nish have nothing to do with

Constantine, as he was an Illyrian and in Illyrian Dardania, there were not yet any Slavic people. In terms of identity, the people of Constantine's era are not the people of today, and it is historically naive to think otherwise. Yet, nothing prevents Serbs or Albanians from trying to recover a glorious past that connects them to times and figures of greatness, like Constantine. Everyday talk among ordinary Albanians, written press, social media, and blogging is constantly full of that. Likewise, Serbian fiction is instrumental to this aim; for example, Dejan Stojiljkovic's novel *Kostandinovo raskršće* (Constantine's crossing),[40] about the quest of Constantine's sword in Nish, remains one of the most widely read books in Serbian public libraries.[41] Even scientific events become a good opportunity to remind others of Constantine's greatness in Serbian land.[42] Greeks and Macedonians do exactly the same in their political claims to Alexander the Great.

Underlying conferences and debates such as those in Prishtina and Tirana are often political agendas hoping to find legitimacy in religious history. For example, the first conference on faiths in Kosovo forwarded the claim that Kosovo and the Albanians are the land and the people who cultivate religious tolerance, given that theirs is the story of Constantine and that the Edict of Milan is ultimately a story of religious tolerance. In his address to the 2013 Tirana symposium on Constantine and religious freedom, Albanian prime minister Berisha proclaimed: "If Constantine was alive today, he would have been among us, not so much because of his Dardan-Illyrian origin, but because this country and this nation has embodied better than anyone else the respect for the other's faith. He could have found the core of his Edict, here in Albania, much better than anywhere else, embodied as it is in the morals of the citizens of this country with different religious faiths and with a perfect respect for religious tolerance."[43] These are not merely neutral characterizations of the past but rather political claims to the moral superiority of one group over another, claims made by all, whether Albanians, Serbs, Greeks, or Macedonians.

Everyday Religious Politics

When we talk about religion, we are dealing with some very different things. We are dealing with religious leaders and religious institutions that are like politicians and patrons of power and authority. The politics of religion can be felt most profoundly at the level of everyday interactions. In 2009, I visited the new St. George Cathedral in Korca and was greeted by a deacon who said, "Kalimera" ("Good morning" in Greek). I asked why he did not greet me in Albanian—*Mirëdita*—to which he replied that he too was Albanian but that here people like speaking Greek more. This is not true, I replied, unless Korca has been made part of Greece. I was born and grew up here as an Orthodox, but I have never seen and heard someone speaking Greek. "You must not have seen very well," he retorted angrily, "but the more you come to church the more you will see, you too!"

Similar arguments that revolve largely around a belief that the church is increasingly a place for Greek influence can be seen in the relationship between identity politics and religious entrepreneurship, for instance, in the situation of the Orthodox Church and the Unity for Human Rights Party (Partia Bashkimi për të Drejtat e Njeriut, PBDJN), a political party claiming to represent Albania's ethnic Greek minority. The fact that PBDNJ played a major role in the Albanian political scene has been largely due to both financial and political support from Greece, which enlarged the footing of both Orthodox followers and PBDNJ voters. In a process of "homogenization" with Greek ethnicity,[44] any Albanian of Orthodox Christian origin can receive a full pension and medical insurance from the Greek government. One simply needs to show a birth certificate—easily fabricated in many cases—as a proof of origin or descent in the south Albanian areas claimed to be Greek by the extreme nationalist ideology of Megali Idea. To prove one's "Greekness," individuals also need to affirm their profession of the Orthodox Christian faith, just as a Muslim must accept and affirm the shahada.[45] The effect of this Greek policy was a dramatic increase both in the ethnic Greek minority and in followers of the Orthodox Church. Indeed, according to independent surveys censusing religious identification, stated affiliation changed dramatically in the 2000s from the traditionally-given distribution of about 70 percent Muslims, 20 percent Orthodox Christians, and 10 percent Catholics, to 38 percent Muslims, 35 percent Orthodox Christians, and the remaining 27 percent being Catholics and non-affiliated others.[46] At the same time, PBDNJ secured an increasing number of seats in the Albanian Parliament.

Greek homogenization was a great opportunity for supplemental income for many Albanians in the harsh days of postcommunist life and came at a time when the Greek government could afford an aggressive nationalist policy, partially thanks to the generous European and international loans. The financial crisis that befell Greece, however, could no longer support a nationalist policy of the Greek homogenization of Albanians. As a result, the numbers of Orthodox followers and PBDNJ voters in Albania declined dramatically. For the first time, the 2011 census asked for religious and ethnic affiliations, but a huge proportion (70 percent) of Albanians refused to declare their religious faith,[47] and only 0.87 percent Greek minority and 6.75 percent Orthodox Christians were found in the Albanian population.[48] PBDNJ and the Orthodox Church,[49] but also the Greek government, officially protested against the census results, which they claimed were manipulated because of such an "impossible" proportion.[50] In the following elections, PBDNJ also lost all seats in the Albanian Parliament. During the summer of 2015, I was watching a TV program on the southwest Albanian coast, which is not only a hotly contested area of Greek politics but also one of the most beautiful holiday places in Albania. A journalist reported that this year people were speaking increasingly in Albanian rather than in Greek, as had been the case a few years before.

This story of the opportunistic and pragmatic relationship between religion and politics is not unique to Orthodoxy but can be seen as well in the recent intensification of Islam in Albania, especially in the increase of Muslim worship buildings throughout the Albanian landscape and in the increasing display of conspicuous religious insignia like the Muslim scarves worn in many Albanian towns. It is

Figure 30.2. "The Albanians" mosaic at the entrance to the National Historical Museum in Tirana tells a story of resistance to invasion and occupation throughout the country's history. Such presentations of the past are among the material ways history incurs upon everyday life, often to political and religious ends, 2006. Photograph by David W. Montgomery.

believed that foreign financial donations support Islamic proselytism in Albania. In particular, Turkish funding from the Gulen philanthropic agencies has been very instrumental in building religious and educational institutions. It is believed by many that they also provide individual pensions for new converts to Islam.[51] Curiously, during a short visit in Albania in the summer of 2015, I could barely notice any women covered with a headscarf in Tirana. There might be many reasons for the observable decline in the display of headscarves, one being that if there is no longer funding provided to support Muslims in Albania, there is no longer reason for some to display Muslim belonging, which the scarf is seen to index.[52]

To better understand the debates at issue, among Muslim Albanians after independence in 1912, the Muslim veil was seldom worn by women in the towns—though it was more widely worn by women in rural Kosovo than in Albania. It is only since the 1990s and the turbulent changes of the postcommunist transition that there has been a rebirth of religion in Albania, including the following of Islam and the return of the veil, in particular among some young women. Interestingly, as I have argued elsewhere, in vernacular Albanian there is no Muslim term for the veil; while the word *havale* is etymologically related to "veil," it is not perceived as a religious Islamic obligation but used more in the sense of "embarrassment" and "discomfort."[53] The distinction is important in the expression *nuk kam havale*, literally "I can't wear the veil," which means the rejection of the "social veil" that confined women to the shelter of the house and courtyard,[54] a seclusion that has been expected from ordinary housewives until recently, despite changes in the position of women. Actually, the expression is often used rather demonstratively by younger women—both Christian and Muslim in Kosovo and Albania—as the unofficial declaration of women's liberation from cultural and religious constraints.

But as we see, both historical incursions and everyday public discussions are windows into the relationship between identity politics and religious entrepreneurs. Throughout the region, there are stories of Catholics, Orthodox Christians, Muslims, and others who claim both religious and moral heritage by selectively drawing on history and politics to infuse everyday life with claims of legitimacy and belonging. How these stories get told significantly affects the everyday of both politics and religion.

Notes

1. The significance of religion balances the rest of social life. See Doja 2000b.
2. Doja 2006a, 2006b, 2006c.
3. Doja 2011.
4. Doja 2000c.
5. Doja 2008.
6. Edwards 2015.
7. Bieber 2002.
8. "Imami i Prishtinës Krasniqi: Do të kandidoj për President i Kosovës," *Shqiptarja*, January 18, 2014, accessed July 22, 2018, http://shqiptarja.com/kosova/2727/imami-i-prishtines-krasniqi-do-te-kandidoj-per-president-i-kosoves-196466.html #sthash.4vM923Fp.dpuf.
9. In April 2012, Kosovo president Atifete Jahjaga refused to decree the appointment of MP Amir Ahmeti as ambassador because of "his religious offences, especially those expressed publicly last year in favor of religious courses and the wearing of Muslim headscarves" in primary and secondary schools. See "Ngarkesat religjioze lënë pa status diplomatin Amir Ahmeti," *Koha Ditore*, April 27, 2012, accessed July 22, 2018, http://koha.net/?id=8&arkiva=1&l-97254.
10. "Irinej: Kosova, e shenjtë për Serbinë," *Top Channel TV*, June 1, 2014, accessed July 22, 2018, http://top-channel.tv/lajme/artikull.php?id=278998.
11. "Shenjtërimi i Katedrales 'Ngjallja e Krishtit' shoqërohet me incidente," *Dita*, June 1, 2014, accessed July 22, 2018, http://www.gazetadita.al/shenjterimi-i-kishes-ngjallja-e-krishtit-ne-ceremoni-kreret-e-ortodoksise-boterore/.
12. "Tirana dhe Prishtina në këmbë kundër kryepeshkopit serb, Berisha e shpall armik, Rama e sulmon ashpër, tension në Kosovë," *Gazeta Express*, June 3, 2014, accessed February 27, 2017, http://www.gazetaexpress.com/lajme/tirana-dhe-prishtina-ne-kembe-kunder-kryepeshkopit-serb-berisha-e-shpall-armik-rama-e-sulmon-ashper-tension-ne-kosove-18533/.
13. "Rama kritikon patriarkun serb: Shpërfille besimin, na ke fyer!," *A1Report-Shqiptarja*, June 2, 2014, accessed February 27, 2017, http://shqiptarja.com/news.php?IDNotizia=217677&NomeCategoria=home&Titolo=rama-kritikon-patriarkun-serb-shp-rfille-besimin-na-ke-fyer&IDCategoria=1&reply=384881&page=1.

14. Judah 1997.
15. Anzulovic 1999.
16. Doja 1999a, 1999b, 2000a, 2000c.
17. "Mesha në greqisht natën e Pashkës, Blushi: Kur do flasë shqip Anastasi?" (Easter office in Greek language, Blushi: When the Archbishop will speak Albanian?), *Panorama*, April 14, 2015, accessed February 27, 2017, http://www.panorama.com.al /mesha-ne-greqisht-naten-e-pashkes-blushi-kur-do-flase-anastasi-shqip/.
18. "Prifti ortodoks akuzon Blushin se ngriti gishtin kundër Zotit: Jo krim që s'është shqiptar" (The Orthodox priest accuses Blushi to raise the finger to God: There is no crime not being an Albanian) *Panorama*, April 14, 2015, accessed February 27, 2017, http://www.panorama.com.al/prifti-ortodoks-akuzon-blushin-se-i-ngriti-gishtin-zotit -per-janullatosin-jo-krim-qe-seshte-shqiptar/.
19. "Kush e vrau Mitropolitin e Korçës?," *E Vërteta*, September 14, 2014, accessed February 27, 2017, http://everteta.al/kush-e-vrau-mitropolitin-e-korces/; "Mitropolitin e Korçës Fotis Kallpidhis e vrau Spiro Kosturi," *Shqiptarja*, October 12, 2014, accessed February 27, 2017, http://shqiptarja.com/m/home/mitropolitin-e-kor--s-fotis-kallpidhis -e-vrau-spiro-kosturi-245374.html.
20. "Prenushi u dënua nga Enveri: nuk donte të ndante Kishën nga Papa," *Panorama*, April 14, 2014, accessed February 27, 2017, http://www.panorama.com.al/prenushi-u -denua-nga-enveri-nuk-donte-te-ndante-kishen-nga-papa/.
21. See Kristo Frashëri, "Tri të vërtetat për të cilat gënjen Janullatosi," *Gazeta Shqiptare*, October 11, 2010.
22. See video of enthronement ceremony at https://youtu.be/zLszHi-MUyc, accessed February 27, 2017.
23. See *Gazeta "Lirija,"* September 4, 1992; *Koha Jonë*, September 11, 1992.
24. See "At Nikolla Marku dhe Kryepeshkopi Janullatos, akuza kundër njëri-tjetrit," *Gazeta Shekulli*, February 5, 2013, accessed February 27, 2017, http://www.shekulli.com .al/p.php?id=15798.
25. See https://www.facebook.com/dorian.koci1/posts/10207599560365760?pnref= story, accessed February 27, 2017.
26. Doja 2015; Abazi and Doja 2016.
27. So far, the tensions raised by radicalization have been confined to vitriolic online debates, with some condemning any display of Muslim identity and others accusing them of not understanding the Islamic faith (see "Toleranca në provë: Shqipëria përballë sfidës së radikalizmit," *Gazeta Mapo*, December 10, 2015, accessed February 27, 2017, http:// www.mapo.al/2015/12/toleranca-ne-prove-shqiperia-perballe-sfides-se-radikalizmit/).
28. "Kryepeshkopi Anastas: Takimi me Tsipras ishte planifikuar shumë kohë përpara," *BalkanWeb*, August 26, 2015, accessed February 27, 2017, http://www .balkanweb.com/site/kryepeshkopi-anastas-takimi-me-tsipras-ishte-planifikuar-shume -kohe-perpara/.
29. "Κι άλλα σύννεφα έφερε το γκρέμισμα του ναού," *Η Καθημερινή*, August 29, 2015, accessed February 27, 2017, http://www.kathimerini.gr/828830/article /epikairothta/ellada/ki-alla-synnefa-efere-to-gkremisma-toy-naoy.
30. See copy of the Greek note at http://www.oranews.tv/wp-content/uploads /2015/08/reagimi.jpg, accessed February 27, 2017.
31. "Athens Condemns Demolition of Orthodox Church in Albania," *Kathimerini* English Edition, August 26, 2015, accessed February 27, 2017, http://www.ekathimerini .com/200908/article/ekathimerini/news/athens-condemns-demolition-of-orthodox -church-in-albania.

32. See https://www.facebook.com/media/set/?set=a.10153174628091523.1073742791.138734771522&type=3 (accessed February 27, 2017).

33. "Jorgo Goro: Kisha e Shën Thanasit do të rindërtohet, varri i Katalanos është pjesë e projektit," BalkanWeb, August 27, 2015, accessed February 27, 2017, http://www.balkanweb.com/site/jorgo-goro-kisha-e-shen-thanasit-do-te-rindertohet-varri-i-katalanos-eshte-pjese-e-projektit/.

34. Lempert 2012.

35. "Gënjeshtra të shenjta," *Gazeta Tema*, August 26, 2015, accessed February 27, 2017, http://www.gazetatema.net/web/2015/08/26/genjeshtra-te-shenjta/.

36. See "Qëllimet ekspansioniste dhe 'megalloidea' e Janullatosit në Shqipëri," *Mapo*, August 25, 2015, accessed February 27, 2017, http://www.mapo.al/2015/08/qellimet-ekspansioniste-dhe-megalloidea-e-janullatosit-ne-shqiperi.

37. Albert Doja, "The Politics of Religion and the Construction of Instrumental Realities and Identities against an Imagined Future of the Balkans," Faiths in Kosovo: Past, Present, Future, International Conference Commemorating the 1,700th anniversary of the Battle of the Milvian Bridge and the Conversion of Emperor Constantine to Christianity, American University in Kosovo, Prishtina, May 15–17, 2012. Video at http://youtu.be/APpTBffsjfc.

38. Konstandini: 1700 vjetori i Ediktit të Milanos dhe Liria fetare, Tirana: Albanian Episcopal Conference, 2014, p. 29.

39. See Press Releases & Media, "Symposium: Edict of Milan—Constantine the Great, 2013," accessed February 27, 2017, http://www.interfaithkosovo.org/constantine-the-great-edict-of-milan-symposium/ (emphasis added).

40. Stojiljkovic 2009.

41. See http://www.konstantinovoraskrsce.com/ (accessed February 27, 2017).

42. See Second Regional Symposium on Electrochemistry: South-East Europe Program & Book of Abstracts, Belgrade, June 6–10, 2010, p. 32, accessed February 27, 2017, http://www.shd.org.rs/RSE-SEE_2/RSE_SEE_2-Book_of_Abstracts.pdf.

43. Konstandini: 1700 vjetori i Ediktit të Milanos dhe Liria fetare, Tirana: Albanian Episcopal Conference, 2014, p. 30.

44. See http://hyllin.blogspot.com/2009/06/natyralizim-apo-homogjenizim.html (accessed February 27, 2017).

45. The shahada is the Muslim profession of faith: "there is no god but Allah and Muhammad is the messenger of Allah."

46. "Raporti i ri: shqiptarët 38% myslimanë dhe 35% kristianë," *Gazeta Shqip*, October 2, 2006, accessed February 27, 2017, http://www.forumishqiptar.com/threads/73218-Raporti-i-ri-shqiptarë-38-myslimanë-dhe-35-kristianë.

47. "Censusi përmbys fetë: 70 përqind refuzojnë ose nuk deklarojnë besimin," *Gazeta Shekulli*, April 25, 2012.

48. Population and Housing Census 2011, 1.1.13-14, p. 71.

49. Deklaratë Zyrtare: Të dhënat e Censusit 2011 për të krishterët orthodhoksë të Shqipërisë janë tërësisht të pasakta dhe të papranueshme," accessed February 27, 2017, http://orthodoxalbania.org/alb/index.php/al/censusi-deklarata.

50. "Rezultatet e censusit: 83% shqiptare 0.87 grekë, Shqipëria ka më shumë katolikë se ortodoksë," *Gazeta Tema*, December 7, 2012, accessed February 27, 2017, http://www.gazetatema.net/web/2012/12/07/censusi-83-shqiptare-0-87-greke-komunitetet-fetare-me-shume-katolike-se-ortodokse/.

51. In his official visit to Albania in May 2015, Turkish president Recep Tayyip Erdoğan denounced Gülen philanthropic agencies as a "terrorist parallel state"

("Erdogan: Bllokoni aktivitetin e Gulen, 'shteti paralel' terrorist," May 14, 2015, http://shqiptarja.com/news.php?IDNotizia=292203#sthash.ROvGttdB.dpuf). In the aftermath of the July 15, 2016, attempted coup d'état in Turkey, any supposed link to Gülen funding is under scrutiny in Albania.

52. For many, the motivation behind wearing the scarf is seen as financially instrumental. At the UN refugee summit of September 20, 2016, for example, the Austrian foreign minister gave a statement urging countries to stop increasing Islamic radicalism in Bosnia and Kosovo or Albania, where "a strong religious and ideological influence is noticeably characterized by women being paid to walk fully veiled in the streets" ("Kurz: Alle Staaten tragen Verantwortung, http://www.kleinezeitung.at/politik/aussenpolitik/5087606/UNFluchtlingsgipfel_Kurz_Alle-Staaten-tragen-Verantwortung). Such sentiments are shared and widely discussed in Albanian-speaking print and social media ("Ministri austriak: Në Shqipëri, femrat paguhen që të mbulohen," http://opinion.al/ministri-austriak-ne-shqiperi-femrat-paguhen-qe-te-mbulohen).

53. Doja 2008.
54. Backer 2003 [1979].

References

Abazi, Enika, and Albert Doja. 2016. "From the Communist Point of View: Cultural Hegemony and Folkloric Manipulation in Albanian Studies under Socialism." *Communist and Post-Communist Studies* 49 (2): 163–178.

Anzulovic, Branimir. 1999. *Heavenly Serbia: From Myth to Genocide*. New York: New York University Press.

Backer, Berit. 2003 [1979]. *Behind Stone Walls: Changing Household Organization among the Albanians of Kosova*. Edited by Antonia Young and Robert Elsie. Peja: Dukagjini Books.

Bieber, Florian. 2002. "Nationalist Mobilization and Stories of Serb Suffering: The Kosovo Myth from 600th Anniversary to the Present." *Rethinking History* 6 (1): 95–110.

Doja, Albert. 1999a. "Ethnicité, construction nationale et nationalisme dans l'aire albanaise: Approche anthropologique du conflit et des relations interethniques." *Ethnologia Balkanica: Journal for Southeast European Anthropology* 3: 155–179.

Doja, Albert. 1999b. "Formation nationale et nationalisme dans l'aire de peuplement albanais." *Balkanologie: Revue d'Études Pluridisciplinaires* 3 (2): 23–43.

Doja, Albert. 2000a. "Entre invention et construction des traditions: l'Héritage historique et culturel des Albanais." *Nationalities Papers: The Journal of Nationalism and Ethnicity* 28 (3): 417–448.

Doja, Albert. 2000b. "Histoire et dialectique des idéologies et significations religieuses." *Europeans Legacy—Towards New Paradigms: Journal of the International Society for the Study of European Ideas* 5 (5): 663–686.

Doja, Albert. 2000c. "The Politics of Religion in the Reconstruction of Identities: The Albanian Situation." *Critique of Anthropology* 20 (4): 421–438.

Doja, Albert. 2006a. "A Political History of Bektashism from Ottoman Anatolia to Contemporary Turkey." *Journal of Church and State* 48 (2): 421–450.

Doja, Albert. 2006b. "A Political History of Bektashism in Albania." *Totalitarian Movements and Political Religions* 7 (1): 83–107.

Doja, Albert. 2006c. "Spiritual Surrender: From Companionship to Hierarchy in the History of Bektashism." *Numen: International Review for the History of Religions* 53 (2): 448–510.

Doja, Albert. 2008. "Instrumental Borders of Gender and Religious Conversions in the Balkans." *Religion, State & Society* 36 (1): 55–63.

Doja, Albert. 2011. "Honneur, Foi et Croyance: Approche linguistique anthropologique des valeurs morales et religieuses." *Anthropos: International Review of Anthropology and Linguistics* 106 (1): 161–172.

Doja, Albert. 2015. "From the Native Point of View: An Insider/Outsider Perspective on Folkloric Archaism and Modern Anthropology in Albania." *History of the Human Sciences* 28 (4): 44–75.

Edwards, Jason A. 2015. "Bringing in Earthly Redemption: Slobodan Milosevic and the National Myth of Kosovo." *Advances in the History of Rhetoric* 18 (supl): S187–S204.

Judah, Tim. 1997. *The Serbs: History, Myth and the Destruction of Yugoslavia*. New Haven, CT: Yale University Press.

Lempert, Hans. 2012. "Das Verhältnis von Religion und Nation in Albanien." *RGOW: Religion & Gesellschaft in Ost und West* 4 : 10–12.

ALBERT DOJA is Professor of Sociology and Anthropology at the University of Lille, France, and Chair of Anthropology of the National Academy of Sciences, Albania.

Section VI: The Art of Everyday Life

"The art of everyday life" is a phrase concerned with both beauty and activity. On the one hand, there is an aesthetics to creative forms of expression that unfold into meaning through film, song, words, dance, and other expressions recognized for their holding more than ordinary significance. On the other hand, how one socially navigates life requires a skill that, with practice, can be felicitous in form. The chapters in this section recognize those aspects of art that are built on repetition and the experience of practice and those that convey meaning within and beyond the everyday.

Art surrounds life, and here we are reminded of the subtlety with which it works. In her chapter on architecture and memory, Alyssa Grossman shows us how everyday places of collective memory aesthetically memorialize the past. Carol Silverman shows how wedding music can become a space for ethnonationalism to emerge as musicians alter between resisting and accommodating the state's attempt to determine its cultural construction. In discussing film, Yana Hashamova writes about how some Balkan female directors have used the genre to portray a more complex picture of motherhood than traditionally depicted. Likewise seeking to show how art shapes, and at times pushes, boundaries of understanding, Ervin Hatibi looks at how literature is used to frame ideas—love, foreignness, sexuality in relation to censorship, and a postsocialist reinventing of society—and how it speaks to both the context of constraint and the creativity that arises in response to such constraints. And lastly, Marko Živković reminds us that behind creations of art is training, hard work, and devotion to excellence in a craft—that art is beauty and activity.

Each of these chapters remind us that the expressions of art have lasting effects in how we see, think, and engage the world. To understand everyday life, we must recognize the beauty, creativity, and art that surround us.

31 Unintentional Memorials: Everyday Places of Memory in Post-Transition Bucharest

Alyssa Grossman

Most contemporary studies of memorial landscapes tend to focus on official landmarks, monuments, archives, and museums as authoritative sites of collective remembrance. This chapter, on the other hand, addresses places of urban memory that are not so deliberately or explicitly commemorational. As Alois Riegl long ago defined such "unintentional monuments," their commemorative value is determined not by their makers but rather by those who happen to recognize it as such.[1] Sidestepping the city of Bucharest's more obvious examples of "intentional monuments" and residual constructions that symbolize and mythologize its long and controversial communist past,[2] I delve into the more ambiguous corners and crevices between such structures. I investigate specific realms that are not always immediately identifiable as memorial: shop windows, construction sites, renovations, street signs. While these types of mundane features are not commemorative in and of themselves, their current manifestations in Bucharest can be tied to powerful and visceral impressions related to the city's complicated trajectories through the past and present.

Encounters with disregarded or marginalized parts of a city can often be highly sensorial and more intense than experiences within its more developed or mainstream arenas, giving rise to strong corporeal processes of remembrance.[3] Walter Benjamin borrowed Proust's term "involuntary memory" to describe the unexpected and unbidden recollections stemming from interactions with such everyday, overlooked cultural spaces and forms.[4] Involuntary memories emerge as spontaneous and fragmented ruptures rather than developed narratives, incorporating aesthetic and haptic qualities that trigger a heightened emotional state.[5] In Benjaminian terms, this type of "suddenly emergent" awareness constitutes a dialectical type of memory, involving a fleeting superimposition of the "has been" and the "now," a constellation of past and future, recollection and expectation.[6] Because involuntary memories tend to be more idiosyncratic and contradictory than most established social and political memorial tropes, they demonstrate individual and collective remembrance schemes that are more complex and nuanced than standard interpretations of memory work prevalent in the media, politics, and academia.[7] Examining such processes within everyday spaces can therefore point to feelings and conceptions about the past that defy easy categorization into nostalgic or sentimentalizing frameworks, and resist the more formalized, regulated rhetoric of the heritage industry.[8]

In post-transition, EU-era Romania, now in the beginning of its fourth decade following the end of forty-four years of communist rule, intense debates continue about how the national past should be remembered and represented. While there is a widespread endorsement of initiatives to condemn and criminalize the previous totalitarian regime and its practices of political repression and economic deprivation,[9] such views are blended with a renewed appreciation for the types of social relationships and material culture connected to the communist past, which have come to be regarded as meaningful and unique.[10] Many academic and popular analyses claim that these disparate opinions ought to be reconciled or resolved in order for Romanians to properly "move on" and embrace their new European, post-transition identity.[11] Yet it is by acknowledging this very composite of fluctuating and contradictory perceptions that such a mandate might be reframed, offering alternative understandings into present-day social and political dynamics as Romanians continue to evaluate their history and look to the future.

Starting in 1999, when I began to conduct anthropological research in Bucharest, my own inquiries into the unintentional memorial spaces of the city have attended to the presence of such multilayered and often dissonant processes of recollection. In this chapter, I examine material settings in contemporary Bucharest, where involuntary memories spontaneously emerge, and trace their contours as they weave in and out of official and everyday discourses and through individual and collective imaginations.

Bucharest as a Porous City

Like any landscape, a city can be viewed as a "terrain of memory," physically shaped by different cultural processes over time.[12] Today's Bucharest covers eighty-eight square miles, with roughly two million inhabitants. On a map, it looks a bit like a bicycle wheel, with a central hub and spokes that divide its six different districts. In the seventeenth and eighteenth centuries, the region underwent a series of occupations by the Ottoman Empire, the Habsburg monarchy, and Imperial Russia. The city's topography and architecture betray all these influences, as well as those of the Soviet takeover during the Second World War; the subsequent four decades of communist rule; and the 1989 revolution leading to the transition, post-communist, and European Union eras.

During his regime from 1965 to 1989, Nicolae Ceaușescu's dogged projects of demolition and construction altered the Romanian capital so drastically that it was frequently referred to as a "scarred" or "mutilated" city riven into two distinct parts: the so-called Civic Center (Ceaușescu's massive and unfinished assemblage of administrative buildings and Soviet-style blocks for the nomenclature, initiated in the 1980s), and the rest of the city.[13] At first glance, today's visitor might see the Civic Center and the other communist-era residential districts built after the 1950s, with their rows of cracked and stained concrete, and think this was all Bucharest had to offer. But the less immediately visible folds of the city reveal an eclectic amalgamation of architectural styles and forms. Byzantine churches and monasteries, nineteenth-century influences from Paris and Vienna, and twentieth-century modernist, Stalinist, and Ceaușescu-ist architecture all coexist, now competing with the waves of bourgeoning skyscrapers. Shiny glass buildings share lots with grimy prefabricated apartments. Rickety kiosks and vending stalls border restored villas with well-groomed gardens. Scaffolding and covered walkways extend down entire streets, their edifices in continuous stages of renovation.

Many local planners and architects have lamented that Bucharest is too full of contrasts to possess any clear or overarching identity.[14] Yet the visual inconsistencies and superimpositions of old and new, deterioration and reconstruction, are part of its dynamic character, and speak to the city's "porous" qualities. As Svetlana Boym notes, drawing on Walter Benjamin's writings, porous cities feature a coexistence of ruins, renovations, and transitional spaces.[15] By provoking people to recollect the past as they look toward the future, they give rise to unique types of remembrance objects, discourses, and practices. A porous city is a palimpsest, containing sedimentary layers of material structures and collective imaginaries that have accrued over time, to be interpreted "historically, intertextually, constructively, and deconstructively".[16] Many parts of Bucharest paradoxically have been preserved by the simple fact that they were for so long neglected or forgotten. These unheeded, ordinary places then serve as porous sites where the past unexpectedly erupts into the present, unsettling the "reified continuity of history" to transform notions of time and our place within it.[17]

The City as Work Site

Throughout the decade immediately following the 1989 revolution, Bucharest's landscape continued to be dominated by dozens of stranded, rusting cranes looming over Ceaușescu's half-finished constructions, along with an urban and social infrastructure badly in need of attention. Publications about Bucharest written during this period describe its crumbling buildings and atmosphere of dizzy sadness and nostalgia.[18] The early 2000s saw increased levels of foreign investment and interest in Bucharest, with new businesses appearing and real estate prices on the rise. The years leading up to Romania's EU accession witnessed a surge of state efforts to rebuild and clean up the city. One article in the *New York Times* travel section featured Bucharest as an alternative tourist destination, with a "quirky" and "gritty" feel, whose quaint and moldering charm must be visited before the city succumbed to the inevitably mainstreaming effects of globalization.[19] The worldwide economic crash in 2008 slowed down many of these changes, but Bucharest continued to be rebuilt and reworked, both literally and in ongoing productions of narratives about the city.

Following the country's accession into the EU in 2007, there were further efforts to revamp Bucharest's local and international image, although palpable doubts remained about the long-term sustainability of its architectural transformations, and its capacity to meet current global standards as a European capital. During my fieldwork, I frequently heard complaints about the dubious logic and general inconvenience of the city's incessant renovations. As one journalist noted, "Under the pretext of accelerated development, the demolitions and constructions have been going non-stop. . . . The real estate boom has transformed our world into a construction site".[20] The local media frequently covered debates about the increasing numbers of tall buildings, particularly those situated in areas of the city now touted as historic. Many criticized the skyscrapers for clashing with the surrounding architecture, suffocating the existing neighborhoods and destroying their charm. People joined protest groups, drafted petitions, and posted signs at building sites calling attention to the disruptions they were causing.

Such passionate responses demonstrated how the contemporary status of the city as work site could serve as an involuntary yet stark reminder of Ceaușescu's extreme demolition and construction policies during the so-called Golden Age of communism. When a series of high-rises started appearing next to several Bucharest churches in 2006, many people recalled the era of the 1980s, when Ceaușescu razed a portion of the city the size of Venice, bulldozing more than a dozen of the city's churches and physically relocating many others behind apartment buildings to hide them from public view. As a colleague remarked to me in 2007, "A new series of equally serious destructions is happening now. . . . a dementia equivalent to the time of Ceaușescu." Ceaușescu may be the most obvious target for Bucharest's previous urban problems, yet pinpointing today's culprits has proven more elusive. Lacking an official, systematic urbanization policy, Bucharest is transforming its contemporary landscapes in silence, mainly through private initiatives.[21] The few urban planning laws that do exist are simply ignored, and people can only vaguely blame the corruption of government officials, and the current neoliberal agenda that allows investors to implement any plan they like, as long as they have the money.

Yet I also encountered a tentative admiration for the city's rapid transformations, with its new construction projects, extended tramlines, and rising real estate values. These changes were regarded as disconcerting yet necessary upheavals; the city–as–work site promised modernization and progress but also a chance to restore to the nation its seemingly rightful precommunist aesthetic and cultural identity. Around the time of Romania's accession into the EU, Bucharest's central district of Lipscani suddenly began to be referred to as the city's "Old Town." Featuring a scattering of historic buildings, including the Stavropoleos church, the National Bank of Romania, and the ruins of the Old Princely Court built by Vlad the Impaler in 1459, this neighborhood had managed to escape Ceaușescu's demolitions. After 1989, it had become a derelict, ramshackle area, inhabited mainly by Roma squatters, scattered with boarded-up buildings, secondhand junk stores, and an assortment of shoe and clock repair shops. In the mid-2000s, however, the newly formed Association of Investors in the Historic Center of Bucharest began actively publicizing the need to revitalize the district, regulate its commercial development, and increase its business value.[22] The city replaced Lipscani's old, uneven cobblestones with new ones that were uniform and straight and installed plaques on its streets detailing the neighborhood's architectural history. Elegant and expensive clothing boutiques, cafés, and bars appeared, and in a few years, this new "Old Town" had become a popular site for tourists and locals, with a flourishing nightlife.

Such practices deliberately invoked nostalgia for precommunist Bucharest as the interwar "Paris of the East," host to French neoclassical and German modernist architecture, an epicenter of culture and prosperity. This appellation, however, is a result of selective cultural memory, as it overlooks the fact that Bucharest was originally called "Little Paris" because of its extensive modernizations during the late 1800s, directly inspired by Baron Haussmann's urban constructions of wide boulevards, straight lines, and open spaces in 1850s Paris.[23] At the same time, the new post-transition face of Lipscani betrayed a disregard for the area's more recent history as home to the numbers of Roma who were once again displaced in the push to fabricate a romanticized vision of a national, historic city center.

In the context of Romania's accession into the EU, such urban reconfigurations and the discourses surrounding them speak to the messiness and incongruity of memories characteristic of the current post-transition era. While there was widespread resistance to the contemporary renovations and transformations of Bucharest that harkened back to Ceaușescu's megalomaniacal schemes, at the same time there was strong support for creating the city anew, with similar goals of reworking its topographies to fit into a distinct set of political and cultural ideals.

Memory Screens

Corporate power and the media became rapidly and blatantly visible in postcommunist Bucharest, appropriating public space and feeding on collective expectations about the future. As early as the 1990s, huge commercial neon signs were placed across the buildings in the central Romana, Unirii, and Victoriei Squares. Over the following years, banners advertising the names of Romanian companies and products competed with digital screens flashing with the logos of multinational corporations. Enormous posters, tacked onto the cracked and dirty sides of communist-era residential blocks, advertised newly constructed Bucharest apartment complexes in improbably glamorous and bucolic settings.

In 2007, Apa Nova, the main private water and sewage utility of municipal Bucharest, initiated a public campaign called "Why we love Bucharest." This operation included a series of advertisements and billboards, as well as a blog on the company's website where people could contribute their own fond memories and anecdotes about the city. On a more visible daily level, it involved the posting of alternative street signs around Bucharest. The Apa Nova signs were placed directly underneath the original ones, using the same layout and font

Figure 31.1. Billboard reads: "Living in a block isn't what it used to be," Bucharest, 2007. Photograph by Alyssa Grossman.

but containing appellations designed to trigger a sense of collective memory by affectively tugging at personal associations with particular parts of the city. "Here I kissed Ana," "The street where my grandmother used to live," and "The street where I banged up Dad's car" were some of the Apa Nova signs I noted during my fieldwork.

This explosion of so many ads and billboards during the EU-accession era in Bucharest prompted public responses that ranged from indifference or humorous toleration to outrage. Many people expressed annoyance at their distasteful presence, but seemed resigned to the notion that such was the price one had to pay for acceptance into the global consumer economy. Cultural historian Andrei Pippidi likened Bucharest's present-day commercial banners to communist propaganda that in previous decades had hung from the rooftops in Romana Square. In his newspaper editorial "Down with the Adverts!", he reminds his readers of the slogans that every citizen used to encounter on a daily basis.[24] "Read Scînteia!" (the national communist newspaper), "The Ileana Sewing Machine!" and "No meal without ocean fish!" were not so different from the messages of their current, capitalist counterparts. "Tolerated for so many years," he writes, "these ads have always been a disease of our city".[25]

The flux of commercial images and slogans in Bucharest's contemporary public space visually documented the extent to which private economic forces were reclassifying the city through their "symbolic languages of exclusion and entitlement".[26] As Șerban, an ethnologist in his sixties who lives in the same house in Bucharest where he grew up, remarked to me, "Things in this city are disappearing at an enormous speed. . . . What annoys me is that I am starting to forget what it was like before, because my memory has fewer and fewer forms of external support." The projected national and institutionalized visions of Bucharest saturated its surfaces, contributing to the formation of unintentional memorials that both reinforced and contradicted existing cultural narratives, provoking individuals to uncover their own counter-memories of the city and its changing configurations.

The Poetics and Politics of Windows

Individual efforts to "remake the urban fabric" of Bucharest turned not only neighborhoods and streets but windows themselves into a striking part of the city's postcommunist, unintentional memorial landscape.[27] As housing prices continued to rise in the early 2000s, so did costs of maintenance and heating, and many people chose to replace their old, wooden-framed, single-pane windows with double-glazed, plastic-framed "thermopane," or PVC. After the revolution, these items became synonymous with ideas of progress and westernization and were fitted into increasing numbers of old villas, communist-era apartments, and new houses throughout the city. Often during my fieldwork, I would awake to the crashing sounds of breaking glass in the courtyard of my block, as yet another customer had their old windows replaced. It was not uncommon for me to see stacks of discarded windows lined against hallway walls, waiting to be taken to the landfill. By the mid-2000s, thermopane installation companies had sprung up everywhere, their own shop-front windows shiny and airtight, draped with vertical vinyl blinds.

The thermopane phenomenon proved to trigger a mixture of enthusiasm and disdain, not only for Romania's past, but also for its present. My interlocutors grumbled about the ubiquity of the ugly new windows but at the same time would pay a great deal of money to have them installed in their homes. It was a practical decision, they told me, and no matter how offensive, it was still an effective and modern means of insulation. Wooden-framed windows were outdated, a sign of the past. As the literary critic Mircea Vasilescu remarked, thermopane offered Romanians a means of discarding and forgetting the Ceaușescu era;[28] it was seen as proof that Bucharest was regaining its status as a European capital and finally "catching up with the times." The incongruous sight of bright white frames fitted into faded old villas was a frequent source of critical commentary, yet hardly anyone I knew rejected this phenomenon entirely.

Business establishments also hurried to renovate their window displays. In my daily excursions around the city, it was not uncommon for me to find handwritten signs posted on shop fronts, containing announcements such as, "Dear Clients! The Casandra Bakery will be closed between January 8 and February 5 for modernization." In such cases, "modernization" usually meant the removal of its wooden-framed windows, along with their characteristic boxlike displays that contained eclectic arrays of objects, sometimes only tangentially related to the merchandise of the shop itself. Often framed by a backdrop of lace curtains, these

Figure 31.2. Shop window, Bucharest, 2007. Photograph by Alyssa Grossman.

exhibitions of plants, clocks, shoes, photographs, mirrors, and other trinkets resembled eccentric museum dioramas or miniature theater sets comprising intriguing assemblages of miscellanea.

As this style of shop window gradually gave way to more up-to-date standardized presentations, I began to photograph those that remained throughout the city. Their perceptible disappearances from the urban landscape underlined their status as antiquated and spatially marginal arenas of the present, unintentional monuments storing powerful yet implicit memories. When I began asking people about the meanings behind these particular features, I was told that they were leftovers from the "authentic" communist style of shops. Many of my colleagues scoffed at such eccentric displays, with their connotations of communist backwardness. Others recalled their resemblance to grocery stores during Romania's extreme food shortages of the 1980s, when establishments struggled to come up with creative presentations of the few pathetic items that were actually in stock. One man in his sixties told me how the state used to assign specialists to decorate shop windows, which had to conform to the specifications of the regime. The displays were once a matter of national pride, and there were even state-sponsored competitions between them. Other people noted that many of the old-fashioned vitrines that still could be found today were often run by craftspeople such as shoemakers, clock and watchmakers, and hatters. With the arrival of disposable capitalist mentalities, these skills were dying out, along with their accompanying modes of window display.

These vitrines indirectly commemorated, rather than explicitly memorialized, a range of individual and cultural narratives about the past. As their existence throughout the city dwindled, these mundane remainders from the past took on a heightened significance. Fallen into their role as inadvertent memorials, they connected to a mixture of implicit associations with a different way of life, and the tangle of values, relationships, and daily routines that were part of the previous political regime. Like Benjamin's "romantic ruins" of the French arcades, these urban features unexpectedly elicited new readings of old forms, giving voice to contradictory and unresolved recollections, assumptions, and expectations underlying Romania's current post-transition period.

Layers of Recollection

The word *topos* is linked to concepts of both space and language, with the notion of urban topography encompassing materials, bodies, and minds.[29] A city's landscapes include not just physical sites but also contingent and subjective arenas of experience connected to a multiplicity of narratives, emotions, and recollections.[30] The interweaving and diverging of different modes of remembrance within such spheres attest to the unstable and ineffable qualities of memory, and the ways in which they can become compressed and embedded within mundane urban realms. Simon Schama once wrote that myths and memories often remain "hidden beneath layers of the commonplace".[31] Yet it is the very layers of the commonplace that also become material conduits for involuntary remembrance work. It is not what lies beneath them but the very surfaces and textures of their everyday, apparently noncommemorative forms that must be taken into account.

As Eleni Bastéa has observed, any city is a complicated "amalgam of official rhetoric, politics, and personal history . . . often at odds with each other."[32] Much contemporary public rhetoric depicts EU accession-era Bucharest as a city in disrepair, badly damaged by its communist past, struggling to regain its dignity and a foothold in the capitalist world economy. But individual narratives, as well as tangible layers within the city itself, convey alternative, more nuanced discourses. Bucharest is not simply a postcommunist city currently now being "re-Europeanized." It is a complex, post-transition metropolis whose residents reveal ambivalent and often conflicting opinions about its past, present, and future transformations.

Notes

1. Riegl 1998 [1903], 623.
2. For examples of literature on this subject, see Barris 2001; Ioan 2007b; Light and Young 2013, 2015b; O'Neill 2009.
3. Edensor 2007, 227.
4. Benjamin 1999, 211.
5. Mace 2007; Van Campen 2014.
6. Benjamin 1999, 462.
7. Grossman 2015.
8. Moran 2004, 57–58; see also Crinson 2005; Rodrigo 2011.
9. Hogea 2010; Tanasoiu 2007.

10. Light and Young 2015a; Marin 2013.
11. Popescu-Sandu 2010; Stan 2013.
12. Ballinger 2003, 15.
13. Cantacuzino 2001, 22; Ioan 2006.
14. Gauriș 1997; Ioan 2006.
15. Boym 2001, 76.
16. Huyssen 2003, 7.
17. Benjamin 1999, 474.
18. Durandin 2006, 41.
19. Rail 2006.
20. Turcescu 2007.
21. Pippidi 2007a.
22. Frolu 2006.
23. Ignat 2007; Ioan 2007a.
24. Pippidi 2007b.
25. Ibid.
26. Zukin 2000, 138.
27. Beldiman 1997, 279.
28. Vasilescu 2006.
29. Boym 2001, 77.
30. See also Casey 1987; Tilley 1994.
31. Schama 1996, 14.
32. Bastéa 2000, 3.

References

Ballinger, Pamela. 2003. *History in Exile: Memory and Identity at the Borders of the Balkans*. Princeton, NJ: Princeton University Press.

Barris, Roann. 2001. "Contested Mythologies: The Architectural Deconstruction of a Totalitarian Culture." *Journal of Architectural Education* 54 (4): 229–237.

Bastéa, Eleni. 2000. *The Creation of Modern Athens: Planning the Myth*. Cambridge: Cambridge University Press.

Beldiman, Alexandru. 1997. "Refacerea țesutului urban." *Secolul 20: Revistă de sinteză: Literatura Universală, Bucureștiul* 4-6: 279–280.

Benjamin, Walter. 1999. *The Arcades Project*. Cambridge, MA: Belknap Press.

Boym, Svetlana. 2001. *The Future of Nostalgia*. New York: Basic Books.

Cantacuzino, Șerban. 2001. "Inns, Churches, Parks, and Avenues." In *Bucharest: A Sentimental Guide*, edited by A. Fabritius and A. Solomon, 15–39. Bucharest: Romanian Cultural Foundation / PLURAL 1.

Casey, Edward S. 1987. *Remembering: A Phenomenological Study*. Bloomington: Indiana University Press.

Crinson, Mark. 2005. "Urban Memory: An Introduction." In *Urban Memory: History and Amnesia in the Modern City*, edited by M. Crinson, xi–xx. New York: Routledge.

Durandin, Catherine. 2006. *București. Amintiri și plimbări* (ediția a II-a). Translated from French into Romanian by H. M. Vasilescu. Bucharest: Paralela 45.

Edensor, Tim. 2007. "Sensing the Ruin." *The Senses and Society* 2 (2): 217–232.

Frolu, Teodor. 2006. "Centrul Istoric: Puține schimbări, multe așteptări." *Dilema Veche* 3 (134): 11.

Gauriș, Marius. 1997. "O lume Art Deco." *Secolul 20: Revistă de sinteză: Literatura Universală, Bucureștiul* 4-6: 69–78.
Grossman, Alyssa. 2015. "Forgotten Domestic Objects: Capturing Involuntary Memories in Post-Communist Bucharest." *Home Cultures* 12 (3): 291–310.
Hogea, Alina. 2010. "Coming to Terms with the Communist Past in Romania: An Analysis of the Political and Media Discourse Concerning the Tismăneanu Report." *Studies of Transition States and Societies* 2 (2): 16–30.
Huyssen, Andreas. 2003. *Present Pasts: Palimpsests and the Politics of Memory.* Stanford, CA: Stanford University Press.
Ignat, Petru. 2007. "La pas prin Bucureștii de odinoară: Bulevardele în cruce din centrul micului Paris." *România Liberă*, January 15: 27.
Ioan, Augustin. 2006. "The History of Nothing: Contemporary Architecture and Public Space in Romania." *Artmargins.* Accessed January 2, 2016. http://www.artmar gins.com/index.php/featured-articles-sp-829273831/156-the-history-of-nothing -contemporary-architecture-and-public-space-in-romania.
Ioan, Augustin. 2007a. "Influențe franceze în arhitectura Bucureștilor." *Adevărul*, May 30.
Ioan, Augustin. 2007b. "The Peculiar History of (Post)Communist Public Places and Spaces: Bucharest as a Case Study." In *The Post-Socialist City: Urban Form and Space Transformations in Central and Eastern Europe after Socialism*, edited by K. Stanilov, 301–312. Dordrecht: Springer.
Light, Duncan, and Craig Young. 2013. "Urban Space, Political Identity and the Unwanted Legacies of State Socialism: Bucharest's Problematic *Centru Civic* in the Post-Socialist Era." *Nationalities Papers* 41 (4): 515–535.
Light, Duncan, and Craig Young. 2015a. "Local and Counter-Memories of Socialism in Post-Socialist Romania." In *Local Memories in a Nationalizing and Globalizing World*, edited by M. Beyen and B. Deseure, 221–243. Basingstoke: Palgrave.
Light, Duncan, and Craig Young. 2015b. "Public Memory, Commemoration, and Transitional Justice: Reconfiguring the Past in Public Space." In *Post-Communist Transitional Justice: Lessons from Twenty-Five Years of Experience*, edited by L. Stan and N. Nedelsky, 233–251. New York: Cambridge University Press.
Mace, John H. 2007. "Involuntary Memory: Concept and Theory." In *Involuntary Memory*, edited by J. H. Mace, 1–19. Oxford: Blackwell Publishing.
Marin, Manuela. 2013. "Between Memory and Nostalgia: The Image of Communism in Romanian Popular Culture. A Case Study of Libertatea Newspaper." *Palimpsest* 5: 4–16.
Moran, Joe. 2004. "History, Memory and the Everyday." *Rethinking History* 8 (1): 51–68.
O'Neill, Bruce. 2009. "The Political Agency of Cityscapes: Spatializing Governance in Ceaușescu's Bucharest." *Journal of Social Archaeology* 9 (1): 92–109.
Pippidi, Andrei. 2007a. "După 80 de ani." *Dilema Veche* 4 (156).
Pippidi, Andrei. 2007b. "Jos reclamele!" *Dilema Veche* 4 (188).
Popescu-Sandu, Oana. 2010. "'Let's All Freeze Up until 2100 or So': Nostalgic Directions in Post-Communist Romania." In *Post-Communist Nostalgia*, edited by M. Todorova and Z. Gille, 113–125. New York: Berghahn Books.
Rail, Evan. 2006. "Going to Bucharest." *New York Times* (Travel Section), October 8. Accessed January 10, 2016. http://www.nytimes.com/2006/10/08/travel/08goingto .html?_r=0.
Riegl, Alois. 1998 [1903]. "The Modern Culture of Monuments: Its Character and Its Origin." In *Oppositions Reader: Selected Readings from a Journal for Ideas and Criticism in Architecture*, edited by K. M. Hays, 68–83. New York: Princeton Architectural Press.

Rodrigo, Russell. 2011. "Between Remembrance and Recreation: Containing Memory in Urban Landscapes." *Memory Connection* 1 (1): 272–282.

Schama, Simon. 1996. *Landscape and Memory*. London: Fontana Press.

Stan, Lavinia. 2013. "Reckoning with the Communist Past in Romania: A Scorecard." *Europe-Asia Studies* 65 (1): 127–146.

Tanasoiu, Cosmina. 2007. "The Tismăneanu Report: Romania Revisits Its Past." *Problems of Post-Communism* 54 (4): 60–69.

Tilley, Christopher. 1994. *A Phenomenology of Landscape: Places, Paths, and Monuments*. Oxford: Berg.

Turcescu, R. 2007. "Orașul si sinucigașii." *Dilema Veche* 4 (162).

Van Campen, Cretien. 2014. *The Proust Effect: The Senses as Doorways to Lost Memories*. Translated by Julian Ross. Oxford: Oxford University Press.

Vasilescu, M. 2006. "Capitala europeană a termopanelor." *Dilema Veche* 3 (137).

Zukin, Sharon. 2000. "Whose Culture? Whose City?" In *The City Reader*, edited by R. T. LeGates and F. Stout. 2nd ed. London: Routledge.

ALYSSA GROSSMAN is an Associated Researcher at Valand Art Academy, University of Gothenburg.

32 Between East and West, Folk and Pop, State and Market: Changing Landscapes of Bulgarian Folk Music

Carol Silverman

Today, Western audiences know Balkan music mainly through women's choirs and brass bands; few realize the complexity and diversity of the region's soundscape.[1] The Balkans have been a crossroads between East and West, a region where language, religion, foodways, rituals, customs, music, and dance trace influences from both the Middle East and Western Europe to create a dense web of rich cultural connections. Focusing on Bulgaria, this chapter explores one popular genre of folk music, "wedding music" (*svatbarska muzika*), in terms of history, contexts, and meanings, in both traditional and contemporary family and community life. I investigate wedding music performers and consumers, noting the important role of Roma (Gypsies). Revered as musicians but reviled as people, Roma provide a significant example of exclusion from state-sanctioned categories of "folk music."

Wedding music has made an indelible imprint on the musical landscape in Bulgaria; it provides a window into the changing roles of the state and the market and the economic challenges of professional musicians during and after socialism. It also raises cultural and political questions: What is Bulgarian folk music? What is culturally authentic? What is Gypsy music? All these issues must be seen in the context of historical definitions and new media outlets. Widening my framework, I trace styles, producers, and audiences, highlighting the emergence of fusion forms of folk/pop. I explore controversies about how tradition is defined and how music is interpreted in economic, political, social, and symbolic realms. Finally, I note the changing relationship between music and the politics of nation/states in relation to nationalism, ethnicity, and cultural rights.

The Balkans as Musical Crossroads

Historically, the Balkans were the meeting point of three religions—Christianity (Eastern Orthodoxy and Catholicism), Islam, and Judaism—and multiple empires: Byzantine, Ottoman, and Austro-Hungarian. This confluence has influenced the vast diversity of styles of Balkan folk music, from older layers of drone-based harmonies, Turkish-influenced melismatic modal melodies, and Western chordal harmonies to more recent folk/pop fusions. Balkan music is played on a wide range of village instruments, such as bagpipes, bowed and plucked strings, drums, and a variety of end-blown and fipple flutes, as well as Western instruments. Some musicians are nonprofessional community members while others are paid professionals. In the latter category, Roma are distinguished for their mastery of improvisation, monopoly of specific styles and instruments, vast repertoires for patrons from diverse ethnic groups, and openness to eclectic influences. Originally from India, Roma are the largest minority in Europe today and continue to face high rates of prejudice and discrimination.[2]

The traditional Balkan economy was agricultural, supplemented by transhumant herding of sheep and goats. Due to the crossroads location, east/west and north/south trade flourished, including the exchange of prized crafts, such as silver filigree, copper, and handmade textiles. The cosmopolitan aspect of the Balkans is striking, with rural economies tied to urban trading centers via markets. The common Ottoman cultural legacy is clearly visible in many aspects of life, including costume, food, architecture, music, and Islam. But older pre-Christian layers are also visible in rituals tied to nature and fertility of the land and women. Eastern Orthodoxy remains the predominant religion (and is experiencing a revival), although all Balkan religions tend to be syncretic, borrowing from each other where layers can be discerned.

Balkan folk culture revolves around the cycle of the land, the extended patrilineal patrilocal family, and the village community. Traditionally, folk music and dance were an integral part of life cycle rituals, such as births, baptisms, circumcisions, weddings, and funerals, and calendrical holidays, including saints' days, carnival, and the movement of herds to seasonal pastures. The weekly Sunday dance after church and agricultural chores such as harvesting and stringing tobacco were also active sites for music. Vocal music tended to be the domain of women and instrumental music the domain of men.[3]

Nationalist and Socialist Frameworks of Bulgarian Music

The terms heritage, tradition, and folk had great weight in nineteenth century Balkan nation-building projects; indeed, heritage and tradition were used to culturally define the nation as a community composed of homogeneous "folk," thereby excluding minorities. Because folk music became a politicized symbol of the Bulgarian nation, its definitional borders were carefully patrolled, and Romani and Turkish music were clearly outside these borders;[4] until recently, these musics were never performed in ensembles, festivals, or music schools under the rubric "folk."

It is no accident that the discipline of folklore arose during the age of romantic nationalism and became a tool for nation building. According to Johann Gottfried von Herder, the architect of "romantic nationalism," every nation was an organic entity with its own native cultural institutions and pure spirit that are best reflected in the folklore of the peasants.[5] Language, religion, customs, and music were central elements of the folk spirit, and they were assumed to be congruent with a singular community. Benedict Anderson showed nations were "imagined communities" constructed through narratives and symbols of identity.[6]

In Bulgaria as well as elsewhere in the Balkans, folklore emerged at the nexus of defining and valorizing peasant culture; thus collecting, cataloging, and classifying folk music (*narodna muzika*) became a central nationalist project of the late nineteenth century and extended well through the twentieth. The preoccupation with language/dialects, rural life, and regional variation surfaced in music, especially in collections of folk song texts. Note that the word *narodno* comes from the Slavic root *narod*, meaning synonymously people, nation, and folk. Donna Buchanan points out that under socialism narodno took on the further meaning of "'people's' in the sense of an undifferentiated mass of workers laboring towards a common ideological goal."[7] As Ivaylo Ditchev writes: "Folklore, largely used under communism, can be considered part of high national culture, because it was the result of a rigorous politics of observation, filtering and control, if not outright invention of practices intended to create the desired image of the people's artistic image."[8] Buchanan further comments that narodna muzika, defined as simultaneously folk, national, people's, and popular music, emerged as both inclusive (of all things Bulgarian) and exclusive (of all things non-Bulgarian);[9] this could be described as ethnonationalism in music.

Bulgarians (and other Balkan peoples) view their prenationhood past as a time of foreign (eastern) domination;[10] the Ottoman period is contrasted with the late nineteenth-century fight for "freedom" for the nation/state. Until 1990, the Ottoman era was depicted in Bulgarian scholarly works as well as common parlance as "Turkish slavery" or "five hundred years under the Turkish yoke." I will not contest here the validity of this depiction but merely note that most of the populace today still assumes it is factual. Suffice it to say that both Western historians and post-1989 Balkan historians agree that at least in the early centuries, the Ottoman Empire was tolerant. The biggest bone of contention is whether the Turks forcibly converted people to Islam. While most Bulgarians believe conversion was forced "by fire and sword," most scholars agree conversions were voluntary in response to various economic, legal, and religious pressures.[11]

Until recently, historians and folklorists depicted Bulgarian folklore as a refuge from Turkish domination; scholars claimed the peasants clung to their language and customs in an effort to maintain their Bulgarian identity. Music was specifically described as a rallying point around which the idea of nationalism grew. Thus a central task of the scholars of the emerging nation/state was proving that Bulgarian culture, especially music, was pure, untainted by years of Turkish domination.[12] In almost every scholarly work until 1989, it is claimed that Turkish music left hardly a trace among the local Bulgarian populace. This claim is clearly absurd, considering not only the history of Bulgaria but also its location as a crossroads between the Middle East and Europe. Todorova points out that the dominant view of the Ottoman past characterizes it as a "religiously, socially, institutionally, and even racially alien imposition."[13]

During the socialist period, village music of the Slavs was reaffirmed as authentic folk music, played on "traditional" instruments and was valorized as the soul of the nation, to the exclusion of urban music and the music of minorities, whether they lived in villages or towns.[14] The music of all minorities was excluded from the public realm. This ideology was enshrined in radio and television media, in folk music ensembles, in schools, and in folk festivals.[15] In addition, the music of minorities was never specifically collected or studied. With this backdrop, we can understand why wedding music created such a scandal.

Wedding Music during Socialism

In the 1970s, wedding music catapulted to fame, causing something close to mass hysteria. The fact that Roma were some of the prime innovators, fueled the controversy around the genre. Labeled "corrupt" by purists, the socialist government prohibited wedding music from the official media and from private celebrations. This absence ironically promoted its success in the unofficial media. Fundamentally a grassroots panethnic youth movement, wedding music struggled against state censorship and became a mass underground cultural phenomenon.

Wedding music encompasses music played not only at weddings but also at baptisms, house warmings, and soldier send-off celebrations;[16] in short, at major ritual events in village and urban contexts, for Bulgarians of all ethnicities. Although its history reaches back to urban ensembles of the nineteenth century that were composed mostly of Roma, wedding music as a distinct genre began to crystallize in the early 1970s when amplification was introduced. The loudness of electric amplification and its affinity to rock music became a symbol of modernity and the West.

What defines wedding music is a combination of instrumentation, repertoire, and style. Instrumentation typically consists of clarinet, saxophone, accordion, electric guitar, electric bass guitar, and drum set, plus vocalists; in the late 1980s, synthesizers were added. These instruments have a greater range and versatility than Bulgarian village instruments. In addition, violin or trumpet or village folk instruments appropriate to the region are added. Note that the core instruments were outside the socialist rubric of "folk." Even today, these instruments are not taught in folk music schools.

The repertoire of wedding music can be divided into two main categories: Bulgarian music and Romani music, primarily, *kyuchetsi*.[17] Eclecticism is the preferred mode of creation. The emphasis is on originality, versatility, and the ability to improvise. Dazzling technique is displayed by complicated rhythmic syncopations, daring key changes, arpeggio passages, chromaticisms, and extremely fast tempi. The vocal style emphasizes rhythmic vibrato and extensive ornamentation, imitating the melodic instruments.

Wedding music is inextricably tied to large, opulent life events that are the pride of Bulgarians of all ethnicities. Weddings are a status symbol; villagers will save for years to invite hundreds of guests for a three-day event. Despite

Figure 32.1. Romani wedding in the village of Bolyartsi, Thrace, Bulgaria, 2014. Photograph by Carol Silverman.

totalitarianism, the socialist period was the apex of community celebration and display. Ignoring government warnings about "bourgeois conspicuous consumerism," villagers insisted on abundant food and drink, expensive gifts, and good-quality music.[18] Thus many wedding musicians had steady professional work in the socialist era despite prohibitions.

The unquestioned guru of wedding music was Ivo Papazov, founder (with his cousin, accordionist Neshko Neshev) of the band Trakiya (Thrace). However, both Roma and Bulgarians had and have decisive roles in wedding music, and bands are often mixed. The background of musicians varies, from conservatory graduates to the majority who play by ear. Romani musicians tend to play by ear, the way most ethnic Bulgarians learned before the 1960s. Ethnic Bulgarians are more tied to the ensembles and the folk music schools that emphasize musical literacy. The wedding music tradition, however, is strictly oral.

Due to the phenomenal popularity of wedding bands, the demand for them in the 1980s became grossly inflated and some musicians became very wealthy. Expensive celebrations and lavish public tipping in the realm of the free market were alarming to the socialist government. In addition, many wedding musicians tried to avoid required state jobs, but the government taxed them heavily for wedding work. In 1985 a system of categories was introduced to regulate prices, but it failed to tame the capitalist essence of wedding music.

Figure 32.2. Orkestar Mania with saxophonist Melyatin performs at a Romani graduation party in Haskovo, Thrace, Bulgaria, 2014. Photograph by Carol Silverman.

As mentioned previously, wedding music was excluded from official government-sponsored media; it was also either neglected by scholars or else condescendingly labeled as "clichéd" or "kitsch." The most common criticism was that wedding music incorporated foreign elements and did not retain the "purity" and "authenticity" of Bulgarian folk music. It was, ironically, simultaneously too Western (like jazz and rock) and too Eastern (like Romani, Turkish, and Middle Eastern music).

This rhetoric about musical purity is directly related to the 1980s state policy of monoethnism and the concomitant regulation of the display of Muslim ethnicity. The Bulgarian government required Muslims to change their names, claimed Roma did not exist as a separate ethnic group, and prohibited circumcisions, the wearing of *shalvari* (wide Muslim pantaloons), the speaking of Turkish and Romani languages, and the performance of the Romani/Turkish instrument *zurna* (double reed pipe). Kyuchetsi were banned entirely, and the jazz, rock, and non-Bulgarian elements in the Bulgarian repertoire were cleansed. Playing and dancing kyuchek was officially prohibited under the legal rubric "hooliganism." Many wedding musicians were fined, and Trakiya members were jailed several times.[19]

Simultaneously, musicians negotiated around and sometimes defied these rules; for example, at village events, family members kept watch for approaching police officers. As soon as the police approached, musicians would either run away, hide, or switch to "pure" Bulgarian music. As Ortner points out, resistance is never simple—it is always paired with collaboration.[20] More precisely, resistance often involves accommodation to the state; moreover, the state is not monolithic. Musicians, though brave, were survivors—they did not seek to become heroes because of lofty antigovernment principles. They defied the state because of economic rather than moral imperatives. Music was their profession, and they made a living by serving their patrons who requested kyuchetsi.[21]

Resistance to prohibitions was sometimes located in the very institutions that espoused them, such as the folk music schools. Although playing wedding music was strictly forbidden, students would regularly sneak out of school on weekends to play or listen to the famous musicians. In fact, many students told the urban legend–like story of being threatened about the evils of wedding music by their music teachers, of ignoring them, of sneaking out to attend weddings to hear the famous musicians, and of seeing their teachers at these same events! Resistance, then, was located at even the most official sites. Ivo Papazov recalled that some of his most ardent fans were police officers, and he even played at their private events. Similarly, when I told folklore scholars that I was studying Roma, they responded with the official line, "They don't exist," accompanied always by an ironic smile.

These examples amplify Michael Herzfeld's point that cultural intimacy between individuals and the state is highly nuanced.[22] Herzfeld commented: "For a brief instant we see the official representatives of state ideology as human beings capable of wincing at the absurdity of what they must nevertheless proclaim."[23] He further explained that despite the external formality of states, they can be viewed in social terms as "intimate apparatuses." The state embodies "potentially disreputable but familiar cultural matter" which is "the very substance of what holds people together.... Some of that substance even includes resistance to the state itself."[24] On both sides, the official and the unofficial, there were cracks in dogma. Police officers arrested musicians but secretly loved kyuchek; wedding musicians not only resisted but also accommodated the state. In the cracks in official ideology, then, wedding music thrived.

In the mid-1980s, the state record label Balkanton released several official versions of wedding music that were sanitized of foreign influences, jazz, and kyuchetsi. Musicians greatly resented these arrangements, claiming they detracted from the music and merely filled the pockets of arrangers with money,[25] yet they recorded them. This brings up the issue of self-censorship. Wedding musicians developed the ability to sense when they could push the limits of the state and when they had to tow the party line. This may help to explain the apparent puzzle of why musicians recorded censored versions. James Scott's work on "everyday protest" suggests that interpreting resistance always requires analyzing power and its effects on the weak.[26] The hegemony of the state does not depend on brainwashing but on how public discourse triggers shifts in consciousness. Both wedding musicians and the state may have perceived "the advantage of avoiding open confrontation."[27] In addition, we can assume neither that musicians had full agency nor that the state had total hegemony. "On the contrary, at times social structures, roles, statuses . . . modify agency and its consequences. . . . Actors may engage in everyday acts of resistance or desist from them under structural pressures.[28] Wedding musicians, then, strategically alternated between accommodation and resistance to the state. In addition, the state itself was not monolithic, and indeed, "different levels of the state may work at cross-purposes."[29] The state was ambivalent about the wedding music phenomenon that was fast becoming a mass movement. Policy was contradictory, and at times, the state even cashed in on the popularity of wedding music—for example, by selling semiofficial cassettes, illustrating Herzfeld's point about cultural intimacy.

The state took a more direct hand in controlling and regulating wedding music via the Stambolovo festivals (1985–88). Within a few years, scholars went from vilifying wedding musicians to lauding their talent; but state policy dictated what could and could not be played at the festival.[30] Stambolovo was organized to police the borders of wedding music—not only to cleanse it of kyuchetsi but also to make sure that the Bulgarian repertoire was "pure." The state would make wedding music conform to the revered category "folk music" and would save it from internal pollution, which was metaphorically, ideologically, and physically located among the Roma and Turks.[31]

Wedding Music during Postsocialism

Ironically, in the 1990s, wedding music garnered effusive praise internationally while at home it faced severe economic challenges. Trakiya became an international sensation (with several Western albums and tours) precisely when communism fell, but it was ignored at home for a decade when new forms of music began competing for the Bulgarian public. The transition to capitalism affected wedding musicians in contradictory ways: though there were new freedoms to play Romani and Turkish music, the economy suffered greatly, and few had money for multiple-day celebrations. Weddings shrank to one day, and DJs replaced live music.

The Bulgarian public, meanwhile, enthusiastically embraced Serbian, Macedonian, and Greek musics and pop/folk fusions (*chalga*),[32] which became the rage in restaurants and taverns. Wedding bands broadened their repertoires to include these musics, and still today they must know the folk/pop repertoire. The opening of the borders permitted musicians to travel, and the best wedding bands toured. Unfortunately, the euphoria of transition was short-lived, and the reality of unfettered capitalism soon soured the populace. Economic crisis gripped Bulgaria in the early 1990s; there were shortages of goods, and thousands of people tried to emigrate. Corruption flourished in everyday transactions as well as in restitution of land and property. A tiny class of "new rich" emerged, flaunting their cars and jewelry, while the middle class sunk closer to poverty and rates of unemployment rose. Discrimination against Roma increased as their rates of unemployment reached 90 percent.

At first, wedding musicians embraced capitalism boldly, as most of them had experience in the free-market realm. Many bands released albums on newly formed private labels. Everyone, including state ensembles, looked for private sponsorship, either local or foreign. Musicians also became concerned about issues of copyright, rampant piracy, and exploitation by record companies. Indeed, the mafia emerged as a force in the 1990s and had its finger in music. The 1990s Stambolovo festivals were financed by private sponsors, but attendance dwindled because people had less disposable cash. In 1994 the Payner company sponsored the first Trakiya Folk festival; attendance was good, but Payner decided to change its direction toward chalga, which was capturing a huge audience. Many wedding musicians went in this direction due to the lure of money and the backing of producers.

However, wedding music still has numerous fans, and every year there are anniversary concerts and festivals in honor of famous musicians. On the other hand, due to the decline in work, some wedding musicians are nostalgic for the socialist period. According to Ivo Papazov, "I had more work back then. People were happier and had a lot of money. I don't think anything good has come of the new democratic Bulgaria. Now it is a place of corruption."[33] Nostalgia, however, should be seen not only as the longing for socialism but also as a critique of capitalism and a desire for order and security. In the "free" market, whatever sells receives the most media playtime; and in the 1990s–early 2000s, chalga, not wedding music, was the best-selling genre.

Today wedding musicians are increasingly seen as champions of Bulgarian folk music. In some respects, they are correct, if we conceive of folk music as wider than the narrow authentic socialist definition, and if we see wedding music as opposed to chalga. Some wedding musicians blame chalga for the decline in the demand for wedding music; they assert that chalga is more pop than folk and that it is technically inferior to wedding music. However, connections between chalga and wedding music exist, and some musicians do both; others distance themselves from it.

Aside from stylistic differences between wedding music and chalga, their respective positions vis-à-vis the state are different. In the socialist period the competitors of wedding music were the ensembles that were the purveyors of "authentic folk music." Wedding music received some of its cache by being oppositional to the state. More specifically, it represented capitalism in the midst of socialism. Now the competitor to wedding music is chalga, supported by unbridled capitalism. The state is weak and wedding music has lost its antistate oppositional positioning; it is emerging, however, as a potential force of nationalism.

One indication of the embrace of wedding music as folk and national music (possibly associated with chalga fatigue) was the 2007 launch of the twenty-four-hour cable TV channel by Payner, Planeta Folk; Payner now regularly sponsors concerts featuring a combination of chalga and wedding performers. Programs on Planeta Folk include not only wedding bands but also shows on the history and folklore of various regions and on Eastern Orthodox liturgical music. Instrumental improvisations are rather short and tame, omitting the wildness of wedding music. Unlike in chalga videos, singers are dressed modestly and do not dance; rather, a folk dance ensemble wearing stylized costumes does line choreographies, often in an outdoor village setting. This staging distances wedding music from chalga and squarely defines it as rural and folk. In addition, Payner regularly recruits many of its chalga stars into wedding band performances; this illustrates the trend of assimilating the allure of chalga into a wholesome folk image of wedding music and simultaneously accomplishes the ideological work of nationalism.

Wedding Music Today

The current fate of wedding music must be seen in the context of the continuing economic crisis and the unpredictability of private markets. Folk and wedding musicians and the music schools still suffer from decreased governmental funding for the arts and decreased incomes of the populace to spend on arts. Bulgarian weddings tend to be just one day, engagements are scarce, competition is fierce, and chalga is still quite popular. Despite this, the quality and quantity of wedding music is impressive. Even though income is meager, wedding musicians display virtuosic technique and improvisatory abilities, play long hours, and create new repertoires. The role of Roma is prominent and new kyuchetsi are regularly composed. In sum, the diversity and vitality of wedding music is still very apparent today in family and community life and in commercial media.

Notes

1. This chapter draws from materials in Silverman (2007, 2012). Fieldwork was conducted in Bulgaria, 1980–2014.
2. Stewart 2013.
3. Rice 1994.
4. Turks and Roma are the largest ethnic minorities in Bulgaria. According to the 2011 census, Turks (who are Muslim) are 9 percent of the population and Roma—about half of whom are Muslim—are 5 percent of the population.
5. Wilson 1973.
6. Anderson 1983.
7. Buchanan 2006, 34.
8. Ditchev 2004.
9. Buchanan 2006, 36.
10. Ibid., 37.
11. Hupchick 1994.
12. Silverman 1989.
13. Todorova 1997, 162–164.
14. Rice 1994, 1996; Buchanan 1996, 2006.
15. Silverman 1989.
16. This celebration (*izprashtane na voinik*) is sponsored by the family of the soldier and can be as elaborate as a wedding.
17. Bulgarian tunes are either traditional or drawn from the standard Thracian wedding repertoire that was composed by famous wedding musicians. Kyuchek, the major genre of Romani music, emphasizes improvisation and features metric variants of 2/4, 4/4, 7/8, and 9/8. Solo kyuchek dancing features hip and shoulder movements;

the tunes for kyuchetsi are often composed by wedding musicians and are inspired by eclectic sources. Wedding songs may be in Romani, Turkish, or Bulgarian.

18. Silverman 1992.
19. Buchanan 2006.
20. Ortner 1995.
21. Silverman 2012.
22. Herzfeld 1997.
23. Herzfeld 2000, 226.
24. Ibid., 224.
25. Buchanan 1996; 2006.
26. Scott 1985, Scott 1990.
27. Sivaramakrishnan 2005, 350.
28. Ibid., 351.
29. Ibid.
30. Peycheva 2008, 249–250.
31. Silverman 2012, 127–148.
32. Although I cannot devote due attention to chalga here, I note that the challenges of wedding musicians must be understood in tandem with the rise in chalga, a huge industry with spinoffs such as hotels, amusement parks, and fashion items. See Buchanan (2007), Rice (2002), Statelova (2005), and Silverman (2012), chapter 9.
33. Cartwright 2006, 38.

References

Anderson, Benedict. 1983. *Imagined Communities: Reflections on the Origin and Spread of Nationalism*. London: Verso.

Buchanan, Donna. 1996. "Wedding Musicians, Political Transition and National Consciousness in Bulgaria." In *Retuning Culture: Musical Change in Eastern Europe*, edited by Mark Slobin, 200–230. Durham, NC: Duke University Press.

Buchanan, Donna. 2006. *Performing Democracy: Bulgarian Music and Musicians in Transition*. Chicago: University of Chicago Press.

Buchanan, Donna. 2007. "Bulgarian Ethnopop along the Old Via Militaris: Ottomanism, Orientalism, or Balkan Cosmopolitanism?" In *Balkan Popular Culture and the Balkan Ecumene: Music Image and Regional Political Discourse*, edited by Donna Buchanan, 225–267. Lanham, MD: Scarecrow Press.

Cartwright, Garth. 2006. "The King Returns." *fRoots* 28 (281): 37–38.

Ditchev, Ivaylo. 2004. "Monoculturalism as Prevailing Culture." *Eurozine*, February. Accessed June 15, 2018. https://www.eurozine.com/monoculturalism-as-prevailing-culture/.

Herzfeld, Michael. 1997. *Cultural Intimacy: Social Poetics in the Nation-State*. London: Routledge.

Herzfeld, Michael. 2000. "Afterword: Intimations from an Uncertain Place." In *Fieldwork Dilemmas: Anthropologists in Postsocialist States*, edited by Hermine De Soto and Nora Dudwick, 219–236. Madison: University of Wisconsin Press.

Hupchick, Dennis. 1994. "Nation or Millet? Contrasting Western European and Islamic Political Cultures in the Balkans." In *Culture and History in Eastern Europe*, 121–155. New York: St. Martin's Press.

Ortner, Sherry. 1995. "Resistance and the Problem of Ethnographic Refusal." *Comparative Studies in Society and History* 37 (1):173–193.

Peycheva, Lozanka. 2008. *Mezhdu Seloto i Vselenata: Starata Folklorna Muzika ot Bŭlgaria v Novite Vremena* (Between the village and the universe: Old folk music from Bulgaria in contemporary times). Sofia: Marin Drinov.

Rice, Timothy. 1994. *May It Fill Your Soul: Experiencing Bulgarian Music*. Chicago: University of Chicago Press.

Rice, Timothy. 1996. "The Dialectic of Economics and Aesthetics in Bulgarian Folk Music." In *Retuning Culture: Musical Change in Eastern Europe*, edited by Mark Slobin, 176–199. Durham, NC: Duke University Press.

Rice, Timothy. 2002. "Bulgaria or Chalgaria: The Attenuation of Bulgarian Nationalism in Mass-Mediated Popular Music." *Yearbook for Traditional Music* 34: 25–47.

Scott, James. 1985. *Weapons of the Weak: Everyday Forms of Peasant Resistance*. New Haven, CT: Yale University Press.

Scott, James. 1990. *Domination and the Arts of Resistance: Hidden Transcripts*. New Haven, CT: Yale University Press.

Silverman, Carol. 1989. "Reconstructing Folklore: Media and Cultural Policy in Eastern Europe." *Communication* 11 (2): 141–60.

Silverman, Carol. 1992. "The Contemporary Bulgarian Village Wedding: The 1970s." *Indiana Slavic Studies* 6 (Balkanistica 8, special issue: Bulgaria Past and Present, edited by John Treadway): 240–251.

Silverman, Carol. 2007. "Bulgarian Wedding Music between Folk and Chalga: Politics, Markets, and Current Directions." *Musicology* 7: 69–97.

Silverman, Carol. 2012. *Romani Routes: Cultural Politics and Balkan Music in Diaspora*. New York: Oxford University Press.

Sivaramakrishnan, K. 2005. "Some Intellectual Genealogies for the Concept of Everyday Resistance." *American Anthropologist* 107 (3): 346–355.

Statelova, Rosemary. 2005. *The Seven Sins of Chalga: Toward an Anthropology of Ethnopop Music*. Sofia: Prosveta.

Stewart, Michael, ed. 2013. *The Gypsy "Menace": Populism and the New Anti-Gypsy Politics*. New York: Columbia University Press.

Todorova, Maria. 1997. *Imagining the Balkans*. New York: Oxford University Press.

Wilson, William. 1973. "Herder, Folklore, and Romantic Nationalism." *Journal of Popular Culture* 6 (4): 819–835.

CAROL SILVERMAN is Professor of Cultural Anthropology and Folklore at the University of Oregon. She is author of *Romani Routes: Cultural Politics and Balkan Music in Diaspora*.

33 Mothers in Balkan Film
Yana Hashamova

In her *Oriental Tales*, Marguerite Yourcenar includes "The Milk of Death" from Albanian folklore. The legend is very popular in Balkan folk poetry and is well known throughout the region. In her story, Yourcenar delivers the legend through the words of a Frenchman, Jules Boutrin, working in Ragusa (the Italian name of Dubrovnik) in the 1930s. Conversing with his English friend, Philip Mild, over a drink in a German alehouse—and in a true orientalizing fashion, admiring and exoticizing the Balkan culture—Jules opens the topic of motherhood and declares that "only in the legends of semi-barbaric countries we still find these creatures, rich in tears and milk, creatures whose children we would be proud to be."[1] He then proceeds to tell Philip of an Albanian mother who was sacrificed by her husband and his brothers to protect the tower which they were building. The brothers built it during the day, but the walls crumbled at night. At the end, in order to finish the tower, they had to wall in a human being alive. Needless to say, the youngest wife who just had a baby was the one placed in the foundations of the walls. She only begged for two holes on the wall, so she could still breastfeed her baby. The legend states that the milk was flowing for two years until the boy weaned himself. Responding to stereotypes about the Balkans as the backward periphery of Europe, Yourcenar added a second ending to her story, in a way contrasting the heroic motherhood of the legend to a mother contemporary to the two western Europeans. In it, Jules chases away a Gypsy woman who carries a blind baby and begs for money. Philip is puzzled at Jules's attitude, but he was told that on purpose she blinded her child with herbs to evoke sympathy. Disenchanted, Jules concludes the story: "There are mothers ... and then there are mothers."[2]

While one should not argue that film has replaced the role of folklore in everyday life in the Balkans, for urban and rural folklore continues to thrive, film has come to occupy a central role in the cultural life of contemporary people in the Balkans and, certainly, not only there. Two additional arguments deserve mention here. It has been studied that film documents moral, political, and economic issues of societies at certain historical periods as well as reflects the collective political unconscious of given communities.[3] In addition, in *Cinematernity: Film, Motherhood, Genre*, Lucy Fischer convincingly explores "the cultural 'fusion' of film and motherhood."[4] In a similar vein, this chapter discusses the diverse motherhood experience of Balkan women as portrayed in contemporary film.

Figure 33.1. A discussion following a film screening at the annual *Pravo Ljudski* (human rights) Film Festival in Sarajevo, 2016. Photograph by Vanja Cerimagic.

Examining two Bulgarian and one Bosnian film created by women and focusing on the modern experience of motherhood in these two countries, I contend that the portrayals of contemporary mothers differs significantly from those of the Balkan legend; Balkan contemporary mothers struggle with brutal social, economic, and political realities and while they overcome many challenges, they do not always succeed in being the self-sacrificial mothers of legends. Although Bulgarian literary and film canons traditionally represent male writers and directors, after 1990 Bulgarian women filmmakers asserted their strong voice on the big screen, recognized nationally as well as on the international festival circuit.[5] During 2015, Bulgarian cinema celebrated one hundred years of its creation and the Bulgarian National Television ran a viewer contest for the best ten films. Unsurprisingly, a film by a Bulgarian female director does not appear among the first ten.

At the same time, the 19 Sofia Film Festival ranked the ten best films after 1990 and two of the ten were created by women. This modest emergence of women directors signifies new cultural conditions, changed public and market tastes, and the deconstruction of the traditional (male) canon. Films of directors such as Zornitsa Sophia (*Mila ot mars* [Mila from Mars], 2004) and Milena Andonova (*Maimuni prez zimata* [Monkeys in Winter], 2006) masterfully portray mothers' tribulations and triumphs in their daily lives. While there are other female directors of note since 1990, such as Iglika Trifonova, Svetla Tsotsorkova, and Kristina Grozeva, here I focus on *Mila from Mars* and *Monkeys in Winter*, for they explore in depth the socialist and postsocialist motherhood experience.[6] Bosnian women directors like Jasmila Žbanić, Ines Tanović, and Aida Begić, too, made their mark on the national culture and international film festivals in the last fifteen years. Žbanić's *Grbavica* (Esma's Secret, 2006) presents a powerful depiction of the most challenging aspects of motherhood that some Bosnian women had to experience, raising children conceived as a result of the Yugoslav war rapes.

Mila from Mars: The Resilient Mother

Written, directed, and coproduced by Zornitsa Sophia (born 1972), *Mila from Mars* marks a new sensitivity toward human kindness and love that can transform one's physical and psychological being, sensitivity that most Bulgarian films of the period, preoccupied with fragmented subjectivity, displacement, and dysfunctional social and family structures, lack.[7] An orphan sold to a drug dealer and a pimp, Mila escapes from her captor at a gas station and settles in a remote border village inhibited by only a group of elderly who make their living by growing and selling (as well as smoking) their own marijuana. Early in the film, the viewer discovers that Mila is pregnant and suspects that she flees the abuse of her pimp because she has her baby to think of. Her son, born on Christmas Day and called Christo, is treated by the villagers as a small miracle. As Mila (reminding the viewer of both Mary and Mary Magdalene) grows lonely, she relates emotionally and sexually to the only young man in the village, an alienated army veteran and a Buddhist teacher. In the isolation from modern civilization, with all its seductive advantages and alienating nature, Mila travels a road of self-discovery both sexually and spiritually. In turn, she empowers the local people who have been abandoned by society in its feverish attempts to escape the past and join the Western world.

Although well received at international film festivals, the film triggered a critical debate, as some accused it of exoticizing the Balkans and advancing the stereotype of the "wacky backwaters," while others praised its innovative exploration of female sexuality in the Bulgarian and, more generally, Balkan contexts.[8] Here I am interested mostly in the psychological portrayal of Mila, who exhibits a wide range of emotions in demonstrating social resilience. The imaginative handheld camera and tilted angles contribute to the presentation of a disturbed and vulnerable young woman and create a strangely moving effect. The viewer sympathizes with the heroine (played by Vesela Kazakova), whose wounded psyche, physical estrangement, and yet warm humanity inexplicably reveal the sad destiny of many Bulgarian orphans while simultaneously showing their admirable strength. Vivid flashbacks of the way she was sold and the abuse at the hands of her pimp ring a true note and call attention to the horrific experience of human trafficking.[9]

Although Mila is mostly silent and withdrawn, the spectator is invited to follow her subtle acceptance of her pregnancy and the quandary as a single mother-to-be. What makes her character appealing, however, is the uncertainty and hesitation with which she deals with her personal crisis.[10] Mila is withdrawn, alienated, and hesitant to open up to her new "friends" and to embrace her new conditions both socially and personally. It takes her some time, as she struggles to accept the elderly and forgotten people in the village as her new family. Being abandoned by her biological parents, sold by the orphanage guardians, and abused by her pimp, she is understandably unable to trust people. These new "grandparents," however, slowly and patiently win her trust and awaken her human kindness, a troubling testament to the lost middle generation of her parents who are absent from the film and who have relinquished their responsibilities.[11] No doubt, this absence speaks of the struggles of the generation that carried the transition to democracy in Bulgaria.

Although she escapes to give birth—and with Christo being born on Christmas, the symbolism of a new beginning is clear—she does not accept motherhood easily. She even abandons her baby, only to return to him at the end of the film and to accept her feelings for her newfound lover and partner. The film ends with a scene in which her lover protects her and her baby from the angered pimp (Christo's biological father), as Mila and the Buddhist teacher (her lover) look into each other's eyes and introduce themselves: Asen and Mila. It is then that the viewer hears Mila's name for the first time, signifying to her opening-up and acceptance of her love.

Zornitsa Sophia attentively and warmly depicts the emotional hesitations, vulnerability, and slow but assuring personal growth of a young, abused, and abandoned woman who has to come to terms with herself, her life, and her social reality. Evoking the Roman god of war in the title, the film represents a disturbed and vulnerable young mother in a place as far and as alien as Mars who nevertheless manages to open up to her adoptive grandparents and her lover, Asen; together they all will raise Christo with love in a better place, one imagines and hopes.

Esma's Secret: Overcoming Trauma

If *Mila from Mars* depicts the trials of a young mother who conceived her child in abuse and violence and who, as an orphan, has to create human bonds and learn how to love herself, others, and her baby, Jasmila Žbanić's film presents a full-blown picture of the challenges a single mother has to overcome to raise her daughter in the aftermath of the Yugoslav Wars in Bosnia. In *Esma's Secret*, Esma (Mirjana Karanović) maintains two jobs to make the most basic ends meet and provide for her teenage daughter, Sara. Material privation, however, is only one of Esma's difficulties, as she has told Sara that her father was a *shaheed*, a Muslim hero who died defending Bosnia during the Yugoslav war of the 1990s, and now she has to prove it by providing a certificate of his death. As a daughter of a *shaheed*, Sara is respected by her friends. Furthermore, this parentage secures her a discount on a school trip. When her mother fails to produce a certificate of her father's heroic past, Sara, a rebellious teenager and tomboy, brutally offends her mother. At gunpoint Sara questions Esma's morality and integrity and demands to know the truth about her father. Esma's outburst is addressed not just to Sara but to a society that substitutes macho myths for reality: "You want to know the truth? Here's the truth! I was raped in the war camps and you're the bastard of a Chetnik!"[12]

Estimates of rapes during the Bosnian war (1991–95) range from twenty thousand to fifty thousand.[13] Unlike the Nuremberg Charter, which did not include special provisions for rape, in 2001 The Hague International War Crimes Tribunal for Yugoslavia identified rape and sexual enslavement as "crimes against humanity."[14]

Enduring the catharsis of voicing the truth, Esma for the first time is able to narrate her devastating experience, to recuperate her memories, to give expression to the trauma, to weep, and to proclaim her hate and then her love for Sara. Esma not only admits the truth to her daughter but also shares her memory of the violation with other women in a social therapy group. This liberating, though long-delayed and excruciating, opening-up is symbolically significant for Esma's life, the first step toward her psychological recovery and healthy, albeit difficult, future.

"I pounded my belly with my fists to make her fall out of me. It was no use. My belly grew with her inside. Even then they came. In twos, threes, every day. In the hospital when I gave birth to her, I said: 'I don't want her. Take her away.'" When she hears the baby crying behind the wall, however, her milk gushes from her breast, and she decides to feed the infant, just once. If up to that point it is the biological-maternal instinct that prompts Esma to have contact with her newborn, the decisive moment comes when Esma sees her daughter, so small and beautiful, and decides to keep her.

The film's concluding sequence, of the students' departure for the trip, testifies to the difficulties that mother and daughter need to overcome in order to (re)establish their bond. Distressed and distant from each other, they walk quietly side by side to the bus. There Esma embraces her daughter, who remains cold and remote. Once inside the bus, Sara appears at the rear window, gazes impassively at her mother, and then after a few moments hesitantly extends her hand, placing it palm up against the window in a traditional gesture of peace. The camera cuts to a close-up of Esma's face, which lights up, and she begins to wave energetically to her daughter as the bus moves off.

In a review of the film, Meta Mazaj observed: "As the school bus pulls away, we see an affectionate moment between mother and daughter, a gesture certainly hopeful and forward looking, yet where this gesture might lead is unclear."[15] Though the gesture certainly cannot and should not be read as a clear sign of Esma and Sara's future harmony and closeness, the song "Sarajevo, lubavi moe" ("Sarajevo, my love"), which the students sing and Sara joins in with a smile, encourages a cautiously optimistic interpretation of the ending. Popular from the Yugoslav period, the song is not about Bosnia but about Sarajevo. It would be misguided to read this ending as a nostalgic reference to Yugoslavia. Rather, it is a reminder of the spirit of Sarajevo as a multiethnic, multireligious, and multicultural city, where Esma and Sara could overcome the trauma of their past.[16]

Monkeys in Winter: Generations of Tribulations

While *Esma's Secret* explores the consequences of Bosnia's recent tragic past, Milena Andonova's *Monkeys in Winter* presents the tribulations of three

Bulgarian mothers in the span of the last fifty years. It portrays the destinies, anxieties, and internal conflicts of three Bulgarian women, whose lives revolve around motherhood and children. Their stories unfold amid Bulgaria's social and political history since the 1960s, which is organically interwoven with the women's personal dramas. In a captivating and challenging way, the director positions motherhood in the center of the film. Motherhood, a source of passions and desires, becomes the driving force in the lives of these women and the cause of both intentional and unintentional murders.

The film opens with a montage of brief scenes presenting the three heroines: Tana (Angelina Slavova), Lukretsia (Diana Dobreva), and Dona (Bonka Ilieva-Bonnie). The years are 2001, 1981, and 1961, respectively. The director then proceeds to show Dona's story. She is a gorgeous woman of Roma ethnicity and viewers meet her at the time of her divorce when her former husband and his new wife come to take some of Dona's furniture. A local authorities-representative (Filip Trifonov) offers her a job in the small town's hygiene department, asking her to become an informant. An insightful cut to the next scene of street washing elicits various associations with communist practices: brainwashing and political cleansing.

The camera then jumps to Lukretsia who is finishing law school in Sofia and hopes to be offered a job in the capital rather than being placed in the provinces. Disorienting and disturbing underwater shots depict Lukretsia's dreams of drowning in a swimming pool and reveal a complex and difficult relationship between her and her mother. Brief scenes showing Lukretsia's roommates from the dormitory hint at the generational conflicts and deep social problems of the 1980s, when Bulgarian youth became disillusioned, lost its moral ground, and dreamed only of empty and easy goals. Lukretsia's, like other young people's, desire was to marry and remain in Sofia. After a position in Sofia is denied to her, she is introduced to an odd Sofia resident with the hope of marrying him. A grotesque and distressing meeting between the two ends with her pregnancy. In the meantime, she meets a young Frenchman (Sava Lolov), and they fall in love with each other, which further complicates her situation as she attempts to abort her baby, to no avail.

The camera jumps again, this time to 2001, and follows Tana, who prays for a child. Around a small isolated mountain chapel at the bank of a lake, there are people gathered to pray and ask God for help. A woman voices the problems of the time: "The world turned around and got confused. God it the only hope for many people." A camera jump returns viewers to 1961, when Dona is blackmailed and forced by the authorities-representative to marry an older invalid (Stefan Mavrodiev). In a succinct scene, Dona learns from her older daughter that the invalid abuses her daughters. She smashes his head with a shovel and runs away with the children. Through a winter long shot the camera presents Dona, desperate and helpless. She decides to leave her children on their own in her old town. Another jump takes the audience to a night view of an apartment block where a baby is crying. In a state of shock, Lukretsia leaves her baby on the street alongside garbage cans.

While Dona's and Lukretsia's stories are almost uncovered, Tana's is at its beginning. Viewers know only that she is happily married but has problems conceiving a child. The drama in this family accelerates when sterility tests reveal the husband's weak spermatozoids. After antagonistic scenes, in which the husband (Valentin Tanev) refuses to accept the tests results, viewers see them reconciled and enjoying a vacation with friends in the country. The happy news of her pregnancy, however, does not bring happiness, for the husband suspects her of sleeping with another man and beats her up. During a violent scandal, he suffers a heart attack and dies. The last two scenes of the film depict Tana with her toddler playing in the snow and Lukretsia, who appears to have lost her mind, seeking her baby around garbage cans. In a long take, the camera follows her disappearing into a winter forest. The winter shot concludes the sad and tragic destinies of these women and visually unites their three stories in an original narrative structure. In my conversation with the director, Andonova mentioned that mothers are like monkeys in winter, capable of high and low deeds and of happiness and sorrow. Through the stories of these three mothers, the film also presents various gender and ethnic inequalities and difficulties that women had to face during socialism and after.[17] The film portrays motherhood as a powerful experience that can lead to tragedies and triumphs and, more importantly, as an experience that is very personal and unique and does not always match the traditional understanding of it as fulfilling and rewarding.

Mothers in Balkan Film

The stories of these Balkan mothers—Mila's escape from trafficking and teenage pregnancy that teach her to trust people; Esma's struggles to raise her daughter, conceived in the Yugoslav Wars' rape rooms, in a society that refuses to acknowledge the traumas of its past; and Tana, Lukretsia, and Dona, who, in various periods of Bulgaria's last fifty years, have had (or failed) to overcome social ostracism and personal burdens in their motherhood struggles—portray the challenges and unfair expectations that societies place on mothers. All of these women's experiences, unique and exigent, defy any traditional view of motherhood as conceiving and raising children with love and care. Contrasted with the Albanian mother's sacrifice described by the Frenchman in Yourcenar's story, these mothers bear triumphs and tragedies in their daily lives, as they remain truthful to their desires and themselves or suffer painfully their fatal decisions.

While one can conclude with Yourcenar's last words—"There are mothers . . . and then there are mothers"—in their realistic and objective portrayals of mothers, the films differ significantly from the exotic and stereotypical depiction of Balkan realty and culture in "The Milk of Death." Different from the Albanian mother's subordination to the word of her husband and his brothers and her sacrifice for her baby (a boy, of course)—in other words, unlike the total erasure of her subjectivity and desire—the cinematic Balkan mothers actively assert their agency and voice in the most personal decisions of their lives that concern motherhood. These images paired with the modest emergence of Balkan women film directors and women's cinema testify to cultural changes in Balkan women's everyday lives compared to the times of the folkloric legend. Although just starting to be more visible and powerful, Balkan women's cinema opens space for imagining a more self-determined everyday life for Balkan women.

Notes

1. Yourcenar 1985, 39.
2. Ibid., 51.
3. For more on this type of film scholarship, see Wood (2003). For a similar approach to particularly Balkan films, see Iordanova (2001).
4. Fischer 1996, 4.
5. By "canons," I mean a list of authors and titles that are most studied and known by the general public. For more on Bulgarian women writers, see Kirova (2004).
6. For a discussion of women's images in Balkan films created by male directors, see Iordanova (1996).
7. My analysis of *Mila from Mars* benefited from a conference presentation by Miglena Ivanova (now at Flinders University, Australia).
8. For more on the film and the conflicting opinions, see Skrodzka (2012), Trifonova (2007, 32–36), and Yotova (2013).
9. Orphans are identified by antitrafficking NGOs as the most vulnerable group of children and adolescents that fall victim to pimps and traffickers. Here, I avoid the complex discussion about the differences between prostitution and trafficking. I will mention, however, that since Mila is kept under tight control by her pimp who refuses to let her go when she demands that he stops the car and she had to escape and hide in the remote village, the case shares aspects of trafficking whose victims are deprived of free will.
10. *Mila from Mars* became the best-selling Bulgarian film for over a decade (Skrodzka 2012, 52).
11. For an intriguing psychoanalytic reading of the film, see Sabbadini (2014, 68–75).
12. *Chetniks* (четници) were members of an organized anti-Axis movement in Yugoslavia during World War II. Although they had a comeback during the Yugoslav Wars of the 1990s, Serb soldiers who abused Bosnian and Croats during these conflicts were also called *Chetniks* by their victims.
13. Boose 2002, 71.
14. Fisher 1996.
15. Mazaj 2007, 61.
16. The impact of the film contributed to the change of the country's legal definition of a veteran and included raped women in it, granting them access to social and financial support.
17. This is not to say that socialism did not advance women's rights, especially in the sphere of education and professional development, but in many respects, the rigid patriarchal mentality governed women's daily life experiences.

References

Boose, Linda. 2002. "Crossing the River Drina: Bosnian Rape Camps, Turkish Impalement, and Serbian Cultural memory." *Signs* 28 (1): 71–96.

Fischer, Lucy. 1996. *Cinematernity: Film, Motherhood, Genre.* Princeton, NJ: Princeton University Press.
Fisher, Siobhan. 1996. "The Occupation of the Womb: Forced Impregnation as Genocide." *Duke Law Journal* 46 (1): 91–146.
Iordanova, Dina. 1996. "Women in New Balkan Cinema: Surviving on the Margins." *Film Criticism* 21 (2): 24–39.
Iordanova, Dina. 2001. *Cinema of Flames: Balkan Film, Culture, and the Media.* London: British Film Institute.
Kirova, Milena. 2004. "To 'Write as a Woman' in Bulgaria in the 90s of the 20th Century." *L'Homme Z.F.G.* 15 (1): 109–116.
Mazaj, Meta. 2007. "Review: *Grbavica.*" *Cineaste* 32 (3): 60–61.
Sabbadini, Andrea. 2014. *Moving Images: Psychoanalytic Reflections on Film.* London: Routledge.
Skrodzka, Aga. 2012. *Magic Realist Cinema in East Central Europe.* Edinburgh: Edinburgh University Press.
Trifonova, Temenuga. 2007. "Stoned on Mars: Home and National Identity in Recent Bulgarian Cinema." *Cineaste* 32 (3): 32–36.
Wood, Robin. 2003. *Hollywood from Vietnam to Reagan and Beyond.* New York: Columbia University Press.
Yotova, Sophie. 2013. "Redefining Female Sexuality; Mila from Mars: A Contemporary View of Gender in Balkan Cinema." May 31. Accessed October 12, 2015. https://sophieyotova.wordpress.com/2013/05/31/redefining-female-sexuality-mila-from-mars-a-contemporary-view-of-gender-in-balkan-cinema/.
Yourcenar, Marguerite. 1985. *Oriental Tales.* Translated by Alberto Manguel. Toronto: HarperCollins Canada.

YANA HASHAMOVA is Professor and Chair of the Department of Slavic and East European Languages and Cultures and Honorary Associate Researcher at the Institute of Culture and Memory Studies at the Research Centre of the Slovenian Academy of Sciences and Arts.

34 Memories of Foreign Love
Ervin Hatibi

Literature creates and interprets, and as such, we can see ourselves within it. It frames understanding, gives form to experience, and allows imagination to have a home. There ideas play out in ways that create new possibilities, new ways of being, and new ways of making sense of suffering and joy. Stories of freedom, constraint, morality, and beauty—in moderation, excess, and absence—become tools that move the reader to other worlds, to other insights. It is seeing the risk in what can be said and imagining the origin of feelings. Stories hold what everyday life was, is, can be, and should (or should never) become, all in conversation with a world that is specific and universal—as all lives are. A repository of meaning and an arbitrator of memory, there is power in creativity that makes the written word—as love exploring boundaries—both dangerous and hopeful.

And yet, literature is not neutral. As Albanian socialist censors worked to sanitize writing deemed incompatible with the ideology of the state—meanings of international authors, like Nobel laureate Heinrich Böll, were transformed in ways that made them compatible while local authors, like Ismail Kadare, were either censored, self-censored, or able to find creative ways to mask subversive views—it was only after socialism ended that new meanings were discovered, including the foreign and feminine voice. This process of discovery came alongside social changes that saw shifting boundaries between the tradition of the censor and more experimental forms of (writing) the body's experience. But it was the experience, even in darkness, that the writers sought to explain.

More than three decades after its first appearance in Albanian, Heinrich Böll's novel *The Clown*—about searching for something in which to believe—was republished in its entirety, reconstituted with passages that had formerly been removed by the Albanian censors. The resurrected passages—described by the publisher as dealing with the triad of "love," "religion," and "politics"—were highlighted with gray coloring in the print, a nostalgic homage to old censorship. The shades of gray, applied to almost fifty different passages of *The Clown*, turn the text into a symbolic map of the mentality of Albanian Stalinist isolationism, a political map that assigned foreignness not only to the outlawed religion and anti-Communist thought but also to love and its paraphernalia. Here, as elsewhere, we can see the social influence of prose on the everyday regions of "love" in literature, myth, and memory as we trace change on the map of "foreignness" after the fall of the old regime and the end of isolation.

Love? Not in Our Books

The second and unabridged Albanian edition of Böll's novel *The Clown*[1] offered a number of typographical surprises that Ardian Klosi, translator and publisher of the book, explains in a note: "We kindly ask the reader of *The Clown* to forgive us for the gray background that accompanies certain passages, serving to distinguish what was censured in the first edition of the book published in 1985.[2] This is perhaps of no interest for the generations that grew up after the 1990s; it might be so, indeed, even for the larger part of a more mature audience who strive to forget that time with all its brutal or sophisticated mechanisms at work to keep Albania isolated." Hence, the ashy stains that we encounter today in the text, similar to hematomas in the process of healing, reveal to us those instances in the book from which, a few decades ago, were removed words and passages deemed unacceptable.

> The removals concern three important subjects: love, religion, and politics. Forty-nine disposals are executed in all, targeting those objectives: thirty removals with respect to love, fourteen religion, and five politics. From a quantitative standpoint, expunged from the text are 260.5 lines that speak about love, 71 lines relating to religion, and 156 lines of a political nature.
>
> As I undertook the moiling task of bringing about a complete translation of *The Clown*, I noticed that the parts removed from the book did not constitute considerable fragments of text; it was not, I may say, a proper censorship that tackles, as the case may be, anticommunist sentiments or rhetoric, erotic descriptions, or parts concerning Catholic priests. It was instead quite a complex procedure, woven, or rather twisted and subtly patterned, something that would first appear for an instance only to suddenly reappear elsewhere, coursing in the meantime between the lines, turning back often, going right, then unexpectedly left, attacking and disposing of with perplexing consistency the word linen or the word stain (as indicative of lovemaking); the same fate was reserved for the word pope any time the occurrence was not painted under a bad light. Despite my fuming against and cursing of the person or people who undertook this pertinacious labor twenty-three years ago, again robbing me today of the energy that would have sufficed to translate another novel of Böll, I nonetheless realized that I had before me a masterpiece of censorship.[3]

No treatise on censorship and freedom in socialist Albania can afford to ignore the museum piece that is this face-painted second edition of *The Clown* with its "forty-nine shades of gray."

However, it must be remembered that translated works of fiction by and in themselves substantiated a gray region of freedom, a realm where the censorship dulled and lacked its dynamic or the usual gravity it exercised on the national literary production, the control and the dialectics of coauthorship inflicted on it. After much domesticating and leveling exertions, however toilsome, of the kind described above by Klosi, the translated literary works, nevertheless, should not and could not have been extricated of their fundamental alterity.

At Home Abroad

Legitimation through translation appears to have also motivated Ismail Kadare to graft the manuscript of his own novel *The Shadow*—for fear of unwarranted searches—and present it in the paratext as a work by the German writer Siegfried Lenz "translated from French," dissimulating in turn the identities of the characters, places, and circumstances with denotations of the German world. With one single step or, more precisely, one tactical jolt, equally distancing him from both self-censorship and censorship, the writer decides to experiment with the dangerous freedom acquired through the agency of transmigration—a theoretical preoccupation on which the novel elaborates extensively. Freedom, not simply that necessary to write, demanded the *la mort de l'auteur* and *la trahison du traducteur*.

Politicizing and intellectualizing the obsession with the image of the Frenchwoman to the extent of claiming its sanctity, the narrator—a filmmaker who feels alive only when outside the prison that his country has become—virtually shouldering a coffin, stalks a Parisian actress on those precious occasions when visiting the city as a member of an official delegation. The inevitable return to the isolated motherland is then experienced as a veritable entombment up to the moment of his next cinematic peregrination. The events take place mainly on foreign land, in Paris, and most of the characters are obviously Parisians. But the manuscript, camouflaged as an overtranslation (from German to French to Albanian), is furthermore complemented with a masquerade of foreign characters and foreign narrators as a consequence of the transfer of authorship to a foreign writer. Last but not least, the work is trafficked by the real writer (practically a ghostwriter), for safety reasons, and kept secure in a bank vault in Paris, the city where the book will ultimately see its first publication, translated this time into French in 1994—a few years after Kadare fled Albania and adopted France as his new home.

While the censors of *The Clown*—practically in the same iconic year, 1984, when *The Shadow* was being written—were paining to domesticate and discipline the translated work of a German writer, sequestering its otherness to the best of their abilities, Kadare *becomes* the German writer and tries to liberate the text.[4] The alterity condenses on many levels within and throughout the text, to the extent that it reaches the point of no return: the shadow novel of a novel that does not exist, in which the narrator enters and emerges from his coffin less and less metaphorically and becomes literally the shadow of the writer himself (a distinctive character in the novel who, in an oblique *mise en abyme à clef*, is suspected of trafficking manuscripts outside the country)—all this strikingly reminiscent of a Borgesian story—all the while aware that the trafficked manuscript was predetermined by the author to be published in Paris only after his death, when it would have become impossible for the state to inflict punishment on him.

The true author of such a novel, during this period of Albanian censorship, is a dead author.

The scorched domains listed by Klosi—*religion, politics,* and *love*—seem to be neither more nor less than the very *gray matter,* the *substantia grisea,* of literature, and it is essential to emphasize this in order to properly understand the asphyxia that afflicted literature and society under Enver Hoxha's regime. What was purged from this gray matter pertaining to the literary translations was already obviated during the creative process of the native literature; moreover, as these activities within the society were forbidden by law and prosecuted, they only reappeared in the full swing of a revanchist sentiment in postdictatorial literature and society.

From Fear to Sex

Ullmar Qvick, a Swedish translator and compiler of several anthologies of Albanian literary works, recalls how, during his first visit in Socialist Albania in 1970, he endeavored to slip past the police cordon surrounding the hotel designated for tourists, determined to discover what was kept hidden behind the decor. His adventure in the small town of Kavaja, however, ends quickly—an obvious casualty of the general vigilance over foreigners or the fear of communicating with them—and he finds himself accompanied to the local Executive Comity[5] to provide the necessary explanations.

> We were met by two unshaven men to whom I politely explained who I was . . . and that I entertained the wish to visit a factory. After hearing my words, one of them made a phone call and talked to a factory administrator.
> . . . In the meantime, a secretary entered from an adjacent room and looked at me with contempt. There was something wrong with her clothes, which prompted a sinister suspicion in my mind: Could it be that she had spent a fiery night with the two officials? My knowledge of Albanian literature produced after the 90s has reinforced this suspicion, enabling me to better understand the delicate predicament of a secretary in socialist Albania.[6]

Of course, this testimony is valid only as a cursory verdict on postsocialist Albanian literary production and its preoccupations with sexualization, intentness that in its fervor assumed traits of punitive sorties against the censured past.

In an interview in the mid-1990s, Ismail Kadare commented on what he perceived to be a straining difficulty that the new literature was experiencing in coping with freedom, precisely because of what he observed as a mechanical excess in revisiting the old prohibitions. In a passing, yet almost clinical, note, the writer regarded even the use of the word *urine* as an affected topical ubiety along the unrelenting erotic raving that marked the usual literary crop of the day. For a predictable length of time, the centrality of these *massive* reconnections with the body, aside from functioning as a natural compensation for the inhibitions suffered—and not only in literature but also in its most literal and scatological aspects—should also be regarded as a carnivalesque revenge against the paternalistic voice of rostrums and political speeches: the body avenging itself through opprobrium.

The persistence and restlessness in the first part of the 1990s to explore sites and nooks of the erotic domain that, until then, were walled up and hence inaccessible by the literary creativity not only account for the tormented struggle to invent anew a language and an identity that were practically never before known by the puritanical Albanian writing but also reflect the pervasive reinventions of the postsocialist Albanian society when confronted with the ceaseless retreat of state and family, the massive onrush of migration (within and out of the country) and globalization. The re-ideologization of sex as the signifier of both the West and newly found freedom, the deterritorialization of the relationship between couples, the rise of intercontinental families, and the new urban anonymity emerging as anomia, gender, and ethnic profiling of capitalistic relations, all appeared concurrently with the liberation of the Albanian writer from his or her educative responsibilities—a direct consequence of the termination of contract with the state: the old and exclusive publisher.

Beyond the Borders

All the new developments that followed the collapse of the dictatorial regime could be very well understood by employing the overused synecdoche of the fall of the Berlin Wall. As the German republics became one and Europe attained its completeness through the other half, so also did the Albanian geography become global at last; it freed its regions—until then under occupation and thus unreachable—one after another to the world and in the same fashion reclaimed as its own the swathed sites of the body that the stern Hoxhaist morality forbade from seeing the light of day. The ash-like pale color of the skin that covered parts of the body—contrasted to the exposed, sun-bathed parts—are the projection of the terra incognita on the map. Although it is true that the Berlin Wall was substituted with the borders of the Schengen Area, and that the bromidic conservative attitudes and the return of the once-penalized religion comfortably and quickly placed themselves in the offices vacated by Hoxhaist morality, nothing in Albania would ever be the same.

Initially it was the younger generation that assailed the world by migrating and to counterbalance its absence, the departed youth was instantly supplanted by the *au naturel* imagery of a youth from abroad on newspaper stands. There arose an explosion of cheap erotic editions in black and white and uncensored movies and video clips that were played on TV and in theaters, which pirated entire acres of premium occidental skin as a social transplant until translated and incarnated in Albanian. The liberated territories relate wholly to one another in the public imagination. They have done so since long ago, officially, from the time when the dictatorial regime proscribed as "foreign acts" a consecution of "degenerate" behaviors and inclinations, most of which gravitated around sex; alien for the "communist" morals, while in fact, after some explanation, they were alien

Figure 34.1. A poetry reading at *E për-7-shme* bookshop in Tirana, 2006. Photograph by Andris Stastoli.

because they were characteristic of the world that belonged to the foreign bourgeoisie and capitalists who dwelled beyond the barbed wire.

Interviewed some twenty years after the demise of the regime, an aged border guard, whose testimony is still marked by effective grotesqueness, relates his experiences during the decades of codified surveillance of foreign land: "[There were] naked people showing their bottoms and swearing at us, but in most cases, right before the eyes of our guards, not far from the boundary markers and in plain open spaces, couples would perform sexual acts. The aim was to propagate the idea that their country was the land of great liberties for the individual, contrary to what our propaganda maintained, dominated as it was by moral conservatism."[7] Further on, the officer describes how Albanians attempting to secretly cross the libidinal and eschatological border of the republic were killed on sight, practically executed.

The same border is described in a different manner in an anecdote of a time whose hero was the renowned writer Dritero Agolli, former head of the League of Writers and Artists of Albania:

> Not long ago I went to see doctor Glozheni and asked his help because we kept having children. For goodness sake, I pleaded, I need a vasectomy, I can't afford any more children. "Lo Dritero" said he, "True, you are a dear friend to me, I love you and all, but alas, cross my heart, what you ask cannot be done, so my advice for you

is to practice withdrawal, *coitus interruptus* only can save you ..." Fuck it, retorted I, what are we supposed to guard more intently, not to trespass the Party line or not to impregnate our wives?[8]

The nudity, the unfettered sexual relations and their facile description or discussion were natural only to the *outside world*: the emblems of freedom enjoyed by Western culture. It does not require much courage to reason that the principal battle cry of the student protest against the regime that cried *E duam Shqipërinë si gjithë Evropa*[9] (Tirana, December 1990) finds its equivalent in both *Jouissez sans entraves* and *La vie est ailleurs* (Paris, May 1968).

The Morality of Foreign Love

Certainly, the realm of Albanian imagination was not waiting for the advent of Communist propaganda to conceive the sexual depravity of the West, or more precisely, that of Europe. The famed grievance of Father Gjergj Fishta expressed in his masterpiece *The Highland Lute*[10]—"Europe, aging whore, it's you that / On your word and God have trampled"[11]—while a synthesis of patriotic despair for the partition of Albania and a sacerdotal denunciation of the next Babylon, seems to carry as well the echoes of popular perceptions at the time with concern to the morality of the continent. These perceptions of the general public are also recorded in the chronicles of Faik Konica[12] who in a satirical piece ridicules a breed of Albanians that define Europe as "all that region where people wear hats, where there are too many cars, whose men do not possess our spunk and the women are indecent."[13] The arousing *otherness* of a triumphant and enticing Europe seems to be construed as a composition of technological discipline and moral laxity in a mannish, artisanal, and ultraconservative Albania, reminiscent of the gynoid character in Fritz Lang's contemporary motion picture *Metropolis* (the same biblical reference as found in Fishta). As the technology comes or, more accurately, descends ready-made from Europe, so does the parody of emancipation of women from the shackles of tradition, breezing in from abroad as a form of migration played by cabaret artists and prostitutes. Thus:

> In the [19]20s (probably even earlier) the shantozas appeared. This word comes from French, chanteuse-singer; however, Albanians would not suffer to translate it, wishing to make it clear that they were foreigners stuck with that appellation. In a special club called Café Chantant Paris in Dibra Street ... were employed twenty-five or thirty young girls from Montenegro, who ... on a specific hour of the night will come down from the second floor.[14]

> In a typical oriental country, like Albania was at that time, prostitution could not emerge except as an import brought by the invading armies and with it came as well the measures that regulated it. Before that, it was permissible for the beys to keep in their courts a small group of female gypsies, who generally performed as dancers, but were known to fulfil the duties of courtesans as well ... so, in the beginning of the past century, both types of this category were common: the courtesans and the regular prostitutes, the latter mainly foreigners.[15]

The historiography and terminology of the above reports—obtained from the retro rubrics of contemporary press—could be discussed endlessly; instead, what is important to observe in these quotations is the continuous refashioning of the matter that constitutes the public memory, and its equivocation by actors, ideologies, and commonplace clichés, framed within "references" extracted from period newspapers. The memo we obtain as a dictum states that prostitution was foreign, and twice so: the first to practice it were foreigners who answered the *needs of the foreigners*, and even when it was local, it remained foreign by virtue of the *racial belonging* of the natives who practiced it. Nevertheless, what comes through the documentary elements of these excerpts is the notion that this new role-playing game was in need of an escapist setting that made it possible to evoke Paris and was in want of characters that embodied an untranslatable identity, like the *shantozas*. Furthermore, the slogans and quips employed in the role-playing game were needed to remain within the limits of a *rendez-vous* where novelty and alterity are consumed. Let us not forget that Paris, or the real Par(ad)is(e), is elsewhere, overseas—as much a domain of imagination and hyperbole as it is of the masculine action and gaze of the students, merchants, diplomats, and emigrants.

"The moral scrupulosity of a conservative society prompted the affluent to embark the ferry to Bari [Italy], where none knew them and where the range of debaucheries they could indulge in was greater"[16]—says the author of vintage rubrics in the contemporary press. Once the dictatorship was installed in the country, the only place left to go and sin—and where one could be no one—was in communist eastern Europe where young people were sent to study. For the longest time, the sole publicly accepted testimonies of the love life of Albanian students abroad came in the form of foreign spouses they would bring home and much less often in literary works such as, for example, Ismail Kadare's novella *The Twilight of the Eastern Gods*.[17] Today they are mainly the subject of interviews and memoirs—especially those about the tragic destiny of ostracized or persecuted eastern European women, ultimately coerced to divorce their Albanian husbands immediately after the severance of diplomatic relations with the other countries of the socialist camp. After the 1990s, the theme of the life of Albanian students abroad would form the backdrop in the semiautobiographical work of the writer Fatos Kongoli, opening a new frontier rarely ventured before and much further East: China. "We were afflicted by sexual esurience. China had ample potential to appease our suffering," claims a student's character in Kongoli's novel *Dragoi i fildishtë* (The Ivory Dragon).[18] "According to the official reports in our possession, it seems that you have raped half of the girl population in Beijing,"[19] a police officer retorts promptly. In Kadare's works published in the 1990s, a former student in Moscow who had fled Tirana after an overprotective brother of his girlfriend threatened to disfigure him with sulfuric acid, dubbed the time of his overseas studies as "the Tartar Mongol erotic march"[20] among the joyful hordes of local girls who wrote their phone numbers on cigarette packs in lipstick.

At home, such impossible scenarios were infiltrated solely through television waves: "People were fracturing arms and legs clambering the rooftops to install

all sorts of antennas, suggestive of pans, potties, harpoons or Jesus's crown of thorns, to watch the erotic movies on private Italian TV stations."[21]

The territory of foreign freedom effected at times, in the form of a tour bus, to permeate as deliverance from the chastity belt of dictatorship. In a short story with strong autobiographical elements, Adhurim Lako begins with a description of the first day of work for a translator and tour guide in his twenties, who by the evening loses his virginity to an Italian girl of the same age in her hotel room.[22] The erotic tension fuses subsequently with the dread of being penalized, which sets the tone for the remainder of the story, until the exposed translator—standardly suspected to be a spy, a contingency for anyone who dealt with foreigners—succeeds in avoiding prison.

Discovering through the Feminine

For decades, the male viewpoint has been the common thread of all descriptive experiences with regard to the erotic otherness, and consequently it converges in feminizing territories, nationalities, and even concepts such as civilization and progress, while alienating the feminine. The predicament changed for the free Albania of the 1990s, where the migration of all genders destabilized the male paradigm: now the world, but mostly the West, was also to be discovered from the feminine experience, and efforts would be made to describe it through the female perspective. Behind the fallen wall, Europe would achieve its wholeness only by joining the East and West together, but for Albanians, it also finally found its balance between the symbologies of gender, accessible to the feminine gaze at last. Moreover, Europe, or the West, as the authentic land of liberty (including sexual freedom)—thereby a fantasy platform (of the erotic as well)—could also serve as a concourse for both sexes to reexamine gender representations. Signs of this mutual effort can be easily recognized in a section of an anthology of short stories—*Albania Tells: 1991–2010*—published by Ardian Klosi and entitled *The New World*.[23]

"Look for Me in the Garbage Cans" by Elvira Dones tells of a prostitute in Italy who encounters by chance an elderly ex-neighbor from her country, now working as a garbage truck driver.[24] When confronted with the paternal embarrassment of the old man, the heroine insists that now she is a *whore* and no longer the child that he knew. When finally the driver crossly accepts to call her by that name, insulted she hollers for her colleagues and clients who hurriedly came and violently beat the *offender*, leaving him unconscious and blood-covered until, toward the end of the story, he is found by the police, leaving the reader uncertain of his fate.

In Yllijet Alicka's "Longing," during a dinner with expensive wines, ending not unintentionally with a glass of Calvados (a mythical brandy featured in *The Arch of Triumph*, a popular novel by Erich Maria Remarque published in 1988), one character asks the wife of his best friend to abandon everything and start a new life with him that very night in the European city where after so many years of being apart they met inadvertently as participants in a scientific conference.[25]

In Teodor Keko's "Two Albanians in Düsseldorf," the protagonist saves money to finance a long journey to the country where an acquaintance of his now lives

Figure 34.2. Friend's Book House, Tirana, 2017. Photograph by Olsi Duzha.

and who years ago had promised him she would be willing to make love but only if they were in Germany ("I can't make love in this squalid country").[26]

In "Veronika," another short story by Adhurim Lako, the Albanian narrator traveling somewhere in northern Italy pretends to be an Englishman when talking with a girl on a train.[27] Later, however, when they undress, suddenly the conversation switches to Albanian. When the time comes for them to go their separate ways, the girl refuses to tell her compatriot her name. Alone again, the narrator decides to christen her Veronika.

We never learn the English name the girl decided to give the narrator. What we learn, however, is that the user guide for escaping to the new world assembles all the abolished and effaced words, reimagined anew after having been lost during the decades of isolation and censure.

Notes

Special thanks to the writer and translator Dritan Xhelo for his generous help with this chapter.

    1. Böll 2008. The novel was translated from the original in German *Ansichten eines Clowns* and published by the late Ardian Klosi.

    2. Böll 1985.

    3. Klosi 2008.

    4. Kadare claims to have finished *The Shadow* in 1986, to have smuggled it out of Albania, and to have deposited it in a bank vault in Paris, having previously left special indications to publish it only should anything happen to him.

    5. City municipalities in communist Albania.

    6. Qvick 2013.

    7. Muho 2013.

    8. Faja 2013.

9. We want Albania to be like the rest of Europe!
10. Fishta 2005 [1937]. Father Gjergj Fishta (1871–1940) was a Franciscan friar and a celebrated Albanian writer and intellectual. His epic poem *The Highland Lute* is commonly regarded as one of the heights of Albanian literature and has been dubbed the Albanian *Iliad*.
11. Fishta 2005 [1937], 111.
12. Faik Konica [Konitza] (1875–1942) was a leading figure of the Albanian National Awakening. He was one of the greatest personalities of modern Albanian culture, a renowned intellectual, writer, and political figure.
13. Konica 2007, 69.
14. Bakiu 2011.
15. Baxhaku 2012.
16. Bakiu 2011, 45.
17. Kadare 1978.
18. Kongoli 1999, 54.
19. Ibid., 135.
20. Kadare 2003 (Albanian edition), 94. Precisely the same term is attributed to Ismail Kadare when he speaks about his life as a student in the memoirs authored by his wife, Helena Kadare (2011, 56).
21. Kadare 2003, 57.
22. Lako 2010a.
23. Klosi and Demo 2010.
24. Dones 2010.
25. Alicka 2010.
26. Keko 2010.
27. Lako 2010b.

References

Alicka, Ylljet. 2010. "Mall [Longing]." In *Shqipëria Tregon: 1991–2010* [Albania Tells: 1991–2010] edited by A. Klosi and E. Demo, 343–352. Tirana: K&B.
Bakiu, Gazmend A. 2011. "Çengitë dhe shantozat." *Revista Klan* 704: 44–45. http://www.revistaklan.com/index.php?id=1369&mod=2.
Baxhaku, Fatos. 2012. "'Mretni,' prostitute dhe çingie." *Gazeta Shqip*, March 4. https://web.archive.org/web/20120306003448/http://www.gazeta-shqip.com/opinion/8f27bd84db36c1ba13cff244c0fb8b51.html.
Böll, Heinrich. 1985. *Me Syrin e një Kllouni* [The Clown]. Translated by A. Klosi. Tirana: Naim Frashëri.
Böll, Heinrich. 2008. *Me Syrin e një Kllouni* [The Clown]. Translated by A. Klosi. Tirana: K&B.
Dones, Elvira. 2010. "Kërkomëni në kazanët [Look for Me in the Garbage Cans]." In *Shqipëria Tregon: 1991–2010* [Albania Tells: 1991–2010], edited by A. Klosi and E. Demo, 191–215. Tirana: K&B.
Faja, Agim. 2013. "*Origjina e Botës*: Pse shqiptarët i skandalizon arti." *Gazeta Shqiptaja*, October 16.
Fishta, Gjergj. 2005 [1937]. *The Highland Lute*. Translated by R. Elsie and J. Mathie-Heck. London: I B. Tauris.
Kadare, Helena. 2011. *Kohë e pamjaftueshme* [Insufficient Time]. Tirana: Onufri.

Kadare, Ismail. 1978. *Muzgu i perëndive të stepës* [Twilight of the Eastern Gods]. Tirana: Naim Frashëri. French edition: Kadare, Ismail. 1981. *Le crépuscule des dieux de la steppe*. Paris: Fayard. English edition: Kadare, Ismail. 2014. *Twilight of the Eastern Gods*. New York: Canongate Books.

Kadare, Ismail. 1986. *The Shadow*. French edition: Kadare, Ismail. 1994. *L'Ombre*. Paris: Fayard. Albanian edition: Kadare, Kadare. 2003. *Hija*. Tirana: Onufri.

Keko, Teodor. 2010. "Dy shqiptarë në Dyseldorf [Two Albanians in Düsseldorf]." In *Shqipëria Tregon: 1991–2010* [Albania Tells: 1991–2010], edited by A. Klosi and E. Demo, 171–190. Tirana: K&B.

Klosi, Ardian. 2008. "Requiem për censurën." *Gazeta Shekulli*, September 28. https://web.archive.org/web/20080930195018/http://shekulli.com.al/news/53/ARTICLE/33066/2008-09-28.html.

Klosi, Ardian, and Elsa Demo, eds. 2010. *Shqipëria Tregon: 1991–2010* [Albania Tells: 1991–2010]. Tirana: K&B.

Kongoli, Fatos. 1999. *Dragoi i fildishtë* [The Ivory Dragon]. Tirana: Çabej. French edition: Kongoli, Fatos. 2000. *Le dragon d'ivoire*. Paris: Rivages.

Konica, Faik. 2007. "Çipi i palaçove." In *Faik Konica: Veprat*, 69. Tirana: Konica.

Lako, Adhurim. 2010a. "Koha [The Time]." In *Shqipëria Tregon: 1991–2010* [Albania Tells: 1991–2010], edited by A. Klosi and E. Demo, 216–222. Tirana: K&B.

Lako, Adhurim. 2010b. "Veronika." In *Shqipëria Tregon: 1991–2010* [Albania Tells: 1991–2010], edited by A. Klosi and E. Demo, 223–227. Tirana: K&B.

Muho, Habib. 2013. "Skena seksi dhe femra nudo përballë ushtarëve të kufirit jugor të Shqipërisë." *Gazeta Shqiptare*, July 10. https://web.archive.org/web/20130711093001/http://www.balkanweb.com/gazetav5/artikull.php?id=135459.

Qvick, Ullmar. 2013. "Në Shqipëri na përgjonin pastruset" (interview). *Gazeta Shqip*, July 23. http://gazeta-shqip.com/lajme/2013/07/28/ne-shqiperi-na-pergjonin-pastrueset/.

Remarque, Erich Maria. 1988. *Harku i Triumfit* [*The Arch of Triumph*]. Tirana: Naim Frashëri.

ERVIN HATIBI is an Albanian poet, essayist, and painter. His books of poetry include *Përditë Shoh Qiellin*; *Poezi*; and *Pasqyra e Lëndës*. He is author of *Republick of Albanania*.

35 The Sound of Charcoal Rustling: Drawing from Life in Belgrade

Marko Živković

The apartment is on the third floor of a typical high-rise apartment building in New Belgrade, a city built in the 1970s according to socialist ideas and Le Corbusier's aesthetics to serve as a "giant worker's dormitory" for Yugoslavia's capital, Belgrade, on the marshy plain across the Sava and Danube rivers. Unlike the old Belgrade, the streets are wide and straight. Concrete skyscrapers in various stages of dilapidation are clustered into "blocks" with their own esoteric numbering system that often confounds even the taxi drivers. The apartment is typical of New Belgrade: a living room, a small adjoining kitchen, a tiny bedroom and a bathroom, a small glass-enclosed balcony. A maximum of eight easels and two benches can fit in the living room around a small raised podium where the model sits. There is usually a still life—a bottle, a kettle, and some fruit—arranged either at the model's feet or somewhere in the kitchen. Students stand in front of their easels, sit on the benches, or around the kitchen table. Each easel is modified to support two drawing boards, one on each side, so that this small room miraculously accommodates up to eighteen students. Most use charcoal to draw the model on two- by three-foot Kraft paper sheets. A few, sitting at the benches or in the kitchen paint the still life. Classes are four hours long with a fifteen-minute break every hour. This is the preparatory drawing school run by a painter we will call Tinker Bell, and a photographer, designer and multimedia artist we will call Sunset, one of about a dozen such schools in Belgrade. There are classes for children, amateurs, and grade school students preparing for the entrance exams to the specialized art and design high schools, but the core mission of the school is to prepare high school students for the extremely demanding and competitive entrance exams for the Belgrade Faculties of Fine and Applied Arts. To have a shot at passing these exams, students must undergo at least a year of rigorous training. It is these exams, which deserve to be called "hellish," that sustain the preparatory schools.

Tinker Bell was a classmate of my wife, Gordana, at the Faculty of Fine Arts (FLU)[1] from which both graduated in 1998. When Gordana passed away in 2012, I decided to spend most of my sabbatical year in my native Belgrade. Coming to Tinker Bell's classes was very soothing—I was immersed in the same exact way of teaching, practicing, and living art I picked up from Gordana during our ten-year-long marriage. It is this immersion in one of the nodes of Belgrade's art world—the preparatory school—that serves as the starting point for this excursion into the everyday life of art in Serbia.

The curious thing about Belgrade preparatory schools is that they are an essential part of an institution that could be seen as an anachronism, a combination of French Fine Art Academy[2] traditions and the socialist art system that somehow survived into a largely inhospitable present.

It is hard to precisely characterize the present moment in Serbia. Once the dominant nation in the old Yugoslavia (1918–41), and one of the six republics in the socialist Yugoslavia established after World War II by the victorious partisans led by Tito, Serbia emerged from the wars of Yugoslav succession (1991–95) as an independent republic. While an active participant in the wars fought in Croatia and Bosnia, it suffered no fighting on its own territory until the NATO bombing in 1999 that resulted in the majority Albanian province of Kosovo winning its independence. Slobodan Milošević, a former socialist who had ruled Serbia since 1989 and a major actor in the Yugoslav wars, was voted out of office in 2000, and extradited to the tribunal in The Hague where he died in 2006. An ideologically heterogeneous, loose, and malleable coalition of parties that opposed Milošević came to power in 2000 and stayed in power with diminishing public support and increasing collaboration with the successors of Milošević's socialists until they were decisively beaten in 2014 by the successors to the ultranationalist-populist parties allied with Milošević in the 1990s.

At least since 1989, the major political actors that still dominate the scene have changed their ideology and alliances so many times that, with a few marginalized exceptions, the politicians could be characterized only by opportunistic populism. Corruption, predictably, is high, and so is unemployment and general apathy. The judiciary is weak, beholden to current power holders, and independent journalism is marginalized by tabloids while socialist institutions, practices, and mentality coexist with varieties of wild and neoliberal capitalism in an amalgam impossible to disentangle.

State funding for culture is at a historic low, and even the meagre funds promised tend to go to those affiliated with the parties in power or simply disappear into private pockets. And while there is work for applied artists—designers, camera operators, sound engineers, and so on—fine arts are in disarray.

As in other socialist countries, freelance writers, theater and film workers, musicians, and visual artists all had their state-funded associations that secured their members' health and retirement benefits, and assisted with workspace and exhibition venues. This function carried over into the postsocialist era, but at the time of writing, in 2014, the visual artists suddenly started receiving notices from their municipal tax offices claiming they owe up to several thousand euros in unpaid taxes. What happened was that the municipal tax offices, taking advantage of the fact that government was sometimes late in paying the artists' benefits, started imposing steep interest rates as penalties for unpaid taxes due on these "earnings." Artists, who generally do not even see these payments, were suddenly treated as tax evaders threatened with property seizure. And instead of reacting as an association through its own lawyers, the individual members were reduced to each fighting their own individual battle.

It is in that environment that the Belgrade preparatory schools still flourish. On average, students spend one to two years taking classes. A monthly fee comes up to approximately one sixth of an average monthly salary.[3] In addition, students are supposed to constantly produce homework sketches. And at crunch time, right before the exams, it all becomes a frenzied rush to prepare portfolios.

Students will also quite often attend several schools and seek advice from several instructors. The instructor's reputation ultimately depends on the success rate of their students at the entrance exams. Tinker Bell and Sunset are very successful and quite popular, so much so that they have to turn students away, mostly due to the space constraints and the limits to their ability to provide individual attention.

For the entrance exam at the FLU—or, as it is popularly called, "Akademija" (The Academy)—students bring their portfolios containing five live nude studies, five small drawings, and five paintings. They spend three days drawing a live model (standing), two days drawing the portrait of a model (sitting) with hands, and one day painting a still life. Entrants are judged by a committee large enough to prevent any single professor from pushing through a "favorite," and the prevailing opinion is that the exams are fair and incorruptible. There is a sense of hard work in Tinker Bell's and Sunset's school. Models are all professionals, another class of people who scrapes some sort of existence from the system of art education that depends heavily on drawing from life and getting human anatomy right. Most of them are veterans who also pose at the Akademija and other art schools. They take pride in their professionalism, and often boast of being "the best model." It is indeed hard work to stand motionless for four hours. Some of them are artists themselves; most are otherwise unemployed or retired. Some are veritable legends about whom generations of artists tell hilarious anecdotes. After spending years in studios, some of them acquire the expertise equal to professors. "Listen to Slavica [one of the famous models]," Tinker Bell advises her students, "her critique is as good as Akademija professors.'"[4]

Tinker Bell is exacting but also soft hearted; Sunset plays the disciplinarian. There is lots of joking and laughter. Gossip and intimacies are shared, especially during the breaks, when most students crowd the little glassed-in balcony and smoke. Tinker Bell and Sunset are strict instructors but also confidantes who worry about their students in a parental way. The funniest remarks get written down on a piece of paper and stuck to the kitchen wall. My favorite: "Ass is the strongest" (anatomically correct since *gluteus maximus* is indeed the largest muscle in the human body). There is playful competition over who gets to choose the background music. Some are listening to their own from their MP3 players.

Tinker Bell makes frequent rounds criticizing work in progress. One student she urges not to shirk careful measurement with the stick, to the other she points that the model is "falling," that the proportions are not right, or that the line should be thicker right here. Occasionally she will shout, quite loudly: "Feet are

Figure 35.1. Tinker Bell in the old studio. Measuring is essential, 2014. Photograph by Marko Živković.

larger than the head! Model leaves, drawing stays! Eraser is evil!" These are all maxims received from their teachers and their teacher's teachers, sometimes creatively amended on the basis of personal experience. It is possible to reconstruct the FLU pedagogy or general aesthetics and ethics from these maxims and from the remarks repeatedly used in the critique. The fraught issue of erasing is a good example. The Belgrade school religiously uses Kraft paper, sturdy, brownish, and cheap. The paper is very tolerant of abuse—you can draw and erase, draw and erase many times without it tearing. The live drawings are called "studies" for a reason. They should ideally show the trials and errors of the "research" needed to arrive at the good "solution to the problem." The orthodox doctrine is that constant erasing and drawing over the erasure is a good thing, a process of searching for the form. Especially if erasure, as it normally does, leaves the faint traces of past mistakes. Nurtured in this doctrine, Tinker Bell has arrived at the seemingly opposite maxim: erasers are evil! She used to think that to erase was the gutsiest thing—you are a "brave heart" indeed if you erase what you just drew and start over again. Now she thinks those who erase actually show fear of imperfection

The Sound of Charcoal Rustling 387

that should be discouraged in students. Rather than erase mistakes, true "warriors" should display bravery in keeping them totally visible. Even though the maxim seems to be malleable, the underlying principle is preserved: live model study is about a painstaking process of searching for the true form through many trials and many mistakes. And it is not only aesthetics that are in question here; the "brave heart" is an ethical category as well.

It is important to try to extract the underlying principles like that one. With such extraction we may arrive at a particular ethos, an amalgam of ethics and aesthetics, a more or less coherent system of values that could be characterized as a "culture" of the Belgrade school of art. This ethos may be at odds with the ethos prevailing in the rest of society at the moment, and their comparison may prove to be illuminating.

The ethos in question is obviously something transmitted from generation to generation, and in the process, just like in any tradition, it is also transformed. The best way to grasp this tradition in the making, its play of conservatism and innovation, is to juxtapose several generations that simultaneously practice it. Fortunately, I was able to record several such incidents. One involves Borislava, a sculptor who prepared Tinker Bell for her own entrance exams in the early 1990s; the other is a series of lectures I gave at the first- and second-year anatomy class at Akademija taught by Vladeta, who was one of Tinker Bell's professors and who also happened to prepare my wife, Gordana, for her entrance exams.

Borislava: Charcoal Rustling and Pain

In July, Tinker Bell and Sunset moved their studio a few blocks down the street to the walk-up space in the high-rise where they live on the seventh floor. It is larger, sunnier, and most importantly, closer to home. One day Tinker Bell and I picked up Borislava, a formidable lady with an impressively large hat, and brought her to the studio. Students had been prepared for Borislava's visit. Those who did not know her from her previous visits, were nevertheless exposed to a lot of Borislava's famous sayings and lore through Tinker Bell. The stereo is playing classical music, and after drinking her Turkish coffee brewed specially for her on the seventh floor, Borislava starts her critique round. The first boy needs to correct the vertical axis and make the hands more alive. The girl who is next is admonished to avoid paying attention to surface details such as the model's chest hairs. "Find the movement, that's where the model's character lies. Every model has something peculiar. This elbow is too high. Knees shouldn't be a gelatinous mass." And then she comes to the third student, a girl with earphones. "Don't listen to the Walkman, please. And don't even think of taking this to the entrance exam. A painterly [*likovna*] emotion must be allowed to work through without distraction. You didn't come here for entertainment; you came here to suffer, to struggle . . . you can't have a little music, a little leisure, a little drawing, as if we were Americans attending some summer camp."

Even classical music is too distracting, Borislava thinks; it is best to work in silence. She turns to the class and utters her legendary phrase: "You should

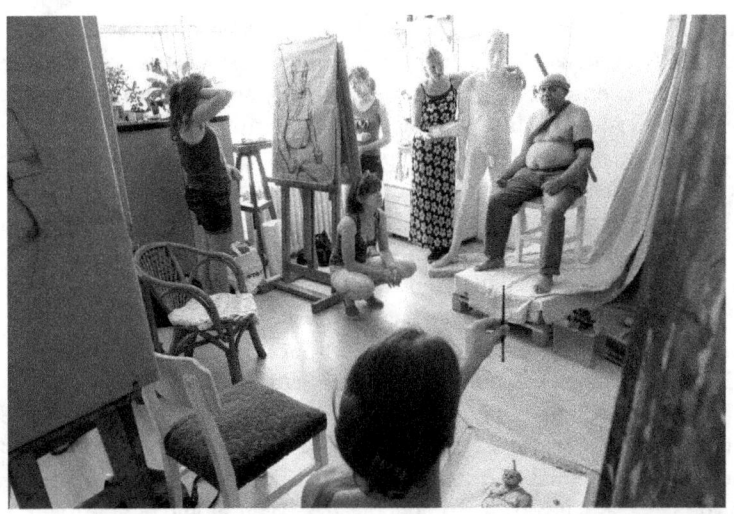

Figure 35.2 a and b. Žika, a legendary model, sits for a live model session in the new studio and afterward departs as students display their sketches, 2015. Photograph by Marko Živković.

listen to the rustle of the charcoal and your pain." "You won't have Mozart and Beethoven at the entrance exam," Borislava warns, "and no air conditioning either; you'll have horrible heat instead."

By the time she had critiqued all eleven students, Borislava has touched on all the main points of old-style Belgrade school pedagogy. It starts with the overall composition, and the way the model is positioned, then moves through the bodily proportions in perspective, the quality of line that should exhibit a good range of thickness, and the evocation of volume or mass through line and shading. Particular attention is paid to hands. "The hand is very alive and it is very painterly [likovna], it shimmers, it is agitated, just like the eye." But although all these criteria of a good drawing are essentially about achieving a precise and accurate likeness, naturalism is in fact a bad word in this pedagogy and must be transcended, even at the level of the preparatory school. Composition and anatomical precision are indispensable, but they are only means to higher ends—the drawing should express the particular, unique character of the model; it should have movement and be alive. Students should find something that captivates them about a particular model and exaggerate it. Hands, feet, and eyes should be alive, shimmering. Borislava constantly warns the students against overdoing the drawing, prettying it up, "killing" or "suffocating it" with excessive shading and details. It is when the "nervature of our being gets cold," as she puts it, that we start making accents "to make it pretty." And at the core of that inexpressible quality teachers are trying to steer their students toward, is the word *likovno*— painterly. It is undefinable. You can only be trained, over years, to recognize it when you see it, and if you are a practicing artist, you should be able to produce it. To lack this quality is to produce kitsch.

But there is more to this training than just aesthetics. Students are also invited to live up to an ethical ideal that combines a certain kind of asceticism (no cot on which to rest, no air conditioner, no music), hard work that amounts to self-torture, willingness and ability to acquire manual skills of a good craftsman, and as Borislava makes quite explicit in her pep talk at the end of her visit, "just work sincerely, sensually, strongly, tenderly and you must succeed." An artist then is a fearless warrior, a self-abnegating monk, a scientist patiently seeking solutions to problems and yet bursting with sensuality and lust for life. This, in a word, is a classical Romantic image of the fine artist. It is a calling, and it is opposite to mere everyday utilitarianism. To be a part of this system that starts in the preparatory school, the students must buy into this ethos which is in many ways at odds with their environment of postsocialist, postconflict Serbia.

Vladeta: The Anatomy of Landscape

In his midsixties, wiry and vital, with silver-streaked beard, Vladeta has been teaching at the Akademija for thirty-five years. A medical student before he switched to fine art, Vladeta is a full professor in charge of the two-year course in plastic anatomy. "We literally torture students for two years," he says as I am preparing to deliver two lectures on the body in traditional Chinese and Ancient Greek medicine—to his second-year students in the morning, and to the first years in the afternoon. First years are twice in number, eager and more engaged than their second-year colleagues. "They are more open and sincere than the second year," Vladeta tells me, "because they are still in the big illusion about everything."

One of the best ways to get at the ethos underlying the Akademija system is to provoke talk about the contrast between fine and applied art. The consensus is that there is more than enough work for designers in Serbia, but surviving on fine art alone is a rarity indeed. However, it is the starving fine artist who commands higher prestige than the well-fed designer. I provoke this discussion in the first-year class after my lecture, and one student who started out in design and switched over to fine art volunteers what I came to recognize as a typical attitude. Designers, for all their talk about themselves as artists, free, and so on, according to the student, are narrow and lack depth. They give no thought to their own culture, let alone to foreign ones. Fine artists, and people devoted to pure art, such as literature, on the other hand, are people with whom you can have meaningful conversations. "They are much more disposed *to work on themselves* than the designers who care only about money and profit." *To work on oneself,* is an old phrase I was surprised to hear from a young person in present-day Serbia. Used in all earnestness and with admiration, it encapsulated neatly the values of what the Germans call *Bildung*, a notion that was born of German Romanticism and sustained, among other things, the modern idea of the university and its mission of nurturing harmonious self-cultivation. In Germany, *Bildung* is contrasted with *Erziehung*, education in useful skills, and this contrast maps neatly on the stereotypical view of fine versus applied art in Serbia. When Vladeta, not without admiration, referred to "the big illusion" the first year Akademija students are still living, he was referring to this Romantic view of art as noble and a nonutilitarian self-cultivation that seems so quixotic in today's world.

Vladeta, himself, of course, is nothing if not even more quixotic than his students in this sense. "You refuse to sell any of your paintings," his wife admonishes him. "It's not a bad position," he responds, "when you don't sell. Then you don't go for easy solutions, no slapping things together just for sale. This is irresponsible. That's why I killed myself doing hard work of all kinds just to survive." Vladeta is an extremist in this regard. But his attitude is the exact equivalent of a "pure" scientist committed to solving scientific problems for their intrinsic interest rather than for their potential material usefulness. And indeed, Vladeta brings this to our discussions in the class.

Vladeta is fascinated with modern physics. Their new ideas are often revolutionary, crazy, he says, but they must ground these ideas in mathematics and prove them in a series of ingenious experiments. "Why can't I be a good physicist? Because I don't know math. I can have a brilliant, crazy idea but if I cannot prove it mathematically and experimentally, I cannot promote it. Similarly with art. [An] artist who knows tradition, but in a way that we study it here, is like a mathematician who has mathematics in his hands. In art, you don't have to have mathematics as a tool, but you have to have skill."

Indeed, in order to see art as solving problems, as the Belgrade school does, there needs to exist something akin to a Kuhnian paradigm, a framework that everyone tacitly accepts.[5] For the Belgrade Akademija school of art, this paradigm consists in a set of skills, perceptive acumen, and a sensibility that is hard to put into words. Rather, like all skills, it is acquired through a long period of apprenticeship. There is "mathematics" in it, in the laws of perspective, the golden rule, Fibonacci series, and anatomical proportions; there is physics in color theory; and there is craftsmanship.

Graduates of Akademija, the "academic artists," tend to be extremely condescending toward any nonacademic art, unless it is a consecrated form of naïve art they tend to admire (and sometimes use to revitalize their own academism). This condescension is particularly reserved for the kitsch sold on the streets of Belgrade. And yet even academic artists will confess to doing often highly lucrative stints of commercial work, the archetype of which is quick portrait drawings done at the seaside for wealthy foreign tourists. Vladeta talks about several of his academic colleagues who were very good at this. "You could buy a car by working on the coast for a summer," Vladeta reminisces. This sort of lucrative art is not necessarily seen as corrupting. "Life is not for purists," Vladeta tells students. "Unless your parents are rich, you should be prepared to do hard work in order to survive. You can do anything at all as long as you separate it from your final aim [which is to produce real art.] But if you cannot make a distinction, you can get stuck [in the commercial art.]"

Vladeta is fully aware of the anachronism of the Belgrade fine art tradition of which he, as a professor of anatomy, is obviously a prime embodiment. "We had a delegation here from the Paris Beaux Art Academy some years ago," he says, "and they said: 'Oh, you are still doing this. We stopped it forty years ago.'"

There is evident pride in this conservative insistence on the rigorous training in drawing. Students and faculty alike are aware that they are probably better at drawing than most of their counterparts in North America. But Vladeta also admits the Belgrade school is not exactly at the top of that hierarchy. According to his experience, the place at the top is taken by the St. Petersburg academy. Russians are even more orthodox than the Serbs.

And yet, Vladeta is at pains to point out that all this rigor and torture of students in anatomy classes is not about naturalism, some sort of skillful translation from objective reality. It is not painting by numbers, not about rigidly applying rules and schemas. This is something that most instructors and students believe "Americans" are guilty of. The Belgrade school of drawing, Vladeta told me in an interview, is after abstraction, not naturalism. It is about finding the philosophical in form. It is perhaps our Byzantine and Orthodox heritage, he ventures, that predisposes us to seek the inner, spiritual, the abstract beyond the surface physical likeness. In that sense, even landscapes have their anatomy. When you solve the landscape problem you are using the same sensibility developed in solving a live model in anatomy class. Drawing the live model is then a skill transferable to anything at all. Even the great abstract artists—Mondrian, Kandinsky, Klee, and others—so the first years students will tell you, have gone through the same process of making whole "mountains of drawings," as one of them in Vladeta's class put it. The road to abstract essences goes through solving the problems of figurative drawing.

Akademija is far from monolithic. It is in fact quite riven with generational, ideological, and aesthetic conflict, some of if quite severe. The major cleavage is seen to be between the "modern" generation who are fully conversant with the world art trends, given to experimentation and leaning away from craft[6] and toward conceptual art. Many of my interlocutors, from different generations of

Akademija graduates emphasized these divisions, and yet, they all agreed that everyone among the faculty, no matter what faction they belong to, ultimately buys into the importance of developing serious drawing skills as a basis for everything. In that sense, Akademija, however imperfect, crumbling, and conflict-ridden it may be, is still a bastion of an old, traditional order. All of those who passed through the system claim that they can tell at a glance whether a drawing was done by a fine art or design student and even whether it was done by a painting, sculpting, or print student (the three FLU specializations). Most importantly, they claim that they all know exactly who is good and who is mediocre, and that implies a stable reference system. It is not "anything goes" in Belgrade art.

The Akademija system is a direct descendant of the French Beaux Art tradition. Ultimately, it could be traced back to the way art was taught in the Renaissance. This kind of institutionalized tradition of academic art thrived in socialism. Communist revolution in Russia produced some of the best avant garde art we know of, and yet this amazing creative outburst was very quickly destroyed by Stalinism and replaced by an essentially bourgeois academic art underlying the so-called socialist realism. Whatever good art got produced under the strictures of this essentially kitsch regime was the one artist sneaked by the censor. But while the official aesthetic line (by no means steady and predictable) favored quite unrevolutionary academism, the socialist system elevated the artist to the position of power, reputation, and influence arguably unrivaled by the capitalist world.[7] It was, however, only the state-certified artists who enjoyed such prestige and influence, and the certification was done precisely through the highly selective state institutions of which Belgrade Akademija is a perfect example. Artists, provided they passed through the gauntlet of hellish entrance exams, rigorous and long studies, and criteria for the membership in the state-run artists associations, were largely exempt from the market pressures and practically guaranteed state support. The Akademija graduates still carry this pride with them. They are academic artists and they feel entitled to a high degree of respect. But socialism is no more, and the position of the artist in today's Serbia seems to be suspended in ambiguity. A student in Vladeta's first year anatomy class put it thus: "It seems to me we don't have a role anymore, as if we are levitating in some sort of interspace."

Akademija Professors' Excellent Doodles

Akademija entrance exams are now less than ten days away. Tinker Bell and Sunset are busy helping students put together their portfolios. Additional models are brought in and students sometimes stay up to eight straight hours instead of the regular four. Even the ethnographer is roped into sitting for a portrait. And then Tinker Bell gathers them around her laptop and shows them a series of sketches. Apparently, there is a long tradition at the Akademija of faculty bringing their sketchbooks to faculty meetings and drawing quick portraits of each other. Oh, this is professor so and so, Tinker Bell excitedly exclaims, and this one was done by professor so and so. Collective sounds of awe are emitted. Students are already quite adept at recognizing a really good drawing. Tinker Bell underlies it with more particular comments: "Look how he draws this eyebrow in pure lines; see how you don't even see the lips here." "Oh, they bicker and argue at these faculty meetings," Tinker Bell assures me, "but they constantly draw each other." Oh, how well these people draw! And it is obvious, too, that for all their differences, they are all ultimately invested in a core of painterly values they can all easily recognize in each other. This is another poignant three-generational moment. A cohort of acolytes getting a glimpse of what the masters who may soon become their mentors can do, all mediated through Tinker Bell who was taught by some of the same professors and is herself a highly accomplished master. Some disillusionment will probably occur later; after graduating, the artists will confront Serbia's realities, but right now, in Tinker Bell's studio they are enchanted. And apart from the romantic notions of art as calling that most of them entertain, I venture that a part of the enchantment lies in an assurance that there exists an institution where high standards are maintained and transmitted—in the midst of a society that does not.

Academic artists I talked to are often critical about Akademija, sometimes even outright bitter. Professors have big egos and produce nothing but clones of themselves; they stop doing art and exhibiting; it is all about vicious clan battles; Akademija is too conservative, even reactionary; it has declined—I heard it all many times. And yet, underneath all the dissatisfaction, I could always detect (and elicit) a common pride. The rigor of the entrance exams and the pedagogy ensures that every graduate of Akademija reaches a high level of skill. They all also know quite well that only a few are truly "talented" and they can spot them with unerring precision. And for all the talk of the "decline," there is also a sense that this undefinable "something" Akademija stands for is still being transmitted reliably—for whatever it is worth.

A Little Orange Flame

Preparing a posthumous retrospective exhibition of Gordana's art at the University of Alberta in Edmonton, I asked some of her close friends to recall an incident, a vignette about her and record themselves telling it in their native tongue accompanied with a silent video portrait of themselves. Gordana first met Vladeta in the most established of the preparatory drawing schools in Belgrade (in Šumatovačka Street). It was not unusual for Akademija professors, such as Vladeta, to also teach there. Later, when Gordana passed the entrance exam, he was her professor in Anatomy and, together with his wife, Ljilja, he took her under his wing—in one telling incident, he walked across half the city to deliver a hot meal to her when she was lying sick at home. He was the first to correct her drawing, the first to recognize her talent, and at our wedding in 2003, Gordana chose Vladeta and Ljilja as her witnesses (a position of high honor). Here's what Vladeta said in the video he made for Gordana's retrospective exhibition:

> When I was a student, I had a wonderful professor—Koka Mihać,
> who told me the following story about what is art:

You think, she said, that art is given to everyone.
No, she said, it isn't.

Art is a little candle flame someone carries,
nurtures, recognizes and preserves.

And wants to give that little flame to someone as a gift
but cannot find the right person who will accept it.

Who can accept it, and will know how to preserve it,
and to carry it, care for it, and nurture it.

So that she could give that little flame to such a person
to carry on fanning it further.

And so, she said, she looks and looks around,
nobody in sight,

and then she sees the fiftieth, and gives to that fiftieth
the little flame, the orange flame, to preserve it, to nurture it,

to keep it from dying and to fuel it with power to endure,
and that fiftieth again, against all odds, finds another fiftieth,

and so it gets transmitted from one right person to another.

Well, I had a sweater—one half of it black.
And the other half was all in squares, lively, multicolored.

Gordana loved it and wanted to wear it,
and I gave it to her to wear.

In return she gave me an orange, flaming jacket.

And whenever I wear that jacket
people tell me, wow, what a beautiful jacket!

And whenever I see something beautiful,
or something that is art,

I can put my hand in the pocket,
and touch Gordana's hand, Gordana's fingers.

Thus I and Gordana talk to each other
to this very day.

She wore that sweater, she wears it,
she carries that little flame,

I gave her that little flame,
just as it was given to me by my professor

and it is orange, just as the jacket is orange,
the jacket I wear to this very day.

Notes

1. FLU stands for the *Fakultet likovnih umetnosti*. The faculty is a part of the Belgrade Art University that also includes the Faculty of Dramatic Arts, the Faculty of Music, and the Faculty of Applied Arts. FLU was founded in 1937.

2. In Belgrade, most people use the shorthand "Beaux Arts" to refer to the Paris École nationale supérieure des Beaux-Arts, founded in 1648 as the Académie Royale de Peinture et de Sculpture (Royal Academy of Painting and Sculpture) modeled on Italian fine art academies.

3. This refers to the average monthly salary of a resident of Belgrade. In general, high school students rarely work and rely on support from their parents for such schools.

4. Slavica would sometimes notice a student struggling at the first day of exams and alert the preparatory school teacher, who would still have time to intervene.

5. See Kuhn 1996.

6. Pride in the ability to make anything at all by one's own hands is very much in evidence in the Akademija world. While privileged Americans can buy any shade or hue of a paint, those in the Akademija world can make them all out of three primary ones. And if need be, they can make their paints from scratch. They can even make their own paper and brushes. An Akademija professor, Zoran Graovac, for example, is held in universal awe in this respect. His papermaking skills are on par with the Japanese artisans at the Living National Treasure level, but he also makes the presses, meshes, and other tools himself at the highest standards of perfection. He has also acquired the secrets of a legendary master of paintbrush making.

7. See Fitzpatrick 1992, 1999, as well as Haraszti 1987.

References

Fitzpatrick, Sheila. 1992. *The Cultural Front: Power and Culture in Revolutionary Russia*. Ithaca, NY: Cornell University Press.

Fitzpatrick, Sheila. 1999. *Everyday Stalinism: Ordinary Life in Extraordinary Times: Soviet Russia in the 1930s*. New York: Oxford University Press.

Haraszti, Miklós. 1987. *The Velvet Prison: Artists under State Socialism*. New York: Basic Books.

Kuhn, Thomas S. 1996. *The Structure of Scientific Revolutions*. Chicago: University of Chicago Press.

MARKO ŽIVKOVIĆ is Associate Professor of the Anthropology Department at the University of Alberta, Edmonton, Canada. He is author of *Serbian Dreambook: National Imaginary in the Time of Milošević*.

Postface

David W. Montgomery

Put provocatively, the task of this collection of essays is subversive. It is subversive in the sense that it aims to facilitate an appreciation of the complexity in which people live—the context of the everyday—to argue that it is from this that we must begin any attempt to understand people. Perhaps on the face of it, this would seem a pedestrian goal were it not for the fact that the predominance of international engagement with and analysis of the region prioritizes the perspectives of elites who often have different struggles than the nonelites discussed here. In fairness, all have everydays—elites and nonelites—with similarities, except that publicly, and often analytically, we value the experience and perspective of elites and nonelites differently. As well, much of what is taught about the region—or any region for that matter—are the highlights of a territory's successes and failures rather than the personal toils of those lost to history. The reality of most is that we fall into this latter category, destined to have subsequent generations not understand how we lived our common days.

But there is a transformative potential in one's ability to see the everyday, for it is in this space that reflexivity has its greatest purchase. Thus an aspired to success of this volume would be that the contextualization of history, home, livelihoods, politics, religion, and art would all come to inform the process by which any place is engaged. We all have biases that influence our understanding of the world and there is a danger in over-universalizing how we believe the world should be contra how the world is from other lived realities. The chapters in this volume have aimed to give the context for appreciating this within the Balkans.

In the introductory chapter situating the contributions of this volume, everyday life theory was given a nod but not interrogated. This is not to suggest that there is no underlying theoretical argument driving this book. On the contrary, one of the biggest challenges faced in the social sciences is how to understand and theorize movement.[1] The everyday is furtive ground for such theoretical engagement because in its repetition we see both linear and circular time represented as movement through life's trajectory.[2] The circularity comes in our seasons of habit—daily chores, holidays, and the ongoing reimaginations of history—while the linear is known in our own walk from birth to death.

The hope is that the strength of a theoretical argument emerges out of narratives that subtly reinforce a view toward the diversity of experience in the world.

Here then, the claim for everyday life is that local understandings are central to getting at any form of understanding. The emic perspective—the starting point of view of many interlocutors throughout the volume—is central to giving context to opportunities for engaging with others. My world is different from someone else's world, and to engage I must consider what the world of the other looks like.

As the Albanian writer Ismail Kadare observes, "There is a lot of talk about the Other nowadays. And, as so often happens when old themes and conversations are rehashed after a phase of oblivion, we tend to believe that it—the Other one—is the object of our attention for the first time."[3] Increasingly, it seems our days are ones filled with the persistent challenge of how to live with the Other.[4] The chapters in this book show the multiple variables that contribute to such challenges, but central to any success is a deep awareness and appreciation of how something is locally valued. To do this, we need to see *everyday life in the Balkans*, and elsewhere.

Notes

1. Montgomery 2016.
2. See Felski 1999 and Lefebvre 2014.
3. Kadare 2013, 113.
4. Seligman, Wasserfall, and Montgomery 2015.

References

Felski, Rita. 1999. "The Invention of Everyday Life." *New Formations* 33: 15–31.
Kadare, Ismail. 2013. "History of the Other." In *The Stranger Next Door: An Anthology from the Other Europe*, edited by R. Swartz, 113–122. Evanston, IL: Northwestern University.
Lefebvre, Henri. 2014. *Critique of Everyday Life*. Translated by John Moore. London: Verso.
Montgomery, David W. 2016. *Practicing Islam: Knowledge, Experience, and Social Navigation in Kyrgyzstan*. Pittsburgh: University of Pittsburgh Press.
Seligman, Adam B., Rahel R. Wasserfall, and David W. Montgomery. 2015. *Living with Difference: How to Build Community in a Divided World*. Berkeley: University of California Press.

DAVID W. MONTGOMERY is Director of Program Development for Communities Engaging with Difference and Religion (CEDAR) and Associate Research Professor at the Center for International Development and Conflict Management at the University of Maryland. He is author of *Practicing Islam: Knowledge, Experience, and Social Navigation in Kyrgyzstan* and of *Living with Difference: How to Build Community in a Divided World* (with Adam Seligman and Rahel Wasserfall).

Index

Adriatic Sea (and coast), 3, 9, 12, 15, 16–17, 280, 290, 300
Albania: Dhermi, 326; Durres, 9, 270, 326; Himara, 205–206, 272; Korca, 323, 328; Tirana, 204, 267–276, 322, 325–330; Vlora, 201–209, 268
Agolli, Dritero, 377–378
agriculture, 17, 68–69, 148–149, 151, 157, 240. *See also* farming.
ajvar, 55, 59n17, 83
alcohol, 26–28, 45, 55, 122, 135, 171, 180–181, 183, 194, 213, 281, 285. *See also*, rakija.
ambiguity, 2–3, 54, 87, 393
architecture, 12, 13, 19, 32, 39–40, 237n1, 254-255, 258, 319n9, 325, 337, 340–343, 352
art, 5, 13, 19, 70, 255, 337, 384–396
austerity, 193–194

Balkan, culture, 3, 45, 46, 96, 363; peninsula, 2–3, 12, 13, 16, 22, 134, 139, 185n2, 190; region, 14, 96, 188, 191, 196n19
Bektashi Order. *See* Islam, Bektashi.
Before the Rain (film), 52, 180
belonging, xi, 3, 87–88, 108, 113, 131, 188–195, 199–200, 220, 253–254, 256–257, 271, 299, 307, 312, 327, 330–331, 379
Black Sea (and coast), 3, 15, 49, 155, 161
Böll, Heinrich, 372–373
borders, 28, 125, 126, 134, 158, 159, 190, 199–200, 202, 206–208, 232, 235–236, 280, 352, 358, 376
Bosnia and Herzegovina: Bihać, 117–126; Mostar, 107–114, 133–136; Sarajevo, 25, 27, 47, 53, 54, 89, 91–94, 133, 135–142, 145, 364, 367; Stolac, 133–142;
Bosniak. *See* Muslim, Bosnian.
boundaries: cultural, 3, 29, 322, 372; ethnic, 221, 227–229; geographical, 3, 233, 322; political, 20, 29, 233, 252–253, 294, 322; religious, 276, 294, 299, 311, 317–318
Bulgaria: Plovdiv, 9, 45, 48; Sofia, 9, 19, 45, 48–50, 156, 192, 240–244, 364, 368; Veliko Tarnovo, 155, 158
Bulatović, Momir, 211

bureaucracy, 12, 232, 235–237
business, 24, 33, 37, 46, 56, 58, 78, 121, 135, 149, 151, 158, 161–163, 173–175, 192, 204, 245, 269, 286, 295, 341, 343, 345
burek, 52–58
Byzantium, 9–20, 208, 218, 253, 326, 341, 351, 392

café, 7, 22, 26, 44–50, 57, 104n6, 112, 138, 156, 171, 173, 201, 251, 255, 276n14, 278, 284, 343, 378
capitalism, 31–32, 52–53, 138, 143n8, 162–164, 358–359, 385
Ceaușescu, Nicolae, 340–343
celebration, 5, 71, 140, 179, 185n2, 215, 224–246, 258, 279, 282, 284–285, 290–296, 297n16, 302, 322–323, 327, 354–360
censorship, 36, 337, 354, 357, 372–376, 393
children, 24, 90, 113, 148, 169, 242, 257, 268, 295, 363–370; care, 61, 64–73, 103, 118–119, 283; education, 107–114, 140, 151, 211, 384
Christianity: Catholic, 11, 13, 18, 87, 103, 147, 265–270, 290, 299–308, 309n10, 324–239, 373; Evangelical, 270; Orthodox, 11–13, 18–20, 87, 105n10, 147, 189, 227, 254, 256, 263, 268–273, 279, 289–296, 297n11, 297n20, 311–318, 321–331, 351–352, 359, 387, 392; Protestant, 265, 268, 270
Christmas, 268, 292, 294, 365–366
church, 10–11, 13, 15, 17–19, 29, 147, 211, 256, 267, 270–276, 276n10, 289–296, 297n20, 301–308, 309n10, 314–318, 322–329, 341–342, 352
cigarettes, 24–25, 56, 76, 88, 138, 194, 213, 255, 379. *See also* tobacco.
The Clown (novel), 372–372, 374
coffee, 2, 24, 26, 44–50, 76, 88, 91, 112, 133–142, 146, 170, 193, 203, 251, 275, 275n14, 388
communism, 31, 35–36, 189, 194, 202, 204, 239–249, 268, 289, 301–307, 342, 353, 358
Constantine, Emperor, 10, 11, 321–322, 327–328
construction (reconstruction), 9, 18, 31–35, 41, 71, 96, 121, 134, 136, 142, 157, 175–176, 180–188, 191, 224, 254–259, 293, 323, 325, 339–347

conversion, 13, 303–308, 311–312, 319n7, 321, 353
corruption, 112, 193, 208, 239–249, 268–269, 342, 354, 358–389, 385
crisis, economic, 68, 148, 151, 163, 188, 190–195, 207, 242, 244, 358, 360; political, 202
Croatia: Dubrovnik, 9, 14, 16, 215, 299, 300, 363; Pula, 181, 185n11; Split, 9, 14, 110, 150, 302; Zagreb, 63, 65–68, 135

Danube River, 10, 13, 15, 16, 293, 384
Dayton Agreement, 121, 133, 232,
Dalmatia (coast), 147, 179
democracy, 92, 162, 204–205, 208, 242, 245–249, 294, 366
development, cultural, 13; economic, 133, 196n19, 242; political, 217, 239
Đjukanović, Milo, 211, 214
Drina River, 230–237
Dushan, Stefan, 280

Easter, 227, 268, 294, 313, 322–323
education, 41, 64, 69, 89, 90, 103, 107–114, 138, 140, 149, 151, 179, 203, 233, 294, 330, 384–396
elderly, care, 64, 67–72, 117–126, 141, 148–149
Epirus, 188, 272, 327
Esma's Secret (film), 365, 366–367
European Union, 42n4, 63, 85n1, 156, 161, 188, 191–192, 194, 195, 199, 202, 207, 252, 274. 340

farming, 12, 13, 78, 148, 158, 161–162, 231. *See also* agriculture.
fashion, 38, 40, 86–94
feminism, 61, 86–94, 380–381
film, 52–53, 179, 319n7, 363–370
Fishta, Gjergj, 378, 382n10
folk, folklore, 326, 352–353, 363; folk music, 351–360
Frashëri, Naim, 267

globalization, 61, 70, 85n1, 91, 162, 341, 376
Greece: Athens, 188–189, 190, 218, 326; Trikala, 188–195

handicraft, 12, 82, 140, 346, 352, 390–392
The Highland Lute (epic poem), 378
hookah, 24, 47
homemade, 55, 76–84, 184
homogenization, 52, 70, 83, 329, 352
homophobia, 92, 98, 100, 102–103, 104n6, 105n10
homosexuality, 27–28, 96–104, 273–274

hospital, 18, 102, 125, 135, 169, 170, 171, 178, 212, 367
hospitality, 56, 292–295, 322; industry, 151, 172
Hoxha, Enver, 201, 266, 268, 274, 276n10, 324, 327, 375, 376
humanitarian assistance, 93, 120, 138, 148–151, 212

icon, 11, 19, 20, 193, 271, 291–293, 318
iftar, 89, 281–285
Illyrian, 12, 201, 203, 207, 209, 267, 327–328
immigrant, *see* migrant
inequality, 56, 162–164, 369
International Criminal Tribunal of the former Yugoslavia (ICTY), 90, 220–229
investigation, 220–227
investment, 35, 71, 73, 131, 134–136, 155–164, 341–343
Islam: Bektashi, 265, 267–269, 271, 276n1, 324; Shi'a, 267; Sufi, 267, 280; Sunni, 265, 267–268, 280, 324
Italy: Bari, 379; Padua, 179, 185n1; Rome, 10, 12, 17–18, 204, 267, 324

Judaism, 24, 45–47, 127n16, 312, 314, 319n11, 351

Kadare, Ismail, 208, 372, 374–375, 379, 381n4, 382n20, 398
Kastrioti, Gjergji (Skanderbeg), 267
Klosi, Ardian, 373–374, 375, 380
kinship, 63–73, 119, 124, 136, 237n10
Kongoli, Fatos, 379
Kosovo: Gjakova, 279; Mitrovica, 279; Prishtina, 279, 280, 282, 327–328; Prizren, 70, 278–287

labor, market, 66–72; work, 12, 83, 134–137, 141, 160, 179–185, 206
LGBT, *see* homosexuality

Macedonia, Former Yugoslav Republic of (FYROM): Ohrid, 19, 220, 224; Skopje, 52–58, 222, 224–229, 251–259, 284
madrasa (*medrese*), 280
Marović, Svetozar, 221
marriage, 13, 68, 71–72, 97, 103–104, 174, 274, 291, 305–506, 317
masculinity, 100, 179–185
memorial, 226, 252, 292, 339–345
memory, 44, 80, 110, 190, 254, 315, 319n7, 320n17, 327, 339–347, 367, 379

migrant, 47, 53, 55, 69–72, 134–139, 142n3, 142n4, 145–152, 156, 159, 192, 206, 223, 268, 323. *See also*, refugee.
Mila from Mars (film), 364–366
Milosevic, Slobodan, 214–216, 322, 385
Milvian Bridge, battle of, 321, 327
monastic, 12, 17–20, 193, 297n11, 317, 322, 341
Monkeys in Winter, 364, 367–369
Montenegro: Podgorica, 140–141, 211–219
morality, 27–28, 159–162, 265–276, 366, 372, 378–380
mosque, 45, 211, 256, 268–275, 278–286, 314
movie, *see* film.
music, 11, 88, 169, 284, 301, 351–360, 386, 388
Muslim, 26, 45–46, 87–90, 135, 256, 265–276, 278–287, 313–318, 322, 329–331, 356, 366; Bosnian, 70, 87–90, 94n2, 107–114, 121, 127n36, 196n29, 232; Bulgarian-speaking, 311–318
myth, 267, 316, 322, 373

narghile, *see* hookah.
National Liberation Army (NLA), 220–227
nationalism, 95, 215, 221, 257, 289, 294, 353–354, 359–360
neoliberalism, 63, 66–68, 126, 138, 155–164, 342, 385
neighbor, 15, 26, 33, 41, 55, 61, 66, 69, 81, 102, 136, 145, 160, 211, 281, 319n11; neighborhood, 33, 45, 48, 55, 66–68, 76, 93, 135, 151, 193, 202, 283, 342–345; neighborliness, 1, 68, 107; 311–318
Neretva River, 107, 133–134
Noli, Fan, 268, 324–325
nongovernmental organization (NGO), 86, 88, 90, 99, 149, 202, 215
North Atlantic Treaty Organization (NATO), 151, 196n29, 215, 242, 253–254, 285, 385

Ottoman, 3, 12, 17, 22–29, 44–49, 189–193, 195, 208, 253–256, 267, 278, 280, 311, 315–316, 322–323, 352–353

pagan, 10, 12–13, 18, 256, 290,
parade, Pride, 100–103, 104n6, 105n9
pilgrimage, hajj, 269, 272
Pomak, *see* Muslim (Bulgarian-speaking).
poverty, 68, 70, 93, 149, 162–163, 188, 191–195, 358
property, 18, 35, 66, 68, 134, 141, 146–147, 155–164, 173, 176, 220, 239, 358, 386

Qosja, Rexhep, 208,

rakija (brandy), 55, 169–170, 178n2, 183. *See also*, alcohol.
Rama, Edi, 326
Ramadan, 269, 278–287
refugee, 87–90, 93, 122, 125–126, 131, 134–135, 138, 141, 143n6, 145–152, 152n9, 212, 253, 334n52. *See also* migrant.
Rhodope Mountains, 311–318, 319n10
Roma (Gypsies), 12, 96, 136, 256, 259n3, 279, 342, 343, 351–360, 368
Roman Empire, 9–10, 13, 253. 321
Romania: Bucharest, 253, 339–347

sacred site, 272, 301, 317–318, 322
Sava River, 3, 384
Schengen Area, 206–207, 376
Serbia: Belgrade, 9, 32, 33, 35, 91, 92, 103, 105n10, 119, 214, 216, 217, 233, 280, 282, 297n16, 384–396; Nish, 321, 327–328; Novi Sad, 169, 175
The Shadow (novel), 374, 381n4
Simeon II, king, 241–242, 249n
Slava, 172, 289–296, 297n16
Slovenia: Ljubljana, 53–55, 100–102, 104n6, 105n10
Solana, Javier, 216
Southeast Europe, 2–3, 188, 321. *See also* Balkans.
Srpska, Republika, 120, 125, 127n36, 232, 236

Tito, Josip Broz, 34, 84, 211, 256, 385
tobacco, 24–26, 45, 49, 352. *See also* cigarettes.
Turkey: Constantinople, 10–19, 267; Istanbul; 10, 45–46, 213

Under the Yoke (novel), 46
United Kingdom (Britain), 156–162, 165n43
UNESCO World Heritage site, 10, 134, 280
United States, 31, 90, 91, 92, 134, 135, 138–142, 174–175, 177, 202, 215, 267, 268

Vasa, Pashko, 266, 269
Vazov, Ivan, 46
VMRO-DPMNE (International Macedonian Revolutionary Organizations-Democratic Party for Macedonian National Unity), 56, 223, 251–258

Yanoulatos, Anastasios, 322, 325–326
Yugoslavia, 31–42, 53, 88, 91–92, 118–120, 180, 211–212, 253, 385
Yourcenar, Marguerite, 363